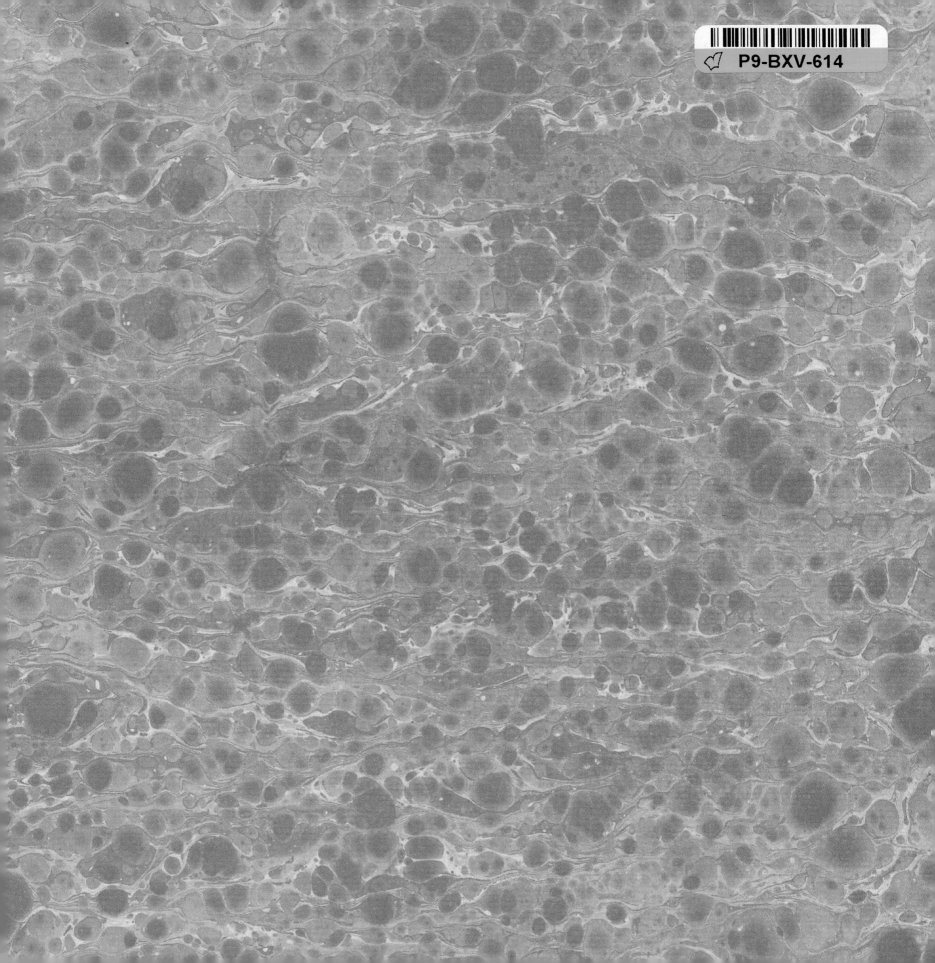

EVERYDAY
LIFE THROUGH
THE AGES

Argentinian
gaucho

Bengal
lancer

Farm worker,
medieval Europe

Fiji
islander

Arab
sheik

American
Indian

READER'S DIGEST

EVERYDAY LIFE THROUGH THE AGES

Published by The Reader's Digest Association Limited
LONDON   NEW YORK   SYDNEY   CAPE TOWN   MONTREAL

Chinese peasant

Tibetan herdsman

Cretan postman

Japanese geisha

Roman senator

English hired funeral mourner

Aztec eagle warrior

Ancient Greek youth

Bedouin tribesman

London policeman

Somali tribesman

Editor
Michael Worth Davison, MA

Art Editor
Neal V. Martin, BA, H.Dip. Des

Contributors

CONSULTANT EDITOR
Asa Briggs, FBA, MA, BSc (Econ)

The publishers would like to thank the following writers, consultants
and artists for their major contributions to this book:

WRITERS

Charles Allen

Hugh D. R. Baker, BA, PhD
Professor of Chinese,
University of London

Keith Branigan, BA, PhD, FSA
Professor of Archaeology and Prehistory,
University of Sheffield

Michael Cannon

Graeme Decarie, PhD (Queen's)
History Department,
Concordia University, Montreal

Alan Duggan

Plantagenet Somerset Fry

Nigel Hawkes
Science Editor, *The Times*

Tim Healey

Kathleen Hulser, MA
Department of History, New York University

Sybil M. Jack
Associate Professor, Department of History,
University of Sydney

Stefan Kaiser, PhD
Senior Lecturer in Japanese,
School of Oriental and African Studies, University of London

Nelson Kenny

Anthony Livesey

Rowena Loverance
British Museum Education Service

Tim Low

Helen McCurdy, BA

Anne E. Millard, BA, PhD

Anne Pearson
British Museum Education Service

Thomas L. Robinson, MA, MDiv, PhD
Lecturer in Greek Studies,
Union Theological Seminary, New York

Richard Tames

Irwin Unger, PhD
Professor of American History,
New York University

Bernard A. Weisberger

| Japanese samurai | British seaman of 19th century | German peasant | Muslim market trader | Solomon islander | Manchu Chinese | Dutch fisherman | Australian Aborigine | Persian water carrier | Turkish apple seller | Hebrew temple musician |

SPECIALIST CONSULTANTS

Jens Firsching, MA
University of Heidelberg

George Hart, MPhil
Staff Lecturer, British Museum

Nick Merriman, MA, PhD, AMA
Head of Department of Early London History and Collections,
Museum of London

David Morgan, BA, PhD
Reader in the History of the Middle East,
University of London

Lorna Oakes, BA

Neil Parsons, BA, Dip Afr Stud, PhD
Honorary Research Fellow, Institute of Commonwealth Studies,
University of London

P. G. Robb, BA, PhD
Senior Lecturer in History, School of Oriental and African Studies,
University of London

Peter Sawyer
formerly Professor of Medieval History,
University of Leeds

Patricia Vanags, BA
British Museum Education Service

ARTISTS

Ian Atkinson
Baird Harris

Richard Bonson

Gino D' Achille
Represented by Artist Partners Limited

Terence Dalley, ARCA

Sarah Fox-Davies

Brian Delf

The Grose Thurston Partnership

Vana Haggerty

Ivan Lapper, ARCA, FCSD

Malcolm McGregor

Robert Micklewright, RWS

Steven J. Smith

David Thorpe

Edward Williams

Maps
Malcolm Porter

Cyclist
of 1850

Masai
warrior

English
bricklayer

Hun
horseman

Mughal
woman

Omani
tribesman

Roman
legionary

Russian
road sweeper

Peruvian
Indian

English woman of
Victorian times

The way it was then

There is much about the history of everyday life that we shall never know. People keep their secrets. Some things, however, we know better than they did. They had at best only a limited knowledge of their world – or worlds. We have a global overview. And we have the great advantage over all our ancestors of knowing what came next, including the disasters and the wars that broke the pattern of everyday life.

This volume, original and ambitious in its global span, is designed to satisfy curiosity. It spans the centuries and covers the continents. There are two kinds of curiosity to which it responds. First is our natural curiosity to learn more about people in the past who had something in common with ourselves, starting with our family ancestors. Second is our equally natural curiosity to learn more about people who were – and are – very different from ourselves. This book covers both the familiar and the exotic. It cannot, however, cover everyday life in all countries at all times. Like all history, it has to be selective.

Some elements of everyday life remain constant through the centuries and across the world. For life to continue, new generations of men, women and children are born. They have all had to find shelter, to eat, to drink, to clothe themselves, to divide their time between different pursuits, to work and to play. Yet they have done all these basic things in different ways in different times and places – and seldom completely of their own choice. The relationship between necessity and choice in any generation has often been complex, though equally often people take choice or necessity for granted. How long and how hard we work or are made to work, and how far we travel – by choice or by necessity – have always varied greatly even within the same generation.

History can be traced through a succession of generations as well as through a sequence of events, and this raises questions about courtship and marriage, and how children are brought up. One crucial question precedes even that of upbringing. How long did people live? The answer to the question lay not only in food and shelter, with work and wages, but in medicine, and it is only recently that medicine has begun to become scientific.

The rise of science is one of the great unfinished themes of this book. It influenced the minds of men and women as well as their behaviour, yet since the volume ends with the beginning of the 20th century it stops before the most transforming phases of a story which already influences how we think about our ancestors and our contemporaries in other places.

A survey of everyday life in any age, including our own, cannot leave out the question of what people were interested in and why, and how they felt as well as

European
nun

Egyptian
drinks seller

Showman with
dancing bear

Dutch soldier in
South Africa

Rumanian
shepherd

Elizabethan
courtier

Japanese
peasant

American
plainsman

English
Puritan

German
grenadier

how they thought, not least about pain and pleasure. What were their values? What part did religion play in the pattern of life? The questions have to be posed not only about ourselves, but about our most remote ancestors, those who lived in caves and hunted for food. There is a drama of every man and every woman in all this, a drama of hardship and sacrifice as well as of ritual and romance.

The drama has always been expressed in pictures as well as in words – from sketches of animals in caves through paintings, silhouettes and studio photographs to family snapshots. This volume is richly illustrated, therefore, but the illustrations are an essential part of the whole. The text employs every device, imaginative and interpretative, to bring vividly to life the everyday past of a wide gallery of characters, familiar and unfamiliar.

On the cover of the book there are pictures of many of these characters, and inside there are accounts of the daily lives of such contrasting people as a Roman centurion, a Saxon ploughman, a Sumerian schoolchild, a medieval nun, a North American trapper, a pilgrim on the road to Compostela, and a Victorian pauper. There is something in the volume to appeal to all interests – and to all ages.

Things inevitably figure as well as people. Some things were simple, such as the first arrowheads.

Some had become complex by the end of the 19th century. The railway was one of them, not only changing ways of getting to work or going on holiday or lowering the costs of travel of goods and people, but also transforming attitudes towards time. Some things were useful, from tools to ploughs and from ploughs to steam engines. Some things were decorative, for everyday life from the beginning had its arts and fashions. Some things were destructive, used in the battles and wars that have occurred throughout human history. Some things were made to last, some to throw away. Some things were for display, some for comfort in everyday life.

Things that have survived always serve as emissaries from the past. They can be more eloquent than documents, public or private. When curiosity is the hallmark of the historian, everything is grist to the mill.

Asa Briggs

Buddhist monk

Slave in sugar field

Russian Cossack

Viking warrior

Bolivian Indian

French army canteen worker

Turkish religious leader

Irish potato gatherer

Swiss mountain guide

Indian holy man

Contents

British soldier of 19th century   Woman of Ancient Egypt   Mexican peasant   Medieval French knight   Maori chieftain   Revolutionary in Paris   Inuit hunter   Moroccan woman   English prize fighter   Hunter-gatherer   Woman of Ancient Greece

Cover picture and below *The rich
diversity of the human race is illustrated
by Malcolm McGregor, in a gallery of
portraits from all over the world and
from many different ages.*

English
chair mender

Russian
milkmaid

Japanese Shinto
priest

English medieval
halberdier

Arab
donkeyman

English
chimney sweep

Woman of
the steppes

Medieval
minstrel

Scottish
clansman

African
woman

Ancient Worlds

The first people in the world were hunters and food gatherers, totally dependent on nature and on their own skills. They had few options as far as the fundamentals of food, clothing and shelter were concerned. Skins were the earliest clothes. There were cave-dwellers before there were householders, fires before farms.

The first great revolution in human history was the development and spread of agriculture, which can be traced back to the growing of wheat and barley in the Near East. Agriculture meant settlement. It required forethought: people had to know when to sow and reap, as well as how. Agriculture demanded hard work. Women found a new place in the system. Soon new crafts developed, such as the making of pottery, textiles and jewellery. Agriculture made it possible to sustain a larger population, and after the introduction of agriculture into Europe the number of people rose tenfold. Where there was no agriculture there was no development.

The word 'culture' is related to the word agriculture, the cultivation of the land, and the word 'civilisation' is derived from the Latin word for city. It was in cities that the art of writing was first developed, making possible the first human record of history in the making – the history not only of events but of everyday transactions between scribes, farmers, craftsmen, priests and officials. The record was set down on stone and in clay, on papyrus, on skins and on paper.

City life, too, brought widening contrasts between the lifestyles of rich and poor. These existed even in the city-states of the sophisticated Greeks, who became the earliest people to ask questions about the human condition, about truth and beauty, and about the quality of life. Violence has been part of the human condition from very early times, as the first cities expanded at their neighbours' expense and grew into empires, soon to find themselves at war with other empires. The effects of war on ordinary people could be devastating. Citizens suffered from their rulers' ambitions; wherever armies were on the move they looted, raped and destroyed.

The last great empire of the ancient world, Rome, offered law and order within the boundaries of the lands its legions had conquered. The wealth of these lands, still largely agricultural, supported an imperial capital which at its height may have had more than a million inhabitants; not until the 18th century did any other city in Europe approach it in size.

In the East there existed another great empire, with ways of life totally distinct from European ways, in country and in city. The civil servants who ran China were bureaucrats, not priests, but they followed a moral code based on the principles of Confucius. Other moralities were preached by the great religions that the ancient world generated. One of these, Christianity, became the established religion of the Roman Empire.

The fall of Rome to the 'barbarians', as the Romans called them, is held to mark the end of the ancient world. Yet Christianity survived the empire's fall, and the Christian chronology is still used over the greater part of the world. Christians were proud of their inheritance, whose impact on everyday life was to prove as great as its impact on the life of the spirit.

HUNTERS TURN TO FARMING

From their first appearance on planet Earth, early humans showed that they were here to stay. They were quick-witted and dexterous, giving them the edge over their competitors in fighting for survival in a harsh and demanding world. They invented the spear-thrower, the harpoon and the bow and arrow – and they used their new weapons to good effect when hunting for food. Men were the armed pursuers of animals; but it was the women who gathered in the nutritious roots, berries and nuts. In addition, early people discovered that two stones struck together made a faster and more effective way of starting fires for cooking, heating and lighting than the previous method of rubbing two sticks together. Later, bands living in the fertile river valleys of the Middle East built mud-and-reed houses grouped in fortified villages. There they became the first people to herd cattle and farm the land – and to trade their produce for other essential goods.

EARLY HUMANS 100,000–2500 BC

STRIKING IT RICH WITH FLINT TOOLS

The world has existed for more than 4000 million years. Primitive life forms first appeared on earth more than 3000 million years ago, but fully evolved, modern human beings, *Homo sapiens sapiens*, have only been on the scene for the tiniest fraction of that time – some 100,000 years.

Modern humans were an instant success. Having evolved in Africa, and possibly Asia too, they spread rapidly across the globe. Some crossed the land bridge that then linked the Old World with the New at what is now the Bering Straits. Others migrated from South-east Asia to Australia, and a final wave fanned out from South-east Asia through the Pacific Islands and eventually reached New Zealand. The only place they failed to reach was the continent of Antarctica; that journey was too difficult.

Big game *The role of the early human male as hunter in quest of food is graphically shown in a rock painting depicting bowmen and prehistoric animals, from Jabbaren, in the Sahara.*

The world our ancestors inherited from the Neanderthals, their close relations, was in the grip of what was to be the last of the great Ice Ages. Ice had moved from the poles towards the Equator, so thick in places that it would have buried the skyscrapers of New York had they then existed, and so widespread that it buried most of northern Europe, Russia and America, as well as Antarctica. The Neanderthals had survived in this harsh environment, but the newcomers did more: they flourished, increased and were so successful that they had leisure to produce ornaments for themselves, to decorate their clothes, to make music, to create works of art and to evolve complex religious beliefs and rituals.

The tools for the job

For something like 1 million years, primitive forms of humans had been making tools and weapons of stone. These have survived, while everything else has decayed. This is why that long early period of human development is referred to as the Stone Age.

Remains of the Neanderthals have been found in Africa, western Europe and as far east as central Asia. Their tools were remarkably alike right across the wide geographical range, and they changed very little over a period of some 100,000 years. Then along came modern human beings and in no time at all, relatively speaking, techniques improved and many new kinds of tools and weapons were invented.

The best stone for making tools and weapons was flint, and to get good-quality flint people would travel considerable distances and trudge home loaded with valuable but heavy stones. At Kostienki in Russia, for example, tools have been found made of flint from some 90 miles (145 km) away. Everyone must have been able to make and care for their own tools and weapons. It was no use for a hunter to find himself in the middle of a hunting trip with a broken spear that could not be replaced, or to be unable to cut up the deer for food because his knife was blunt and he had no idea how to sharpen it.

Modern humans became skilled shapers of flint. Some of the more skilled practitioners among them may have made fine tools for their friends, in return for a gift or a favour. Only an elite few, however, could have produced such superb pieces as the so-called 'laurel leaf' blades, some of which are nearly 12 in (300 mm) long and not quite 1/2 in (13 mm) thick.

The use to which these masterpieces were put is something of a puzzle. They are too long and fragile for use in hunting. Possibly they were highly prized possessions that gave their owner prestige, and which could

then be exchanged for other goods. The burin, or borer, was one of the most versatile tools in the early humans' kit. Used both as a chisel and an engraver, it was the first tool designed to make other tools – in fact, the machine tool of its day. Among the most important inventions was the spear-thrower. This was a piece of wood or antler up to 2 ft (610 mm) long, with a hook at one end. The butt of a spear was engaged in the hook and the spear was thrown. The impetus given by the spear-thrower

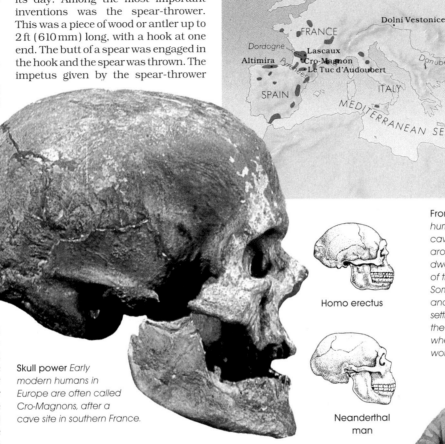

Skull power *Early modern humans in Europe are often called Cro-Magnons, after a cave site in southern France.*

Homo erectus

Neanderthal man

meant that the spear would travel farther and faster, and penetrate far more deeply than one which was thrown by hand alone.

Another weapon of early humans was the harpoon, made of bone or antler. The barbs on one or both sides of the slim blade held fast in the flesh of a prey, preventing it from struggling free. In addition, some bone spearheads were made with grooves down the sides. This increased the flow of blood from a wounded animal, killing it more quickly.

One of the most startling examples of early human beings' inventiveness was found at Dolni Vestonice, a site in modern Czechoslovakia. There some ingenious craftsmen mixed earth with ground-up bones and fashioned it into figures of animals and humans, particularly women, and then baked them rock-hard in a kiln.

From cave to farm *The first traces of early humans in Europe have been found in caves in Spain and France, and date from around 40,000 years ago. Hundreds of cave dwellings have been found on both sides of the Pyrenees, and in southern Spain. Some Cro-Magnons lived in eastern Europe and Russia. Early humans also settled in the fertile valleys of the Tigris and the Euphrates, where they became the world's first farmers.*

AN EYE TO THE MAIN CHANCE

The keynote of human evolution has been our ability to adapt and invent, and to solve problems – in short, our ingenuity. *Homo erectus*, who lived half a million years ago, used tools and mastered fire, and Neanderthal man, who emerged 120,000 years ago, developed more advanced skills. But once modern humans, *Homo sapiens sapiens*, appeared in Europe, they rapidly displaced other human forms. Modern humans are taller and more slightly built than the Neanderthals, with less pronounced brow ridges. Their skulls are more domed and their chins are more pointed. Though the Neanderthals' brain was as big as that of modern humans, or bigger, Neanderthals had become stuck in an evolutionary rut. They could not compete with the sharper, graceful newcomers with their superior tools and their eye to the main chance, exploiting every opportunity that came their way.

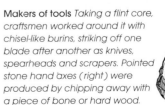

Makers of tools *Taking a flint core, craftsmen worked around it with chisel-like burins, striking off one blade after another as knives, spearheads and scrapers. Pointed stone hand axes (right) were produced by chipping away with a piece of bone or hard wood.*

ANIMALS AND PLANTS TO FILL THE POT

As with all living creatures, the most pressing daily need for our early human ancestors was to obtain an adequate supply of food. This food was obtained by a mixture of hunting, fishing and gathering from the larder provided by nature.

The Cro-Magnons – the early humans of Europe and Russia – were nomads. This does not mean that they wandered aimlessly day after day. It is more likely that bands of a few families would travel regularly through a fairly well-defined territory on seasonal migrations. They might have summer and winter bases and move between the two in spring and autumn, drawing on different food resources according to the season.

Large game, small game

Bones found on their camp sites reveal that the Cro-Magnons hunted a wide variety of game including reindeer, bison, horse, deer, elk, wild cattle, ibex, and even the majestic woolly mammoth and woolly rhino. To these must be added smaller game such as hare, and birds such as ptarmigan, grouse and water fowl. The

Caveman art *A wounded bison, its entrails hanging out, dominates a cave painting at Lascaux in France. It was painted 17,000 years ago, by flickering lamplight, in colours mixed from natural pigments such as red and yellow ochre. The painters ground the minerals, then blended the colours on stone palettes and applied them with brushes made of twigs with chewed ends, animal hair, feathers, or pads of fur or moss. Other animals hunted for food included the auroch, or wild ox (below), an ancestor of modern cattle.*

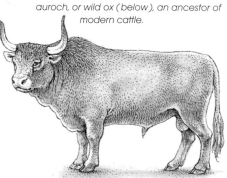

THE FAST AND FURIOUS HUNT FOR REINDEER

Moving stealthily through the long grass and shrubbery, a band of hunters closes in on its prey – a herd of reindeer. With their long, slim, wooden spear-throwers, the hunters quickly pierce a likely victim – already made vulnerable, perhaps, by age or injury. The spear-thrower, tied to the hunter's wrist by strips of leather or sinew, is a short notched baton in which the butt of the spear is lodged before throwing. It works on the lever principle and, in effect, increases the length of the hunter's throwing arm, giving him a better chance of an outright kill. In case the animal does escape, a hunter with a bolas is ready to send his weapon swirling around the reindeer's legs and bring it to the ground. The noise and fury of the hunt sends birds shrieking into the air.

Hook and line *To catch fish, double-pronged hooks of bone were fastened to a long leather line.*

Deadly devices *No amount of twisting could free a fish from the barbs of the deer-antler harpoon (above, right). The wooden spear-thrower (above, left) increased a spear's range and penetration.*

Cro-Magnons were highly skilled and inventive hunters, who varied their techniques according to the season and the prey. Probably the men did most of the hunting, for the very practical reason that most adult women would have small children to care for – a crying baby would scare off the game before the hunt had even started.

A band of hunters might sneak up on a herd of reindeer, bison or horses, pick out a likely victim, run it down and spear it to death. However, a lot might go wrong with this approach. A slight change of wind or a tiny sound would betray the hunters' presence, and the herd would run. To get really close to a large animal, particularly one with horns, was especially dangerous; approaching a wounded one was doubly so.

The Cro-Magnons' chances of success and safety were increased by the invention of the spear-thrower and the bow and arrow. Both enabled the hunters to launch their attack from a greater and safer distance. Moreover, whereas running down a quarry required the combined efforts of all the men of a band, it was possible with a spear-thrower or bow and arrows for one or two men successfully to hunt even the largest animals.

Being opportunists, on such expeditions the men would take advantage of whatever chances were offered to them. However, some hunts were planned with a special quarry in mind, and were executed with military skill and precision.

Mammoths to the slaughter

For example, pits would be dug along well-used trails and covered with branches. The victim would crash into the trap and be unable to climb out. Even a mighty mammoth could then be dispatched, though it might be a long and bloody business.

Reindeer follow set routes on their twice–yearly migrations. Hunters would ambush them at vulnerable moments, such as when they were crossing a river. Herds of grazing animals such as horses and bison are always on the alert, charging off at a hint of danger. This could be exploited. Hunters would position themselves round three sides of a herd, creep in close, then, at a given signal, leap up yelling, throwing stones and perhaps waving flaming torches. The herd would then head for the one open path that apparently led to safety, but in fact they were being driven over the edge of a cliff or into a blind canyon where they were duly slaughtered.

People who lived near the sea or who visited the coasts had another rich source of food – fish, seals, sea birds, shellfish and seaweed. Those who dwelt inland could enjoy freshwater fish such as salmon, trout, eel and pike. One of their ingenious inventions was the gorge – a baited sliver of bone attached to a line of leather or sinew. When a fish took the bait the gorge stuck in its throat and it was hauled in. Nets, made from plant fibres or leather, have not survived, but the existence of small, grooved stones that could have been net weights suggests that nets were in use.

Fishers also invented the leister, a three-pronged spear. A fish was impaled on the central straight prong and the curved prongs on either side stopped it wriggling off.

In the spring the salmon raced upstream to spawn. This was a gastronomic bonanza for the Cro-Magnons, as huge deposits of scales and bones found in some places confirm. Salmon could be speared as they struggled through the shallows, and the crafty Cro-Magnons may well have piled up stones to form a trap. The fish would swim through the funnel-like entrance into a pool from which there was no exit, except on the prongs of a leister. Much of the catch was then dried or smoked and stored.

All members of the band, regardless of age or sex, could contribute to such an expedition.

Body and soul *Powerful drawings of horses and wild goats decorate a wall in a cave at Lascaux. The grid-like patterns may represent animal traps, by which the artist symbolised the capture of the quarry physically and spiritually.*

A SPECIAL ROLE FOR WOMEN

As well as eating large quantities of meat and fish, Stone Age people were apparently fond of vegetarian foods – as the minute scratch marks on their teeth show. It was as gatherers of nuts, berries, roots and the like that the women and young girls of a band came into their own. Every day or two, groups of them would set out with flint axes or wooden digging sticks, hardened by careful treatment in the fire, knives, and leather bags or reed baskets. They had a vast inherited knowledge of the leaves, grasses, roots, flowers, berries and nuts that were good to eat, where they were to be found and at what times of the year. The women looked out for anything else that could be eaten, such as birds' eggs, young birds and animals, lizards and honey. They may have carried spears to defend themselves against wild animals.

Versatile tool *A flint axe was used for felling trees, shaping timber and digging up edible roots. The head of the axe fitted into a bone holder, and this was tied to a wooden handle by a strong leather thong.*

HEAT, HOMES AND THE HEREAFTER

Early humans had been using fire for thousands of years, but it was the Cro-Magnons – named after the cave in southern France in which their bones were found – who discovered that if a certain stone, iron pyrites, is struck with a flint it gives off a spark hot enough to ignite tinder. So a quicker, surer way of starting a fire than striking two sticks together was at hand.

The hearth was the focus of family life, both in the summer – when many people lived in tents of wood and hide – and in the winter, when they sheltered in caves. As well as providing heating and light, the hearth was used for cooking food, and fire was used to ward off hungry predators which might attack the communities. Gathering fuel for the fire and building up a good stock for the winter were essential chores. In most places this meant collecting wood, but on the plains of eastern Europe and Russia, where trees were scarce, bones were used instead. Bones do not burn easily, so shallow channels were dug to draw more air into the bottom of the hearth.

For part of the year our ancestors were probably on the move, travelling between their summer and winter camps. The reindeer hunters, for example, would spend the winter months sheltering in caves of the Dordogne area of France and in the Pyrenees, and then follow the migrating herds to their summer pastures, some to the Atlantic coast, others to the Mediterranean. With the approach of autumn, the herds and their followers would return to the winter grazing lands.

When on the move, people had to be able to carry all their possessions and their young children. There would therefore be very few heavy or fragile objects. Once settled in a base camp, the hunters and gatherers would fan out over the surrounding countryside so as not to deplete the resources or frighten off the game by making too many kills.

Cro-Magnons may even have taken the first steps towards the taming of horses. Some bands may have captured and raised young foals, treating them virtually as pets and then using them as decoys to attract wild horses into the hunters' traps. Another companion joining the hunters was the domestic dog. For centuries some Cro-Magnons must have adopted and reared wolf cubs, which interbred and subtly changed until a clearly recognisable dog evolved. A typical band of hunter-gatherers would consist of some four to six families, numbering in all 20-30 people. There were very few such bands about. The population of Europe could be counted in tens of thousands, rather than millions, but this does not mean that the bands hardly ever saw each other.

Since several bands would exploit the same food source – reindeer or bison, for example – they would naturally be drawn together at certain times in places where their prey regularly congregated. In winter, several bands would head for areas with good caves.

Life expectancy was short, judged by modern standards. Few people lived into their thirties, and those who survived beyond the age of 40 were truly old. A young girl of the period sat for one of the world's earliest-known portraits – a tiny ivory head whose features, still well-defined, show what at least some of the people of Stone Age times looked like. Found in south-west France, the head was carved by a primitive craftsman more than 20,000 years ago.

Many women died while giving birth, and those who survived breast-fed their babies for at least three years, or until the infants had teeth that could cope with adult food. Mortality among small babies and young children was high, and so the population increased very slowly indeed. One estimate puts the entire human population of the world at between 5 and 10 million at the end of the Ice Age, around 10,000 BC.

As boys practised the making and using of tools and weapons, and learned the lore of hunting, so girls followed the older females, learning the business of food gathering and many other tasks; these would include child-rearing, cooking, scraping and treating animal skins, turning the cured hides and furs into clothes, containers and tents, weaving baskets, the correct ways of storing food for the winter, and probably brewing herbal medicines.

An Ice Age rock band

In leisure moments, especially in the evening and during the long days of winter, there were stories to be told that passed on to future generations the traditions of the band and knowledge of the spirits which guided and guarded them, besides reliving the triumphs of past hunts. People would certainly have enjoyed singing and dancing, particularly when there was a meeting between two bands or some ritual to celebrate.

There was certainly music for such occasions. Flutes and whistles made from leg bones have been found, and an object excavated in a French cave resembles the Aborigine 'bull-roarer', making a roaring sound when whirled. At Mezin in the Ukraine were found a 'drum' (a mammoth's shoulder blade, struck by an antler), 'castanets' and 'rattles' (mammoths' jawbones), and a 'xylophone' (a mammoth's hip bones, which gave off different 'notes' according to the area struck).

Thanks to their skill as hunters, and to their inventiveness, our ancestors did not have to spend all their time struggling to survive. They had the leisure and the brain power to think, to consider abstract concepts about life

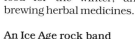

Stone Age portrait

HOME SWEET HOME

Within the mouth of a spacious cave, a group of Stone Age families have pitched their tents for shelter during the winter months. A skin windbreak draped on poles opens briefly as hunters fresh from a kill come in out of the cold. In front of the hunters, two women crouch over a hearth lined with stones and prepare food for the evening meal. Beside them a man stretches a length of cord across a wooden framework as he starts the laborious stringing of a fishing net.

Hand raised in the centre of the cave, a storyteller holds children enthralled with traditional tales of hunting, fighting and playing – in this world and the next. Some of the adults also listen to his accounts – while behind the children a woman weaves a rush mat. Around the oil lamp in the foreground two men play on flutes made from the leg bones of reindeer. Pegged to the ground beside them is an animal skin ready to be treated – a valuable prize from the hunters' last trip into the harsh world outside.

Oil light *Animal fat was burned in a stone lamp with a moss wick.*

Bodies of clay *Stone Age sculptors made their way hundreds of feet underground, along a small river and through a maze of cramped tunnels, in order to carve clay models of two bison, each about 2 ft (610 mm) long. The bison are in a low-ceilinged chamber in the cave of Le Tuc d'Audoubert, in the Pyrenees in south-western France. They were found at the start of this century by three boys who explored the cave by raft and on foot, carrying lamps. Why the sculptors chose so dark and inaccessible a site for their work is a mystery: it is possible that the figures served some function in religious rites.*

Heads of bone *Early hunters used spear-throwers made from deer antlers to catch their prey. Imaginative carvings of birds and animals were particularly common, as this weapon shows. It features a realistically carved young fawn, its head turned to examine two birds perched saucily on its rump. The spear-thrower, which is more than 6 ft (1.8 m) long, comes from the French Pyrenees.*

Fertility figure *A preoccupation with fertility is shown in the so-called 'Venus of Willendorf', a limestone figure 4 in (100 mm) high carved in Austria some 30,000 years ago. The swollen breasts, buttocks and abdomen convey sexuality and pregnancy, and may represent a mother goddess worshipped by Stone Age people.*

and death and to question what supernatural powers ruled the world and everything that happened in it.

Art in nature's cathedrals

As the intellectual and spiritual side of life developed there was another dramatic development: people adapted the manual dexterity they had acquired while making tools, and became artists. Their paintings – mostly hidden away in the darkest and most inaccessible areas of the caves – were possibly an integral part of some long-forgotten religious ritual, performed in hushed whispers in the depths of these natural cathedrals in the bowels of the earth.

The most spectacular examples of the Cro-Magnon peoples' artistic impulses (and probably their religious belief, too) are to be found in the caves of south-west France and northern Spain, where animals arc painted on the walls and ceilings, sometimes in great profusion – as at Lascaux and Altimira. By contrast, there are relatively few human figures.

Some pieces of bone and antler have been found engraved not with pictures of animals but with dots and lines in apparently random doodles. One expert who examined the tiny dots under a high-powered microscope found they had been made at various times and with the use of different tools, and suggested that they recorded the days of each phase of the moon; in other words, these apparently random marks may be in fact a system of notation, representing the world's first calendar.

While some authorities remain sceptical about this, a calendar based on the moon, whose rhythmic phases are readily observable, and on the seasons, would be a useful aid to hunter-gatherers, and quite in keeping with their other achievements and their intellectual development.

Respect for the dead

When a Cro-Magnon died the body was not simply abandoned and left to rot in the open. Even the Neanderthals seem to have had some concept that death was not the end, and that care must be taken of the body. The Cro-Magnons buried their dead in or near the caves and huts in which they lived. Clearly they were anticipating a new life in the world beyond this one, because they were buried in their beaded clothes, along with their tools, weapons, jewellery and favourite possessions. In many burials, red ochre has been found scattered over the corpse. Possibly this was to give the deceased a more lifelike appearance, or else to represent birth blood, as the deceased was reborn, through Mother Earth, into eternal life.

Gradually the ice lost its grip and retreated towards the poles. By about 10,000 BC the animals and plants of northern Europe, Russia and North America were changing dramatically. Some large species died out, including woolly rhinos, giant elks and large deer. At the same time, others retreated with the ice and were replaced by new and smaller species, such as red deer and fallow deer.

Thanks to their ability to adapt and invent, our ancestors stayed put and learned to exploit the new animals and plants in order to survive and prosper.

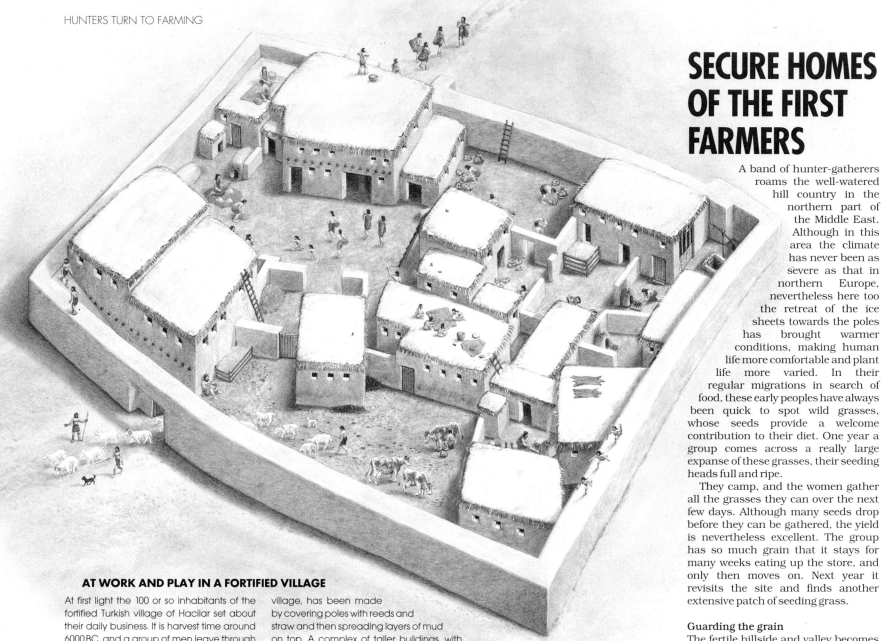

SECURE HOMES OF THE FIRST FARMERS

A band of hunter-gatherers roams the well-watered hill country in the northern part of the Middle East. Although in this area the climate has never been as severe as that in northern Europe, nevertheless here too the retreat of the ice sheets towards the poles has brought warmer conditions, making human life more comfortable and plant life more varied. In their regular migrations in search of food, these early peoples have always been quick to spot wild grasses, whose seeds provide a welcome contribution to their diet. One year a group comes across a really large expanse of these grasses, their seeding heads full and ripe.

They camp, and the women gather all the grasses they can over the next few days. Although many seeds drop before they can be gathered, the yield is nevertheless excellent. The group has so much grain that it stays for many weeks eating up the store, and only then moves on. Next year it revisits the site and finds another extensive patch of seeding grass.

Guarding the grain

The fertile hillside and valley becomes a regular stopping place for the group. So valuable a source of food is 'their' grain that they are tempted to stay for longer and longer periods to make sure no one else takes it.

The women, with the inheritance of thousands of years of observation of plants, recognise that when grains are dropped on the earth they will grow into new plants. Then, one year, the

AT WORK AND PLAY IN A FORTIFIED VILLAGE

At first light the 100 or so inhabitants of the fortified Turkish village of Hacilar set about their daily business. It is harvest time around 6000 BC, and a group of men leave through the north gate to gather in wheat and barley from the outlying fields. From the roof of a two-storey mud house, a lookout watches them depart. Close by, on the roof of the corner granary, two women are grinding corn ready for baking in the oblong oven below. In the courtyard, two more women prepare to dry grain in the oven, so that the husks can be peeled off before the seeds are stored.

Meanwhile, a group of men and women cross the north courtyard, and potters tend their wares in the pottery courtyard, where a ladder leans against a mud-built defensive wall about 5 ft (1.5 m) thick. Some half-dozen red-and-cream-striped clay pots stand drying in front of a small, single-storey house – whose roof, like all those in the

village, has been made by covering poles with reeds and straw and then spreading layers of mud on top. A complex of taller buildings, with their own inner courtyard, house the pottery. On the roof of the main building, rugs and some pots await the women who will soon climb up to spread out fruit to dry in the sun.

Across from the pottery, in the north-east corner of the village, is one of two shrines in which the faithful worship their gods. The other shrine is placed in the south-west corner of the village, diagonally opposite. The villagers draw their water from a stone well to the side of the north-east shrine. In front of the shrine a woman prepares some food in a beehive-shaped outside oven with a smoke hole in the centre; over the wall a villager carries a locally made jar of provisions into a single-storey, communal kitchen. Two pelts are drying in the sun on the roof of the two-storey kitchen, and in the

kitchen courtyard a woman prepares a meal for baking in another outside oven. Above her, on top of the wall, three high-spirited youngsters dash down towards the kitchen in the south-east corner.

In the south courtyard a cow is being milked, while two others docilely await their turn. Meanwhile, staff in hand, a shepherd boy drives his flock of goats through the south gate, where two more shepherds stand by, and out into the country for a day's grazing. Beside the gate a villager takes his ease, sitting against a wall. He alone in the village seems to have time to spare from the daily routine of toil in field and village which was the early farmers' lot.

Building brick *Sun-baked mud bricks were used for building many early homes. This one was made in Jericho more than 5000 years ago.*

women perhaps drop a large quantity of gathered grain by accident, and notice the results when they return the following year. Later still, some of the women deliberately put some of their gathered grain back into the earth to guarantee a crop the next year.

Now the group members have a vested interest in this spot. It is their crop, their land. They take the monumental decision to stay and to

concentrate their efforts into tending their precious asset. They still hunt and gather, but they have settled and are growing a crop. This is one of the great turning points of human history. Unknowingly, they have become the world's first farmers.

Due to a natural mutation, some of the grasses 'sown' by these early farmers did not shed their seeds quite as quickly or easily as the rest. Genetically, they were subtly different. Inevitably, the grain of these plants formed a disproportionately large percentage of the crop gathered and resown by the women. Each year the proportion of the mutated grain increased until, over the years, a new domesticated strain emerged. Similar processes of exploitation and domestication occurred with other grasses, vegetables and fruits.

Food on the hoof

Dogs had already been domesticated, but now they were joined by other animals – sheep, goats, cattle and pigs – taken by the hunters when very young and raised in the camp to provide a guaranteed meat supply. Some unsung genius had the bright idea of allowing some of these walking larders to live long enough to breed, so removing the necessity of seeking out new young from the wild.

In this way the herding side of farming evolved. Large, aggressive animals were killed off quickly before they got too dangerous and before they could breed, so the domesticated

strains that emerged were smaller and more docile than their wild ancestors – and less well-endowed with horns or tusks. Although hard work was required to grow grain and look after the stock, nevertheless a family could now grow more than enough to meet its needs for a year and have milk and wool as well as meat and leather from its animals. A small area that would have only supported one hunter-gatherer could now support a community of about 150 people. The population began to expand much faster, and people stayed together in larger and larger groups, forming the first villages.

Reaper's tool *A bone-handled sickle with saw-like teeth of flint was used by the earliest farmers in the Middle East around 4000 BC to reap their wheat and barley.*

The new Middle Eastern villagers produced new tools to meet new needs – flint-toothed sickles to cut the grain and eventually ploughs to till the land, replacing their old digging sticks. They learned how to build ovens to bake bread and cook other kinds of food. Soon the principle of the oven was adapted to build kilns in which to fire clay bowls and jars for the storage of grain and other foods.

People discovered how to extract linen thread from the flax plant, and how to spin flax and wool and weave it into cloth for clothes, bedding and other domestic purposes. They eventually also made cloth sails for little rafts, canoes and reed boats. They learned that their barley could also be used to make an agreeable drink – beer – and that the juice of grapes could be turned into an

Pots from the kiln *These brightly coloured clay pots grouped around a model of a Hacilar kiln have decorations ranging from traditional red-and-cream stripes to abstract patterns and a four-petalled flower motif.*

even stronger and headier brew. Since people were no longer obliged to move, carrying all their possessions with them, there was no limit to the quantity of goods they could acquire. So they began accumulating personal belongings – including not only basic equipment such as tools, weapons and pottery vessels but also items of furniture.

Now that villagers could produce more food than they needed for themselves they could pay people, in food, to produce the goods they wanted. People also took the goods they had made themselves and exchanged them with other villages which had some useful natural resource of their own – volcanic glass for making knives, for example – or who produced some particularly fine items such as high-quality cloth. The farmers had branched out as traders.

ART OF THE POTTER

Potters living in the Turkish farming village of Hacilar produced ornamental vessels which reflected their fascination with the world around them. Starting around 6000 BC, they drew on two main resources: an established tradition of skilled pottery-making, and the rich and malleable local clay. Using their imagination and flair they ensured that no two products were alike in shape or design.

Among the most popular designs were flowers shaped like Maltese Crosses – which probably symbolised fruitfulness – and human and animal figures, faces and gestures. Large-horned bulls, for example, are thought to have represented the god of fertility, and hands with three and four fingers held up may have been warding off evil spirits.

Wild wheat *The first harvests came from a species of wheat called Einkorn, which grew wild in Turkey and the Middle East 10,000 years ago.*

CITIES IN THE RIVER VALLEYS

Flat plains watered by great rivers were the sites of the world's first civilisations. The Tigris and the Euphrates, the Indus and the Nile flowed through regions with a similar climate, where warm river mud, nourished and replenished by flooding, brought bumper crops. These fed booming populations, and allowed for larger urban settlements than had been possible before.

In Mesopotamia, the land watered by the Tigris and Euphrates, by 3500 BC the world's first cities were already functioning, with workshops, schools, brick-built houses, majestic palaces and temples. Their people used the wheel, the plough, a system of arithmetic and an annual calendar. Above all, they developed the skill of writing. In the Indus Valley, the area of modern Pakistan, a tightly organised society arose, with planned towns and a religion which may have been the precursor of Hinduism.

THE FIRST CITIES
3500–1500 BC

WHEELS FOR THE POTTER AND THE CART

A flood river was a capricious mistress. In Mesopotamia, for example, the Euphrates had a tendency to change its course, turning fields to deserts and causing villages to be abandoned. The floods came in the spring, and farmers learned to build dykes to protect their crops. They also dug out basins and canals so that water could be stored and distributed to fields some distance away from the river itself.

Banking up the river and scooping out the ditches was a continuous task. Year after year dams had to be kept in good repair, and canals had to be dredged to prevent them from choking with silt. The irrigation systems covered whole districts, eventually uniting thousands of villagers in a collaborative effort.

Strong and lasting forms of government were needed to keep the enterprise going and to ensure fair distribution – so that no farmer stole the water destined for another, for example. Irrigation works did more than boost crop yields. They bred the habit of obedience to political authority, out of which city-states would develop and flourish.

A plough for the farmer
Date palms lined the canals, while wheat and barley were grown in fields that produced two harvests a year. The Mesopotamian peoples were good pastoralists too, keeping dairy herds and raising sheep in numbers: the sheepskin kilt was traditional costume. But cereal crops above all accounted for the region's prosperity, and the plough was invented as an aid to cultivation. It probably developed from weighted wooden digging sticks as a kind of large hoe, the first examples

Silent worship *A Sumerian peasant woman sits holding a small pot – made, perhaps, on the newly invented potter's wheel. Vessels in which to store the fruits of the harvest were a basis of early city life. The alabaster sculpture, almost 7 1/2 in (190 mm) high, dates from about 3000 BC. The Sumerians were often depicted with their arms clasped in homage to their gods.*

being pulled by men, women and even children. By 4000 BC, however, a more efficient instrument had been introduced, pulled by two oxen with a driver walking behind it to guide the plough and drive its wooden blade into the earth.

At first the plough beam was fastened by ropes to the oxen's horns. The yoke came as a further improvement, and in due course the bronze share replaced the wooden blade. For all its floods, Mesopotamia had little rainfall, and the soil baked hard in summer. Ploughs allowed vast new areas to be broken up and sown, further boosting grain supplies.

For sowing itself, an ox-drawn seed drill was devised. This was an instrument for planting seed in rows instead of 'broadcasting', or scattering by hand. The plough-like device made a groove in the soil, while seed trickled into it by means of a funnel and tube. School and reference books of the past habitually credited an early 18th-century English farmer, Jethro Tull, with the invention of the seed drill. Yet it is clearly shown in a carved stone seal from ancient Sumer, the most southerly part of Mesopotamia, whose 12 or more city-states formed the core of the Middle East civilisation.

Wheels for the cart

To and from the cities plodded oxen and asses pulling another brilliant invention: the wheeled cart. The wheel itself – the basis of so much subsequent technology – seems first to have appeared in Mesopotamia in the form of the potter's wheel, a hand-spun disc that permitted speedier production of vessels.

The earliest evidence for a pottery wheel dates back to about 3500 BC, but it was not until some 250 years later that the wheel was adapted for use in transport. The earliest type of cartwheel was a solid affair, without spokes, formed by shaped planks of wood and protected with leather. The carts themselves were four-wheeled vehicles used to trundle goods from farms to markets, or to carry officials in ceremonial processions; they were pulled by oxen or wild asses, as horses, though known elsewhere, were not yet in use in Mesopotamia.

The great Sumerian cities – Ur, Eridu, Lagash and Nippur among them – frequently warred among themselves and never merged into a strong unified state like Egypt. Each was set amidst fertile and irrigated land, and prospered by agriculture and cattle breeding. Building stone, metals and good timber were all scarce in the Mesopotamian mud plain, but with copious supplies of grain and wool available for export, the Sumerians were able to bring in from other regions whatever vital raw materials they were lacking .

Ur – the Biblical 'Ur of the Chaldees', situated by the Euphrates river – was a great warehousing centre to which goods came by land, river and sea. Hundreds of clay tablets show graphically how the vital foreign trade was organised. Silver and lead were brought down the Euphrates from the mountain edge of present-day Turkey. Timber came from Syria, and from heights to the north-east. From Afghanistan, traders brought semi-precious stones such as lapis lazuli.

Stone and copper arrived from Oman, while ships from Ur plied down the coast of Arabia bringing back gold and incense. A thriving trading post was set up at Dilmun, on the island of Bahrain in the Persian Gulf, to handle some of these commodities. Thus the so-called 'sea kings' of Ur did a prosperous annual trade in imports and exports.

Sumerian vessels included heavy barges and ships with mast, deck, cabin and oarsmen. Some could carry up to 36 tons of goods, and seamen were adventurous enough to voyage beyond the Strait of Hormuz and around Iran to do business with the people of the Indus Valley.

In 1977, the Norwegian anthropologist Thor Heyerdahl built a large reed boat along Sumerian lines and sailed the vessel, called *Tigris*, across the gale-torn Indian Ocean to prove that such a long and arduous voyage was possible.

PROGRESS OF THE WHEEL

The first people to use the wheel were probably Mesopotamian pottery workers who, around 3500 BC, built up pots on hand-operated turntables. About 250 years later they had carts with solid wooden wheels. The earliest vehicle wheels consisted of two or three sections of plank cut to form a disc and fastened together with wooden or copper brackets. They were fixed in place with linchpins through the ends of the axles. Lighter spoked wheels arrived around 2000 BC. The spokes radiated from the hub, and they were held together by a one-piece rim made of wood.

In harness The wheeled cart drawn by oxen, in a model from Mohenjo Daro, resembles the bullock carts used in modern Pakistan.

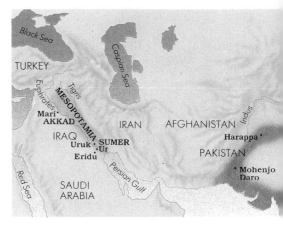

Where city life began *The world's first cities were built in two distinct and similar areas: the valleys of the Tigris and Euphrates rivers in the Middle East (coloured green), and to the east the valley of the Indus (coloured orange). Both well-watered lands were ideal for farming.*

Corn cutter

A bronze sickle with a sharp cutting edge was used by early farmers in the Middle East to harvest the cereal crops. The handle is a modern reconstruction.

Workers on the march *A parade of fishermen and herdsmen and their animals forms one of the mosaic panels of the Royal Standard of Ur. The 'standard', a wooden box about 18 in (460 mm) long, was probably the sounding board of a musical instrument used around 2500 BC at the court of Ur, one of the leading Sumerian city-states. The figures are made from an inlay of shell against a background of lapis lazuli and red limestone set in bitumen. The workmen's role was to serve the gods by providing the ruling leisured class with meat and fish, and by looking after the working animals which pulled carts and carried burdens.*

In the round *A clay model shows a circular, Sumerian building, which was probably a fort or a shrine.*

BEER, BRONZE AND BODIES BEAUTIFUL

To tent-dwelling desert nomads whose long wanderings brought them into Mesopotamia, ancient Ur must have appeared a metropolis of astonishing grandeur. Rising from the fertile plain of the Euphrates, with its plush quilt of cultivated fields, the city was visible for miles around. Ringed by canal and rampart, Ur was built on a mound to prevent flooding, and had at its heart a stepped pyramid of mud brick rising to a soaring temple.

Around the sacred precinct spread the houses of more than 24,000 inhabitants, closely packed along narrow, winding streets with scattered shops, bazaars and taverns among them. Exotic wares were unloaded at the wharves of Ur's two harbours, while through the unpaved streets passed wealthy merchants and slaves, busy craftsmen, palace staff and processions of priests who worshipped the city's patron deity, the powerful moon god Nanna.

Bare chest and fitted dress
In the early days, Sumerian men went barechested and barefooted through town, clad only in one form or another of the traditional ringed kilt. Later, a long shirt-like garment was worn, often with a fringed shawl. Women went clad in a draped garment or fitted dress, and their headgear was rich in variety. Hair might be worn in braids coiled around the head, free-flowing with a headband, or topped by a helmet-like hat.

For ornament, Sumerian jewellers produced fantastically elegant work in gold, silver and semiprecious stones. Bright beads of azure-blue lapis lazuli were particular favourites, often worn with reddish carnelian for contrast in bracelets and necklaces.

At night, people generally slept on mats, for although some homes had beds the furnishings of most of the mud-built houses were relatively sparse, consisting chiefly of chests, low tables, stools and chairs. Crockery – in the form of pots, jugs, vases and so on – was by contrast abundant, mud again furnishing the vital raw material.

With their vast grain harvests, the Sumerians had loaves of unleavened bread for their staple diet. Wheat and barley were pulped to make a kind of porridge. Other food stuffs included onions, leeks, cucumbers, beans, garlic and lentils. From the herdsmen's

'WELCOME TO MY HOME!'
Arms outstretched in welcome, the white-robed master of the house greets an early morning caller in the reception room of his two-storey home in Ur. The windowless, mud-brick house built around a central, open-air courtyard is a typical residence of a well-to-do businessman such as this jewel merchant. To the side of the two men is a small family tomb, a feature of every such home. Next to this is the household chapel, with the shrine tucked against the whitewashed dividing wall. From the shrine, steps lead down to a large storage cellar.

In the tiled courtyard another recently arrived visitor has his feet washed over a drainage hole by a bearded slave. Beside them stands an oil storage jar, one of several spread about the house. Near the blue-clad visitor another servant sweeps the tiles.

Meanwhile, in the long narrow kitchen two slave girls prepare to cook a meal, using locally produced pottery bowls. Near the kitchen is a small bedroom. On the floor above there is more activity as the mistress of the house gets dressed in her bedroom. As soon as she is ready she will go downstairs and help her husband to entertain his guests. In the corridor a maid carries towels to the bathroom at the back of the house. Then she will tidy up the bedroom of the young son of the house, who left in a hurry as he was late for school. Beyond the bedroom, steps lead up to the flat roof where the family often sleep out beneath the stars.

Kitchen contrasts *A cheap clay sieve pot could be found in even the humblest of Sumerian kitchens. But only the well-to-do could afford expensive items such as this bronze water vessel with a decorated spout-head. Although it resembles a modern kettle in shape, the vessel was probably used for filtering unboiled water.*

goats and cattle came milk, butter and cheese. The palms which grew so abundantly along the irrigation canals yielded dates, which might be eaten fresh, dried, or pressed into a thick syrup. Beef and mutton added further variety, and fish was very popular. There were numerous fish sellers, and even restaurants where fish could be bought ready-fried.

Beer was the great Sumerian drink. Brewing may have started soon after the production of cereal crops, for it was originally a job done by house-wives making the staple porridge or bread. Mesopotamian texts refer to 19 different types of beer, varying according to the grain (wheat, barley, or blended), the aromatic plants used as flavouring and preservative agents, and the honey and malt they contained. Wine was available in much more limited quantities, and was strictly for the well-to-do. The leisured classes also enjoyed more refined entertainments such as poetry and music played upon the lyre, harp and drum. There were board games too: a delightful gaming board has survived from ancient Sumer, having 20 squares of shell, incised with patterns in black and red paste. The so called 'Game of Ur' had an in-built drawer for the tokens which were moved after casting dice, or throwing sticks.

The Game of Ur, for two players

Master and mistress

In the homes of rich and poor alike, the father was very much the master. He had the legal right to divorce a barren wife, to take concubines and even, under certain circumstances, to sell his wife and children into slavery. These rights were enshrined in the earliest-known code of written laws, compiled under Ur-Nammu in 2111 BC. Nevertheless, a woman in Ur had some rights. She was permitted to own property, for example, and was allowed to give testimony in court cases.

The Sumerians also had a liking for high-minded, homely proverbs such as: 'Pay heed to the word of your mother as though it were the word of god.' On a more cynical note there was the reflection: 'For a man's pleasure there is marriage; on thinking it over there is divorce.'

Proverbs, again, made frequent references to people's wealth. 'We are doomed to die; let us spend. We shall

live long; let us save', was one old saw. Another, alluding to the headaches that come with ownership of property, observed, 'He who possesses much silver may be happy. But he who has nothing at all can sleep peacefully at nights.'

The rise of farming and city-dwelling led to great possessions of goods and money, and to surpluses of commodities such as corn. These surpluses supported specialist crafts-men whose improving technologies transformed everyday life. Potters mass-produced vessels upon the wheel, while full-time metalworkers developed vital new skills through experimenting in their workshops and exchanging ideas. Using improved kilns to smelt their imported supplies of copper and tin, Sumerian smiths discovered how to produce bronze, a material much harder than copper alone. The Bronze Age began around 3500 BC in Mesopotamia, and here too smiths learned the art of making bronze castings by the lost-wax method. In this procedure a wax model was covered in clay. The wax was then melted and drained away so that the mould, or hollow it left behind, could receive the metal. Goldsmiths mean-while mastered the art of beating their precious metal into wafer-thin sheets, and spinning it into threads of delicate filigree work. Sumerian carpenters used saws and drills to shape their timbers. In turn, using wedge-shaped bricks, the builders developed some of the first arches – spanning small culverts in the water and sewage systems.

Jewels of glass

Ever inventive, the Sumerians also exploited their country's oil reserves, using the bitumen, or pitch, that seeped from the ground as bonding for brickwork and waterproofing for boats. No one knows who first stumbled on the secret of making glass from sand, soda and limestone. But it may well have been a jeweller in Mesopotamia or there-abouts, while he was experimenting with beads and glazes. Certainly the skill had been acquired, both in Sumer and Egypt, before 2000 BC.

It was not until the next millenium that the first glass vessels were made, however. Pieces of glass at this stage seem to have been treated much like rare artificial gemstones.

BLACK EYES AND FALSE BEARDS

The height of beauty among the Sumerians was considered to be heavily made-up eyes, faces and hands – with the emphasis on the eyes. Both men and women used bluish-black antimony to line and highlight their eyes; in addition, they blackened their eyebrows and eyelashes, giving them a dramatic and, to modern eyes, a somewhat sinister appearance. Occasionally, Middle Eastern kings wore false beards to make them seem more dignified and grave.

Sumerian women – and sometimes men – were also fond of painting their faces with white lead, so that they resembled masks. In stark contrast they coloured their lips and cheeks blood red with henna, and applied henna to their fingernails and the palms of their hands. They smoothed their skin with pumice stone, curled and perfumed their hair, took perfumed baths, and, to repel vermin, anointed their bodies with oil.

Among the women's toilet articles were shell-shaped gold cosmetic cases, eyebrow tweezers, metal toothpicks, and small metal rods for pushing down cuticles.

Beauty aids *Sumerian men and women used paints in such colours as charcoal, blue and brown to make up their eyes. The cakes of paint were kept in gold cosmetic pots and small shells, found in tombs near Ur dating from 5000 BC.*

Gold earrings from an Ur tomb

Leaves of gold *A headdress with gold leaf pendants is suspended from a double row of carnelian and lapis-lazuli beads. The headdress, dating from about 2600 BC, was found in a grave at Ur.*

A DAY IN THE LIFE OF A SUMERIAN SCHOOLBOY

Shunnu runs at breakneck pace through the alleys leading to the great palace and its adjoining school. Arriving in the classroom just in time, Shunnu takes his place at a mud-brick bench. All morning, he and his class-mates work at their writing exercises. The teacher has prepared their clay tablets with neat lists of words down one side. Their task is to copy them to the best of their ability.

Today the list is of gemstones. Since Shunnu is the son of a jewel merchant he recognises some of the words. Yet still his fingers become numb from pressing the reed stylus into the clay, and his eyes blur from concentrating on the dancing patterns of wedge-shaped markings. All the while, the teacher moves among the benches. 'Come, Shunnu, you can do better than that', he grumbles at one clumsy effort, and the boy

feels the tap of the rod across his shoulders. At lunchtime Shunnu eats the bread rolls and dried figs that his mother has prepared, and he chats to the other pupils – many of them sons of palace officials. In the afternoon there are oral tests in multiplication. Two of the palace boys receive canings for getting their sums wrong; Shunnu's heart pounds as his turn comes round; but the teacher's nod tells him his answers are correct. By evening Shunnu is tired – and there are still three days to go before the next holy day. Wearily he walks home to tell his father how the day has gone.

DEATH OF KINGS, BIRTH OF LEARNING

When a king of the Sumerian city-state of Ur died he did not go alone to his tomb. His entire household of some 70 people was buried with him, having taken poison in order to follow their sovereign into the next life – where they would continue to serve him loyally as before.

The preparation for this mass burial was meticulous. First a long, sloping shaft was dug down to a pit that would serve as the tomb chamber. This was filled with rich offerings, and the king's corpse was placed in it, with a handful of personal retainers. The chamber was then sealed, and a great procession of attendants moved down into the shaft. These included court ladies in resplendent golden headdresses, guards with sheathed daggers, musicians strumming bulls'-head lyres, grooms with ox-drawn chariots, and soldiers bearing copper spears.

All carried a small cup from which they drank a lethal drug before lying down by the tomb chamber to prepare for eternity. The musicians continued to play their lyres until the end, when they too took poison and succumbed. The shaft was then filled in with several layers of earth and clay, amid further ritual offerings and libations. The lack

MAN-MADE LINK WITH HEAVEN

The monumental ziggurat, or pyramid-shaped religious complex, at Ur was built in about 2100 BC to the glory of the moon god Nanna. The ziggurat was seen as a link between heaven and earth; the god was believed to alight in the temple on its summit and to descend to mingle with his followers in a larger temple at the base.

The ziggurat – from the Assyrian word *ziqquratu*, or 'mountain top' – had a steep, triple staircase leading from the ground to the 80 ft (24 m) summit. It had a core of solid mud bricks, reinforced with wooden beams and bound with reed matting, and a casing of fired bricks set in bitumen. It measured some 700 ft (213 m) around the base and its three tiers contained the living quarters of the temple staff, as well as shrines and storehouses,

The ziggurat was the centre of Ur's religious life, and there was a constant coming and going of priests, temple officers, slaves and worshippers. As it rose above the highest imaginable water level, it also served as a place of refuge in time of flood.

Bringer of war *Bearded and brooding, this hollow copper head found near Ninevah represents one of the rulers of Akkad, the dynasty which from around 2300 BC conquered the whole of Mesopotamia, including the Sumerian city-states. The warrior dynasty, founded by King Sargon, set up the first powerful, unified empire between the Tigris and the Euphrates.*

of resistance on the part of the attendants indicated a fatalistic obedience both to their sovereign and to their gods. Certainly, all the evidence suggests that religion was very important to the Sumerians. They believed that the gods ruled the earth and that men were created to be their servants. Each city was regarded as belonging to a particular god or goddess, whose earthly home was the city's temple, the scene of elaborate rituals conducted by a hierarchy of priests.

Hundreds of other deities looked after every aspect of life and death. The greatest was An, the sky god who remained aloof in the heavens taking little interest in earthly affairs. There were complex rankings of priests, as well as armies of secular workers and slaves to support them. For a city's patron deity owned not only the urban community but also the cultivated fields and villages which made up the whole city-state.

> 'You can have a Lord,
> you can have a King, but
> the man to fear is the
> tax-collector.'
> SUMERIAN PROVERB

Some land was worked by villagers directly for the gods, under supervision by temple officers. Some was allotted to temple staff as a reward for their services, and much was let to farmers who surrendered part of their produce to the temple as rent. The priests were the leading collectors of taxes – already, by 2500 BC, burdensome features of everyday life.

Words and figures

The Sumerians were the first people to develop a system of arithmetic. Adding, subtracting and multiplying were important skills when handling goods such as sacks of grain or heads of cattle in quantities. The Sumerians also developed an efficient system of weights and measures, and their supreme invention – that of writing – arose from the practical need to keep records of goods for the purposes of trade, or tax collection.

Those records began in the simplest way with picture images of the item – an ox head, for example – and a number of dots to indicate the quantity. Symbols were drawn on a soft clay tablet using a sharpened reed. The tablet was then baked in a kiln to harden it.

Originally, lists of items were arranged in vertical columns starting from the top right-hand side. Around 3000 BC, however, scribes found that they could write better by turning the tablets and writing from left to right, in horizontal rows.

At the same time, the original, pointed stylus was abandoned in favour of one with a wedge-shaped tip. Scratching with a point was prone to leave untidy ridges; the new wedge-shaped stylus could be pressed into the clay to leave a crisper impression. Stylised images, composed entirely of cuneiform, or 'wedge-shaped', marks made up the writing system used in Mesopotamia.

Signs and syllables

By about 2500 BC, however, the original picture signs were reduced to such stylised symbolism that the original objects could hardly be recognised. Scribes also started to use characters to represent ideas, actions, feelings and so on, rather than concrete objects alone. Ambiguities sometimes resulted, however. The picture image of a foot, for example, might mean to come or go or stand and so on. Thousands of different characters would have to be invented to encompass the full range of words in use.

The eventual solution was to use signs phonetically – that is, to indicate sounds rather than actual objects. By this method, in English, an abstract concept such as 'treason' might be represented by placing the image of a 'tree' alongside that of , say, the 'sun'.

Using a fairly limited repertoire of syllables it was possible to build up any word. The Sumerian system included some 600 signs which had to be memorised. The scribes failed to condense the system further by breaking syllables down into the two dozen or so letters that make up the modern alphabet. Nevertheless, their own method proved remarkably flexible, permitting a rich literature to flourish alongside workaday texts such as legal contracts and bills of sale. The Sumerian system of arithmetic was based on the unit of 60 – unlike our unit of 10 – and has survived

through the centuries in our hour of 60 minutes and circle of 360 degrees.

In early times, Sumerian doctors relied heavily on the driving out of demons by magical rites, but practical remedies were also available. There were dressings, plasters and poultices to bind wounds and reduce infection. Many of these included the use of salt as an antiseptic and saltpetre as an astringent, to harden the skin and reduce bleeding. One of the world's earliest prescriptions, for an infected limb, dates from 2100 BC: 'Pass through a sieve and then knead together turtle shells, salt and mustard. Then wash the diseased part with good beer and hot water, and rub with the mixture. Then rub again with oil, and put on a poultice of pounded pine.'

Much attention was given to astrology and the casting of horoscopes. By studying the heavens to discover the seasonal patterns that were all important to farmers, astronomers also worked out a calendar, based on the behaviour of the moon in the night sky. Its 28 day cycles gave a year of 12 months – with a few odd days left over. The moon goes through four phases in each month; these quarters produced the concept of the seven-day week.

ESCAPE FROM THE FLOOD

Among the earliest inscriptions made on clay tablets by Sumerians using their new skills in writing were epic tales of their legendary heroes. They include the story of the quest by King Gilgamesh to learn the secret of eternal life. He sets out in search of a sage called Utnapishtim, and finds him after crossing the Ocean of Death. Utnapishtim tells Gilgamesh how a great flood, sent by the gods because mankind had so displeased them, had destroyed all his fellow men. Helped by Ea, the god of wisdom, Utnapishtim saved himself and his family by building an ark and floating for seven days and nights until they reached their present home. This episode clearly shared a common source with the Biblical story of Noah and the Flood. From Utnapishtim, Gilgamesh learns that immortality is a gift bestowed by the gods.

Folk hero *A wall sculpture of Gilgamesh, the legendary hero-king of Sumer, shows him bearing an axe and a young lion, symbol of power. The sculpture comes from Khorsabad.*

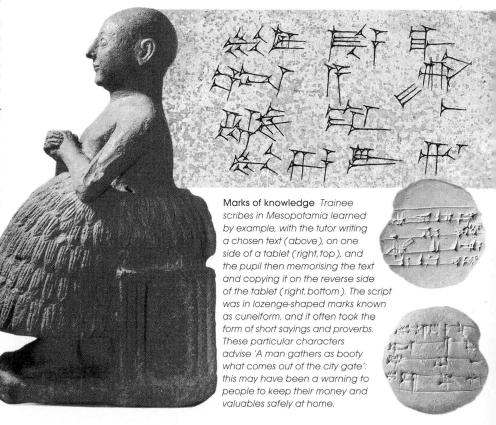

Man of learning *A clay model of a Sumerian teacher-scribe from the city of Lagash reflects the dignity and propriety for which the schoolmasters were renowned.*

Marks of knowledge *Trainee scribes in Mesopotamia learned by example, with the tutor writing a chosen text (above), on one side of a tablet (right, top), and the pupil then memorising the text and copying it on the reverse side of the tablet (right, bottom). The script was in lozenge-shaped marks known as cuneiform, and it often took the form of short sayings and proverbs. These particular characters advise 'A man gathers as booty what comes out of the city gate': this may have been a warning to people to keep their money and valuables safely at home.*

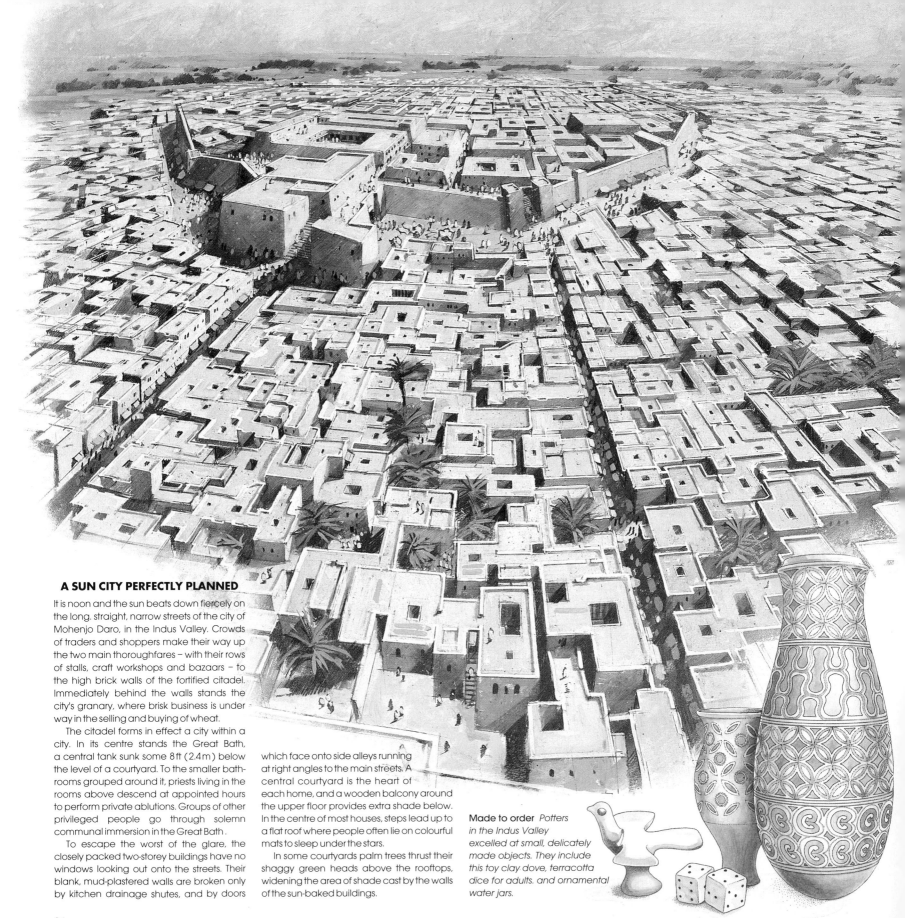

A SUN CITY PERFECTLY PLANNED

It is noon and the sun beats down fiercely on the long, straight, narrow streets of the city of Mohenjo Daro, in the Indus Valley. Crowds of traders and shoppers make their way up the two main thoroughfares – with their rows of stalls, craft workshops and bazaars – to the high brick walls of the fortified citadel. Immediately behind the walls stands the city's granary, where brisk business is under way in the selling and buying of wheat.

The citadel forms in effect a city within a city. In its centre stands the Great Bath, a central tank sunk some 8 ft (2.4 m) below the level of a courtyard. To the smaller bath-rooms grouped around it, priests living in the rooms above descend at appointed hours to perform private ablutions. Groups of other privileged people go through solemn communal immersion in the Great Bath.

To escape the worst of the glare, the closely packed two-storey buildings have no windows looking out onto the streets. Their blank, mud-plastered walls are broken only by kitchen drainage shutes, and by doors which face onto side alleys running at right angles to the main streets. A central courtyard is the heart of each home, and a wooden balcony around the upper floor provides extra shade below. In the centre of most houses, steps lead up to a flat roof where people often lie on colourful mats to sleep under the stars.

In some courtyards palm trees thrust their shaggy green heads above the rooftops, widening the area of shade cast by the walls of the sun-baked buildings.

Made to order *Potters in the Indus Valley excelled at small, delicately made objects. They include this toy clay dove, terracotta dice for adults, and ornamental water jars.*

GRID-PATTERN TOWNS BY THE INDUS

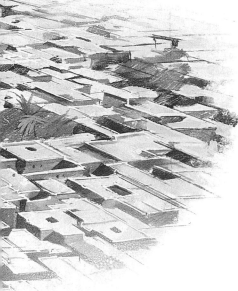

When people started living at close quarters in towns instead of villages they faced a new set of problems. To get rid of household slops or to answer the call of nature a town-dweller could not simply use the nearest field or ditch, as before. At Mohenjo Daro, one of the great cities of the Indus Valley civilisation, the rulers came up with an ingenious solution: they built the world's first drainage system.

The houses of Mohenjo Daro had bathrooms and toilets. Water and sewage ran out of them through earthenware pipes into the city's drains, which ran under the streets. Sumps and manhole covers were placed at intervals, allowing the municipal cleaners to climb down and clear any blockage. Eventually, all waste found an outlet at disposal points outside the city.

The Indus civilisation arose around 2500 BC, after small communities of hill farmers started to colonise the fertile valleys of the River Indus, in what is now Pakistan. Here, as in Mesopotamia, the climate was swelteringly hot, and the low rainfall meant that irrigation was essential for farming on any scale.

Like the Euphrates, the Indus was prone to flood – and with a particularly terrifying, erratic force fuelled by the melting snows of the Himalayas. Dykes and canals to control the floods and distribute the life-giving waters needed constant attention, and perhaps this was what led to the especially strong form of central government that developed.

The earliest town planners

Certainly, everything suggests that the rulers had immense power: power not just to rule over their towns but to create them from scratch. For besides main drainage, the Indus peoples also achieved another breakthrough – as the world's first town planners. Whereas

Mesopotamia's great settlements grew up in more or less haphazard fashion, those of the Indus were laid according to set patterns.

The titanic work must have involved supervisors directing the efforts of thousands of builders and engineers. More than 100 towns have been identified, the most impressive being built on gigantic mounds of earth and rubble to raise them above the flood plain. Biggest of all were the great cities of Harappa and Mohenjo Daro, each more than 3 miles (4.8 km) in circumference, including a fortified citadel and lower town. Each was also designed according to a grid system, much like that used in many North American cities today.

Police in the streets

Ruler-straight streets running north-south were crossed by others running east-west. The main streets could be up to 33 ft (10 m) wide, suggesting swarming traffic and opportunities for great parades. The side roads were much narrower, though, with many back lanes and alleys winding between the main housing blocks.

One-room huts situated at the main intersections may have been guard posts for some sort of police force. There are tantalising gaps in our knowledge about the civilisation, for although the Indus peoples invented a system of writing, only short examples of their script have survived and no one has been able to decipher them.

Their form of government is an enigma. They may have had kings – but no royal tombs have been discovered. Some historians have suggested that an all-powerful priesthood held sway, others that the rulers acted like a military junta. Certainly, a great deal about the known sites suggests soldierly discipline and regimentation.

Spinning stone *A terracotta spinning wheel from the Indus Valley was used in the making of vividly coloured dresses and cloaks. The flat, round stone was used to weight the base of a hand-operated wooden spindle.*

Even the innumerable mud bricks came in standard sizes, with kiln-baked bricks for foundation work and civic buildings, and sun-dried mud bricks for private houses.

Regimented as they may have been, the people of the Indus still enjoyed life. They liked playing dice, for example, and they tootled on clay whistles shaped like birds. Toys for children included ceramic monkeys that danced on strings, while real monkeys were kept as pets. Caged birds twittered away in many a home, and it seems that the Indus peoples may even have kept singing insects in small pottery containers. Dogs and cats were other popular pets. A telltale find at one Indus site was a brick – obviously laid out fresh in the sun to dry – which bears the footprint of a cat, slightly overlapped by that of a dog that was chasing it at full speed.

Transport by water and land

Shapely boats, with high prow and stern, central mast and long steering oar, plied the rivers. Camels and pack-horses trudged the overland routes, and the biggest loads were carried in lumbering, two-wheeled ox carts just like those seen in Indian villages today. They had the same high sides, with no back or front, and even the same standard gauge of 3½ ft (1.06 m) between the wheels.

The surplus wealth these hard-working farmers produced meant that their traders did a brisk business with Mesopotamia. They brought copper from Baluchistan; lead and silver from Rajasthan; gold, tin and lapis lazuli from Afghanistan; lead and rare shells from southern India; turquoise from Iran, and jade from the Far East.

No rich temple buildings have been found, and there is little evidence of the religious beliefs of the Indus peoples – who seem to have collapsed before Aryan invaders around 1500 BC. Some baked clay figures of a fertility goddess have been found, as well images of a seated male figure in a horned head-dress. This may be an early version of Shiva, the god of destruction and renewal in the later Hindu religion.

Dancing girl *A bronze statuette of a dancing girl, hand provocatively on hip, was found at Mohenjo Daro. The figure, 4½ in (115 mm) high, is naked except for a necklace and rows of metal armlets.*

RAZORS, MIRRORS, BANGLES AND BEADS

The people of the Indus Valley were no strangers to personal vanity. Men shaved with the help of copper razors and polished copper mirrors. Women decked themselves out with elaborate hairstyles and wore bangles, necklaces and anklets, beads of soapstone or paste, and ear-rings and finger rings of copper. The Indus people were the first to grow cotton, from which they made fabrics which they dyed in bright colours.

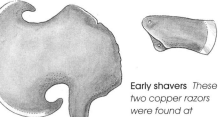

Early shavers *These two copper razors were found at Mohenjo Daro. Originally they were attached to handles.*

GOOD LIFE AS A GIFT OF THE NILE

The Ancient Egyptians knew they were the special favourites of the gods. Every year, the waters of the River Nile flooded over their land and deposited rich silt that turned desert into farmland. The river gave them fish and waterfowl to eat, mud for bricks and paper from the papyrus reeds that grew on its banks, and a broad highway on which people and goods could travel. Beyond the river valley lay deserts which protected the Egyptians from all but the most determined invaders. Those apparently barren wastes were actually a source of natural riches – gold and copper, semiprecious stones for jewellery, and a variety of stones for building. With the exception of good-quality timber, it seemed that the gods had lavishly endowed the people of Egypt with everything they needed.

Egypt's history is a long one. The Nile valley had already been settled for centuries before the states of Upper and Lower Egypt were united under one king around 3000 BC. From then on, Egypt retained its distinctive culture until in 30 BC it became part of the Roman Empire. This long history – one and a half times as long as the present age of the Christian era – included several distinctive periods of greatness. During the 500 year period known as the New Kingdom, which began around 1570 BC, Egypt reached its greatest extent and the height of its prosperity.

ANCIENT EGYPT 3000 – 30 BC

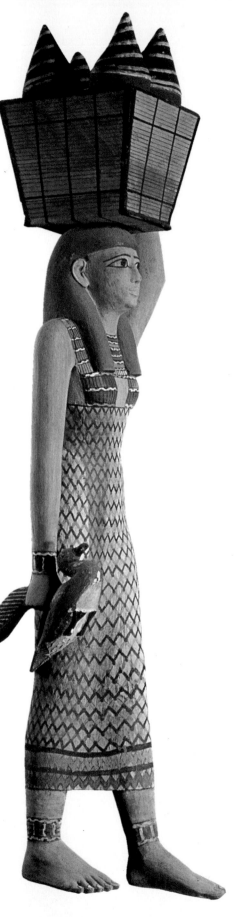

ALL THE KING'S MEN, WOMEN AND CHILDREN

The Egyptian people held their king in such awe that they felt it was disrespectful to refer to him directly. So they would say 'The Great House has decided...', rather in the way that Americans and Britons now say 'The White House' or 'Buckingham Palace'. The Egyptian words for 'Great House' were pronounced something like *per a'o* – hence our word pharaoh.

The pharaoh had absolute power. He owned the whole land, headed the country's administration, commanded the army, and initiated all policy, foreign and domestic. He was the fount of all law and justice, head of the cults of all the gods, and the intermediary between heaven and earth.

The pharaoh was no mere human. Egyptians believed that the land's first kings were the sun god Re and his descendants Shu, Geb, Osiris and Horus. Kingship subsequently passed to humans, but the king was still a unique being. When he sat on the throne, arrayed in his full ceremonial regalia, the spirit of the god Horus entered him and he became god incarnate on earth, a ruler whose pronouncements had all the weight of divine utterances. So the king and, to a lesser extent, his family were set apart from the rest of humanity, and to keep the divine blood pure, kings preferred to marry their sisters or half-sisters.

Setting up home

Family life for more humble folk started with marriage at about 20 years of age for men, and slightly younger for women. Parents were expected to choose their children's spouse, but the abundance of Egyptian love poetry suggests that young people also had ideas on the choice of partner. The provision of the family home was usually the husband's responsibility,

Land of plenty *A servant girl supports a basket of wine jars with conical stoppers, and carries a bird for her master's table. She displays the Ancient Egyptians' delight in adornment: jewellery decorates her wrists, ankles and neck, and she gazes ahead with eyes enhanced by make-up.*

although some couples lived with the parents of one of the partners, or in a house belonging to the wife.

A wife brought a dowry of personal goods and furniture to the new home, and the husband settled a maintenance allowance on his wife. The couple set up a marriage fund, to which the man contributed two-thirds of the value and the woman the rest. The fund passed to the children on their parents' death or divorce, and ensured their security.

Continuing the line

Egyptians longed for children, and not only for the love and happiness that they brought. Children supplied a form of insurance: they worked for their parents, and cared for them in their old age. Most important of all, they would give their parents a proper burial and make regular offerings at their tombs, ensuring their smooth passage into the next world and a contented eternity.

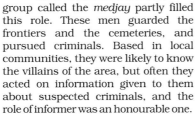

Scarab beetle amulet

A childless couple would try a variety of medicines, spells and prayers to secure the longed-for baby. If these failed, they could adopt one – a young relative, or the child of a couple who had more offspring than they could provide for. Once the longed-for child arrived, either by natural means or adoption, the anxious parents guarded it with all the amulets, prayers and spells they could muster.

Rights for women

In Egypt a wife was called the 'Lady of the House'; she ran the home and family and was entitled to respect and consideration. Even if a man kept concubines the wife's rights, and those of her children, were unassailable.

While she was married, a wife's personal property remained under her own control. She might allow her husband to administer lands for her, but he could not dispose of them. Women could make wills and leave their personal property to anyone they chose.

Divorce proceedings could be started by both wives and husbands. A divorced wife had her personal property and her dowry returned, and retained custody of her children, who received the marriage fund. Widows and divorcees could remarry at will.

Women did not hold government office, but the wife of an official absent on government business could keep the office running in his absence. Women could hold positions at court and in temples, could own and run

estates and farms, and could follow careers in skilled trades such as that of weaver or perfume maker, as well as more obvious callings such as dancer, musician and nanny. Any debts they ran up in business deals were their own responsibility, and they could witness contracts.

The frequency and enthusiasm with which ordinary Egyptians went to court shows that they had a remarkable degree of faith in their legal system. At its best, the standards of Egyptian justice were very high, with no bribery or favouritism; rich and poor had equal rights, and women went to law on the same terms as men. Egypt had no police force in the modern sense, but a group called the *medjay* partly filled this role. These men guarded the frontiers and the cemeteries, and pursued criminals. Based in local communities, they were likely to know the villains of the area, but often they acted on information given to them about suspected criminals, and the role of informer was an honourable one.

Most cases were tried before the courts that were held in all settlements

of any size, but appeals could go to higher courts. There were no lawyers, so both plaintiffs and defendants would present their own cases. The accused pleaded guilty or not guilty, and was presumed to be innocent until proved otherwise. Witnesses took oaths in the name of the god Amun and the king, and the judges, of which there would be several, cross-examined the witnesses and examined documents.

Punishments for those found guilty included reprimands – and in cases of theft, the restitution of stolen property to several times its original value – beatings, and hard labour. For more serious offences judges could order exile or mutilation, or the death sentence for crimes such as tomb robbing, murder or treason.

Under sail *Nile boats had both sails and oars, and a steering oar at the stern. The wind blew from the north, so boats travelled south under sail, and were rowed northwards with the river's current. Most boats were made of wood, and the best were of cedar, from Lebanon.*

Valley of plenty *In the New Kingdom years, the Nile created a 1200 mile (1930 km) strip of fertile land in the midst of barren desert.*

FLOOD OF WEALTH

Egyptians sang hymns praising the 'creator of all good', for all water for people, crops and animals came from the Nile. Every year, melting snow and rains in the Ethiopian highlands sent huge quantities of water down the river, whose water level rose higher until in mid-July it spilled over its banks.

Egypt's very existence depended on this annual inundation, which soaked the fields and deposited silt that enriched the soil. The water at Aswan usually rose 25 ft (7.6 m). A rise of 3 ft (1 m) less brought hardship, and 5 ft (1.5 m) less meant famine. If the river rose 12 in (300 mm) more than usual the water damaged irrigation canals; an extra 4 ft (1.2 m) drowned villages and crops.

The flood water was stored in basins and canals for use through the growing season; the ditches that carried water from storage basins to the patchwork of fields could be opened or blocked off as required.

Watering can *After the inundation, the soil gradually dried out, and Egyptians then used a shaduf to water their garden crops. They pulled the bucket down into the irrigation ditch, and allowed the weight at the other end of the pole to raise the full bucket.*

Map labels: Mediterranean Sea; LOWER EGYPT; Memphis; Cairo; Nile; Sinai; Tell el Amarna; UPPER EGYPT; Red Sea; Deir el Medinah; Thebes; Aswan – 1st Cataract; NUBIA; 2nd Cataract; KUSH; 3rd Cataract; 4th Cataract; Napata; 5th Cataract; Khartoum

Groundwork *Cows, oxen or humans drew ploughs.*

Reaping the rewards *Ears of wheat and barley were cut with wooden sickles set with flint blades. The straw was left standing, and gathered later to make mats or bricks. Women and children took food and drink to the men in the fields, and picked up the grain left behind. Donkeys carried baskets of grain to a circular threshing floor, where cattle trampled on it to loosen the grain, to a background of farmers' singing. Women then used wooden paddles to toss the grain in the air so that the chaff blew away.*

Harvest home *A granary like the one shown in this wooden model could store different varieties of grain in separate containers, each of which had a sliding hatch at the bottom. Before it was stored away, scribes recorded the amount of grain produced.*

HARVEST OF THE FERTILE RIVER BANK

Neat parcels of farmland bordered the Nile, and it was there that nearly all Egyptians worked. The boundaries between farmers' fields were marked with special stones, and during the annual inundation the Nile's waters obliterated all landmarks except the stones. The dishonest farmer then had an unparalleled opportunity to move boundary stones in his favour, but stealing precious land in this way was considered one of the worst sins an Egyptian could commit.

When the river water started to recede, the farmers' first tasks were to reinstate any migrant boundary stones, and to repair flood damage to dykes. Then Egypt's yearly round of cultivation began in earnest. Peasants with digging sticks broke up the larger clods of earth; then came ox-drawn ploughs followed by sowers scattering seed by hand, and sheep or goats to tread the seed in.

During the growing season, farmers worked hard weeding and watering the crops. They also had to protect them from birds, and from straying cattle and even the odd hippopotamus.

A visit from the tax man

Egypt's most important crops were wheat and barley, and flax which they grew for linen and linseed oil. Farmers paid part of their tax in grain, so when the crops were ready for harvest, they faced an unwelcome visitation from tax assessors. These officials estimated the probable yield of the crops in the fields and set the amount that had to be handed over in taxes. Grain was harvested in March or April. All work in the fields and at the threshing floor was a communal effort, and landowners often provided musicians to play flutes while the peasants worked. The tax collectors arrived and what was left after their visit was carefully stored in granaries and silos. The beehive-shaped silos each stored one type of grain, and a small farm would have several of them. Then everyone celebrated in honour of Renenutet,

guardian goddess of the harvest. The middle of March marked the beginning of the summer season of drought and heat. During this period it was vital to repair any damaged irrigation canals before the soil dried out and became too hard to dig. For a few weeks farmers enjoyed a brief rest before the floods came again.

The wheat that the Egyptians grew in such quantity was made into about 40 different sorts of bread, pastry, cakes and biscuits, but grinding the grain was very hard work. It was usually done by women using two stones, and as it was done in the open air, grit and other foreign bodies found their way into the flour. These impurities caused extensive wear on the teeth, and Egyptians often suffered from tooth infections and abscesses.

> ' . . . in the land of Egypt, when we sat by the flesh pots, and when we did eat bread to the full'.
>
> EXODUS 16:3

The Egyptians' bread dough was made from flour and water – but without yeast, so the bread did not rise. It was cooked as flat loaves or in moulds, and different flavourings could be added, such as honey, milk, eggs, fruit, butter and herbs.

Barley was the other major grain crop, and the Ancient Egyptians used it to make the beer that everyone drank everyday – even the gods. The brew had an alcohol content of about 8 per cent. To make it, the Egyptians first moistened barley with water, and left it to stand. Then they mixed the moist grains with lightly baked barley loaves in a large jar, poured on more water, and let the mixture ferment. When the beer was ready it was very thick and had to be strained before drinking.

Wine for the wealthy

Unlike beer, which everyone drank, wine was the rich person's drink. The best vineyards were in the Delta, and the Egyptians made red and white wines, both sweet and dry. The juice of the first pressing, by foot, produced the best wine. Then the grapes, pips and stems were put in cloths attached to poles and twisted to extract lower-quality juice from the remainder.

The juices from the various pressings were put into jars and allowed to ferment, then the jars were plugged with a wad of leaves capped with mud. A small hole was left until secondary fermentation had taken place, then that too was sealed. Each jar was labelled with details of the quality, the year and the vineyard. The Egyptians relished their wine and served it neat. They also made wines from dates, pomegranates and palm sap.

So plentiful and fertile was the land that growers could afford to spare space for flowers. They were widely cultivated to beautify gardens and, twisted into garlands, to adorn people

Day's catch *The Nile teemed with fish, which the Egyptians enjoyed fresh, dried or salted.*

and houses. Flowers were also offered to deities, and used to make perfume.

The broad expanses of the Nile Delta made excellent grazing land, and the Egyptians kept cattle for their milk, meat and leather, and to pull ploughs and sledges. They had several different breeds – short horns, long horns and hornless – and during the New Kingdom humped-back zebu were imported from Syria. In Upper Egypt fertile land was limited and grazing scarce, so cattle destined for the table were fed in stalls. Some of these beasts were fattened to the point where they could hardly stagger along: one carving shows monstrous beasts intended for sacrifice being transported from the stall on wheeled platforms.

Sheep and goats flourished on lower-quality pasture such as the stubble in fields and the desert fringes, and provided wool and hair, milk, meat and hides. The native Egyptian sheep had horizontal horns, but by the time of the New Kingdom it had been replaced by an imported curly horned variety.

Pigs were kept in large numbers and pork was a popular dish even though it was forbidden, at least to priests,

because it was thought to be unclean, a beast of the wicked god Set.

The native beast of burden was the donkey – camels had not yet been domesticated. Horses were introduced to Egypt by Asiatic invaders a century or more before the New Kingdom, but they were expensive luxuries used solely for pulling chariots.

Vintage year *Grapevines were grown on trellises. The fruit destined for top-quality wine was trodden by foot, which gave the best juice as it did not crush the stems or pips. Five men work in the vat here, but some vats were big enough to hold six men.*

Bronze jar *As well as pottery, a rich household owned gold, silver and bronze tableware such as this bronze vessel.*

FRUITS AND FLAVOURS

So rich was the Egyptian soil that farmers could grow many types of crop, and most people enjoyed a varied diet. Wheat and barley gave the Egyptians bread and beer, and in addition, farmers also grew a host of different vegetables and fruits. So meals could include onions, leeks and garlic, peas and beans, celery, lettuces, radishes and cucumbers. Grapes and dates were eaten both fresh and dried. Then there were figs and melons, pomegranates, gourds, and the fruit of the dôm palm, with its gingery flavour. Other flavourings were the herbs cumin, marjoram, coriander, dill, mint and parsley. Saffron and sesame oils were widely used in cooking, but olives were little used.

The Egyptians' only sweetening agent was honey, and the beehives were cylindrical pots. A multitude of Nile fishes and water birds added variety to the dinner menu, along with hares, gazelles, and antelopes caught by hunters in the desert.

Texts that have survived mention soups and sauces and the use of oil, milk and butter. Food was cooked using braziers, tripods which supported cooking pots over fires, and ovens fuelled with wood. The well-equipped kitchen had grinding stones, a range of pots, pans and jars, ladles, spoons and knives, sieves, strainers and whisks.

Headcount *The Egyptians kept aviaries full of geese, ducks and pigeons, and ate both the birds and their eggs. In this painting geese are rounded up for a census. The chicken was introduced from Syria in the 15th century BC, and was described as a 'bird that reproduces itself everyday'. It remained a curiosity rather than a source of food for a long time. Hunters snared wild ducks and other birds with nets and throwing sticks.*

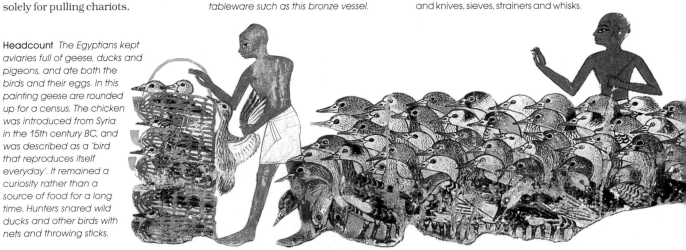

JEWELS, WIGS, AND WALLS OF MUD BRICK

Egyptians, both men and women, were most particular about their appearance. Hair, jewellery and make-up were all important, and so were clothes. Nearly all clothes were made from linen, which came in a range of qualities from coarse material almost like sacking to a very fine, lawn-like fabric. Wool was considered impure, and cotton was not widely used until 2000 years later.

Early Egyptian clothing styles were very simple. Men wore loincloths and kilts of various lengths, and women wore straight dresses which were suspended by two straps and fell to just above the ankles. By the time of the New Kingdom, however, garments had become more elaborate. For a formal occasion, men wore a full pleated tunic – a folded length of cloth with openings for head and arms, held in place by a broad sash round the waist. Women wore pleated dresses fastened by brightly coloured ribbons. When they were hard at work, men wore a loincloth or nothing at all, and women wore only a short kilt, for the Egyptians had no inhibitions about nudity. Children often wore no clothes at all.

When the temperature dropped, the Egyptians wore a light shawl or wrap. Both men and women might put on a headcloth to keep the dust out of their hair, and use fans of reeds or feathers to alleviate the heat. Sandals were made of reeds or leather with a strap between the toes; leather sandals were sometimes lavishly decorated.

Instant hairstyles

Egyptians of both sexes, all ages and from every walk of life were addicted to jewellery. For those who could afford it, there were pieces made from gold, silver and copper, used alone or with inlays of semiprecious stones and enamels. The less well-off could buy jewellery made from pretty banded pebbles, shells and ivory.

The fashionable ensemble was completed with a wig made from human hair. Women's wigs were longer than those for men, but both had elaborate arrangements of plaits and curls. On less formal occasions Egyptians might dispense with a wig, but if their own hair was thin it could be padded out

In vogue *New Kingdom fashion dictated sharply pleated clothes for both men and women.*

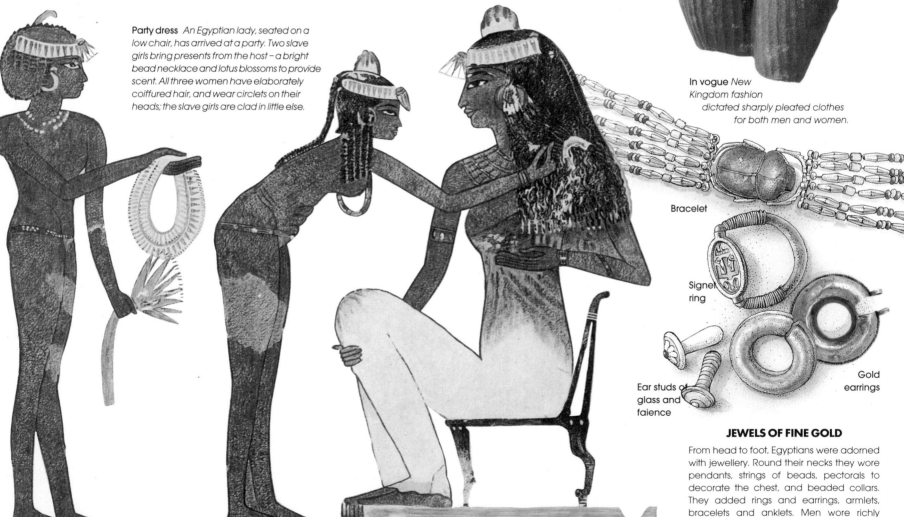

Party dress *An Egyptian lady, seated on a low chair, has arrived at a party. Two slave girls bring presents from the host – a bright bead necklace and lotus blossoms to provide scent. All three women have elaborately coiffured hair, and wear circlets on their heads; the slave girls are clad in little else.*

Bracelet

Signet ring

Ear studs of glass and faience

Gold earrings

JEWELS OF FINE GOLD

From head to foot, Egyptians were adorned with jewellery. Round their necks they wore pendants, strings of beads, pectorals to decorate the chest, and beaded collars. They added rings and earrings, armlets, bracelets and anklets. Men wore richly decorated belts, and women could buy strings of beads to wear round the hips.

with false tresses. Children's hair was arranged in a distinctive style with a plait hanging down one side of the face, the so-called 'sidelock of youth'.

Finishing touches

The Ancient Egyptians went to great lengths to care for their skin, and to embellish and improve the features provided by nature. To clean the skin, they used a cleansing cream made from oil, lime and perfume, and they regularly rubbed oil on their bodies to combat the drying effects of the sun. They had pastes to remove unsightly hair, and to do battle with unacceptable body odours.

To keep themselves smelling sweet, the Egyptians' other weapon was perfume, which they made from flowers and aromatic woods steeped in oils. At banquets, cones of perfumed animal fat were placed on the heads of the guests; as they melted they ran down the face and neck and had a cooling effect.

An Egyptian's cosmetic box – itself a specially designed item – contained a mirror, razors for removing body and facial hair, and tweezers to pluck eyebrows. Both men and women wore eye paint, which they applied with little sticks. The paints were made from malachite (copper ore) or galena (lead ore), which were ground to a powder, mixed with oil to form kohl, and stored in small jars. Eyepaint not only made the eyes look beautiful, it also helped to ward off flies. Rouge and lipstick were made from red ochre, which was ground and mixed with fat to form a paste, and then applied with a pad and a brush respectively.

To keep their hair in good condition, there were lotions to prevent hair loss, and to deal with dandruff and baldness. Egyptians dyed their hair with henna, which women also used to dye their palms and the soles of their feet. For the Egyptian adolescent there were formulas to cure spots, while ageing beauties had recourse to anti-wrinkle creams.

Down to earth

In sharp contrast with the elaborate ingredients the Egyptians applied to their bodies, their houses were built from the simplest materials. Stone was reserved for temples and tombs that were meant to last for eternity, but houses, from peasants' huts to royal palaces, were built of bricks of mud and straw, dried in the sun. Houses in country areas usually had one or two storeys, but in towns they sometimes rose to three storeys, or even four.

Egyptians who could afford it used fine imported cedar for pillars and doors, and stone for steps and door jambs. The rest used local palm timber, and made pillars from bundles of reeds plastered with mud. In the bright sunlight only small windows were needed, and they were usually at ceiling height. Rolls of matting attached to the lintels above windows and doors could be let down to keep out flies and dust, while still allowing air to circulate.

Another way of encouraging air to circulate was a vent in the flat roof. Families spent a great deal of time on the roof in order to catch every cooling breeze, and a kiosk or awning gave some shade. On summer nights many people slept on their roofs.

Walls, outside and in, were plastered and painted. Outside walls were usually white, but decorations inside varied from plain colour washes to elaborately decorated scenes. Houses of the wealthy might have plastered and painted floors, or even floors of glazed tiles, but the poor made do with stamped earth. The lamps which Egyptians used to light their homes ranged from the very simple – shallow pottery vessels with wicks floating in the oil – to beautiful alabaster vessels.

Baths and a portable lavatory

Some Egyptians were lucky enough to have their own well, but most people got their water directly from the river or from public wells in the street. Each household had to dispose of its own refuse and sewage. They could dig a pit and bury it, throw it in the river, or leave it in a spot where scavenging birds and animals, and the drying effects of the sun, soon took care of it.

Personal hygiene was very dear to the Egyptians. The poor washed in the river, but anyone who could possibly afford it had basins for washing at home. The wealthy even enjoyed the comfort of a bathroom. A pipe carried the waste water out through the wall and into a jar for re-use on the garden.

The rich also had lavatories a wooden seat on brick supports, under which was a pottery vessel that could be emptied after use. In other homes people used a portable lavatory – a wooden stool with part of the seat cut away and a pottery vessel underneath. More basic arrangements prevailed in the country, where most people relieved themselves out of doors.

Garden of Eden *It was every Egyptian's dream to own a shady garden. In the painting, date palms and fruit trees ring a pool, and shade its wealthy owner's house.*

Plain living *Home for the majority was a very modest structure, like the one shown in this clay model found in a tomb. Stairs lead to a flat roof with an air vent.*

HOME FURNISHINGS

Furniture in the Egyptian home was sparse, but it was practical and often decorative. Most was made from local woods and reeds, but there were also more expensive pieces of imported cedar and ebony, inlaid with gold, silver, semiprecious stones and faience, a glaze of powdered quartz. People usually sat on stools and cushions, and spread their bedding on the floor, but the better-off had chairs and beds. Most Egyptians had tables, and stored their belongings in chests, boxes and baskets, and there were special boxes to hold jewels, cosmetics and wigs. Kitchen equipment was functional, but they had tableware ranging from pottery to gold and silver. Knives and spoons made up the cutlery.

Folding stool *Some Egyptian stools had leather seats, like the one on the right; others were rush-seated. Beneath the stool are sandals and a reed brush.*

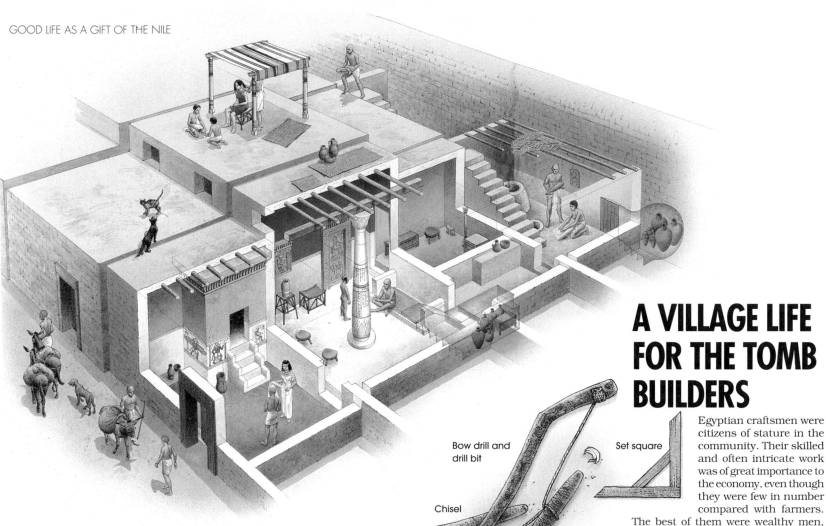

A VILLAGE LIFE FOR THE TOMB BUILDERS

Woodwork tools *Using set square, drill and adze, the Egyptian carpenter joined wood with joints similar to those used today, and decorated objects with inlays and veneers.*

Bow drill and drill bit

Chisel

Adze

Set square

Egyptian craftsmen were citizens of stature in the community. Their skilled and often intricate work was of great importance to the economy, even though they were few in number compared with farmers.

The best of them were wealthy men, and among them were weavers, painters and jewellers, workers in metals, leather or glass, and sculptors who carved the many stones found in the desert.

A trainee craftsman, normally following his father's trade, started as an 'apprentice', rose to be a 'junior', and finally graduated to full craftsman status. The more skilled workers could find full-time jobs in the workshops of nobles, temples and kings.

Shift work, and a strike

For several hundred years a community of craftsmen on the Nile's west bank at Thebes worked on the royal tombs in the Valley of the Kings. The men and their families lived in the village of Deir el Medinah, which was specially built to house the tomb makers. The village had its own temple, court, doctor and scorpion charmer, and a wall round it to keep out desert raiders.

The Egyptian 'week' was ten days long – eight days of work, followed by two days off. On working days the men of Deir el Medinah lived in a village close

HOMES WHERE THE ROOF WAS AN EXTRA ROOM

Deir el Medinah, the village built to house men working on the royal tombs, was a prosperous place and its residents lived in some comfort. The flat-roofed houses were built of mud bricks; the roof was supported by a wooden pillar in the main room, and was reinforced by date-palm beams. Most houses had three rooms, plus an outside kitchen and two small cellars where the family kept their valuables, wine and oil jars.

The main entrance to the house opened from a narrow street into a room where work such as weaving was done; this room also contained the family shrine, reached by a flight of steps. The main room of the house led off it and was sparsely furnished with stools, tables and chests, and a platform 'couch' where the family sat to eat. The man of the house, sitting cross-legged on the platform, talks to a naked child whose hair is worn in a sidelock. Beneath the platform there was access to one of the cellars. To the

child's left are a false door decorated with a god and hieroglyphs, and a carved stone, which both played a part in the family's worship of gods and ancestors.

Behind the main room was a combined storeroom and bedroom, whose furniture might include a lamp on a tall support, a headrest used while sleeping, and storage chests. The roofless kitchen at the back of the house had a circular oven, and steps to the roof where an awning provided some shade. In the kitchen a servant kneads bread.

In the workshop *Craftsmen offer wares for inspection, while colleagues pack jewels in a box and a metalworker adorns a sphinx.*

34

Tools of the trade *Etched on the wall of his tomb, a senior official records the offerings he expects to continue to receive from his estates, season by season, in the next world. He writes with a brush made from a reed or palm-leaf rib, using ink from a dish. To create carvings such as this, artists planned designs on papyrus, transferred the outline to a grid on the wall and then added the details.*

Painter's palette *The Egyptians ground minerals to make brightly coloured paints.*

Cartoon animals *A cat herds geese and a lion mummifies a donkey in a topsy-turvy world which could be a political parody.*

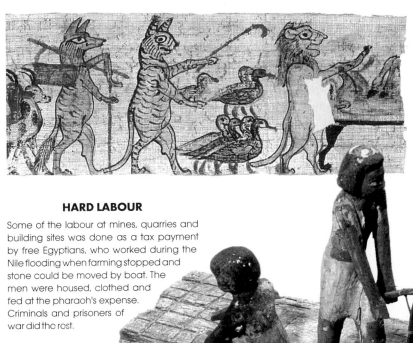

HARD LABOUR

Some of the labour at mines, quarries and building sites was done as a tax payment by free Egyptians, who worked during the Nile flooding when farming stopped and stone could be moved by boat. The men were housed, clothed and fed at the pharaoh's expense. Criminals and prisoners of war did the rest.

Model of brickmakers digging and moulding mud

to their work, and rose early to start work while it was still cool. The tools, lamps and materials that they needed were drawn from a central store. They were logged in and out by scribes, who also supervised the collection and payment of wages, wrote letters and legal documents for the villagers, and sent progress reports to the vizier, the pharaoh's highest official.

'His fingers are like crocodile hide. He stinks more than fish eggs.'
METALWORKER, DESCRIBED *c.* 1300 BC

The men worked one shift in the morning, broke for a meal and a rest during the heat of the day, and returned for the second shift when it was cooler. Far from being downtrodden, as they have sometimes been portrayed, the builders of the royal tombs were well paid, had plenty of leisure and could be downright militant. History's first recorded strike is that of the men of Deir el Medinah, who downed tools when their wages were late.

High day and holiday

Wages were paid in kind, and consisted of food, oil, linen and firewood, and special bonuses of salt, wine, extra meat and silver. There were slaves to do the heavy work such as grinding grain, bringing water up from the valley and chopping firewood.

Over the 'weekend' the men rested, held parties and worked on their own tombs. 'Holy days' gave them a further 65 or so days off work each year and included four days for the local feast and five days of New Year celebrations. But the official holidays were still not enough for some workers, and absenteeism was widespread. Scribes noted the excuses: illness, a row with the wife, brewing beer for a festival, attending a funeral, hangovers and a child's birthday.

Desert stonecutters

In the Valley of the Kings, royal tombs were cut into cliff faces. Elsewhere in Egypt, temples and tombs were built of lime-stone and sand-stone quarried from cliffs and deserts. Granite and alabaster,

which were more difficult to work, were used for decorative elements such as pillars and floors. Blocks of stone were left at the quarry until the waters of the inundation were at their height. The stones were then transported as far as possible by boat.

To make bricks for buildings for the living, brickmakers dug Nile mud with a wooden tool, put it in a pit with water and chopped straw, and trod it with their feet to mix it. The mixture was shaped in wooden moulds, then left to bake hard in the fierce Egyptian sun.

Building stone was not the only commodity transported by water, for the Nile provided the easiest means of carrying goods and people up and down Egypt. Small ferryboats took peasants, their produce and their animals to and fro while larger, faster vessels sped officials on Government business. Barges carried heavy goods, and sleeker trading vessels set off to foreign parts.

On land, the rich were carried in chairs, but most people travelled on foot. Farmers and traders loaded their goods onto donkeys, or carried them in baskets hung from yokes across their shoulders. Wheeled carts were hardly ever used: they were equally ineffective in desert sand and in the mud of the cultivated area during the inundation.

Buying and selling in local markets and small shops was carried out by barter, with goods valued against copper weights called *deben*. By the time of the New Kingdom some purchases were paid for in deben, though Egyptians never took the final step of making them the official currency.

Concubines in exchange for gold

Most overseas trade was organised by the pharaoh as part of his foreign policy. Kings wrote to pharaohs begging for Egyptian gold, and one pharaoh demanded in return 40 concubines 'in which there is no blemish and none with shrill voices'.

Temples and independent merchants also traded overseas, exporting gold, wheat, linen, papyrus and a wide range of manufactured goods. They ventured out in all directions – south into Africa, west to the Saharan oases and Libya, north to the Aegean Islands and Greece, and east to the lands round the eastern Mediterranean shores. They brought back timber – especially cedar from Lebanon and ebony from the African interior – silver, copper, slaves, horses, incense, wine, cattle and a host of luxury goods.

TIME OFF WORK AND A VISIT TO THE DOCTOR

It is sometimes thought that the Ancient Egyptians were a sad and solemn people, because of their elaborate funeral rituals and the time and energy they spent preparing for death. In fact, the opposite is true. The Egyptians enjoyed this life so much that they wanted to continue the earthly delights throughout eternity, and made thorough preparations to ensure their future happiness.

From early childhood onwards, the Egyptians had many ways of filling their spare time. While they were not at school, or learning their future trades, children played with model boats and animals, balls, slings, whips and tops, and dolls, some of which had jointed limbs. They also had ingenious toys with moving pieces, such as a lion that snapped its jaws, and little dwarfs who 'danced' when a handle was turned.

Carvings show children running, jumping and twirling each other around, and playing what appear to be team games. One painting shows girls riding piggyback on their friends' shoulders and playing ball games.

Sport on the river, and a quiet read

Once they had left such childish pursuits behind, there was no shortage of other ways for Egyptians to spend their leisure hours. Adventurous noblemen might go out hunting with other men, or take their families out on the river. There they could fish, hunt wild birds, enjoy a picnic and perhaps even swim, if the area was free of crocodiles.

Men of lower ranks took part in wrestling contests and fenced with wooden swords. There were boating competitions on the river: teams of men, armed with poles, stood in boats which were rowed towards each other at great speed. Each team tried to knock the opposing one into the water.

An Egyptian lucky enough to have a garden could relax among flowers and trees by a pool where lotus blossoms floated. If this delight palled, then out would come the gaming board. Board games were almost a national sport in Ancient Egypt, and there were several different ones to choose from, such as Hounds and Jackals, and Twenty Squares. But the favourite game of all was Senet. Everyone in Egypt had a Senet board – there were humble ones of mud and reeds for peasants, faience and wooden boards for the better-off, and luxurious boards of ebony, ivory and gold for the rich.

Those who could read, and could afford to own books, might settle down with a papyrus scroll and enjoy travel stories, the adventures of the Shipwrecked Sailor, or even tales of a risqué nature. Whether they could read or not, everyone in Egypt enjoyed listening to professional storytellers. Other quiet moments could be spent watching the antics of family pets, for Egyptians kept cats and dogs, monkeys, geese and gazelles. When pet dogs died, their collars were buried with them ready for when they were reunited with their owners.

Noblemen and women would learn to play musical instruments and to sing, but there were also professional musicians who, like dancers and acrobats, entertained at

Family outing *The Nile teemed with fish and game birds, and this family, all beautifully dressed, are out for a day's sport on the river. They stand on a papyrus raft, with fish swimming underneath. The man holds a throwing stick in one hand, and birds that he has already caught in the other. The cat was probably used to flush out the game.*

HUNTING AND FISHING

Hunting was a favourite sport among Egypt's noblemen, and it provided them with excitement and danger, as well as animal skins and interesting extras for the table.

Armed with spears and bows and arrows, and accompanied by long-legged hunting dogs, they went to the Nile marshes in pursuit of wild bulls, and to the desert fringes for gazelles, lions and hares. Some hunters made sure of success by building an enclosure of nets and posts and driving the game into it, so that they could kill the animals at leisure. The Nile was a fruitful source of prey of all sizes. Hunters on papyrus boats harpooned hippopotamuses and crocodiles, fished with rods and hooks, harpoons and nets, and used throwing sticks to bring down game birds.

Harpoon

Huntsman's weapon *The Egyptian sportsman used a wooden throwing stick when he was out hunting game birds. Some, like the one in the painting above, were shaped like snakes, and complete with a snake's head; others were shaped more like boomerangs. The aim was to throw the stick at the bird and break its neck or wings.*

Board game *A husband and wife play Senet, moving pieces along a board like the one above, with 30 squares. To determine the pieces' movements, players used the Egyptian equivalent of a dice: a handful of sticks, flat on one side and curved on the other. They threw the sticks, and counted the flat and curved surfaces.*

parties and religious festivals, and in the streets. Musicians were often blind people; music was not written down, so they were not at a disadvantage.

Egypt had no public games or theatre, but great royal and religious processions provided colour, glamour and excitement. At large temples, priests and priestesses performed sacred dramas about episodes in the lives of the deity they served. Going on a pilgrimage to one of the great cult temples offered not only a spiritual and emotional outlet, but also the attractions of a nonstop party.

The Egyptians loved parties and entertainment, and relished fine food. They were also very partial to beer and wine, and drank both in large quantities. Liberal amounts of alcohol were a feature of religious festivals, as the Egyptian gods were thought to approve of their worshippers enjoying themselves. There were wine shops and brothels, and, associated with them, rowdy young men who had to scramble over walls to escape arrest after disturbing the peace or starting a brawl.

Doctors in demand

Revellers who enjoyed themselves to excess might feel in need of a doctor the following day. Egyptian medicine reached a very high standard, and its reputation spread to neighbouring countries. A student doctor learned from an established physician, perhaps his father, but there also seem to have been medical schools attached to temples, and there was at least one school for midwives.

Many Ancient Egyptian doctors were 'general practitioners', working in the community, but others specialised in one part of the body. Medical texts that have survived give clues to the extent of the Egyptians' knowledge. There were specialist books about every part of the body, texts specifically on gynaecology, books for surgeons, dentists and vets, and books giving recipes for medicines.

Doctors were instructed that when making a diagnosis they should first observe the patient closely, then ask questions, inspect, smell, feel and probe. If they were then confident they could cure the patient they would say 'An ailment I will treat'; if it was a more difficult case with an uncertain outcome they would say 'An ailment with which I will contend'.

A course of treatment

Egyptian doctors were well aware of their limitations, however, and were told not to inflict unnecessary suffering on their patients, so there were many cases where they had to say – at least to themselves – 'An ailment not to be treated'. They were recommended to take note of the treatments and

Music and dance *Two scantily clad dancing girls move in time to the music of a flute played by an impeccably groomed lady. Other musical instruments were lyres, cymbals, drums and harps with anything from four to more than 20 strings.*

Dinner party *A table piled high with food stands ready for the guests at this banquet; the cones of perfumed wax on their heads will melt during the evening and cool them. The slave girl will serve the food, and wine from the jars under the table.*

medicines they used and of their effects, so that they had a record for similar cases in the future.

There were medicines to be taken internally, others to be applied to the outside of the body, and others still to be inhaled. Egyptian ingredients that can be identified today appear to be sound herbal remedies. However, some medicines had ingredients such as mice, beetles and dung, which aimed to drive out the demons causing the illness.

The Egyptians had a remarkable knowledge of the way the body worked, and knew about its internal arrangements through mummifying the dead. For them, the heart was the most important organ; they knew that it pumped blood round the body, and that the pulse 'spoke the messages of the heart'. They also knew that injuries to one side of the brain affected the opposite side of the body.

Doctors sometimes used surgery as well as medicine to treat patients, and opened injured skulls to relieve pressure on the brain. Before an operation the surgeon gave his patient a drink, presumably a painkiller, 'to render it agreeable'. In the New Kingdom the painkiller might have been opium, imported from Cyprus. Because of the importance the Egyptians attached to ritual purity the surgeon and his assistants washed themselves and purified the instruments in fire before the operation. Both of these would cut down the risk of infection.

The Egyptians were a deeply religious people, and prayers would always be used as well as medicines, even for the simplest ailments. In difficult cases, magic might be employed. It was also possible to visit the temple of a deity associated with medicine, such as Imhotep, which had priests trained as doctors. At some temples the sick could spend a night close to the god's sanctuary. During such a stay, called 'incubation', the patient might be cured by the deity, or dream of the god and receive instructions for treatment. Even if no help was forthcoming, the sufferer was spiritually comforted.

GODS WHO GAVE A FINAL JUDGMENT

Religion played a part in every aspect of Egyptian life. There were gods of the earth, the air and water, and deities responsible for every aspect of life from birth to death. The greatest and most powerful gods, such as Amun, Hathor and Osiris, were worshipped throughout the land and had huge cult temples in their 'home' towns. Others, such as Meretseger who lived on the Western Peak above the Valley of the Kings, had a local following in their own district.

There were also lesser deities, often concerned with the domestic scene and events such as childbirth. These gods and goddesses had no temples but were loved by people of all ranks, and Egyptians paid homage to them at the small shrines in their homes.

The numerous Egyptian gods and goddesses took many different forms. Some were shown in human form but with distinctive dress and regalia. Others were shown either as the animals or birds specially associated with them or with a human body and their sacred animal's head. Sobek, the god of water, was represented by a crocodile, and Anubis, the embalmers' god, had the head of the jackal that frequented cemeteries.

An Egyptian temple was not like a church, mosque or synagogue where people congregate to hold services. It was the deity's home on earth, where gods and goddesses made contact with humans through cult statues which were tended by faithful servants.

Round the temple, with its sanctuary where the god lived, were offices, the 'House of Life' where books were stored and copied, workshops and a sacred lake, from which pure water was drawn for ceremonies. A high wall surrounded the whole complex to keep out pollution, impurity and evil.

Servants of the god

Temples were run by priests. They did not live apart from the community, but could marry and hold secular posts as well as religious ones. Large temples had a permanent high priest and several deputies, but at small village shrines, local craftsmen and farmers often acted as priests.

Priests served for one month, three times a year. While he was on duty the priest had to be absolutely pure; he shaved off all body hair, bathed several times a day, avoided wearing wool and refrained from eating certain foods. When they were not actually performing rituals, priests had other work to do such as running the god's estates and his workshops, and organising his mining and trading ventures. Some priests were specialists in fields such as astronomy or astrology, or the interpretation of dreams.

Temples had other staff. There were priestesses who sang hymns and shook metal rattles, called sistra, during

Amulet representing the girdle of Isis

services, and there were also professional musicians, and singers and dancers. Bakers, brewers, butchers and cooks prepared food to offer to the god; craftsmen laboured in the workshops; maintenance men, cleaners and a host of slaves did manual work. The revenue to pay staff wages, taxes and maintenance costs came largely from rents paid by tenants who farmed temple lands.

Ordinary Egyptians were only allowed inside the temple under very special circumstances, and then they had to be ritually purified. Normally people prayed at the temple gate where they addressed their prayers to huge statues of the reigning king. As the child of the gods, the king acted as intermediary between them and his people. But even the most humble petitioners were confident that great deities would listen to and grant their pleas. Often they set up against the temple

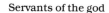

Tears of sorrow Weeping professional mourners sully their bodies with dust. Just as dirt was the reverse of cleanliness – which was so important to the Egyptians – so death was the reverse of life.

Ship to carry the dead
The Nile and ships were of such major importance to the Egyptians that symbolic ships also played a part in their rituals. The dead were ferried over a river of death to reach the underworld, and Egyptians often left a model funeral barge, like the one above, in the tombs of their relatives. The dead man's son used two large oars to steer the barge whose sides were painted green, the colour of growing crops, to symbolise life in the future. The mummy lies under a canopy, and at its head and foot are mourners representing the sister goddesses Isis and

Nephthys. Isis was the wife of Osiris, the god of the underworld and also of the Nile's inundation. He gave all Egyptians, however humble, the hope of life in the next world. Egyptians also believed that the sun god sailed across the sky during the day, and that he disembarked at dusk and travelled through the underworld on a different ship, bringing light to the realms of the dead.

Jackal judge *At the final test against the Feather of Truth, a heart heavy with sin unbalanced the scales; the sinner would be devoured by a fierce monster and condemned to eternal desolation. But for those whose lives had been virtuous the scales balanced, and eternal bliss with loved ones in the Fields of the Blessed followed.*

wall a small stone slab decorated with ears; it served both as an offering to the god, and a reminder to him to listen attentively.

Every Egyptian, from king to peasant, consulted oracles: it was a way of solving problems about their family or job, or settling legal disputes where neither side could be broken or made to yield. They went to the temple gate, where a scribe wrote down the petitioner's question, carefully phrasing it so as to require a yes or no answer. A priest took the question to the god's statue in the sanctuary and the god replied.

At festival time the god's statue was placed in a boat and carried out of the temple so that anyone could ask it a question. The answer was given by the boat swaying backwards or forwards, or becoming so heavy that its bearers sank to their knees.

Some people preferred to question a sacred animal. If a deity was closely associated with a particular animal or bird, a living creature of that species was kept in the god's temple. Answers to petitioners' questions were interpreted from the creature's movements.

Faith such as this gave priests the opportunity to manipulate answers, but in most cases the system worked well. Priests saw the petitioner's problem objectively and, in local temples, were likely to know the people involved and the background of the case. Some priests may have taken bribes, but most were honest believers who prayed and fasted, and were thoroughly purified, before they went on duty. When they gave advice they believed that their movements and gestures were inspired by the gods.

Religious festivals brought spiritual and emotional release, whether they were local affairs or the rites of great state gods which attracted pilgrims from all over Egypt. People took part in processions; they worshipped the god to whom the festival was dedicated, made offerings to him and perhaps consulted his oracle. Attendance counted to one's credit in the next world, and for the sick there was always the chance of a miraculous cure.

Into the next world

Egyptians devoted a great deal of time, energy and resources to preparations for the next world. They saw earthly life as a dream, over in a flash, while life in the west – the Kingdom of Osiris, god of the dead – was eternal, so careful preparation for it was essential.

To enjoy eternity to the full the body had to survive. When an Egyptian died, embalmers collected the body and carried it by boat or litter to their workshops, where they treated it with one or more of the processes that would preserve the body.

Embalmers could remove the brain, take out the internal organs which were then stored in canopic jars, dry out the corpse by packing it in a salt called natron, or anoint it with preservatives. To make the corpse ready for the tomb, they packed it with linen, beautified it, and finally wrapped it in long bandages.

Food and drink, and the dead person's personal possessions, were placed in the tomb to ensure the deceased's comfort in the next world. The tomb ranged from a simple hole in the sand to an elaborate stone building, or a rock-cut suite of rooms decorated with scenes of daily life, of the funeral, and of the world to come. These painted scenes would work by magic to provide the deceased with daily needs in the next world, if their heirs failed to maintain a supply of offerings. The funeral itself was a great ritual effort aimed at launching the deceased safely into the next world.

The deceased, meanwhile, had been ferried over the river of death, and now had to pass through the underworld braving many dangers and demons on the way. To help them negotiate these hazards, the dead used the spells and instructions in the 'Book of the Dead' that had been buried with them. Those who could assure the 42 assessors that they had not committed any of Egypt's 42 'deadly sins' could enter the judgment hall of Osiris. There the deceased's heart was weighed against a feather representing truth, and the final reward or punishment made.

GODS AND CHARMS AT HOME

Many of the prayers of Egyptians were directed not to gods in temples, but to the statuettes of their favourite deities that they kept in their homes, in little shrines. Two popular deities were Bes, who was the god of the family and newborn children, and Taweret, goddess of pregnant women. Taweret took the form of a pregnant hippopotamus, and Egyptians prayed to her for a safe delivery.

To protect themselves from harm, in this life and the next, Egyptians wore amulets, or charms. They were made in many different materials and represented deities or sacred symbols. Some of the semiprecious stones from which amulets were made, such as lapis lazuli, had protective properties themselves. The Egyptians also indulged in magic, casting spells to protect their children, or to attract a desired lover to their side.

Family god *The god Bes was a grotesque creature, part dwarf and part lion. Balanced on a lotus flower, he holds a tambourine in his left hand. Bes was sometimes shown carrying a sword to protect the family.*

CAREERS FOR BOYS: SOLDIER OR SCRIBE

The high-spirited young man of Ancient Egypt had an outlet for his energies that promised excitement and a path to advancement. For the Egypt of New Kingdom times had a large and well-trained army, which protected the frontiers and patrolled the pharaoh's outlying lands. The king was the army's commander in chief and often took to the field in person, with a bodyguard of chosen men, and officials to advise him.

Each division of the Egyptian army consisted of about 5000 men. Four thousand of them were infantry troops who were subdivided into companies of 200 men. Companies, with names such as 'Bull in Nubia' and 'Manifest in Justice', were divided into units of 50 soldiers. The division's

Chariot of war *The pharaoh, as chief of the army, often went into battle in person, and even if he did not, it was usual to portray the king as a warrior. King Tutankhamun, who died in about 1323 BC at the age of 19, can have had little active campaign experience, but a painted casket from his tomb shows the young king crushing Asian enemies from his chariot. The scene is more like a hunt than a battle, for the pharaoh's dogs are taking on the bearded enemy. Behind him, fan-bearers and the vulture goddess above the king's head offer some protection from the perils of war.*

Edge of death *A sword with a gold hilt was the weapon of an Egyptian officer. The hilt was shaped so that it fitted comfortably into the palm of the hand.*

Prisoners of war *During their victorious campaigns in the New Kingdom the Egyptians took many prisoners. Captives like these fettered Peleset, or Philistines, became slaves.*

remaining 1000 men formed a chariot wing of two-man teams. There were also foreign mercenaries, often lightly armed skirmishers, who were particularly useful on frontier and desert patrols. Because of the good prospects it offered, the army was not usually short of volunteers. In emergencies,

Armed attack *Soldiers were trained to use spears, battle-axes, javelins, swords, maces and bows and arrows. The army unit went into battle accompanied by a standard-bearer, and a trumpeter who gave orders with coded calls on a long trumpet. A soldier armed with a scimitar, a curved sword, follows one who carries a battle-axe; the rest carry spears.*

however, men could be conscripted, and then one in a hundred were usually called up. New recruits had their hair cropped, and were issued with leather body armour, helmets and shields. They learned to use all the army's weapons, but tended to specialise in one in particular, so that there were companies of spearmen, companies of bowmen and so on.

The young recruits were sent on long training marches, for when it was on campaign the army covered an average of 12 miles (19 km) a day over desert terrain. To prepare them for war, the men were ruthlessly drilled. As battles usually consisted of a succession of precisely executed tactical manoeuvres, soldiers had to be able to respond on command to directions given by trumpet. In battle, the young, inexperienced troops formed the second ranks and reserves, while hardened soldiers made up the front line. Shock troops called the 'Braves' were the army's elite. Chariots played an important part in Egyptian army tactics; they were built for speed and manoeuvrability, and formed a mobile firing squad that dashed into the fray, scattering the enemy. Chariot warriors needed special training; most of them were young noblemen and the job had a certain glamour.

Donkeys on the march
The Egyptian army was well organised, and so were its back-up services. Heralds carried messages and made reports, scouts explored the terrain, and grooms cared for the horses and for the donkeys that carried baggage. There were doctors for men and animals, scribes to deal with supplies and wages and to record the campaign, priests and magicians to give spiritual and magic support, astronomers and astrologers, armourers, cooks, spies and a host of servants.

Away from their home barracks, the soldiers lived in tents erected within rectangular earthworks with sentries posted on the ramparts. The king's tent, and that holding the portable shrine of Amun, the chief New Kingdom god, stood in the centre of the camp, with the remainder arranged in orderly rows. Officers' tents were commodious and comfortable, with two or more rooms and furniture including folding 'camp beds' and stools.

Retiring veterans might be eligible for a land grant, and outstanding bravery was rewarded. There were decorations – 'medals' in the form of gold lions and gold flies – or the prospect of promotion when bravery drew the attention of a general or the king. On campaign the king, normally a remote figure hedged around by protocol, could get to know his officers and plan appointments for his favourites.

Khety, a scribe writing in the New Kingdom, painted an appalling picture of army life. According to him, soldiers were subjected to brutal training, life in camp was a constant round of quarrels, rivalries, drunkenness and gambling, and campaigns meant hunger, thirst, flies, and wounds that lead to death or permanent disablement.

'Be a scribe, that you may be saved from being a soldier.'

ANONYMOUS SCRIBE, *c.* 1300 BC

But in writing his black report of the Egyptian army, Khety intended to deter his pupils from enlisting, and therefore abandoning Khety's own profession. A scribe in Ancient Egypt had a good, secure job, and it was one that offered the bright boy a golden opportunity to make his way to the top. Scribes kept the whole machinery of government and society working, and there were jobs at all levels. A peasant's son was unlikely to reach the highest ranks of government, but his grandson might make it. The key was education.

Happiest days
Poor families made great efforts to send a son to school, hoping that it would make the boy's, and therefore the family's, fortune. Village schools were usually run by the local priest, or by a scribe who added to his income by teaching the basic skills. Large temples had bigger and better schools, and foundations such as that of Amun at Karnak gave top-quality teaching in more advanced subjects.

School, for boys only, began at about seven years of age; girls were taught at home. Discipline in Egyptian schools was fierce. 'The ear of a boy is in his back: he listens when he is beaten,' said the papyrus *A Warning to Schoolboys*. Teachers probably had to be stern, for the task of learning hundreds of hieroglyphs and their shorthand forms must have been boring and repetitive.

The pupils copied texts again and again on ostraca – pieces of stone or broken pottery – or on wooden boards covered in wax that could be smoothed and re-used. Once he had mastered reading and writing, the pupil learned other skills such as composing letters in the correct form, doing accounts, and drawing up legal documents.

Able boys whose parents could afford it could go on to more advanced studies – mathematics, history, geography, foreign languages, drawing, surveying, engineering, astronomy, medicine and literature. Eventually they might specialise in one or two subjects. They might even have taken examinations, for surviving documents that pose problems demanding solutions have all the hallmarks of examination papers.

After their schooldays, professional scribes continued to make notes on ostraca, but the final document was copied onto scrolls of papyrus, which was made from a reed which grew up to 10 ft (3 m) high. The white inner part of the reed was cut into strips, which were thoroughly soaked and arranged side by side. A second layer was laid on top, with the strips running at right angles to the lower one. The two layers were pounded and pressed until they fused together, and the sheets of 'paper' were trimmed and smoothed ready for the scribe with his brush and inks.

Written word *Inscriptions on tombs and monuments were written in hieroglyphs, using hundreds of different symbols. Most of them represented consonant sounds, but some were pictures with no sound value that were added to make the meaning clear. The passage below includes, in the oval shape, the name of Nefertari, wife of Ramses II.*

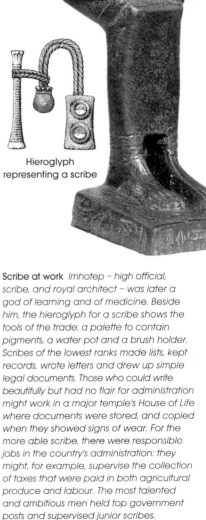

Hieroglyph representing a scribe

Scribe at work *Imhotep – high official, scribe, and royal architect – was later a god of learning and of medicine. Beside him, the hieroglyph for a scribe shows the tools of the trade: a palette to contain pigments, a water pot and a brush holder. Scribes of the lowest ranks made lists, kept records, wrote letters and drew up simple legal documents. Those who could write beautifully but had no flair for administration might work in a major temple's House of Life where documents were stored, and copied when they showed signs of wear. For the more able scribe, there were responsible jobs in the country's administration: they might, for example, supervise the collection of taxes that were paid in both agricultural produce and labour. The most talented and ambitious men held top government posts and supervised junior scribes.*

MASTERS OF THE AEGEAN

Europe's first civilisation developed around 2000 BC on the Mediterranean island of Crete. Around sprawling, brilliantly decorated palaces lived a community of farmers and seafarers who loved religious rituals and joyous games, colourful dress and glittering jewellery. This early civilisation is called Minoan after its legendary King Minos, in whose maze-like palace at Knossos was said to roam the Minotaur, a creature half-man and half-bull, which was slain by the Greek hero Theseus.

The Minoans were peaceloving people who grew rich by trading with other Mediterranean peoples. Only after a sudden widespread disaster – possibly the effects of the eruption of the volcanic island of Thera, 75 miles (120 km) to the north – and the disruption of their trade routes did the Minoans lose their mastery of the seas to Mycenaean colonists from Greece.

MINOANS AND MYCENAEANS 3000 – 1100 BC

THE FIRST MERCHANT MARINERS

As the first naval power recorded in history, the Minoans developed skills in seafaring which protected them from pirates and gave them wealth from trade and fish to eat. Like many an island people, they loved the sea around them and used it to their advantage.

The Cretan coastline, with its string of sandy beaches in little bays protected by low peninsulas, suited the Minoan mariners. Harbour towns grew up on the peninsulas, and ships could draw up on whichever side was protected from the prevailing winds at the time. Usually the ships were drawn stern first up onto the beach; but if a vessel was not going to be unloaded at once it could be anchored offshore, attached by ropes to heavy stones with holes through them. There were no piers, though breakwaters of large boulders were built around some harbours to give additional protection from rough seas.

Once a Minoan boat had been beached, the crew went ashore by a gangplank attached to the stern, and a throng of porters came aboard to take off the cargo, then load it onto wagons or onto mules to transport it to towns inland. There was usually no need for extensive warehouses at the water's edge: one exception seems to have been at Kommos, the port which served the palace and town of Phaistos, where excavations have revealed the foundations of a large,

Bounty from the sea *The pride of an Aegean fisher boy in his catch of mackerel shines out from the plaster of a wall from the island of Thera, present-day Santorini, as brightly as when it was painted 4000 years ago.*

strongly constructed building at the back of the beach. By power of oars or sails the Minoans used a wide variety of ships for different purposes, and their artists lovingly carved these vessels on seal-stones and painted them in frescoes. The first Minoan ships were propelled by 20 or 30 oarsmen, but by 2000 BC traders were putting to sea in ships with central masts carrying rectangular sails. They were steered from the stern by means of large oars.

On a fresco of 1500 BC found at Akrotiri on Thera the variety of shipping is remarkable. Many of the boats seem to be ceremonial barges with 30 to 40 oarsmen, naked except for loin-cloths, seated below an upper deck on which eight or ten figures are seated. These boats have masts, but no sails are hoisted and the rigging is strung with decorations. Other ships are smaller, with only eight or ten rowers and no mast. The most important boat, however, looks to be one with an oblong white sail and no oarsmen. On its deck stand large brown containers, and the ship is clearly a merchant vessel bearing its cargo towards a town on a hillside overlooking the sea.

Gifts for the pharaohs

In vessels like these, Minoan seamen crossed the Mediterranean to trade with distant lands. They sold wine, olive oil and luxury products outstanding for their craftsmanship and beauty. Examples of painted Minoan pottery found in Cyprus, Lebanon, Syria, Jordan and Egypt are almost certainly

Bees at a sunflower, on a golden pendant

the survivors of a much larger range of exports including perfumes, woollen goods and fine metalwork. In return for such exports, the Minoans brought back to Crete raw materials not found on the island: tin from Persia, gold and pearls from Egypt and ivory probably from Syria.

Along with these raw materials came smaller quantities of manufactured luxuries, including trinkets, pottery from the Cyclades and Cyprus, and stone vases from the workshops of Egypt. Some of these vases carry the seals of Egyptian pharaohs and were probably gifts from one head of state to another. Tomb paintings in Egypt show emissaries bringing gifts for the pharaoh; these visitors include some, called *Keftiu* by the Egyptians, who are believed to be Cretans. Ships carrying Minoan envoys, merchants and goods to the Near East would have travelled south-eastwards to Egypt, then up the coast of the Levant before crossing to Cyprus, and along the southern coast of Turkey back to the Aegean.

In some places, the Minoans who went abroad as traders stayed as settlers, establishing themselves in many coastal towns on the islands of the Aegean and around the coasts of southern Greece and Turkey. In settlements on Thera, Melos and Kea have been found architecture, frescoes, statuettes, pottery and stone vases of Minoan inspiration or manufacture. Also found on these islands are samples of Minoan writing, known as Linear A, and evidence of the Minoan system of weights and

measures, suggesting that business in the islands was done according to traditions set by Minoan traders.

Food from the waters

While Minoan traders were returning from long Mediterranean voyages to beach their ships and unload their cargoes in Cretan harbours, other Minoans would be offshore fishing from small rowing boats. The tools of their craft were trident-headed spears, nets weighted by perforated stone rings, or simple hook-and-line.

The seas around Crete are well stocked with fish, and Minoan frescoes and seal-stones show tunny, mullet, parrot wrasse and mackerel. In addition, crab, cuttlefish and above all octopus were caught and eaten.

Trade centre *By the 15th century BC, Minoan traders spanned the eastern Mediterranean. A century later, Mycenaeans took over Minoan colonies and markets.*

ART THAT MIRRORED NATURE

The Minoans had an almost childlike love of colour and ornamentation in their daily lives. Goldsmiths and silversmiths created brilliant items of jewellery, amazing in the intricate detail fitted into a tiny space. Craftsmen were also close observers of nature: even the most delicate gold necklaces were ornamented with papyrus flowers, lilies or shellfish. Realistic images of sea creatures, birds, plants, beasts and insects appear on countless designs. Seaweed and shells were almost as plentiful on vases, jugs and other vessels of clay, obsidian and rock crystal as they were on the shores of Crete.

Octopus jar *On a storage jar from eastern Crete, an octopus swims among shells and seaweed.*

Necklace *Gold and glass form a delicate pattern.*

Crystal jug *The rhyton, for pouring libations, has a crystal handle.*

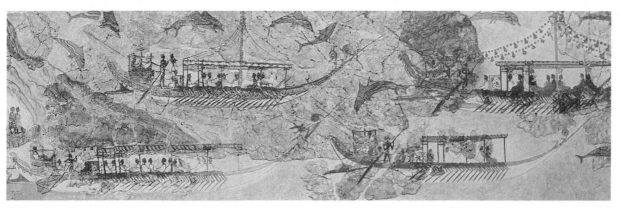

Naval power *The glory of Minoan maritime might is shown in a frieze from Akrotiri, on Thera. A variety of ships – some with masts and rigging festooned with decorations – are surrounded by playful dolphins. The ships are powered by banks of rowers and steered by large oars.*

MARKET DAY IN ANCIENT CRETE

A palace stands at the top of the hill, and from the courtyard in front of it a road leads off in each direction to encircle the little Minoan town. Down from the palace descends a stepped, cobbled street some 6 ft (1.8 m) wide, with rows of houses pressing close on either side. Made of rough stone and mud, plastered and painted, each home has a single door facing the street, with a stone threshold leading into the ground-floor rooms. Stairs lead to an upper floor, which is topped by a roof supported on wooden beams and columns.

A dog lies stretched out in the shade of a wall, too sleepy to investigate the passer-by. Now and then a narrow alleyway runs off between the houses, leading to further homes set back behind those facing the road. Through an open door the passer-by can glimpse a potter working at his wheel, or a farmer pressing the olives he has just gathered from his trees.

In Gournia, a little town set on a low hill on the northern coast of Crete, the visitor today can still walk the line of the Minoan streets and imagine them as they were 4000 years ago, thronged with the comings and goings of the town's 700 inhabitants. The roads are still stone-paved, and low walls mark the outlines of the houses.

An offering at the shrine

Along these ancient roads it is easy to imagine a farmer passing on his way home with a donkey carrying panniers full of grapes or olives. If a ship had just put in, a procession of people would be wending their way up the street with supplies of copper, ivory and other materials destined for the palace stores. At one corner a carpenter might be observed hurrying along with his tool kit

Piped water *Segmented terracotta pipes, interlocking and roped together through loops, carried the water supply in Minoan palaces.*

to do some minor repairs on the cargo ship, or to a neighbour's fishing boat. Meanwhile, the ship's captain would have reached the town and turned up a small cul-de-sac to where a simple, one-roomed building up a short flight of steps housed the town's only public temple. A safe and speedy journey called for a thank-offering to be made at the shrine.

Gournia was typical of the small towns in which one in three of Minoan Crete's 150,000 inhabitants lived. They were unfortified, because the sea around the coasts provided protection enough from enemies. The remainder of the population lived in villages, hamlets and isolated farmsteads.

Gracious living in the palace

Knossos, always the largest and most important town in the island, had a population of 20,000. Its palace was the seat of the island's government, the scene of ceremonies and religious rituals such as bull-leaping, and the residence of the island's ruling families. The living quarters of the palace at Knossos must have been on the upper floors of the palaces, since the number and size of living rooms on the ground floor are very limited.

The rooms that do survive, however, give the impression of gracious living. Light-wells and folding doors between piers allowed plenty of light and air into cool rooms, which were paved with smooth gypsum slabs and brightened with colourful frescoes. The palace residents bathed in tubs made of painted clay, filled by servants using pitchers. The water, carried through clay pipes, was also used to flush an efficient system of toilets.

Many of the retainers and officials lived in houses just beyond the walls of the palace, and not surprisingly these houses emulated the palatial living quarters in both their design and decoration, but on a smaller and less lavish scale.

Farther out in the 'suburbs' of towns such as Knossos and Malia the houses were less elaborate, without the fine paving and artistic frescoes, but they still offered comfortable accommodation for a Minoan family. Many were still built on two or three storeys; a fine mosaic found at Knossos depicts houses with timber-reinforced walls, doors at street level and windows on the first and second floors. Other houses had only one storey, but still possessed seven or eight rooms. A typical Minoan house had separate

HUSTLE AND BUSTLE IN THE BAY

The harbour rings with a cacophony of street noises. It is market day and a butcher tries to extol the quality of his meat, vying with a visiting eastern merchant showing off a roll of rich purple cloth. Behind them a scuffle breaks out among a gang of young men outside a local brothel, and to try to calm them down, the madam hurls water from a second-storey window.

This is Gournia, a thriving Cretan harbour town, around 1500 BC. Across the bay, a stately palace lies tiered on a hillside in the morning sun, while the townsfolk go about their daily business. Sheep graze on the slope above the fishing boats moored in the bay, a group of boys play on the grass, and some other youngsters throw stones out over the water. Beyond them, in the shade of a Mediterranean umbrella pine, women sit, serenely spinning. A porter helping to unload a recently docked merchant vessel down in the harbour passes by carrying a tusk of ivory – a precious import from Libya, one of the widely travelled Minoan traders' many ports of call.

Bare-breasted women squat on the grass, with their fishermen-husbands' latest catch of assorted fish and octopus. Beyond them, an olive and fig dealer has been unloading the contents of his baskets from his donkey. to display his wares on the street. Beyond an open window on the ground floor of the corner house, a potter is busy turning a storage jar: no fewer than five potters' wheels have been unearthed at Gournia. Today, only a labyrinth of ruins of the lower layers of the town walls remain as testimony to this once busy and bustling little jewel of the Aegean.

rooms for eating and sleeping, and either a kitchen or a small yard in which cooking was done. Here there might be an olive press in one corner and a millstone for grinding flour in another. A large *pithos*, or earthenware storage jar, might also stand here to collect and store rainwater. The living rooms might have wooden or stone benches built against the wall, as well as folding stools and small, low tables. Bedrooms were furnished with low couches or simply mattresses on the floor, and wooden chests for storing clothes and other possessions.

Meals were served on pottery plates and in bowls which were usually brightly decorated with abstract designs. Mutton was the commonest meat on the table, although pork, beef and seafood were also available. There was no shortage of herbs to flavour the dishes, nor of beans, peas and other

Night light *To light their way about their homes, Minoans had portable lamps of red clay with ring or loop handles.*

vegetables to accompany them. Grapes, figs and pears made up the second course, and the Minoans loved honey. Ancient Cretans, like their modern successors, washed their meals down with plenty of wine.

In the towns, some householders were craftsmen who would have a workshop in their house, but many other townsmen and the vast majority of villagers made a living from the land. The mill, the oil press and the collection of simple tools – axes, sickles, chisels and all-purpose knives – found in the remains of their homes testify to their daily occupations.

PRETTY AND PRACTICAL

Minoan craftsmen added the touch of artistry to the humblest of everyday objects. Wine cups, tumblers, pitchers, jugs and jars of clay were painted in white, orange, red or brown, sometimes with banded neck and base and sinuous bands following the vessel's contours. To keep themselves warm when the Aegean sun went down, the islanders used clay fire boxes, vessels with holes in the sides, like miniature braziers, which they could carry from room to room. For lighting their homes they had portable oil lamps of burnt red clay. To grind food, such as cereals, the Minoans used a pestle and mortar; the pestle was simply a convenient lump of natural rock, but the stone mortar was carefully cut, with feet to keep it steady. Knives of bronze were often curved, and bevelled to a sharp edge on both sides; one end was then bent over to serve as a handle.

Ritual pan

Four-handled storage jar

Clay water jug

Pestle and mortar

Portable heater and bronze knife

Homes in miniature *Plaques in faience, or glazed limestone paste, which decorated a chest, give an idea of the appearance of the homes of ordinary Minoans. Built of unbaked brick, the houses rose to two or three storeys, and the outside walls were colourfully painted. Inside, the homes even of the less well-off were lavishly furnished.*

Olive press *Fruit was put into the upper jar, then boiled. The juice trickled through the spout into the lower vessel, to be ladled into storage jars. The three-legged clay pot (right) was used for cooking.*

LEAPING IN HOMAGE TO THE GODS

Religion for the Minoans was a joyous affair, its ceremonies accompanied by vigorous acrobatics, dancing and wrestling. The deities worshipped by the Minoans were predominantly female, a group of proud goddesses who are depicted bare-breasted but extravagantly costumed, like the priestesses who conducted the many ceremonies in their honour.

The rulers of the city-states of Minoan Crete were spiritual as well as secular leaders, and the palaces from which they administered their realms were also the scene of frequent religious rituals and ceremonies. The most extraordinary of these was the amazing ritual of 'bull-leaping', in which young men and women clad only in loincloths attempted to somersault over the backs of charging bulls.

The bulls, trapped in the countryside in nets, were let loose in an arena marked out in the central court of the palace. One after another, young men and women approached the bull face to face, then grasped it by the horns and turned a handspring over its back, landing on the ground behind the bull where a companion steadied them. The young leapers must have required strong muscles and immense courage. Modern bullfighters doubt whether such a feat was possible, yet many surviving frescoes and models show it being safely accomplished, and none depicts any mishaps. The risk of death and injury for the participants must, however, have been high.

Originally, princes and princesses are thought to have been the performers in these bull-leaping ceremonies; in later times, however, specially trained athletes took over their roles. The origin and exact significance of the ceremony is unknown; however, the male potency of the bull may well have been seen as conferring fertility and strength on the celebrants.

Knuckle-dusters in the ring

Boxers and wrestlers also competed to honour the Minoan gods and goddesses. Some of these contests could be violent: one contemporary illustration shows boxers wearing

Leaping the bull
A fresco from Knossos shows a youth in mid-somersault over the back of a bull. A girl waits to steady him.

Hunting the bull *Catching Cretan bulls was as dangerous as bull-leaping. A Minoan gold cup shows a bull knocking down and tossing his would-be captors.*

what appear to be knuckle-dusters and protective helmets. Another spectacle attracting large crowds to the palace courtyards was the dancing display, in which troupes of Minoan women in colourful flounced dresses and tight bodices performed disciplined formation dancing – and sometimes more hectic displays in small circles consisting of three or four dancers. The dancers whirled around to the music of pipes, lyres and tambourines.

The same priests and priestesses who supervised these public religious ceremonies also officiated at more private rituals. In the darker recesses of each palace were tiny shrines lined by plaster benches on which were arrayed sacred symbols such as bulls' horns, the *labrys* or double-headed axe, figures of birds and statuettes of the deities. Here the priests and priestesses came, sometimes accompanied by musicians, to pour libations of milk or wine. The principal deity worshipped at these shrines was the protectress of hearth and home,

often known as the Snake Goddess from the serpents she is depicted grasping in both hands in frescoes and statuettes of ivory and gold. Some of the dances performed before the crowds may have been dedicated to the Snake Goddess. Others may have honoured other Minoan goddesses, including those whose role it was to guard the islanders' animals and crops. Many Minoans wore amulets or charms to ensure divine protection.

A shrine on the hilltop

Away from the towns, farmers and peasants flocked eagerly to informal religious ceremonies which were held in the countryside – in caves, on mountain peaks, in forest clearings and beside tumbling streams. Natural caves, of which there are many in Crete, became the focus of particular myths and legends, while many hilltops became the site of open-air shrines – simple enclosures surrounded by rough walls, within which offerings were made and fires lit. Fragments of thousands of

figurines have been found at these sites. Most of them represent cattle, sheep and goats, and were probably left there, or tossed onto a blazing pyre, by farmers seeking protection and blessings for their valuable animals.

Down in the villages, different rituals were performed, particularly at harvest time. The elaborately carved Harvester Vase found at Ayia Triadha, the heart of a major corn-growing area, shows one of these ceremonies in progress. The young men of the village are performing a celebratory dance, prancing along in processional ranks of three and four, their pitchforks and flails over their shoulders. More sober, but equally joyful dances were performed by the men of the village on other occasions, including perhaps

Boxing boys *Sparring boys, each wearing one glove, are shown on a Thera fresco.*

Snake cult *The goddess in glazed limestone paste is garbed as a Minoan noblewoman. She grasps snakes, symbolising the renewal of life by shedding their skin.*

'Now the dancers ran ever so lightly with cunning feet. . . A big crowd stood around enjoying the passionate dance; and two tumblers spun around in their midst, setting the rhythm of the performance.'

HOMER, *THE ODYSSEY*

weddings. The circling men, arms on each other's shoulders, seen on a clay model from Kamilari appear similar to modern Cretan dancing. Symbolic bulls' horns set on the wall of the court in which they perform suggest that the dance had a ritual function – perhaps associated with funerals, as the model was found in a tomb.

To what extent the Minoans believed in an afterlife is not known, but some of them were certainly buried with the objects they might need or desire in another world. In the case of the wealthy elite among the islanders, such grave-goods included golden jewellery and trinkets, while a carpenter at Knossos was buried with his saw and chisels. The mass of the population, however, could expect no more than a pottery vessel or two for company in the grave. Similarly, while the rich and powerful were buried in specially built tombs with carefully laid masonry, ordinary folk could hope for, at best, space in a rock-cut chamber along with the rest of the family.

Dancing girls *Bell-shaped dresses adorn the dancers in a clay model, as they wheel round a lyre player.*

Model temple *Two shepherds look on from above, as the snake goddess performs a ritual.*

Blood sacrifice *A bull lies trussed on a table, its throat cut and its blood flowing into a jar. Two goats await a similar fate. A robed figure plays a flute, and a woman in an animal skin offers fruit at an altar.*

LION-HUNTERS, CIVIL SERVANTS AND KINGS

Hilltop cities ringed with stout walls of stone were the homes of the Mycenaeans, a warlike people who flourished in mainland Greece from about 1500 BC and superseded the Minoans as the dominant power in the Aegean. They were ruled by warrior-kings living in great palaces, their throne-halls bright with frescoes, looking out across the countryside they dominated. The great city-states included Argos, Pylos, Tiryns – and Mycenae itself, after which the entire civilisation is named.

The ruins of Mycenae still tower today above the Argive Plain in southern Greece. Visitors enter, as the defenders of the fortress did 3500 years ago, through the imposing Lion Gate, named after the sculptures of two lionesses which face each other on top of it. From the gate a road led to the royal palace. This consisted of out-houses and a main building with a series of anterooms, bedrooms and storerooms built around a *megaron*, or main hall, supported in the middle by four fluted pillars.

Painted walls and a tiled floor

The hall was dominated by the throne and by a flat, circular hearth and smoke hole – complete with wooden chimney and earthenware flue. On the walls were vividly coloured pictures of hunting scenes, and the floor and ceiling were tiled.

Here the monarch lived surrounded by courtiers, bodyguards, beautiful bare-bosomed women, servants and slaves. Many of the men wore beards – though not moustaches – and had shoulder-length hair.

Just below the palace, a series of houses of two and three storeys were built in terraces on the side of the hill. These were occupied by administrators, tax officials, merchants, wealthy landowners – and by the Followers. These noblemen were the monarch's closest friends, and his dining companions for feasts of venison and Mediterranean shellfish, washed down with large quantities of locally produced wine. The Followers were provided with chariots and charioteers

Fortified citadel *Built on a rocky spur lodged between two deep ravines, Mycenae consisted of two towns. The upper town lay between the palace and a ring of walls made of massive stone blocks; these walls were believed to have been built by the mythical one-eyed giants, the Cyclops, for Perseus, the founder and first king of Mycenae. The lower town spread across the slopes outside the walls.*

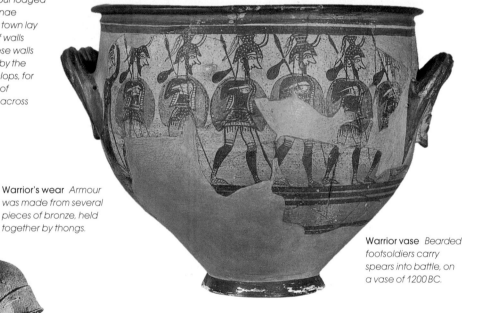

Warrior's wear *Armour was made from several pieces of bronze, held together by thongs.*

Warrior vase *Bearded footsoldiers carry spears into battle, on a vase of 1200 BC.*

WHEN LIONS ROAMED ANCIENT GREECE

Hunting wild game was among the favourite pastimes of the wealthier, land-owning Mycenaeans. Lions, which roamed the countryside, were pursued by huntsmen in chariots, and on foot by teams of hunters bearing bows and arrows and long-pointed spears. Lion-hunting was also a popular pastime among off-duty warriors of the Mycenaean army. Stags and wild duck were also fair game; wild boars were hunted for meat and also for their tusks which were cut, shaped and pierced as decorations for warriors' helmets. The leading Mycenaean warriors also wore bronze armour consisting of a cuirass protecting the chest and back, a high collar or neck guard, shoulder pieces and broad bands that covered the abdomen and groin. Weapons included bows and arrows, javelins, spears, slings, swords and daggers. Full armour was also donned by noblemen when they charged into battle in their two-horse chariots.

Noble pursuit *Huntsmen stalk lions, on a bronze dagger decoration.*

to transport them about the area, and were given slaves and sometimes arable land – which, like the king himself, they rented to tenant-farmers.

House of a merchant

Among the buildings at Mycenae whose remains have been unearthed in modern times are the House of the Oil Merchant – an impressive building with 12 rooms on the ground floor, and a basement beneath. In the ruins of the house were found several large *pithoi*, or storage jars, filled with oil and ready for dispatch. Similar houses that have been uncovered in the area include the House of the Warrior Vase, the House of Shields, the House of Sphinxes, the House of Columns, and The Granary – all being named after the main objects, products or frescoes found in them.

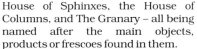

Gold death mask of a Mycenaean king

Like the palace, the flat-roofed houses grew around spacious main halls. The walls had wooden frames, covered with plaster, to help withstand earthquakes, and wooden staircases led to the upstairs bedrooms. Except for rural shrines, the Mycenaeans had no temples or communal places of worship. In most sizable homes, however, one room was set aside as a shrine for the worship of a variety of gods – including Poseidon, the god of the sea, of the horse, and of earthquakes, Demeter, the earth goddess of harvests and corn, Ares, the god of war, Dionysus, the god of wine, and Apollo, the sun god.

Toasts to the deities were drunk from stag-shaped gold cups, and tablets found at Pylos and Thebes suggest that human sacrifices were offered to the gods along with pigs, goats and sheep.

Two rings of graves, part of a large hillside cemetery, were also excavated at Mycenae. The first ring was located inside the city walls, near the Lion Gate; the second ring was situated outside the walls. These were the burial places of the king and members of his family. The king was laid out in his state robes and gold crown, and his face was covered with a death mask of beaten gold. Around him were placed his favourite belongings, such as a bronze dagger inlaid with gold and silver leaf.

The dead lay with their heads on stone pillows. Beside them were placed such personal possessions as were deemed necessary for life in the next world. These included bowls, daggers, shields and mirrors, all made of bronze, gold drinking cups, stone arrowheads, and religious statuettes fashioned from ivory. In later graves, shaped like beehives and called *tholos* tombs, a long stone corridor, or *dromos*, led to the burial chamber, and here the deceased's friends drank wine to his memory before the entrance to the tomb was sealed.

Farming played a major role in the Mycenaean economy, with most of the population living and working on the land. Sheep-rearing was a major activity, and the production of wool enabled many farmers to live in modest but comfortable stone houses, while the peasants lived in one-roomed dwellings made of unfired brick.

A herdsman's food ration

Along with gold and linen-making, olive oil was a main source of wealth, and it was used in vast quantities for cooking and lighting. Wheat, barley and grain formed the basic diet, and peasants were often paid in kind. Their 'rations' were recorded by the palace scribes, and it was decreed that, say, a herdsman's share of cereal should not be more than five times a boy's. For the table, cereals were spiced with coriander, fennel, or cress; strong-tasting milk and cheese from goats and honeyed wine were also popular.

Noblemen among the Mycenaean soldiers were protected by armour, by figure-of-eight shields made of oxhide stretched across wooden frames, and by a variety of helmets – including some made of leather and capped with the tusks of wild boars. The kingdom's sea-raiders seized Minoan colonies and trading posts. On slaving raids to the outlying islands it is thought they frequently put the men to death and brought back the women and children, whom it was easier to keep in a state of permanent slavery.

The fall of Troy

Around 850 BC the Greek epic poet Homer immortalised the warrior-kings of the Mycenaean Bronze Age in his *Iliad*. Written 400 years after the events it describes, this tells how in about 1200 BC the Mycenaeans, under the rule of their legendary king Agamemnon, captured the city of Troy after a ten-year siege.

But the days of the Mycenaeans were already numbered. About this time bands of central Mediterranean pirates known as the Sea Peoples – whose raids on Egypt had been repulsed – cut off the trade routes from the Greek mainland. This, together with a series of inter-state wars, weakened the civilisation. Its cities were gradually destroyed and largely abandoned; and by about 1100 BC the Mycenaean Age was over. The Dark Age of Greece – lasting from the 11th to the 8th centuries – was about to begin.

Scribe's scribble *Some writing tablets bear doodles, such as this maze drawn by a scribe bored with his repetitive work.*

BUREAUCRATS WHO RULED BY THE WRITTEN WORD

The Mycenaean rulers were among the world's earliest bureaucrats, using a huge 'civil service' of scribes to regulate and record every detail of citizens' lives. These scribes kept a tally of taxes paid and of people exempt from tax; of how much wool a farmer was expected to produce and how much bronze a smith was to be allocated for making arrowheads; of how many children lived in a town and how many chariots were kept in the palace. Scribes also acted as the channel through which the orders and demands of state officials were sent around the kingdom. To keep records, a new form of script was developed – known as Linear B because it was one of the world's first known scripts to be written in regular lines. Deciphered in 1952 by the cryptographer Michael Ventris, the script uses symbols, developed from earlier picture writing, to represent the syllables of early Greek.

TI   RI   PO   DE

Keeping the records *Sitting on a low, three-legged stool – the basis of the symbols (above) which were used to form the word* tripode, *'tripod' – a scribe holds a tablet of soft, damp clay in one hand and a sharply pointed thorn stylus in the other. Carefully he writes down information dictated by a vineyard inspector. The scribe corrects mistakes as he goes along – once the tablet has dried in the sun it will be too hard to alter. Finished tablets are stored on shelves.*

Bronze bounty *A clay tablet from Pylos, in the south-west of Greece, is inscribed with a list of contributions of bronze from 32 officials throughout the kingdom of Mycenae. Short upright bars represent units, horizontal bars represent tens, and circles signify hundreds.*

PEOPLE OF BIBLE TIMES

The Near East has seen civilisation after civilisation rise in splendour and crumble into ruins, leaving only traces in the desert sands. Tribes seeking safety or a better life journeyed to and fro along the Fertile Crescent – a green swath linking the Persian Gulf with the eastern shore of the Mediterranean by way of the Rivers Tigris and Euphrates. Here in the land of Canaan there developed the world's earliest alphabet which, in various forms, traders spread throughout the known world. To this same land the Hebrews came from Mesopotamia, to found a kingdom and proclaim their belief in the one true God.

One Babylonian empire rose, and fell to the might of the Assyrians; a second Babylon became the most splendid city of its time before falling to the Persian conquerors. A governor of the Roman Empire ruled Judaea by the time Jesus Christ preached a Gospel which was to spread to the ends of the earth. Through it all, as armies marched and battles raged, farmers and craftsmen laboured on in a pattern of life that changed little with the passing centuries.

HEBREWS, CANAANITES, BABYLONIANS, ASSYRIANS AND PERSIANS 2000 BC – AD 150

MARKS OF THE PAST IN HOLY LAND OF JESUS

Palestinian society in the days of Jesus of Nazareth already bore the traces of layer upon layer of earlier history. From the Mediterranean coast to the River Jordan, from Galilee to Judaea, the complex and colourful history of the land was evident in the varied ways of everyday life among the people.

In villages such as Nazareth in Galilee, couples like Joseph and Mary struggled to keep their pious ways – while in Scythopolis near the Jordan, Greek teachers drilled into their charges the epics of Homer. Scribes in synagogues, zealot rebels in the hills, Samaritans, priests, Roman soldiers, Phoenician traders, peasants – all met at this crossroads of the world.

Tools used in Jesus's day had changed little over the centuries. As a child, Jesus would have helped Joseph in his carpenter's shop, using adze, mallet and saw, before joining other boys at the synagogue to be taught the scriptures. The synagogue, centre of village life, grew out of a painful past. When the Babylonians destroyed Jerusalem and the Temple and drove the Jews into exile, the dispossessed found places to meet for prayer and mutual support. These meeting places or synagogues served so well that they were introduced into Palestine when the exiles returned.

Another result of the Babylonian conquest and the centuries of Persian domination that followed it was that Jesus and his countrymen spoke the Aramaic language of Mesopotamia in everyday life, rather than the Hebrew of King David and their Israelite ancestors. The remnants of history lay all around Nazareth. As Jesus travelled through Samaria, in the heart of Palestine, he conversed with a woman

Exotic northerner *The aquiline features of a Philistine are captured on glazed brick by an Egyptian artist of around 1180 BC. The Egyptians were fascinated by the strange clothes and ways of these sea-raiders who, coming from Crete, settled on the southern coast of Palestine and became the constant enemies of the Jews. They also attacked Egypt, but were defeated.*

Fertility symbol *Bulls were revered for their strength and potency. Canaanites buried this gilded bronze in a sanctuary at Byblos.*

drawing water at Jacob's well. She was performing the regular task of women in the region, but her words that day reflected the beliefs of the Samaritans, a group whose existence grew out of a disaster. In 722 BC an Assyrian army captured the capital of Samaria, deporting many of the inhabitants and substituting deportees from elsewhere under an Assyrian governor.

A distinctive way of life evolved in Samaria, incorporating the law of Moses but rejecting many practices of Judaism. Samaritans and Jews lived side by side but conflict was never far from the surface. All that painful history lay behind the woman's astonishment that Jesus would even speak to her – as St John's Gospel says: 'Jews have no dealings with Samaritans.'

> *'For the Lord is bringing you to a rich land...a land of olives and honey.'*
>
> DEUTERONOMY 8:7,8

Neither community would have had much to do with pagan Greeks nearby, a reminder of another conqueror, Alexander the Great, whose army had subjugated the region in 332 BC. In Caesarea and Ptolemais on the Mediterranean coast, in eastern cities such as Pella, Scythopolis, Gadara, Philadelphia and Gerasa, or even in Sebaste built on the ruins of Samaria, Greeks and Greek speakers could live much as they would in Greece itself or in Hellenistic cities in territories where Alexander had triumphed. Their culture was consciously cosmopolitan, proud of a long tradition of local government, art, literature, theatre and education that people everywhere envied. A merchant in Scythopolis or Pella might worship at the temple of

Dionysus, participate in the city assembly and hope to send his son to university in Athens. He might be friendly with wealthy Jews or with Samaritans who spoke Greek and who shared his commercial interests.

Many Jewish aristocrats, including the royal Hasmonean and Herodian families and the high priests and their clans, were attracted to Greek culture and education, particularly its athletic side. They shocked more traditional Jews by wearing the short Hellenistic tunic. Some young priests adopted the *petasos*, or Greek hat, and even set up a gymnasium near the temple where they exercised in the nude. The rich indulged in banquets while the peasantry saw meat – roast lamb or goat – only on festive days, relying for their everyday diet on bread, dried or salted fish, vegetables, fruit and cheese. Brooding over their daily life lay the might of Rome. Herod Antipas, a Jew, governed Galilee at Caesar's pleasure and kept it pacified with his tax collectors, such as Matthew who became a disciple of Jesus, and soldiers such as the centurion whose servant boy Jesus cured of paralysis. Samaria and Judaea were ruled by Roman governors such as Pontius Pilate.

Roman troops had the right to compel Jewish citizens to carry their burdens for up to a mile. Jesus urged his followers to show extraordinary service to the Romans by going a second mile.

Legionaries often came from far-off lands such as Germany or Gaul and were impressed by Roman civilisation. They doubtless wondered why Jews should want to fight this benevolent power. But fight they did. In the hills dwelt warriors who harassed the occupiers while biding their time for full-scale revolt. One zealot named Simon became a disciple of Jesus.

Many conquerors had tramped the roads where Jesus walked. Each left some mark that continued to shape how people thought and struggled and hoped. Nebuchadnezzar of Babylon, Sargon the Assyrian, Alexander the Great and Pompey the Roman were all gone, but their imprint remained.

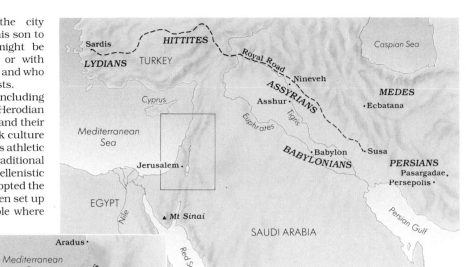

One from many *Persian kings of the 6th century BC welded all the peoples of the Middle East into one empire, stretching from the Aegean to the borders of India. Through the realm ran the 1677 mile (2698 km) Royal Road used by the kings' pony express mail service.*

Cradle of the faith *Though small in area, the Holy Land has been the scene of momentous events over many thousands of years. Its early inhabitants were among the first to benefit from the discovery of farming around 10,000 BC, and this encouraged the growth of cities that still thrive today.*

Graven image *The Israelites were surrounded by pagans who venerated idols, such as this Phoenician ivory carving of a seated goddess. Moses warned his people that if they wished to enjoy God's mercy and the promise of a new land, they must turn aside from the worship of idols. The prophet Jeremiah told them that wooden gods gave no better protection 'than a scarecrow in a plot of cucumbers'.*

Royal lawgiver *With the blossoming of civilisation came the need for laws to regulate the growing complexity of human activities. A patchwork of laws was collected by Hammurabi, who ruled Babylon for 42 years from 1792 BC and ordered copies of his laws to be set up in public places. Carved into this 7 ft (2 m) slab are 282 laws fixing penalties for numerous offences, some based on the principle of an 'eye for an eye'. At the top Hammurabi stands before the sun god Shamash.*

THE HEBREWS, PEOPLE WITH A SINGLE GOD

Three times a year the routine of life among the ancient Hebrews came to a halt. Roads became rivers of humanity as farmers and craftsmen, rich and poor, headed for the great temple that Solomon had built in Jerusalem. All were thronging to celebrate festivals that marked their history, and also the seasons of planting and harvest.

The Hebrew nation had gained a new pride and self-confidence in the days of Solomon's father, King David, who ended foreign domination and transformed the rickety structure of the Hebrew tribes into a kingdom. He gave them a new capital in Jerusalem.

But nothing so symbolised their unity and strength as the temple that Solomon completed in about 953 BC. Resplendent in polished cedar and glittering with beaten gold, it was an unearthly vision to ordinary folk used to the drabness of village life.

Above all, it contained the Holy of Holies, a hidden room where God was present and where rested the golden Ark of the Covenant, containing the Ten Commandments on stone tablets. The temple inspired the people to imagine the glory of their God and the importance of their covenant with him. Throughout most of the one thousand years or so of their existence before the time of Solomon they had worshipped at movable altars and in tents – because they had been a people on the

Winged guardian *This creature from an 8th-century BC ivory plaque has wings and a human head on an animal's body. Two similar figures flanked the Ark of the Covenant.*

A MIGHTY TEMPLE IN JERUSALEM

Worship at the great limestone temple built by Solomon started outside the building itself. In the broad courtyard, servants bring water to refill an enormous bronze bowl used for ritual cleansing. To the right a priest officiates at an altar for burnt offerings. The temple's eastern entrance is flanked by 40ft (12m) bronze pillars; inside, the main sanctuary, 180ft (54m) long, soars to a height of 50ft (15m). At the west end is the windowless Holy of Holies, entered just once a year by the High Priest. The temple stood for eight centuries, and in the 1st century BC Herod the Great turned it into one of the world's glories. Colonnades and courtyards were crowded with worshippers, and markets sprang up outside. The temple supported hundreds of priests and functionaries and gave work for many artisans. But the war which began when the Jews rose against their Roman oppressors, in AD 70. resulted in the destruction of the temple, and most of Jerusalem with it.

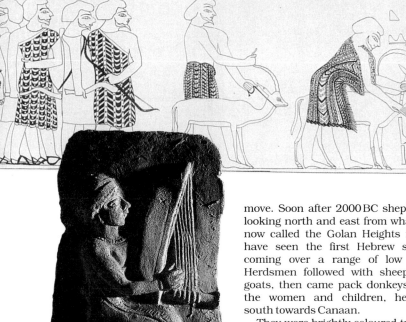

Caravan on the move *The Nile Delta acted as a magnet to peoples living in western Asia and the Fertile Crescent, either as a source of plunder or for lawful trade. An Egyptian tomb painting of about 1900 BC shows a tribe of Semites on their way to Egypt in the days of the patriarchs. The caravan includes women, children and animals. The men are armed with typical Canaanite weapons of the period – chiefly spears and double-convex bows. The warrior on the extreme left also carries an axe with a 'duck-bill' blade. Ahead of him strides a man playing a stringed instrument to lighten their step.*

Heavenly music *The harp was played only by nobles and priests, never by women. It was used in temple worship and was believed to provide the music in Heaven.*

Ark of God *The tribes carried the tablets of the Ten Commandments in the Ark of the Covenant, usually borne on poles but carried to Jerusalem by David on a cart.*

move. Soon after 2000 BC shepherds looking north and east from what are now called the Golan Heights might have seen the first Hebrew scouts coming over a range of low hills. Herdsmen followed with sheep and goats, then came pack donkeys with the women and children, heading south towards Canaan.

They wore brightly coloured tunics, knee-length for men, slightly longer for the women. Men wore sandals or went barefoot, the women leather shoes. Most of the adult males had neatly trimmed beards and hair hanging to the neck; the women's tresses flowed down their backs.

When these nomads camped, they grouped round a tent belonging to their patriarch, an elderly Amorite named Abram, later to be known as Abraham. He was leaving behind the clan of his father and brothers at Ur in southern Mesopotamia and migrating into unknown territory.

Abraham's journey launched the history of the new Hebrew people, a moment of incalculable consequence for the world. Leaving the Euphrates valley with its dark, thick-walled houses, Abraham's growing clan moved to the dry but open wilderness and pasture land of Canaan. In the times of Abraham, his son Isaac and grandson Jacob, known also as Israel, they prospered as semi-nomadic herders moving like shadows among the villages and towns.

Worship of one god

As patriarchs, Abraham, Isaac and Jacob were rich, hospitable, powerful and generous. To the Canaanites they were always outsiders. They never owned the land where they camped or fed their flocks. At most they bought grave sites in which to bury their dead. Even without land the Hebrews were a

force to be reckoned with. In time of danger Abraham was able to raise 318 trained men from among his own servants. The clan's wealth lay in flocks and herds, but when they came to a fertile spot they would stay for some time planting crops to supplement the meat provided by their animals.

The tribal folk kept their identity by discouraging intermarriage; Isaac and Jacob sought wives from among their kindred in Mesopotamia rather than the local people. Their most striking characteristic was their religion of a single deity, distinct from the gods of the Canaanites: Abraham's descendants told how the 'God of Abraham', *Yahweh*, had promised to give the land of Canaan to his descendants.

> '*Get thee out of thy country, unto a land that I shall shew thee.*'
>
> GENESIS 12:1

The Hebrews were vulnerable to the drought and dearth that struck the land time and again. The Book of Genesis tells how Abraham, soon after arriving in Canaan, went to Egypt to escape famine. Later, hunger forced Jacob to take the Hebrews to Egypt, where they remained for generations.

They adapted their shepherd life to the settled ways of the Nile Delta, remaining together in the Goshen region where their numbers grew. The Egyptians used this alien population as forced labour to make bricks. Pharaoh's taskmasters 'made their lives bitter with hard service'.

Bondage in Egypt continued until Moses led the Hebrews into the desert between the forks of the Red Sea. They were forced to spend years as unwilling nomads in a harsh wilderness, facing the demands of a freedom they had

never known. Early in their wanderings Moses led his people to the holy mountain of Sinai, where they renewed their covenant with God and received a fresh set of laws, the Ten Commandments. This laid down the weekly cycle of six days of work and a holy day of rest; it affirmed the sanctity of human life, marriage, justice under law and basic property rights.

The Hebrews worshipped in a movable shrine, an elaborate tent structure called the tabernacle. With them they took the Ark of the Covenant, believing that it not only contained the laws governing their behaviour, but that it also symbolised the presence of God among them.

Into the Promised Land

By now the single clan of Abraham had evolved into 12 great tribes. The Hebrews continued their travels until they came to the River Jordan, the border of Canaan, ready to enter the land which had been promised to Abraham centuries before. Led by Joshua, Moses's successor, they came gradually to dominate the region.

They maintained a loose tribal confederacy with no central authority except faith in their shared law. It was freedom to the point of anarchy; as the Book of Judges says, 'every man did what was right in his own eyes'. Rivals harassed them with devastating raids: crops were destroyed, villages wasted. Finally the elders were ready to surrender authority to a king who could unify the nation and maintain an army powerful enough to throw off foreign domination.

Saul, the first king installed over the nation, was only partially successful because his bouts of depression and apparent paranoia alienated some of his most able supporters, such as the young commander, David. When Saul was killed in battle, the nation fell into civil war from which David emerged as a strong and victorious king.

David unified his people, overcame surrounding nations and extended the boundaries of the kingdom of Israel. David's accomplishments enabled his son Solomon to enjoy prosperity and replace the tabernacle with the magnificent temple in Jerusalem – around a thousand years after Abraham had first entered Canaan.

The lives of the Hebrews had seen many wanderings and sufferings, many defeats and triumphs. Yet for ten centuries their ways and beliefs had survived.

THE HEBREWS AS VILLAGERS AND CITIZENS

Armies tramped through the village streets, governments changed, empires rose and fell, but life among the Hebrews in the villages of Palestine hardly noticed their passing. The life and work of a shepherd, farmer, vineyard keeper or weaver changed little, as sons took up the crafts of their fathers and daughters learned their round of continual labour from their mothers.

Though walled cities dotted the land of Palestine and were important for the culture and history of Israel, the great majority of men and women lived in small unwalled villages and laboured on the land. The cycle of seed time and harvest is mirrored in the Hebrews' calendar and religious festivals.

Farms were run by peasants and combined a small field – planted with wheat if the soil was fertile, otherwise with barley – a vineyard that provided raisins and wine, and an olive grove for oil. Fig trees would be planted and vegetables grown between the vines.

Most peasant houses comprised a single room of stone or more probably mud brick. Part of the beaten earth floor was covered by a platform where the family slept. The rest was a shelter for animals. A stone-lined pit in the floor stored grain, and a fire pit for cooking kept the room smoky.

Families and clans tried to maintain ownership of ancestral farms, but by Jesus's day most land was owned by landlords living in cities and worked by tenant farmers. Donkeys and camels were raised to carry burdens, and oxen were kept for ploughing; but the herding of sheep and goats predominated, especially where soil was too poor to grow grain. Little changed in the hard and lonely life of the shepherds. At night they brought their flocks into folds, stone enclosures with open gates. Crook and club beside him, a shepherd would lie across the opening and try to sleep, becoming a human gate to protect his charges from wild animals. In most villages the basic necessities of life determined the common occupations. The potter sat making containers from red clay for everyday needs, while the smith hammered by a charcoal fire. Working in bronze and iron, he supplied tools, ploughshares, vessels and fittings.

In some periods smiths were treated as a vital strategic industry, since they alone were capable of making weapons and armour. When the Hebrews were trying to establish their monarchy, the Philistine overlords were effectively disarming them by banning all their smiths. Hebrews had to go to Philistia to have a plough or an axe sharpened.

Near the smithy one might hear a carpenter sawing or the whirr of his hand drill, turned by a bow and leather thong. He provided for the needs of the village folk, usually working in a room open to the street. He sat on the beaten earth floor as he shaped the wood held with his feet and knees. He carved yokes, ploughs and other farm tools; for the village households he made furniture, doors and roof beams.

> '*He shall feed his flock like a shepherd: he shall gather the lambs with his arm.*'
>
> ISAIAH 40:11

Many occupations were tied to particular locations. Most fishermen were to be found around the Sea of Galilee; masons and construction workers flocked to the site of any royal building project; Jerusalem and its temple were the centre for large clans of priests.

Women clothed and fed the nation and reared its children. They carded and spun wool, dyed the thread and wove it on vertical looms; they sewed family garments and cleaned clothes by 'treading' them in streams or public pools. The mistress of a large household would manage many servants, and might even manufacture clothing that city merchants could sell.

Women helped men in harvesting, threshing and winnowing grain. In the villages, milling of flour was done primarily by women using a hand mill or even a basic mortar and pestle. They fetched water, mixed and kneaded dough, baked bread in clay ovens and were responsible for other cooking, rising before dawn to light the fire.

Patriarch's resting place *Modern Hebron, high in the Judaean hills, probably gives a good idea of what a Palestinian town looked like in Biblical times. It is the site of Abraham's tomb.*

Peaceful pursuit *A servant fans an Elamite woman as she winds thread on to a spindle. This 7th or 8th-century BC relief was found at Susa in Iran. The Elamites were defeated by Abraham when they invaded the Jordan Valley.*

Working alongside the freemen and women were frequently slaves or indentured servants. Often these were war captives or their descendants; but many were poor people forced to sell themselves into slavery to make good the debts they could not pay, or who had as children been sold into bondage by their own parents.

A widow whose husband had died in debt begged the prophet Elisha for help because 'the creditor has come to take my two children to be his slaves'. To escape such servitude, men fled to join outlaw bands such as the one David led when in hiding from Saul.

In most communities, authority was held by elders who sat in judgment at the town gate. These heads of clans and families settled all community affairs, from economic decisions to civil disputes and criminal cases. It was simple but effective, though the prophets often condemned bribery and injustice. There were no prosecutors or attorneys: each side presented its arguments, along with witnesses and exhibits. Both law and tradition favoured the accused, requiring at least two eyewitnesses to support conviction for a capital crime. Difficult cases were heard by the king or by an appeals court which comprised both religious and civil leaders.

A hard existence left little time for amusement. The Hebrew Bible makes no mention of sports or pastimes, though archaeologists have uncovered game boards of wood, stone and even ivory. Relaxation probably took the form of feasting, singing and dancing, along with storytelling and contests in concocting and answering riddles.

A tunnel for fresh water

From village simplicity to bustling Jerusalem was a vast change. After David had made it his capital, the city became a major centre of commerce. A secure supply of water was provided through a tunnel, constructed in King Hezekiah's time, that ran inside the wall from a protected spring outside.

The capital was destroyed by the Babylonians in the 6th century BC, slowly coming back to life in the next century as Jews returned from exile in Babylon to rebuild the temple and the city walls. Later, as communities of Jews sprang up in cities from Babylon to Rome, Jerusalem became ever more cosmopolitan, because many of these people returned to the holy city for festivals such as Passover or to spend their final years near the temple.

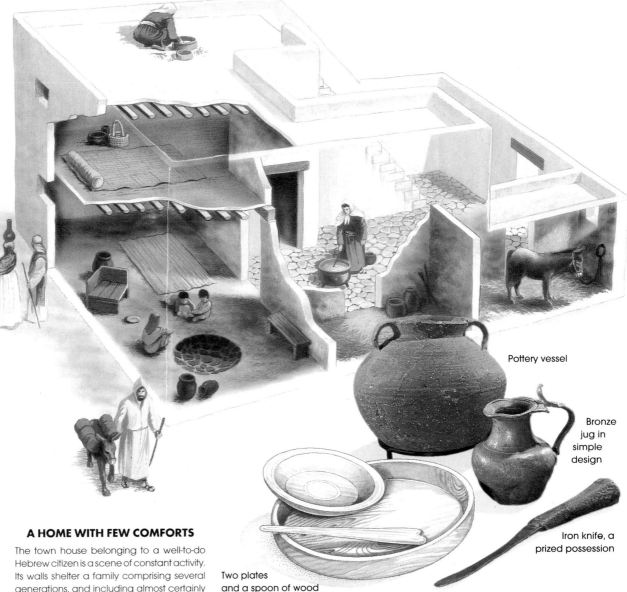

Pottery vessel

Bronze jug in simple design

Iron knife, a prized possession

Two plates and a spoon of wood

A HOME WITH FEW COMFORTS

The town house belonging to a well-to-do Hebrew citizen is a scene of constant activity. Its walls shelter a family comprising several generations, and including almost certainly a slave or two. A door from the street leads into a paved courtyard where a woman is stirring a pot: the warm climate encourages people to live largely in the open air. A donkey stands patiently in its stall while the animal usually kept in the next stall is out helping its master in the fields or carrying goods to market.

The large family room on the ground floor is sparsely furnished with a mat and a crudely made chair. Children squat round the fire pit, where some of the cooking is done. On the upper floor, which is reached by a ladder, the family sleeps, wrapped in cloaks, on mats and bolsters. One woman has climbed up onto the flat roof to carry out a few of her household chores in peace. On summer nights the family will take their mats up here and try to catch a cooling breeze.

HARD LIFE FOR THE WOMEN

Tableware was basic: plates and bowls of wood or earthenware, a bronze jug or two, knives and spoons, produced by craftsmen who usually worked in separate quarters – potters in one, woodworkers in another, smiths in a third. Their designs were more practical than artistic. Women had little to make their toil easier; much of the cooking was done in the courtyard and water had to be fetched from the wells. Lamps of animal fat gave only a flickering light.

Housewife's chore *A clay model, discovered in a tomb in Galilee, shows a woman kneading dough.*

55

REVOLUTION FOR WRITING IN CANAAN

Every child who recites the ABC is continuing a tradition going back more than 3500 years to the Canaanites. It was these creative people, who lived on the east coast of the Mediterranean, who first developed an alphabet to represent spoken sounds. The word 'alphabet' comes, through the Greek, from the Canaanite names of the first two letters of this new system – *alpu* and *betu*.

The region's name of Canaan, it is believed, may have meant 'land of purple'. This referred to the purple dye which the Canaanites extracted from a shellfish called the murex, and used to colour the wool they exported from ports such as Tyre. From the Greek word for this red-purple colour, *phoenix*, derived in turn the name Phoenician for the people who later inherited Canaanite land and culture.

The dye was obtained from a gland in the murex. Each gland yielded a drop or two of liquid which was processed by lengthy simmering in a pan. It took the glands of 60,000 murex snails to produce 1 lb (450 g) of dye, which explains why material dyed in the 'Tyrian purple' was so expensive – and highly esteemed. Papyrus made from the pith of an aquatic reed was distributed in the coastal cities of Canaan to be used as writing material and scrolls for books. The traders of Byblos, one of these cities, became so noted for their high-quality papyrus reeds imported from Egypt that the Greeks used the name Byblos to mean 'book' – and the word 'Bible' is derived from the name of that ancient city.

Flowing locks for a member of the Phoenician aristocracy

Civilisation in Canaan extends deep into the past. Jericho, near the river Jordan, is the oldest walled city known, dating from 7000 BC, and over the next 4000 years many others sprang up, protecting farmers in their fertile valleys and connecting them to trade routes. Farmers left the city in the morning to work in the vineyards and fields, while inside the walls traders arriving from other towns pushed their goods on barrows through a warren of narrow streets to the bustling marketplace. Buyers could shop for wine, olive oil, grain, wool, imported pottery, cedar, ivory, jewellery made from shells or silver and decorated glassware. By the time the Israelites invaded in the 13th century, the city of Hazor had a population of 30,000 to 40,000. Canaanite people were fiercely independent; the towns often quarrelled with each other, failing to achieve that political unification which could have given them the strength to repulse invaders. The tribes and cities were unified by culture and a religion based on myths, which are known through inscribed clay tablets found in the city of Ugarit.

Every town was dotted with shrines and altars, and the ritual included an offering of grain, wine or olive oil at a temple. The principal Canaanite god was Baal, meaning 'Lord'. This expressed Baal's ownership of the land and people and his care for their life and prosperity. He was part of a family of deities under the high god and creator El, meaning simply 'god'.

In myth, Baal was the son of El's brother Dagon, whose name means 'grain'. Baal had gained his standing as principal god by saving the people from destruction wreaked by raging waters and from death brought by drought. Baal himself died, but was restored to life through the love of his sister Anat. Baal's return to life marked the fertility of nature, a mythic

HOW THE ALPHABET BEGAN

Merchants of the ancient Near East who were seeking a quicker way of recording their deals helped to inspire one of history's most revolutionary advances – the invention of an alphabetic system of writing based on the use of one symbol for each sound. Egyptian hieroglyphics and Mesopotamian cuneiform script both used a variety of ways of representing words and syllables, which meant that a huge number of signs had to be memorised. The breakthrough came in the 16th century BC among the Canaanites, early Hebrews and Phoenicians, when it was realised that words are made up of a relatively small number of elementary sounds. Using this phonetic principle a new script was evolved, based on the Semitic speech of the region. Traders took this new script to the western Mediterranean and a variation used in Greece by the 8th century became the basis of all modern alphabets.

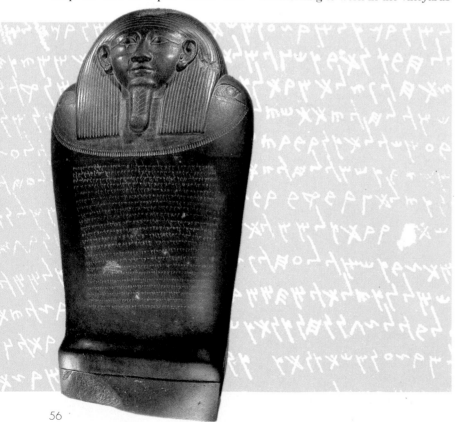

Fit for a king *This Egyptian-style sarcophagus of Eshmunazar of Sidon bears an inscription in praise of the king carved in the newly invented alphabetic script.*

story played out in the cycle of the seasons. For a people who lived between the restless sea and the sterile desert, the myths captured the longing of the people for a stable life on a fertile land. Certain passages bear a striking resemblance to parts of the Psalms.

The early 12th century BC brought disaster for the Canaanites. While Israelite tribes were infiltrating from

Timber trade *Curved Phoenician galleys carried logs of cedar felled in the forests of Lebanon to ports up and down the coast for use in boats, palaces and temples, including Solomon's temple at Jerusalem.*

the east, other groups known as the Sea Peoples moved down the coast from the north and took the cities of Tyre and Sidon. Another branch of the Sea Peoples, the Philistines, occupied south-western Canaan after an attempt to invade Egypt failed. A victory relief carved by the Egyptians on a temple at Medinet Habu depicts the tall, slender Philistine warriors wearing short kilts and feather headdresses and wielding straight swords with round shields. They organised their newly won territory under five allied cities – Ashdod, Ashkelon, Ekron, Gath and Gaza – and became the strongest military power in the region until the time of King David.

The Canaanites could not resist the Israelites and Philistines who fought each other for possession of the land. Gradually they were pushed northwards until only cities such as Tyre, Sidon, Berytus (Beirut), Byblos and Aradus remained as heirs of the ancient culture, now in the keeping of their Phoenician descendants.

The Phoenicians built on their long-standing tradition of sea trade, using their resources of wood and their skill as shipbuilders and woodworkers. They provided timber and craftsmen for such projects as Solomon's temple in Jerusalem. To protect their merchant vessels they developed warships powered by banks of oars-men and armed with rams which pierced hostile vessels below the water line; the rowers then backed away so that the enemy sank.

Phoenicians traded round the Mediterranean in copper from Cyprus, papyrus, ivory and linen from Egypt, and wool from Asia Minor. They mastered navigation and learned to use the North Star to guide their ships at night. By 850 BC they had founded outposts that became major cities, notably Carthage in North Africa. They pressed on to Spain and through the Pillars of Hercules (the Strait of Gibraltar) to trade southwards along the coast of Morocco and northwards to Cadiz and possibly Britain, building profitable long-term markets. They were the first people to sail right round Africa.

Their independence ended in 572 BC when Tyre fell to Nebuchadnezzar of Babylon after a siege of 13 years. Trade carried on and colonies such as Carthage prospered, but the coastal lands of the former Canaan would ever after belong to some larger empire. The 4th century BC saw the destruction of Sidon by the Persians and of Tyre by Alexander. In 146 BC even Carthage fell to the growing might of Rome.

Woman in the window *This ivory carving of a woman in an Egyptian wig may allude to the worship of the Phoenician fertility goddess Astarte in the role of a sacred prostitute.*

CREATORS OF BEAUTIFUL OBJECTS

Despite political upheavals the Phoenicians managed to remain prosperous, and were renowned for their luxurious style of living. There was a great demand for the products of Phoenician craftsmen, and their fine glass, pottery, textiles, ivory ware and metalwork found their way all over the Mediterranean world and the Near East.

Apart from dyes, timber, wine, dates and grain, their merchant vessels carried high-fashion items for the boudoirs of rich women. The silver mirror from Byblos dates from 1250 BC; its lotus-shaped handle shows Egyptian influence. The duck-handled bronze razor from Carthage of around

250 BC reflects the Hellenic taste of later centuries. The Phoenicians had acquired their techniques in glassmaking from Egypt and Mesopotamia, and developed great skill in making beads and ornamental objects. The necklace found in a tomb in Sardinia typifies the widespread traffic in small, delicately modelled glass items. The glass jug was moulded from blue paste, and decorations were added to the surface.

WAR MACHINE THAT SEIZED AN EMPIRE

One of the most feared empires of the ancient world originated in a Semitic peasant people who farmed the fertile northern valley of the River Tigris.

The rise of the Assyrians began as villages looked for protection to the city of Ashur, named after their principal god. The land had productive plains, pastureland and mountains rich in copper ore, limestone, alabaster and marble. It lay athwart caravan routes from the Hittites in Anatolia to southern Mesopotamia, or eastwards across the Zagros mountains to India.

At first, war played little part in the life of the Assyrians, who were busy acquiring wealth. Merchants travelled freely, trading textiles from Ashur. They produced and sold copper, the raw material for tools and weapons. From the east they imported tin essential for turning copper into bronze.

Under King Shamshi-Adad I (1813-1781 BC) the Assyrians enjoyed a brief flowering, but with their good fortune acquired enemies. Pressure from the Babylonians under Hammurabi and from the expanding Hittite Empire to the west was followed by four centuries of foreign domination.

By the time they had shaken this off, their attitudes towards outsiders had changed. The farmers and traders had become warriors. Looking north and east they saw a continual threat from the mountain peoples, and

against them adopted a policy of attack and extermination or forced resettlement. During the 13th and 12th centuries, Assyria's kings pushed their boundaries ever outwards, with campaigns of conquest every summer. Their use of brutality to intimidate enemies was to become the distinctive stamp of Assyrian warfare.

The state developed as a pyramid with the king at the top, a stratum of lords beneath him, and at the base the common folk who shared little of the wealth of conquest but were bound to the land where they had been born and where they laboured all their lives. If the land was sold, they went with it.

Society was organised on the basis of the village. There was no tribal system, nor clear social classes except for the division between slave and free. Even as the empire expanded, village life went on remarkably unchanged. The village paid its lord for protection with goods and services, while he might spend his life at court or in one of the principal cities such as Ashur, Nineveh, Erbil and Nimrud.

> 'I conquered the towns of Luhuti...I destroyed them, tore down the walls and burned the towns with fire; I caught the survivors and impaled them on stakes in front of their towns.'
>
> ASHURNASIRPAL II. *c.* 840 BC

Kings and nobles strove to outdo each other in the opulence of their buildings. Nineveh and Nimrud show the skills of their artists. Walls were lined with stone bas reliefs portraying royal exploits. Sargon II (721-705) used tens of thousands of workers to build a new capital north of Nineveh. Only a few public buildings had been completed when he was killed while on a campaign; the new metropolis was never inhabited.

Urban populations were mixed and included many foreigners brought in as captives. Only force could hold such volatile mixtures together; under a weak king the cities faced crisis and even collapse. These periods of internal turmoil made the Assyrians less of a mortal plague to their neighbours.

Success or failure depended on the king, who controlled the entire society. He was not considered divine, but his body was believed to emit a radiance which put fear into his enemies.

Access to him was rigidly controlled. Even the crown prince had to go through elaborate rites to make sure all omens were auspicious before he could see his father. As regent of the gods, the king lived amid a throng of deities and demons with priests, diviners, astrologers and exorcists. His actions were beset by auguries to make sure they accorded with tradition and did not offend the gods. In religion, the Assyrian kings and their courts were intensely conservative.

Will of the gods

Like many other peoples of the ancient world, the Assyrians believed that once a goal of conquest had passed all the tests of oracles and omens it was deemed to be the will of the gods and could be pursued with ruthlessness, as a divine mission. When kings returned from war they recorded their successes in inscriptions that glow with pride. King Tiglath-Pileser wrote in the 11th century: 'At the command of my lord Ashur I was a conqueror...'

Ashurnasirpal II (859-833 BC) gave a ten-day feast for 70,000 people to celebrate the rebuilding of Nimrud. He kept a private zoo of wild bulls, lions, ostriches and monkeys. Sargon II's son, Sennacherib (704-681 BC), who had quarrelled with his father, campaigned in Babylonia and rebuilt Nineveh with prisoner-of-war labour. He laid out streets, squares and gardens inside a wall 8 miles (13 km) in circumference. For irrigation he diverted water from mountain springs through 6 miles (10 km) of canals.

Assyria reached its height under Ashurbanipal (668-627 BC), a man known as much for his culture as for his ruthlessness – his library of clay tablets was renowned. But his successors were weak and the empire collapsed. Assyria's place was taken by the resurgent Babylonians.

Few wept for the Assyrian Empire's passing. From within it had seemed glorious. But its terror aroused in its victims the loathing expressed by the Hebrew prophet Nahum, writing on the fall of Nineveh: 'Ah! City of bloodshed, utterly deceitful, full of booty – no end to the plunder! The crack of whip and rumble of wheel, galloping horse and bounding chariot!

'Horsemen charging, flashing sword and glittering spear, piles of dead, heaps of corpses, dead bodies without end – they stumble over the bodies!'

At full gallop *The skills of the chase helped the Assyrians to perfect the arts of war. This stone relief from his palace at Nineveh on the River Tigris shows the empire-building King Ashurbanipal leading a hunting party.*

Captives' agony *Assyrians were notorious for their bloodlust: prisoners were often impaled on stakes or flayed alive. In the mid-13th century BC King Shalmanaser I boasted that he had exiled 10,000 enemy soldiers to Assyria as slaves – but first he took the precaution of blinding them all to make them easier to handle.*

TRAINED IN TERROR

It is not difficult to imagine the terror that an Assyrian attack inspired. Its army was vast, well trained and disciplined; it had expert commanders, and plentiful supplies of equipment for all types of combat. By 800 BC, the Assyrians could field an army of 20,000 infantry, 12,000 light cavalry armed with bows and spears, and 1200 two-horse chariots.

The heavy infantry, clad in coats of mail, wielded daggers and swords of iron – the new metal which made the Assyrians' weapons stronger than those of their opponents. The cavalry, in the early days, rode into action on two-horse chariots and dismounted to shoot from behind tall wicker shields. Gradually, archers mastered the tactics of shooting accurately from horseback at full gallop.

Hot pursuit *Fugitives use inflated goatskins to cross a river in a desperate attempt to flee the Assyrians. But the remorseless archers are already drawing their bows.*

Engines of war *Assault towers mounted on six wheels (above) were used to breach the walls of cities. The battering rams at the front were tipped with iron, and could be levered left and right. A carving from King Ashurbanipal's palace at Nineveh (left) shows the conquering troops using picks and levers to send walls tumbling, as flames burst from the turrets. Meanwhile, cowed citizens are being driven off, forced to carry away the booty for their new masters.*

59

AGE OF GOLD FOR MIGHTY BABYLON

In the days of Nebuchadnezzar, at the beginning of the 6th century BC, Babylon was like a city reborn. Fresh conquests and new wealth had restored its long-lost lustre. The great city astride the River Euphrates had known days of glory for more than a thousand years, but it had also suffered disasters and had even been completely destroyed a hundred years earlier, after promoting resistance to the Assyrian Empire under Sennacherib.

Babylon's first flowering during the long reign of King Hammurabi (1792-1750 BC) was by Nebuchadnezzar's time ancient history. By the end of Hammurabi's reign, the city dominated an empire stretching northwards almost to the sources of the Euphrates and southwards to where the river disgorged its silt into the Persian Gulf. After Hammurabi's time, Babylon – the name means 'Gate of God' – enjoyed 400 more years of independence until a period of conflict brought it under the sway of mightier overlords, such as the Assyrians. In 612 BC Nabopolassar, the father of Nebuchadnezzar, took advantage of weakness in Assyria to conquer its empire and elevate Babylon once again to the status of an imperial capital.

A new golden age was born. There was work for all, as wealth flowed into the city. Nebuchadnezzar determined to make his capital a jewel of art, sparing no expense in its adornment. The results must have dazzled all those visitors who entered the city by the new Ishtar Gate. Here people passed between walls richly decorated with glazed bricks and enamelled tiles whose surfaces of blue, yellow, white and red glittered in the brilliant sunshine of Mesopotamia.

Just inside was the supposed site of the fantasy world of the Hanging Gardens of Babylon, which rose nearly 82 ft (25 m) and were built, according to legend, to please one of the king's Persian concubines who pined for the mountains of her homeland. The Hanging Gardens were considered by the ancients to be one of the Seven Wonders of the World; throngs of visitors marvelled at the lofty terraces planted with trees and foliage which were kept lush and green by water pumped from wells and springs.

The Ishtar Gate opened onto the wide processional street known in the native tongue as: 'May the Enemy not have Victory.' It led past the palace of Nebuchadnezzar and on towards the heart of the city, the great temple called Esagila which was dedicated to Marduk, the patron god of Babylon.

East and west of the great temple, on both banks of the River Euphrates, stretched more than 1000 acres (405 ha) of densely packed homes, dotted with smaller temples and markets. As many as 150,000 to 200,000 people may have lived within this fortress city, which was further protected by a canal fed by the Euphrates and by walls 18 ft (5 m) thick at the base and 11 miles (17 km) in circumference.

It was a diverse population, reflecting the history of both conquerors and conquered. The native Babylonians mingled with communities of Hittites, Assyrians, Aramaeans, Chaldeans, Cassites, Hurrians, Elamites, and now the thousands of Jews deported from Jerusalem by Nebuchadnezzar.

Priestly landowners
As in most other cities, sharp class divisions existed, especially between slave and free. In Babylon there was also a great division between the vast numbers of temple personnel and the secular society. Priests of Marduk at

Dazzling entrance *The Ishtar Gate, named after the goddess of love, rises 50 ft (15 m) above the northern entrance to Babylon. The towers are clad in glazed blue bricks with rows of bulls, symbols of the lightning god Adad, and dragons, emblem of the chief god Marduk.*

A TOWER OF BABEL IN BABYLON, 'GATE OF GOD'

The great *ziggurat*, or pyramid, dedicated to the god Marduk soars above the bustling wharves of Nebuchadnezzar's capital on the River Euphrates. Laden camels plod through the narrow street, while builders on a rooftop busy themselves with construction work in the 'new town' that is rising on the west bank of the Euphrates to house the city's growing population. So mighty did the city become that the outer wall which enclosed it was 11 miles (17 km) long. On another rooftop women are busy dyeing fabrics.

Beyond the camel caravan a party of soldiers, their shields shining in the sun, marches out of the city and across a bridge over the Euphrates. The bridge is supported on piers of baked brick and asphalt, faced with stone, and its construction across the deep and swift-flowing Euphrates represents a major engineering achievement. The river, which has changed its course since ancient times, formed a natural line of defence for Babylon as well as a waterway for vessels bringing goods to the city from far-off countries.

Across the bridge, the newcomer enters the city by a gate in the inner wall, which rises to 90 ft (27 m) and has towers at intervals. Beyond, a further wall rings the sacred enclosure containing Marduk's temple, at the base of the great ziggurat.

Built of millions of mud bricks, the ziggurat towers seven storeys high, an awe-inspiring presence, visible for many miles across the flat Mesopotamian plain. The Babylonians call it Etemenanki, meaning 'the house of the foundation of heaven and earth'. At its summit, more than 300 ft (91 m) above the ground, stands a shrine where Marduk is believed to descend from the sky and meet his people. On holy days the king and high priests, watched by thousands of citizens, ascend the long staircase to this shrine to seek the favour of the gods, especially that of Marduk to whom Babylon and all its people and territory belong.

It was the ziggurat in Babylon that gave rise to the Biblical description of the Tower of Babel when, according to the Book of Genesis, the descendants of Noah tried to build a tower that would reach up to Heaven. Hitherto the whole earth had been 'of one language and of one speech'; but to punish the tower builders' presumption God confounded the peoples' language, so that they could no longer understand one another. The outline of the vast rectangular base of the tower in the ground has survived to modern times.

the Esagila temple controlled as much as half of the land and much of the empire's economy, including all kinds of traders and craftsmen. Thousands of farmers worked temple lands for a share of its produce. Slaves also formed the work gangs that kept in good repair the canals on which shipping and the irrigation of the country's fields depended.

Parallel to the temple economy was the secular work force, with many of the same professions and crafts. The masses of surviving business documents – written in the wedge-shaped cuneiform symbols pressed into wet clay tablets – mention apprentices, master craftsmen and guilds in such trades as those of confectioners, boatmen, coppersmiths, brickmakers, leatherworkers, canal diggers, fowlers, brewers, and many others. Formal schooling was limited for the most part to those boys who were preparing to become scribes at the temples or even at the royal court.

The Babylonians treasured privacy for their families, and most houses were built around an enclosed courtyard with only a single door opening onto the street. Adjoining the courtyard was a large family room with several small bedrooms attached. On the opposite side of the court was the kitchen and, if the family was prosperous, quarters for two or three slaves.

Babylonians usually rose early, and dawn would find the men and boys of a pious family already bathed and dressed and on the rooftop bowing on their knees to the rising sun. With these rites completed they came down to a big breakfast.

After the morning's round of activities, which might well include making or participating in a routine sacrifice at one of the numerous small temples, the family would reassemble at midday for a light luncheon followed by a siesta through the heat of the day. Work continued from mid-afternoon until nearly dusk, when people returned

home for their second principal meal. Evening activities might include storytelling, any of the many religious festivals of dancing and singing, and conversation. The day concluded with a light supper before bed.

The Greek historian Herodotus recounts that the prosperous and elegant Babylonian gentleman 'wears a linen tunic, reaching to the feet; over this...another tunic, of wool, and wraps himself in a white mantle. He wears the shoes of his country...His hair is worn long and covered by a cap. The whole body is perfumed.'

'The king spake, and said, Is not this great Babylon, that I have built for the house of the kingdom by the might of my power, and for the honour of my majesty?'

BOOK OF DANIEL 4:30

Despite its prosperity, the city was plagued by unrest and intrigue, especially in the decades after the death of Nebuchadnezzar. Periods of weakness left an opening for others, such as Cyrus the Persian, to take over the empire just as Babylon had once taken over Assyria's.

Two centuries later, when the army of Alexander the Great overcame the Persians, the citizens of Babylon welcomed the Macedonian conqueror. As new cities were founded, however, its strength was steadily sapped, and by the 1st century AD the glorious metropolis on the Euphrates was almost totally deserted.

Guardian gods *Priests and stargazers recorded all celestial phenomena, which they saw as omens for events on earth. Symbols carved on this boundary stone invoke the gods to protect the property: the moon stands for the god Shamash, and the eight-pointed star for the goddess Ishtar. The lore of the Babylonian stargazers survives today in the signs of the Zodiac.*

PERSIANS, THE GENEROUS CONQUERORS

Bearded soldiers of Cyrus the Great of Persia, many in parade finery of gold and white robes, marched into Babylon as conquerors in 539 BC, carrying spears before them and bows and quivers slung over their shoulders. The army had taken the city by a stunning surprise attack. The Greek historian Herodotus describes how they came along the riverbed while the Babylonians were celebrating a festival. Cyrus had diverted the water by draining it into a lake outside the city.

When Cyrus entered Babylon he was preceded by a reputation for clemency gained during his spectacular 20 year rise from being a local ruler of a Persian region within the kingdom of the Medes to dominate all the Medes and Persians. When he attacked the mighty Babylonian Empire he was welcomed as a liberator. A chronicler of the time tells how the people spread green twigs on the ground before him and felt 'like prisoners when the prisons are opened'. Cyrus used tolerance and gentleness to build his empire.

Even in his boyhood, Cyrus was admired for his wisdom, spirit and good looks. Like most Persians, he was convinced of the superiority of everything his country produced. According to Herodotus, wherever he went he drank only water from the River Choaspes near the city of Pasargadae, which he had founded to mark his victory over the Medes. Supplies were carried in silver jugs on campaigns. At the climax of his conquests, he gained the allegiance of the Babylonians by worshipping their deity Marduk, but also showed clemency towards nations Babylon had despoiled. He returned sacred images to their owners and restored temples throughout his empire. Most notably, he authorised the exiled Jews to return to their homeland carrying the temple vessels that Nebuchadnezzar had confiscated, and allowed them to rebuild Jerusalem. It is no wonder that a Biblical prophet spoke of Cyrus as God's 'shepherd' and told how God would go before him 'and level the mountains'.

The empire continued to grow during the troubled reign of Cyrus's son Cambyses (530-522) and the long and distinguished rule of Darius I, the Great (522-486). It seemed to its

VISITORS FOR THE GOVERNOR IN HIS PALM-FRINGED PALACE

A group of people makes its way up a flight of steps and heads for the entrance to the villa of a Persian governor at Lachish, near Jerusalem, some time in the 5th century BC.

Soldiers with spears guard the gateway, which leads to a courtyard with a pool in the centre. Guest accommodation, rooms for storage and servants' quarters are grouped around two sides of the open space. Columns flank the lofty portals leading to the inner rooms of the villa. The section at the rear, to which several people are being granted admittance, was the setting for official business. Both it and the grand reception room in front of it have barrel-vault ceilings, an architectural device which the Persians learned from the Assyrians; its great advantage was that it enabled builders to span greater areas than was possible with flat ceilings, without any need for central support.

This reconstruction is based on the ruins of what was probably the residence of a satrap, or governor, of one of the provinces into which the Persian Empire was divided.

Travel gear *Dressed for a long, dusty journey to a distant governor, a noble modelled in silver in the 5th century wears a long tunic, Persian trousers and a headdress like a monk's hood.*

Still on guard *This life-size archer in richly ornamented robes stands proudly on the wall of Darius the Great's palace at Susa, part of a frieze in glazed bricks created by specialist craftsmen imported from Babylon.*

the official, standardised coin, and found that it facilitated both trade and taxation. Attention was given to commercial waterways throughout the empire, including an early version of the Suez Canal, constructed under Darius I. Persian engineers directed thousands of labourers equipped with shovels in cutting a 125 mile (200 km) channel between the Gulf of Suez and an arm of the River Nile.

Prosperity through trade

International trade grew, and with it prosperity and tax revenues. Egyptian glass could be traded for Indian spices, Anatolian silver, Phoenician purple dyes and textiles, perfumes from Arabia, ivory from Ethiopia, timber from Crete or hundreds of other commodities that filled the trading ships and camel caravans.

Even food products such as grain, wine, oil, dried fish and honey were shipped far and wide. The garb of diverse peoples was familiar in the expanding cities, and the conical cap and leggings traditional among the Persians were known everywhere. As

little chance of change or escape. Many nobles who owned these fiefs, especially parcels in provinces far from the empire's centre, collected income as absentee landlords while they enjoyed the pleasures of the cities.

The Persians made one remarkable contribution to religious life. In an age that produced Confucius in China, Buddha in India, and some of Israel's greatest prophets, Persia was home to the prophet Zarathustra, or Zoroaster. He challenged traditional polytheistic religion and proclaimed instead the monotheistic worship of a supreme god, Ahura Mazda, 'Wise Lord'.

Zoroaster saw life as a battle between light and darkness, good and evil, truth and falsehood. Humans, he taught, were caught in the struggle between spiritual forces on each side, but had the free will to choose good or evil and would be judged after death

Gifts from afar *As tribute to the Persian king, an African brings an elephant tusk, while other peoples bring cloth from Ionia, metal from Lydia and gold dust from the Indus Valley, in containers hung from a yoke.*

and rewarded or punished on the basis of their choice. From the time of Darius I, Persian rulers were strong advocates of the faith of Zoroaster and spread its influence throughout their realm.

The empire's size placed a strain on the administration, especially under later kings who lacked the personality and organisational skill of a Cyrus or Darius I. In spite of difficulties the empire survived more than 200 years. Under Darius I's successor Xerxes the Persians in 480 BC invaded Greece with a huge army, but were driven out when normally fractious Greek states united against them. The Persian fleet, too, was almost wiped out.

In the 4th century BC, a military genius hardly out of his teens burst upon the scene. Alexander swept out of Macedonia with a disciplined army and new tactics. Nothing could stand before him. Darius III faced him in two battles but was no match for the Macedonian, who entered Susa in 331 BC to find 270 tons of gold coins and 1200 tons of silver ingots in the king's treasury. The Persian Empire had new rulers, and a new future.

peoples to encompass the entire world, ultimately stretching from Egypt, Libya and Macedonia to the borders of India and China. Darius was a strong administrator who perfected Cyrus's system of 20 provinces ruled by local governors. He tried to put right any fiscal injustices and kept taxes at 20 per cent on fishing, farming, mining, and clothing manufacture. Native Persians were exempted from taxes.

Darius and his successors were interested in making their empire a vast free trade zone. They made extensive use of a new invention recently developed among the Lydians,

in almost all ancient societies, the wealth, mobility and accomplishments of the upper classes rested on a foundation of farming and village life that hardly changed from one generation to the next. For every nobleman or international trader there were scores of artisans, tenant farmers, field labourers, serfs and slaves, most of them closely tied to the soil.

In theory all land belonged to the monarch, but Darius and later kings parcelled it out to nobles in feudal fiefdoms, the size of each fief corresponding to the military responsibility of its master. The holder of 52 acres (20 ha), an amount called 'bow land', had to supply one archer for the army. Larger holdings were designated 'horse land', 'chariot land' and so on. Serfs and labourers worked estates that were largely self-contained worlds with

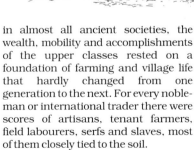

COURIER ON THE ROYAL ROAD

A Persian rider at full gallop carries a vital message along the Royal Road from the imperial city of Susa to Sardis in Lydia. Darius the Great set a high value on good communications as a means of keeping his sprawling empire together. Teams of engineers built sturdy roads over barely discernible caravan trails to make a Royal Road, 1677 miles (2698 km) long. Along it were 111 post stations where relays of fresh horses awaited the messengers, so enabling them to cover the distance in a week instead of the three months taken by a camel caravan. Alexander the Great, and later the Romans, adopted the system. Chains of hilltop fire towers could flash urgent messages even more quickly, and these remained in use until the 19th century.

A WORLD BEHIND WALLS

The Chinese ate with two straight sticks at a time when most Europeans ate with their fingers. They shook hands with themselves before people elsewhere shook hands at all, and they had soup at the end of a meal long before Europeans ate their meals in any set order. In other parts of the world, constant contact between peoples led to an exchange of ideas. But in China, seas, mountains and deserts isolated the people from other cultures during the centuries when settled agriculture, government and writing were coming to the fore.

By the time the Chinese came into contact with other major civilisations, they had developed a culture that was perhaps the most distinctive in the world, and a way of life that they saw no reason to change. So they continued to smile when they were sad, pay doctors when they were well, and in bigger matters, to believe simultaneously in more than one religion. By AD 220, China's distinctive way of life was so firmly established that the empire founded in the Qin and Han dynasties successfully resisted all major cultural invasions for more than 2000 years.

ANCIENT CHINA 221BC–AD220

HARD WORK THAT BUILT AN EMPIRE

The Chinese call themselves 'Men of Han'. They speak 'Han language', and they praise a man as 'a good Han' if he is heroic or 'a good chap'. Han was the name of the great and glorious dynasty which ruled China between 202 BC and AD 220. But more than that, the name Han is used to mean the Chinese people of China as opposed to the many other peoples who have lived there.

The earliest Han Chinese settled in the fertile lands around the Yellow River about 10,000 to 12,000 years ago. All around them, a multitude of other tribes, some of very different physical stock, spoke quite dissimilar languages and had very different ways of life. By about 4700 BC the Han people – hunters and fishermen – had started to cultivate millet, rice and other grains. They domesticated the dog, kept pigs, chickens, sheep, horses and cattle, and made pottery which they decorated with paint and impressions of cord. By 1500 BC the Han had mastered the technology of bronze-making, learned how to make silk and invented the chariot. The unique way they devised of writing their language proved so useful that it survives in modified form today. They worshipped ancestors as gods, and communicated with them by a method of divination that involved interpreting cracks in specially treated animal bones. Settlements surrounded the palaces and offices of their rulers, and were protected from attack with walls of stamped earth.

From then on Chinese civilisation developed rapidly. They settled more land, and new technologies, such as ironworking and high temperature pottery kilns, constantly altered living conditions. By the 5th century BC, their soldiers were using iron weapons and crossbows, and cavalry horses

Guard duty *A life-size clay warrior protects the first Chinese emperor's tomb, ready to jump to his leader's defence in the next life. He was modelled on soldiers whose ruthless fighting united the Han people.*

Spirit signs *The Chinese used tortoise shells, like this one, and shoulder blades of animals to communicate with their ancestors. They asked questions about the family, and the outcome of harvests and of illness. Then they applied heat to a bone, or bored holes in it, and interpreted the cracks that appeared. They inscribed a record of the divination on the shell, and the symbols they used are the earliest known Chinese writings.*

instead of clumsy chariots. With equipment like this, and their large infantry forces, petty rulers of small parts of the Chinese world began to hunger for conquest of all of it.

In 221 BC one such ruler, the King of the Qin state, fought his way to victory over all the neighbouring states and set up a strong government. He became known as Shi Huang Di, 'The First Emperor', and is remembered by the people of China as a tyrannical ruler.

The First Emperor believed in the overriding importance of the state, and he forced his subjects to serve its interests by his rigid system of laws and harsh punishments. The hundreds of thousands of men who broke the many laws were sentenced to forced labour on state projects such as irrigation works and road building. Those who were innocent of any crime were also required to contribute regular labour as a kind of tax payment. China's First Emperor allowed no opposition; he burnt all books which did not conform with the doctrines he relied on, and slaughtered scholars who dared to think unorthodox thoughts. Teachers could work only in state institutions.

On the positive side, the First Emperor unified the Chinese world. To keep it together, he built trunk roads, 50 paces wide, radiating out from his capital city of Xian-yang. He standardised weights, measures and coinage, revised and standardised the Chinese script, and even insisted on a standard axle length for carts so that they could all travel in the same ruts in the roads.

During the 11 years when the First Emperor ruled over China, officials ran the country. All the hereditary privileges and ranks were abolished – except the rank of Emperor, which he expected to remain in his own family for ever. Large families found their power and wealth broken by taxation, and by a law insisting that when a man died his estate should be divided equally among all sons. Farmers benefited from irrigation schemes and were released from serfdom to become more productive – but heavily taxed – freeholders. Books giving advice on agriculture, medicine, and other practical subjects, were exempted from burning.

A wall to keep the barbarians out

In earlier centuries, the Han Chinese built defensive walls against nomad 'barbarians'. Shi Huang Di linked these walls to create 'The Wall of Ten Thousand Li,' along China's northern frontier. A li is about a third of a mile. Folk history says that as many as a million labourers died during the construction work and that some were sacrificed and buried under the foundations to strengthen the wall. Made of earth packed inside wooden moulds, this wall quickly succumbed to wind and weather, but the idea of a wall was taken up by later emperors.

'Cracking his long whip, Shi Huang Di drove the universe before him...He ascended to the highest position and ruled the six directions, scourging the world with his rod, and his might shook the four seas.'
CHINESE HISTORIAN, 2ND CENTURY BC

In spite of the benefits of the First Emperor's rule, however, the Chinese people did not tolerate his harsh living conditions for very long. Shi Huang Di's Qin dynasty survived him by a mere four years, before collapsing into anarchy in 206 BC.

A fitting memorial to Shi Huang Di lies near his tomb, where a whole army of life-size clay warriors, lined up in battle formation with their horses and chariots, guards the emperor in the next world. Infantrymen, cavalry troops and crossbowmen stand in silent ranks. Some wear armour made of iron slats, with a scarf at the neck to prevent it rubbing; others have light cotton clothes, and hairstyles, moustaches, padded trousers and belts are modelled in fine detail. Each clay warrior's head was made separately, capturing more than 7000 individual faces.

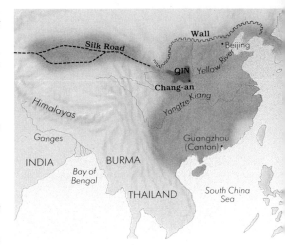

From homeland to empire *The Han Chinese originally lived in the Yellow River plains. At the height of the Han dynasty, their culture had spread far beyond the original Qin lands, and even into central Asia.*

RULERS OVER THE EARLY CHINESE

While other empires of the Ancient World rose and fell, China's culture survived through a succession of different dynasties, or families of rulers, which maintained their hold over a vast area of land for more than 3500 years.

Xia dynasty *(2205 – 1766 BC) This dynasty may be totally mythical: there is no hard evidence for its dates, or even its existence.*

Shang dynasty *(1766 – 1122 BC) Rulers of North China only. A great Bronze Age.*

Zhou dynasty *(1122 – 256 BC) Rulers of North China only. For most of this era Zhou kings had only nominal authority over the many states.*

Qin dynasty *(221 – 206 BC) The first true unification of the Chinese world.*

Han dynasty *(202 BC – AD 220) Most of China came under unified control.*

Ox power *A farmer adds his weight to a harrow so that its teeth bite deeper into the soil to break it up. Advances in farming led to iron tools and draught animals, such as oxen and water buffalo, gradually replacing wooden tools and human muscle power.*

Feeding the empire *The backbreaking task of planting young rice shoots in paddy fields was the everyday lot of millions of Chinese peasants, especially in the south of the empire. Vast amounts of food were grown to feed the army and conscripted workers.*

In the kitchen *A kneeling cook prepares fish for the stove, which his companion is stoking with fuel. Birds and fish for future meals hang behind them, and other cooks work at a bowl.*

In the street *Two friends greet in the traditional way – they shake hands with themselves. To their left, a scholar carries a book written on bamboo strips joined with thread.*

RICH MAN, POOR MAN AND SOLDIER

Respect for ancestors has a long history in China, and in early imperial times families took great care to see their loved ones comfortably settled in the afterworld. The well-to-do decorated the brick and stone walls of tombs with scenes from everyday life, and left bolts of cloth, and food in urns and jars, for the departed to use in the next life. They added pottery models of familiar objects: miniature houses, mills and pigsties, musicians and dancers, and ponds and paddy fields. These models, brought back to the light of day nearly 2000 years later, give a vivid impression of life in Ancient China.

The four centuries from 202 BC, when China was ruled by emperors of the Han dynasty, were a time of invention and development, experiment and

expansion. They were also a time of great contrasts between rich and poor. The wealthy wrapped their dead in rich silk, and placed them in expensive wooden coffins. The poor were buried in clay coffins in shallow pits, and in hard times were even left unburied, at the mercy of wild animals.

At the head of society stood the imperial family, and the nobility. Beneath them came the officials and scholars, followed by the farmers, then the skilled craftsmen, the merchants, and finally the slaves. But as the Han dynasty wore on, classes became less rigidly defined, and people moved from one to another with increasing ease.

Behind the palace walls

The imperial family lived in vast palaces in the capital city Chang-an, the Xian-yang of the First Emperor. These were partly built of brick and stone, but cheaper materials, such as wood or wattle and daub, were used even in the grandest buildings. Roofs made of decorated tiles covered the complex of audience chambers and living quarters, and their brightly

coloured walls were screened from public view by high outer walls with watchtowers and imposing gateways.

The emperor occupied the innermost recesses, surrounded by his wives and concubines, attended by servants, slaves and eunuchs, and guarded by advisers, officials and soldiers. Ceremonial duties kept him a virtual prisoner in the palace, though he made occasional visits to the great imperial pleasure gardens outside the city wall, where exotic plants and animals were kept for his entertainment. The emperor was held in great awe by the people. Although he was not himself regarded as a god, he alone could worship Heaven, and a commoner who looked on his face was liable to be executed.

Wealthy families built wooden houses several storeys high, and decorated them with carvings and paintings. The vast majority of the people, however, lived in one-room shacks of wattle and daub, with thatch roofs and perhaps only sacking for a door. They dressed in the coarsest clothing made of hemp, few had any kind of footwear, and they ate from

HOME AND HARVEST

Home for most Chinese was the village, and the pottery models above show the type of buildings that formed the background to their lives. Some buildings, such as granaries and wells, were used by the whole community. The granary on the right, with its outside staircase, stored surplus grain from good years; it was then sold at government-controlled prices when the harvest failed. To the left of the granary is a substantial wellhead.

Many houses at this time were similar to the building on the left – one-storey structures arranged around the north side of a courtyard. This one has a heavy tiled roof overhanging the flimsy wattle-and-daub walls. Windows, where they existed at all, were very small and were set high in the walls under the roof's eaves. The low winter sun could enter, but the eaves shaded the windows from the summer sun. Foundations were usually made of beaten earth.

In the simplest houses, the cooking was done in the courtyard, sometimes using urns supported by a tripod over a fire. The house was one of a group of buildings which could include a storehouse, pigsty and latrine, and a watchtower to guard the compound.

wooden or earthenware dishes. In good years they could get by, but bad weather or social disorder might force them to sell their few possessions, or even to sell their children into slavery.

The contrast between rich and poor was particularly noticeable in what people ate. The wealthy had a rich and varied diet. They could buy pork, beef, lamb, venison, chicken, duck, goose, quail and pigeon, and also ate dog, owl, sparrow and magpie. Freshwater fish and green vegetables were plentiful, and the well-off could season their food with cinnamon, ginger and garlic as well as salt, sugar, honey and soy sauce. The poor seldom ate meat, and then probably only chicken, and their normal diet consisted of little more than the coarsest grains such as millet and wheat, vegetables, and salted soya beans for flavouring.

> ## 'The law honours the farmer, yet the farmer is poor and despised.'
> CHINESE HISTORIAN, 1ST CENTURY AD

Farmers were the producers of grain – the staple food and the basis of China's economy. But despite their high social position, farmers' living conditions were often quite humble. An owner-cultivator farmed, on average, 17 acres (7 ha), and even in a good year his yield of grain was not enough to keep a family of five,

So they earned money to buy clothes, extra food and other necessities by rearing silkworms or gathering herbs. An extra burden, such as drought, or a family wedding or death, might mean the farmer selling land, and renting fields to grow crops. But with rents as high as 50 per cent of the crop, this made matters worse, and many farmers were reduced to the status of wage labourers. The government, however, gave farmers some help, with manuals of agricultural techniques and advice on crop rotation.

The place of women was clear: they belonged in the home, and the skills they needed were domestic ones. The duties of women from wealthy families were described by a Han writer as 'sewing, weaving and preparing food and wine for guests'. Women from poor homes also had to make items such as straw and cloth shoes to supplement the family budget, and farmers' wives helped in the fields as well. A few professions outside the home were open to women: they could run small shops, practise as doctors, and become sorceresses who were in great demand to cure illness and cast out evil spirits. There were also singers, dancers and prostitutes. But women, even from wealthy families, were barred from government service, and very few women of any class learned to read.

Relief from the daily routine came in the form of festivals such as New Year, and the annual ceremonies to worship

ancestors and gods, all carefully timed so as not to interfere with the agricultural cycle. The markets held in cities and towns also provided welcome diversion, with storytellers, fortune-tellers, medicine men, musicians and pedlars rubbing shoulders with local tradesmen and craftsmen, and with strangers from other parts of the great empire which the Han ruled.

Peace-keeping force

The empire's long northern frontiers were vulnerable to attack by nomad barbarians, and the Han dynasty army tried to keep the nomads out by maintaining garrisoned strongholds at key positions. Roughly one in three of the soldiers were in arms at one time. The others farmed the land, to try to make the garrisons self-supporting, or carried out engineering and building works that included the construction of watchtowers from which they signalled to each other with beacons.

The Han army's biggest problem was the nomads' mobility and skill in fighting from horseback. The Han troops were nearly all conscripted foot soldiers, and the few regular cavalry units were no match for the barbarians. So the army sent expeditions westwards to find horses that were large enough to carry the heavily armed soldiers, and the contact with new peoples eventually opened up the 'Silk Road' trade route.

Guards of empire *The emperor's soldier (above) was likely to be a conscript serving the two years expected of men between the ages of 23 and 56. His weapons are a sword and halberd; the bronze halberd blade (left) has its matching guard for the lower end of the staff. Other soldiers used crossbows and some wore iron armour. They lived on rations of dried, compressed grains.*

Gracious living *The gentlemen depicted in a tile painting, dressed in wide-sleeved robes, would have lived in houses similar to this ornate clay model. Members of such households ate off lacquered tableware, and wore silk and fur clothes, silk-lined leather shoes, and gold, silver and jade jewellery. Animal skins, embroideries, cushions and woollen rugs covered the floors, and they travelled in highly decorated carriages.*

Bronze sword *Weapons could be attractive as well as functional: silk braiding round the hilt of this sword improved the grip. A jade-tipped scabbard was found with it.*

MERCHANTS ON THE ROAD TO MARKET

In early China there was no doubting one's place in the social order – and those involved in trade were almost at the bottom of it. Merchants were considered unproductive parasites, superior only to slaves. But in spite of their lowly status many became very wealthy and kept sumptuous establishments with retinues of slaves.

This flouting of the natural order of things angered one official so much that in 178 BC he wrote to the emperor to complain. 'The law says that merchants are inferior, but instead they are rich and respected', he wrote. 'Even though their men do not plough or weed and their women do not rear silkworms or weave, they dress in the finest silks and eat the best grains and meats.' In case the emperor wonders how merchants can afford to live like this, the official explains: 'They insist on 100 per cent profit.'

Yet despite the official scorn poured on merchants, the Chinese empire flourished on trade. Goods of every description moved round the empire by road and canal, and caravans crossed Asia to the Mediterranean Sea on the 'Silk Road' trade routes.

Money made from deerskin

Some merchants traded by barter, and much of the silk route trade was probably carried on in this way. Within China, however, traders used money. During the Han dynasty the government set up mints to produce large quantities of the copper coins known as 'cash', which remained the basic unit of currency until the end of the 19th century. One ingenious emperor created a unique form of currency – he sold squares of white deerskin for 400,000 copper coins each. The only white deer lived in the imperial park, so this 'paper money' was safe from forgers who became rich by minting their own coins.

The government needed money to pay the huge bills for its military activities, and to finance mass movements of people. At the end of a century of Han rule an estimated 700,000 people were moved into recently conquered land in the northern bend of the Yellow River, and huge numbers of people were transported to the under populated lower stretches of the Yangtze River.

Money was also needed to pay bureaucrats and troops, although some were paid in kind – one army officer received as his month's pay two rolls of silk worth 900 cash altogether. The purchasing power of this sum, in terms of everyday necessities, is hard to estimate, but at about that time a farm horse cost about 4000 cash, an ox cart about 2000 cash, and a female slave a hefty 20,000 cash.

Goods on the road

Taxes were usually paid in grain, rather than money. Much of it had to be moved from outlying regions to the capital at Chang-an, or to the northern frontiers to feed army garrisons which were not self-supporting. Water transport was the most convenient way of moving grain, and canals were built in many parts of the country with the aid of convict gangs and conscripted labour battalions. The Cheng Kuo canal, to the north of Chang-an, was opened in 246 BC; it created a 'short cut' between two rivers and irrigated vast areas of land. A century later, the Chang-an canal provided a direct route for grain from the Yellow River to the capital.

The government also built and maintained a network of major highways and minor roads. Along them travelled horses and oxen, carriages and wagons, and men labouring under heavy loads which they carried on their backs or on shoulder poles. Others took advantage of the newly invented wheelbarrow, and loaded their goods, and passengers, around

Carriage folk *State officials would have travelled in chariots like this one, a half-size bronze model with more than 3000 components.*

Bearing the load *Chinese wheelbarrows preceded Western versions by 1000 years, and were well suited to negotiating rough and hilly ground.*

TRADERS IN SILK

Precious cargoes of silk, the secret of its production held firmly in Chinese hands, were by the 2nd century AD travelling halfway round the world to adorn the wealthy in the other great empire of the time, that of Rome. Long caravans of camels crossed sandy deserts and wind-swept steppes, stopping at towns such as Kashgar and Samarkand on their way to the Mediterranean Sea. As well as silk, merchants carried lacquerware, and iron and bronze goods. For the Chinese, horses were the most important commodity, especially the magnificent animals they found in Fergana and Bactria in central Asia. Traders also brought in jade, furs, musical instruments such as the Bactrian lute, and grapevines from Iran. Some travelled to the Indian coast and sent goods to the west by sea. It was this contact with India that brought Buddhism to China in the 1st century AD.

On the 'Silk Road' *Heavily laden camels form part of a caravan of traders. On their way through a city the party passes an ornate screen which was put up to prevent evil spirits entering a house.*

New technology
The world's first known rudder hangs beneath the steersman's cabin of this model boat, made in the 1st century AD.

Water transport *Canals were vital to China, for transport, irrigation and flood control. The first dated from the 5th century BC, and early canals are still in use . The design of canal boats, and the waterfront scene, changed little over the centuries, to the time they were captured in this busy 12th- century scene.*

Copper 'cash'
Coins called cash with square holes could be strung together, 100 to the string. Ten thousand cash equalled one gold ingot, though gold was rarely traded. The forerunners of round coins were shaped like knives and spades.

its central wheel. The Chinese barrow, which was probably first used to carry army supplies, could be pulled as well as pushed. A strap attached to the handles and passing round the shoulders helped to maintain balance.

Merchants travelling from the north carried furs and precious stones, and more mundane cargoes like melons, coal, hemp, copper and coarse grains. From the south and the west came bamboos and exotic fruits such as lichees and 'dragon's eyes' (lungans), as well as oranges, rice, pearls, tin and cinnamon. East-coast traders brought fish, and much of the salt that inland China lacked. Salt was so important for cooking and preservation, that its production and distribution was largely state controlled.

Not surprisingly, the markets of the empire were well-stocked with goods, most of which were produced within China. Traders brought live animals to sell at the markets, along with meat, fish, clothing, vegetables, and tools for the kitchen. Also displayed for sale were jewellery, leather goods, metalware, textiles – and even slaves. The marketplace was also the haunt of moneylenders. Their eagerness to lend was matched only by the rapacity with which they foreclosed on those who could not pay their high interest rates. One man is said to have received 1000 per cent interest in three months – he had lent gold to the government when it was needed to put down a rebellion. Government officials supervised the markets, and tried to maintain the standard weights and measures, and to collect taxes on all transactions.

BRONZE, SILK AND A CHOICE OF BELIEFS

Chinese legend says that silk was discovered in about 3000 BC by the wife of the mythical emperor Huang-di. A silkworm cocoon accidently fell into some boiling water, and when the empress took it out, she found that it was made of an enormously long and very delicate thread. Whatever the truth about its origins, by the time of the Han dynasty the Chinese were weaving silks of a high standard, with many-coloured abstract designs and patterns of birds, trees and flowers.

The same sort of care was applied to other arts. Craftsmen made multi-coloured lacquerware bowls covered with intricate floral patterns; they painted on silk, and carved friezes on tombs and ornaments from jade. Their glazed pottery was a forerunner of the

porcelain of later dynasties. As early as the 16th century BC the Chinese had mastered the art of bronze-making, and they excelled in making vessels to hold food and wine. They were made in a variety of forms – some stood on three legs, and others were shaped like animals. All were highly decorated, and some were inlaid with gold and silver. Later bronze craftsmen made mirrors by giving bronze discs a highly polished surface, and plaques decorated with animal figures.

Around the 5th century BC, Chinese metalworkers turned their attention to iron. In the Han years iron was so important that for a time its manufacture was a state monopoly, with 48 foundries staffed largely by forced labour. The Chinese made cast iron 15 centuries before it was possible in the West, and even produced steel by combining pieces of iron with different carbon levels. Their success with cast iron came from their knowledge of bronze working, and the invention of a bellows that gave very high furnace temperatures.

The Chinese had wider interests, beyond making useful and ornamental objects. They designed elaborate landscaped gardens which they filled

with rare plants; the musically gifted developed their skills with the help of imported musical instruments, and those of a literary bent wrote poetry.

The Chinese people, high and low, were superstitious and fatalistic – if they noticed an eclipse or a comet, they feared that ill-fortune was on its way. Han emperors employed court

Bronze mask *Craftsmen of Shang times were skilled users of bronze, sometimes even portraying human faces.*

Iron founders *Molten iron from the circular furnace above could be cast in moulds to give mass-produced tools and weapons, or one-off, high quality ornaments. The 'box' in front houses a double-action piston bellows, which forced a continuous stream of air into the furnace and created enough heat to melt the metal. To make wrought iron, iron workers mixed molten iron with other substances in a square trough.*

magicians, at great expense, to journey to the spirit world in search of the elixir of immortality, or to discover the secret of making gold. A number of them were put to death when they did not produce the required results, or when faked results were detected – one man wrote messages on silk and pretended that they had been written by the gods.

Hand in hand with shallow superstition, at this time of awakening and progress, went a great eagerness to explore the nature of man and the universe. In their attempts to outwit fate or to predict the future, the Chinese played with numbers and symbols, and developed mathematics and astronomy almost as a by-product.

Recording hours and earthquakes
Wang Chong, a philosopher who lived in the 1st century AD, showed that the movements of the stars and the moon, and eclipses, were predictable and could have no magical effect on people's lives. Other scholars

Full gallop *Neighing with tilted head and tail aloft as it flies through the air, this 2nd-century bronze horse was modelled on the tall central Asian animals that the Chinese valued so highly. It was found in northern China on the 'Silk Road' route, and is 18 in (460 mm) long.*

were at work on mathematics. Zhang Heng calculated a value for pi – the ratio of a circle's circumference to its diameter – which matches closely the figure used today. In a land where earthquakes were a constant threat, he also made the world's first seismograph to detect and record them. At about the same time, the Chinese invented a water clock, and made accurate sundials marked off into 100 equal units. They calculated correctly the phases of the moon and the length of the solar year, and had a system for writing decimal numbers.

Not all Han ideas were quite so scientific, and most people shared the traditional belief in the forces of Yin and Yang. Yin is weak, passive, female and dark, where Yang is strong, active, male and bright. One could not exist without the other, and all things are in a constant state of flux between the two. The moon is Yin, the sun Yang; day becomes night, but night will give place to day. The forces were symbolised by a circle divided into dark and light halves by a curved line, each half containing a spot of the other's colour. Yin and Yang give rise to the five elements of Earth, Wood, Metal, Fire, and Water, which also follow each other in a never-ending cycle. These traditional beliefs were reflected in Chinese medicine and its concern with balancing Yin and Yang and the elements in the body by means of diet and herbal treatments.

The Han state was run on the principles of Confucius, a Chinese philosopher born about 551 BC. His code valued an orderly way of life, and the advantages of all people knowing their place in society, but did not cater for spiritual needs. And neither did the native Chinese beliefs – in stern ancestor spirits and nature gods – offer any hope of personal salvation. So there was a spiritual vacuum, and after the 1st century AD the religion of Taoism (or Daoism) moved in to fill it.

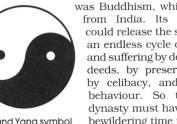

Yin and Yang symbol

Early Taoists tried to avoid death by methods which included breathing techniques, special diets, magic and drugs. In Han times they gradually separated out the ideas of body and soul, and began to look for life of the soul after the death of the body. This afterlife, they believed, could be achieved partly as a reward for good behaviour on earth, though magic, prayer and attention to diet were still involved.

At about the same time, travellers brought new ideas back from abroad, and the most important of them was Buddhism, which came from India. Its followers could release the soul from an endless cycle of rebirth and suffering by doing good deeds, by preserving life, by celibacy, and selfless behaviour. So the Han dynasty must have been a bewildering time to live in. Confucianism, Buddhism and Taoism all had their followers, and many people, unable to sort out right from wrong and sense from nonsense, must have found it hard to know what to believe. The answer was not too difficult – why not believe in them all at once? And many Chinese did just that.

MAKERS OF FINE THREAD

This 8 in (200 mm) long fragment of silk was found on the caravan route in the far west of China. Silk was of prime importance in international trade, and the Chinese kept the means of its production a closely guarded secret. Silkworms fed on the leaves of mulberry trees, whose cultivation was a full-time job for many men, while women reared the worms, reeled off the silk, dyed it and wove it. But it was a precarious livelihood. The trees could become diseased, and the silkworms were fragile creatures, disliking noise and bright light. They were thought to be frightened by strangers, and the women warned them of visits by unfamiliar people.

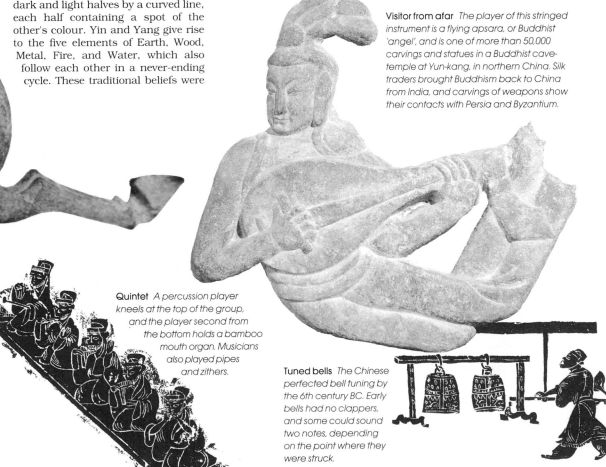

Visitor from afar *The player of this stringed instrument is a flying apsara, or Buddhist 'angel', and is one of more than 50,000 carvings and statues in a Buddhist cave-temple at Yun-kang, in northern China. Silk traders brought Buddhism back to China from India, and carvings of weapons show their contacts with Persia and Byzantium.*

Quintet *A percussion player kneels at the top of the group, and the player second from the bottom holds a bamboo mouth organ. Musicians also played pipes and zithers.*

Tuned bells *The Chinese perfected bell tuning by the 6th century BC. Early bells had no clappers, and some could sound two notes, depending on the point where they were struck.*

GREEK AGE OF GOLD

From a group of small city-states, isolated among high mountains, arose a surge of creative brilliance that laid many of the foundations of European civilisation. A broad range of human activities, from sport to drama, from medicine to philosophy, still follow a pattern derived from the Ancient Greeks whose Golden Age, dawning around 800 BC, reached its pinnacle in 5th-century BC Athens. Memories of an earlier Greek civilisation based on Mycenae had survived through a 500-year Dark Age, to live again in the epics of gods and heroes recorded by Homer. At a time when most people were regarded by their rulers as no more than chattels, one of the great achievements of the Greeks of the Golden Age was to assert the dignity and rights of the individual human being, in a pattern of government from which true democracy was to spring.

ANCIENT GREECE 800–300 BC

THE WORLD'S EARLIEST DEMOCRATS

The land is a mountainous, deeply indented mass thrusting south into the Mediterranean. The climate is benign, but arable soil is scarce and scattered; as a result, early settlements developed as small, independent communities, isolated by the difficult terrain from their neighbours – with whom they were often at loggerheads. Often the only means of communication was by sea.

These factors gave a strongly individual identity to the emerging towns of Ancient Greece. As the towns grew, they developed into separate city-states whose inhabitants showed an intense loyalty to their own community. They called the state the *polis*, meaning a community acting together in the belief that every citizen should share in the government. So the Greek became a 'political animal', who devoted much of his time to public affairs. This was particularly the case among the citizens of Athens, the largest of the city-states.

Votes for the few

In its early days Athens was ruled by kings and tyrants, but in 510 BC, Cleisthenes drove out the last of them and established the world's first democratic government. The word comes from the Greek *demos*, 'the common people', and *kratos*, 'power'. This was not, however, a democracy in the modern sense. Only a minority of the population was allowed to vote – the freeborn Athenian males. Women were not regarded as citizens, and therefore had no vote; neither did foreigners or their descendants, or slaves and their descendants, even if they had become free. The city was divided into ten blocks, called tribes. Each tribe elected 50 men over the age of 30 to a 500-strong Council which carried out

Thrill of the chase *A spear-carrying hunter and his dog go in search of prey, probably wild boar. He wears a hat against the sun.*

the daily function of government. The councillors served in turn on a committee which produced ideas for discussion by the Assembly of all the citizens. During their service, for which they were paid, the councillors took their meals at the state's expense in the administrative headquarters, the Tholos, a round building on the west side of the *agora*, or market.

It was the Assembly, or *ekklesia*, that made laws and decided on great issues such as whether to go to war. All the thousands of citizens could attend, paying a small admission fee, and could speak and vote. Promptness was encouraged: slaves holding a rope dipped in red paint rounded up late-comers, and anyone found with red paint on his clothes was fined.

> 'Here each individual is interested not only in his own affairs, but in the affairs of state as well ... we do not say that a man who has no interest in politics is a man who minds his own business, we say he has no business here at all.'
>
> PERICLES *c.* 450 BC

The Assembly met about 40 times a year on the Pnyx, a hill near the Acropolis, or 'high city' – the rocky plateau which was the birthplace of the Athenian city-state. Men sat on the ground, or on folding stools they brought with them. After prayers and the sacrifice of a black pig the debates began, members voting by a show of hands. Order was kept by a police force of Scythian archers, whose original homeland was north of the Black Sea.

Officials called archons, who were selected by lot, prepared legal cases for trial in the Assembly, and also organised religious ceremonies. The highest-ranking officials were the ten *strategoi*, or generals, elected from the ten tribes by the people. Holding office for a year, they wielded immense power over both the army and the economy, and made far-reaching decisions on behalf of the state.

Power of the courtesan

The most famous *strategos* was Pericles, leader of Athens in the middle of the 5th century, who won re-election no fewer than 15 times. Pericles owed his success largely to his powers of oratory; his mistress, Aspasia, an *hetaira*, or courtesan, is said to have helped him to write his speeches, giving her a political influence rare among women in ancient Greece.

Pericles took power after the Persian Wars, and forged a league of friendly cities into an Athenian empire. Known as the Delian League, because its treasury was initially kept on Delos, an island sacred to Apollo, it embraced many Greek states round the Aegean. Each contributed ships or money for mutual defence, though Athens used much of the wealth to rebuild the temples of the Acropolis destroyed by the Persians in 480 BC. The splendour of the new Parthenon and the other buildings enhanced the influence and fame of the city throughout the Greek world. Their glory endures to this day.

Punishment in a pot

Exile from Athens for a period of years was a common method of punishing criminals and getting rid of unpopular figures. Each citizen attending the Assembly scratched on a piece of broken pot or *ostrakon* the name of the man he thought should be thrown out. The *ostraka* were placed in a pot and the man whose name appeared on the majority was banished, or 'ostracised'.

The citizenry exercised great power through the law courts. Generals who lost battles could be brought to trial to account for their failure. Small-scale litigation was widespread, with many quarrels over property. Every citizen

Time to learn *A teacher called a grammatistes taught reading, writing and arithmetic. Here he unrolls a scroll from which a pupil will read a passage.*

over the age of 30 could serve on a jury, and the modest payment of three obols a day enabled poor people to perform their duty. There were at least 201 jurors at a trial and often many more; a presiding magistrate saw that the case was tried properly but gave no opinion on the matter being heard.

Time-limit for the speaker

Each side was allowed equal time to plead its case. This was measured against a water clock; once a vessel filled with water had emptied through a spout at the bottom into a lower one the speaker had to stop. The accused person, or parties to a litigation, were expected to speak on their own behalf but could if they wished employ speech writers to prepare their cases. Some of these men eventually developed into successful attorneys: it was said of the famous 4th-century orator Demosthenes that he could prepare briefs for either party with equal ease. Jurors were handed voting pebbles which they dropped into one of two pots. The pot that held the majority of the pebbles decided the outcome of the case. Jail was rare: the usual punishments were exile, or loss of citizenship or property. Judges, council members and city officials held office for a year.

Every citizen, rich or poor, had a chance of playing his part. The system may seem amateurish today, and even at the time it was criticised by some well-born Athenians, but it did allow participation by large numbers of people in the affairs of the community.

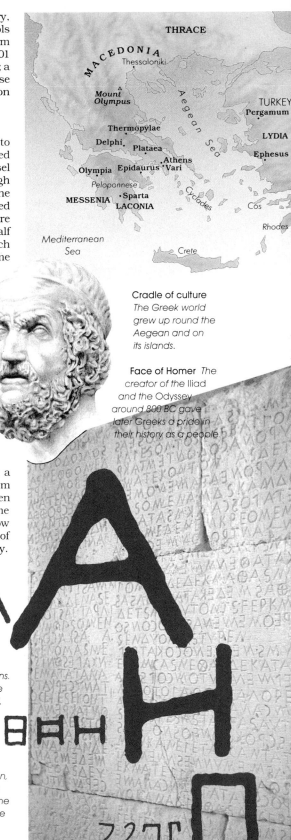

Cradle of culture *The Greek world grew up round the Aegean and on its islands.*

Face of Homer *The creator of the Iliad and the Odyssey around 800 BC gave later Greeks a pride in their history as a people*

Keeping the records *Greek is still a living language, the oldest recorded in Europe with a written history which goes back 34 centuries, to the time of the Mycenaeans. At the close of the Dark Age, in about the 8th century BC, an alphabet was created, based on a Semitic model developed by the Canaanites in the Near East. Beside the large Classical Greek letters on the right – alpha, eta and pi – appear the North Semitic, Early Phoenician, Cretan and Early Greek forms from which they developed. In the background are the laws of Gortyn, in Crete, inscribed on stone tablets in the mid-5th century BC.*

HOPLITES, PHALANXES AND TRIREMES

Two armies advance towards each other, going into battle to the sound of pipes. The sun glitters on crested helmets and iron spearheads, while the roar of opposing war chants rises from thousands of throats. Trumpets blare a shrill signal. The armies raise their spears in readiness for the charge, then break into a run. They rush onwards to engage in close combat,

Shock of battle *Greek infantry tackled their foes from behind a wall of bronze shields. Round and leather-lined, they were held firm by a loop in the centre and a grip near the rim.*

Battle array *A hoplite wears a crested helmet, a shaped metal cuirass, and greaves on his legs. Originally the figure brandished a spear.*

sparking off a deafening clatter of swords on upraised shields. To the people of Ancient Greece the tumultuous clash of armies in the field was a familiar aspect of life. The city-states warred with one another continually, often on the smallest pretext. All male citizens were obliged to fight, though only Sparta had a full-time professional army. The battle season lasted from March to October, allowing the men to return home to bring in the wine and olive harvest. Indeed, in the agriculture-based economy of the city-states, the main method of provoking an enemy into battle was to destroy his crops, or merely to threaten to destroy them. In spite of their squabbles the Greeks were capable of forming an effective national army when they felt themselves under external threat. In the classical period the main enemy was the Persian Empire; this struggle dominated the early 5th century BC. In later times the Greeks were to look back with pride to their victories over the Persian army at Marathon in 490 BC and over the Persian fleet at Salamis ten years later.

In Athens, young men between 18 and 20 were known as epheboi and were trained in military skills. Any man between 18 and 60 could be called up, though after 50 he was usually assigned to garrison duty. In an emergency both trainee soldiers and veterans were called on to fight. The soldier bidding farewell to his wife and family as he leaves for war is a scene that Greek artists portrayed with tenderness and idealism on countless vase paintings and sculptures.

A slave as armourbearer

The backbone of the fighting forces was the infantry. A rich citizen who could afford the armour became a hoplite or 'armed man'. He had to buy his own bronze helmet, body armour and bronze greaves which covered his legs from knee to ankle. He wore a cloak and leather sandals and carried a short iron sword, an iron-tipped

Forest of spearheads *The phalanx was the standard Greek battle formation, constantly evolving with advances in tactics. The front ranks level their 21 ft (6.5 m) spears as they advance on the enemy, while the upraised pikes at the rear help to ward off arrows.*

spear and a shield bearing the device of his tribe. On long marches a slave would carry this heavy gear for his master. In battle the hoplites were grouped in phalanxes – blocks of men drawn up in ranks one behind the other, their spears pointing forwards. In earlier times spears were thrown at the enemy; later they were used for thrusting. Hoplites formed the centre of the army. On either side were lightly armed soldiers, while the flanks consisted of poorer men who could afford only bows and arrows or slings.

In earlier times – the 8th and 7th centuries BC – cavalry warfare was common, but as time passed, the infantry took over the leading role. Horsemen are never mentioned in accounts of the Persian Wars, but during the Peloponnesian War between Athens and Sparta, cavalry became prominent again.

Economic factors probably played their part, as cavalrymen had to be wealthy enough to buy and maintain their own mounts. The horses were not fitted with saddles or stirrups: the men rode bareback, or on blankets or animal skins, and wore boots with spurs. Cavalrymen and horses wore protective armour of small metal scales attached to leather or cloth.

> *'The enemy came round us in a ring and charged. Our vessels heeled over; the sea was hidden, carpeted with wrecks and dead men; all the shores and reefs were full of dead men.'*
>
> AESCHYLUS, *THE PERSIANS*

Besides fighting battles outside their cities, the Greeks strongly fortified the cities themselves. Most of their towns had begun life as Bronze Age citadels, on hilltops chosen for their easily defended position. The most familiar example is the Acropolis of Athens, where the natural contours of the rocky hill were emphasised by massive stone walls inside which the population could shelter in time of war. After the Persian Wars the Athenians built a stone wall round their port of Piraeus and linked it with the walls of Athens by means of a 4 mile walled 'corridor'.

Sometimes the Greeks laid siege to walled towns by building huge mounds beside them. Thucydides, in his history of the Peloponnesian War, describes how in 429 BC the Spartans built such a mound against the walls of Plataea in central Greece and from it attacked the battlements with spears, sulphur, pitch and blazing brushwood. After a two-year siege the Plataeans surrendered and were put to death. The town was then laid waste.

Missile guided by oars

Unlike the landlocked states of inland Greece, Athens based her power mainly on her navy. After the final defeat of the Persians at Plataea in 479 BC, Athens joined with other Aegean states to form the Delian League, named after the island of Delos, to raise funds for their collective defence against Persia. With this wealth Athens built up her vast fleet.

Warships were of three main types, known as penteconters, biremes and triremes. The penteconter was a galley with 50 oarsmen; the bireme had two banks of oars, one above the other, with one or more men on each oar; while the trireme had three banks.

First used in the 6th century, the trireme had become the standard warship by the time of the Persian Wars. About 120 ft (36 m) long, it had a figurehead or painted symbol on the prow and a large square sail on a forward mast; it was steered by a pair of paddles at the stern and rowed by 170 oarsmen – citizens, not slaves – with one man to each oar.

When cruising with a following wind, the trireme hoisted its sail; in a calm or when the wind was contrary it was rowed by the lowest bank of oarsmen. In battle all three ranks rowed, kept in time by the ship's piper, blowing on a double-reed *aulos*. Rowing at full power, they aimed their trireme's ram square at the enemy ship.

The ram wrought fearful carnage at Salamis in 480 BC, when the Greeks inflicted a crushing defeat on the Persians. Salamis set the seal on the naval power of Athens; it was with her triremes that she held her empire.

Deadly punch *Two or three banks of oarsmen rowing at ramming speed could thrust a Greek bireme or trireme through the water at 9 mph (15 km/h). Each vessel had at its prow a bronze-plated ram 10 ft (3 m) long, which splintered the enemy oars, then pierced the hull as soldiers hurled their spears.*

HARDSHIP AND HEROISM

The Spartan was the most formidable fighting man of Ancient Greece. This 6th-century bronze statuette of a cloaked adult warrior shows him wearing a transverse crest on the helmet – possibly a sign of high rank.

At seven years of age, a Spartan boy was taken from his family and placed in barracks. Here he led a tough life, going barefoot and kept hungry.to encourage him to steal food from farms – a skill he might well need in enemy territory. At the age of 20, he was elected to a military club of about 15 members. Here he lived a rigorous life until he reached 30, when he was allowed to marry. The food at the clubs was so bad that a visitor is said to have remarked: `Now I know why the Spartans do not fear death.'

The Spartans' greatest moment of glory came at the pass of Thermopylae in 480 BC, when a small Spartan force under Leonidas held the mighty Persian army at bay, before being killed to the last man.

HIDDEN HEART OF A FAMILY'S HOME LIFE

A caller on his way to visit a well-to-do family in a Greek town of the 5th century BC would turn off the street down a narrow passage, where the sound of voices would guide him into the heart of the household, the courtyard. Here, concealed from casual observers, children played, dogs scratched in the dust, slaves cooked meals on braziers, women talked and washed fleeces, and sacrifices were offered at stone altars.

Surrounding this secluded courtyard were separate quarters for men, women and slaves; the rooms were usually all on one floor, but some wealthier homes had bedrooms on an upper floor. In contrast to the splendour of the Greek temples and public buildings, their houses were modest structures, made of sun-dried brick on a stone foundation. They had tiled roofs, and floors made of mortar or beaten earth.

The day began early. First to rise were the slaves, who were paid for their services and often treated kindly. They lit the kitchen fire, drew water from the courtyard well – or the fountain in the marketplace – and saw that the children were up and dressed. Breakfast consisted of bread dipped in wine and water, followed by dried figs and olives.

Later in the morning the men left for the *agora*, or marketplace. It was they who shopped for daily requirements such as fish, oatmeal, cheese, olives

PRIVACY BEHIND MUD WALLS

The Greeks called a burglar a 'wall-digger'. This was because the outside walls of many houses of the 5th century BC were blank and windowless, so that a thief wishing to break in would simply burrow through the insubstantial mud-brick wall. Even in this country house of a fairly well-to-do family, only a few small windows, closed by shutters, pierce the outer mud-coated, whitewashed wall. The corner tower provides a lookout point.

In the open courtyard, a woman stirs a cooking pot, while children play with a dog. Shade is provided by overhanging eaves supported on slim wooden pillars. Beyond, a woman stands working at a loom leaning against the wall, making clothes for the family. Other women attend to hangings in the largest room, the *andron* or dining room.

In the kitchen, a slave chops vegetables in front of the oven, and the master of the house takes an early meal before going out on his daily tour of work in progress around the estate. Bales of woven cloth lie with vases in a storeroom at the top of the tower, while in the room below a slave helps the young man of the house to take a bath. Outside, a donkey waits while large vases are filled with wine, or with honey from the beehives in pots in the thatched lean-to against the wall.

Time to talk *Household work left time for a matron to advise a young bride before her wedding. Both wear loose tunics, with swirling folds.*

Bread maker *Flour had to be ground for the daily bread.*

Wine drinkers *Revellers at a dinner party, such as those depicted on a wine jar, usually drank from the kylix, a two-handled cup.*

Toilet training *Babies were placed in a potty mounted on a tall base, their legs dangling out of the side. This child is waving a rattle, perhaps wanting to be let out.*

and vegetables, and luxuries such as jewellery and trinket boxes. Women, accompanied by male slaves, might also go shopping, but spent most of their time spinning and weaving at home. They made all the clothes, hangings for walls and windows, blankets and cushions; this was regarded as a noble task, even for aristocratic women. Young girls spent the day with their mothers, learning how to run the home and to spin and weave. In wealthier homes they learnt to read and write, to sing and play the lyre, but formal education was considered important only for boys.

Learning by heart
Highly educated slaves taught the sons of rich families at home, but by the 5th century BC Athens had many schools accommodating about a dozen pupils each. From the age of seven, boys were escorted there each morning by personal slaves, who were responsible for their good behaviour. They sat on low wooden benches, writing on wax tablets with a sharply pointed stylus and reading from rolls of papyrus.

Arithmetic was taught with the aid of an abacus, rows of beads fitted into a wooden frame. Emphasis was placed on learning by heart and reciting Greek poetry, on music – especially the ability to play an instrument – and on athletic skill. The men and boys returned home for lunch, a light informal meal of bread, dried fish and fruit, accompanied by water and goat's milk.

Later on they often went to the gymnasium, a public sports ground where young men exercised on the *palaestra*, an open sanded area, while the older ones watched or strolled among the running tracks and olive groves.

Here basins, plunge pools and steam baths were provided; at home, however, women and children washed in bronze basins mounted on pedestals, using scented water but not soap. Some homes also had terracotta hip baths.

The family spent the day in the courtyard, but as evening approached or when the weather was cold, the scene shifted indoors to rooms lit with clay or bronze oil lamps. Jugs, perfume bottles and other household objects hung from whitewashed walls.

Furniture, made from woods such as cypress and olive, included elegant, colourfully draped couches, high-backed formal chairs, a curved chair with arms called a *klismos*, and tiny, ivory-encrusted three-legged tables.

There were wooden cupboards and chests to hold lengths of woven material, and small portable stools, some folding with fabric seats. Wooden-framed beds had interlacing leather thongs supporting a mattress, on which were laid cushions, blankets and coverlets. The most richly furnished room in the Greek home was the *andron*, the dining room where the men frequently enjoyed a *symposion*, or formal drinking party, in the company of male guests. The men reclined on couches on their left elbows; to recline gracefully was the mark of a civilised man.

Slaves served food on small tables placed next to each banqueter. No knives or forks were used – the food was cut up in the kitchen and everyone helped himself with his fingers, using a spoon only for sauces and shellfish.

Fish, eels and quail were popular dishes. Vegetables such as lettuce, peas, beans, cabbage, onions, leeks and olives were abundant, and cooked in sauces or honey. Meat, however, was rarely eaten. The land was too dry to support beef cattle and meat caught by hunters, such as deer and boar, was eaten only at festival times.

The second course consisted of nuts, figs, grapes, cheeses and honey cakes, and was accompanied by wine. This was mixed with water in a large bowl, into which the slaves dipped jugs to fill their masters' cups. After dinner the men often enjoyed a game called *kottabos*, the object of which was to hurl the dregs from a wine cup at a target placed on a stand, with bets placed on whose eye was keenest.

Father's word was law
The head of the family, invariably a man, exerted total control over his household, which included grandparents, widowed aunts, orphans and spinster sisters. Women had no legal power, even over the fate of a newborn child. If it were sickly, or the father felt that the family's budget could not support the costs of its upbringing, he could decide to leave the infant on a remote mountainside to die. Girl babies were much more likely to be abandoned than boys. A woman's principal role combined the functions of housekeeper and mother. Many women were responsible for the organisation of the family budget, and had a strong influence on family decisions. Children played with tops, hobby-horses, dolls, miniature ox carts and horse-drawn chariots. Clay figures of women making bread prepared girls for adult life; at a ceremony marking the end of childhood they offered their toys to Artemis.

Yellow was a favourite
The basic garment worn by men, women and children was the chiton, a large rectangle of wool or linen cloth fastened at the shoulders with pins or brooches and sometimes worn with a belt. Saffron yellow seems to have been the favourite colour, but they were also dyed purple, red or violet. When they went out the Greeks put on a cloak called a *himation*, and leather sandals; indoors they usually went barefoot.

Women always covered their heads out of doors, pulling up the himation or wearing a special veil. Hair was worn long, and often dyed; girls favoured ringlets or flowing styles. Married women piled their hair on top of their heads and secured it with pins or diadems. Earrings, bracelets, rings and cosmetics gave more adornment.

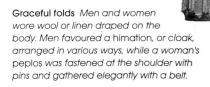

Graceful folds Men and women wore wool or linen draped on the body. Men favoured a himation, or cloak, arranged in various ways, while a woman's peplos was fastened at the shoulder with pins and gathered elegantly with a belt.

Keeping in fashion *The art of hairdressing was well advanced, and women spent hours achieving elaborate coiffures such as this elegant braidwork of tiny, tight plaits. The lady is further adorned with a necklace and pendant earrings. Many women wore wigs, and the hair was often dyed.*

Hoping for a catch *Fish was considered a great delicacy, much prized for banquets; the modern Greek word for fish, psari, is derived from the Ancient Greek opsarion, 'delicacy.'*

BARGAINING BUSTLE BEGINS AT SUNRISE

Early morning was a time of frantic activity in the Athens *agora*, or marketplace. Farmers set up stalls of cheese, grain, pork, fruit, eggs, sheepskins and olive oil for sale. As the sun rose, working women set out to buy food and other household needs; highborn ladies preferred to stay at home.

Later, husbands came to do the bulk of the family shopping, to hire workmen or to buy slaves. If they had a lawsuit in hand, they would attend the courts nearby. Then they relaxed with friends in the shade of colonnades, listening to philosophers disputing, and buying lunches of sausages and honeyed pancakes from fast-food sellers. In the lanes round the agora were workshops where bronzesmiths, tanners, potters, cobblers, makers of shields and lyres sweated over their crafts. Most of the work was carried on in small businesses of 12 to 20 people.

A scramble for fertile land

Once they had sold their produce the country people walked back to their modest farms. Their main crops were grain, grapes and olives. Vineyards and olive groves flourished on the lower slopes of the hills round the city, while wheat and barley were grown in the lusher valleys.

Fertile land has always been in short supply in this mountainous country. Greeks were never able to grow enough wheat for their people and had

Wealth from hardship *The coins of Ancient Greece were minted from silver dug by slaves who toiled on their hands and knees, risking their lives. The best known coin was the Athenian* tetradrachma, *a four-drachma piece bearing an owl, sacred to Athene, the patron goddess of Athens.*

to import grain from Egypt and the Crimea. Land hunger sent many of them overseas to set up colonies. Greek farmers did not practise crop rotation. They sowed crops one year and left the land fallow the next. Oxen pulled wooden ploughs, seed was broadcast by hand, and reaping was done with a sickle. Grain was harvested in July.

Though few farmers had enough pasture to keep many horses and cattle, they all kept oxen, mules and donkeys as draught animals, and got milk and cheese from sheep and goats. Hill farmers kept bees, producing the honey which was the main sweetener. Lentils, peas, beans, onions, cabbages and garlic were abundant. Greeks varied their diet with fishing and hunting, wild boar being a favourite quarry.

Treading the grapes

Vines and olives were the Greeks' main sources of agricultural wealth. They were often grown on terraces cut into the hillside to get the maximum sun, and large numbers of workers were needed to cultivate and harvest them. Ripe grapes were picked in September and taken to a treading floor made of wood or mortar which sloped down to an outlet. As workers trod the grapes, juice ran into a vat sunk into the ground. It was left to ferment in clay vats lined with pitch or resin – the origin perhaps of *retsina*, the resin-flavoured wine still popular in Greece.

These vats were kept in cool cellars for six months, after which the wine was poured into large amphorae for ease of transport.

Proof of large-scale export of wine comes from sunken wrecks of merchant vessels laden with amphorae for Greek colonies in southern Italy or on the Black Sea. The ships returned with perfumes and precious stones from the East, timber from Macedonia and woollen goods from Asia Minor.

Olive oil was another money-making export, basic to the Greek economy. The olive itself was sacred and was believed to be the gift of Athene, patron goddess of Athens, to the people of her city. Olive oil was used for cooking, for washing instead of soap, and as fuel for lamps. Olive trees grow slowly, taking 16 years before fruit can be harvested

Balancing act *The ruler of Cyrene, a Greek colony in North Africa, keeps a careful eye on his workmen as they weigh and store sacks of produce.*

Breaking new ground *Every patch of stony soil was cultivated. This peasant steers two oxen pulling a wooden plough. Another man would have followed, sowing the seeds.*

and 40 years before reaching maturity, so only richer farmers could invest in such a long-term enterprise. Olives were gathered as they still are today: workers shook the branches to make the olives fall into nets or baskets. The fruit was pulped in a hand mill, then crushed in a screw-press to extract all the oil.

Most farmers relied on family help, but the more prosperous would have had several slaves for heavy work. In towns, however, the economy depended on slaves. By the 5th century BC there may have been 100,000 slaves in Attica, the region around Athens, alone, nearly twice the number of free citizens. These slaves were usually treated well; some became doctors, teachers or architects, highly educated and paid enough to enable them to save up and purchase their freedom.

A 4th-century slave called Pasion bought his freedom and became a rich banker. He lent large sums to the city, was made a citizen in return and left a huge fortune.

Hard life in the mines

A slave had no rights and could neither marry nor own property. The philosopher Aristotle defined slaves as 'possessions that breathe' and 'tools that happen to be alive'. The unluckiest slaves were those in the mines at Laurion, south-east of Athens, source of silver for the city's coinage. Coins were introduced from Lydia in Asia Minor early in the 6th century BC.

Variety in the coinage meant plenty of work for moneychangers, many of whom became bankers. They dealt in loans at an average annual rate of 12 per cent in mortgages and in insurance, conducting their business on little tables. The Greek word for a bank is still *trapeza*, or table, as it was when Athenian householders haggled over the price of fish in the agora or farmers handed over their hard-earned obols for a new pair of sandals.

Time to choose *Cleaver poised, a fishmonger waits patiently while a customer ponders how much fish he will need for the evening's dinner.*

Best foot forward *A boy stands on a table while the shoemaker cuts out a pattern to fit his feet.*

79

KEEPING THE FAVOUR OF THE GODS

On a spring morning in Athens a group of little boys aged about three, with flowers in their hair, stand near the door of a temple on the Acropolis. Their families wait nearby. The door opens, and out come white-robed priests and pipe players. The priests hand the boys small clay jugs, from which they take their first sip of wine.

This ceremony of *Choes,* or Jugs, was part of the *Anthesteria, a* spring festival held in honour of Dionysus, the god of wine. As each child sipped in celebration of spring and the new wine, he passed symbolically out of infancy.

Religious rituals marked other key stages in children's lives. At the age of 12 or 13 girls would dedicate their toys to the goddess Artemis at a shrine or temple, as part of a ceremony which celebrated the end of their childhood. Often this ritual took place on the eve of a girl's wedding: girls married young, as soon as their fathers found them husbands, often twice their own age.

An anonymous writer describes the toy ceremony: 'Maiden, to thee before her marriage Timarete gives her cap, her tambourine, her favourite ball – as is meet. O Artemis, the maiden brings her dolls, her childhood playthings, her all.' Terracotta toys such as hobby-

Final journey *A vase painting shows men in dark robes bearing the body of a friend to the cemetery, accompanied by a hired mourner. The dead were anointed with precious oils before burial or cremation.*

horses and jointed dolls have been found among temple ruins. Others have been found in the graves of children, apparently left there by parents as tragic symbols of the playthings their children never lived to enjoy. For a wedding, Zeus and Hera, the guardians of marriage, had to be invoked. The bride had first to take a ritual bath of purification, the water for which was drawn from special fountains by young boys.

On the day of the wedding itself it was customary for the bride to cut off a lock of her hair, wrap it round a spindle and place it on an altar. This was followed by sacrifice and feasting in the homes of both the bride and groom. The bride was driven by the bridegroom in a horse or mule cart to her new home where she was greeted by her mother-in-law carrying a flaming torch with which to light the newlyweds across the threshold. The couple were then led to the hearth where they knelt and were showered with nuts and sweetmeats, tokens of prosperity.

> '*Man made his gods and furnished them with his own body, voice and garments.*'
> XENOPHANES, *c.* 500 BC

To the ordinary Greek, religion was more a matter of ritual practice than of morality. The community believed in the importance of good behaviour, in accordance with high moral standards, but the motives for such conduct were primarily social: one behaved well for the sake of one's family and reputation, rather than for the sake of the gods and goddesses themselves. Worship and

Warding off evil *A woman pours a libation of wine onto an altar in the courtyard of her house to enlist the protection of a god, a custom dating back to earliest times.*

sacrifice were undertaken almost as a binding contract with the gods, a way of ensuring divine favour. Correct performance of ritual to achieve the desired effect was therefore a dominant feature of Greek religion. Many ceremonies were conducted not in a temple or sanctuary by a priest or priestess but by ordinary people in the privacy of their homes.

Hestia, as goddess of the hearth, was believed to protect the very centre of the home. Keeping the home fire burning was therefore a religious act in itself. Most houses also had a herm – a stone pillar with a human head and phallus. This was dedicated to the god Hermes and placed at the entrance to the house to ensure his protection. In the courtyard there was often an altar to Zeus and Apollo, on which offerings of food were set each day by the head of the household. In the countryside, deities such as the goat-legged Pan were

worshipped, and each locality, fountain or stream had its own guardian nymph. Prayers for a good harvest of olives were offered to Athene: grapes were in the gift of Dionysus, while Demeter ensured a supply of corn. All these deities were believed to live on Mount Olympus, the highest mountain in Greece, whose peak was thought to touch the sky. Yet although they set their gods and goddesses in this remote mountain home, the Greeks still saw them as influencing human affairs, often intervening in the lives of cities and individuals.

Rule by a thunderbolt

The gods were thought to resemble humans in appearance and character, differing in one important respect; they were immortal. Supreme among them was Zeus, ruler of the heavens. Sculptors and painters showed him as a mature, bearded man, sometimes holding a thunderbolt and seated on a throne to emphasise his sovereignty. Hera, both wife and sister to Zeus, was patroness of women and of marriage.

The brother of Zeus, Poseidon,

Killing a monster *The goddess Athene watches as the hero Perseus makes off with the head of Medusa, whose glance could turn people to stone. He used a bronze shield, the gift of Athene, as a mirror in which to watch Medusa as he cut off her head.*

ruled the sea. Resembling Zeus in appearance, he carried a trident or fishing spear and was sometimes accompanied by dolphins. Other deities included Ares, god of war; Aphrodite, goddess of love and beauty; Hermes, the messenger god; Hephaestus, god of the smithy; Athene, goddess of wisdom; Demeter and her daughter Persephone, concerned with the earth's fertility; and Apollo, god of healing and music. All these gods and goddesses had sanctuaries and temples dedicated to them. These provided a focus for community worship, and certain deities became associated with particular cities, as in the case of Athene at Athens.

The important role played by religion in Greek life is shown by the beautiful temples, built as houses for the gods. The splendour of temple architecture was a way of honouring the god, and at the same time demonstrating the

wealth and prestige of the community which had created it. Temples were also treasuries for offerings of gold, jewellery and other precious objects which were made to the deity.

In an inner room stood a statue of the god, sometimes lavishly decorated with gold and ivory. This was not for public view, and would have been seen only by priests and temple attendants: ordinary people were never permitted to enter the interior of the temple, which was regarded as the private domain of the deity. Its rooms were windowless, and lit only by oil lamps.

All important public ceremonies, such as the state sacrifices, took place in the open air outside the temple. They were conducted by a priest at an altar – a sacred piece of ground marked with a stone or, in the case of richer sanctuaries, with a more substantial marble structure, and usually situated just beyond the east end of the temple.

The priest, when offering a sacrifice, wore a long tunic and stood with his back to the temple, the doors of which were open to allow the deity to witness the ceremony. Cattle, sheep, goats or pigs would be led forward, adorned with garlands and with their horns gilded. The throat of each animal would be swiftly cut, after which its body was divided up, part of it being placed on the altar to be ritually burnt and the remainder roasted for the sacrificial meal shared by the priest and the other worshippers.

A festival for Athene

Every town held an annual festival for its patron deity. Athens paid tribute to Athene every fourth year in the week-long Great Panathenaea festival. A procession wound up the slope of the Acropolis, bringing a new *peplos*, or tunic, to clothe the ancient wooden statue of the goddess kept in a shrine close by the Parthenon, the great temple dedicated to Athene. This procession is shown on the Parthenon frieze, or Elgin Marbles, now in the British Museum.

On the frieze the Olympian deities are seated on stools or thrones, waiting for the procession to arrive. This is led by women with wine vessels for the pouring of libations. Behind them men lead sheep and cattle to be sacrificed. A priest and a child hold up the peplos just before giving it to the goddess who sits, like the other deities, in a relaxed manner, as if oblivious to the actions of the mortals nearby.

Greeks believed in an afterlife but thought it inferior to life on earth and were in no hurry to get there. Corpses had coins placed in their mouths as the fare for the boatman Charon, who ferried the souls of the dead across the River Styx to the underworld, the realm of Hades. Sometimes a body was buried, but usually it was cremated and the ashes buried, with possessions to be used in the next world.

A feast followed the funeral.

Healing hands *Hygeia, daughter of Asclepius, looks on as Asclepius appears to a patient in a dream. Remarkable cures spread the cult of the god of medicine.*

PRAYING FOR A CURE

The Greeks regarded sickness as an affliction sent by the gods and prayed to them for a cure. From the 5th century BC the cult of Asclepius, the god of medicine, spread throughout the Greek world. Sick pilgrims stayed at his sanctuaries, principally on the island of Cos, at Pergamum in Asia Minor, and at Epidaurus – where a temple, theatre and ritual buildings survive. The god appeared to pilgrims in dreams. These were then interpreted by priests who prescribed treatment, usually diets, gymnastics and baths. From these treatments there developed a system based on scientific observation, which remains the foundation of modern medicine.

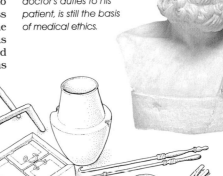

Medicine man *The Oath of Hippocrates of Cos, enshrining a doctor's duties to his patient, is still the basis of medical ethics.*

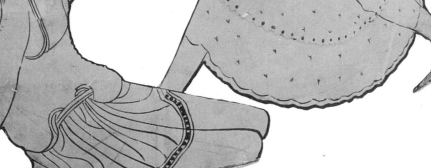

Tools of the trade *Surgical skills progressed steadily, aided by careful study of the workings of the human body. Medicine was beginning to lose its elements of magic, and anatomy and inquiry were playing an ever larger role.*

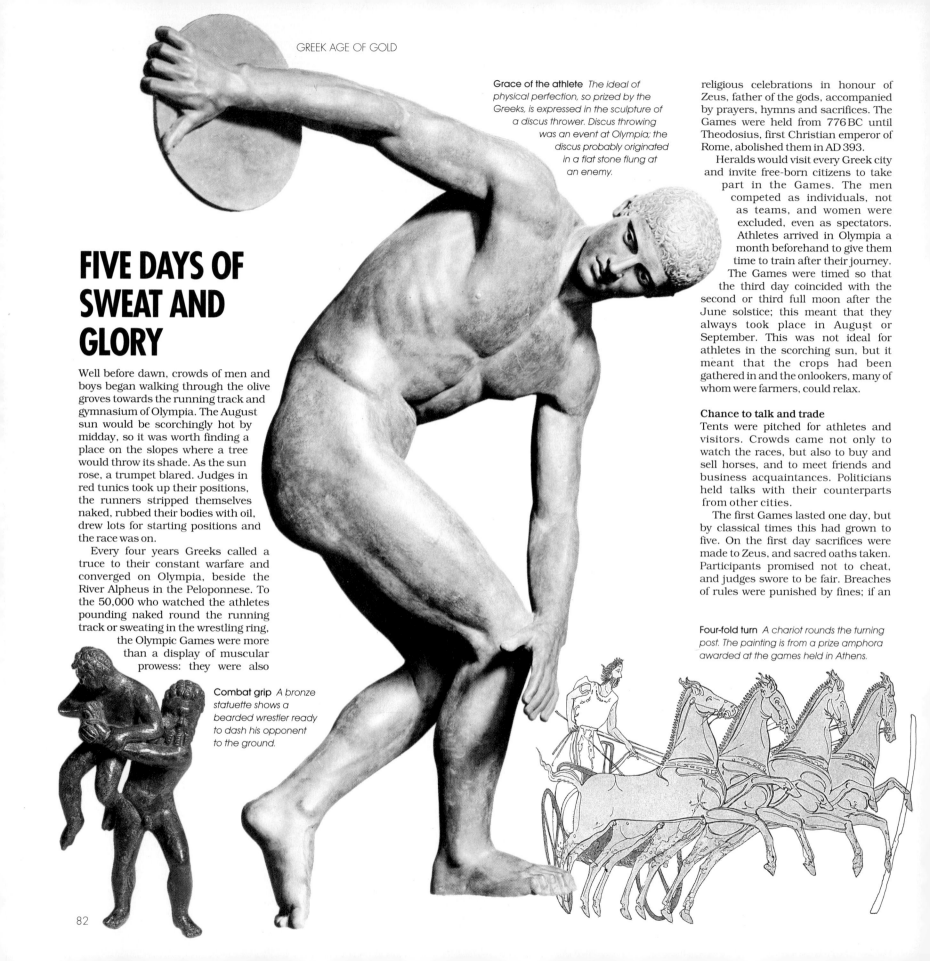

Grace of the athlete *The ideal of physical perfection, so prized by the Greeks, is expressed in the sculpture of a discus thrower. Discus throwing was an event at Olympia; the discus probably originated in a flat stone flung at an enemy.*

FIVE DAYS OF SWEAT AND GLORY

Well before dawn, crowds of men and boys began walking through the olive groves towards the running track and gymnasium of Olympia. The August sun would be scorchingly hot by midday, so it was worth finding a place on the slopes where a tree would throw its shade. As the sun rose, a trumpet blared. Judges in red tunics took up their positions, the runners stripped themselves naked, rubbed their bodies with oil, drew lots for starting positions and the race was on.

Every four years Greeks called a truce to their constant warfare and converged on Olympia, beside the River Alpheus in the Peloponnese. To the 50,000 who watched the athletes pounding naked round the running track or sweating in the wrestling ring, the Olympic Games were more than a display of muscular prowess: they were also

Combat grip *A bronze statuette shows a bearded wrestler ready to dash his opponent to the ground.*

religious celebrations in honour of Zeus, father of the gods, accompanied by prayers, hymns and sacrifices. The Games were held from 776 BC until Theodosius, first Christian emperor of Rome, abolished them in AD 393.

Heralds would visit every Greek city and invite free-born citizens to take part in the Games. The men competed as individuals, not as teams, and women were excluded, even as spectators. Athletes arrived in Olympia a month beforehand to give them time to train after their journey.

The Games were timed so that the third day coincided with the second or third full moon after the June solstice; this meant that they always took place in August or September. This was not ideal for athletes in the scorching sun, but it meant that the crops had been gathered in and the onlookers, many of whom were farmers, could relax.

Chance to talk and trade

Tents were pitched for athletes and visitors. Crowds came not only to watch the races, but also to buy and sell horses, and to meet friends and business acquaintances. Politicians held talks with their counterparts from other cities.

The first Games lasted one day, but by classical times this had grown to five. On the first day sacrifices were made to Zeus, and sacred oaths taken. Participants promised not to cheat, and judges swore to be fair. Breaches of rules were punished by fines; if an

Four-fold turn *A chariot rounds the turning post. The painting is from a prize amphora awarded at the games held in Athens.*

athlete could not pay, his family and native town were held liable. The second day started with processions of officials and competitors with horses and chariots. Contestants and spectators were then plunged into the most dramatic and dangerous of the events – the four-horse chariot race. Up to 40 chariots sped round the track, wheeling round the pillars at each end as tightly and speedily as possible. Accidents were frequent at the turn; few starters completed the 12 circuits. A horse race followed, riders contesting bareback without saddle or stirrups.

Next came the pentathlon, an all-round trial that combined running, long jump, discus, javelin and wrestling. Long jumpers held lead or stone weights, which they swung forward as they jumped to give them extra impetus, and then swung backwards as they landed to provide a final

thrust. The third and fourth days brought foot races, boxing and more wrestling. One form of unarmed combat called the *pankration* was particularly vicious: few tactics were barred except biting and gouging out the eyes. Running events took place in a stadium 218yds (200m) long, covered in sand. The starting line, made of stone slabs with grooves that acted as toe grips, can still be seen at Olympia. Boxing contestants did not wear gloves, but had leather thongs tied round their hands.

On the fifth and final day the winners received their prizes – crowns of wild olive cut from a sacred grove near the temple of Zeus. Afterwards they were given a victory banquet. Further honours awaited them in their home towns: they were excused from paying taxes, received free meals in the town hall and were allowed to wear purple robes. A champion might have a statue put up to him at Olympia.

Though the Olympic Games had the greatest prestige, it was only one of four series of games which attracted sportsmen from all over the Greek world. The other three were the Pythian Games at Delphi, the Nemean Games at Nemea near Argos, and the Isthmian Games at Corinth, all held on a four-year cycle.

> *'The clatter of the chariots filled the arena, and the dust flew up as they sped along in a dense mass, each driver goading his team to draw clear of the rival axles and panting steeds.'*
>
> SOPHOCLES, 5TH CENTURY BC

Apart from these major events, many cities held their own games in honour of their patron deity. Athens venerated Athene as part of the Great Panathenaea festival. Men from all over the region around Athens took part, and winners were awarded large jars of olive oil, bearing on one side a painting of the appropriate race.

Around AD 100 the philosopher Epictetus said: 'Aren't you scorched by the fierce heat and crushed by the crowd? Doesn't the rain soak you to the skin? Aren't you bothered by the noise and general discomfort? But you gladly endure all this, when you think of the gripping spectacle you will see.' The Games remained an enthralling experience for nearly 12 centuries.

War casualty *Polykleitos broke new ground by endowing his wounded Amazon with both grace and the pathos of a victim.*

DRAMA IN HONOUR OF THE WINE GOD

Going to the theatre was for the Ancient Greeks a festival occasion and a day out. People spent the day watching three or four tragedies followed by a comic play. Theatres were bowl-shaped, carved out of the side of a hill. Originally the audiences sat on grassy slopes, but from the 4th century BC stone seats were fitted; the audience brought cushions for comfort.

The front seats would be occupied by judges, priests and important visitors. In front of them was a flat paved arena called the *orchestra*, where the actors performed and a chorus of about 20 singers danced to the music of the pipe. At the back was the *skene*, which originally served as the scenery and also housed the dressing rooms; the skene eventually developed into a stage. Drama had a religious origin, deriving from dances and songs performed in honour of Dionysus, the god of fertility and wine. Playwrights chose

as their subjects well-known legends, and there was plenty of audience participation, with cheering, booing, and even the hurling of missiles. All the actors were men.

The finest playwrights were all Athenians: Aeschylus, Sophocles and Euripides among the tragedians, and Aristophanes among the comic writers. At the close of the drama festival, winning writers and actors were given garlands of ivy. In Athens, all business was suspended during the festival; prisoners were freed from jail to attend.

Mask of terror *A bronze votive mask copied from those worn by tragic actors of the 5th century BC.*

Masks of mirth *Terracotta models show actors wearing masks to emphasise their roles: a comic character (left), and a pair of roistering drunks (right).*

WINE, WOMEN, SONG – AND PHILOSOPHY

For all their interest in matters of the mind, the Greeks were a fun-loving people. Leisure was plentiful, thanks to the availability of slaves and servants, and citizens – particularly men – made the most of it.

At home the main diversion was the *symposion*, or drinking party, attended by men. Good conversation was held in high regard, and a symposion began with serious talk of politics and philosophy. Later the evening grew hilarious under the influence of the food and drink.

Singers, sword dancers, jugglers, musicians and acrobats would go through their paces. The performers were mainly girl slaves, often captured in war and chosen as entertainers for their beauty and skills. Men fell in love with them and had children by them – but they were not permitted to marry them. Vase paintings show these girls dancing with guests and being embraced by them, and serving wine to men lying tipsily on couches. The writer Xenophon gives a graphic description of a typical cabaret turn:

Unguarded moments *Greeks were not always dignified intellectuals: their parties often got out of hand. A vase painting shows two men reeling while a third helps himself to wine. The cup (below, right) shows a courtesan comforting a youth who is being sick.*

'The girl began to accompany the dance on the flute. Then a hoop set around with upright swords was brought in; over these she turned somersaults, into the hoop and out again, as the diners looked on in amazement, afraid she might injure herself. But she completed her performance fearlessly and safely.'

Riddles were popular. A guest who could not solve one had to drink a bowl of wine mixed with brine. Guests sang drinking songs accompanied by the lyre; these short pieces were called *skolia*. The subjects were often political; one refers to the assassination of Hipparchos in 514 BC. 'With my myrtle wreath I will wear my sword, like Harmodios and Aristogeiton when they killed the tyrant and gave Athens equality.' Wine, song and dance went together; at the annual festival of the wine god Dionysus each of the ten tribes of Athens entered a

Graceful gown *A swirling dress gives movement to this statuette of a woman as she sways to the hypnotic rhythm of a dance.*

chorus of 50 boys in a competition. They sang, danced and mimed in a circle while their families looked on proudly. No festival was considered to be complete without music. Pan, the goat-legged god, was said to have made his pipe, or *syrinx*, from reeds of increasing length fastened together with wax and cords. Lyres had seven strings attached to pegs or leather thongs used to tune the instrument. One found in an Athenian tomb had a sound box made from the shell of a tortoise and uprights made from sycamore. Homer, in the *Iliad*, describes one particularly striking instrument:

'Now they came beside the shelters and the ships of the Myrmidons and they found Achilles delighting his heart on a lyre, clear-sounding, splendid and carefully wrought, with a bridge of silver upon it, which he won out of the spoils when he ruined Eetion's city. With this he was pleasuring his heart and singing of men's fame.'

Soldiers' music, children's toys

The *kithara* developed from the lyre and was similarly shaped, but had a wooden sound box which gave a deeper, richer sound. It featured on public occasions in the hands of professional musicians. Trumpets were heard mainly in battle, while tambourines and cymbals were associated with processions and dances in honour of Dionysus.

Musical contests were an important part of the Great Panathenaea festival at Athens: singers and flute players stood on stages with their tutors and the judges ranged below.

Romantic moment *A guest at a banquet embraces a slave girl as the wine takes effect. Solemn discussions on the meaning of life that began the evening are forgotten.*

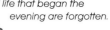

Like parents throughout history, the Greeks gave their children presents, including ingenious toys bought from sellers in the *agora*, or market. Simpler toys were made at home, frequently by the children themselves. In *The Clouds*, a comedy by Aristophanes, a proud father tells how clever his son is at making houses, ships, wagons and frogs out of pieces of leather. Other play-things included swings, seesaws, kites, hoops with bells, model carts, hobby-horses, whipping tops and wheels which were attached to poles for pulling along. Tiny items of model furniture made of lead have been found; perhaps they were meant to go inside wooden doll's houses.

Babies had rattles with pebbles inside them – one lovely surviving example is in the shape of a pig. Jointed clay dolls have turned up in ruined temples, where they had been left as offerings, and also in the graves of children. Many more rag dolls and wooden items probably also existed, but being made of perishable material they have not survived.

Balls were made of pigs' bladders for team games resembling hockey. A carved relief in an Athens museum shows two players with their curved sticks in the act of bullying-off. Vase paintings, which are such a rich source of information on life in Ancient Greece, show leapfrog, piggyback and a form of blindman's bluff.

One beautiful terracotta figurine shows two women absorbed in a game of knucklebones, played with the ankle bones of cloven-footed animals. Five bones were tossed into the air, one at a time, and each had to be caught and held on the back of the hand. Board games, said by the historian Herodotus to have been invented in the state of Lydia, in Asia Minor, were played with dice and counters of glass and bone. The Greeks most often indulged in

Sounding strings
The kithara was a deeper-voiced version of the lyre.

Watch my style *An Athenian boy with long hair shows his dexterity by bowling a hoop while carrying a food tray covered with a cloth. The painting appears on a kylix, or drinking cup.*

these pastimes when they were relaxing with their friends at home. Outside in the agora, however, they could choose from a wide range of more dramatic public entertainments. These included spectacular displays in the sunshine given by magicians, sword-swallowers, conjurors and fire-eaters.

Animals were both indulged as household pets and exploited for hunting and brutal bouts of fighting. Cats seem to have been less common as pets than dogs, pigs and tortoises. Tame cranes and geese strutted about the courtyards of better-off families.

'The girl then began to accompany the dance on the flute; a boy handed her flutes until he had given her twelve. As she danced she threw them into the air and caught them again...'

XENOPHON, *c.* 400 BC

Fashionable young men liked to keep exotic animals such as leopards and panthers as pets. Doves, often associated with Aphrodite, goddess of love, were given to young women as love gifts, and hares were given to young men. Cats, dogs and cocks were set to fight each other, and spectators gambled on the result. A relief shows youths setting a dog to fight a cat. The rich enjoyed hunting, using various dogs according to the quarry. Hunters in search of deer and hares went in ones and twos; but a boar hunt would involve larger groups venturing into thickets with javelins, nets and spears. `

Music and movement *A girl gyrates to castanets while a youth plays the aulos; the strap round his face was apparently intended to keep the double pipes in place. The terracotta figure probably depicts a poet accompanying himself on the lyre.*

EDUCATION FOR THE SOUL

The Ancient Greeks enjoyed music at public and private occasions, both religious and secular. The philosopher Plato said that education had two divisions: gymnastics for the body and music for the soul.

Little is known about how Ancient Greek music sounded. Hardly any examples of notation have survived, and these give no indication of the pitch used. However, there would not have been the complexity of modern arrangements for orchestras and voices: people sang together in unison, and instruments followed the same melodic line. Since Greek music was closely linked with poetry and the dance, rhythm must have been all-important. Music defined the dance steps, and into it a poet wove his words. Poetry was not meant for private reading: the lines were written to be sung or chanted before an audience, often accompanied by musicians and dancers.

The Greeks had songs for all occasions: love songs and chants to celebrate weddings or births, to lament a death or provide a background to repetitive work such as the grinding of grain. There were even songs for curing illness. Women seem to have enjoyed dancing together at home or in the fields, perhaps as a fertility ritual. They are never shown dancing with their husbands.

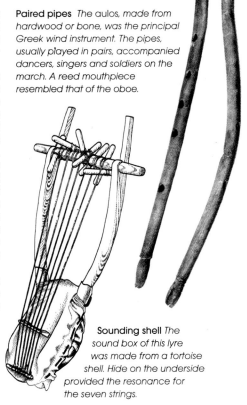

Paired pipes *The aulos, made from hardwood or bone, was the principal Greek wind instrument. The pipes, usually played in pairs, accompanied dancers, singers and soldiers on the march. A reed mouthpiece resembled that of the oboe.*

Sounding shell *The sound box of this lyre was made from a tortoise shell. Hide on the underside provided the resonance for the seven strings.*

CITIZENS OF PROUD ROME

According to legend, the city of Rome was established by Romulus beside the River Tiber in 753 BC. It began as little more than a village of mud huts set on what is known today as the Palatine Hill. Settlements on six other nearby hills merged with it to create a single city, whose people quickly united Italy under a republican government and began to expand overseas. In 31 BC the large and complex state passed into the hands of Augustus, as first emperor. Under a succession of energetic leaders, frontiers were pushed farther outwards to incorporate a vast realm stretching from the surf-beaten Atlantic shores of Spain and Britain to the scorching deserts of Syria and Judaea.

For four centuries the empire flourished, but as provincial armies gained in might, civil war broke out. In 293 the empire was divided between East and West. It was reunited in 324 under the first Christian emperor, Constantine the Great, but fell apart again later when Rome itself was sacked by waves of Visigoths, Huns and Vandals. Finally, in 476, the last emperor of the West was deposed by the German warrior Odoacer.

IMPERIAL ROME 31BC–AD476

THROBBING HEART OF AN EMPIRE

Rome under the dynamic emperor Trajan (AD 53-117) was the heart of the known world – rich and powerful, a sophisticated metropolis of a million and more people. At its centre, from Trajan's eagle-crowned, 92 ft (28 m) triumphal column to the immense Colosseum games arena, magnificent public buildings and temples stretched for almost a mile (1.6 km), flanking elegant squares, arcades and terraces.

Statues of gods and heroes stood everywhere, and all could share in their glory, for there was no 'best part of town' in Rome. All over the city, instead, opulent villas rubbed shoulders with humble terrace homes and workshops. Huge, warren-like apartment blocks reared four and five storeys high, usually with shops, wine booths, grocery stores, vegetable stalls and other businesses at ground level.

Grandeur and graffiti

The grandeur of the Romans' public buildings is well enough known. But the vast mass of city-dwellers lived in ill-lit, sparsely furnished homes, most of which were rented premises. Apartment blocks and other dwellings were covered with signs advertising vacant accommodation. The advertisements were usually painted in tall black letters, and the last line, giving the owner's name, was in red to attract attention. With shop signs and graffiti also covering the walls, Roman buildings were scruffier than architectural studies often suggest.

All these buildings were served by a network of sewers, of which the Cloaca Maxima is the largest surviving example. But most families were not plumbed into it. Instead, they carried their slops and sewage to a neighbourhood disposal point – or simply tipped them out of their unglazed windows

An eye to the future *Gazing fondly at his infant son, a proud Roman father looks forward to the day the boy reaches the age of seven. Then he will pass from his mother's care into the hands of his father to be educated in earning his living as a free citizen of Rome.*

directly into the street. Claims for compensation were often filed by luckless citizens who had household dirt and foul-smelling rubbish poured over them in this way.

Gamblers and gossips

The Romans lived, traded and ate in the street. The poor even cooked food out-of-doors, on portable stoves and braziers. Cooked food was also sold at stalls known as *popinae*, and for a couple of copper coins, slaves and other members of the lower orders could eat their fill in the cramped, musty little taverns which abounded in the city. These were great centres of gossip where, clustered around benches, labouring men played dice, gnawed at cakes of cheese and meal, and quaffed cheap wine from Crete, which was often warmed to suit the Roman taste.

> '*There's nowhere a poor man can get any quiet in Rome... The laughter of the passing throng wakes me and Rome is at my bed's head.*'
>
> MARTIAL (AD 40–104)

The day-to-day noise in Rome was appalling. In the streets boy vendors of sausages and men selling pease pudding yelled out their wares, their strident cries mingling with those of peddlars, snake charmers, courtesans and street entertainers.

The Roman poet Martial complained that the citizens were woken at the crack of dawn by the loud bawling of schoolmasters. All day long, he added, coppersmiths banged away with their hammers. And at night the city's bakers continued the din.

'On one side of the street,' he wrote, 'there's the moneychanger idly rattling his coppers on a dirty table, while on the other side the goldsmith's beating gold plate with his mallet. There's an incessant stream of soldiers, high as kites, shipwrecked sailors with their bodies swathed in bandages, Jewish beggars and salesmen selling sulphur with the tears pouring down their cheeks.'

As the working day began early, many officials and businessmen had completed their duties by around noon. After a break for lunch came the obligatory, hot-weather siesta. The afternoons were then spent in socialising, relaxing, visiting one of the many public baths, attending the gladiatorial games and chariot races, or touring the shops.

The Romans may have been masterly engineers, but jerrybuilding was rife too. The apartment blocks, known as *insulae*, or 'island houses', were especially notorious, with their heavy floors supported only by timber beams. The orator Cicero – who was also a slum landlord – wrote: 'Two of my buildings have collapsed, and in the others the walls are all cracked. Not only the tenants but even the mice have left.'

Ordeal by fire

Fear of fire, above all, preyed on people's minds. With candles, oil lamps and smoky torches providing lighting at night, accidents were common. Despite the proximity of the Tiber and a fairly sophisticated water-supply system, few ordinary homes had water piped in; usually it was drawn from wells or fountains.

The city had seven fire brigades, but their equipment ran only to axes, buckets, hand pumps and hooks – so that anxieties ran high whenever a blaze started in the neighbourhood. The wealthy kept teams of slaves drilled to rescue their marbles, bronzes and other treasures at an instant's notice. For the poorest, crowded into the topmost garrets of the tenements – with a narrow staircase as their only escape route – the nightmare of being trapped and roasted alive became a hideous reality all too often.

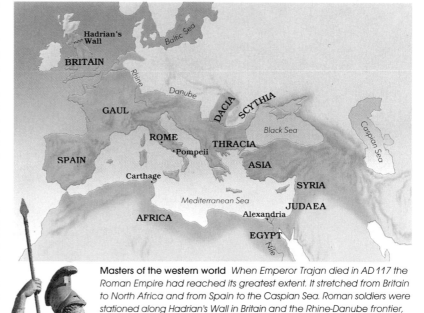

Masters of the western world *When Emperor Trajan died in AD 117 the Roman Empire had reached its greatest extent. It stretched from Britain to North Africa and from Spain to the Caspian Sea. Roman soldiers were stationed along Hadrian's Wall in Britain and the Rhine-Danube frontier, and had garrisons in Gaul, Spain, Thracia, Egypt, Judaea and Syria.*

The world in her hand *A statue of Roma, the armed goddess of war, victory and plenty, shows her holding a globe symbolising the world over which Rome triumphantly ruled. The goddess was regarded as the guiding spirit of the city of Rome, and was worshipped by townsfolk and country people alike. Her head also appeared on many Roman coins.*

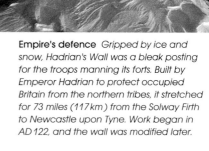

Music in the home *Musicians and actors were hired as entertainers at family celebrations. In this fresco from Pompeii, a woman plucks a lyre with her left hand and a small curved harp with her right hand, while a group of actors wait to perform.*

Empire's defence *Gripped by ice and snow, Hadrian's Wall was a bleak posting for the troops manning its forts. Built by Emperor Hadrian to protect occupied Britain from the northern tribes, it stretched for 73 miles (117 km) from the Solway Firth to Newcastle upon Tyne. Work began in AD 122, and the wall was modified later.*

Empire's foe *A statue shows a prisoner seized in Dacia, present-day Romania.*

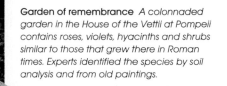

Garden of remembrance *A colonnaded garden in the House of the Vettii at Pompeii contains roses, violets, hyacinths and shrubs similar to those that grew there in Roman times. Experts identified the species by soil analysis and from old paintings.*

Design for living *Style and comfort are captured in this reconstruction of a Roman living room, with its elegant couch, basketry chair, footstool and occasional table. A clay oil lamp (right) illuminated dark corners.*

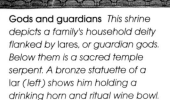

Gods and guardians *This shrine depicts a family's household deity flanked by lares, or guardian gods. Below them is a sacred temple serpent. A bronze statuette of a lar (left) shows him holding a drinking horn and ritual wine bowl.*

HOME COMFORTS AND CLOTHES

A DESIRABLE FAMILY RESIDENCE IN ANCIENT POMPEII

Compared with the poor, who slept on bug-ridden mats in their stifling and rickety tenements, wealthy Romans lived lives of the utmost elegance. Festoons of flowers and the green foliage of climbing plants covered the porticoes and balconies of their spacious mansions. Inside, slaves did all the housework, moving through vistas of cool marble columns, across floors agleam with mosaics. Furniture was of bronze, ivory and rare wood; windows were hung with expensive fabrics; vivid frescoes enlivened the walls with splashes of colour.

Well-to-do citizens often possessed two such homes – a town house and a country villa – both sharing the same basic layout. Visitors came in by way of a vestibula, or entrance passage, whose double doors led into the atrium, or hall. This was the family's main living room, where sunlight, streaming in through an opening in the roof, glimmered on the waters of a central pool. In the atrium, too, was often

A caller at the front door of the wealthy merchant's House of the Vettii waits to be let in. Inside in the atrium, or central courtyard with its rainwater pool, the master of the house chats to another visitor. The family strongbox stands on the tiled floor. On the other side a staircase leads to the upstairs

bedrooms – below which is an indoor horse stall, a lavatory, a rest room and the dining room, where two members of the family are seated. In the rear of the limestone house is the peristyle, or colonnaded garden, with its fountains, sundials, statuary, flowers, shrubs, walks – and lewd wall paintings.

found the shrine to the household gods. These were the *penates* who were thought to protect homes from evil spirits. The whole family would worship at their shrine every day.

Leading off the atrium were the kitchen, dining room, study, bedrooms and other chambers. At the back of the house was a colonnaded garden known as the peristyle, bordered by flowerbeds and shrubs. The Romans were keen gardeners, and especially fond of roses. Wealthy Romans drank rose wine and powdered their bodies with dried rose petals. The luxury-loving Sybarites (from Sybaris in southern Italy) even made mattresses

from rose petals – hence the saying 'a bed of roses'. The poorest citizens tended little window boxes, while the grander suburban mansions had terraces looking down on lawns, fancifully clipped hedges and walks among bay laurel, cypresses and ivy-clad plane trees. Garden seats were placed under vine-covered pergolas for shade against the blistering heat of the Italian high summer. The big country villas had their own extensive vine-yards, olive groves and orchards.

Fountains played in the gardens of the big private houses, which had mains water laid on. Some homes also had central heating. The system,

known as a hypocaust, consisted of furnaces stoked by slaves with wood or charcoal, from which hot air was channelled by ducts to provide under-floor heating – usually for a bathroom. Most homes, however, were heated by means of portable braziers burning charcoal. Fireplaces and chimneys were almost unknown.

Roman furniture was often beautifully made, but there was not much of it – even in wealthy homes. The main item was the bed on which a citizen slept at night and reclined during the day for a siesta, or to receive visitors. The best beds were of wood, finely inlaid with ivory, tortoiseshell and

Make my day *Fierce guard dogs were popular among well-to-do Romans, who had mosaics set into the fronts of their houses warning would-be thieves* cave canem, *or 'beware of the dog'.*

gold, and spread with multicoloured damask quilts. The wealthy had beds in their studies, on which they read and wrote. They dined on couches in the same reclining position.

Tables, by comparison, were very lightweight affairs, often with folding legs. Chairs were uncommon, though wealthy women favoured a seat called a *cathedra*, with a sloping back: the word is the origin of the modern name for a bishop's official chair. Valuables were kept in strongboxes fitted with a lock and key, and mansions were lit at night with bronze oil lamps, hanging lamps and candelabras.

The Romans burned olive oil, a costly and not particularly bright form of lighting which left a pall of smoke hanging in the air – good reasons (along with fire risks) why people made the most of daylight hours.

Most men rose at dawn and breakfasted on nothing more than a cup of water. They often made straight for a barber's shop, where the barbers used iron razors and water to provide close shaves. A young man's first shave amounted to a religious rite: the cuttings were put in a glass phial offered to the gods in thanksgiving for the youth reaching manhood.

Roman men generally favoured a short, no-nonsense haircut, but more fanciful coiffure was also affected: hair was artificially curled, dyed and perfumed. Such foppishness, barely tolerable even in young people, was thought ludicrous in older citizens.

Tunics versus to gas

At home most men wore a woollen or linen tunic, with shirt and loincloth underneath. But for public functions, a Roman citizen (not a slave) was entitled to wear the toga, a semicircular garment made of woollen fabric which was draped in flowing folds over the tunic. Voluminous and immensely stylish, the toga was also awkward to move about in. In vain did emperors pass decrees trying to force citizens to wear their distinctive, ceremonial garb. In the country, especially, Romans took to wearing more practical forms of cloak, while for formal evening meals a smart, loose gown called a *synthesis* was widely adopted.

Roman women wore a flowing garment called the *stola* over their tunics. Belted at the waist and often dyed blue, green, red or saffron yellow, it was worn with an overcloak and became as much a kind of national costume as the toga was for men. Women's underwear was strikingly modern in style: a two-piece bra and girdle is shown in mosaics.

For fashionable women, the daily toilet process was a vital and incredibly time-consuming affair done with the help of slave girls. It began with the lengthy dressing of the hair, which was worn in various elaborate styles, often heaped up on top of the head and fixed with a scaffolding of pins and combs. The satirical poet Juvenal complained of one lady: 'She heaps tier on top of tier, storey upon storey on her head until it is piled high. From the front you'd think she was a queen; behind she's shorter...you'd swear it was a different person.'

Wigs were so popular that some sculpted portrait busts had removable stone wigs, like lids, to anticipate fashion changes. Prostitutes were required by law to wear a yellow wig in Rome, or to dye their hair yellow. In the days of Rome's decadence, fashionable ladies took up this raunchy style, sporting various shades of yellow hair themselves. To meet their demands, large quantities of flaxen hair were imported from Germany.

Easy on the feet *Leather openwork sandals and stout, hobnailed town shoes were sold both ready made and made-to-measure by Roman cobblers. Sandals were normally worn indoors, especially at mealtimes, and at ease in the country.*

Best of friends *Cuddling a pet cat to her chest, a chicken at her feet, this figure of a young girl on a tombstone is one of the earliest representations in Europe of a domesticated cat.*

CROWNING GLORY

Both men and women were conscious of their hair in Roman times, and styles frequently changed. Fashion-conscious women arranged their hair with the help of an *ornatrix*, who specialised in creating fanciful frameworks of hair. 'Every day, so it seems, brings a different style', said the poet Ovid. The three women on the left favoured elaborate, carefully contrived hairdos. By contrast, men's hairstyles were simpler and less changeable – though beards went in and out of fashion over the centuries. Even so, men of fashion relied on the assistance of professional barbers, known as *tonsores*, to help them to look their smartest.

Beauty box *A Roman woman's toilet box held chalk and white lead to lighten the complexion, ash or antimony for eye make-up and red ochre for the lips.*

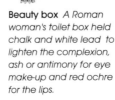

Keeping fit *Young women clad in two-piece garments resembling the bikinis of modern times use dumbbells, a discus and simple exercises in order to keep in trim.*

'With this ring...' *Many Roman brides wore a chunky wedding ring of gold on the third finger of their left hand as a pledge of loyalty to their husbands. The design of this ring, dating from around AD 200, has a symbolic design showing the dextrarium iunctio, or joining of hands. In addition, couples exchanged mutual vows of fidelity.*

CEREMONIES FROM BIRTH TO DEATH

The sanctity of the family was one of the cornerstones of Roman society. People were encouraged to marry young and to have as many children as possible. Most parents took their responsibilities very seriously and tried to make sure their children grew up to be respectful sons and daughters – and model citizens of the future. Some mothers and fathers, however, put their offspring in the charge of servant girls or slaves, and this infuriated the historian Tacitus, who wrote of such a youngster that: 'Its tender, unformed mind is steeped in the stories and lies of these slaves, and no one in the whole house cares a jot for what he says or does in front of the young master...Indeed, the peculiar vices of this city seem to me to be conceived almost in the mother's womb – devotion to actors and obsession with gladiators...'

By tradition, a Roman child's upbringing was very much the responsibility of the parents. There was no public education system, as in Greece. The mother played the major role during infancy, after which schooling began at home, originally under the stern eye of the father as teacher. In later years, though, it became common to maintain a *paedogogus* – a slave who acted as a tutor – or a child might go to a fee-paying school. This was rarely a big establishment – often little more than a single room, a shop or house, simply curtained off from the street.

Children went to school at the age of seven, and learned to write in Latin on wax tablets with a bone stylus. Discipline was harsh, and slackers risked frequent thrashings with the cane, leather thong or eel-skin strap. The endurance of pain was, after all, good training for the future soldiers of the empire. But there were plenty of amusements for children too. School finished in mid-afternoon, and pupils might go on to the public baths or play games such as hoops, leapfrog, knuckle-bones and blindman's buff. Now and again a boy might be seen scudding about the streets in a model chariot drawn by goat or donkey.

Housewives in the making

Rag dolls were favourite toys with girls, who went to schools of their own, though their education was more basic and ended at around 12 or 13 with the onset of puberty. After that they learned to be good housewives. Boys went on to a secondary stage of schooling. These were, of course, the children of the wealthy. The mass of the people – as in every ancient society – were unschooled and illiterate.

At about 16, when privileged Roman youths left school, they went through a ceremony to mark their coming of age. This was held at the forum where, watched by family and friends, boys exchanged the purple-edged toga, or *toga praetexta*, of boyhood for the plain white toga, or *toga virilis*, which was worn by adults.

Manhood was a proud estate in ancient Rome. The father had complete power, not only over his children but over his wife – at least in theory. In reality, women were much more than chattels, for Roman matrons exercised great influence over the households

Parents and offspring *The love of a father and mother for their baby is touchingly illustrated on this sarcophagus of a wealthy Roman named Cornelius – who is shown with his wife and only child. Although large families were the ideal, the infant mortality rate was high, and many parents had to be satisfied with two or three children at the most. Those youngsters who did survive had a normal, healthy liking for games; a child's sarcophagus (right) shows a group of boys playing with a slide and some nuts, and a line of girls throwing balls against a wall.*

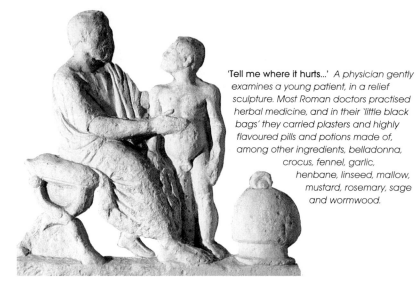

'Tell me where it hurts...' *A physician gently examines a young patient, in a relief sculpture. Most Roman doctors practised herbal medicine, and in their 'little black bags' they carried plasters and highly flavoured pills and potions made of, among other ingredients, belladonna, crocus, fennel, garlic, henbane, linseed, mallow, mustard, rosemary, sage and wormwood.*

and their husbands, too. Human love was celebrated. Our St Valentine's Day customs go back to a February festival of the pagan Romans, in which boys drew girls' names from a love urn.

An orange veil for the bride

Marriage was an important institution, often carefully arranged by match-making parents, and the wedding service was loaded with symbolism. The bride wore a traditional wedding dress and her hair was dressed in archaic style with a veil of vivid orange. The service was held at her home, or in a shrine, where sacrifices such as pigs were offered, the couple exchanged vows and sealed their union with a clasping of hands.

After the service the bride was taken in procession to the threshold of her husband's home, where she smeared the doorposts with oil and fat, adding wreaths of wool. Then she was carried across the threshold – just as brides are today – in an act of ritual abduction. The ceremony marked the girl's transition from virgin to wife, and the nuptial bed was often kept afterwards

in the atrium, or central hall, of the newlyweds' home. A girl at the time of her marriage was often no more than 14 or 15 – sometimes younger. Having a baby was something she looked forward to with apprehension, for miscarriages were common and many women died in childbirth. With disease common and a lack of real medical care, about one in three Roman children died in infancy.

Soon after the birth, the proud father took the baby in his arms and lifted him or her up to demonstrate his paternal bond. A few days later a baby was given a good-luck charm, known as a *bulla*. This was hung around the neck to ward off evil spirits and worn throughout childhood. Boys only surrendered their bulla when they took up the toga of manhood.

A saw for the surgeon

Charms and supernatural cures played a big part in Roman medicine. Surgeons used a wealth of precision instruments such as scalpels, catheters and fine-toothed saws (for amputation), but since there were no true anaesthetics an operation can only have been a bloody ordeal of stark terror and excruciating pain.

The Romans worshipped gods very similar to those of the Greeks. Their sky god, bearded Jupiter, was much like the Greek Zeus, for example; their Venus, goddess of love, resembled Aphrodite; Mars, the war god, was comparable to the Greek Ares. Temples

were devoted to the traditional gods, and many Romans also came under the spell of foreign mystery religions which arrived with the spread of the empire. Some people worshipped the falcon-headed and jackal-headed gods of Egypt; others, especially soldiers, revered Mithras the bull-slayer and Persian god of light; others worshipped Cybele, the Asiatic mother goddess, whose adherents might castrate themselves in their frenzies of devotion.

In due course, Christ also became known. His fervent following was found initially among slaves and the families of the poor. The Christians were persecuted chiefly because of their refusal to acknowledge any other god than their own.

For the great mystery of death, the Romans had traditional rites. The poor might be deposited at night in a common grave with no ceremony, but wealthier citizens were mourned in style. The anointed body of the head of a household was laid on a funeral couch in his lamp-lit atrium, where people paid their last respects.

A coin for the boatman

The Romans shared the Greek belief that dead souls were ferried across the River Styx to Hades, so a coin was often placed in the dead man's mouth to pay the boatman. A funeral dinner was given, and hired mourners wept and wailed as the *pompa*, or funeral procession, led by musicians, accompanied the slave-borne bier to the place of burial or cremation. Portraits of family ancestors were often brought along, so that they might be present in spirit.

But all was not total solemnity. The Romans were realists at heart, and a big funeral procession often included capering clowns who were hired to make jokes about the dead man, reminding mourners that even the great were only human.

WRITING THE ROMAN WAY

The Latin alphabet was generally used throughout the Roman Empire and, as it spread beyond the borders, it became the alphabet of Western civilisation. It had, however, only 23 letters. During the Middle Ages the Roman 'I' was divided into i and j; their 'V' became u, v and w.

Most adult writing was done on scrolls of papyrus and vellum, but bound pages appeared during the later years of the empire, when they found their way into school libraries. Children were taught the basics of writing, reading and arithmetic even before they started school.

In wax and stone *A girl (top) uses a bone stylus to write on a wooden tablet coated on one side with wax. The distinctive capital letters (above) with their fine proportions, evolved by the Romans to engrave on their monuments, are still in use today.*

Funeral march *Reclining as if at ease, a deceased Roman is borne on a bier to his funeral. The procession is led by musicians, while the dead man's family comes behind.*

FEASTS, COLD BATHS AND HOT GOSSIP

Six hundred ostrich brains and peas mixed with grains of gold were among the dishes served up at one feast for Emperor Elagabalus, and he is said to have had so many roses cascade down through apertures in the ceiling at another feast that several of his guests were suffocated. The extravagance of Roman banquets is legendary, and though not all hosts were as profligate as Elagabalus, big dinner parties were among the great pleasures of life in every wealthy home.

While the mass of the poor were sustained chiefly by bread and a wheatmeal porridge known as *puls*, the rich turned feasting into something like an art form. Their banquets lasted for hours, often beginning at three or four in the afternoon and going on well into the night, with acrobats, dancers, dwarfs, musicians and clowns offering entertainment between courses.

Fanned by peacock feathers

Armies of slaves took care of all needs: they removed guests' shoes on arrival and replaced them with sandals; brandished peacock-feather fans to keep flies off food; brought perfumed water to wash guests' hands; and transported glistening, aromatic dishes to the central dining table. It was customary for the most handsome slaves to serve

the wine and cut up food, while the guests themselves reclined, often three people to a couch, with their left arm supported on a cushion. With so much laid on for their delight, it is a curious fact that the guests were expected to bring their own napkins. An aggrieved host said of one miserly guest: 'Hermogenes has never yet brought a napkin of his own to dinner, but always manages to take one home with him.'

The banquet was held in the candle-lit dining room, or *triclinium*, and commenced only after invocations to Jupiter and the household gods. It was generally a three-part affair consisting of hors d'oeuvre, main dishes and dessert.

The writer Martial, planning a modest meal for seven guests, shared his thoughts about the planning of the menu in the following invitation to a friend: 'Now let's see – Stella, Nepos, Canius, Cerlialis, Flaccus and myself make six. My semicircular dining couch seats seven, so add Lupus. Now

Likely lad *Many young slaves would start their working lives serving food at banquets. If they pleased their masters they might be adopted by them and later granted freedom.*

then, the menu. Well, there are marrows that my bailiff's wife has brought, plus the produce – things like lettuce, leeks, some mint and chicory. Then we'll have sliced eggs and mackerel served with parsley, and sow belly done in the brine of salted tuna fish. That's for starters. For a main course, a piece of lamb (one that's been mangled by a fox is cheap!), meatballs (no need for carving!), beans and tender sprouts. On top of that there'll be a chicken and the remains of the ham we ·had the other day. When we've had our fill, we can have ripe apples and a wine that's matured a year or two. To crown the lot there'll be a comic turn – nothing in bad taste mind you. People can let their hair down without regretting it

Feasting at leisure Reclining on a dining couch, the head of the family takes time off from eating to listen as his wife, seated in an armchair, plays a stringed instrument. Meanwhile, their children play at their feet as slaves bring in a rich choice of meat, fish, vegetables and wine.

tomorrow, and no one need worry what he says. They can talk about the Greens and Blues, or any other chariot-racing team: nobody's going to haul them off to court for being drunk in my house!'

Egg dishes, olives, lettuce and figs were popular starters, but in other respects Roman food had little in common with Italian food of today. Tomatoes and pasta were as yet unknown, for example, and garlic was not much used. Instead, the chief ingredient of many dishes was a pungent sauce known as liquamen, distilled from the juices and entrails of fish. It tasted something like anchovy essence and was used to flavour a wealth of gastronomic delights, from milk-fed snails to suckling pig and hot boiled goose.

Dormice as a delicacy

The Romans had a special fondness for dormice – a delicacy for which special containers were built, in which the tasty rodents were battery bred, before being fattened on walnuts, acorns and chestnuts in custom-built earthenware pots. For the table, the gourmet Apicius recommended stuffing dormice with minced pork, pepper, pine kernels and liquamen.

Many Roman recipes have survived in the *Art of Cooking*, written by Apicius in about AD 15. For a Fricassee

Haircuts and hearsay *Barbers' shops were a mixture of men's club and gossip shop. Clients loitered in them to hear the latest rumours and scandal. The iron scissors or shears had some critics, however: 'If you don't want to go to an early grave, stay clear of Antiochus, the barber,' said the poet Martial.*

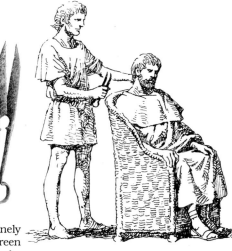

of Sea Food, for example, he suggests: 'Put fish in a saucepan, add liquamen, oil, wine, stock. Finely chop leeks with their heads (ie, green and white parts) and coriander, make tiny fishballs, and chop up fillets of cooked fish, add sea urchins, having washed them well. When all this is cooked, crush pepper, lovage, origano, pound thoroughly, moisten with liquamen, and some of the cooking liquor, and put in the saucepan. When it bubbles, crumble pastry in to bind, and stir well. Sprinkle with pepper and serve.'

A feast for the eye

For banquets, food was artfully prepared to delight the eye so that a wild pig, for example, might be served up surrounded by an arrangement of sweet cakes in the form of suckling pigs. There were surprises for diners, too: boars and sows were sometimes served whole, and then roast thrushes, larks or nightingales were drawn from

their bellies like rabbits from a magician's hat. Mounds of fresh or dried fruit and ingenious pastries were popular desserts. Dishes were served on silver salvers or bright red ware from the popular potteries of Gaul, and much eating was done with the fingers, even though knives and spoons were available – but no forks as yet. Belching was considered to be polite behaviour, and food was washed down with flagons of wine. This was sometimes flavoured with honey and almost always mixed with water – unmixed wine being thought a barbarian taste.

Drunkenness and over-eating made vomiting such a common hazard that certain slaves were specifically allocated the task of clearing up the couches, tables and floors. The uglier

side of Roman nature also revealed itself in the fact that some banquet entertainments included gladiators, summoned to fight and kill each other, the blood, sweat and stench of slaughter being laid on for the pleasure of guests. Sometimes, too, a drunken meal degenerated into an orgy, lustful appetites being aroused by the lewd cavorting of dancing girls, often Spanish and clicking castanets.

Under the rose

But these were excesses. On the whole, banquets were given much as dinner parties are today, for the pleasures of the table and of good company. Gossip was always a particular attraction, and indiscretions flowed as freely as the wine.

It was customary for a rose to be hung from the ceiling to commemorate Cupid's gift of a rose to Harpocrates, the god of silence, to bribe him against disclosing the indiscretions of Aphrodite. Suspending a rose from the ceiling showed that everything said beneath it was not to be repeated: hence the Latin phrase *sub rosa*, or 'under the rose', meaning something said in confidence.

High stakes *Gambling was officially against the law, but Roman men often played dice in the privacy of the baths or in taverns. Large sums were recklessly wagered on would-be games of chance, and unscrupulous gamblers sometimes cheated, as is shown by the loaded dice that have been found. 'Men come not now with purses to the hazard of the gaming table,' said the poet Juvenal, 'but with a treasure chest beside them.'*

A DAY AT THE BATHS

With their gymnasiums, shops, libraries and gardens, Roman baths were popular meeting places. Wealthy citizens often spent the whole day there, exchanging news, playing board games, wrestling and taking exercise with dumbbells and medicine balls. Even the poor could attend, as entry fees were low – and children got in free.

The bathers might pass through three or four different kinds of bath in succession, from tepid to hot and dry, then to warm and steamy, before returning to the frigidarium for a final invigorating cold plunge. There was no soap. Instead, bathers rubbed oil into their skin then scraped it off with the dirt and sweat using a curved, razor-like implement known as a strigil. The wealthy brought their own slaves to help them, or attendants would do it for a fee. The baths were notoriously noisy; people shouted and sang, or grunted and groaned as masseurs pummelled them. Men and women attended, and for many years mixed bathing was allowed.

Keeping clean *The bathhouse mosaic (above) bids visitors to 'Have a good bath' – and reminds them to remove their sandals on entering and to put them on again when they leave. The toilet set (left) has a flask with oil for spreading on the body and bronze strigils with which to scrape off the dirt.*

Baths and bathers *When building their baths – such as the one at Bath in southern England (above) – the Romans utilised the district's natural warm springs. Although mixed bathing was allowed, some public baths had mornings for women only. The lamp-top (left) shows two ladies combining gossip with the call of hygiene at the baths.*

SHOPKEEPERS, CRAFTSMEN AND SLAVES

A colourful and noisy profusion of shops crowded the streets and public squares of ancient Rome. There were the bakers, butchers, poultry sellers, fishmongers, tavern keepers, barbers, booksellers, perfume merchants, furniture sellers, blacksmiths, shoemakers and countless others. Some premises were prosperous, but most were no more than cramped and ill-lit shacks, leaning against people's homes and spilling out into narrow alleys and large covered markets alike.

low rate of interest and lend at a high one. To try to combat speculation in imperial times, a legal rate of interest was set at 12 per cent per annum – equal to 1 per cent per month. Land ownership was far more respectable, and through it some citizens became multimillionaires. The rich politician Marcus Crassus was quoted as saying that a man could not call himself rich unless he could pay for the upkeep of a legion (about 6000 men) out of his year's income.

Banks flourished in the capital, while poorer citizens might keep their meagre savings in an earthenware 'piggy bank'. The basic currency unit was a bronze

Balancing the books *Bankers, tax collectors and moneylenders spent long hours in their counting houses, making sure that their daily transactions were scrupulously entered in their accounts ledgers.*

History on coins *Romans embossed their coins with the heads of emperors, and events such as Caesar's murder.*

Vespasian

Vespasian

Claudius

Ides of March

Hadrian

Julius Caesar

Painted boards were set up to attract people's attention, and goods were often displayed on the pavements – which, being thick with strolling vendors hawking their wares on foot, became at times almost impassable. Congestion was so bad at one point that Emperor Domitian banned wares from the pavement, forcing shopkeepers back into their premises.

In Rome, the great Forum was the main business centre, with a huge complex of stalls, market squares and meeting places. The moneychangers had their shops in this quarter, and would make their heaps of coins flash, jingle and dance to attract custom. There was plenty of cash to be made in moneylending, though it was a trade frowned on by high-born Romans, who had a soldierly contempt for all forms of commerce. 'No gentleman would be a moneylender', wrote the conservative statesman Cato.

Nonetheless, even aristocrats did succumb at times to the lure of easy profits. The object was to borrow at a

coin called an *as*; a *sestertius* was worth four *asses* and a silver *denarius* was worth 16 *asses*. An ordinary soldier was paid 225 *denarii* a year; a small sack of wheat cost half a denarius.

Among the everyday trades, one of the most flourishing was that of the olive-oil vendor. His product was used not only for cooking, but in lamps for lighting and as a substitute for soap to wash the body. Colossal volumes of oil were bought and sold every day; by AD 300 there were 2300 oil sellers in Rome. Large potteries turned out oil and wine jars by the million, and cheap glassware was also mass-produced once the technique of glassblowing was introduced, probably by immigrant Syrian glassworkers, in the 1st century AD.

Another distinctive craft was that of the mosaic worker who, tapping away with hammer and chisel, cut pieces of sandstone and marble to make coloured cubes, or tesserae. These were later set in cement to create the mythological images, pictures of

animals, sporting scenes and so on, for Roman wall and floor mosaics.

Rome was not, of course, the only commercial centre in Italy. Modena was famed for the production of bricks, Bergamo for bronzeware, and Padua for woollen textiles. Luxuries flooded in from the exotic margins of the empire and beyond: silks from China, papyrus from Egypt, emeralds from Scythia and perfumes from Arabia.

From the cold shores of the Baltic came amber in large quantities. This was carved especially at the town of Aquileia to make ornaments cheap enough even for poor women to wear, while fashionable ladies might be seen carrying a ball of amber in their hands, and rubbing it to catch its light

Thoughts of freedom *An oil flask depicts a young slave squatting pensively on a bucket, in a rare moment of leisure. He wears a disc, similar to the one on the left, on which is inscribed his name, that of his master, and the place to which he was to be returned if captured while fleeing.*

fragrance as they passed through the smelly thoroughfares of the capital. Shops in Rome opened early in the morning and closed at midday. They opened later in the afternoon and did not shut down until dusk. Though the mistress of a household might sometimes do the shopping for herself, it was a job generally done by slaves. Most shopkeepers were, in fact, slaves or ex-slaves, members of the vast class who provided so much of the muscle power in daily life. Some were reared at home, and many

A CROSSROADS IN ROME

Standing on the steps of a public building at a busy city crossroads, a red-garbed merchant watches the mid-morning scene. To his left, a high-ranking lady is carried to the baths in a canopied litter guarded by soldiers. In the street below the merchant, a butcher in his open-fronted shop weighs meat for a customer, while on an upper floor people gather upon a flower-bedecked balcony to view the procession.

Covered stalls lining the streets attract customers for a range of goods from fruit and flowers to the latest fashions in jewellery. Porters bear away rolls of cloth and barrels of wine for their purchasers. Farther along the main street, lofty arches bear the great aqueduct, built by Emperor Nero, that brings a regular water supply into the city.

Public buildings around the square include pillared temples, in front of which stand flaming torches showing that they are open for prayer. In the centre, a narrow column marks a public fountain, while several walls are daubed with trade symbols and graffiti scrawled by idlers.

Hard at work *Using a long-handled slice to take loaves from the oven (left), a baker produces one of Rome's daily needs. Knives, choppers, chisels and saws were among the tools made by the blacksmith (below) in his smithy.*

Goods for sale *Bread, oil and wine are among the goods sold by a shop-keeper (left), who points to the various items on his shelves. The streets of Rome were lined with open-fronted stores such as this.*

imported from Britain, Greece, Egypt, North Africa and elsewhere. At the time of Trajan, about a third of the population in Rome were slaves – a total of some 400,000 of them. Men, women and children were bought and sold like animals at public auctions, with placards hung around their necks to advertise their merits.

Slaves were expected to do whatever they were told, and if they failed or displeased their masters they might face ferocious punishment, or even death. A cook who produced a below par meal might be flogged in front of the guests at a dinner table; a clumsy girl attendant might be skewered with a hairpin at a lady's toilet. Runaways, after recapture, were branded on the forehead with the letters FUG, for *fugitivus*. Of course, some masters were more humane. The author Seneca wrote: 'Please reflect that the man you call your slave was born of the same seed, has the same good sky above him, breathes the air you do, lives as you do, dies as you do. Treat your slave with kindness, and with courtesy, too; let him share your conversations, your deliberations and your company.'

Often household slaves were treated with real affection by the families they served. They might be rewarded with freedom for loyal service, or buy their liberty by savings from the wages they were paid. Even as slaves they might become doctors, teachers and, in some cases, government officials.

Under the lash

Slaves in town fared better than those put to work in the fields. There they laboured under the lash of the overseers, often as victims of the hard-nosed bailiffs who managed the landed estates with an eye for nothing but maximum yields and high profits.

Worse still was the plight of slave labourers who toiled in the Roman mines for lead, iron, copper and silver. Gnawed by hunger, shivering in the long, dark subterranean galleries, these living spectres might not see daylight for months on end, and were literally worked to death.

PIPED WATER, AND ROADS TO THE COUNTRY

Goods to market *Ox-drawn wagons trundled along the Roman roads at harvest time, when vast loads of grain had to be moved from the corn-growing country estates to markets in the towns. The drivers used goads to spur the muscle-straining oxen into greater efforts; but the heavily laden and slow-moving wagons clogged the roads and caused some of history's earliest traffic jams.*

Built to last *Roman roads, noted for their durability, were generally built in layers, starting from a base of levelled sand. Above was spread hardcore of lime concrete and broken stone. A third layer might include coarse sand and lime. The surface consisted of blocks of stone set in concrete, and packed with flint and pebbles.*

Straight and true *Roman surveyors employed an instrument called a groma to plot their straight roads and their grid-pattern towns. The groma was also used to check the level of sites for new building works.*

Every day of the year, more than 220 million gallons (about 1 billion litres) of fresh water gushed into Rome to feed its wealth of baths and fountains. The colossal flow was borne by 11 great aqueducts – stone-built watercourses often carried on arches high above ground. The remains of one of them, the Aqua Claudia, can still be seen, once 43 miles (68 km) long and bringing water from a system of underground channels in the hills to serve the imperial capital's vast system of reservoirs, cisterns and pipes. The Romans were above all a practical people, remembered for great engineering projects not only in the neighbourhood of Rome but throughout Europe.

The arch used to support the aqueduct was also the great structural feature of the Romans' monumental buildings. This load-bearing device, more efficient than the simple beam, was further developed to create vaults and domes. The Romans also perfected the use of concrete. The Pantheon, a circular temple in Rome, has a dome with a diameter of 142 ft (43 m), made from a single span of concrete. Erected about AD 118 under Emperor Hadrian, this daring roof is as safe today as when it was first built.

Concrete was also used to make the Romans' celebrated roads. They gave their empire an astonishing network of broad, clear highways that ran ruler-straight across country, uniting the far-flung corners of the realm with the imperial capital.

The Romans' first great public road was the Via Appia, built in 312 BC between Rome and Capua, and later extended to run south as far as Brundisium (present-day Brindisi) at the 'heel' of Italy. It was a highway that came to be used simply for the pleasure of 'going for a spin' or taking the air, borne by a litter, riding on horseback or drawn by a carriage.

Some vehicles were very swankily furnished, upholstered with silk and drawn by mules in gorgeous livery. Slave runners, or dogs, were often sent ahead of carriages to clear a path through the crowds, while the very ostentatious might have a troop of African horsemen riding in front.

Roads for the legions

Wherever the Romans went they imprinted the landscape with their roads. In Britain, for example, within 40 years of their conquest they had laid down a 6000 mile (9600 km) network. Slave labourers working in chain gangs provided manpower for road-works as they did for other engineering projects, but many roads were built by Roman soldiers simply following the shortest distance between military camps or towns. The roads were, in fact, designed more for marching men than for wheeled carts.

Mastering communications was a key to power, and every dozen or so miles there were halts where couriers carrying official dispatches from Rome could get fresh horses. If the roads were first built to meet the legionaries'

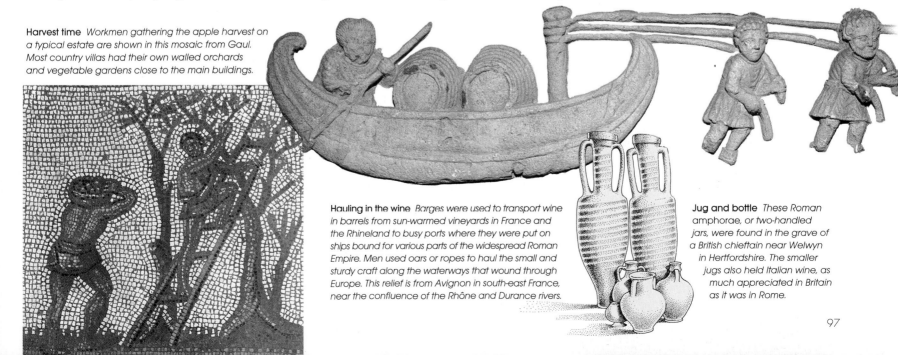

Waterway wonder *A great aqueduct running across the plain of northern Tunisia brought water to the Roman city of Carthage from the mountains of Zaghouan, some 25 miles (40 km) away. The stones were raised into position by cranes and pulleys – Greek inventions, developed by the Romans for huge engineering projects.*

needs, they also fostered trade and prosperity, knitting together the empire's enormous hotchpotch of peoples and provinces through bonds of commerce. They linked the city and the countryside, and goods including wine and farm produce were carted in wagons, borne by mules slung with panniers and on the backs of all-enduring slaves travelling on foot. Travellers could hire two-wheeled cabs or four-wheeled carriages at rental firms found in every sizable town.

Whole households were often seen on the roads, as well-to-do citizens moved with their bedding, servants and provisions, from their town houses to take vacations at their country estates. In hot weather the leisured classes often retreated to villas in cool hill country. In addition, they might visit the seaside to go boating and to take the sun. The Bay of Naples had several popular resorts, including the city of Pompeii, which was destroyed on a hot summer day in AD 79 when Mount Vesuvius erupted with appalling ferocity, burying the city under titanic volumes of pumice and ash. The statesman Pliny the Younger, an eye-witness to the disaster, described how: 'the buildings around us were tottering...we saw the sea sucked away...a dense cloud spreading over the earth like a flood...you could hear the shrieks!'

During long journeys people often stopped for the night at one of the inns along the way – although they were notorious for their mosquitoes, noise, indifferent food and bad water, and the drunken carousing of some of the guests. Brigands and highwaymen ambushed many a traveller in Italy itself – the malarial Pontine Marshes along the Appian Way were particularly dangerous. In foreign lands there were barbarian tribes to contend with.

Piracy was a constant risk for sea travellers, but the worst perils came from the weather. Between November and March, navigation more or less ceased. Tourism never became an industry, in the modern sense, among the Romans. However, guidebooks and maps were available, and some, like modern maps, show the distances between towns and inns. Diplomats, soldiers, merchants and others were keen sightseers and often took time off, in foreign lands, to inspect the local monuments. Some Roman visitors to Egypt even left their graffiti on statues of the pharaohs.

Working the land *A ploughman and his team of cattle are depicted in this bronze model preparing the ground for sowing crops.*

Reaping the harvest *An iron sickle was used for cutting the grain. Farms flourished around the villas in which the rich spent the summer months, away from the gruelling heat of cities such as Rome. The estate-owners and their families travelled to their country retreats along the magnificent roads which ran arrow-straight across the countryside.*

Harvest time *Workmen gathering the apple harvest on a typical estate are shown in this mosaic from Gaul. Most country villas had their own walled orchards and vegetable gardens close to the main buildings.*

Hauling in the wine *Barges were used to transport wine in barrels from sun-warmed vineyards in France and the Rhineland to busy ports where they were put on ships bound for various parts of the widespread Roman Empire. Men used oars or ropes to haul the small and sturdy craft along the waterways that wound through Europe. This relief is from Avignon in south-east France, near the confluence of the Rhône and Durance rivers.*

Jug and bottle *These Roman amphorae, or two-handled jars, were found in the grave of a British chieftain near Welwyn in Hertfordshire. The smaller jugs also held Italian wine, as much appreciated in Britain as it was in Rome.*

INTO BATTLE WITH THE LEGIONS

No ancient people took the profession of soldiering more seriously than did the Romans. They battled their way from the shores of Galilee to the drizzle-soaked moors of northern England, and the security of their vast empire, encompassing 60 million people, depended on strong and efficient fighting forces, ready at all times to swing into action. The Roman army, in the heyday of the empire, was a devastating and hugely successful war machine the like of which the world had never seen.

The key unit was the legion, consisting of about 6000 men. Almost all of these were infantry troops. A legion might include 100-200 cavalrymen used as scouts, standard-bearers and harriers of fleeing foe; but the Romans themselves were not enthusiastic horse riders. When they did raise cavalry regiments they generally employed foreign auxiliaries, among them Gauls and Thracians.

Foreign auxiliaries served as javelin throwers, archers and slingers, too. But the legionary – the archetypal Roman soldier – had to be a Roman citizen, and recruits had to undergo a rigorous screening programme before being accepted into the ranks.

All recruits had to be at least 5 ft 8 in (1.7 m) tall, and they were given a medical examination to ensure that they were physically sound, with good eyesight.

Rage of battle *When Roman troops clashed with their enemies at close quarters, it was a violent and bloody business. Men fought hand-to-hand with swords and spears, and horses reared wildly, often trampling to death the fallen. Those who survived the carnage carried the physical and mental wounds for life.*

Safe keeping *Soldiers carried money in bronze 'bracelet' purses. The catch could not be released until the purse was removed.*

Man of bronze *Resolute soldiers such as this legionary had the power to make or break Roman emperors. He wears a crested helmet of bronze or iron, a cuirass made of overlapping bands of iron, and a kilt made of hanging strips of leather, plated with metal. Despite the cumbersome appearance, flexible leather straps left the wearer free to march and fight with ease.*

Deadly weapon *Thrusting spears with jagged iron heads were once standard equipment for Roman foot soldiers. This spear has its original head, but the shaft is a modern substitute. The spears were later replaced by javelins of varying weights.*

Shoes for marching *Strong, well-ventilated sandals were worn by Roman soldiers on the move. Leather loops laced across the foot and up the ankle. The hob-nailed soles could survive hundreds of miles of fast marching as troops hurried to trouble spots.*

Hard hat *No soldier went into battle without a sturdy iron helmet to protect head and neck.*

Sword of death *The legionaries' principal weapon was the gladius, or short sword. Although the sword had two sharp cutting edges, it was mainly used to stab opponents to death in lightning thrusts from behind a wall of shields. The grip was made of wood or bone, and its handsome leather scabbard was decorated with medallions and scenes of Roman official and everyday life.*

A legionary signed on for 20 years, which was no small commitment. Yet all were volunteers. Men joined for the pay; for the glory; for a chance to see the world; or in hopes of bettering themselves. Through the army a simple ploughboy or blacksmith might rise to the rank of centurion, with 80 men under his command. However, no legionary of humble birth could expect to enter the officer class. Education, wealth and rank – the 'old-boy' network, operating among established families – were the keys to promotion to the upper levels.

Training for combat

On acceptance, a recruit was sent straight to camp for training which continued, with unrelenting pressure, throughout his period of service. Soldiers were put through their paces on the parade ground every day, under the rasping command of a centurion wielding a vine staff, symbol of rank and a weapon of punishment. One man earned the nickname of 'Fetch me another' because he broke so many staffs across the backs of his men.

For exercises, soldiers attacked 6 ft (1.8 m) high wooden stakes, punching at them with their shield boss and stabbing at them with a sword. New recruits had to do this with double-weight practice weapons. Wearing full kit, men were also required to run, jump and vault over wooden horses. There was swimming in the summer months. There were route marches and mock battles, too, all preparing soldiers for the real combat to come.

A life of footslogging

Equipment changed over the years, but in the 1st century AD the standard outfit for a legionary included an iron helmet, body armour of iron rings or laced metal strips, a plywood shield, two heavy *pila*, or javelins, a dagger, the distinctive short, stabbing sword called a *gladius*, and strong sandals made of leather. Footslogging was the

legionary's lot: soldiers had to tramp through desert, mountain or forest at a rate of about 18 miles (29 km) a day.

Roman soldiers were burdened with much more than armour and weapons; they also carried a basket, pick, axe, saw, cooking pot, two stakes for the palisade which made a stronghold of their camp and enough grain to last for about 15 days. The full weight was 90 lb (40 kg) – nearly double the weight carried by modern soldiers in full kit.

Safe beneath the 'tortoise'

In pitched battle, the resolve of the legionaries was awesome. Writing in AD 77, the Jewish historian Josephus commented: 'Their perfect discipline welds the whole into a single body; so compact are their ranks, so alert their movements in wheeling, so quick their ears for orders, their eyes for signals, their hands for tasks.' Again and again, legionary discipline triumphed over the onslaughts of bold but reckless barbarians.

In sieges the Romans were also impressive. To take city gates, groups of 27 legionaries would form themselves into *testudos* or tortoise formations, tightly packed with shields held overhead to form 'shells' of armour against enemy missiles. For siege warfare, too, the Romans used mobile towers, ramps and scaling ladders, with giant catapults called *ballista* to hurl rocks and flaming darts against the enemy.

Victory would be celebrated in style. It was customary to hold 'triumphs' in Rome, public celebrations to welcome successful commanders and their troops, with glittering processions of floats, standard-bearers, horn blowers, parades of wretched captives and the ritual execution of enemy leaders, at a spot near the Forum. Failure was frowned upon. Any unit considered disobedient or cowardly in battle was subjected to 'decimation'; this meant that one soldier in ten was selected by lot to be savagely clubbed to death by his former comrades. Patrolling frontiers, providing

Transporting the troops War galleys powered by banks of oarsmen carried the legions into action overseas. In addition, heavily armed troopships regularly patrolled the frontier rivers of the Danube and the Rhine ready to quell rebellion.

A GOD FOR SOLDIERS

Mithras, the Persian god of light and wisdom, had many adherents in the Roman Empire – particularly among the soldiers of the Roman army. He was often shown slaying a sacred bull (right), whose lifeblood fertilised the world. Mithras, who was born with a sword in his hand, was often depicted with his loyal dog, Silvanus, and with two torchbearers, representing light and darkness. For a time Mithraism was a powerful rival to Christianity in the empire; but Emperor Constantine suppressed it in the 4th century after his own conversion to Christianity.

escorts, building camps, bridges and roads – these were all routine duties throughout the empire. Legionaries spent much of their time doing fatigues in or around the forts which were erected wherever the armies marched. Built of stone according to regular patterns, the forts included barrack blocks, a headquarters building, granaries, latrines, a hospital, armouries and so on.

A wall across England

In Britain, Emperor Hadrian marked the northern limits of the empire with an 80 mile (129 km) long wall which stretched across the neck of England, with 16 garrison forts strung out at intervals. More than 27 million cubic feet (764,000 cubic metres) of stone were used by the soldier-builders for this amazing fortification.

Here and elsewhere, settlements quickly grew up near the forts, with shops and taverns where soldiers gambled at dice and spent their pay on women and drink. Not all was debauchery, however, and they also relaxed by soaking in hot, steamy baths – and by writing letters home. A legionary was not supposed to marry, but many took up with local girls and started unofficial families, so helping to spread Roman ways of life and the Latin tongue across their vast and diverse realm.

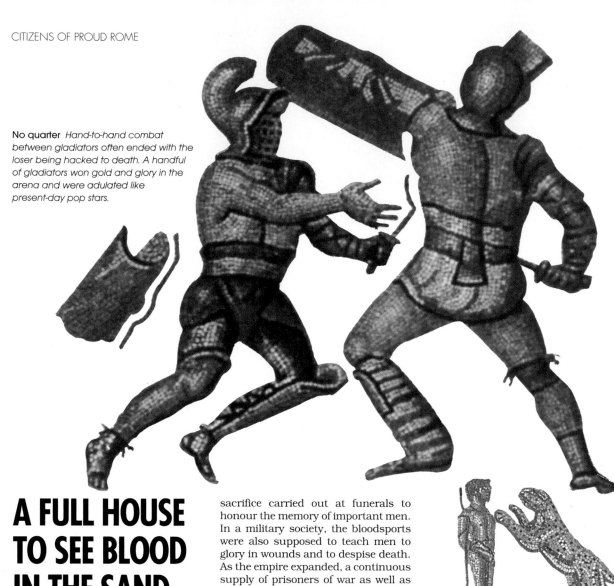

No quarter *Hand-to-hand combat between gladiators often ended with the loser being hacked to death. A handful of gladiators won gold and glory in the arena and were adulated like present-day pop stars.*

A DAY IN THE LIFE OF A GLADIATOR

Aroused at dawn by security guards, Flavius, a gladiator at Emperor Trajan's imperial school in Rome, assembles with his comrades for roll call in the central courtyard. He then breakfasts in the mess on barley bread and goat's-milk cheese, and reports to the armoury where he is issued with a shield, a helmet, leather shinguards and lightweight, steel practice weapons.

Training takes place in the school's own practice arena, under the eagle eye of the chief instructor – a scarred and sinewy former gladiator, the victor of numerous contests. It is his job to ensure that Flavius and his comrades are good enough and tough enough to satisfy the emperor and the crowds in the arena. The instructor gives his sharpest attention to the first-class fighters – the darlings of the crowd. Graffiti scrawled on walls at Pompeii reveal that a Thracian gladiator named Celadus was the local girls' current hero and heart-throb.

As the sun climbs towards noon, Flavius sweats and curses as he is drilled in the art of parry, thrust, riposte and feint. As his life will depend upon his skill and agility, he endures the training stoically. Midday brings a break for lunch and a siesta, after which Flavius has a wash and visits the school's barber for a shave. Next he attends physical training, which includes weightlifting to build strength and tone up the muscles. Then comes the evening meal. As darkness falls, he returns to his cell under the eye of the guards. Tomorrow Flavius has to face the bloodbath in the arena.

A FULL HOUSE TO SEE BLOOD IN THE SAND

Aware of their impending fate, the gladiators roared 'We who are about to die salute you!' to the emperor at the outset of a murderous contest in Rome. The entertainments were staged at the Colosseum, an astounding building of tiered arches with a seating capacity of 45,000 people and standing room for 5000 more. Wild beasts were kept in cages underground, where there was also a water system capable of flooding the arena for mock sea battles.

As many as 80 separate entrances allowed the mass of spectators to arrive and depart without too much crush, and a vast canvas awning was sometimes stretched over the top for shade against the sun. No trouble was spared in mounting these grisly spectacles of blood, pain and death. The public slaughter in gladiatorial fights began as a religious ritual – a form of sacrifice carried out at funerals to honour the memory of important men. In a military society, the bloodsports were also supposed to teach men to glory in wounds and to despise death. As the empire expanded, a continuous supply of prisoners of war as well as condemned criminals provided fodder for the shows.

Foreign captives were expected to fight according to their own customs with their own distinctive weapons. These set some classic gladiatorial styles: Thracians, for example, carried a curved scimitar and a small shield, while Samnites fought with the short sword and a hugely vizored and crested helmet. Another type was the *retiarius*, a lowly figure who fought bareheaded and armed only with a fisherman's net and trident.

So popular did the shows become that professional gladiators were trained at special schools to stiffen with skilled displays the

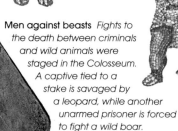

Men against beasts *Fights to the death between criminals and wild animals were staged in the Colosseum. A captive tied to a stake is savaged by a leopard, while another unarmed prisoner is forced to fight a wild boar.*

Faceless fighter *A gladiator's bronze helmet (right), completely covered his head and face, giving him a sinister and unearthly appearance.*

wretched performances of reluctant prisoners. At Trajan's imperial school, the Ludus Magnus in Rome's Via Labicana, most of the gladiators slept in the windowless cells of a 100 room barrack hall. There was more comfortable accommodation for the top-class gladiators, but even within their hall security guards kept constant watch to make sure there were no escapes.

A few freemen signed on for the prize money, which could account for a quarter of their contract price, but they had to swear an oath of submission for the duration of their contracts, agreeing to be 'burnt with fire, shackled with chains, whipped with rods and killed with steel'. Both in training and in combat at the games, *lorarii*, or floggers, were at hand brandishing scourges and red-hot irons to force laggards into the fray.

Death by a thumb signal

A major event in the Colosseum began with a parade of gladiators decked out in robes of purple and gold, riding chariots into the arena. The fighters were paired by lot and fought to the death before the excited onlookers. The grim figure of an official costumed as Charon, ferryman of the Underworld, would dispatch a mortally wounded loser by smashing his skull with a mallet. If a victim fell only slightly wounded an appeal for mercy might be made to the emperor, watching in his box, who listened to the verdict bayed out by the crowd and then indicated with a thumb signal whether the man should live or die. Crueller even than the duels between trained gladiators were the mass executions of criminals and the wild beast shows, which were

Music at the games A call on the trumpet heralds the start of the gladiatorial games. Musical interludes are played on a hydraulic organ, and horn players urge on the combatants. At the centre of the mosaic, a trainer restrains a gladiator who has just downed his opponent. Beside them a lightly clad net-fighter takes on a foe with leather armbands, and on the right two opponents with leg armour fight it out.

also held in the arena. In these hideous displays, unarmed, shrieking human beings were thrown to lions and bears. Alternatively, an armed man might be sent into the arena to chase and kill a defenceless man, only to be stripped of his weapons and hunted down by an armed pursuer in his turn. Beast shows and executions were generally staged in the morning, sometimes in a half-empty arena. There was a break around noon when the maimed corpses were removed and clean sand was laid down for the main events – the gladiatorials – which took place in the afternoon.

Not all the Roman Games were such gruesome events, although chariot races, too, offered their taste of spills, bloodshed and death. In Rome the races were staged in the Circus Maximus, a long oval stadium with a track split down the centre by a barrier. There were different events for vehicles drawn by two, three or four horses.

Hazards of the chariot race

As many as 12 chariots might burst from the starting gates to thunder around the track, clouds of dust billowing around the rushing vehicles. Crashes were frequent, especially at the turns; if a chariot was overturned the driver might be dragged along after his galloping horses for the remainder of the race, constituting a bloody and mangled hazard for the remaining high-speed charioteers.

Fans went wild with excitement as they urged their teams and their favourites on. People gambled feverishly on the results, and four great racing factions were distinguished by their stables' colours: the Reds, Whites, Blues and Greens. Charioteers who pleased the crowd were hero-worshipped, even though they were not technically required to finish a race. Victory went to the winning chariot – whether it had its driver or not.

To the victor the spoils With the gladiatorial races at their height, an agitator (bottom right) spurs the horses on, while a sparsor (top left) sprinkles water on the chariots' overheated wheels. In the centre of the track, officials mark the end of a lap by turning over one of the bronze dolphins on the outer rods, and removing one of the eggs on the inner rods. Other officials hold up the palm and wreath (centre) for the victorious charioteer, who was also honoured by a statue (left).

NIGHTS OF APPLAUSE AND BOOS AT THE THEATRE

Like the chariot races, the first Roman stage plays were mounted as part of religious festivals. The productions owed much to Greek tradition. Masks were worn and all the parts were played by men – except in the *mimus*, or mime. This was a kind of low farce in which women were permitted to play the female roles, and the actors were not masked. Most audiences showed a preference for comedy and political satire, rather than tragedy.

Masked faces Actors with stiff linen masks played both sexes.

One of the most popular playwrights was the earthy poet Plautus. He specialised in adapting fast-moving comedies written by Greek playwrights in which slaves bossed their masters about, boastful and licentious soldiers were outwitted, parents were hoodwinked by grasping sons, and mistaken identities led to a riot of misunderstandings.

Plays were staged in the open air, and

there were set rituals of applause for different degrees of appreciation. Modest approval was expressed by snapping the finger and thumb, and greater enthusiasm was shown by clapping. Playgoers showed wholehearted delight by waving the flap of the toga, or a handkerchief.

Many performances were paid for by well-to-do citizens hoping to gain popularity. This was sometimes foiled by audiences booing when they were meant to applaud. To counter this it became common practice to pay some playgoers to applaud loudly whatever they really thought of the actors or the play.

Unmasked feelings When Roman actors and actresses appeared in comic mimes they did not wear masks. The mimes were broad comedies performed on rough stages in the street, to the delight of ordinary townsfolk.

BEYOND ROME'S BORDER

As Rome sought to push the boundaries of her empire ever farther outwards, her armies clashed with tribes scattered widely over north Europe. Prominent among them were the Celts, by then living to the west of the Rhine, and the Germans to its east: warlike peoples with bloodcurdling battle cries, grisly funeral rites and gruesome sacrifices. Julius Caesar conquered the Celts in Gaul in the 1st century BC, then crossed the English Channel in 55 BC to confront their British cousins descending from hill-fort strongholds.

Farther east, nomadic horsemen ranged across the steppes of central Asia. From around the 7th century BC the Scythians had set up a kingdom north of the Black Sea. A thousand years later, the marauding hordes of Attila the Hun swept westwards from Mongolia, pushing before them Germanic tribes who poured across the crumbling boundaries of the Roman Empire.

GERMANS, CELTS, SCYTHIANS AND HUNS 700 BC – AD 400

GRIM SECRETS OF THE BOG BURIALS

One early spring day in 1950, at Tollund Fen in Jutland, Denmark, the 2000-year-old body of an Iron Age tribesman was discovered. His features were astonishingly well preserved in the umber-brown peat. The Danish scholar Peter V. Glob has described how 'he lay on his damp bed as though asleep, resting on his side, the head inclined a little forward, arms and legs bent'.

Further examination, however, was to reveal that the man's death had by no means been peaceful. The skin of his throat was creased by a braided leather noose: he had been hanged.

The bogs of northern Europe have, over the years, yielded the remains of several hundred Iron Age people. Many have been remarkably preserved by the chemical action of the acid peat, and many display evidence of death by violent means. The most numerous finds have been made at sites in north and central Jutland, where the famous Tollund Man was uncovered.

From the Alps by toboggan

Another exceptional discovery was that of so-called Grauballe Man, found in 1952 only 11 miles (18 km) away. More misshapen than his neighbour by pressure of the peat, he also wore a more anguished expression. His throat had been cut from ear to ear.

What was the meaning of these grim discoveries? And who were these ancient people? Jutland was the home of an early Germanic tribe called the Cimbri. Their warriors were known to classical writers for being tall, blond and blue-eyed, somewhat simple-minded but ferocious in battle. They once threatened Rome itself, swarming into northern Italy towards the end of

Art of the sacred dance *This graceful figure of a slender dancing girl was among a hoard of sculptures made by Celts living on the banks of the River Loire and buried around the time of the Roman conquest of Gaul. The figure, in which the artist has skilfully captured the suggestion of movement, is thought to represent one of the stages in a ritual pagan dance.*

the 2nd century BC. It is said that when the Cimbri crossed the Alps they tobogganed down the snowy slopes on their shields, giving out deafening yells as they descended.

Little was known about the Nordic giants' daily lives at the time. But from the middle of the 1st century BC, when Caesar had conquered Gaul, much more information became available. The Roman historian Tacitus, in particular, compiled a book called *Germania* in which he distinguished clearly between the Germans and their Celtic

Chariots of war *Wild-haired Celtic warriors, shrieking bloodcurdling cries as they drove their two-wheeled war chariots into battle, were sometimes enough to unnerve even the most battle-hardened Roman soldiers.*

neighbours. The Rhine, he said, was the great divide, the Celts living to the west of it and the Germans to the east. Celtic influence was strong in Germanic culture; nevertheless the Germans maintained a separate identity – perhaps because, as Tacitus reports, they did not intermarry with other peoples.

Governed by tribal chieftains, the Germans were, it seems, a generous and open-hearted folk who, like the Celts, were much given to feasting and drinking. They would stupefy themselves with home-brewed beer, and they gambled at dice so recklessly that losers might have to submit to slavery.

The bodies found in the Jutland bogs connect us in the most intimate way with the Germans' physical appearance. For example, many items of clothing have been recovered in an extraordinary state of preservation. Tacitus speaks of the Germans often going naked except for a short cape, and this is confirmed by the finds. The men seem often to have worn a skin shoulder cape, pinned by a brooch,

and little else, though optional extras included a cap, woven coat, kilt-like garment, leggings and shoes. Female costume was more elaborate. Women's outfits have survived, including woven skirts and scarves which display advanced textile skills. Even hairstyles have survived through the preservative action of the peat bogs. One fascinating find was the severed head of a man found at Osterby, in Germany, wrapped in a cape made of deer skins. The man's greying hair had been tied up at the right side of the head in an elaborate knot similar to those depicted in Roman carvings of Germanic warriors and described by Tacitus as a speciality of the Swabian tribe – hence their name of 'Swabian knots'.

'His face wore a gentle expression – the eyes lightly closed, the lips softly pursed as if in silent prayer. It was as though the dead man's soul had for a moment returned from another world.'

PETER V. GLOB, *THE BOG PEOPLE*

Why, though, had this head been severed? Germanic law, as described by Tacitus, provided for varied punishments, which may help to explain the gruesome aspect of the relics. For example, traitors and deserters were hanged on trees. Cowards, shirkers and homosexuals were pressed under a hurdle into the slime. Adulterous wives were taken from their house, stripped, shaven and flogged by their husbands. It is easy to interpret the bog finds in the light of these details. There is the noose around Tollund Man's neck, for example.

At Winderby in Domland Fen the body of a 14-year-old girl was found naked in a 1st century AD peat grave, her hair shaven off and a blindfold around her eyes. The girl's body had been weighted down with branches and a large stone. She had either been pressed down or drowned in a bog.

Sacrifice to Mother Earth
In Haraldskjaer bog in Jutland the body of a 50-year-old woman was discovered pegged out, apparently to be buried alive. Wooden crooks had been driven

Rome's adversaries *Tribes of Celts were scattered throughout northern Europe as far west as Spain, northwards to Britain and eastwards to Denmark. Their neighbours across the Rhine were known as Germans. North of the Black Sea lived hordes of nomadic horsemen known to the Greeks as Scythians.*

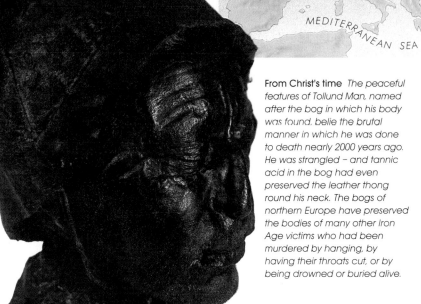

From Christ's time *The peaceful features of Tollund Man, named after the bog in which his body was found, belie the brutal manner in which he was done to death nearly 2000 years ago. He was strangled – and tannic acid in the bog had even preserved the leather thong round his neck. The bogs of northern Europe have preserved the bodies of many other Iron Age victims who had been murdered by hanging, by having their throats cut, or by being drowned or buried alive.*

down tight over each knee and elbow joint, fastening her to the peat below. In addition, strong branches had been clamped across her chest, similarly fixed in place by crooks driven deep into the bog. Given the reports by Tacitus it is easy to believe that these and others were executed criminals. But there is another theory: some, at least, of those killed may have been victims sacrificed to the fertility goddess Nerthus, or Mother Earth. It was a widespread Iron Age practice to make ritual deposits of valuable objects in lakes, marshes and pools. Such offerings ranged from gifts of food in pots to magnificent silver vessels and weaponry seized as war booty. The treasures seem to have been deposited in watery places to propitiate the gods,

ensure a good harvest, or thank the deities for their help. Perhaps human beings were offered as sacrifices too. Pointing to this possibility is the evidence of the stomach contents of Tollund and Grauballe Man. Both victims seem to have been given as their last meal a sort of gruel made from grains and wild-flower seeds. In Tollund Man's case, these included barley, linseed and willowherb seeds.

The absence of either summer or autumn foods in both these bodies suggests that Tollund and Grauballe Man may both have been sacrificed in winter in rites honouring the fertility goddess, to hasten the onset of spring.

Mounted warrior *The huge leather shields borne by Celtic horsemen almost hid them from their foes' view. This stylised figure from the 7th century BC was discovered at Strettweg in Austria.*

INTO BATTLE WITH SHOUT AND TRUMPET

Fighting was an obsession with the Celts, whether in bands against enemy forces, or in the brawling combat that erupted incessantly between individual warriors. Drunk on strong beer and lust for glory, the Celts did battle with a fierce exhilaration that seasoned Roman soldiers even found alarming. They were careless of life and limb, often going into battle naked but for a torque or neck ring.

The Roman historian Tacitus, describing an attack by the legions on Anglesey, wrote: 'On the shore stood the opposing army with its dense array of armed warriors, while between the ranks dashed women in black attire like the Furies, with hair dishevelled, waving brands.'

Red-haired rebel queen

Celtic men were tall by Mediterranean standards; the skeleton of a warrior discovered near Milan in Italy was 6 ft 5 in (1.9 m) in height. Even the women were large and fiercesome brawlers. Boudicca, the rebel queen of the Iceni who died in AD 60, was described as huge of frame, harsh-voiced and with a great mass of bright red hair falling to her knees.

Ammianus Marcellinus, a Roman author, writes of the Celt being virtually invincible with his wife fighting by his side: 'stronger than he by far, and with flashing eyes, she...begins to rain blows mingled with kicks like shots discharged by the twisted cords of a catapult'.

Celtic warriors often cut off the heads of their foes and dangled these grim spoils from their belts and saddles, or bore them aloft on spears. Singing in triumph they would carry the heads back to their

Thrust or throw *Spears were either hurled at an enemy from a chariot or used at close quarters to stab. An iron spearhead with bronze decoration (right) is believed to have belonged to a chieftain.*

HAND-TO-HAND COMBAT

Celtic warriors armed themselves with spears and swords. They wore elaborate helmets and protected themselves with shields, which were often ornamented with distinctive swirling, abstract loops and patterns.

The early Celts went to battle in war chariots – lightweight vehicles drawn by a pair of fast ponies. The chassis was wicker-work and the harnessing was often splendid. Two men rode them – the leather-coated charioteer, and the warrior. Both would hurl spears as they rode, then leap from the chariot to engage in hand-to-hand combat with daggers and swords.

As time passed, cavalry supplanted chariots in warfare. The Gaulish Celts were especially noted for their skill as horsemen, and units of their riders, clad in gaudy tunics and tight-fitting hose with flowing cloaks, were incorporated into the Roman army.

To face the Celts in war was a terrifying experience. Often they went into battle with their faces 'tattooed' with blue dye. Their Druid priests and priestesses hurled insults at their adversaries, accompanied by a bloodcurdling cacophony of battle cries and the blaring of war trumpets, which were decorated with bronze boars' heads.

Showcase shield *Most shields were fashioned of wood or leather, but this shield, found at Battersea in London, is faced in bronze and far too ornate and delicate to have been used in battle. It may have been used as a chieftain's ceremonial shield.*

Horned helmet *A chieftain wore this headgear around the 1st century BC.*

Cut and thrust *The long sword was the warrior's main weapon.*

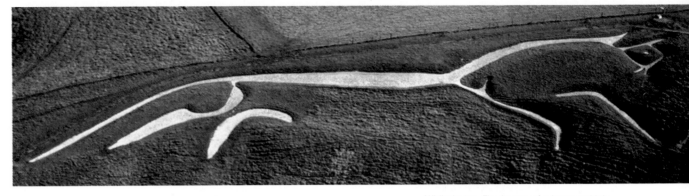

hill-forts and homes, nailing them up as highly revered trophies. In Celtic shrines found at Roquepertuse and Entremont in southern France the skulls of many young men were displayed in specially carved niches.

With such savagery matched by their fighting and riding skills, the Celts presented Rome with a formidable foe. Their weaknesses, though, lay in lack of strategy and discipline – and in the weakening effects of their constant feuding.

The characteristic Celtic settlement was the hill-fort, a fortified upland site. Grass-grown earthwork ramparts enclosing hilltops survive in their thousands around Europe today, extending from Hungary to Spain. Their building seems to have started around 700 BC – about the time when the use of iron began to develop. Originally places of refuge, they only later developed into fixed settlements. To create a hill-fort, a shallow trench was first dug around the site, leaving gaps for the entrances.

> '*Their trumpets are of a peculiar barbaric kind. They blow into them and produce a harsh sound which suits the tumult of war.*'
>
> DIODORUS SICULUS, c. 50 BC

Then began the piling up of earth for the ramparts, the faces of which might be strengthened with stone or timber. Some forts were simple stockades of wood, while others were stone-walled, without bank or ditch.

Towards the later period the Celts also built fortified towns, called *oppida*, in plains and valleys. Most settlements, however, were on hilltop sites, with their obvious advantages for defence, such as that at Maiden Castle in southern England. The weakest spot was the gate, and this was sometimes protected by labyrinthine systems of walled corridors, with watchtowers, bastions and inner and outer gates.

Alongside the world in which the Celts lived there existed another, supernatural realm. This place of magic was peopled by gods and goddesses who could change their form at any time to interfere in human affairs. The power the deities wielded made it necessary for the Celts to placate them with rites and sacrifices. The extent to which beliefs and myths affected the daily lives of the Celts impressed even the Romans. Declared Caesar, observing the Celts who faced him as adversaries in Gaul: 'The whole Gallic people is exceedingly given to religious superstition.'

The Celts worshipped their various gods in the form of sculpted stone images, bronze statuettes, carvings in wood and other effigies. Among at least 400 deities that have been identified are Cernunnos, the horned stag-god; Sequana, goddess of healing; and Taranis, lord of thunder. Their images were worshipped in forest clearings, hilltop groves, and springs, as well as in wooden temples.

Druids keep the peace

Mediating between the natural and supernatural worlds was the priesthood of the Druids. The Druids recited history, explained the law, studied the heavens and trained the sons of nobles. Above all, they read the omens – in the flight and calls of birds, for example – and performed sacrifices.

Some accounts have survived to give a glimpse of the rites. The Roman author Pliny, for example, described a sacrifice in which mistletoe played an important part. This plant was highly revered, especially when found growing on the equally sacred oak. 'They call the mistletoe by a name meaning the all-healing. Having made

Horse's bit in bronze, with enamel decoration

preparation for sacrifice and a banquet beneath the trees, they bring thither two white bulls, whose horns are bound. Dressed in a white robe, the priest cuts the mistletoe with a golden sickle. Then they kill the victims, praying that God will render this gift of his propitious to those to whom he has granted it.' Human beings too were offered to the gods, according to Caesar. The macabre features of Celtic religion can be explained in part by their belief that death had no finality. The Celts buried their dead with articles needed for their journey to the Otherworld: the burial chamber of a Celtic princess near Vix in central France contained fine Celtic goldwork and other treasures from Greece.

The Celtic year was divided into four parts, each beginning with a great celebration. The first, by the modern calendar, was observed on February 1, and known as the Feast of Imbolc. It was dedicated to the goddess Brigit, and linked with the birth of spring lambs. The second was on May 1, known as Beltane, and dedicated to Belenus, god of herd and harvest: it was the origin of our May Day.

The third festival, the Feast of Lughnasa, occurred on August 1; this was dedicated to Lugos and concerned with the cereal harvest. The Feast of Samhain, celebrated on the eve of November 1, was a time of magic and sorcery, when spirits were made manifest to the living, the dead walked, and supernatural forces had to be propitiated with rites and sacrifices. This festival has survived as Halloween.

White horse *The image of a horse cut into a chalk hillside at Uffington, in southern England, may have been dedicated to the goddess Epona, often depicted riding.*

Bear goddess *Celtic deities were often associated with animals. The goddess Artio is shown with a bear.*

Woodland goddess *A figure on a cauldron may represent the goddess Medb, who had her own sacred tree.*

FUN AT THE FEAST, TOIL ON THE FARM

Feasting was a Celtic passion second only to warfare, and the two activities were closely related. After a battle, successful warriors quickly sought the opportunity to boast about their exploits, and festivities lasting for days on end gave full rein both to their gluttony and their vainglory. Heroes were rewarded at the feast with a choice cut of meat – often thigh of roast boar or even an entire piglet – known as the 'hero's portion'.

Wine was enjoyed by the Celtic nobility, who obtained their supplies from Italy or from the Marseilles area of France, and quaffed from bronze tankards. Ordinary tribesmen generally contented themselves with barley ale or wheaten beer prepared with honey, often drunk from a communal cup.

Drunken dagger fights

The Celtic thirst for alcohol was legendary among the ancients, and drinking certainly contributed to their volatile temperament. 'When they become drunk they fall into a stupor or into a maniacal rage', commented Diodorus, a Sicilian of the 1st century BC. The rival boasts of drunken warriors at a feast often led to dagger fights – sometimes to the death.

For more tranquil entertainment, poets sang and bards chanted to the music of instruments which resembled lyres. The Celts delighted in music,

Straight edge
Iron slashers were in use by 550 BC.

Toothed edge
Celtic tools included this serrated saw.

Curved edge
The axe-head was probably used to cut meat.

HOUSES THAT IRON AGE FARMERS BUILT TO LAST

Smoke filters lazily through the thatched roof of a conical Iron Age roundhouse. The roof rests on a wooden framework atop walls of wattle and daub – a mixture of clay, chalk, straw and animal hair. Inside, a woman watches over a bubbling cauldron of meat. The air is heavy with the damp smell of burning wood from the fire. Beside it is a beehive-shaped clay oven. When the food is prepared the family will gather around a table that is little more than a raised wooden palette. Plates and spoons are also of wood; the only metal 'cutlery' is the dagger. The walls are hung with various tools, such as shears and saws, and personal armour, such as shields. A loom, on which women weave the family clothing, stands by the door.

This impression of a Celtic dwelling is based on an actual building reconstructed on the chalk downs of southern England. The house, some 42 ft (13 m) in diameter, is the centrepiece of Butser Ancient Farm, a re-created Iron Age farm of 300 BC, near Chalton in Hampshire. The continuing project has proved the extraordinary resilience of such a basic building. For years, the simple structure has withstood the elements, including hurricane-force winds and torrential rain.

Wheels for war and peace *Lightly built but strong, the two-wheeled chariot held two warriors and was hauled by ponies. Sturdier vehicles, also using spoked wheels held by wooden pins and probably drawn by oxen, served for civil transport and farm work. A wheeled vehicle was used in Gaul for reaping grain.*

and at some festivals held to mark the seasons there were contests on instruments and in verse. Held in the open air, these popular events also included horse and chariot races – thrilling events in which a charioteer moved acrobatically back and forth on the bar between his ponies. Brawling at these festivals was strictly forbidden; they were held under the auspices of the gods, and a breach of the divine peace was punishable by death.

For everyday pastimes there were games such as fidchell, 'wooden wisdom', which was similar to chess in having two sets of men pegged onto a board. It was sometimes played for stakes, and the Celts also enjoyed gambling at dice. Among their field sports was a game resembling hurling, played with curved sticks and a set of balls. Hunting was still a source of food, but it was also a popular pastime. The pursuit of wild boars from chariots was a kingly occupation.

Salt from Alpine mines

There was more to life than feasting, warfare and games, however. The Celts farmed like other ancient peoples, tending herds of cattle and flocks of sheep, and also raising pigs. 'Their pigs are allowed to run wild,' observed the Greek geographer Strabo, 'and are noted for their height, pugnacity and

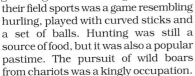

swiftness. It is dangerous for a stranger to approach them.' Salted pig meat was one of the Celts' most valued exports to the Mediterranean world. Another was salt itself, which was vital, both as a flavouring agent and as a preservative.

One of the most important Celtic sites in Europe is at Hallstatt in the Austrian Alps, where ancient salt mines formed the centre of a great and flourishing industry between 700 and 500 BC. Equipped with pickaxes, mallets and pine torches for flares, the Celtic miners burrowed as deep as 1000 ft (305 m) into the mountainside. Leather gloves protected their hands as they slid down ropes leading to the

galleries; cowhide backpacks brought the prized salt to the surface. To do business with their southern neighbours, the Celts borrowed the idea of coinage from Greece and Rome, producing coins of their own which bore cult images of animals and stylised faces instead of classical heads. In bartering among themselves, however, the Celts usually calculated in commodities. Slaves, for example, were an important unit of value. According to one Irish scale of reckoning, a *cumal*, or female slave, equalled three milk cows. Equally impressive was the ability of the blacksmiths. The Celts used iron ploughshares for farming lands that were too poorly drained for earlier peoples to cultivate. The Celts were the first to shoe horses, and they invented a technique for forging seamless iron tyres for chariot wheels, using red-hot iron bands that were cooled with water to shrink them into place. Iron chisels, handsaws, shears and tongs were among their tools.

Beautiful jewellery and other personal items were fashioned by metalworkers too. The characteristic ornament was a gold or silver neck ring, called a torque, which was symbolic of high rank in society. Exquisite mirrors, bracelets and brooches have also survived. The artistry is typified by swirling, semi-abstract patterns that evoke curling vine tendrils, branches and leaves.

The Celts, it seems, were show-offs – another fact noted by Strabo, who wrote that 'to the frankness and high spiritedness of their temperament must be added the traits of childish boastfulness and love of decoration. They wear ornaments of gold, torques on their necks, and bracelets on their arms and wrists, while people of high rank wear dyed garments besprinkled with gold. It is this vanity which makes them unbearable in victory and so completely downcast in defeat'.

Beauty and bells that jingle

The women must have spent hours before their polished bronze mirrors, washing, combing and plaiting their abundant tresses which embodied the ideal of feminine beauty. Fastidious in matters of personal hygiene, the Celts washed using water and soap – a commodity not used by the Romans.

Bodies might afterwards be anointed with oil and sweet herbs. For cosmetics, women used a herb known as *ruan* to rouge their cheeks, painted their fingernails, and dyed their brows with the black juice of berries.

Men also took pains over their personal appearance. Hair was braided or limewashed and combed back to give it the look of a horse's mane, favoured by warriors. Beards were sometimes worn, but the most characteristic facial feature was the moustache, grown long and drooping over the upper lip while cheeks and chin were shaved clean with razors.

In their clothing the Celts were just as keen on eye-catching effects. Men wore trousers in everyday life; this was a custom which the Celts seem to have borrowed from the horse-riding nomads such as the Scythians. It certainly fascinated the toga-clad Romans. Above, men wore fringed linen tunics with a long cloak over the top, thick for winter, lightweight for summer.

'The Gauls are tall in stature and their flesh is very moist and white...their hair is not only naturally blond, but they also use artificial means to increase this natural quality...the hair is so thickened by this treatment that it differs in no way from a horse's mane.'

DIODORUS SICULUS, c. 50 BC

This woollen cloak, known as a *sagum*, was a celebrated item of apparel. It was patterned with gaudy stripes and checks, sometimes being further adorned with gold or silver embroidery. Highly prized, and bearing a special tax within the Roman Empire, the Celtic cloak was worn both by men and women.

Tall figures, brightly clad, bangled, braided and with manes of red-gold hair, the Celts moving through the streets of Roman cities must have presented an exotic sight. They even brought with them exotic sounds, too, for they walked to the jingling of little bells – a final vanity – stitched to the edges of their clothes.

Vanity ware *Celtic women of high rank had treasures such as elaborately engraved bronze mirrors buried with them.*

Fancy fastener *Safety pins or pins of bronze, sometimes set with coral, were used to fasten women's dresses.*

Warrior wear *Celtic fighting men wore distinctive torques, or neck rings, made of gold or gold alloy.*

Swirling, abstract designs on a pottery vessel

HORSEMEN SWARM IN FROM ASIA

The steppes of central Asia in ancient times provided a vast belt of grazing land for tribes of nomadic herdsmen. They were highly mobile people who lived according to the rhythm of the season, following the wandering of their sheep, goats, horses, cattle or yaks. Theirs was a cold and forbidding landscape of mountains and bare plains. They had no writing, and they made no stone-built cities. Moreover, as wanderers they had no use for cumbersome furnishings, using only lightweight household items, chiefly of wood, hides and cloth.

What is known of the nomads survives in a scattering of graves, and in texts written by observers from the settled civilisations to east and west. The Greeks knew the Asian nomads loosely as Scythians, applying the term more specifically to a group who, from the 7th century BC, set up a kingdom north of the Black Sea.

Trousers for comfort

The Scythian women were rarely seen, but kept confined to their wagons and circular tents; these tents, made of felt stretched over a wood framework and known as yurts, can still be seen in central Asia today. The men wore kaftans, distinctive pointed headgear and trousers – a major invention of Asian horsemen and one that made riding more comfortable. They also carried swords, shields and a bow and arrow case.

Notorious among ancient peoples for their cruelty, the Scythians were said to blind their slaves to make them easier to manage, and to drink from cups made from enemies' skulls.

The Greek historian Herodotus described many of the Scythians' outlandish customs, especially their burial rites which included the ceremonial slaughter of wives, servants and animals. The burial of kings, he said, took place in a great square pit. The royal corpse was embalmed, its belly slit open, cleaned out and filled with chopped frankincense, parsley

Parthian shot *A bronze figure shows a mounted warrior turning to loose an arrow at a pursuer. Through this feat of horsemanship the Parthians, who came from Scythia, gave their name to a missile or comment delivered in retreat.*

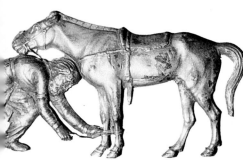

Horse in training *A Scythian hobbling a horse that has been saddled decorates a humble storage jar.*

Horse in action *Two foot soldiers and a mounted warrior go into battle, and a dead horse lies at their feet. The scene, cast in gold, adorned a Scythian comb found in a burial site of 500 BC. Scythians were often enlisted to fight in the armies of the Greek city-states.*

and anise before being sewn up again. With the bodies of slaughtered attendants and horses were piled mounds of golden vessels.

Scythian tombs excavated at Asian sites confirm many details, including the square burial pits, embalmed bodies, skeletons of sacrificed horses and splendid gold objects. But the most fascinating tombs were found at Pazyryk on the Altai steppes near the Mongolian border of western Siberia. Snow had seeped into these tombs and never melted, so that bodies and a wealth of normally perishable articles were preserved virtually intact. Fabrics, especially, were vibrant with colour and as richly textured as when they were made, around 500 BC.

Stools and a portable table

As well as tapestries, magnificent saddlecloths and richly decorated horse trappings, the finds at Pazyryk included many small domestic items that help to build up a picture of the daily lives of the people. Though they sat chiefly on rugs and cushions, the nomads also had low wooden stools covered with fur or hide. Additionally there were several small, collapsible wooden tables: the top served as a tray or plate when detached from the legs, the components being easy to pack when the nomads moved on.

Stone oil lamps provided light for log huts and birch-bark tents. Indications about the nomads' food and drink came from earthenware bottles discovered in one tomb, which held the dregs of fermented mare's milk – a drink known as *qumis* – and a pouchful of cheese. Hemp seed and equipment for smoking hashish were also found. The Pazyryk nomads wore beautifully stitched and

braided shirts. Other items found in the tombs included luxurious kaftans of sable hide and squirrel fur, felt stockings and red leather boots. Of course, this must have been the apparel of tribal royalty. The most remarkable discovery was the body of a tattooed man, interred with his wife or concubine. A tribal chief, he was covered from head to foot with tattooed designs of winged cats, griffins and other fabulous beasts.

The man had died in battle, from a head wound that had smashed his skull, and he had been scalped. For his burial, though, a wig had been sewn onto his head. A false beard, made of horsehair dyed black, had also been attached to his chin. Both tattooing and scalping were referred to by classical authors as practices of the Asian barbarians.

> *'It is on horseback that all Huns remain day and night, to buy and sell, to eat and drink, and, leaning forward on the narrow necks of their mounts, they collapse into a sleep deep enough to allow all manner of dreams.'*
>
> AMMIANUS MARCELLINUS, c. AD 380

Scholars believe that the nomads who made the Pazyryk tombs were eventually overcome by a migrant people of Mongol stock, perhaps the ancestors of the Huns. This savage folk originated in Mongolia and burst onto

the stage of world history in the 4th century AD, with refugee tribes flooding before them. To ancient writers, the Huns represented the ultimate Asiatic horror. One author wrote: 'They have a sort of shapeless lump, not a face, and pinholes rather than eyes', while Attila, their great war leader, was referred to as 'a hideous dwarf'.

Meat beneath the saddle

From Hunnish graves comes evidence that the Huns purposely played on other people's terror of their physical appearance, by bandaging the heads of children from infancy to deform their skulls. The Huns took a fierce pride in their own poverty, and in the austerities of their lives. They wore only coarse linen and skins and used them until the garments dropped in tatters from their backs. Their diet was

said to consist of the root of wild plants, with half-raw meat which they tenderised under their saddles.

Primitive and uncouth in so many ways, the Huns were unparalleled horsemen. They had no nobility of birth; chiefs were chosen purely for their fighting ability. In warfare they relied above all on speed. Lightly armed, and riding horses of lighter weight than was common in Europe, they swarmed down on their enemies in a loose wedge formation, yelling horribly as they came. After hurling spears and firing bone-tipped arrows with deadly accuracy, they would lay into the enemy with swords in hand-to-hand combat.

Violent, volatile and (according to the Romans) deceitful in their dealings, the Huns lived without any home base, legal system or formal religion.

Cleansing ritual *As part of their funeral rites, according to the Greek historian Herodotus, the Scythians put up conical tents in which they inhaled the smoke of hemp seed, cast onto hot stones. Herodotus said the hemp gave off 'a vapour unsurpassed by any vapour bath one could find in Greece. The Scythians enjoy it so much they howl with pleasure'.*

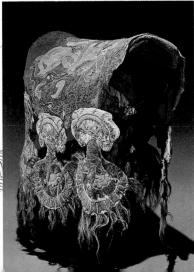

Stylish saddle *A felt saddle found in a Siberian tomb is stuffed with deer hair, decorated with appliquéd figures, and edged with horsehair and fur.*

Old Worlds, New Worlds

The fall of the Roman Empire was accompanied throughout Europe by a huge movement of people, some of them already Christian converts. They spoke different languages, dressed in different clothes and ate different kinds of food, yet all depended for their livelihood on the land, the rivers and the seas. The land was cultivated with hard toil, and the amount of cultivated land increased as forests were cleared. By AD 1000 the most enterprising and vigorous of the migrant peoples, the Norsemen, had become settlers, builders of castles and founders of kingdoms.

As order slowly returned to Western Europe, life became more secure, more prosperous and more sophisticated. The population continued to grow, until pressure on land and epidemic disease reduced numbers in the 14th century.

Both in Asia and Europe the proportion of people living in towns and cities grew from the 12th century onwards. From dependence on their lords in the countryside, men and women escaped to lives of greater freedom in the cities. Trade crossed frontiers – in Europe in wine and wool, and between Europe and Asia in silk and spices. Where trade routes met there were crowded market centres and colourful fairs.

Everyday life in the country followed the seasons. In the cities it was enlivened by religious festivals; and architecture, art, music and literature caught the spirit of vibrant, sometimes violent, times. Cathedrals built and beautified over several generations still survive in their magnificence, and old-established universities such as Bologna, Paris and Oxford testify to the medieval interest in learning. Learning was even more prized in the countries of Islam, and by the 10th century, cities such as Cairo, Cordova and Baghdad were as renowned for their libraries as for their palaces. Islamic scholars excelled in philosophy, science and medicine.

Most men and women, however, never saw a city, and most men and women could not read. Their rules of behaviour were laid down by religious authorities. Unlike Islam, the Christian Church was governed by a hierarchy, headed by the Pope in Rome. The Church built monasteries and convents within which ways of life were strictly disciplined. Chastity, holy poverty and prayer were proclaimed as virtues, but so also was work. Christendom and Islam clashed, particularly at times of crusade, but there was conflict within Christendom too, and Asia and Africa had their share of violence.

The 15th century in Europe was a century of extravagance, heresy and superstition – but a century, too, during which the material lot of most people improved and the arts were pursued with great imaginative power. Three innovations helped to usher in a new age. Printing, already known in China, came to Europe when Johann Gutenberg pioneered the use of movable type. The most famous of his books was a Bible, but romances and business documents were printed as well. Gunpowder, another Chinese invention, made the castle of the Middle Ages obsolete. The compass made possible the voyages of the first European explorers; among them was Christopher Columbus, who in 1492 'discovered' America – which in fact already had a long history, unknown to the Europeans.

ON THE GOLDEN HORN

The world's first Christian empire came into being in AD 330, when Emperor Constantine the Great proclaimed Constantinople (present-day Istanbul) the new capital of the Roman Empire. Built like Rome itself on seven hills, the city rose in tiers around the imperial palace and the cathedral-church of Hagia Sophia. A coastline studded with walled harbours protected a patchwork of towns, villages, farms and orchards.

The empire reached its cultural and financial peak during the reign of Justinian 1, from AD 527 to 565. Its wealth and artistic treasures made it the goal of a succession of attackers from Arab seamen to Persian soldiers, and in 1204 Constantinople was captured and looted by troops of the Fourth Crusade. It was reoccupied by Emperor Michael VIII in 1261; but from then on it went into a steady decline. From the mid-14th century onwards it was a prime target for the Ottoman Turks, and in 1453 it finally fell to Turkish attackers under Mehmet II. The civilisation that had preserved the Christian faith for more than 1000 years was no more.

BYZANTIUM AD 330–1453

BUSY HUB OF A CHRISTIAN EMPIRE

Anyone walking along the exotic main thoroughfare of Constantinople could be forgiven for thinking he saw the whole world go by. For more than 2 miles (3 km), the avenue wound through the centre of the city from the imperial district in the east, branching off towards the massive Golden Gate in the west – the entrance for travellers and merchants from the Adriatic coast and northern Greece. Middle Street, or the Mese as it was properly called, contained a seething mass of citizens and visitors talking in a babel of tongues, including Greek, which was the everyday language used by the people. The throng surged along the marble thoroughfare, passing by elegant porticoes and two-storeyed arcades, crowding around shops crammed with luxury goods such as locally crafted gold ornaments and jewellery, and spilling out into the surrounding spacious squares and narrow, winding streets.

Fair-skinned sailors mingled with swarthy Hebrews from Palestine and muscular Ethiopian Negroes. Like most visitors, they were bound for the open-air bazaars which sold everything from religious images to grapes, and the arcades where shoemakers and other leather workers displayed their handmade wares.

Some merchants offered cloaks of brocaded silk to those who could afford them. Originally, bales of silk were brought overland from China on journeys lasting up to 230 days. To save time and expense, Justinian persuaded two Persian monks to

Guardian of the empire *An elite body of fierce, heavily armed soldiers formed the guard for the Byzantine emperors. Many of the men were highly paid foreign mercenaries, including Saxons, Russians and Vikings. Military service was compulsory for all able-bodied men under the age of 40, and at its peak the Byzantine army was about 120,000 strong.*

smuggle a few silkworm eggs into the city in a hollow bamboo stem – and so established Constantinople's silk industry. Some of the brocaded garments, made exclusively in the imperial workshops, were kept as gifts for visiting rulers.

In the street, moneychangers sat at tables loaded with bags of gold and silver coins. Entertainment was provided by jugglers, clowns, performing monkeys and corner orators, while prostitutes and pickpockets plied their trades. Here and there were seen the coloured robes of various professions and sects. Among them, mercenaries in the pay of the emperor pushed their way, while condemned criminals were taken to places of torture or execution seated back-to-front on mules, their hands tied behind their backs, while their captors lashed them ceaselessly.

Every now and again servants with cudgels forced a path through the crowd for their wealthy mistresses, who were borne in litters by eunuchs on their way to the fashionable Baths of Zeuxippus. There, society women met their friends. exchanged gossip, compared jewellery and clothes and discussed the forthcoming games and chariot races at the Hippodrome.

Rich merchants and court officials cantered by on white horses resplendent in magnificently embroidered saddlecloths. By contrast, paupers and beggars covered with sores abounded, and there were not enough hospitals, hostels, orphanages and workhouses to shelter the sick and the homeless among the city's million or so inhabitants. Vagrants sought refuge in the covered colonnades, and in the winter the authorities fixed boards across the spaces between the columns to keep out the cold winds.

Perfume against the plague

Sanitation was almost unknown in the poorer quarters away from the city centre, and the cramped, refuse-strewn alleys, crowded inns and busy stables gave rise to plagues which took a deadly toll. It was not uncommon to come across the corpses of diseased down-and-outs, sometimes lying in the shadow of the imperial palace itself, near the site where the perfumers put up their sweet-smelling stalls. Some people even claimed they saw the ghosts of the dead haunting the area.

To try to remedy the situation, Justinian decreed that tens of thousands of extra loaves of bread be given to the hungry each day. In addition, he launched an ambitious programme of public building works, ranging from churches to schools, using for labour the unemployed citizens, peasants and immigrants.

'Those who are sound in body and have no means of subsistence,' he pronounced, 'will be sent immediately to the organisers of public works, to the heads of bakeries, and to those who maintain the gardens and public places. If they refuse, they will be expelled from the city.'

Bustle on the quayside

The new buildings did not entirely solve the ever-growing problem of homelessness, poverty and unemployment. They did, however, help to make the city one of the marvels of its time. Not the least of its wonders was the series of walled harbours in which anchored the warships, fishing vessels and cargo boats which daily pumped fresh blood into the city's arteries. The quaysides themselves were crammed with seamen, sailmakers, porters, carpenters and caulkers. Everywhere was the smell of fish, the staple diet of the dock workers who lived in the dark cluttered alleys.

As protection against the constant threat of invasion, the sea approach was barred by a strong chain stretched across the Golden Horn. This – coupled with some 13 miles (21 km) of triple walls up to 25 ft (7.5 m) thick, 50 fortified gates, numerous watchtowers and the moat that encircled the city – strengthened the inhabitants' belief that they were 'God guarded'.

This was just as well, for Justinian was frequently warring with various nations, including the Persians, Turks, Huns and Goths. In addition, civil uprising threatened whenever taxes were raised or if there was a poor harvest. These protests were often sparked off by one or other of the two rival political factions in the city: the Blues and the Greens, named after the colours they wore upon their shoulders. As well as managing many city affairs, such as maintaining roads and walls, they brought complaints to the emperor' s attention.

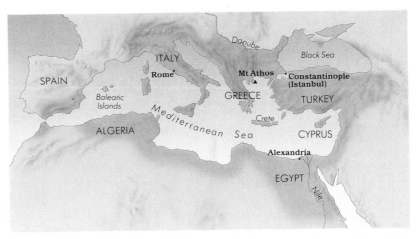

Christian realms *At its height, in AD 550, the Byzantine Empire included much of North Africa, Greece, Italy and southern Spain. It also embraced Cyprus, Crete and the Balearic Islands.*

THE INTERNATIONAL LANGUAGE OF THE EMPERORS' GOLD

By land and sea, Byzantium's trade routes linked the continents of Asia, North Africa and Europe. For more than 700 years its booming economy was based on a gold coin called by foreigners the *bezant*, after Byzantium itself. The handsome bezant contained some 65 grains (4.2 g) of pure gold, and its intrinsic value and stability ensured its use internationally, from China to Britain. When in the 8th century the English historian and theologian the Venerable Bede sought to praise a chaste British princess, he described her as being as 'pure as a bezant'. Introduced by Constantine I in the 4th century – and known within the empire as the *nomisma* – the coin held its value until the 11th century.

Crowned heads *Byzantine gold coins bear the images of Emperor Anatasius (top), the co-emperors Justin I and Justinian (centre), and the King of Italy, Theodahad.*

Pastoral scene *Carved ivory boxes may have held the bread for the Communion service.*

Night of the big catch *Fish were a staple food in Constantinople, and fishermen worked day and night to meet the demand. Here a fisherman and his young assistant haul in their bulging net, while a light at the stern shines on the water.*

PRAISING GOD IN CHURCH AND AT HOME

Jewelled Bible looted during the Fourth Crusade

Excited citizens lined the flower-strewn way that led to the great church of Hagia Sophia, or Holy Wisdom. Choirs sang hymns as the procession, headed by attendants dressed as the 12 apostles, solemnly drew nearer. As soon as the white-robed emperor himself came into view, the people prostrated themselves before him. It was Easter Day and the emperor – regarded by his people as Christ's vicar on earth – was on his way to preside over the annual festival commemorating the resurrection of Jesus from the dead. The interior of the church was dominated by the ornate gold altar, inlaid with precious stones. Crimson-robed musicians accompanied male choirs hundreds strong, whose voices reverberated from the mighty dome. The smell of incense mingled with the smoke from thousands of candles.

Christianity was the official religion of the state, and the church was an awesome symbol of God's kingdom on earth. Masterminded by Emperor Justinian, Hagia Sophia rose 180 ft (55 m) in the air, dwarfing the other domed churches in the city. It took 10,000 workmen only six years, from AD 532 to 537, to build.

The citizens needed little encouragement to follow the faith, and echoed the sentiments of Justinian – who, like every emperor, played a leading role in religious ceremonies throughout the year. 'The greatest gifts which God in his love of mankind has given to men,' he stated, 'are the priesthood and the empire; for the one ministers to things divine, while the other guides and takes care of human affairs.'

Every home was blessed and dedicated to God. Each fishing boat was blessed before it set sail, and farmers had their land and cattle blessed. Poems were written in tribute to God's glory. Frescoes and mosaics showed scenes from the life of Christ and the saints. Huge processions celebrated the Christian festivals.

Heated religious discussions took place daily in private houses, in the marketplaces, arcades and bazaars, on street corners – wherever, in fact, people debated the topics of the day. 'This town is full of craftsmen and slaves who are all deep theologians and preach in the shops and in the streets,' wrote a 4th-century chronicler. 'If you want a man to change some money for you, he will first teach you in what way the Son differs from the Father; if you ask the price of bread, he will tell you by way of answer that the Son is inferior to the Father; and if you want to know if your bath is ready, the bath attendant will reply that the Son was created from nothing.'

The controversy which for long split the city centred on the nature of Christ. To the orthodox church Christ was both flesh and spirit, human and divine. This view was held by the emperor, by most of the wealthy citizens, and by the monks and priests. However, an heretical group called the Monophysites maintained that Christ was pure spirit and had no bodily form. This belief was supported by many of the slaves, peasants and poor people. For a solution, the

populace looked to Justinian, who set up the Council of Constantinople in AD 553, at which a complicated compromise was hammered out. But it pleased neither side, and the controversy continued.

Despite the sway of Christianity, superstitions abounded. People of all ranks, including even the emperor, consulted astrologers and fortune-tellers, while pagan rites played a significant part in the daily lives of the less sophisticated and well educated. To celebrate the gathering of the grape harvest, countryfolk indulged in drunken revels in homage to Bacchus, the Roman god of wine. Gradually, the priests transformed the Bacchic feasts into harvest festivals.

Each month churches displayed a different mosaic or statuette of a holy person in specially dedicated chapels. And most homes had icons – from the

Good Shepherd *Seated on a pile of rocks, Christ, in his role as the Good Shepherd, tends his flock. Mosaics of pastoral scenes decorated the walls of Byzantine tombs.*

THE EMPEROR'S CHURCH PARADE

Emperor, patriarch and common people of Constantinople unite in worship at the church of Hagia Sophia. Beneath the huge dome, the principal celebrants have taken their place and a solemn service is about to begin. Earlier, onlookers have watched scenes of elaborate ceremonial as stately processions converge on the church. The emperor, first to arrive, has an escort of formations of the Imperial Guard. From the opposite side of the church another

procession escorts the clergy, led by a deacon with the Gospel and a censer. Behind them come the patriarch and the rest of the clergy. The emperor and the clerics meet in the vestibule and proceed into the church – the emperor and patriarch through the central door and the remainder through the side doors. The congregation, waiting in the courtyard, then pours into the church through the side doors and the women take their place in galleries. The patriarch then leads the procession across the nave, and past the circular pulpit with its flanking guard of honour, towards the sanctuary at the east end. Then he walks down a strip of carpet to his throne at the side of the church. The clergy take their places on terraces of raised seats with the patriarch in the centre. The service is ready to begin.

Greek word *eikon*, or 'image' – above the bed, in a corner of the living room, or in a miniature chapel. The icons were seen as having miraculous powers; some people made little distinction between the icons themselves and the saintly figures they represented. This came close to idolatry and led to many icons being smashed or defaced by the emperor's troops. The word iconoclast, or 'breaker of images', derives from this practice. The controversy lasted for more than a century, and resulted in a series of clashes and riots in Constantinople. Harmony was finally restored in AD 843, when the Empress Theodora reintroduced and legalised the images. However, this was on the understanding that a distinction was made between the worship of God and the veneration of icons. Veneration was also bestowed

Silver Images *The faces of Christ and five of his disciples adorn a six-sided silver incense burner, dating from the 7th century.*

Golden skull *Mounted in gold, this relic of the skull of St John the Baptist, with its jewel-encrusted cover, was a gift to the Byzantine court from Bulgaria.*

Art in enamel *A 10th-century cross depicts the Virgin at prayer. The ornamentation is in cloisonné enamel.*

on the Virgin Mary's robe and belt – seen as the holiest of Constantinople's many religious relics. The belt in particular was seen as the city's palladium, or safeguard.

After the emperor himself, monks, priests and nuns were held in the highest esteem. One monk in particular, named Daniel, was one of the daily sights of Constantinople in the 5th century. He lived on top of a slender pillar some 66 ft (20 m) high in imitation of his master, St Simeon Stylites. The word stylites, or 'pillar-dwellers', comes from the Greek *stylos*, or pillar.

Daniel mounted the column in AD 460, when he was 51 years old, and – apart from occasions when he was forced off by high winds – stood there almost naked until his death 33 years later. During that time he was baked by the blazing midday sun, and coated with ice on winter nights. His emaciated body was encrusted with foul-smelling filth, his matted hair and beard were infested with lice, and his feet were almost eaten away by disease. Each evening a disciple climbed a ladder to the top of the column and gave his long-suffering master his one simple meal of the day. One of Daniel's most devoted admirers, Emperor Leo I, persuaded him to have a small roof placed over his head, to protect him from the worst of the elements.

Music and mosaics

Most monks, however, lived in monasteries, which also housed some of the empire's finest composers, writers and artists. They provided the words and music for many of the hymns, produced a wealth of dazzling illuminated manuscripts, and created the golden-hued frescoes and mosaics of saints and holy men which gave added beauty to the magnificently decorated churches. Of all their works, none was more awesome than the figure of Christ as Ruler of the Empire, which was placed in the centre of a church's main dome.

The belief in life after death lay at the heart of Byzantine religious thought. The threat of invasion and defeat by the barbarian hordes was never far away, and people therefore looked to the promise of the next world for a far less threatened existence.

Most commoners were buried in cemeteries set outside the city walls, where their tombstones often showed their portraits. For funerals, family members and friends wore black robes – only the emperor donned white for mourning – and professional mourners were hired. Laments were ritually uttered around the tombs three times after burial – on the third, ninth and fortieth days, according to a time scale intricately worked out by the astrologers of ancient Babylon. To the end, the people of Byzantium continued to mix their orthodox faith, which remained distinct from that of Rome in liturgy and in doctrine, with the remains of their pagan belief.

High living *The earliest and most renowed pillar-dweller was a Syrian, St Simeon Stylites. He spent 70 years perched on top of a series of pillars – each one taller and more precarious than the last.*

TOIL AND FUN IN TOWN AND COUNTRY

Since dawn, large crowds had waited expectantly before the gates of the Hippodrome. This was one of the days for chariot racing – the highlight of Constantinople's sporting and social life – and as soon as the gates opened thousands scrambled for a place in the tiers of stone seats. Entrance was free for any man from the emperor down to the humblest dockland porter. Women, except the empress, were not allowed to watch the regular contests of skill, strength and daring.

Soon, roared on by some 60,000 spectators, the charioteers urged their horses along the course. The noise was tremendous, with the thunder of the horses' hooves and the frenzied cries of the contestants' supporters sounding far beyond the stadium itself.

Seven times the chariots raced around the *spina* – a line of monuments that formed a spine up and down the centre of the course. The race, covering about 1 1/2 miles (2.5 km), was soon over and the victor received his rewards: the adulation of his fans, and a palm or crown from the officiating prefect.

Dancing girls and bear fights

Four races were held in the morning, and four more in the afternoon. For light relief, entertainment was provided in the intervals. Acrobats, jugglers, clowns, actors, singers and comedians all had their turn, as did troupes of dancing girls wearing hip-length tunics.

The Hippodrome, modelled on the famous Circus Maximus in Rome, was about 550 yds (500 m) long and 130 yds (119 m) wide. Chariot races were not the only events held in the Hippodrome. It was also the scene of animal hunts and bear fights – and

of the torture and sometimes the execution of dishonest officials. Important public announcements were made there by the emperor, and it was the venue for heated political meetings and civil uprisings.

But life in Constantinople was not all thrills and excitement. Most people's lives revolved largely around their homes and work places. Many of the well-to-do lived in two-storey houses of wood or stone with blank street walls and windows that looked onto enclosed inner courtyards, some with ornamental mosaic floors. Most houses were built around a central hall, with wooden staircases leading to the main living rooms on the first floor.

Indoors, colour and comfort were provided by carpets, cushions and curtains. The dining room was dominated by a large oblong table at which meals were eaten, surrounded by wooden benches and stools. Most families had breakfast and two three-course meals a day – usually of fish, meat and a pudding. As well as knives, forks and spoons, fingers were habitually used. It was considered courteous and hygienic to remove one's shoes before entering the room

Emperor's-eye view *From the imperial box the emperor kept a keen and expert eye on the chariot races. His appearance there was greeted by a storm of cheering, followed by silence as he blessed the spectators. When the emperor dropped a white handkerchief, four quadrigas, or four-horse chariots, charged into the sand-covered arena to race round and round the line of tall monuments down its centre.*

and sitting down to eat. Domestically, the head of the house was the wife. She saw to it that the indoor lavatories and baths were kept clean, that the garden shrines were well tended, and that the hot-air, underfloor heating was functioning properly. She was helped in her work by paid servants and unpaid slaves, some of whom were children aged under ten. Outside the home, however, she was not the social equal of her husband. She was not allowed to take part in processions or protests, and all women, even the empress, had to cover their faces in public.

Many marriages were arranged by parents – and some engagements were announced when the couple were only four or five years old. The law, however, forbade marriage under the age of 14 for boys and 12 for girls, so engagements could last for a decade or more. A wedding was one of the highlights of a family's year. On their way to the church the happy couple were showered with rose petals by white-clad guests and well-wishers. Later, at the wedding banquet in the home of the bride's parents, men and women sat at separate tables. When it was time for the newlyweds to retire, the guests accompanied them to the bridal chamber. There they were awakened the following morning by the guests singing outside the door.

By contrast, the lives of the poor were drab and often cheerless. Many of them dwelt in tiny flats in blocks up to nine storeys high, often built in cramped alleys cheek by jowl against the homes of merchants and city officials. Constantinople did have some hard-and-fast planning regulations: the stone-paved main streets had to be at least 12 ft (3.6 m) wide, while the balconies of private houses had to be 15 ft (4.5 m) above ground and 10 ft (3 m) from the opposite wall. Among the most ornate and luxurious buildings were the public bath-houses in which the water-loving citizens often had two or more baths a day. Dotted around the city there were broad parks and spacious gardens in which people went to relax and exchange news and gossip. In addition to the Hippodrome there were carnivals and theatres for dancing, music and spectacles, while jousting tournaments were periodically held in the various circuses.

Daily life was governed by strict laws, some of which were barbaric by present-day standards. For example, thieves could be condemned to the loss of a hand; fire-raisers were sometimes burned alive; people who spread cruel gossip or slander might have their tongues slit, and those found guilty of incest faced death by being drowned in a sack.

Hippodrome horse *The bronze horse is one of four which today grace the front of St Mark's Cathedral in Venice. It is believed they once decorated the Hippodrome in Constantinople, drawing a triumphal chariot, and were brought to Venice as loot by the Crusaders.*

However, the death sentence was seldom imposed and imprisonment was almost unknown. In the 10th century, Constantine VII allowed murderers and traitors to become monks and to serve life sentences in monasteries. Prostitutes were encouraged to become nuns. At the beginning of the 15th century, however, a Spanish traveller observed the punishment given to those 'convicted of heinous crime', and to shopkeepers who sold underweight meat and bread. 'All such,' he recorded, 'are exposed in the stocks, where they remain night and day at the mercy of the rain and wind.'

Although emperors were not above the law, they had the power to change it to their own advantage. Justinian I did this in AD 525 in order to marry Theodora, whose past as a courtesan and actress would otherwise have prevented her from becoming empress. Four years later Justinian set about revising and updating the Roman laws governing the empire in the Codex Justinianus, or Justinian Code – a labour of love which took 36 years.

Among his reforms, Justinian abolished the right of parents to sell their children into slavery. He also championed women's rights, allowing wives to have property of equal value to their dowries, giving mothers equal say with fathers in the upbringing of their youngsters, and permitting widows to be the guardians of their children. The enlightened, liberal new code formed the basis of civil law in the empire until its downfall 900 years later.

THE YEAR THE TAXPAYERS REBELLED

High taxation was a major cause of discontent in Constantinople and in the surrounding countryside. In town, people paid their taxes in gold, and in the country they paid with produce such as cereals.

A 'people's rebellion' took place in the capital in January 532, after Justinian I had increased taxes to pay for his campaigns against the Persians. Rioting sparked off among the crowds in the Hippodrome by the rival Blue and Green political factions spread throughout the city, with the rebels shouting *Nika!*, 'Victory!' Shops were looted and many buildings, including the imperial palace, were set on fire and severely damaged. The emperor's first thought was to flee from Constantinople. But his empress, Theodora, refused to go with him, declaring that death should come before dishonour. 'If you wish to lengthen your life, O Emperor, flight is easy,' she told him. 'There are your ships and there is the sea, but consider whether, if you escape into exile, you will not wish every day that you were dead. As for me I hold with the ancient saying that the imperial purple is a glorious shroud!'

His courage restored, Justinian turned his army on the rebels. A few days later some 30,000 troublemakers were slaughtered in the Hippodrome, and the rebellion was over.

Pay as you earn *Peasants worked hard in the fields on behalf of the landowners. When tax collectors came they were allowed to pay their dues with the crops they had nurtured.*

INTO BATTLE WITH FLAMES AND SWORD

Carefully holding catapults containing their 'secret missiles', the Byzantine troops advanced on the enemy fortress. Once within firing distance, the catapulters hurled the missiles – clay pots filled with an incendiary liquid called 'Greek fire' – over the battlements at the opposing forces. The pots exploded on impact, sending out tongues of flame which scorched the faces and hands of the victims, and sometimes burned them alive.

Time and again Byzantine troops captured enemy strongholds by using the fire, and they also employed it to defend their own forts and cities. 'It should be turned against any tower that may be advanced against the wall of a besieged town', proclaimed Emperor Constantine VII in the 10th century.

Effective as it was, the mysterious and volatile Greek fire was apt to explode when being carried over rough ground, injuring if not killing those transporting it. After a time the army stopped using it, but it was then adopted as the Byzantine navy's most feared weapon. It caught fire spontaneously when wet, and the more water that was thrown on the flames the more fiercely they burned; they continued burning even on the sea.

Top-secret ingredients

Although it was manufactured under the greatest secrecy in Constantinople – where most of the empire's munitions factories were situated – Greek fire was not a Byzantine invention. It was said to have been invented in the 7th century by a Greek-speaking Syrian refugee, Callinicus of Heliopolis. Its top-secret ingredients apparently contained naphtha, sulphur, saltpetre, quicklime and petroleum.

In AD 941 Greek fire is said to have destroyed some 10,000 ships sent by the Russian Prince Igor; the defeated Russian sailors compared it to 'lightning from heaven'. In the following century it was used by Emperor Alexius I Comnenus to set fire to a fleet from Pisa, in Italy.

'The Emperor knew that the Pisans were skilled in sea warfare,' recorded the Princess Anna Comnena, 'and was

Cavalry charge *Riding in tight formation, their long spears forming a deadly fan, Byzantine cavalrymen attack. The helmeted troops were noted for close-quarter fighting.*

apprehensive about having battle with them. So on the prow of each of his ships he had fixed a head of a lion, open-mouthed, made in bronze or iron and gilded all over, so that just the sight of them was terrifying. He made the fire that was to be directed against the enemy through tubes pass through the mouths of the beasts, so that they looked to be vomiting fire.'

Military service was compulsory in Byzantium for all able-bodied men under the age of 40. Highly paid foreign mercenaries – many of them British and Russian – were also employed, and at its peak the imperial army was about 120,000 strong. It was divided into regiments of some 3000-4000 men, which were sent to defend the various military districts or

provinces. In some areas generals were expected to raise, equip and maintain their own regiments, which were duly named after them. To encourage recruits, many of the soldiers posted to distant provinces or frontiers were paid in plots of agricultural land. They often had servants and slaves to help them on their smallholdings. In addition, they received taxes from the peasants working on the estates.

Most of the soldier-farmers held their estates for life, but to help keep the army up to strength, they were sometimes allowed to pass their holdings onto their sons. In turn, the new owners had to be prepared to ride, fully armed, to the defence of the province.

Byzantium's first military manual was published in AD 590. The emphasis

was on caution, and generals were urged to avoid pitched battles where possible. In the event of warfare they were to spare the lives of any prisoners they took and to treat captured women with courtesy and respect.

The Byzantines were also pioneers in psychological warfare. Generals were told to boost their soldiers' morale by inventing stories about victories won by other imperial regiments, and a widespread intelligence network of spies and scouts was established. Agents arranged for letters containing false and incriminating information about enemy leaders to be intercepted by their staff. In addition, truce negotiations were often started although the emperor had no intention of honouring them. All this caused

Flames and ladders *Byzantine soldiers perfected several techniques for storming enemy strongholds. Among them were the use of scaling equipment and of the incendiary liquid known as Greek fire. Scaling frames were placed against the fortress walls, and soldiers carrying piston-like 'flame guns' climbed to the top. They fired the guns by means of a hand pump, shooting streams of liquid flames at the defenders. As ladders could be pushed over, the besiegers swarmed to the top up nets held in place by grappling hooks.*

Price of power *For a Byzantine emperor, it was often a short step from enthroned splendour to assassination – with his head cut off and shown to the public on a spike.*

TOUGH AT THE TOP

Most Byzantine emperors came to power by so-called 'divine right' rather than by birth or natural succession. This meant that virtually anyone was free to declare himself 'God's choice' and to try to seize the throne – often by murder. The penalty for failure was instant execution – and even successful usurpers were often quickly ousted. Plots and counter-plots, of the type that made 'byzantine' a byword for intrigue, brought one emperor after another to a violent end. Of the 88 emperors between AD 324 and 1453, no fewer than 29 were butchered. They included Basilicus, starved to death in 477; Phocas, dismembered in 610; Constans II, bludgeoned to death in 668; Romanus III, drowned in 1034; Alexius II, strangled in 1183; and Andronicus I, tortured to death in 1185.

upsets and delays which allowed the Byzantines to bring up well-drilled reinforcements. These consisted of infantrymen armed with bows and arrows, daggers and short broadswords for hand-to-hand fighting, as well as maces, slings, javelins and spears. Cavalrymen carried battle-axes, lances, long broadswords and bows and arrows which they used skilfully and accurately while riding their horses at high speed.

Whenever battle was joined, the Byzantines proved to be fierce and courageous fighters. The troops were led by regimental standard-bearers holding up the Roman *vexillum*, or standard, as well as good-luck banners. Marching shield-to-shield came the infantrymen, encouraged by

army chaplains and groups of morale boosters, who read patriotic verses and exhorted them to 'do or die'. When the encouragement reached its height, the soldiers rushed headlong at the foe, yelling: 'The Cross shall conquer!'

For centuries, the Byzantines had lived under the threat of invasion. The risk of siege was so great that in the early 8th century each citizen was ordered to hoard enough food to last for at least three years. In 1204 the Crusaders sacked Constantinople and set up a 'Latin Empire' which lasted for more than 50 years, until the city was recaptured by Emperor Michael VII.

Byzantium never fully recovered from this blow, and in 1453 the empire fell. The Sultan of the Ottoman Empire, Mehmet II, advanced on Constantinople

Marching to war *Agile foot soldiers armed with bows and arrows and spears made them redoubtable hill-fighters.*

with 100,000 troops – outnumbering the defenders by about ten to one. Scouts had reconnoitred the outer wall and engineers laid mines at the weak spots. To circumvent the chain across the Golden Horn, some 70 Ottoman vessels were taken overland on rollers and launched against the northern wall. Meanwhile, the walls were pounded by gunpowder and cannon.

Seven weeks later the sultan's troops surged into the city. Emperor Constantine XI died fighting alongside his men, and Sultan Mehmet rode on his white horse to Hagia Sophia. He proclaimed the cathedral a mosque, dedicated to the glory of Allah. After 1000 years of Christian rule the empire was to be governed by those whom Christendom abhorred as infidels.

INVADERS MAKE A NEW EUROPE

On the hot night of August 24, AD 410, barbarian armies led by the Goth, Alaric, burst into Rome. For three days the Germanic warriors sacked the imperial capital, bringing the epoch of Roman greatness to a symbolic end. 'The whole world perished in one city', wrote St Jerome. In the hectic centuries that followed, tribes of Germanic pagans, including the Saxons and Franks, overran the crumbling remnants of the once-proud empire, then settled down only to be ravaged in turn by Vikings from Scandinavia.

In this huge upheaval the Celts were swept ever westward, and their culture survived only at the Atlantic margin of Europe: in Cornwall, Wales, Brittany and Ireland. This whole chaotic period was dubbed the Dark Ages by later writers. Yet to European culture the warrior tribes brought arts and energies of their own: a pioneering spirit, vigorous farming skills – and heroic myths that celebrated their own achievements.

SAXONS, CELTS, FRANKS AND VIKINGS AD 400 – 1000

TRIUMPHS OF THE SAXON WARLORDS

When Rome fell, rough-hewn Germanic tribesmen swaggered into the cities and villas of the decaying empire, plundering their treasures, laying waste their buildings, lighting camp fires on their mosaic floors. They were warriors and farmers, with a strong feeling for nature but no taste for civic life. The great Roman road system soon began to fall apart. Roman law gave way to ancient tribal codes. Native peoples who had for long been accustomed to dealing with toga-clad governors now found themselves taking orders from spear-wielding chieftains wearing coarse-woven shirts and cross-gartered leggings.

Some Germanic tribes such as the Franks, who had lived on the margins of the old empire, had absorbed a smattering of Latin culture and Christian teaching. But those whose destination was Britain were of the roughest pagan stock. 'A race hateful to both God and men', was how one Briton later described them.

The tribes flooded into Britain when the Romans left in the 5th century AD. They came by longboat, and included a host of different peoples: Angles, Saxons, Jutes and Frisians among them. For simplicity, though, the newcomers are remembered as the Anglo-Saxons or – more simply still – as the Saxons. Some settled peaceably enough alongside the native Celtic Britons, but there is ample evidence also of battles and bloody repression. The Church chronicler Bede,

Armed attacker *Some of the native Celts of 5th-century Britain were allowed to go about their everyday lives in peace when hordes of Germanic tribes – known collectively as the Saxons – swarmed in. Others came under attack by armed warriors like this one, shown on a carved whalebone box made in Northumbria.*

A jewel fit for a king *Alfred, ruler of Wessex, who waged hit-and-run warfare against the invading Danes, owned this jewel made of gold, crystal and enamel. The inscription, in Latin, reads: 'Alfred had me wrought.'*

writing around AD 700, describes how 'the priests were everywhere slain before their altars; the prelates and the people, without any respect of persons, were destroyed with fire and sword; nor was there any to bury those who had been thus cruelly slaughtered'.

Some Britons, it seems, took to the hills only to be butchered there in heaps. Many others, starved and dishevelled, gave themselves up to face a lifetime of slavery.

A hero king in Camelot

It is thought that the original King Arthur was a leader of the Britons in their doomed resistance to the invaders, and that the ancient hill-fort of Cadbury Castle in Somerset may have been his Camelot. Certainly the Arthurian legends borrow heavily from ancient Celtic myth. But the concept of knighthood owes more to the invaders' own traditions. The word 'knight' derives from the Anglo-Saxon *cniht*, meaning a boy or servant, and it is known that the German tribes admitted young men into their warriors' ranks with a great deal of ceremony, involving, for example, the ritual presentation of a lance and shield.

The fighting instinct was in the Saxons' blood, and heroic combat was celebrated in poems such as *Beowulf*. Some 3200 lines long, the epic concerns a great warrior who does battle with monsters in a tale of seafaring, blood-feud and treasure hoard which must have been told countless times around the fire of the warrior-farmers' smoky halls.

Face mask of a king

Superb examples of Saxon arms and armour have been found among the Sutton Hoo treasures, recovered from the ship burial of a Saxon king. The find, near Woodbridge in Suffolk, eastern England, dates from about AD 625: within a huge, open long-ship were discovered numerous relics including the king's axe, shield, jewelled sword and ornamental helmet, made of bronze and iron and fronted by an extraordinary face mask.

What with overcoming the native Britons, fighting among themselves and fending off attacks by later waves of Scandinavian invaders, the Saxon warlords had plenty to occupy themselves. But they brought more to the British Isles than Dark Age violence. In time their multitude of little kingdoms became unified under a single Anglo-Saxon dynasty. Kings governed an increasingly orderly realm with the help of a *witan*, or council of wise men, and the population converted to Christianity following St Augustine's mission to Canterbury in 597.

One outstanding relic of the Saxon kings is Offa's Dyke, an earth rampart and ditch which originally ran 170 miles from the estuary of the Severn to that of the Dee. It was built by Offa, King of Mercia from 757 to 796 to mark the boundary between his own English realm and the Welsh tribes beyond. Reaching 10ft (3m) high or more, it may once have been topped by wooden palisades. A footpath follows most of the route to this day: the few gaps in the dyke were once blocked by forest. Offa also introduced a new form of

Historian monk *The quill of a Jarrow monk, the Venerable Bede (673-735), recorded life in contemporary Anglo-Saxon England.*

currency, composed of silver pennies, which set a standard for English coinage which was to last for 600 years.

Greater still, as a national figure, was Alfred, ruler of Wessex from 875 to 899. A scholar and lawyer, he came to power when the divided kingdoms of Saxon England were threatened by Danish attack. It was Alfred who prevented their conquest of England, after a campaign waged from the Isle of Athelney, in the Somerset marshes.

Eventual victory came at the Battle of Edington, in Wiltshire, in 878, when Alfred, according to his biographer Bishop Asser, 'closed his ranks, shield locked with shield, and fought fiercely against the entire heathen host in long and stubborn stand'. Later, however, England was partitioned along the line of Watling Street; beyond this, to the north and east, lay the Danelaw, settled by the Scandinavians, where Norse customs and law held sway.

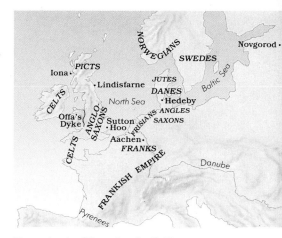

War and order *Tribes of earlier Celtic immigrants were firmly entrenched in the British Isles when the Saxon warrior hordes swarmed in. Four centuries of continual turmoil created a new Europe on the fringe of the former Roman Empire.*

King's frontier *Marked out by the King of Mercia at sword's point to delineate the boundary between his kingdom and the Welsh, the great earthen bank called Offa's Dyke can still be seen stretching for 80 miles (128 km) through the Welsh border hills.*

King's helmet *Unearthed at Sutton Hoo, in eastern England, this protective headgear with a face mask is made of decorated bronze and iron. Such helmets were worn only by kings in Anglo-Saxon England.*

FARMING AND FEASTING IN THE 'SHIRES'

For more than 600 years, Anglo-Saxon patterns of living imprinted themselves on the country that they occupied. To this day, it owes its very name to them: England is the land of the Angles.

As farmers, the new arrivals left one immensely important legacy in the form of the English village. The great majority of these date back to the Anglo-Saxon period, when isolated farmsteads began to give way to communal settlements. Place names of Anglo-Saxon origin tell much of the story. Those ending in -ham refer to settlements or enclosures, for example. The land-hungry invaders cleared vast tracts of Britain's primeval forest: -den, -ley, -hurst and -field all indicate clearings in the wood.

Rimmed by boundary ditches and fencing, the villages were constructed of timber, wattle and thatch. Lords or thanes lived in large halls; churls, or free peasants, lived in smaller halls, while the poorest – who included slaves – dwelt in the rudest of hovels.

Most buildings were rectangular, unlike the circular homes of many Celts, and some were cruck-framed

Toil in the fields *Peasants had to plough an acre of their lord's land a day. In return they had their own small patches to cultivate.*

Saxon king *The gallery of monarchs on coins includes Alfred.*

Mint tradition *For centuries after Alfred's reign, coins were stamped out with crudely made dies. This example from the early 10th century was discovered during the excavation of a house in York.*

with A-shaped timbers supporting the roof. Some homes had sunken bases for wooden flooring. Two-storey halls emerged in the later period. Most villagers had their own small kitchen gardens where they might raise fruit and vegetables, and grouped around their homes were assorted barns and pens for livestock. There might be workshops, too, for weavers, metalworkers, cobblers, woodworkers and the like: village tradesmen were coming into being. Another development was the widespread use of water mills for grinding corn.

After the conversion to Christianity, the church became a focus for village life, serving as a meeting hall as well as a place of worship. Saxon churches were built from wood, or from masonry taken from Roman ruins, and they were fairly simple in construction. To farm the land, the Anglo-Saxons

introduced a massive, wheeled plough with an iron ploughshare, capable of cutting into previously unworkable soils. Six or eight oxen were needed to draw it, however, and it was a hard job to turn at the end of each furrow.

To reduce the number of turns necessary, strip-farming was introduced, the plough being driven along long, strip-like tracts of land. The furlong of 220 yds (201m) derives from this practice; it was originally a 'furrow long', the distance the ox team could pull without a rest.

The strips owned by individual peasants were laid out in two or three large, open fields, and each year one of these would be allowed to lie fallow to restore its fertility. The villagers would share some pasture for grazing, and have some access to woodlands for timber and fuel. The woodlands still kept an ancient air of mystery and fear, however, as the realm of outlaws and of wolves. Wolf-hunting was a favourite pursuit of the Anglo-Saxons; indeed, it was not until Tudor times that wolves finally became extinct in the British Isles. In the woodlands, too, children

Scars of the past *Straight, parallel ridges made by the ploughs of Saxon farmers can still be seen today, even though the fields have long been used for grazing.*

A WINTER'S DAY BEHIND THE PLOUGH

Aelfstan rises before dawn, casting off his coarse sheepskin blanket. His wife is already awake but his boy is still asleep, huddled in a corner of the sunken-floored hut. Waking him with a cuff, Aelfstan reaches for his heavy woollen mantle. Before long, man and boy are outdoors, facing the cold of a November morning. A rutted track leads to the fold where Edgar the oxherd has been keeping watch all night – there have been reports of outlaws in the neighbourhood. Aelfstan yokes the oxen and harnesses them to the plough. The beasts belong to his lord, like the land he must work today. All morning Aelfstan follows the lurching, iron-shod plough, while the boy urges the beasts on with raw-voiced cries and prods from a hazel stick goad. At midday Aelfstan's wife brings dark rye bread and skim-milk cheese, which man and boy swill down with watery ale from an earthenware jug. They return to their labour; by dusk they have ploughed a full acre. In the evening the exhausted pair warm themselves at the open hearth. There is bread and ale again, this time with a hot bean stew from an iron cooking pot. By the fading firelight, all lie down to sleep.

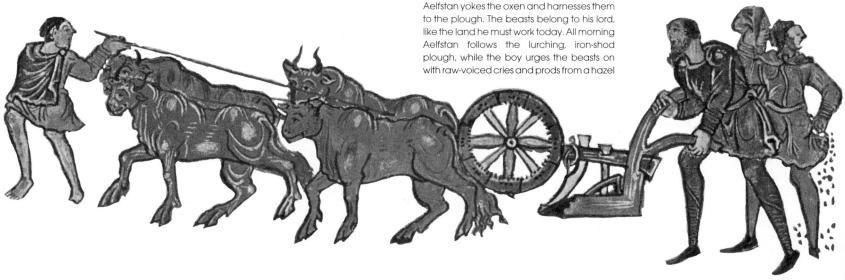

might gather acorns to make coarse bread in years of bad harvest, or go bird-nesting for eggs to relieve the monotonous diet of the average peasant family. Cereals with a little dairy food were standard fare. Fish and salt meat offered some rare variety – but fresh meat was a luxury known to very few, except on special occasions when peasants might be invited to the lord's hall to share a feast.

The feast given in the lord's hall was one of the great joys and rewards of a Saxon's life. Ale, wine and mead, made with fermented honey, were served in plentiful quantities; tales were told, minstrels played, and the company regaled themselves with games and riddles, for which the Anglo-Saxons had a passion. Some of the riddles have survived, such as: 'My nose is downward: I go on my belly and dig into the ground, moving as directed by the grey enemy of the forest and my master and protector, who walks stooping at my tail.' The answer is a plough, the grey enemy of the forest being the ox.

To be banned from the mead-hall was one of the great sorrows expressed in Anglo-Saxon literature, indicating the breaking of a bond between the man and his lord. This was a vital bond, dating back to a time when fighting men expected to be well armed and feasted by their chief in exchange for their readiness to die for him in battle. With village life in more settled times, the same bond survived in different form. The churls or freemen gave service to the thane by working in his fields and surrendering a share of their crops to him. In return they were granted small plots of land – and the comforts of the mead-hall on occasion.

Trial by the shire court

Bonds of kinship were also important in Anglo-Saxon society. A murderer brought upon himself the vengeance of the victim's kinsmen who might kill him with the sanction of the law. But vengeance did not always take the form of a life for a life. Money or land might be accepted instead – the rate of compensation depending on the dead man's social standing. Every man had his *wergild* – his death price – which became a way of defining his rank. Under laws codified by King Alfred,

Daily bread *Meals in a peasant home were based on the simplest ingredients. Home-baked bread was made from flour ground beneath a flat round stone. Milk and cheese were daily fare, and sometimes the diet might be varied by fish or birds' eggs.*

Game counter

a miscreant caught sleeping with the wife of a man of the highest class would be required to pay the husband 120 shillings, a sum equivalent to 20 oxen. A cuckolded churl, however, received only 30 shillings in recompense. Crude as such calculations might appear, they did represent an attempt to set up a systematic rule of law. The Anglo-Saxons, under a single royal authority, made major advances in this field. The country was divided into shires, many of which survive little changed from Saxon times. Legal and administrative affairs were dealt with by a shire court, or moot.

Trial was sometimes by ordeal, held in the nave of the village church. An accused man might have to carry a red-hot iron in his hand. The hand was then bandaged, and if the wound had healed after three days he was cleared of the charge. Alternatively, a man might have to plunge his hand into boiling water. Convicted criminals might be punished by a fine, mutilation or death. Justice was clearly rough but there was little to be gained by evading its procedures. A defendant who failed to answer a summons could be killed by any villager with impunity.

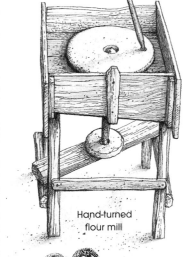

Hand-turned flour mill

Beauty aids *An elaborate dress fastener using hook and eye (above) was used by Saxon women. Among other aids were tweezers that could be hung from a belt (below), a device for cleaning out the ears, and the medieval equivalent of a nail file.*

Saxon fireside *A central, low, circular open fireplace is the dominant feature of the Saxon family hut. By the open door is a foot-operated wooden lathe. Beneath the rough-hewn wooden floorboards is a pit that might have prevented rising damp. This hut is part of a village reconstructed at West Stow, in eastern England.*

Arm of the law *Hanging was the usual form of execution, the penalty for crimes such as murder, arson, theft and treachery to a lord. The gallows was often placed at the boundary between settlements. Major cases might come before the king himself, advised by a council of nobles and churchmen known as the witenagemot.*

MONKS WHO KEPT THE FAITH ALIVE

The celebration of Christ's birthday on December 25 owes nothing to the known facts of Christ's life: it simply coincided with the winter solstice of Europe's pagan peoples. The word Easter has no root in the Bible story; it derives from Eostre, a Germanic goddess whose festival was celebrated in the spring.

In reality, a wealth of words, customs and practices associated with Christianity have heathen origins. And they date back to an extraordinary period of cultural interaction, when fervent missionaries moved among the rough tribes who inherited Europe when Rome fell. Almost everywhere, bands of lawless warriors brought death, chaos and suffering. Territories once governed by Christian emperors lapsed into paganism, with its spirit worlds and fertility rites. The early church fathers made the inspired decision not to try to annihilate the accepted shrines and rituals but instead to adapt them to Christian purposes.

At Europe's north-westerly margin, Ireland escaped the worst tide of tribal unrest, and its monasteries preserved both classical scholarship and the Christian faith. Ireland's conversion is traditionally credited to St Patrick, a Briton who founded a church at Armagh in the 5th century. The Irish Celts developed their own distinctive brand of Christianity, rooted in the traditions of their land. Most of their monasteries were situated in defensible places such as abandoned hill-forts, fortified promontories or small islands.

'Beehive' homes *Monks on islands facing the wild Atlantic lived in tiny stone cells set on bare shelves of rock. The blocks were partially overlapped to bring each course further inward until they met overhead.*

Often enclosed by earthen banks, these windswept sites were sparse in their comforts, for Irish Christianity placed great stress on the frugal life.

The monks lived in clusters of wickerwork huts or stone cells. Besides the monks' dwellings, monasteries also included a small church or oratory, a guesthouse, a refectory where meals were served, and perhaps a school where young monks – often unlettered ploughboys and herdsmen – scratched out their first lessons on wax tablets.

From the Irish monasteries, missionaries set out to convert the people of Britain, preaching, baptising and confirming the superstitious tribes of Picts and Saxons. The performance of miracles was often ascribed to the monks, who cured illnesses and cast out evil spirits almost as routine duties. In about 563

Making music *Under the less ascetic rule of St Benedict, monasteries became centres of a more secular culture – producing manuscripts on music, art and literature and transcribing old tales and poetry.*

the missionary St Columba set up a monastery on the Hebridean island of Iona, and from there his disciples carried the faith into Northumbria and over to Europe. The prime purpose of this and other monasteries, however, was to provide Christian rites and services. Pilgrims were given hospitality, and there was a constant coming and going of visiting churchmen.

A monk's life on Iona revolved around the daily disciplines of prayer, penance, work and learning. The brethren had the Celtic tonsure – the front of the head was shaved in a line from ear to ear, unlike the more familiar Roman tonsure which was a circle shaved from the crown. Coarse woollen garments were worn above a cowled white tunic and leather sandals. The community of about 150 monks was self-supporting, so that duties included herding cattle, sowing crops, milling corn and sea fishing. Wednesdays and Fridays were reserved for fasting. There was rest on Saturday, but from Saturday night through the whole of Sunday the monks knelt or walked in prayer. The faith and devotion of the

Guardian demon *The early church offered sanctuary to all. At Durham Cathedral, fugitives hammered on a knocker recalling pagan worship of monstrous beasts.*

Solitary scribe *Working in the loneliness of his simple cell, illuminating the capital letters and borders of one book may have been a lifetime's work for one monk.*

Celtic missionaries was legendary, and one of them, St Columbanus, set up communities as far afield as Gaul and northern Italy. His rule was a harsh one, incorporating such punishments as six strokes of the cane for speaking at table, laughing during prayers or singing poorly, even though suffering from a cough. But perhaps the sternest tests were faced by those monks who went off to live as hermits on far-flung islands.

Austere as it was, the Irish tradition was not wholly unworldly. The illuminated manuscripts display the artists' evident love of nature, particularly of animals, which are drawn with great vitality. There are human touches, too, in the way that weary scribes sometimes scribbled complaints in the margins of their manuscripts. 'Twenty days to Easter Monday and I am cold and tired', grumbled one. 'The ink is bad, the parchment scanty, the day dark', wrote another.

Nunneries were also established, and it seems that their inmates were not immune from human vanities. Of a community in Scotland, a 7th-century monk, Adamnan, complained that the nuns were 'either sunk in unprofitable sleep, or else awake only to sin'.

There was, in addition, a milder monastic tradition which came to British shores from Rome. The story has often been told how Pope Gregory was inspired to send missionaries, after he saw some fair-complexioned pagan slaves for sale in the imperial capital. Told that they were Angles, he is said to have replied that they were 'Not Angles but angels'. In 596 the pope sent Augustine and a party of monks to Canterbury to convert the English, and they brought the monastic rule of St Benedict which was less ascetic than the Celtic tradition.

One pint of wine a day

Benedictine monasteries usually had a mill, a garden and a bakery. The monks slept on mattresses with pillow and woollen blankets. Two cooked dishes were provided for the daily meal, and wine was considered acceptable. 'We read that wine is not suitable for monks,' wrote St Benedict, 'but because, in our day, it is not possible to persuade the monks of this, let us agree at least that we should not drink to excess. We believe that one pint of wine a day is enough.'

The Celtic and Roman churches, differing in such details as the shape of the tonsure and the date of Easter, found themselves at loggerheads in the 7th century. Their differences were settled in Rome's favour at the Synod of Whitby, a council convened by King Oswy of Northumbria. As a result, the English Church was brought into line with the continent, and the rich Celtic tradition fell into a decline.

ARTISTS FOR GOD

A unique art form developed in early English and Irish monasteries, as scribes copied the Latin text of the Gospels on parchment or vellum and artists then painstakingly decorated the manuscripts, adapting the spiralling, plaited and interlacing patterns of pagan Celtic art to the sacred texts. The colours were very rich, although no gold leaf was used. On treeless Iona was begun the Book of Kells, a 680 page masterpiece containing an illuminated text of the four Gospels. Missionaries from Iona founded a monastery at Lindisfarne, off the coast of Northumbria, where monks produced another exquisite version of the Gospels.

Biblical bestiary *Manuscript illuminators liked to weave animals, both real and imaginary, into their painstaking work.*

Sun-wheel cross *The amalgamation of the paganism of earlier days with the newer faith of Christianity is represented by the design of the familiar Celtic cross. The circle, a heathen depiction of the sun found in many pagan cultures, was incorporated with the cross, the instrument of Christ's crucifixion, to link old and new faiths.*

Monk in the making *A Benedictine novice undergoing tuition still lacks the tonsure of his superior.*

CULTURE AT THE COURT OF CHARLEMAGNE

A people who were 'wise in council, noble in physique, radiant in health, excelling in beauty, daring, quick, tough' – this was how the Franks described themselves, in a code of tribal law dating from the 6th century. A boastful self-image, no doubt; but it is true that the Franks' story belies conventional ideas that peoples of the period once called the Dark Ages were merely uncouth marauders.

The Franks created the nucleus of modern France. Their emperor Charlemagne founded an empire whose influence shaped 1000 years of European history. Furthermore, Charlemagne's court at Aachen became a brilliant centre of European culture, fostering a flowering of art and learning so spectacular that it has been called the Carolingian Renaissance.

The Franks were a people of Germanic origin who advanced from the Rhineland between the 3rd and 6th centuries AD, making themselves masters of all Gaul, and adopting Christianity. They were formidable warriors, often very tall, with fair or red hair combed forward in a style that left the nape of the neck bare. Cloaks, tunics and knee-length breeches were typical wear, with the bandaged leggings characteristic of so many Germanic tribesmen. Around the tunic, warriors wore a leather girdle from which hung a very distinctive weapon: a throwing axe known as the *francisca*, which had a curved blade and curved handle.

From the warrior's belt hung such items as a knife, scissors and comb, as well as a sword. The common soldier used a broad-bladed sword known as a *scramasax* that was wielded with both hands.

Horsemen against the Moors

In AD 732 the Frankish leader Charles Martel repelled a Moorish invasion by recruiting armed horsemen and giving them grants of land in return for their pledge to serve in his armies when summoned. Such a land grant was known as a fief, or in Latin *feudum*, from which the term feudalism derives. As king of the Franks for 46 years, Charlemagne campaigned

against Lombards, Saxons, Avars, Gascons, Basques, Muslims and others to create a realm that spanned Europe from the Baltic to the Mediterranean. Perceiving him as a staunch defender of the faith, the pope crowned him Roman Emperor on Christmas Day in AD 800, at St Peter's in Rome.

Charlemagne's realm covered an area almost as extensive as the Roman Empire had covered in Europe. Ruled through a variety of subordinate counts, bishops and abbots, it encompassed the greater part of European Christendom. Lacking a true bureaucracy, Charlemagne used envoys to convey his wishes over his immense realm,

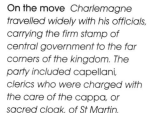

Price of pride A blast on a richly ornamented magic horn was supposed to call Charlemagne to the aid of Roland, the commander of his rearguard on a campaign in Spain. Ambushed in a mountain pass, Roland scorned to use the horn until too late. Charlemagne arrived to find him slain.

On the move *Charlemagne travelled widely with his officials, carrying the firm stamp of central government to the far corners of the kingdom. The party included capellani, clerics who were charged with the care of the cappa, or sacred cloak, of St Martin.*

Frankish law *An illuminated manuscript depicts the secular law as a man and the authority of the Church as a woman. The hands above them are thought to represent those of God, looked upon as the ultimate authority in both spheres.*

Harvest time *Autumn in the countryside: a Frankish manuscript of the 9th century shows peasants scything the corn on the land of their feudal lord and winnowing his grain.*

Stylish script *A reformed handwriting known as Carolingian miniscule, 'small letter', was introduced by Alcuin. Its rounded design became the basis of modern printed letters.*

and granted fiefs to forge personal bonds of loyalty. Lay officials included the *comes stabuli*, or count of the stables, from which the word constable derives. His job was to organise transport for both court and military purposes.

Charlemagne and his royal household spent much of their time moving from one estate to another, following the old Roman road system. His favourite residence was the palace he had built at Aachen – the marvel of its day, with a great domed octagonal chapel, graced by marble columns imported from Rome and Ravenna. There was also an immense reception hall 160 ft (49 m) long, a library and a marble swimming pool served by warm water from thermal springs. The pool could hold 100 bathers, and the hot springs were also tapped to provide luxurious central heating for the palace. An impressive complex, it must have astonished the Frankish people who were little used to stone buildings.

Parties beside the pool

Charlemagne was a burly man over 6 ft (1.8 m) tall. He had an unusually large head and a voice that was curiously weak for someone of such stature. Physically active, he enjoyed swimming in his pool, where he often threw parties. He also loved to hunt in the vast woods of the neighbouring Ardennes. Apart from some over-indulgence at the open-air banquets that followed the chase, he seems to have been moderate in his eating and drinking habits. He also preferred simple, Frankish clothing to Roman costume, which he wore only in Rome.

A 9th-century cleric who was his biographer describes how Charlemagne once played a trick on a group of overdressed courtiers returning from a fair in Venice. They attended Mass

Frankish fighters *Horse-riding knights formed the backbone of the feudal system. It was under Emperor Charlemagne that heavily mailed cavalry appeared, using stirrups for purchase and control when fighting on horseback. From this time, cavalry dominated medieval warfare.*

'strutting in robes made of pheasant skins and silk; or of the necks, backs and tails of peacocks in their first plumage. Some were decorated with purple and lemon-coloured ribbons; some were draped round with blankets and some in ermine robes'. So Charlemagne took them hunting clad just as they were, driving them through muddy thickets on a foul, rainy day. Afterwards he compared the state of his own sheepskin with their bedraggled condition.

Charlemagne was no puritan: on the contrary, he displayed a marked fondness for the ladies. It was said that only one unmarried woman at his court ever refused his advances, and he took several wives, at least four of whom are known to posterity. Some churchmen complained about the emperor's multiple marriages, but the mood of his court was relaxed.

Charlemagne was prepared to use mischievous methods to make points. He is said once to have asked a Jewish merchant to teach a proud bishop a lesson. The Jew did so by persuading the bishop, a collector of curios, to buy

Ruler's cup *Bavaria became part of Charlemagne's empire in 788, when its duke, Tassilo, owner of this chalice, was charged with conspiring with the Avars.*

a stuffed mouse wrapped in silk in the belief that it was a costly treasure. Convivial by nature, Charlemagne also showed authentic Christian piety. Einhard describes him as a constant worshipper at his chapel in Aachen. At meals he often liked a work of theology read to him. He founded elementary schools, and higher schools, attached to monasteries and cathedrals. The palace school in Aachen, where his own children were taught, attracted the greatest scholars. Among these was

Alcuin of York, who joined the court of Charlemagne in 782. He taught by means of dialogue: 'What is life?' 'The joy of the blessed, the sorrow of sinners, the expectation of death.' 'What is death?' 'An unavoidable occurrence, an uncertain journey, the tears of the living, the confirmation of the testament, the thief of man.'

Charlemagne's empire was divided at his son's death among feuding successors. It was restored in 962, as a realm centred around possessions in Germany, in the Low Countries and in northern Italy. This became known as the Holy Roman Empire, in recognition of the twin influences that had permeated the realm of Charlemagne: classical tradition and the Christian faith.

Sacred weapon *The iron lance belonging to successive Holy Roman Emperors carries extra spiritual protection: the gold sheath at its centre is stretched over a nail reported to come from Christ's cross, as an inscription down the centre records.*

FURY OF THE SEABORNE WARRIORS

'From the fury of the Northmen, good Lord deliver us!' The prayer is said to have been offered by Christians all along the coast of Dark Age northern Europe. And though scholars have come to doubt whether this was the precise wording, the sentiments were widespread. Viking raiders burst onto the scene towards the end of the 8th century, fierce sea warriors lured from their Scandinavian homelands by lust for plunder. And where the Vikings went, terror went too. The origin of the word Viking is disputed, but one

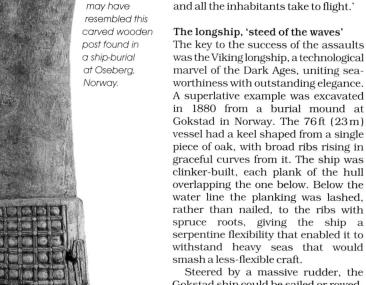

Lion's snarl
The prow of a Viking boat may have resembled this carved wooden post found in a ship-burial at Oseberg, Norway.

suggestion is that *vik* meant bay, creek or fiord, and that to go *i viking* meant to quit one's own fiord and go adventuring abroad. Some of these adventurers may have been farmers, supplementing their income by seasonal raiding, but many were professional warriors prepared to spend long periods abroad.

Some Norsemen went as traders, and many went as colonists; but it was as pirates that the Vikings had the most impact. The sight of Norse warships, long and low, with square sails and dragon prows, brought panic as they loomed over horizons, slunk around headlands and raced up estuaries. For 200 years the emblems of their pagan gods – Thor's Hammer and Odin's Raven – symbolised fire, rape and pillage. Churches and monasteries were particular targets, furnished as they were with gold and silver ornaments, and often left undefended except by monks and priests.

The Vikings' assault on Lindisfarne in northern England in 793 was one of the first raids, and many more assaults followed. During the next century London, Paris, Lisbon, Cadiz and Pisa were among the towns sacked. 'The number of ships grows larger and larger, and the great host of Northmen continually increases,' complained the French monk Ermentarius. 'There is hardly a monastery which is respected, and all the inhabitants take to flight.'

The longship, 'steed of the waves'

The key to the success of the assaults was the Viking longship, a technological marvel of the Dark Ages, uniting seaworthiness with outstanding elegance. A superlative example was excavated in 1880 from a burial mound at Gokstad in Norway. The 76 ft (23 m) vessel had a keel shaped from a single piece of oak, with broad ribs rising in graceful curves from it. The ship was clinker-built, each plank of the hull overlapping the one below. Below the water line the planking was lashed, rather than nailed, to the ribs with spruce roots, giving the ship a serpentine flexibility that enabled it to withstand heavy seas that would smash a less-flexible craft.

Steered by a massive rudder, the Gokstad ship could be sailed or rowed. Parts of the sail had even survived; it

Iron cap *The Viking helmet had a spectacle-like guard for eyes and nose. The wooden shield had an iron boss at the centre to protect the holder's hand.*

Axeman's assault *The Viking battle-axe derived from the woodman's tool. One notorious Viking king, Erik Blood-axe, hacked his way to the throne of Norway with this axe, and adopted his name from it.*

The Viking's armoury *The principal weapons used by the Viking warrior included a slashing sword, a stabbing spear, and a fearsome battle-axe.*

was made of pale woollen cloth, striped or chequered with red. Oarsmen pulled at 16 pairs of oars, suggesting a crew of 32 men. However, the Gokstad ship had 64 shields, which could be hung from a rail running round the outside of the ship. So either the ship was rowed by two men to an oar, or else half the crew rested while the other half rowed. Capable of speeding at 10 knots under sail, the longship was revered by Norsemen almost as a living thing. 'Steeds of the waves', they called their vessels; and the prows carved with dragons and other beasts added to the impression of animation.

Mystique of the sword

Viking warriors have been stereotyped as wearing hugely horned helmets. In fact, no such headgear has been uncovered by archaeology. Though horned figures do sometimes appear in Viking art, it seems likely that these

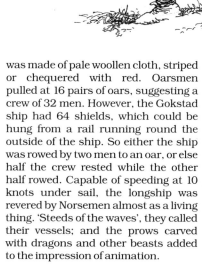

North Sea crossing *After crossing the North Sea in longships with menacing carved heads at the prow, a 9th-century fleet of Norse sea-raiders wearing conical helmets and carrying spears prepares to land on the English coast.*

Legendary longship *The ship found at Oseberg was powered by 15 pairs of oars and steered by a side-rudder. The spirals on prow and stern represent a serpent's head and tail. Friezes show fabulous beasts.*

had a religious significance. Metal helmets of any type were rare; those that have survived were rounded or conical, sometimes with eyepieces that gave them a sinister, mask-like look. Mail shirts made of interlocking iron rings offered body protection to some warriors, but padded leather jerkins were more commonly worn.

Bows and arrows, spears and round wooden shields formed part of the Viking's armoury, but it was to the warrior's sword that the greatest mystique attached. This was a heavy weapon, used in sweeping blows with the cutting edge, rather than thrusting. The Viking also used a battle-axe; this was derived from the farmer's axe, and early examples served both as tool and weapon before specialised axes were devised for use in battle.

'Bear-shirt' fanatics

In battle the Norsemen fought with an awesome savagery. Most ferocious of all were the warriors known as *berserkrs* – from whom the word berserk derives. The name means 'bear shirt', and the fanatics went naked but for the skins of wild beasts, fighting with a frenzy so intense that they might bite their shields. Often they wore wolf skins, perhaps giving rise to the first tales of werewolves.

On a coastal raid the Vikings generally made a fortified encampment where they beached their ships, then quickly erected a rampart and stockade to protect the landward approach. When serious opposition was encountered they attacked their foes in a massive phalanx many ranks deep, or in a wedge-shaped formation known as the 'swine array'. The Norsemen fought almost entirely on foot, rarely using cavalry – though captured horses were often employed for mobility on the march. It would be wrong to think of the Vikings only as hit-and-run specialists. Following their raids they settled large tracts of land, including the area of eastern and northern England known as the Danelaw. Here Norse customs and laws prevailed for 200 years. In Russia, the Vikings were known chiefly as traders and bringers of order. Russia in fact owes her name to a group of Rus – Swedish Vikings – who were invited by the Slavs to rule their anarchic land in the 9th century.

Riding with the Valkyries

Nevertheless, warfare unquestionably loomed large in Viking life. To die in battle was thought a glorious thing. The chosen slain were conveyed to Odin's heavenly hall of Valhalla, where they spent their days in friendly battle and their nights in feasting. The Valkyries selected the favoured dead. Originally conceived of as demonic scavengers, they were later depicted as Odin's warrior handmaidens, who flew on horseback over the battlefield to carry chosen warriors to the afterlife.

The idea of death as a voyage was common, too. Ship burials were a widespread funeral rite. Fully equipped craft were interred in earth mounds, with food supplies and a wealth of everyday objects. The Gokstad ship held the body of a dead king, laid on his bed in a little tent with his weapons arranged around. Among the accoutrements were the bodies of horses, dogs – and a peacock. Cremation was also widespread, and burials provided apocalyptic spectacles, as the vessels blazed on the open sea.

THE RAVEN AND THE HAMMER

The principal deities of the Norsemen were the one-eyed Odin or Woden, wise ruler of the gods, who was armed with a spear and symbolised by a raven, and Thor, the god of thunder, whose symbol was a hammer. Their names live on in our Wednesday and Thursday. Almost as important was Frey, the god of fertility, who fell in love with the giantess Gerd, but was furious when she kept him waiting – hence he is often depicted twisting his beard in impatience. The Valkyries served as handmaidens to Odin, while gods as well as mortals were subject to the Norns, goddesses of fate.

Bronze of Thor, god of thunder

Silver pendant of a Valkyrie

HOME FROM THE SEA TO FARMING TOIL

Back in calm waters after days on the storm-tossed North Sea, the Viking raiders came home to their small farming villages dotted round the Scandinavian shores. But they were not returning to a life of comfort and leisure. All of them had work to do ashore – for the typical Norse settlement was a cluster of self-sufficient farmsteads, on which practically every hour of daylight between raids was needed for tending the cattle and growing the crops necessary for survival in a cold northern climate.

For shelter from the weather, the Vikings built timber-framed houses which were little more than barn-like halls. Here men, women and children slept on straw-filled mattresses and ate on wooden benches. The floors of compacted earth were strewn with reeds, and in the centre of the hall women cooked at a long hearth made of stone or clay.

Smoke from the fire thickened the air and blackened the rafters with soot before billowing out

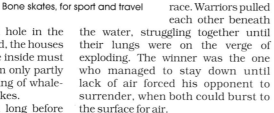

Bone skates, for sport and travel

through a single central hole in the ceiling. Because of the cold, the houses had no windows, so those inside must have lived in a hazy gloom only partly brightened by the flickering of whale-blubber lamps on long spikes.

The day's work began long before the Vikings broke their fast. At dawn men would go out into the fields and do several hours' work before returning to the village and eating their first meal, at mid-morning. They ate barley or oatmeal porridge and buttermilk together with crusty loaves of bread made from barley or rye.

The other meal of the day, eaten at nightfall, was a little more elaborate. The Vikings bred cattle, sheep, goats, pigs and poultry, and ate huge quantities of meat, either roasted on a spit or boiled in vats, perhaps with peas, onions and leeks to make a stew. Fish was wrapped in leaves, to preserve the juices, then cooked

between hot stones. The Vikings ate from wooden bowls and dishes, using spoons, knives and fingers – forks were unknown to them. At the evening meal they washed their food down with beer from tankards and drinking horns. To while away the hours on long, dark evenings they listened to poems and sagas telling of heroic exploits. They played dice and board games, some using pieces resembling draughts, others using bone pegs. Music came from harps and boxwood pipes, while women spun wool with distaff and spindle, or wove at upright looms propped against the wall.

Most of the Vikings' sports and games were as tough and rumbustious as the people themselves. Some were not so much sports as a form of training for combat – a chance for a man to develop or show off his courage, strength and cunning. Skiing and skating were among the gentler winter pastimes: the skis and skates were made of bone, fastened to the boots with thongs, and were also used for speedy travel across icy lakes and rivers. Ball games were rough and brawling, and no holds were barred when one Viking challenged another to all-in wrestling. In the same way, when the Vikings staged a swimming match it was more of a battle than a race. Warriors pulled each other beneath the water, struggling together until their lungs were on the verge of exploding. The winner was the one who managed to stay down until lack of air forced his opponent to surrender, when both could burst to the surface for air.

As with men, so with animals. The Vikings enjoyed the danger and excitement of horse racing, but what really set the adrenaline flowing was a horse fight. They would tether a mare in season, then goad specially bred stallions into fighting over her. The rearing, whinnying, snorting, biting and kicking of a good horse fight could always be counted on to draw a crowd of spectators.

Keys on a bronze brooch

For everyday wear, Norse women wore a linen shift under an outer tunic that consisted of two lengths of wool joined at the shoulders by straps fixed with a

pair of bronze brooches. The brooches were not simply ornaments: from one of them hung household necessities such as keys, knife, comb and purse.

Men wore shirts of linen or wool, with a tunic called a *kyrtil* on top. Their woollen breeches varied in cut, from a drainpipe style to huge, baggy-trousered affairs gathered in below the knee. Linen pants might be worn as underwear, while men and women wore heavy cloaks, which doubled as blankets. Their laced, leather boots were fur-lined for winter, and on sea voyages the Vikings often wore oiled animal skins over their clothes.

'Any man who slaughters a sacrificial animal – whether it is an ox, ram, goat or pig – fastens it up on poles outside his house to show that he has made his sacrifice in honour of the gods.'

A TRAVELLER FROM CORDOBA, AD 950

Another important building was the boat shed, into which vessels were dragged for the winter. There was often a stone-flagged bathhouse, containing a peat fire where stones were heated so that water cast onto them filled the air with vapour – an early form of sauna.

When men were away on a raiding party it was left to the women to manage the farms single-handed, or with the help of older villagers left at home, and children. The adventuring spirit of the Vikings meant that many raiders left their bones on foreign shores. Many a farmstead was left without a master or a male heir, and widowed women became landowners in their own right.

Viking comb

Room for living *Wooden planks and wattle and daub form the walls of this reconstructed Viking room. Low earth platforms for sitting and sleeping flank a hearth of stones topped with clay, with its cooking pot. A loom stands by one wall.*

Gaming board

Tableware *A graceful glass beaker of funnel shape contrasts with a roughly carved bowl of birchwood.*

Spiked lamp

Oak-wood pail

LONGSHIPS IN SAFE HAVEN AT THE HEAD OF THE FIORD

The people of a Viking farming settlement on the deeply indented Norwegian coast gather at the water's edge to watch the bustle of activity around two ships involved in journeys of raid and trade. Seagulls add their raucous clamour to the scene. From the beached longship, with its tall mast and gracefully curving prow, returning warriors carrying spears and shields head towards one of the trackways of tightly packed logs that lead into the heart of the settlement.

A smaller vessel called a knorr, used for fishing and carrying cargo, lies at the jetty, loading up with skins and other produce from the surrounding farms, to be taken to trade with other settlements. Away to the left,

carpenters are swarming over another longship which is nearing completion. Wood also forms the framework of the farmers' homes, the upright planking often filled in with clay for extra warmth. The roof thatching is held down with bands of hide anchored by stones. On some older houses the thatch has become so thickly matted with turf that a cow (far right) is nibbling at it.

A stream runs down the hillside, where foresters are hauling in logs to fire the stone furnaces for the smithy, where the blacksmith and his team work iron smelted from the local bog ore. Large settlements might have specialist ironworkers, but in some homesteads the farmer served as his

own blacksmith, hammering out farm tools, chains, nails, rivets and weapons alike. The smith's role was a heroic one in Norse mythology – the great god Thor himself was depicted carrying a forge hammer – and the smith enjoyed a high status in Viking society.

In the foreground, horses drink at a pool; behind them, women are storing dried herrings in barrels for winter food. Over an open doorway, a dead cow has been hoisted into place on a platform built of poles: a farmer would periodically sacrifice one of his rare livestock and display it in this way in honour of the gods. Stables, haystacks, storehouses, muckheaps, barns and other outbuildings complete the settlement.

TRADE LINKS FROM ICELAND TO THE VOLGA

As masters of the northern seas and rivers, the Vikings trafficked across a vast expanse. Arab merchants and diplomats met them in Russia, and one of these – Ibn Fadlan, an ambassador from the Caliphate of Baghdad – left an eyewitness report of Viking traders abroad. 'Never have I seen a people of more perfect physique; they are tall as date palms and reddish in colour', he wrote, adding that they moored their ships along the Volga and built wooden houses on its banks.

The Arab observer lamented the Vikings' lack of social graces: 'Ten or twelve of them may live together in one house, and each man has a couch of his own where he sits and diverts himself with the pretty slave girls whom he has brought along to offer for sale. He will make love with one of them in the presence of his comrades. Sometimes this develops into a communal orgy.'

Slaves were, in fact, one of the Vikings' main commodities; many of these were females, used and sold as concubines. Other goods offered by Viking traders included cattle, swords, Baltic amber and the pelts of otter, marten and beaver. Sealskins, walrus hides and walrus ivory were additional exports, brought from the Arctic.

In return, the Vikings brought back wines from the South, silks and spices from the East, Byzantine brocades, Persian leatherwork, jewellery, toiletries and glassware. Tens of thousands of Arabic silver coins, dating from the 9th and 10th centuries, have been found at sites scattered around Scandinavia. They testify to a Viking thirst for silver, which was accepted just as readily in the form of ingots and ornaments. Scales for weighing quantities have often been found in Viking graves, and the fact that coins have often turned up cut in half indicates that they were valued more as bullion than as currency in the strict sense.

The Viking traders were, it seems, notably superstitious. Ibn Fadlan describes them flinging themselves to the ground before carved wooden effigies, with offerings of bread, leeks, milk, beer and even slaughtered sheep and cattle. Offerings would also be made on such occasions as surviving an ambush or negotiating rapids.

By canoe and horse sledge

Russia was penetrated chiefly along the great arteries of the rivers Volga and Dnieper. The traditional seagoing vessels of the Vikings were ill-suited to the rapids, marshes and gorges along these rivers, so the Vikings carved out canoes of their own or bought small local craft and travelled downstream in flotillas. Winter ice presented no problem to the sturdy northerners. They had their goods hauled on sledges drawn by horses wearing crampons, enabling them to cross frozen swamps at speeds impossible in summer.

For seagoing trade, the Vikings used a cargo vessel called a knorr, very different from the warriors' longship. Built for bulk carrying rather than for speed, it was deeper and broader than the fighting vessel. Like the longship, the knorr was basically a one-sailed, open boat in which cargo and crew travelled exposed to the elements. Using such vessels, mariners covered nearly 4000 miles (6400 km) to reach the New World. Though the Vikings had no compasses, they were skilled navigators who could follow a course for many days without sighting land.

The position of the stars and knowledge of tidal currents also helped in direction-finding. If a Viking seaman was lost at sea, he might make landfall by studying the flight of sea birds and stationary cloud formations, which form over land rather than water. As basic rations, seamen

Coins of conquest *Silver pennies were minted in the Viking trading settlement of Jorvik (modern York). They bore such figures as a raven, the symbol of Odin, a sword and a bow and arrow.*

Buried treasure *Silver was highly prized by Viking traders. This hoard of ornaments and coins was buried for safekeeping around AD 975 at Birka, in Sweden.*

Start of the journey *A knorr, or cargo ship, loads up for a voyage to a distant colony.*

Before Columbus *Around AD 1000, the Viking adventurer Leif Ericson sailed west from Greenland and, after ten days, made landfall in what he called Vinland, the 'Land of Wine'. A Viking colony survived briefly in what was almost certainly present-day Newfoundland.*

Fair dealing
After the invaders came the traders. These bronze scales and linen bag (above), and lead weights (below), show that deals were precisely measured.

might take dried fish and meats, curds, hard-baked bread and barrels of ale. Kitchen and cooking gear included kegs, cauldrons, dishes, and hand mills for grinding corn. Adzes, hammers and other Viking ship-building tools have been recovered, used for on-the-spot repairs or for building small craft in foreign parts.

The Vikings' successful trading created some flourishing commercial centres. Hedeby, on Jutland's Baltic coast, was among the most prosperous communities, with a population of about 1000 people on its 60 acre (25 ha) site. Enclosed by ramparts, it was built on a lake at the head of a fiord, and its wealth of mooring posts indicate how it must once have bustled with cargo vessels.

Hedeby was by no means unique. At Novgorod and Kiev in Russia the Vikings founded trading posts that would grow into great cities. Dublin was just one of the fortified harbours which Norse traders set up on Irish shores, as bases for trips to the west coast of France and Spain. York in England and Rouen in France had existing settlements before the Vikings arrived, but were notably stamped by their presence. Active and prosperous as these little centres may have been, however, they never became true cities

in Viking times. The Norsemen were not town-dwellers by nature; they were farmers with a taste for adventure, and their pioneering spirit led them to colonise the islands of the Atlantic Ocean.

Democracy in Iceland

Storms drove the first Vikings off course to the shores of Iceland. The early settlers found the island far from barren. Well wooded with birch, rich in fish and birds, it also held plentiful supplies of bog iron ore to feed the smithies' forges. A flood of immigrants in the 9th and 10th centuries created a community of fishermen and farmers known for their sturdy and independent spirit. The Icelandic Vikings set up an assembly, the Althing, where all free men could speak and cast their votes, in the first rudimentary democracy since Ancient Greece.

Westwards lay the ice-bound immensity of Greenland, discovered in 982 by Eric the Red, a hotheaded Icelander outlawed for manslaughter. Having wintered for three seasons on its rugged coast, he named the place Greenland as a lure to further settlement. In due course a Viking community of some 3000 people managed to scratch out an existence here, living in dank huts on the distant rim of the Arctic wastes.

Treasures from the East *A wealth of luxuries from far-off lands flowed back to the Vikings' homeland. They included this Arabic glass found in Sweden, and an axe-shaped silver pendant, possibly manufactured in Russia, found in Norway.*

133

CASTLE, TOWN AND CHURCH

Good order in Europe, which had crumbled under the onslaught of Islam and the Vikings, was slowly restored from the 10th century onwards. Castles dotted the landscape, dominating the countryside which obeyed them, and from them local lords defended their people from external attack and settled internal disputes. Mounted knights swore loyalty to their feudal masters, to their ladies' honour – and to God.

The Church and its bishops ruled over matters of morality, and parish priests officiated at the rites of birth, marriage and death. Cathedrals towered skywards, and new monasteries replaced those burned by earlier marauders or fallen into decay. All these great buildings were added to constantly, as the skills and technology of masons developed. A new spirit of self-confidence inspired lords, common people and even children to embark on pilgrimages to martyrs' shrines, and on Crusades to rescue the Holy Land from Islam.

WESTERN EUROPE AD1000–1450

SLOW CHANGE FOR BARON AND PEASANT

As daily life in northern Europe became more organised and orderly, the numbers of people increased. Expectation of life at birth was low; women frequently died in childbirth and men in war; medical skills were limited; and the Biblical span of three score years and ten was an age rarely attained. Yet slowly, inexorably, the population rose. In England alone, in the two centuries from 1100 to 1300, it grew from around 2 million to between 4 and 5 million.

Most people continued to live in the countryside, dependent on their lords – barons, counts, dukes and princes – and their armed retinues. Changes to the traditional ways of cultivation, according to local custom and the rhythms of the seasons, were slow, but pressure on resources brought new practices. In the past, land had usually been left fallow for one year in two; now it was left fallow for only one year in three, by crop rotation that included spring and winter corn.

Forests yield to the plough

Horses in some places replaced oxen; tools became more specialised and achieved more efficient forms. The people brought ever more marginal land under the plough. In England, more land was under crops in 1300 than at any time before the Second World War. On the edge of the Holy Roman Empire the Germans pushed

Songs of love *Troubadours attached to the courts of European lords sang of the love of knights for their ladies. They accompanied their songs with the gentle notes of the lute, newly introduced from the Middle East. A skilled player could pluck elaborate melodies from its five pairs of strings.*

ever farther eastwards, levelling the forests and draining the marshes.

Towns remained small. Only the largest communities, such as Paris, exceeded 100,000, while communities of 10,000-20,000 people were considered towns of major importance. They acted as market centres for their areas, and were the places where specialised craftsmen were to be found.

The central town of the diocese, with its narrow streets clustered round the cathedral, came to be called a city. Cathedrals could be symbols of order as well as of religion. The mighty Durham Cathedral crowned a hilltop dominating a countryside subdued by Norman soldiers; its prince-bishops had special powers from the king and ruled as uncrowned monarchs of north-east England, to keep the marauding Scots at bay. Throughout Europe almost every major town had its castle. Other castles were built at important river crossings and passes between one valley and the next. In England, in the 40 years following the conquest of 1066, no fewer than 500 Norman lords had been given permission to build castles – to 'crenellate', or surround with battlements, was the technical term. In Italy, in the countryside around Florence, two castles are mentioned in documents that go back before 900. In 1050 there were still only 52, but by 1200 their numbers had risen to 205.

Towns and trade expanded together. The Mediterranean trading zone, based on Venice, Pisa and Genoa, exporting and importing eastern goods, was the source of exotic novelties. The northern trading zone centring on the Rhine and the Baltic dealt in heavier goods – the forest products of timber, pitch and tar, iron and grain and cloth. The two zones were not linked by sea until after 1300, for navigating the Strait of Gibraltar was beyond the ships and seacraft of most shipmasters. Instead, traders passed between the zones using either the rivers, navigable in flat-bottomed barges beyond present limits, or expensive overland cartage.

Fairs sprang up at strategic meeting points, and from them gradually

Defeating the 'clipper' *Coins gradually became worn, or lost a great deal of their value, by being clipped around the edges for the value of the silver. The English 'Short Cross' penny (top), introduced in 1180, was withdrawn in 1247 and re-minted as the 'Long Cross' (lower left), the longer arms making the coin harder to clip. The 'Sterling' penny (lower right) was minted from 1279.*

developed long-distance banking and financial structures. At first, silver coins minted by local rulers who took a percentage for their trouble were exchanged by moneychangers at the fairs at rates governed by their silver content. From the mid-13th century, however, settlement by bills and letters of credit slowly became common.

The roads were used by travellers not only on their way to fairs but also on pilgrimages, most of them travelling in groups to reduce the risk of attacks by bandits and brigands. Even on foot, a population used to walking long distances to market could cover 25 miles in a good day's journey.

Soldiers, couriers of the monarch and law officers would pass to and fro on the roads. Groups of monks might be travelling from one house to found a new establishment, while an individual monk might be on his way from one monastery to another to teach skills, to learn them, or to seek out the records of earlier knowledge lost during a long period of destruction. It was the monks who chronicled the events of their area, year by year – the names of the

rulers, the battles, the droughts, famines and diseases, the ominous appearance of a comet. They were often critical of their rulers. William of Malmesbury complained that the lords were not defending their neighbourhoods but laying them waste.

War, whether public or private, was still frequent. Internecine strife often overrode opposition to a common enemy: at the Battle of Sluys in 1340, the first major engagement of the Hundred Years' War between England and France, seamen of Yarmouth and the Cinque Ports deserted the English fleet to fight each other. By the 14th century, after a long time of expansion, pressure of population was breaking

Continent of kingdoms *Europe in the early Middle Ages was a mosaic of kingdoms squabbling for power. The Holy Roman Empire consisted of some 300 states.*

down the old system of service and agricultural life. Famine, plague, sword and fire – the Four Horsemen of the Apocalypse, foretold in the Book of Revelation – were altering people's ideas. Many criticised the Church for its privileges; some, significantly, for its doctrines. Ways of thinking as well as ways of living increasingly diverged in medieval Christendom.

Divided society *The lifestyles of noblemen and peasant were in sharp contrast throughout the Middle Ages. The title of The Effects of Good Government which Ambrogio Lorenzetti gave to his painting of a falconer and a swineherd suggests that he saw the distinction as a virtue.*

Gold by the bagful *Profiting from new opportunities in trade, a moneylender extracts bags of coins from his strongbox for a client who has overreached himself.*

NORMAN KNIGHTS RIDE TO CONQUEST

The long coastline of north-west France drifts into a mixed countryside of fertile pastures, woodlands and gentle hills. This was a seductive landscape to the marauding Vikings of the 9th and 10th centuries. They ravaged towns and monasteries with such freedom that the French king Charles the Simple made a historic deal with one of the invaders, a Viking warlord named Rollo. In AD 911 he offered the warrior large tracts of land at the mouth of the Seine as a duchy, clearly hoping that the outlander would screen his realm from further Viking incursions.

The gamble worked. Rollo and his son not only held but expanded the original land grant, which acted as the required buffer. In due course the Vikings intermarried with the local population and adopted French as their tongue. Through linguistic contraction, the Norsemen, or Northmen, came to be known as Normans. And their duchy was Normandy.

The Normans also converted to Christianity – though it has to be said that, in the early days at least, such conversions often lacked a basis of burning faith. Some Vikings are said to have gone through the rite of baptism ten or 12 times in order to obtain the white garments given out after the immersion ceremony.

An elite of armoured riders

Success in land battles came when the Normans, already masters of the sea in their Viking longships, now became formidable warriors on land as they rode into battle on Frankish warhorses. Normandy had rich pasturelands where warhorses, known as destriers, were raised in numbers, so that armoured, horse-riding knights came to form an elite class among the warriors. Horsemen wore knee-length mail shirts, or hauberks, made of interlocking iron rings. These were often hooded and were split at the knee to facilitate riding.

The iron helmet worn on top was conical, with a protective nose piece. A lance was the knight's chief weapon, mainly used for thrusting. For protection the horseman carried an elongated shield, tapering like a kite, and made of leather over a wooden frame, with metal reinforcement. A strap inside allowed the knight to sling it round his neck, leaving both arms free.

Horsemen rode standing almost upright in their stirrups, and a mass of cavalry riding at full tilt was said to be virtually irresistible. The horsemen generally rode in squadrons under their lords, and their charge was often preceded by volleys of arrows fired by archers to soften up the foe. For close combat the knight had a broad-bladed sword, designed for slashing. Some warriors laid about them with the mace – a weapon which even the clergy were permitted to use because it could crack skulls without 'shedding blood'.

It was their cavalry that brought the Normans success at the Battle of Civitate (1053), by which they defeated an army of Pope Leo IX. And it was their cavalry that won eventual victory against Saxon infantry at the Battle of Hastings in 1066.

Across the Channel to victory

A fleet of square-sailed ships, much like the Viking vessels of earlier times, transported Duke William's army across the English Channel for the famous encounter near Hastings. By no means all the invaders were horsemen; the cavalry was supported by leather-jerkined archers and foot soldiers, as well as cooks, carpenters and other craftsmen.

Master Wace, the Norman poet, tells how the archers 'touched the land foremost, each with his bow bent and his quiver full of arrows slung at his side. The knights landed next, all armed; with their hauberks on, their shields slung at their necks, and their helmets laced. They formed together on the shore, each armed upon his warhorse. All had their swords girded on, and passed into the plain with their lances raised.'

The Normans followed up their successes in battle by extensive castle-building, and through castles and cavalry they built up a scattered dominion that eventually extended from the Scottish borderlands to the Mediterranean and the Levant. At the same time the feudal system took classic shape. In this system, which derived from the Franks, a lord parcelled out units of land – known as fiefs – in return for homage and a commitment to a defined amount of military service. Society was essentially a pyramid: the king or duke relied on the homage of his leading lords, who in turn ruled through lesser nobility. At the lowest level were the serfs, whose name comes from the Latin *servus*, meaning slave. Although the king stood at the head of the pyramid, real power in practice started at the level of dukes and counts who, in Europe, often owed only the most limited service to

Battle tapestry *The Saxons, with luxuriant moustaches, brandish their spears against Norman cavalry charging their hilltop at Hastings in 1066. Slaughtered knights edge the foot of this scene from the Bayeux Tapestry showing the victory of Duke William over King Harold.*

Bible on a bowl *The Warwick ciborium, made about 1175, held the consecrated bread for communion.*

their king. Each of them was effectively an independent ruler, and the difference between a royal court and a ducal one was often very slight.

In both, household officials formed their master's ruling council. The chamberlain, for example, who looked after the king's bedchamber, became responsible for finance because the bedchamber was heavily guarded and hence the safest place for treasure. The chancellor was the principal household cleric, perhaps the only literate servant available in many households; originally he sat behind a screen, or *cancella*, writing and sealing the king's letters for him.

RULED FROM A WOODEN CASTLE

After their conquest of England in 1066, the Normans set about an extensive programme of castle-building. Duke William's conquering army brought prefabricated castles with them. A contemporary chronicler recorded that teams of carpenters came ashore carrying their axes, planes and adzes, and that the castle was 'all shaped, framed and pierced to receive the pins, which they had brought with them, cut and ready in large barrels'.

In England, as elsewhere throughout Europe, the Normans followed up their victory by building castles all round the country. The commonest type consisted of a motte, or earth mound, topped by a stockaded fort, and a bailey, or fortified enclosure, at its foot. With forced labour, motte-and-bailey castles could be built in a fortnight, and by 1100 at least 500 had been built in England alone. A defensive moat was sometimes added to provide an extra line of defence, as at Berkhamsted (right) in southern England. With the coming of more settled times, the bailey was occupied

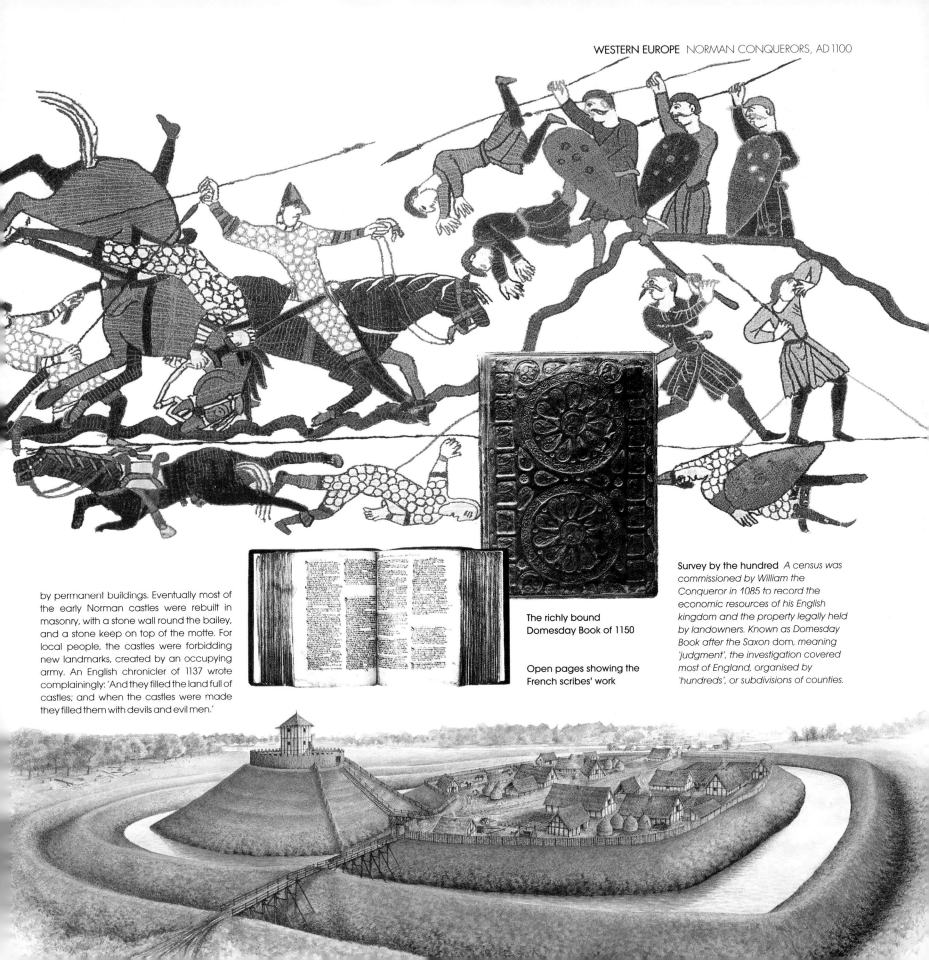

by permanent buildings. Eventually most of the early Norman castles were rebuilt in masonry, with a stone wall round the bailey, and a stone keep on top of the motte. For local people, the castles were forbidding new landmarks, created by an occupying army. An English chronicler of 1137 wrote complainingly: 'And they filled the land full of castles; and when the castles were made they filled them with devils and evil men.'

The richly bound Domesday Book of 1150

Open pages showing the French scribes' work

Survey by the hundred *A census was commissioned by William the Conqueror in 1085 to record the economic resources of his English kingdom and the property legally held by landowners. Known as Domesday Book after the Saxon* dom, *meaning 'judgment', the investigation covered most of England, organised by 'hundreds', or subdivisions of counties.*

WHEN WALLED TOWNS MEANT FREEDOM

'Town air makes men free', was a saying of the Middle Ages. In an era when most people were tied to the land, the property of their feudal lord, towns emerged as cradles of liberty. Within these colourful, exciting – and sometimes corrupt – hives of activity, life was lived according to rules very different from those of the countryside. Residents of a town obeyed an elected mayor and other officers. Instead of toiling to support nobles in castle or manor they paid taxes to the king, and raised from among themselves any money needed for their town's defence.

Town life revived during the 11th century, as the great wave of Dark Age unrest at last died away and something like orderly government settled

Ring of elegance *By the early 15th century, music and dance had become more popular, and their rhythms and patterns increasingly elaborate. These courtly Italians are performing a round dance, of a type still performed today.*

on European realms. Princes played their part in the urban reawakening. Ever short of funds, they allowed sizable settlements to become free boroughs, disconnected from the rule of the local manor, in exchange for cash payments. The granting of the town charter was the great symbolic event in this process. Once it was granted, the town council took up responsibility for administration. The towns themselves might be Roman cities reborn after

barbarian destruction, or wholly new communities, perhaps growing up at the gates of a medieval castle. Many developed in higgledy-piggledy fashion around the paths and boundaries of village field systems, which helped to account for their narrow, winding streets. The builders clearly liked them this way, however: a snug jigsaw of buildings served as a windbreak at a time when glass windows were rare. Among the major towns of Europe,

Paris was unusual in having not a mayor but a provost, who was representative of the king. But it was typical of many larger cities in beginning as an assemblage of scattered villages which connected up. This helps to account for its profusion of churches and abbeys. The intervening pasturage, vineyards and marshes bordering the Seine were only gradually built over.

The Parisian bridges were always of great importance, as in many medieval towns, and were early centres of commerce in their own right, having shops and stalls set up on them. The moneychangers occupied a bridge known from 1142 as Pont-au-Change. It was later, in the reign of Philip II Augustus (1180-1223), that the city was organised as a single unit, within a town wall and gates.

The thick, defensive town walls rose sheer from the fields, and the gates were locked at dusk to keep intruders out. There was no street lighting. A

Close-packed for defence *Medieval towns such as Cordes, in southern France, were built with their houses crammed together, both for ease of defence and to break the force of the wind. In spite of the risks of fire and disease, this type of town plan lingered on well after the Middle Ages.*

night guard of ordinary citizens patrolled the streets with flickering torches, and those found walking at night without good reason would be locked up. A town crier raised alarms.

Traders who named streets

Trading started at dawn; the market square, with the cathedral or great church, was the focus of town life, the point to which most roads from the town gates led. The shops of specialist tradesmen often led off the market square, related businesses being grouped together. This accounts for the names by which many streets are known today: Butchers' Row, Brewers'

Mixed bathing *In medieval towns, having a bath involved more than a good wash. Here couples eat and drink as they bathe.*

Street, Cornhill, Rue des Cordeliers, (street of leatherworkers), Rue de la Poissonnerie (fishmarket) and so on. The shops of fishmongers and tanners were usually situated on the outskirts of towns because of the pungent stenches issuing from them. On market days the wares of local tradespeople were supplemented by goods brought in from the countryside.

Shops were generally open-fronted, with shutters for night-time security which dropped down to form counters during the day. Many goods were made on the premises, and there were many trades in which customers brought their own materials; they might arrive with their own evening meal to be baked at the bakery, for example. Traders often hung signs outside their shops to indicate their business: a boot, say, or a fish. The barber's pole, painted red and white to symbolise his double role as shaver of beards and letter of blood, is a legacy of this time, when symbols served a largely illiterate public.

Among the privileges conferred by the town charter was the right of tradesmen to form guilds – associations designed to protect members' interests and to maintain standards. The guilds did much good work: assisting widows and orphans, and members who were sick. They helped to build churches and schools, and contributed to the upkeep of town walls and bridges. At festivals they staged morality plays. Townspeople had to take care when picking their way through the streets, for the filth was

appalling. People hurled rubbish and slops out of their windows into alleys that swarmed with rats and flies. Pigs scavenged through the squelching mud, and horses and dogs defecated freely. People, too, often relieved themselves in the streets; public latrines might be built on platforms over a river, or on ditches emptying into it, but such precautions only increased the risk of contamination to water supplies. Disease was rife. Many towns had a hospital sited well outside the city walls for the reception of poor people who were suffering from leprosy and other contagious diseases. Bathhouses, which were common in many towns, had large pools with heated water. A visit to these baths was a regular family practice, and in many cities bathing money was a regular part of a worker's salary. The baths were run by a guild, whose apprentices and journeymen were trained as rigorously as in any other guild. The baths had stringent rules regarding behaviour, but after mixed bathing became popular, promiscuity followed and by the 14th century the *bagnio* (Italian) or 'stew' (English) was often a brothel.

Despite much squalor, however, most towns had their fragrant areas, too. There were orchards and gardens scented with herbs and flowers, as well as green spaces for archery and ball games.

Morris man *A carving from Munich of a travelling showman dancing at carnival time has the bells round the legs associated with morris dancing throughout Europe.*

FUN AND TRADE AT THE FAIR

One big event for townsfolk in medieval Europe was the annual trade fair, which took place just outside the town walls and lasted for several days. Monarchs encouraged such fairs, both to foster trade and also to make a profit from tolls levied on the goods that merchants brought in for sale.

The commerce of the fair takes place in a carnival atmosphere. A stilt walker towers over the crowds, acrobats go through their paces, and lute-playing musicians amuse the onlookers. One merchant displays cloth and silks which may have come from China, and another has brought enough pots to keep the town's vintners supplied for the coming year. At other stalls customers will be haggling for wholesale supplies of Russian furs, French wines and Italian glass.

The fair is rigidly controlled. A mounted guard patrols, and the brightly painted tent houses a special court known as *pied-poudre*, where disputes can be settled while the disputants are still 'dusty-footed'.

GUILDS FOR MERCHANTS – AND ROBBERS

Burgess, burgher, bourgeois – all three words have the same root in an ancient German word, 'burg', meaning a fortified place. This was also the origin of the medieval walled town in northern Europe. Its burghers – solid citizens of the merchant class – acted as a dynamic force in medieval society. Separated from the land, and dealing in cash and commodities, they were looked down on by the feudal nobility, and mistrusted by churchmen, too, as usurers and frauds.

The merchant's daily round often included a visit to his guildhall. Many well-to-do townsmen were members of guilds, which became increasingly exclusive as the centuries passed. A rigid system developed, by which parents would make a payment to a master-craftsman to train one of their children as an apprentice for a period of up to seven years, beginning at 11 or 12. During this time the youth was unpaid, or lived on very low wages, but was given board and lodging in his master's house, perhaps sleeping on the workshop floor.

> 'When I see the draper in his house, methinks he hath no clear conscience. Dark is the window where he bargaineth with thee, and scarce canst thou tell the green from the blue.'
>
> JOHN GOWER, 1330-1407

After training, the apprentice became a journeyman, working for wages on a day-to-day basis. Then, after a further period of years, he would be required to produce a top-quality test piece of his work, known as a 'masterpiece'. If sufficiently skilled, he was accepted into the guild and permitted to have a shop and apprentices of his own.

The wealthier families gradually came to control the guilds, so that many craftsmen without influence were condemned to spend their lives as journeymen, and were never able to achieve admission to the rank of master. Life as a medieval merchant

was comfortable, but only a small number of townsfolk enjoyed this lifestyle. Below them a layer of people lived in poverty, untrained for work of any consequence. Their lot was sweated labour and the dirtiest carrying jobs, or scraping a living as pimps, scavengers, beggars, swindlers, street-cleaners, or thieves. Even among these a form of guild system operated: there were illegal associations of robbers and beggars.

This dispossessed rabble formed a disquieting element in the lives of the solid burghers on whom the town's wealth was founded. From its menacing tenements came the 'cutpurses', so called because they cut off the purses that dangled from the belts of the wealthy, at a time when sewn-in pockets were still unknown.

To live inside a town meant living in a largely self-governing community. Every freeman was a member of at least the lowest congregation or great council, while the better-born and

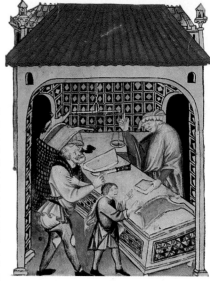

Signed and sealed *Every wealthy merchant had his own seal, often with a religious design. These English seals show (top) the Virgin and Child, and (bottom) the Lamb and Flag.*

well-to-do belonged to the higher echelons of government. Being a member of this community might involve unpaid services for the public good – as one of a force of nightwatchmen and street patrols, for example. There were paid officials, too, their jobs financed by rates and taxes, who were charged with improving and defending the city, enforcing the law and providing a range of services. There were varied forms of tax assessment. Among the most unusual and effective systems was the one practised in Nuremberg: individuals assessed their own liability to tax and paid over

Only the best cuts *A farmer brings his haunches of meat to the butcher, who bargains to get them at the lowest price.*

All services provided *The medieval town crammed its shops into a small space. In this French street the traders include tailor, furrier, barber and grocer.*

Drapers' forum *A shrine in a street of drapers ensures their honest dealing. Their wares are laid out on counters and trestles.*

the requisite sum. While there were many poorly paid labourers who toiled at heavy, dirty work, and were not freemen, many of the craftsmen were literate, intelligent and highly skilled. Luxury craftsmen flourished in cities such as Paris, which was famous for silk weaving, furniture making, gold and silver ware, musical instruments, illuminated manuscripts and printing.

Nuremberg was known throughout Europe for its prodigious industrial skills. Among its specialist craftsmen, belonging to 140 separate guilds, were gunsmiths, locksmiths, makers of scientific instruments, scales and spectacle lenses, playing-card illuminators, makers of spigots for barrels, and producers of gut strings for viols.

Some of the names of these craftsmen are still remembered today. Hans Lobsinger, for example, designed and built sawmills and stamping mills, hydraulic fountains and polishing machines operated by foot treadles. Hans and Leonhard Donner made jacks and other lifting devices. Georg Weaver made counterweights, while Hans Eheman devised a keyless lock.

Courted by kings and princes

Such cities were full of entertainment and culture. They had their own plays, music, balls and dances, and they built magnificent churches and public buildings to compete with their neighbours and rivals. A merchant from such a city had a full, satisfying life. If he was a member of the small inner power elite, not only would he decide on matters relating to his own craft or trade but he might also be able to influence city policy, and even take part in decision making at a national level. Wealthy merchants were courted by kings and princes, who often needed help in raising money, or arranging for a supply of weapons.

At all levels of society, life in medieval towns was patriarchal. It was a husband's duty to control his household, which meant chastising wife, children and servants whenever he thought it necessary. Failure to do so might lead to a public shaming, by means of the 'skimmington' ritual: accompanied by a procession banging drums, a man representing the husband, wearing horns and seated back-to-front on a mule, was struck with a ladle by a woman representing the wife, while the crowd shouted and jeered outside the victim's house.

Women were expected to obey their male kin. Their principal role was the management of hearth and home – cooking, cleaning, bearing children, and caring for the sick and elderly. The most important decisions taken on their behalf were the choice of a husband and the details of their marriage contract, which made provision for their maintenance. Their commonest employment was the spinning of wool or flax, which gave the unmarried girl her name of 'spinster'.

Women as brewers and bakers

From the age of about nine or ten, most girls were sent away from their families to work as domestic servants. But women also worked at various trades, alongside male relatives or on their own. They worked in the textile and clothing business, in brewing and baking and in the provisioning trade. They made shoes, gloves and hats, and ran inns and taverns. They might be apprenticed to trades as different as pin-makers and printers.

A widow often carried on her late husband's business in her own right, when she would employ her own apprentices and journeymen. Women's beliefs about the world they lived in strongly influenced the moral fabric of medieval town life. Gossiping as they worked, they kept an eye on the comings and goings of people in the community, and passed their own effective judgment on them.

FROM SCOLD'S BRIDLE TO BURNING AT THE STAKE

Enforcing the law in a medieval town was the task of specially appointed town courts. A woman who abused family or neighbours in public might be convicted as a 'scold' and sentenced to wear a bridle whose bit held her tongue still. Public brawling and drunkenness might land an offender in the stocks, or see him whipped. Whores were whipped at the cart's tail, often followed by a mocking crowd who threw rotten fruit.

Punishment was intended to match the crime. Long-term imprisonment was rare; instead, retribution was usually sudden and dramatic. A thief might have his hand cut off, and a malcontent who wrote against the government might lose the hand that held the pen. Slanderers might have their ears cropped. Hanging was common not only for murder, but for rioting and serious robbery.

Suspected witches often had to undergo trial by water. This involved being thrown into a pool: if the accused floated, she was judged guilty and executed, while if she sank she was deemed innocent – but died anyway. Witches, like heretics, were burned at the stake; this form of execution was held to cleanse the earth of the witches' evil influence by the purifying effect of fire.

The town council took great care to maintain the quality and quantity of the food supply. The use of false weights and measures was punished by the ducking stool. A butcher who sold horseflesh as venison, or a baker who weighted his loaves with stones to cheat the customer who paid by weight, would be put in the stocks. A dishonest brewer might be forced to drink massive quantities of his own ale – and have the remainder tipped over him.

Lesser offences would be punished by a fine, which helped to pay for enforcing the law. For offences against ecclesiastical laws, the Church held its own courts; fornicators and adulterers might find themselves shamed in public, wearing the garb of a penitent and carrying candles.

Rough justice *Cutting off the hand was the penalty for serious and persistent theft.*

Wife beater *A husband had the right to beat his wife as a discipline, but not while under the influence of drink, or in an outburst of bad temper. Such aggression was often held to be the result of unsuitable diet.*

FOOD AND FINERY IN A TOWN HOUSE

Shortsighted saint *Glasses for myopia were invented around 1280. This 14th-century miniature is the earliest-known picture of spectacles.*

Houses in medieval towns were built with two or more floors, with storeys jettied out, or projecting one above the other. This increased the floor space upstairs – but it also darkened and narrowed the thoroughfares outside, contributing to the dark and airless atmosphere of medieval town streets.

Individual plots were often narrow and ran back from the street with long back gardens or yards. In the early Middle Ages, when towns were less congested and village traditions still very much alive, pigs, chickens and even cows might be kept at the back. A hole dug here might also serve as a privy, though many merchants' houses had cellars with a cesspit beneath. These needed regular cleaning out, a noxious job often done by operators in the 'night cartage of filth'. Homes had no water on tap. For household purposes water was fetched from river or well, or bought from water carriers in the street. Nor were there bathrooms; for a full immersion in warm water, people went to the public bathhouse.

The kitchen was often erected as a separate building in the yard, again as a precaution against fire. Medieval kitchen equipment included pestle and mortar, bunches of twigs for whisking, and quantities of scouring sand, used in washing up. There were long-handled pots and long-handled pans, though frying was less common than boiling. One reason for this was the relative scarcity of animal fat, which was more urgently needed for soap, candles and axle grease than for cooking. Not all cooking was done at home, for few homes had ovens. Wives and servants often took ingredients to a specialist: pie materials to a piemaker, for example.

Merchants dined very amply and clearly enjoyed pastries, whether crammed with fruit or berries, or with savouries such as chopped ham, soft cheese, lark or eel. Already, French wines from the Bordeaux region were prized, sometimes bought in leather 'hoses' shaped like a man's leg. Householders' furnishings became more elaborate as the years passed. By the 13th century,

Difficult labour *Though many medieval women died giving birth, the mother and baby in this picture, from a sequence of six childbed scenes, both survived the ordeal.*

Toby jug's ancestor *This 14th-century pottery jug is crudely modelled as a head.*

Eating in style *By 1400 pewter dishes were used for serving food.*

A SHOP AT THE FRONT AND A HOME AT THE BACK

The medieval merchant's house is family home, workshop and shop combined. On the ground floor, the cloth merchant and his assistant display wares which have been made on the premises. The shop front is open, with a shutter to close it at night. The shutter is built on a pivot, and during the day can be hinged downwards to serve as a trestle on which to display goods.

At the back of the house a cauldron of soup bubbles over an open fire; the smoke finds its way out through the gaps between walls and roof. A servant keeps an eye on the pot, while a wet nurse is cradling the latest addition to the family. At the rear of the house is the scullery. Upstairs, in the main bedroom, the merchant's wife lies in bed, having recently given birth. The doctor doses her with a herbal tonic, watched from the doorway by the obligatory chaperone. An image of the Virgin on the wall testifies to the wife's piety. Some merchants' houses were built of stone, but most were wooden and therefore very vulnerable to fire. The spaces between the timbers were filled with wattle, or interlaced branches, and daub, or clay. Houses were draughty, as the windows had no glass and only wooden shutters.

Winter warmer The cold months of winter were the traditional time for eating and drinking more than usual. Here a wealthy merchant, well wrapped in a fur-lined coat, warms himself by the fire, while his servants bring in soup and meat from the kitchen.

well-to-do people slept in wooden beds decorated with carvings and painted ornaments, and used linen sheets, pillows and embroidered coverlets. To give privacy in shared bedrooms – and also to keep out the draughts – curtains were hung around beds from ceilings, or from iron arms projecting from walls. The first four-posters developed from this tradition. With hanging lamps, these curtained beds were rooms within rooms.

Glass was still rare for household cups and vessels, but glass windows started to appear in merchants' houses in the 14th century. The small panes were set in a latticework of lead or wood mullions within an iron frame, and could often be removed by their owner and taken to a new home. Glass mirrors were among the wealth of new artefacts brought back by the Crusaders. The Arabs had made glass lenses as early as the 11th century; two centuries later spectacles came to Europe.

Increased contact with the East, which came through the Crusades, also changed home interiors. Tapestries, for example, began to replace plain baize in richer merchants' houses as wall hangings and as covers for cushions, stools and benches. Carpets appeared on floors, and not all of them were imported. From the 12th century onwards, European manufacturers started to make their own carpets, copying Turkish and Persian originals.

Rich fabrics and bright colours

Fabrics became richer as the Crusaders introduced cotton, diaphanous muslin (the word is derived from Mosul), patterned damask (from Damascus), and gauze (from Gaza). All these helped to transform medieval costume, which became ever more fanciful and exotic. Married women, for example, were expected to cover their hair, and in the early Middle Ages they generally wore a plain white wimple – a cloth framing the face and drawn into folds under the chin. At a later period, horned, mitred and steeple-shaped headdresses appeared, hung with gauzy veils. Pied and striped colours were used in men's costume, and in the

14th century, garments were often decorated by 'dagging' – ornamental cutting at the edges, with zigzags and various other shapes.

Noblemen often wore ultra-short tunics, exposing much more of the tightly hosed leg than churchmen thought proper. Dandies' ludicrously long, pointed shoes became so slender that to make walking possible the tips had to be chained up and fastened at the knee. These 'devil's clawes, snouted and piked', were abominated by the Church, and laws were passed to try to limit their length.

Keeping merchants in their place

Wealthy burghers vied with the nobility for showiness, edging their garments with expensive furs and going about sparkling with jewellery. However, such extravagance by commoners seemed to threaten the stability of the established feudal order, so laws were passed to keep them in their place. By the 14th century, in many countries, merchants were distinguished by the long dark robes they were required to wear so as not to compete with the vivid styles of their aristocratic superiors.

A garment favoured by commoners rich and poor was the capuchon, a hood with a short cape extending over the shoulders. Merchants often wore this twisted up on their heads like a turban. Both men and women wore their master's livery, for clothing was part of a servant's remuneration. Men wore the garments of their trade, such as a chef's hat, and the needy sometimes earned clothes by acting as mourners at great funerals. The monarch provided his judges and officers with clothing twice a year, in winter and summer, and merchants' wills often mention gifts of clothes to aid the poor.

Upstairs toilet By the late 15th century, latrines were becoming common even in ordinary houses. Here a communal latrine is perched high up between the upper storeys of two buildings; but the man at ground level is making use of a convenient corner.

Safe-keeping Doorlocks meant a burden of keys.

Portable cutlery Early spoons were so precious that they folded for carrying to meals.

HERBS FOR DUBIOUS FOOD

Medieval cooking relied on strong flavouring to improve the taste of dubious food, especially meat kept in a larder that was often none too clean and none too cool. So the burgher's wife grew a wide selection of herbs at her kitchen door. Besides home-grown seasonings such as thyme, garlic and peony seeds, salt was readily available, mustard and saffron were farmed, and pepper from the East was brought to towns in quantities by merchants.

Sugar, however, was a scarce commodity. The taste for it was brought back by returning Crusaders, along with maize, lemons and melons, but cones of cane sugar were so costly that they were kept locked away.

Fish was a widespread food, since the Church had decreed that no one should eat meal on Fridays (or on Saturdays and Wednesdays in the early Middle Ages). Meat, eggs and other dairy foods were banned throughout Lent, so that about half the days of the year were regarded as 'fish days'. Fish was cooked with parsley and fennel, and herrings were popular fare.

SERMONS IN STONE, WOOD AND GLASS

For a medieval European community, the decision to build a cathedral was an enormous undertaking, calling for a staggering investment in resources and labour. Most cathedrals dwarfed the settlements around them; a fair-sized town in medieval times had a population of around 5000 people – and a cathedral such as Chartres could hold them all.

Little wonder that many cathedrals took a century or more to complete. 'Happy he who will live to see the church completed!' yearned the poet Henri d'Avranches. Yet in France alone, 80 cathedrals as well as several hundred abbeys were completed between 1180 and 1270; and in Europe as a whole 500 cathedrals were raised within four centuries.

Even in an age of economic prosperity, the task of raising the money to buy the materials and pay the workers to build a cathedral provided a challenge for local ingenuity. Often the bishop and his chapter of monks or canons bore the main burden; they diverted revenues from estates, and ran fundraising campaigns to tap royal and other benefactors. At Rouen, in

Lifting by muscle power *The crane's hand-operated wheel needs the strength of two men to control it. Thongs hold the scaffolding together.*

HIGH SKILLS IN AN AGE OF STONE

Building a church or cathedral called for all the technology of the Middle Ages. Masons carved stone for the walls and for the window tracery, letting their fancy run riot in sinister gargoyles or graceful statues of saints. Woodcarvers worked oak into choir stalls and altars, while artists in stained glass filled the vast spaces of the windows with glowing depictions of scenes from the Bible.

A mason's training usually began in the quarries, where he hammered in wooden wedges to tear out the stone, or shaped it roughly before it was carried to the building site. Later the apprentice was promoted to laying shaped blocks in position, and finally to carving. At this stage he acquired his own personal mark, often a simple, angular

shape such as a star or a cross. A finished block normally bore three different marks, showing who had carved it, which quarry it came from (so that the owner could receive payment), and where it should be placed.

Even senior clerics often lent a hand with the manual work. One chronicler praised St Hugh of Avalon, a 12th-century Bishop of Lincoln, for his enthusiasm and toil: 'He supplied not only his own wealth, and the labours of his servants, but the sweat of his own brow; for he oftentimes bore the hod-load of hewn stone or building lime.'

Shaping *Skilled masons, daggers ready to hand, use adzes, rulers and T-squares.*

Mixing *A labourer prepares a load of lime mortar.*

Normandy, the cathedral's south-west tower, known as the Tour de Beurre, was paid for with proceeds from the sale of indulgences allowing people to eat butter during the Lenten fast. Siena, in Italy, required every owner of a beast of burden to provide an annual load of marble. Some benefactors gave stone, timber or labour.

The first Freemasons

Unskilled labour was recruited locally; many volunteered for the work, expecting special grace as their reward. The serious business, however, was left to the professionals. Carpenters were required in large numbers: their first tasks were to make carts and barges for transporting materials to the site, and to erect a stout shelter, often a lean-to against an existing wall, where the masons could continue to carve through the winter months. Called a 'lodge', this was the origin of the lodges of the Freemasons' Order. Carpenters also made the tools, scaffolding, platforms, ramps and pulleys.

Standing at the top of his profession was the master mason, who combined the roles of architect, supervisor and materials contractor. He oversaw the progress of work in the quarry, in the lodge and on site, as well as liaising with his patron. Successful master masons, such as Henry Yevele

at Canterbury, were well-paid figures who mingled with the powerful and educated. The vast Gothic cathedrals of the late 12th and 13th centuries are notable for their immense window spaces. Made to fill these spaces was stained glass of superb artistry, its brilliant colours achieved with a palette only of white, blue, yellow, green, red and purple. The themes chosen for these windows showed how this world and the next are linked, and explained the Bible to the illiterate.

The shrine of Thomas Becket at Canterbury was adorned with no fewer than 200 scenes of his life, martyrdom and miracles. Windows at Chartres depict 43 city trades, including the guild of barrel-makers – whose window shows Noah as the first vine-grower.

Kings, saints and Noah's Ark

The cathedrals were also embellished with magnificent sculptures. Wells had 400 statues on its west front, and Chartres had more than 2000. While kings and saints adorned prominent niches, small-scale carvings in less obvious places often dealt with more down-to-earth or humorous subjects. Salisbury's chapter house has a frieze showing Old Testament scenes such as Noah's Ark and the fall of Sodom and Gomorrah, while a carving at Wells portrays a man with toothache. Sculptures at Amiens show virtues and vices. Cowardice is shown as a knight fleeing a hare, and Rebellion as a man snapping his fingers at a bishop.

Paintings were used on walls and on the ceilings of side chapels – William of Malmesbury wrote of Canterbury's 'coloured pictures that led the wandering eye to the very summit of the ceiling'. The crucifixion depicted on the wall of a side aisle provided an altar at which to celebrate the eucharist on busy days. The adornment of the high altar, however, was

of major importance. When Duccio finished a 92 panel altarpiece for Siena cathedral in 1311, the entire city took a holiday.

As the town's largest building, a cathedral was the natural place for public meetings; the entrance area often acted as an informal labour exchange, the crypt as an overnight shelter for pilgrims and the walls a base for traders. But a cathedral was, above all, the focus of a town's religious life, a setting for worship. Behind the bishop loomed a spiritual hierarchy which extended to the Pope, to St Peter, and to Christ. The bishop's palace was usually next to the cathedral, and from it he and a household of officials presided over the spiritual and temporal welfare of the community. A chain of command ran downwards through archdeacons and rural deans to rectors and vicars. Below them served the unbeneficed clergy who sang masses for the dead, and the attendants not in holy orders – deacons, vergers, incense-bearers.

Many priests were accepted as the arbiters of village disputes, and as the community's representatives in their dealings with the outside world. Most pastors worked their own 'glebe' – the land assigned to a church to provide the priest's living. Toiling at backbreaking work in the fields on weekdays, priests were only distinguishable from their parishioners on Sundays when, robed in simple vestments, they performed their office.

Joined in marriage *A priest joins the hands of a couple during a 14th-century wedding. As the Middle Ages progressed, the Church played a greater part in marriage, which became less secular.*

Priest's vision *A priest prays over his psalter before a miraculous appearance of the Virgin and Child. Priests were expected to teach the village children their prayers, to carry out the sacraments of baptism, marriage and burial, and to hear confession.*

Time past *Mechanical clocks gave monks a means of marking the hours of darkness, so that they could perform their devotions at the correct hours. Wells Cathedral, in western England, had this clock around 1390.*

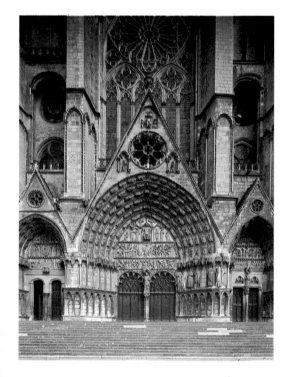

Gothic glory *Huge trade fairs helped to raise money to build the great medieval cathedrals. The decorated portals of Bourges symbolise the idea of the cathedral as a 'Gateway to Heaven'.*

FROM THUG TO KNIGHT ERRANT

The Norman knights who landed on the Sussex coast on that fateful day in October 1066 were tough, hard-bitten warriors, with little appreciation for the refinements of life. The Hastings locals thought that they were priests because of their close-cropped hair – the mark, in England, of a man in holy orders. However, it was not long before the younger Normans began to copy the long, curled hairstyles of the English nobles, which moralists found effeminate; while their clothes became more flowing and elaborate.

Side by side with this increasing sophistication went a development in the concept of knighthood. As the Middle Ages progressed, knighthood became a vocation surrounded by a mystique that took it far from the brute realities known to the first armoured horsemen. To qualify as a knight, candidates had to embark on a long apprenticeship at the age of seven, when they were sent away to serve as pages in a great lord's castle. Training in swordsmanship and horse riding followed. At the age of about 14, the page became a squire and ran errands and did chores for a particular knight. It was not until he was about 21 that he was formally dubbed knight.

Chivalry is the name given to the idealised qualities of knighthood, which included honesty, courtesy and a readiness to defend the weak. Though loutish realities often belied these virtues, gallant standards were at least set and followed by many. One area in which the ideal quickly became

Holding the horse *For about seven years, from the age of 14, a squire attended his knight, carrying out such tasks as looking after his horse and weapons, and running errands.*

submerged by brutal reality was the tournament. This started out as a free-for-all melee among hot blooded young members of the military caste, who formed teams and engaged in bloody mock battles. At one such event, at Lagny-sur-Marne in France in 1180, more than 3000 mounted knights took part, and the field was left littered with dead and wounded at sundown.

In vain did the church fulminate against such diversions, and try to direct young knights into such pastimes as hunting with hawks and hounds. The games were regarded as necessary rehearsals for warfare. 'A knight cannot shine in war if he has not prepared for it in tournaments,' wrote one chronicler. 'He must have seen his own blood flow, have had his teeth crackle under the blow of an adversary.' A losing knight, even if he survived, still paid a heavy penalty: he forfeited horse and armour, and might be taken prisoner and held for ransom.

As time passed, however, more orderly forms of combat gradually came to replace the original free-for-alls. Jousting became a favourite form of entertainment, for example. Two armoured knights with blunted lances met one another at a headlong gallop, before crowds who watched from stands decked with pennants. And true to the traditions of courtly love, ladies bestowed on their favoured knights personal tokens, such as a handkerchief or ring.

Wild birds for the table

From the thrill of the tournament, knights and nobles returned to lives of isolation within their castles and fortified manors. Families attended chapel every morning, and for pastimes there were chess, backgammon and dice. Cooking was done in stone-floored kitchens with wide fireplaces, and much roasting on the spit. This was mounted on firedogs and turned by apprentice cooks, by boy scullions who might sleep on the kitchen floor at night, or by dogs which were trained by having live coals put beneath their feet.

Poultry, game birds and all kinds of fowl were particularly popular among

Deadly stroke *The tournament was nothing less than practice for real battle, and often led to serious wounds or even death. These early contestants in the lists battle in chain mail; in later years, jousts were fought in full plate armour. The personal insignia on the knights' surcoats and shields were the origin of coats of arms.*

the Normans. Many a manor had its own dovecote and poultry yard, whilst wild birds were also trapped or hunted with falcons. Dishes might include birds, from blackbird to heron, and also rabbits – warrens were a prized and protected right of the lords. At banquets, dressed swan was a favourite.

Although the great hall was still the central feature of all manors and castles, more specialised rooms were coming into being. By screening off one end, for example, the lord made a small private room, called a solar, for himself and his lady. And as buildings became more elaborate, the lady herself, secluded in her chamber, became a focus for the illicit passions associated with courtly love.

This romantic concept was spread by travelling troubadours in the 12th century. It glorified the love of a knight for his chosen lady, who might be anybody but his own wife. Sir Lancelot's love for King Arthur's Guinevere was in this tradition. The villagers lived in poorer conditions. Only low, windowless hovels built of earth and sods under a rough bracken thatch sheltered them and their cattle from the cold and rain. After nightfall peeled rushes dipped in goose fat or tallow provided light when necessary. Not until the 13th century did their housing improve, sooner in France than in other countries. Some village folk might themselves be free persons, or hold freehold land. Many, however, were unfree villeins, or

Into the woods *A squire seeks to persuade a maiden that experience in courtly love is a necessary part of his training in chivalry.*

Thirsty work *A knight making do-it-yourself repairs to his armour is offered a pie and a goblet of wine by a girl attendant.*

cottars, holding their share of the village fields and the rights to run animals on the commons and to take firewood from the forest in return for services to their lord. These services included prescribed days of labour on the land of their lord – with or without their own animals – the carting of the lord's goods, various chores, and fixed payment of their own produce, such as hens and eggs.

The church was an important focus of activity, with its calendar of holiday festivities. Built at first of wood or wattle and daub, churches were later rebuilt in stone, with solid rounded arches. At the lord's mill and bakehouse, people gathered to have their corn ground and their bread baked, handing over a proportion in return. Daily life followed its time-honoured patterns, with back-breaking toil in the farming of fields and the tending of livestock. At fair times the monotony would be broken by travelling entertainers: acrobats, jugglers, puppeteers and storytellers.

A lord governed through agents such as his bailiff, and the reeve – usually one of the villeins, who supervised the men at work. The Normans policed their lands with some vigour, and they brought to England the continental practice of trial by battle, in which two freemen would settle a dispute by fighting until one submitted. Accusations and counter-accusations were voiced first, and the men fought under oath, it being assumed that God would grant victory to the one who had sworn truly.

A SQUIRE'S GREAT DAY

For Gilbert who had been in training – first as page, then as squire – since the age of seven, this was the long-awaited day, when he would receive his sword and spurs in the ceremony of knighthood. On the evening before, he had been ritually cleansed in a bath of rosewater, then stayed all night at prayer alone in the church. In the morning he attended Mass amid the smoke of incense and the glow of candles. Now, with heart pumping, he walked slowly before a large congregation of wellwishers towards the altar where the priest stood waiting, holding the blade he was to consecrate.

'Bless this sword, that thy servant may henceforward defend churches, widows, orphans, and all those who serve God, against the cruelty of heretics and infidels. Bless this sword, Holy Lord, Almighty Father, Eternal God...', the priest's words echoed around the choir where Gilbert knelt. When the blessing was over, his lord stepped forward and delivered the *colée* – a light blow to the cheek – before girding the sword around the youth's waist. Spurs were attached to his heels. Gilbert was now a knight; he brandished his sword three times to acknowledge the honour, then returned the blade to its scabbard.

SLAUGHTER BY KNIGHTS AND BOWMEN

Head first *A knight struggles into his chain-mail armour. Though it weighed 30 lb (13.5 kg), the thousands of links of which it was formed made it surprisingly pliable.*

During their heyday in the 12th-13th centuries, bands of mailed knights, galloping at poorly trained foot soldiers, made themselves masters of medieval warfare. They were terrifying figures, made all the more awesome by the great cylindrical helmet which protected the head, and the heraldic devices blazoned on their shields and linen surcoats.

Knightly codes of elegant combat may have counted for something in a handful of set-piece engagements. But most fighting in the days of chivalry was, in reality, small-scale and squalid. Knights made armed raids into enemy territory, and civilians unprotected by castle fortifications or city walls were beaten and plundered.

The most common form of engagement was the siege. To the defeated, knights often showed no mercy. The French chronicler Froissart, for example, described how Edward, England's Black Prince, commanded his troops to massacre the citizens of Limoges after taking the city by siege in 1370. More than 3000 people perished, amid much piteous weeping.

Mounted men-at-arms, of whom knights were the elite, provided the cutting blade of early medieval armies; infantry were kept back to form a secure base in battle.

Knights and nobles led their own formations of armoured men, each man-at-arms being served by a squire and pages, and often an archer. The group was called a 'lance'.

A charge by a formation of knights was terrifying and usually conclusive, but knights were at risk in one respect: having weighed themselves down with

Turmoil at the gate *A besieger hauls on a trebuchet, or giant catapult, to hurl boulders against a city's walls. An archer using a longbow fires at attacking knights, while defenders make a sortie from the city gate. Swords and battle-axes slice through armour, and the dead fall underfoot.*

full armour, they were vulnerable if unhorsed. It is a myth to suppose that fallen knights lay helpless, like beetles on their backs, but it did take effort and time, particularly for the elderly, unfit or obese, to arise – and time was not always available. Many knights, fallen on their faces, had their helmets battered into their skulls with clubs, while the last sight for those fallen on their backs was of the visor being raised and the glint of steel before an enemy dagger was plunged through an eye and into the brain.

The era of heavy cavalry was to pass, however. The beginning of the end was signalled in 1392 by the Battle of Nicopolis, in which a western army of mounted knights was overthrown by a Turkish force strengthened by highly disciplined janissary foot soldiers. By the time of the Battle of Agincourt in 1415, though mounted knights still staged spectacular charges, infantry played a much more important role.

> '*The French were boasting that they would cut off three fingers of the right hand of all the archers that should be taken prisoners, to the end that neither man nor horse should ever again be killed with their arrows.*'
>
> FRENCH KNIGHT AT AGINCOURT, 1415

Before the introduction of artillery, the knights' worst enemy was the might of the bowmen. There were two types of bow: the crossbow, favoured by continental armies, and the longbow, favoured by the English and Welsh. The crossbow was an extremely accurate weapon, and the speed and impact of a crossbow bolt enabled it to penetrate armour impervious to other missiles.

The longbow, a weapon of Welsh origin adapted by the English, could produce a much greater rate of fire than the crossbow – up to ten arrows a minute in the hands of a skilled bowman. Its range, however, was some 280 yds (256 m), slightly less than that of the crossbow. It was less accurate, too, but its rate of fire compensated for these disadvantages.

Longbows were made of staves of yew or elm, 6 ft (1.8 m) long, tensioned by a bowstring. So highly valued by English kings was the experienced longbowman during the Hundred

Years' War (1338-1453) that he was given the high rate of payment for the time of sixpence a day.

For the longbowman, as for the lowly foot soldier, life on campaign was a gruelling existence. A day's march, even without military action, might cover 12 miles, the distance being set for the convenience of the horses, not the soldiers. Moreover, soldiers were subject to brutal military discipline, including summary punishment ranging from flogging to hanging, to fines or additional duties for lesser offences, such as theft or sleeping on watch.

Disease the worst enemy

Food was minimal, uncertain in delivery and unappetising; soldiers had to forage for extra supplies. Pay for a foot soldier on campaign amounted to little more than a civilian received for a day's labour, and it was often paid in arrears. Soldiers had to endure intense heat in summer and freezing conditions in winter. They were more likely to die from plague or dysentery than in battle. The commissariat had to find grain for the soldier's daily loaf, hand mills to grind it and portable ovens to bake it, and also beer, salted fish and cheese. All this, as well as tents and soldiers' personal gear, had to be transported, so that carts and wagons were added to the train. An English campaign in France might entail 50,000 people on the march, including whores and others in search of easy pickings.

Why, then, did any young civilian enlist and take the 'king's shilling' – the sum which, once accepted, was deemed to bind a recruit to the army? In many cases he was forcibly recruited; in others he volunteered because of famine at home. There was, too, always the prospect of profit through plunder or ransom. As well as its recruits, every army had its mercenaries, who fought under a contract for anyone who was willing to employ them, and acknowledged no authority but that of their elected leader.

Safety helmet *The hinged visor, shaped to deflect missiles, is bordered by a Biblical blessing to protect the wearer.*

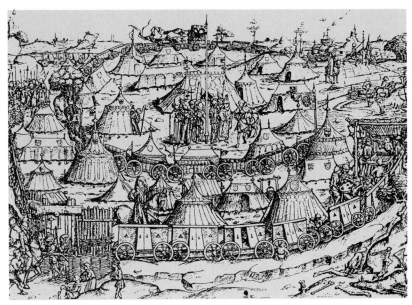

Fortress of wagons *The wagenburg, a ring of wagons linked by a chain and defended by cannons and bowmen, evolved in Bohemia in the 15th century. It foreshadowed the tactics used 400 years later by American pioneers defending themselves against hostile Indians.*

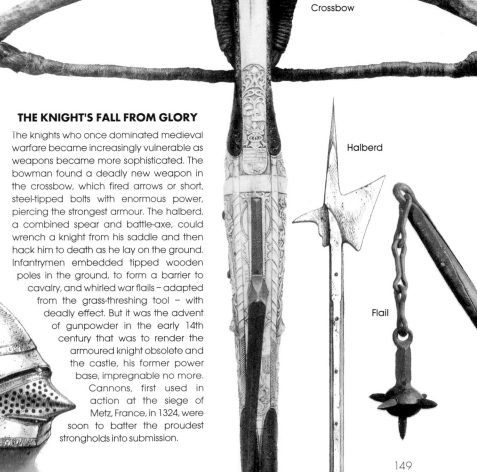

Crossbow

Halberd

Flail

THE KNIGHT'S FALL FROM GLORY

The knights who once dominated medieval warfare became increasingly vulnerable as weapons became more sophisticated. The bowman found a deadly new weapon in the crossbow, which fired arrows or short, steel-tipped bolts with enormous power, piercing the strongest armour. The halberd, a combined spear and battle-axe, could wrench a knight from his saddle and then hack him to death as he lay on the ground. Infantrymen embedded tipped wooden poles in the ground, to form a barrier to cavalry, and whirled war flails – adapted from the grass-threshing tool – with deadly effect. But it was the advent of gunpowder in the early 14th century that was to render the armoured knight obsolete and the castle, his former power base, impregnable no more. Cannons, first used in action at the siege of Metz, France, in 1324, were soon to batter the proudest strongholds into submission.

HORROR DANCE OF THE BLACK DEATH

'My brother! My brother! alas what shall I say? Whither shall I turn? On all sides is sorrow, everywhere is fear. I would that I had never been born, or, at least had died before these times. When before has it been seen that houses are left vacant, cities deserted, fields are too small for the dead, and a fearful and universal solitude covers the whole earth?'

So wrote the Italian poet, Petrarch, from Parma on May 19, 1348. The bitter lament was addressed to his brother – the sole survivor of a monastery that had once contained 35 people. They were victims of the Black Death, a cataclysm that had reached Europe in 1347. It claimed many of Petrarch's closest friends as well as the lady who inspired some of his finest poems, the young and beautiful Laura, who died in April 1348.

Death and disease were no strangers to the filth-ridden towns and villages of medieval Europe. But the Black Death was a visitation of annihilating ferocity. It is believed to have begun in central Asia, spreading to China and India, then into the Crimea and Europe. The plague was carried along trading routes by the black rat; this creature played host to *Ceratophyllus fasciatus*, the flea that harboured the plague bacillus.

One route by which the pestilence entered Europe was through Tatar warriors who in 1346 laid siege to the port of Caffa on the Crimean coast. Their own forces were riddled with the plague, and they used giant catapults to lob corpses high over the town walls, thus contaminating the inhabitants. Merchants fleeing the city of Genoa sailed home, bringing the pestilence with them. The most common form of the disease was the bubonic plague, characterised by painful swellings known as buboes in the groin and armpits. Vomiting, fever and delirium were other symptoms, but it was possible for victims to recover from it after some days. More virulent were the pneumonic and septicaemic plagues, which afflicted the lungs and bloodstream. In the septicaemic plague, a perfectly healthy person might become infected during the day and be dead by nightfall.

Italy was among the first European countries to be hit, and the poets Petrarch and Boccaccio are just two of the writers who have left accounts of the plague's tragic effects. In the early days, when proper funerals were still being held for victims, no bells were allowed to be rung from the churches for fear of spreading panic. Later, though, deaths were so widespread that corpses were dumped without ceremony in mass pits.

Rituals of the Flagellants

Above all, the plague seemed to embody the wrath of God brought down on sinful humanity. In Germany, Flanders and parts of France bizarre rituals were enacted by self-punishing Flagellants – men and women who whipped themselves to a frenzy with metal-tipped scourges to atone for their sins. Processions of up to a thousand black cowled figures, men in the lead, women behind, wound their way through the countryside and into towns and villages. Here, before the rapt gaze of the populace, they formed a large circle and stripped to the waist, piling their discarded clothes inside the circle. Then, at a signal from their leader, they prostrated themselves on the ground,

'Many died daily or nightly in the public streets: of many others who died at home the departure was hardly observed until the stench of their putrefying bodies carried the tidings.'

GIOVANNI BOCCACCIO, 1351

Angel of death *Superstition held that someone in every household died when a 'bad angel' struck the door with her lance. Each blow of the lance heralded a death. This fearsome image is from one of many 'Dance of Death' pictures and sculptures made during the plague. Twin carriers of the plague were the black rat and the flea that lives on it (below). Flea-bitten rats died, and the fleas on them transferred to humans, so spreading the disease.*

Under the lash *A procession of Flagellants marches on 'pilgrimage'. Where they stopped they whipped themselves to a frenzy with scourges, to atone for sins and so avert God's wrath and the plague.*

Burial for the victims *In the early stages of the plague, coffins were still available, as in this burial at Tournai in Belgium. Later on, as the victims grew more numerous and wood ran short, the dead were bundled into pits.*

often with arms outstretched, as though crucified. The leader passed among them wielding a multi-thonged, metal-tipped scourge, thrashing those who had adopted certain postures specially designed for sinners – face to the ground for adulterers, lying on one side holding up three fingers for perjurers, and so on. Then, at another signal, all started whipping themselves with similar scourges, beating their backs and breasts, urged on by three or four of their fellows standing in the centre of the circle.

In June 1348 the Black Death crossed the English Channel, gaining its first foothold in England at Melcombe Regis, which is now part of Weymouth in Dorset. Though the cult of the Flagellants never caught on in the British Isles, the pattern of death and depopulation occurred much as elsewhere. Without harvesters or herdsmen to tend to them, crops rotted in the fields while livestock strayed. Priests succumbed to the disease along with everyone else – or fled their stricken flocks. As elsewhere, parents carried their own dead children to mass graves. 'From these pits such a stench was given off that scarcely anyone dared even to walk beside the cemeteries', wrote William Dene, a monk of Rochester in Kent. Nobody knows just how many people the Black Death wiped out in Europe – one estimate puts the toll at 20 million or more. In England, one-third of the population may have died in the first onslaught, and subsequent recurrences brought the population down to around 2 million by 1400.

The result was a wages explosion for those among the labouring classes who survived. Workers were

No mercy for the peasants *The Black Death resulted in labour shortages throughout Europe, and led peasants to assert their rights more vocally than they had dared to do in earlier feudal times. In France, the 'Jacquerie Rising' of 1358 was suppressed by the nobles, who hunted down the rebellious labourers and massacred them.*

so hard to find that they could demand, and win, large rises. Many farmhands doubled their pay at a stroke, deserting their landowners for better money elsewhere, and so accelerating social changes already in progress, as traditional relationships between lord and vassal were eroded.

The disappearing village

During the late Middle Ages tens of thousands of European villages disappeared. In England, some 20 per cent of the villages were abandoned and forgotten, showing up centuries later through aerial photography. The Black Death was by no means the only cause of this. Periods of famine had already done damage, and with the rise of the wool trade, landlords converted many arable fields to pasture, so that old farming communities were wiped out. Nonetheless, the Black Death was a contributing scourge that caused depopulation on a scale that is almost beyond imagining. It was not until around 1600 that the continent recovered its pre-Black Death level.

It was a global catastrophe, too. The plague ravaged the Muslim world and decimated the nomad population of the Eurasian steppe lands. China's population halved between 1200 and 1393. Chinese historians blamed Mongol invaders – but the real cause was probably the Black Death.

HOW PLAGUE EXPOSED THE DOCTORS' DILEMMA

The Black Death revealed the ineffective character of medieval medical practice. The ordinary practitioner of the time was often hardly more than a herbalist, skilled in gathering plants from the fields or roadside, but with little knowledge of the causes of disease. Faced with a serious epidemic, all he could do was to look on and hope not to catch the infection himself.

Bewildered physicians were as much at a loss as everyone else to account for the calamity. Some supposed that the plague resulted from some evil and noxious mist, arising from an unusual conjunction of the planets. Others claimed that the Jews had been poisoning the wells. Hysterical anti-Semitism was widespread, and much cruel persecution followed.

One important practice which resulted from the Black Death was quarantine, whereby ships arriving from the East were isolated for 40 days – in Italian *quaranta giorni* – and their crews were prevented from coming ashore. In Mediterranean ports this was to become a widespread precaution during the 15th century.

Smell of death *A 15th-century doctor holds a pomander to his nose in self-protection as he feels the pulse of a plague victim.*

Cripples' plight *Medieval medicine was as incapable of dealing with crippling maladies as with plague.*

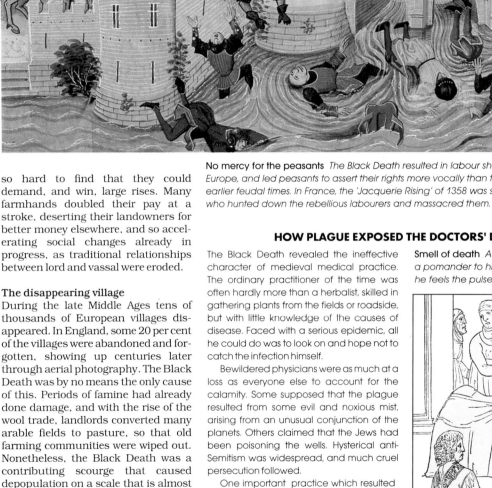

A MONK'S LIFE OF PRAYER AND TOIL

A place of peace *At the heart of even the largest monastery stood an oasis of open space. This central square, often grassy, was separated by open colonnades from the cloisters in whose shelter monks walked, heads bowed in private prayer. Around the cloisters were arranged all the major buildings of the monastery.*

Archive and library, treasure house, college and craft centre all rolled into one, the monastery at its best represented the core of Christian culture. But its principal purpose was prayer and the praise of God, in a self-contained community whose members made a total lifelong commitment to poverty, chastity and unquestioning obedience to a superior.

Monks also took a vow of stability, pledging themselves not to move from one house to another unless sent by an abbot. Some monasteries, however, were bases from which missionaries spread the faith into surrounding pagan areas. Some became centres for reclaiming waste land and improving agricultural techniques. Some, such as Reichenau and Fulda in Germany, became famous for schools of painting. Some monasteries, such as Bobbio in Italy, were famed for their libraries, while St Gall in Switzerland was the most important centre of education north of the Alps, until the rise of Paris.

Almost all monasteries provided hospitality for the wayfarer, and many cared for the infirm. The cycle of daily life in a monastery was organised around the regular pattern of divine service, which occupied at least five out of every 24 hours. In summer it began at midnight with Matins, lasting about an hour; in the winter months Matins started at 2am, in an unheated stone church, lit only by candles. There was time for further sleep until the half-hour service of Prime at 6am. After a sparse breakfast of bread and ale, the monks dispersed to work or study. They gathered again for Mass at 9am, after which they met to discuss matters of business in the chapter-house before a second Mass at 11am.

Dinner, the main meal of the day, was at noon and consisted of soup, bread, vegetables and fruit with cheese or eggs. Meat or fish might be available if it were not one of the fast days which, for the more zealous orders, made up half the year. During the meal the monks listened to a reading from the Scriptures, and afterwards rested until Nones at 2pm. The afternoon's work, broken by Vespers at 4pm,

lasted until supper at 6pm, and the last service of the day, Compline, followed at 7pm. After quiet reading the monks went to bed, still in their habits, and slept with a candle burning in dormitories where silence was observed at all times.

The father of western monasticism was St Benedict of Nursia, who established a monastery at Cassino, south of Rome, in 529. His 'Rule' set the basic pattern for monastic life, dividing the hours into balanced portions devoted to labour, rest, study and devotion. St Benedict's ideal was of a disciplined but compassionate community set apart from the troubles and temptations of an uncertain world. New orders were founded, with different rules, but Benedict's ideal remained the basis of their way of life.

Finding a tax loophole

Most monks worked hard, and managed well the estates given to them by the newly converted rulers of Europe. They also benefited from the donations of the wealthy, and of the guilt-ridden who hoped to redress sins with gifts, and they were skilful in exploiting tax exemptions and trading privileges. Great abbeys along the banks of the Loire, Seine, Rhône, Rhine and Moselle ran their own transport fleets, and engaged in highly profitable commerce. But material success all too easily bred arrogance and corruption, and threatened the pure pursuit of the monastic ideal.

> *'The monastery itself ought to be built so as to contain all necessities within it...so that monks shall have no need to wander abroad, as this is not helpful to their souls.'*
>
> ST BENEDICT, *c.* AD 535

The Abbey of Cluny, established in Burgundy in 910, was the spearhead of a revival of monastic discipline throughout western Europe. By 1130, however, the monks had grown proud and built for themselves a basilica so huge that for four centuries it was the largest church in the world.

The layout of monastery buildings usually followed a standard plan. The church formed one side of the cloister, where the monks exercised and studied. Other buildings round the cloister included the kitchen and

Taking the habit *Repudiated wives and unwanted daughters were among those who entered a nunnery, where the first sacrifice was the loss of their hair (above). When a novice monk took his final vows and was accepted into the brotherhood, the abbot put the habit over his head (below).*

MONKS AT THEIR TOIL

As members of a self-supporting community, monks had to engage in a variety of tasks, from heavy manual labour to delicate craft work or administrative and housekeeping chores. Lay brothers helped as specialised craftsmen, or farmed outlying estates or 'granges'. Although set apart from the world, monks were by no means isolated from it. The monastery was landlord and employer to the local community, a place of care for the poor and infirm, of rest for the traveller and of education for the children.

Division of labour *Two monks split a tree-trunk. One holds an axe, while the other strikes the axehead with a wooden mallet.*

Into bad habits *Not every monk kept rigidly to his vows. A satirical drawing shows a backslider set in the stocks with his mistress.*

refectory, and, a little apart, the infirmary which sometimes had its own cloister, and the latrines. By the standards of the day monasteries provided their inhabitants with good health care and sanitation, and some had sophisticated water supply and drainage systems. Some had a separate abbot's lodging, a dormitory for lay brothers, a guesthouse and stables for visitors, and a gatehouse.

At the head of the monastery was the abbot, who might be absent for long periods attending the bishop or the monarch, participating in synods, visiting outlying estates or inspecting subsidiary houses. In the absence of the abbot, the prior ran the monastery.

Among the monastic officials was the precentor, who oversaw music and the organisation of ceremonies. The chancellor supervised the library, archive and conduct of correspondence. The sacrist looked to the fabric of the buildings, while money and supplies were in the hands of the bursar and cellarer respectively. New recruits spent at least a year as novices before taking their final vows. One of the peculiarities of monastic life that they had to learn was the sign language of

more than 100 signals which monks employed to communicate with each other during periods of silence. For example, moving the forefinger up and down the end of the thumb at eye level meant 'pass the wine, please'.

In addition to their community of monks, larger monasteries often had dozens or even hundreds of lay brothers who took vows of poverty, stability, chastity and obedience, but did not commit themselves fully to monastic life. Needing texts for study, refectory readings and services, the monks spent many hours in the laborious and costly task of copying them by hand, using only pen, ink and parchment.

Preserving the written word was so important in this age of mass illiteracy that St Benedict's rule allowed the monks, otherwise vowed to poverty, to own their own pens. They also wrote new works, and acted as scribes for local nobles. It was a short step from copying texts to embellishing them; some monasteries became renowned for exquisitely decorated manuscripts.

At a time when most men's horizons were bounded by the fields they worked, the monasteries formed part of an international framework. And the dispatch of ordinary monks across Europe helped to spread new skills, from herb-growing to metalwork, and from music to estate management.

Carved riddle in a cathedral *Medieval woodcarvers lavished their craft on the misericords found below the choir seats in churches large and small. This example from Worcester Cathedral, carved about 1380, illustrates a riddle. It shows a woman dressed in a net, half riding on a goat, with one foot on the ground and with a hare under her arm. The riddle concerns someone 'not driving, walking or riding, not dressed or naked, not in the road or out of it, and bringing a gift that is no gift' – for the hare runs away as soon as it is given.*

Inside the convent *The abbess, bearing a crozier, leads a procession through the cloisters of a convent, followed by the priest and his assistant and nuns with music books. Above, the priest celebrates Mass, as the sacristan pulls the bell ropes. Novices look on from a window.*

A DAY IN THE LIFE OF SISTER URSULA

Sister Ursula groaned as she knelt to pray. Getting up in the middle of the night to sing divine service became more of a trial with every passing winter. She glanced towards the abbess to see if the tiny outburst had been detected. For the abbess was new, zealous and foreign, being the cousin of the French bishop within whose diocese the nunnery lay. She probably came with a mandate to bring lax provincials up to the best continental standards. The usual daily meeting was therefore punctuated with icy reprimands and fiery exhortations on every subject from sloppy dictation to wasting food by feeding scraps to stray animals. Some of the new abbess's innovations had been welcome – hot towels in the refectory were a boon to rheumatic hands. Had Ursula not been passed over for promotion she might have made this innovation herself. Seeing this thought for what it was she made a mental note for evening confession: 'Father I have been guilty of uncharitable thoughts....'

THE PILGRIM'S PATIENT PROGRESS

Many of the great pilgrimage centres of the Middle Ages could be glimpsed from miles away. Towering over the communities which lived off them, the first appearance of their spires on the horizon lifted the spirits of the weary as they passed the brow of a hill or emerged from deep forest into open country. Drawing closer, the pilgrims would soon be assailed by those who, in one way or another, depended on the shrine for their living. Beggars and keepers of hostels and stables touted for custom on the approach roads. Closer to the shrine, vendors sold charms and souvenirs – leaden badges to be sewn onto the hat, or small metal flasks, embossed with scenes from the saint's life and used to carry water from a holy spring, or oil from the lamps burning around his tomb.

At the entrance to the shrine, pilgrims would pass under the scrutiny of the monks. These sharp-eyed guardians classified all who passed beneath their gaze – the fashionable lady with hair demurely covered but remarkably unstained by travel; the true penitent, gaunt and ragged, with bare and bleeding feet; the chronically sick, borne in litters by hopeful relatives; the murderer, shuffling in chains, sentenced to wear the weapon of his crime hung around his neck as a perpetual accusation.

Once inside they might by stages approach the objects of their veneration – an elaborate marble tomb, a candle-lit altar twinkling with offerings, or a gem-studded box called a

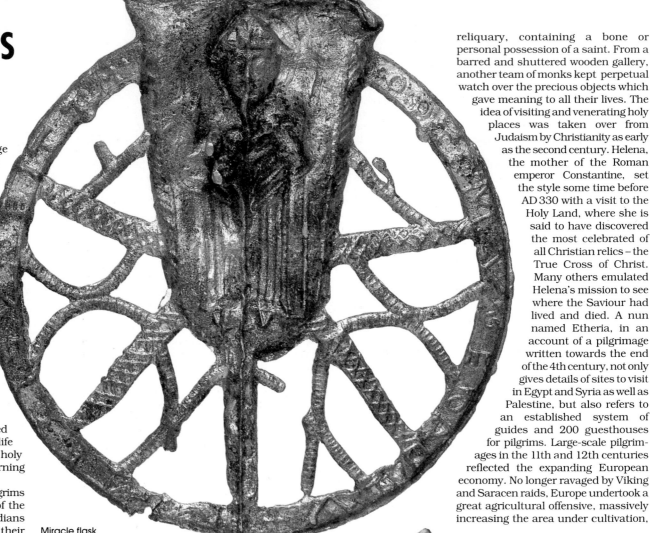

reliquary, containing a bone or personal possession of a saint. From a barred and shuttered wooden gallery, another team of monks kept perpetual watch over the precious objects which gave meaning to all their lives. The idea of visiting and venerating holy places was taken over from Judaism by Christianity as early as the second century. Helena, the mother of the Roman emperor Constantine, set the style some time before AD 330 with a visit to the Holy Land, where she is said to have discovered the most celebrated of all Christian relics – the True Cross of Christ. Many others emulated Helena's mission to see where the Saviour had lived and died. A nun named Etheria, in an account of a pilgrimage written towards the end of the 4th century, not only gives details of sites to visit in Egypt and Syria as well as Palestine, but also refers to an established system of guides and 200 guesthouses for pilgrims. Large-scale pilgrimages in the 11th and 12th centuries reflected the expanding European economy. No longer ravaged by Viking and Saracen raids, Europe undertook a great agricultural offensive, massively increasing the area under cultivation,

Miracle flask
Pilgrims to the shrine of Thomas Becket, murdered at Canterbury in 1170 and later canonised, could buy an ampulla, or flask, supposed to contain the diluted blood of the saint, capable of working miraculous cures. This example of 1270 is inscribed, in Latin, 'Thomas makes the best doctor for the worthy sick'. The pilgrim hung the flask round his neck on the way home, then placed it in his church.

A cripple wheeled to the shrine

Horseback pilgrims *For the wealthy pilgrim who could afford a horse, a pilgrimage was a companionable experience enlivened by storytelling on the way and overnight stops at taverns. A vivid picture of the ride to Canterbury is given by the poet Geoffrey Chaucer in his Canterbury Tales, written in the late 14th century. One of his characters, the Wife of Bath, had already made pilgrimages to Jerusalem and Santiago de Compostela.*

and thus creating the wealth that built cities and financed hazardous journeys and costly military expeditions. Another stimulus to pilgrimages was provided by the Crusades. It was the interruption of pilgrim traffic by militant Seljuk Turks which provoked the preaching of the First Crusade in 1095. The resulting capture of Jerusalem prompted thousands more to visit the 'golden city', and two military orders of soldier-monks, the Templars and Hospitallers, were set up to provide security for the pilgrims.

At one end of the scale a pilgrimage might mean no more than a hike to a local shrine to mingle with the crowd on an auspicious day. At the other it might mean perpetual pilgrimage, a form of atonement reserved for the most heinous of crimes, or a burden taken on as a vocation similar to that of a monk or a hermit. Between the two extremes came the once-in-a-lifetime visit to one of the three great shrines of western Christendom – Canterbury, Rome and Compostela.

In Rome, pilgrims could visit the supposed burial sites of the Apostles and other martyrs. According to a 14th-century pilgrim guidebook, a call on St Vitus and St Modestus would bring pardon for a third of a lifetime's sins, while the sight of St Veronica's relic – a handkerchief bearing the imprint of the face of Christ – could wipe out 3000 years of purgatory.

A fisherman in Spain

After Rome itself, the most important focus of pilgrimage in Europe was Santiago de Compostela, in north-western Spain. Santiago is the apostle known as 'St James the Great' who, according to legend, preached the gospel in Spain before being martyred at Jerusalem around AD 44. In 813 a tomb discovered near Compostela was claimed to be that of the saint.

The uncovering of the relics gave an immense boost to the morale of Spanish Christians, then confined to a narrow strip of territory along the north of the Iberian peninsula. An earthen church over the tomb was soon replaced by a stone one. After the whole

town had been destroyed by the Moors in 997, a cathedral was begun in 1078 and completed in 1211. So famed was Santiago that the scallop shell of St James, the fisherman saint, became a symbol adopted by pilgrims throughout Christendom. Another widely used device was a palm, symbolic of the Holy Land – hence the surname 'Palmer' taken by many pilgrims.

By sea to the Holy Land

Beyond Europe lay the Holy Land itself, which most reached by sea. Venice was a major port of embarkation, so much so that the senate of the republic enacted a series of detailed regulations to prevent the overloading of passenger vessels, to specify the arms their crews should carry and to detail the luggage and provisions to be allowed per person. Galleys left twice a year, once to arrive in time for Easter, and the other to return before winter.

Pilgrims could also travel overland, across the huge plain of Hungary and down through the harsh mountains of the Balkans. A large party might make it in six months. While the pilgrims themselves were not permitted to bear arms, an armed escort was permissible, and the ranks of the company might be further swollen by merchants seeking safety in numbers. Pilgrimage was by far the safest way to travel in medieval times, especially for women, and this fact may help to explain its survival long after the beliefs that inspired it had begun to wane.

A PILGRIM'S DAY ON THE ROAD

Rising early for Mass, the pilgrim Jacques has a special reason to look cheerful about the day's walking that lies ahead. For at last he is nearing the end of a long journey which started three months ago when he joined a band of fellow pilgrims at Chartres. Their destination is the shrine of Jacques's namesake – 'St James' in English and 'Santiago' in Spanish – at Compostela in north-west Spain.

At a shrine in Chartres, Jacques had knelt in prayer before starting on the journey through the mountainous Auvergne. He was glad of company, for wolves and bandits lay in wait for the lone traveller. At the end of each day's 20 mile walk, he looked forward to the warmth and food provided by a hostel endowed by the wealthy Abbey of Cluny. With his companions, Jacques had sung to enliven the journey, and stopped to pray at wayside crucifixes. Now the goal of Santiago lies no more than a day's walk ahead. Jaques bathes in a local river, imitating the practice of pilgrims to Jerusalem who immerse themselves in the River Jordan as a form of baptism. He also picks up a block of limestone to carry on the last stage of his journey, both as a symbol of his burden of sin and as a practical contribution to the building or repair of a local church or hostel. This evening Jacques will sleep within sight of the gleaming spires of Compostela.

Staging post *The church at Conques in southern France was one of several built for pilgrims on the route to Compostela.*

Symbol of a saint *Pilgrims who had been to Santiago de Compostela wore lead scallop-shell hat badges in honour of St James the Great, patron saint of the shrine.*

Dangerous journey *The hazards of life on the road are shown by a 15th-century artist. Armed men attack a band of pilgrims outside the walls of a town, then rob them of their few possessions before leaving them for dead. Pilgrims were advised to travel in groups, with an armed escort.*

RISE OF ISLAM

In the century following the founding of the first Muslim community by the Prophet Muhammad in AD 622, Islam conquered an empire which stretched from Spain and Portugal to the borders of India. The lands won in the name of Allah became a single civilisation united by religion and the Arabic language – the language of the Koran in which Muhammad's revelations were collected. Muslims also created a new form of art based on geometric patterns, plant motifs and calligraphy. They preserved and revitalised the classic texts of the Ancient Greek philosophers and scientists, and they elaborated a vast code of law.

The occupation by Muslims of the Holy Places of the Christian faith gave rise to two centuries of bitter struggle between Islam and militant Christendom. The religious zeal of the Crusaders was fanned by the hope of new lands and greed for the spoils of war, and both Christians and Muslims fought with great ferocity. Christian states established in the Holy Land became a channel by which Muslim learning and eastern influences on food and fashion reached Europe. Gradually Islam expelled the Crusaders; in 1291 the last Christian stronghold of Acre fell to Muslim forces.

ISLAM AD 622–1350

WHERE THE KORAN RULES EVERY DEED

The year is 1350, and for a quarter of a century the Arab traveller Ibn Battuta has been journeying round the Islamic world, from Spain in the west to India and beyond in the east. In Baghdad he finds the city's 2000 bathhouses are plastered with the sticky black substance which we now know as oil. In the Maldive Islands, where he has been a *qadi* or religious judge, he has tried in vain to stop the local girls going topless. And in Timbuktu, on the southern edge of the Sahara, he notes that the locals observe Friday prayers so keenly that slaves have to reserve places in the mosque by spreading their masters' prayer mats well in advance.

Wherever the travels of Ibn Battuta take him, after he has climbed stiffly from the back of a horse or camel, or walked thankfully down the gangplank from a creaking dhow, he heads for the mosque, which stands near the heart of every Muslim city. Its arched and columned hall is dim, cool and quiet after the hubbub of the streets outside, where traders cry their wares, from paper to peaches, from silks to elegant brassware. A moment's pause, and the silence

Fountainhead of knowledge *A Muslim mufti, expert in religious law, expounds a passage of the Koran, the sacred book of Islam. Believed to have been dictated to Muhammad by the angel Gabriel, inspired by Allah, the Koran provides a framework for every aspect of life, from religious doctrine to personal behaviour. Some Muslim scholars know the Koran by heart.*

gives way to soft sounds appropriate to a place of prayer and contemplation. From the courtyard comes the splashing sound of running water, as a pool or fountain is essential for the ritual washing of hands, feet and face which precedes the five daily periods of prayer. But water is also, to a desert people, a symbol of Allah the life giver, and a preview of paradise.

Near the *mihrab* – the empty wall niche, found in every mosque, that indicates the direction of Mecca – a man rocks gently back and forth, passing a string of beads through his fingers and murmuring an incantation. Those who pass him, barefooted on the rich carpets, respect his sincerity.

Islam's 'Five Pillars'

Ibn Battuta is a devout observer of the 'Five Pillars', the obligatory duties of Islam. The fundamental pillar is the creed: 'There is no god but Allah, and Muhammad is the messenger of Allah.' Next come the five daily periods of prayer, always recited in Arabic and carried out regardless of where the believer may be. Third, the Muslim should give charitable alms, to be spent largely on relieving the poor. Fourth, he must keep the annual fast of the month of Ramadan. From dawn until dusk, the believer must not eat, drink, or even swallow his saliva.

The final requirement is to make the *hajj*, or pilgrimage to Mecca, in the 12th month of the Muslim lunar calendar. Arrived in Mecca, the believer performs simple rites which recall incidents in the life of Muhammad himself, and of Abraham, believed to have been the first guardian of the Ka'ba – the huge granite cube in the centre of the city, which is Islam's holiest shrine.

Progress of a scholar

From a corner of the mosque comes a rising and falling chorus of piping voices, as a class of boys recite passages from the Koran. The most gifted pupil may become a *hafiz*, one who has memorised the entire Koran.

When they have mastered the sacred text, the brightest boys may go on to study grammar and rhetoric, since the Koran provides the model for all literary style. Scholars may then progress through every realm of knowledge, from medicine to music and from astronomy to agriculture. Their final goal is the highest realm of human thought – theology, and its social expression, religious law. By the gate of the mosque a small group of

men talk over a question of religious law with the imam, or prayer leader. Unlike a Christian priest, the imam claims no sacramental powers. His functions are closer to those of a Jewish rabbi: to lead communal worship, to preach a sermon after the Friday prayers, and to give guidance on conduct.

The imam wears his beard clipped, in the style attributed by tradition to Muhammad himself. After the Koran itself, the sayings and deeds of the Prophet, as preserved in *hadith*, or 'traditions', are the prime source of Islamic law. For centuries after the Prophet's death, as the Muslim empire expanded to embrace an immense variety of peoples and places, Muslim jurists strove to produce a code of behaviour which classified every act or sentiment into one of five categories:

compulsory, permitted, neutral, discouraged or forbidden. This body of law governs the lives of Muslims today, as it did when Ibn Battuta roamed the world 650 years ago.

Allah triumphant *A century after the death of Muhammad, the Muslim empire was already vast, stretching from Spain and North Africa to the borders of India.*

Pilgrim goal *A minaret rises above the houses of sun-baked Kairouan, in Tunisia. From it a muezzin, or crier, calls the faithful to prayer. Kairouan is one of Islam's holy cities, founded less than 40 years after Muhammad's death.*

Camel-back caravan *The sounds of trumpets and kettledrums accompany a cheerful pilgrim cavalcade. This 13th-century painting from Baghdad shows a Muslim version of the pilgrims of Chaucer's Canterbury Tales. The main centre of pilgrimage was Mecca, as it still is today, but there were many other shrines and holy places for the pilgrim to visit.*

The beauty of the word *The revelations of the Koran are recorded in exquisite calligraphy, honouring their source in Allah. The strict rule of Islam forbids the portrayal of the human form, so Muslim calligraphers devoted all their skill to perfecting the graceful flourishes of the Arabic script, decorating the margins of the sacred text with designs based on plant forms, and stylised, often abstract patterns.*

PEARLS, SLAVES AND BUNK BEDS

There were occasions when a Baghdad pearl merchant, during the reign of the great 8th-century caliph Harun al-Rashid, might find it hard to talk. This was not because there was any fault with his voice, normally raised in incessant bargaining and gossiping, but because he was testing a fresh consignment of pearls by sucking them to check their taste.

Sweet-tasting pearls from Oman commanded a high price. A batch that tasted of salt, on the other hand, would be inferior pearls from the Red Sea, fit only to banish to the back of the shop. At least both these types were genuine – unlike some offerings which floated on water, showing them to be fakes.

The pearl merchant's shop might be little more than a hole in the wall in the Baghdad souk or bazaar. Every sizable Muslim city had its souk, often covered against the weather and sealed from the street by a strong gate. Crammed with traders in every commodity, the souk was the gathering place for imports from all over the Arab world and beyond. From Arabia came tanned hides, from the Yemen incense, indigo and turmeric, from India sandalwood, ebony and rubies. Africa sent gold, ivory and slaves. Isfahan produced foodstuffs – honey, apples, quinces, saffron, salt and fruit drinks – with bunk beds by way of contrast.

Fair deal for the customer

Byzantium, the capital of its own Christian empire, supplied ready-mixed medicines for the apothecary and lyres for the seller of musical instruments. Along the Silk Road from China, the oldest and greatest of the world's civilisations, came not only brilliantly dyed silks for the drapers, but paper and ink for the stationers, cinnamon for the sellers of spices, and exquisite porcelain. The far north also contributed: Scandinavia supplied furs, armour and falcons.

Since the traders were all gathered together in the souk, it was easy for them to maintain quality control by keeping an eye on one another, and for customers to compare prices and make sure they were not overcharged. Unlike Christian countries, where

Food for thought *A 10th-century Persian nobleman ate from this dish, one of a set, inscribed with proverbs. This one says: 'Only modesty points out the action of a noble man.' Households owned sets of such edifying dishes.*

Happy homecoming *A wealthy merchant, accompanied by his friend, returns home for the birth of his son. Worried slaves meet him at the door. A large house, with balcony and elaborate decoration, was a merchant's reward for success in business.*

Caravan club *A booted merchant mounts his camel for a desert journey. Caravans of merchants plodded for days across the sands, guarded against bandits and spending the night at a caravanserai or desert hostel.*

TREASURE HUNTERS OF THE SOUK

Pungent with the smell of spices and noisy with haggling and the screams of trussed livestock, the souk or bazaar lies near the heart of every Muslim town. Here, under cover from the noonday sun, traders cater for every worldly need. Shoppers, mostly men, pause to chat, to sip fruit juice, to watch craftsmen at work making pottery, metalwork and carpets and textiles with bright patterns. There are arrowheads and falcons for the desert sportsman, intricately carved combs for his wives, and a wealth of other goods, from mercury to pomegranates and from woollen coats to saffron. There may even be horses, camels and ostriches from Arabia, coconuts and leopard skins from India, peacocks and rhubarb from China. Past the fretted wooden balconies the souk plunges into a tunnel-like warren, lined by more kiosks and craftsmen's workshops and lit by holes in a long, many-domed roof. Beyond, the minaret of the mosque rises above the bustle of the city, its stonework sculpted with intricate friezes of geometrical patterns. From its balcony five times a day the muezzin, or crier, summons the faithful to pray and to hear the message of the Koran, and a brief calm descends on the souk.

trade tended to be looked down upon, the Muslim trader was a highly respected member of the community. As a young man, the Prophet Muhammad himself had been engaged in long-distance commerce, organising camel caravans which crossed the Arabian desert, and winning the nickname Al-Amin, 'The Trustworthy', by his honest dealing.

The high standards of the souk were maintained by the *muhtasib*, or market inspector. A typical code drawn up in the 12th century in Seville – then a Muslim city – lays down detailed regulations. Butchers were forbidden to hang their bloody joints beyond the ends of their counters, in case they soiled the clothes of passers-by. Olive oil was not allowed to be sold near the mosque, because spillages might permanently stain the walls and the passageways. Egg sellers had to keep a bowl of water ready to hand, so that customers could make sure the eggs were fresh by floating them. Counters, containers and surfaces used in food preparation had to be scrubbed daily.

Fast food was as popular in the 13th century as it is today, and standards of hygiene were rigidly controlled. One regulation stipulated: 'Sausages and grilled rissoles should only be made with fresh meat and not with meat coming from a sick animal and bought for its cheapness.' Another stated: 'The leftovers of the cooks and fryers must not be offered for sale.' The muhtasib was told to watch out for fraudulent practice, such as mixing flour with the cheese used for fritters. The

Sold into slavery *A customer makes a choice from among a group of black and white slaves, while a merchant weighs his coins to make sure he is getting full price.*

souk was not only a place where goods were offered for sale: it was also a place where they were made, or at least went through their finishing processes. Unpleasant-smelling businesses, like tanning, were relegated to the outskirts of town. But any trade which offered highly skilled craftsmen the chance to show off to potential customers would take advantage of the opportunities offered by a shop in the souk.

Skilled cutters carved rock crystal into delicate scent bottles, leatherworkers tooled hides to make covers for sacred texts, and goldsmiths inlaid metal writing cases with gold and semiprecious stones. The souk was also home to a wide variety of service industries. Laundries, bathhouses and massage houses, barber shops, bloodletting practitioners and letter writers were all to be found there.

The importance of Muslim commerce can be gauged from the number of English business terms derived from Arabic. Our tariff comes from the Arabic *ta'rif*, meaning literally 'information'; while magazine, in the sense of 'storehouse', derives from *makhzan*. Fine textiles, valuable in proportion to their bulk, were a staple item of trade. Cotton, from the Arabic word *qutn*, damask, from Damascus, and muslin, from Mosul, have hardly altered. The most unlikely derivation is that of the tabby cat, whose name comes from Attabiya, a Baghdad suburb famous for multicoloured fabrics.

Made in the souk *This graceful jar from Syria was designed to hold grain or dried fruit.*

ARISTOTLE AMONG THE ARABS

As the scholar al-Kindi strolled through the crowded streets of Baghdad to the shady colonnades and fountain-filled gardens of the House of Wisdom, his absent-minded appearance gave no clue to the keenness with which he studied the world around him. The sight of a man staggering and falling on the cobbles inspired him to write a treatise on 'The Cause of Vertigo'. As he looked up at the cloud-filled sky above the city, he wondered why rain fell often on the lush river valleys of the Euphrates and Tigris, but seldom over the desert. The outcome was a study called 'The Reason Why Rain Rarely Falls in Certain Places'.

Al-Kindi (801-73) was one of the first teachers at the House of Wisdom, the university founded by Caliph Ma'mun, son of Harun al-Rashid, early in the 9th century. By about 900, the knowledge of the Ancient Greeks, forgotten for centuries in the West, had been rediscovered by the Arabs.

The thoughts of the philosophers Plato and Aristotle had been translated into Arabic, as had the mathematical observations of Ptolemy, Euclid and Archimedes, and the medical writings of Galen and Hippocrates. The House of Wisdom produced other brilliant

Next move *Chess reached Persia from India shortly before the Islamic conquest. It was popularised in the West by a book translated from the Arabic in 1238, and published in Spain.*

Temple of learning *Islamic scholars study in the book-lined library of a mosque. As early as the 9th century, the main library of Cordoba, in Muslim Spain, held some 500,000 books, approximately one for every inhabitant of the city – at a time when the richest Christian monastery would number its books in dozens.*

For caliph and camel driver *The astrolabe, devised by the Greeks, was the principal aid to navigation used in the Islamic world. Along a disc marked with degrees along its edge, the user could calculate the altitude of the stars, and thus his latitude. He could also determine the five daily times for prayer.*

scholars, such as al-Biruni, who lived some 70 years later. He was not only a linguist and an expert on religious history but also the author of works on drugs, minerals and astronomy.

Above them all towered the figure of Ibn Sina (980-1037), known to the West as Avicenna. Credited with 500 published works, in subjects ranging from meteorology to mathematics, he is also said to have discovered the contagious nature of tuberculosis and understood how epidemics are spread. Avicenna was to remain a standard authority for six centuries, in the West as well as the Arab world.

Drawing upon a core of knowledge inherited from the Greeks, Muslim physicians believed that a person's health depended upon the correct balance of the four 'humours' or main body fluids – blood for the sanguine humour, phlegm for the phlegmatic, choler or yellow bile for the choleric, and black bile for the melancholic. The prime task of the healer was to restore harmony by drugs, rest or diet.

'Fix your fee with the patient when his illness is at its worst, for when he gets better he will forget what you have done for him.'
DOCTOR IN MUSLIM SPAIN, AD 900

The Muslims' ophthalmic skills were highly developed, as were their osteopathic techniques, and they passed on their knowledge through teaching hospitals with permanent paid staff. Baghdad, for example, had more than 1000 certificated doctors, as well as a specialist mental hospital where the therapies included playing music.

Muslim interest in astronomy was stimulated both by religion and by practical necessity. The requirement for Muslims to pray at specific hours of the day, and to face Mecca while doing so, led them to master accurate calendric calculations, and work out techniques of determining directions and distances. During their travels over trackless wastes they found the stars a surer guide for navigation than shifting sand dunes, or watercourses.

Included among the sciences most revered by the Arabs were history and geography. Their greatest historian, Ibn Khaldun who died in 1406, formulated a theory of the rise and decline of dynasties, which he saw as governed by alternating vigour

and decadence, as conquerors who emerged from the desert became softened by civilisation. Muslim trade contacts stimulated an interest in geography. In 1138 the scholar al-Idrisi compiled a geography of the known world, consisting of an atlas, a gazetteer and a solid-silver model of the earth's surface. His survey included information on Britain, 'a considerable island, whose shape is that of the head of an ostrich... Its inhabitants are brave, active and enterprising, but all is in the grip of perpetual winter'. Eight centuries later, inhabitants of that same island use words such as 'algebra' and 'alkali' without pausing to remember their origins in the rich legacy of Islam.

Strings in harmony
The gentle lute, whose name derives from the Arabic al-'ud, 'the wood', was probably brought back to the West by returning Crusaders.

Herbs for healers *The practice of medicine was one of the triumphs of Islamic science. This picture from The Book of Antidotes, which appeared in 1199, shows gardeners gathering medicinal plants, supervised by a physician seated at top left. Arab doctors were skilled in the use of drugs, many of them derived from plants, and were advanced in surgery and eye treatment.*

Saws for surgeons *The Arab surgeon had a wide variety of saws and other cutting instruments at his command. However, surgery was normally a last resort, as the Arabs recognised the dangers of infection. They also had religious scruples about performing dissections and surgical operations, since Muslim doctrine believed in the resurrection of the body.*

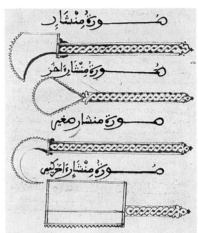

FIGURING IT OUT – WITH THE AID OF THE ZERO

The Arabs derived much of their mathematical knowledge from Ancient Greek thinkers such as Euclid and Archimedes. But they revolutionised Greek methods of calculation, which were based on letters of the alphabet, by the simple expedient of using a dot for zero – a concept unknown either to the Greeks or to the Romans. The dot developed into a small circle or *sifr*, the origin of the modern word 'cipher'. The Latin translation of *sifr* was *zephyrum*, from which 'zero' derives. From arithmetic the Arabs advanced to the more abstract world of algebra, producing in the 9th century the first textbook on the subject. The word algebra itself comes from the Arabic *al-jabr*, which means literally 'the bringing together of separate parts'. Arabic numerals, brought from India by Arab scribes, became the basis of the numerals in common use today. Some have become simplified over the centuries (below), but the symbols for 2 and 3 remain little changed. Even computer digits derive ultimately from Arabic numerals.

١ ٢ ٣ ٤ ٥ ٦ ٧ ٨ ٩ ١٠ ٠

1 2 3 4 5 6 7 8 9 10 0

CRUSADERS FOR GOD AND GLORY

A group of 43 adventurers set out from Cornwall in the year 1280 to journey to the Holy Land. Calling themselves Crusaders, they included two women, two tanners, two chaplains, a miller, a shoemaker, a tailor, a smith and a merchant – not by any means a typical military unit. But by this time crusading had been going on for two centuries, and it had changed greatly from its original character.

Over those two centuries there had been more than half a dozen huge expeditionary forces led by kings and princes. The first, in 1099, had succeeded in wresting Jerusalem from Muslim control – and massacring the city's entire Muslim and Jewish population, perhaps numbering as many as 70,000 people altogether. The first Crusaders also conquered a broad strip of territory along the eastern coastline of the Mediterranean, but they were pushed out gradually as the Muslims regrouped, then brought their superior local fighting ability to bear. The last great Christian stronghold, the port of Acre, was retaken by the Muslims in 1291.

There were also expeditions of ordinary peasants and townspeople – and even, in 1212, a march by children. These mass marches inevitably ended in disaster before they got anywhere near the Holy Land, as may well have happened to the group from Cornwall. Their members were whittled away by hunger or bandits, or else cut to pieces by the inhabitants of the lands through which they tried to force their way, living off the land as they journeyed. Some went by water, sailing from southern France or northern Italy; many, however, went overland all the way, like the first Crusaders.

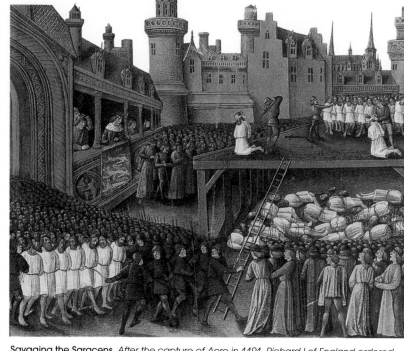

Savaging the Saracens *After the capture of Acre in 1191, Richard I of England ordered the slaughter of 2600 Saracen prisoners of war. A French manuscript illustration of 1490 shows the king watching from a balcony while his executioner swings at a prisoner.*

Seal of the Templars, an order of crusading knights

The motives of the would-be redeemers of the Holy Places varied very widely, from the sincerely pious to the openly venial. They went for salvation, for plunder, for land and for fame. They went to escape debt or punishment or even damnation. By the 12th century Pope Calixtus II was already promising to soldiers fighting against Muslims in Spain 'the same forgiveness of sins which we have given to the defenders of the eastern church'. A Crusade became any war against the enemies of the pope – Muslims, pagans or even heretical Christians. Even the highest religious ideals did little to restrain Crusaders from atrocities.

During the First Crusade the chronicler Ralph of Caen recorded that 'our troops boiled pagan adults in cooking-pots; they impaled children on spits and devoured them grilled'. The local commander did feel impelled to explain this away to the pope in a letter which pleaded 'cruel necessity' in the face of 'terrible famine'.

The typical Muslim attitude to the invaders was summarised by the 12th-century scholar and warrior Usamah ibn Munqidh. He wrote: 'All those who were well-informed about the Franj (the Franks, or Western Europeans) saw them as beasts superior in courage and fighting ardour but in nothing else, just as animals are superior in strength and aggression.'

Trial by ordeal

Closer acquaintance did little to revise his opinion. Usamah recorded with evident contempt this instance of Christian judicial procedure: 'A large cask was set up and filled with water. The young suspect was tied up, then hung by a rope from his shoulder-blades, and plunged into the cask. If he was innocent, they said, he would sink into the water, and they would pull him out by the rope. If he was guilty, it would be impossible for him to sink into the water. When he was thrown into the cask, the unfortunate man tried as hard as he could to sink to the bottom, but he could not manage it, and thus had to submit to the cruelty of their law, may God's curse be upon them! He was then blinded with a red-hot silver spike.'

In the long run, it was the Crusaders who changed. Those who settled locally adopted local lifestyles. Not only did they wear loose robes and open sandals, they even took to wearing turbans and adopted such alien customs as steam baths, shampooing and the use of perfumes. Spicy foods and ice-cold 'sherbets', made from fruit juice and snow, were new delights. Music,

Knights in transit *Aboard their cart is a mysterious lady throwing flowers.*

Peasants on the move *It was not only knights in armour who made the hazardous journey to the Holy Land. Many ordinary people set out on personal crusades in the hope of salvation, either singly or in groups. One early expedition in 1095-9, known as the People's or Peasants' Crusade, was led by Peter the Hermit, a fanatic from Picardy in northern France, who rode through Europe on a donkey rallying peasants to his cause. They descended on the countryside through which they passed like locusts, pillaging the local peasants and plundering villages and towns. In their turn, stragglers (left) were set upon by troops in the countries through which they passed. The People's Crusade dispersed before it reached the Holy Land.*

Blessing the children *This French stained-glass window shows a priest giving his blessing to the Children's Crusade of 1212.*

Cash economy *Having no regular currency, the Crusaders solved the problem by using either imitation Saracen coins (left) or genuine Byzantine coins (below).*

INNOCENTS ABROAD

The Crusades attracted people of all ages and social classes. In 1212 two boys in their early teens, Stephen in France and Nicholas in Germany, began a Children's Crusade. They promised their followers that the sea would divide in front of them and that angels would guide them to Palestine. Stephen led his children through the streets of Paris and headed south, his procession of some 9000 children being joined on the way by priests, prostitutes and vagrants. In Marseilles they were offered passage to Palestine by two villainous shipowners, who sold them into slavery in North Africa. Nicholas's band crossed the Alps and got as far south as Brindisi, where they too ended up as slaves.

dancing, poetry, hawking and the joust were established pleasures that could be enjoyed in new ways.

Over the years many of these changes began to feed back to Europe itself, most noticeably in matters of fashion and personal grooming. The use of new designs and novel fabrics and an interest in hairdressing were the first obvious signs of change.

A new silhouette
As early as 1130 – within a generation – Western women had acquired a new shape, a silhouette. Clumsy, cover-all draperies gave way to garments which were pinched in at the waist and cut to fit tightly from shoulder to hip and then to flare out in folds. Their hair was washed and plaited, and the plaits were decorated using beads and tassels

or interwoven with strips of fine materials. Aristocratic men took to curling their hair and trimming their beards. And whereas the first Crusaders had favoured a severe 'pudding-basin' hairstyle to cushion their conical helmets, their descendants began to grow luxuriant shoulder-length locks.

By the 13th century the military dress of the Crusaders was becoming more civilian in style, and some of its features were being adopted in women's dress. The chain-mail hood, for instance, inspired a cloth hood which framed the female countenance to advantage. The surcoat or tabard, with its wide armholes and loose waist, could cover a long gown for ornament as well as warmth. Less obvious, but no less lasting, was the influence on gardens. In much of southern Europe

new plants such as citrus fruits were introduced. The design of gardens was affected by the Muslim taste for pools and fountains, welcome features in a desert world and symbolic of paradise.

On a more sinister note, the word 'assassin' came to Europe, from a sect of fanatical Muslim killers crazed on the drug *hashish*, or cannabis, who terrorised the Crusaders.

The meaning of the maze
Mazes acquired a new popularity in the Christian world. To the medieval mind everything stood for something else, for all creation echoed the divine and supernatural. Thus labyrinths, well known in the classical world, were re-interpreted to represent the Church as the Ark of Salvation, reached at last through the tortuous paths of sinful

life. The journey of the soul to Heaven, of Christ to Calvary or of the Crusader to the Holy Land were brought together in symbolic patterns which could be reproduced in plants or on a church floor, and had immediate meaning for the warrior returning from Palestine.

Leakproof agreement *An Arab inscription from the time of the Crusades affirms: 'We make no treaties that hold no water.'*

HUMAN TANKS FIGHT FOR HOLY PLACES

Bracing himself in his stirrups, a crusading knight charged full tilt at his opponent, his lance couched closely into his side until the time came to skewer his opponent with a single unstoppable thrust.

In many ways resembling a tank, a mounted knight suffered from many of the same limitations, depending for his effectiveness on the nature of the terrain and the tactics of his enemy. Hit-and-run harassment, which took advantage of wooded or mountainous country, could prove very damaging, especially against men struggling under the effects of an unfamiliar and punishing climate, often weakened by fever or dysentery and anxious for the health and fitness of their horses.

The basic protection of a Christian knight was a hauberk, or shirt of mail reaching to the knees and split at the crotch so that it could be worn on horseback. Mail shirts were composed of thousands of ringlets, each one being joined to four others by a painstaking process of hand labour. Mail in itself was poor protection without a gambeson, a padded undercoat made of leather thickly stuffed with wool. This would prevent a blow from a sword or mace driving the ringlets deep into the flesh.

In the Holy Land knights wore a long, flowing surcoat to reflect heat from the sun and protect them from the cold of the desert night. A mail hood might also be worn to protect the head and throat, as well as a leather-lined steel helmet. Add on the weight of a metal-rimmed wooden shield, a belt with sword, dagger and scabbards, a lance and an axe or mace, and the total burden for a knight going into combat would be well over a third of his own body weight.

Thus burdened, a knight had little scope for fancy sword play. Cutting, not thrusting, was the main technique of fighting. Rather than piercing vital organs the sword usually inflicted long gashes which would bring unconsciousness through loss of blood and, unless skilfully dealt with, death from infection. Until the later development of plate armour, swords therefore terminated in a rounded slashing edge, rather than a point. A full-strength blow from a heavy sword could break a man's arm, disabling him from further combat, without even penetrating the protection of his armour. Muslim soldiers, by contrast, were lightly armoured, relying on greater agility for their protection. Although they also wore mail, it was often of a lighter construction. Unlike Christian knights, they did not scorn to use the bow, a composite weapon of wood, horn and sinew. This had a range of 550 yds (500 m), and it could pierce mail at 160 yds (145 m) when firing heavy arrows with an arrowhead triangular in cross-section.

Aid for an unhorsed king

Mounted knights were the elite of the crusading armies. The bulk of their forces, however, usually consisted of infantry armed with spear and crossbow. Used in the right combination by a skilful commander they could be very effective, as Richard Coeur de Lion showed in his last significant crusading battle, fought near Jaffa in August 1192. By then his force had been reduced to 2000 foot soldiers and just 54 knights. A Muslim force of 7000 cavalry came to finish them off,

Impregnable stronghold *The mighty Krak des Chevaliers, in the mountains of Syria, is the most magnificent of Crusader castles. Garrisoned by the Knights Hospitallers, it served as monastery as well as fortress.*

Assault and battery *During the prolonged siege of a castle, many types of device were employed by both defenders and attackers. In this dramatic scene some attackers are being raised in a basket to enable them to fire down on the castle, while others are undermining the walls with pickaxes. On the right, a group of besiegers protected by screens approach the castle, while a battering-ram is wheeled towards the wall. The defenders are equally active. Some are firing crossbows or hurling down missiles from the ramparts, while defenders on the right are lowering a grappling hook and a padded fender against the battering-ram.*

but reckoned without Richard's tactical skills. Protecting his front with a line of shield-carrying spearmen, Richard arranged behind them two ranks of crossbowmen, which fired alternately.

Held back by the bristling spear points, the lightly armoured Muslim horsemen milled about in confusion, an easy prey to the crossbowmen. Pressed together they made a compact target for Richard and a shock group of knights who suddenly charged through from the rear. Only 15 of the knights were mounted, but they were enough to overwhelm their stunned opponents – until Richard's horse was killed under him. Whereupon a Muslim galloped up with a choice of horses, sent by the chivalrous Saladin.

Such dramatic incidents were less typical of crusading warfare than the long, unglamorous grind of a siege, the outcome of which usually depended more on weather, morale, disease, food supplies or treachery than on military technique. Nonetheless, as time went on, both sides employed increasingly sophisticated devices for attacking increasingly sophisticated defences.

Outsize slings could be employed to hurl not only solid rocks but also incendiary missiles. Muslim armies appear to have been thoroughly familiar with these and to have used them to great advantage against the Crusaders. Natural seepages of *naft*, or petroleum, occur throughout the Middle East and special incendiary units called *naffatun*, protected by fire-proofed uniforms, featured in many Muslim armies. Numerous formulae for incendiary mixtures have survived, using blends of petroleum, quicklime, pitch, resin, saltpetre and sulphur. Some of these substances were designed to ignite on contact with water, others to cling to the shaped stone of a castle wall, or the armour of a knight. These mixtures could be delivered in large quantities, by means of siege engines, to burn buildings. In close combat they could be used in small quantities, in glass or ceramic pots hurled by 'grenadiers'. There were even siphon-like devices acting as primitive flamethrowers.

Incendiary weapons were to prove particularly effective in destroying the Crusaders' siege artillery and assault platforms, and may well have played a decisive role in ensuring their defeat in the course of the 13th century.

Missile heads *Normally, the trebuchet or giant sling was used to hurl huge stones. But in 1097, during the siege of Nicaea in Turkey, the Crusaders cut the heads off prisoners and fired them at the defenders.*

IN A CASTLE UNDER SIEGE

Back to the castle races a scout, bringing the alarming news that an enemy force is approaching. The garrison commander at once sends messengers on horseback for help, insuring himself against their falling into enemy hands by loosing carrier pigeons with the same appeal. Then he sends out troops to scour the countryside for grain and live-stock, both to bolster his own supplies and to deny them to the enemy.

Built into the design of his castle are two vital elements for its defence – an internal supply of water, and a clear field of fire all round. The commander has also to consider the nature of his garrison. A disciplined body of knights, such as the Templars, would be ready to accept the hardships of rationing, or sleeping and eating at irregular hours to keep the walls manned. The presence of strangers, or large numbers of women and children, could lead to friction; and if many fell sick, morale would be weakened.

The worst threat which the besieged commander has to fear is 'mining', when an enemy tunnels under a wall, then burns out the supporting props so that the wall collapses into the void. This is, however, a slow procedure, frustrated by bad weather or where a castle is built on solid rock. Instead the attackers might hurl dead animals into the besieged castle to spread disease – an early example of germ warfare. The more usual tactic, however, is to try to batter a breach, using the trebuchet. This siege engine, originally from China, could throw a 100 lb (45 kg) stone for 55 yds (50 m).

Defender of Islam
Nimble and lightly armed, Saracen warriors, carrying bow, sword and shield, were often more than a match for the heavily armed Crusaders.

Spanish steel *This ornate sword and scabbard (right) were worn by Boabdil, sultan of Granada and the last Moorish ruler in Spain.*

TRADERS IN THE DARK CONTINENT

On a summer's day late in the 11th century, Abu Ubayd al-Bakri was invited to a royal audience given by the King of Ghana. Impressed in spite of himself, al-Bakri watched as the king heard and adjudicated on his subjects' complaints, seated in a pavilion ringed by ten horses caparisoned in gold, in front of pages holding gold-mounted shields and swords, and flanked by the sons of princes resplendent with gold plaited in their hair. Even the guard dogs at the doors of the pavilion wore gold collars, from which hung gold bells that tinkled gently in the breeze.

Al-Bakri, a Muslim from Spanish Cordoba, was on a journey to compile a general survey of Bilad al-Sudan, the 'Land of the Blacks', as the Arabs called the vast swathe of territory south of their own area of settlement. During the first decades of its existence, as far back as the 7th century, Islam had stormed westwards along the coastline of North Africa. But its penetration into the African interior was more gradual, and was achieved as much by trade as by conquest.

'Ships' of the desert

Covering perhaps 200 miles (320 km) a week, the Arab camel caravans plodded across the Sahara, trekking 1000 miles (1600 km) southwards with bolts of luxury cloth and blocks of salt, used as a desert currency. These they exchanged for African slaves, for finely tooled leather goods and for kola nuts, the source of a narcotic prized in countries where Islam prohibited the drinking of alcohol.

The Sudan, as the Arabs at that time understood the term, extended from the Atlantic through the upper

Refuge from sun and sand *For countless centuries the oasis has been the source of life-giving water for desert dwellers and travellers. In earlier times trading camel caravans would refresh themselves at such spots of greenery in the arid wasteland.*

White gold *Salt was a valuable trade commodity in the hot African interior.*

Sharp practice *Spearheads could buy food and clothing.*

Hard currency *Copper ingots were a common medium of exchange.*

Chain currency *As many as 100 cowrie shell 'coins' could be linked.*

Riding the sands *Muslim traders, such as this merchant depicted in a 13th-century manuscript, crossed the Sahara to trade with the kingdoms of the Sudan, which then stretched from West Africa to the Red Sea. They rode 200 miles (320 km) a week.*

reaches of the Niger, on to Lake Chad, and ultimately to the Red Sea. (Present-day Sudan is only the eastern part of this whole immense region.) In al-Bakri's day its leading state was called Ghana: this embraced present-day Gambia, Guinea, Mali and parts of Senegal – though not, surprisingly, modern Ghana. In 'The Book of Roads and Kingdoms', as al-Bakri's African survey was called, he tells us that Ghana boasted stone buildings, rare in Africa, and practised religious toleration, with both Muslims and pagans in important posts.

Soon after al-Bakri's visit, the glory of Ghana was brought to an end by the powerful Muslim state of Mali, which rose in its place. Its wealth came from large-scale gold mining; and it grew so rich that when its king, Mansa Musa, made the pilgrimage to Mecca in 1324 he distributed so much largesse that he depressed the value of gold in Arabia for a decade.

Two centuries later the Moroccan diplomat Hasan ibn Muhammad, who was later to become better known by his westernised name of Leo Africanus, visited Mali when it was well past its peak. All the same, he found its inhabitants 'superior to all other Africans in wit, civility and industry'. At the capital city of Timbuktu he was dazzled by the royal palace, which had been decorated by crafts-men from Spain, and even more by the splendour of the king, who rode out attended by 3000 cavalry and a bodyguard of bowmen who were armed with poisoned arrows.

Mali was succeeded in turn by Songhai as the leading state of Islamic West Africa. Like Mali, it based its economy on revenue from trade, and extended its authority northwards, to control the import of salt, and also southwards to control the purchase of gold. It was divided up into clearly defined provinces, and its army was largely a feudal host whose captains owed allegiance to the king. There were also specialised ministries to deal with finance, agriculture, forestry,

justice – and with 'white people', meaning Arabs and Berbers. In 1591 Songhai was overthrown by Morocco, and the West African empire was at an end. Islamic scholarship flourished throughout these king-doms. So also did the toleration of traditional religious practices, which were allowed to continue alongside Islam. Many of those who attended the mosque also underwent tribal initiation rites, or used the services of sorcerers and witch doctors.

Spread of Swahili

Islam also gained a foothold in East Africa, where Arab traders settled along the coast. These newcomers intermarried with the local Bantu women and were known as 'Sawahila', 'coast people'. Their Arabised speech, Swahili, became the adopted language of the whole region. The Muslims' settlements were, however, confined to the coast, and to the offshore islands, such as Zanzibar, centre of the clove trade. They made no attempt to annex the interior, where their agents traded fine cloth from India and porcelain from China for ivory, slaves, gold, copper and iron.

By the 13th century the coastal city of Kilwa, now in Tanzania, was minting its own copper coinage. By the 17th century, under its Portuguese name Quiloa, it was famous enough for its fabulous wealth to be mentioned in Milton's *Paradise Lost*. The remains of its Great Mosque, the largest on the East African coast, can still be seen, as can the ruins of its fortress-palace, which cover 2 acres (0.81 ha).

One part of Africa alone resisted the expansion of Islam. This was Ethiopia, which had been converted to Coptic Christianity as far back as AD 333, but in the 8th century was isolated from contact with the wider world by the tide of Muslim conquest which swept across the lands of the Sudan. For 800 years, until it

Cooling system *Such ornamental fan-holders were a sign of high office. The holes held tufts of horsehair or feathers, waved to keep the face cool.*

was visited by a Portuguese explorer in 1520, Ethiopia stayed largely cut off from Western Christianity; it was known only vaguely in Europe as the domain of the fabulous ruler Prester John. The Europeans dreamed that some day Prester John would unite with them in a crusade against victorious Islam; ironically, when they finally arrived in Ethiopia in force in the 19th century, they did so not as allies but as hostile invaders.

Rock of Ages *The rock-hewn churches of Lalibela, in Ethiopia, are among the wonders of Africa. Ten such churches were hewn from the rock around the year 1100.*

ZIMBABWE'S STONES OF MYSTERY

More than a century after their discovery, the huge granite ruins of Zimbabwe are still shrouded in mystery, as no doubt their builders meant them to be. Their name means 'Great Place' in the Shona language, a fitting title for the only ancient stone buildings of significance surviving in southern Africa. In 1980 the name was adopted for the former Southern Rhodesia.

Consisting of a hilltop fortress-palace and a temple in the valley below, the complex was probably built by successive Bantu-speaking peoples between the 11th and 16th centuries. The buildings are of drystone construction without mortar, and the blocks are skilfully shaped and laid in courses with great precision. Zimbabwe was the centre of the Monomatapa trading empire, which exported gold via the coast to the Muslim world. Besides being a defensive strongpoint

it was also a burial site and a royal residence, built so as to shield the divine king from the gaze of his people.

The empire of Monomatapa was succeeded in the 16th century by a new dynasty, the Rozvis. They constructed some of the largest of Zimbabwe's buildings. Their rule survived until the 1830s, when they were overthrown by warriors from Zululand, the kingdom founded 20 years earlier by Shaka.

Royal etiquette in Zimbabwe was complex. Even close courtiers had to approach the monarch crawling on their stomachs, and were obliged to cough when he coughed, and so on. But the royal prerogative had its drawbacks. Once the king became diseased or senile, and could no longer project the aura of virility on which the prosperity of the state was thought to depend, he was obliged to poison himself.

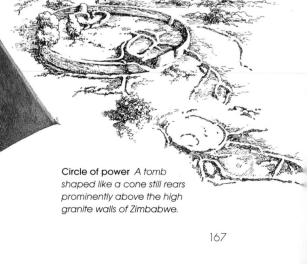

Deadly missile *Knives with twin blades were common weapons in West Africa, their knife edges hurtling through the air in deadly sequence.*

Circle of power *A tomb shaped like a cone still rears prominently above the high granite walls of Zimbabwe.*

LANDS OF ISLAM

In the middle of the 11th century, nomadic Turkish tribesmen known as Seljuks swept into the central Middle East. Zealous converts to Islam, the Seljuks were the forerunners of several fierce warrior peoples who brought a new vigour to the lands which they made their own. A century later, Genghis Khan transformed the scattered Mongol tribes of the central Asian steppes into a united and powerful empire, which Tamerlane was to carry to further conquests. Two other Islamic peoples – the Ottomans in Turkey and the Safavids in Persia – reached their cultural and artistic peaks in the 16th and 17th centuries. By this time, descendants of Tamerlane had swept into India and created a Mughal empire distinguished by the extravagance of its court life, art and architecture.

SELJUKS, MONGOLS, OTTOMANS, PERSIANS AND MUGHALS AD 1050–1700

WHERE THEIR CARAVANS RESTED

Shimmering across the desert sands like a broad, battlemented fortress, the caravanserai dominated the horizon. As the group of travellers came up to its welcoming shelter, they and their horses and camels were dwarfed by the cliff-like walls, with their lines of small windows at the top and a scattering of air holes at the bottom.

The caravanserai stood near the Iranian town of Ribat-i Sharaf. It had been built in the 12th century by Sanjar, the last of the Great Seljuk rulers of Iran, as a stopping place for the merchants, scholars and pilgrims who journeyed together – often for mutual protection – along the royal road into Iran from the north. It was one of many such 'guesthouses' which the Seljuks introduced and which came to be erected throughout the Middle East for travellers and their pack animals.

Once inside the huge, heavy-doored gateway – through which fully loaded camels could comfortably pass – the travellers found themselves in the paved central courtyard, with a refreshing fountain in the middle. The courtyard, open to the sky, had room for about 400 donkeys or camels, in addition to squads of attendants and porters, and it held a large brick cistern in which to collect the winter rain. In addition to the usual sections of a caravanserai – such as stables for the travellers' horses, apartments, and a mosque – there was a magnificently decorated upper audience chamber, approached by a flight of stairs. Here, when he was in residence, the sultan would receive honoured guests. Many of the caravanserais situated along the trade routes were

Mounted might *The Mughal emperor Aurangzeb personifies the warrior skills of the Muslim invaders who swept into India in 1526 and established an empire that endured for two centuries.*

erected outside the walls of a town or village. They were built to encourage commerce. Business, however, was lightened by pleasure, and some of the larger establishments employed their own teams of musicians to entertain the select mixture of guests.

Charges for accommodation varied, and few of the inns provided food. Indeed, when the sultan was staying at the Ribat-i Sharaf caravanserai he alone was fed, while the other guests were expected to cook their own meals in a corner of the courtyard outside.

Afterwards, the guests might take a bath, check that their goods and belongings were safely stored away in cell-like rooms on the ground floor, and then make their way up a stone staircase to their lodgings on the arcaded first floor.

Any traveller who became ill was looked after by a resident doctor, in an infirmary. A guest unfortunate enough to die on the premises would be ceremoniously buried in a mausoleum attached to the caravanserai, where the family could later visit the tomb.

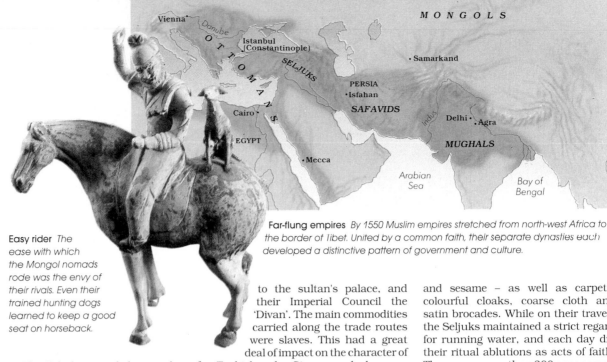

Easy rider *The ease with which the Mongol nomads rode was the envy of their rivals. Even their trained hunting dogs learned to keep a good seat on horseback.*

Far-flung empires *By 1550 Muslim empires stretched from north-west Africa to the border of Tibet. United by a common faith, their separate dynasties each developed a distinctive pattern of government and culture.*

A tide stemmed *In 1529 Suleiman the Magnificent led his troops to the gates of Vienna. It was the farthest west that the Ottoman forces advanced.*

The Seljuks provided a number of Turkish dynasties which ruled over central and western Asia from the 11th century to the 13th century. Even after they became a settled community they retained many of their nomadic habits. The sultan met his tribal chieftains at the entrance to his tent, and when they passed into the tent they sat on divans set around the walls to discuss their business. Both customs were later adopted by the Ottoman Turks, who called their reception hall the 'Sublime Porte', after the gate or entrance to the sultan's palace, and their Imperial Council the 'Divan'. The main commodities carried along the trade routes were slaves. This had a great deal of impact on the character of Turkish rule. Since people born as Muslims could not be used as slaves, rulers such as the Ottomans rounded up young Christian males into their armed forces and civil service. Once these recruits entered the palace school they were brought up as Muslims; but this did not automatically free a non-Muslim from slavery.

From their days as nomads the Turks had strong trading contacts with the wider world. Even after they themselves had adopted a more settled life, they continued to encourage trade across their lands. A Seljuk merchant meeting a Tatar trader at the Crimean port of Sudak, for example, might want the livestock or dairy produce provided by the nomadic peoples roaming the northern steppes. Even more than that, he might require some of their vast range of furs – beaver, ermine, fox, hare, grey squirrel, mink, sable, weasel and wild goat. In return, the Seljuk merchant would offer confectionery, fish, grapes, raisins, yeast

Holy mat *This Ottoman prayer mat has an arched design which must point to Mecca when the mat is in use.*

and sesame – as well as carpets, colourful cloaks, coarse cloth and satin brocades. While on their travels the Seljuks maintained a strict regard for running water, and each day did their ritual ablutions as acts of faith. There were more than 200 spas spread throughout the empire, equipped with sumptuous bathing establishments and drinking fountains. Some springs were reserved for the use of horses and other valuable work animals. And at the sultan's court there was a special post of Master of the Water.

The Turks were a warrior people who worshipped the skills of fighting and horsemanship. Seljuk soldiers were expected to play polo at least once a week as a way of keeping themselves alert and in trim. The sport of archery was also highly regarded, and the sultans themselves, as men of action, set good examples.

From slave to sultan

Baybars, the 13th-century Sultan of Egypt, for example, led the way in encouraging proficiency at archery. He was a Mameluke – a member of a powerful military caste originally made up of slaves which ruled Egypt from 1250 to 1517, and which remained the dominant political power there, even under Turkish rule, until early in the 19th century. In Cairo Baybars laid out a special archery field, with marble markers to record the distances achieved – the farthest, in his time, being 636 yds (581 m).

Baybars had originally been a Turkish-speaking slave who was sold to a military leader for a small sum because of an eye defect. However, this did not stop him from following his own distinguished career as an army commander. He seized the throne in 1260 and ruled Egypt and most of Syria for the next 17 years.

TENTED HOMES FOR MONGOLS ON THE MOVE

When the 13-year-old boy who was to become Genghis Khan succeeded to the leadership of his small Mongol clan, his father, a minor chief, named him Temuchin but bequeathed him little else. Temuchin had to fight for his meagre inheritance. His small group of people owned horses, goats and sheep, but lived in a harsh terrain, and they were surrounded by Tatar enemies who had repeatedly inflicted defeats on them. The Mongols were scattered, leaderless and militarily impotent.

Temuchin was to change all this. By forming prudent alliances and defeating his rivals in battle, his reputation grew so rapidly that individuals, then whole clans, soon flocked to his side, not only to secure Mongol unity and safety but to enjoy the booty that his wars of expansion offered. By 1206 he had taken the name Genghis Khan, or 'Supreme Ruler', God's representative on earth. By the time of his death in 1227 Genghis Khan held sway over the greater part of northern China, westwards to Afghanistan and as far as the Dnieper River in eastern Europe.

Pardons for prisoners

Throughout this vast area Genghis Khan's word was absolute. Yet despite his reputation among foreigners as a man of extreme violence and cruelty, among his own people Genghis Khan was considered a benign and liberal ruler. He spared the lives of prisoners who could read and write, which he could not, and protected any captured craftsmen who could be of service.

However, the death penalty was imposed for a wide variety of offences. A Mongol could be executed for something as trivial as stepping on the threshold of a commander's *yurt*, or tent, and for giving comfort to prisoners without special permission. Adultery and gluttony were also capital offences. Mongols were obliged by law to share their food with any fellow citizens who were hungry.

Even so, the rights of the individual were protected by a body of traditional laws, which may have been supplemented by rulings made by Genghis Khan himself. These laws may even

Portable homes *The Mongols' circular tents, or yurts, were built on light wicker frames, making them easy to dismantle when it was time to move on.*

Camps old and new *Gathered around their camp fire, a group of 14th-century Mongols and their animals (above) rest and make ready for the next day's journey. Present-day tribesmen (left) still spend the winter in their traditional yurts, with their sheep and goats safely penned in.*

have been enshrined at some time in a written legal code. In addition, he allowed the practice of alien religions such as Islam and Buddhism, which stemmed from his conquests of Persia and China. The Mongols' own religion was Shamanism, a mixture of magic and sorcery which taught that all aspects of human life were controlled by a hierarchy of good and evil spirits. These were ruled over by a supreme god called Tengri, next to whom in importance came Itugen, an earth goddess who controlled the fertility and health of herds and crops.

White-robed shamans, or witch-doctors, could communicate with the spirits. The shamans, who carried staffs and drums as their symbols of office, claimed that they consorted with the spirits during dreams, or while in deep, self-induced trances.

There was no public worship among the Mongols. Instead families kept images of Itugen and their ancestors in their yurts, smearing the mouths of the images with food and drink before sitting themselves down to eat. Wine was poured daily as a ritual offering to the four points of the compass, as well as to the winds and to the sun. The Mongols believed that running water was a materialisation of higher powers,

Skill in the saddle *Brilliant horsemanship was the key to the Mongols' success. Vigorous and highly competitive games of polo were regarded as ideal training for the warlike tribesmen.*

which therefore must not be polluted. For instance, anyone caught urinating in running water, or washing in water during a thunderstorm, faced the death penalty.

Wives and concubines

The Mongols were divided into tribes, each with a certain number of tents and an appropriate amount of grazing land. In turn, the tribes were split into *oboks*, or clans. The clansmen were believed to be the descendants of a common ancestor, and were forbidden to marry within the clan, so abolishing the risk of incest. Wives bought from other clans were paid for with animals, goods and grazing land – as well as luxuries judged to be appropriate to the status of the families of the brides-to-be. As well as a wife, or wives, rich men often had a collection of concubines. Whenever the head of a family died, his concubines then became the legal property of his son-and-heir, who often married one of his father's widows. This ensured the future well-being and security of the women and their children.

> '*It is better to be drunk in Hell than to be sober in Paradise!'*
>
> JAHIR, COURT POET, *c.* AD 1100

The Mongols' nomadic way of life followed a set seasonal routine. After having spent the winter in their own sheltered grazing grounds in the valleys, each clan travelled to the high plateau of the steppes. As shepherds, the Mongols mainly ate mutton, as well as beef and horse meat and the flesh of any animals they could catch, such as foxes, wolves, rats and mice. Normally meat was either roasted or boiled, then eaten with the fingers from a communal food pot. A mounted messenger, or soldier out on patrol on his own, would place his meat under the saddle of his horse; thus it became tender with the day's riding, and was then eaten raw. The main drink among the Mongols was mare's milk; when fermented, the milk formed their staple alcoholic drink, *qumis*, which was often drunk to excess and caused

a great many early deaths. Although heavy drinking was admired as a manly quality, the abuse of alcohol was so prolonged and persistent that it came to be regarded as the hereditary vice and weakness of the Mongols.

It was the fashion for high-class Mongol women to paint their faces white – originally to protect the skin from the sun and the wind. They painted their eyebrows black, so that they met in the middle, and also dyed their hair and wore large and elaborate headdresses. Mongol princesses were even more magnificently attired, in robes made from Chinese silk, and caps adorned with threads of gold. By contrast, women occupying the lower ranks of Mongol society usually wore baggy trousers. They sometimes padded their trouser pleats with cotton in order to create the impression of plump hips, a physical attribute much admired by their menfolk. Small noses were seen as another sign of feminine beauty. Despite the great importance of jewellery and fabrics, the Mongols manufactured none of these articles themselves but had them specially imported from Samarkand and the central Asian city of Bukhara. Gold earrings were so highly prized among women that they were brought from the East in camel trains guarded by armed horsemen.

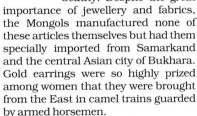

Gold earrings

When Genghis Khan died in 1227 he was buried near the River Onon in Mongolia, at a spot he had earlier chosen. In accordance with his wishes, every living thing which lay in the path of the funeral procession, including all the vegetation, was ruthlessly laid to waste.

Other great Mongol rulers followed in his footsteps – notably Kublai Khan (1215-94), Genghis Khan's grandson, who made China his power base, and Tamerlane (1336-1405), who set up his capital in Samarkand. From the city, in which his palace and mausoleum now stand, Tamerlane launched his successful conquest of Persia.

However, the days of Mongol glory and supremacy were growing shorter. By the end of the 15th century the Mongols' power had entered into an irreversible decline and they gradually reverted to their nomadic pastoral ways, and disappeared for ever into the mists of history.

AN EMPIRE FORGED BY HORSEMEN

Children of the Mongols were taught to ride even before they could walk, and they grew up in the saddle. Mongol boys' skills on horseback often decided their careers, and the most adept of them became cavalrymen or mounted messengers. Indeed, the horse was so important to the Mongols, and to the conquest and control of their vast, unruly empire, that horse thieves were regarded as among the worst of criminals and were invariably sentenced to death.

To keep in touch with the remoter parts of their realm, Mongol emperors used a system of highly paid 'arrow riders', who rode in relays to bring them information about their enemies and the concerns of their scattered people – with most of whom they otherwise had little or no contact. From a small core consisting of the finest regular soldiers, the riders grew into a force some 10,000 strong, which formed an elite legion.

'The greatest delight for man is to inflict defeat on his enemies, to drive them before him, to see those dear to them with their faces bathed in tears, to bestride their horses, to crush in his arms their daughters and wives.'

GENGHIS KHAN, c. 1220

By eating and sleeping in the saddle, each arrow rider aimed to cover at least 100 miles (160 km) a day – so bringing in the space of a day and a night news and reports which otherwise could have taken a month to deliver. On the main routes, rest stations were some 25 miles (40 km) apart. To save time in changing mounts, bells on the riders' saddles announced their approach. Everything was held in readiness for them, including food, and they were soon on their way again, their bodies bandaged against saddle sores and the freezing winds or blazing heat of the steppes. Altogether, the arrow riders may have used as many as 250,000 ponies. The horse played an equally important role in the Mongol army, a highly organised force armed with a formidable array of weapons. Every light cavalryman carried a short bow with a range of some 350 yds (320 m). He had two quivers, each holding about 30 arrows including both light,

Attack and defence
Mongol warriors wore iron helmets with iron mesh face pieces, and carried hide shields. Steel axes were used for savage hand-to-hand fighting.

long-range arrows and also heavily tipped arrows for use in fighting at close quarters. Each warrior carried also a small sword, an axe, two and sometimes three javelins, and a dagger strapped to the inside of the left forearm. Heavy cavalrymen wore the added protection of iron helmets and armour of layered leather, stretching from just below the chin to the knees. They were also provided with shields of skin or lacquered wickerwork, and with lariats. For mounted soldiers, trousers which buttoned below the knee had to be worn. Ordinary soldiers wore shirts made of heavy, raw silk, which lessened the impact of any arrows that pierced the body. Strong enough to resist tearing, the silk went into the wound with the arrow, making it easier to remove. Each man carried a waterproof saddlebag of hide which could be inflated for crossings of deep rivers. This bag contained clean clothes, a needle and thread, a fish-hook and line, a hatchet, an iron cooking pot and two leather bottles, one for water, the other for milk. Rations consisted of smoked meat, millet and yoghurt. So, if necessary, each warrior had the supplies to act as a self-sufficient unit when he was sent into action.

There were few male civilians in Mongol society in the 13th and 14th centuries. Any male who was fit and aged between 14 and 60 was liable to be called up for military duty, particularly in an emergency. Like other successful armies before it – such as those of the Arabs, Byzantines, Parthians and Persians – Genghis Khan's military might was based on a combination of armoured lancers and archers on horseback. In addition to this, the soldiers' flexibility and speed foreshadowed the tactics of armies to come – including the use of German tanks in the Second World War. Above all, however, the army's success was due to its strict organisation, based on units of ten.

The smallest unit, the *arban*, or troop, contained ten men with an elected leader. Ten troop formations made up a *jagun*, or squadron, whose

Headlong flight *The Mongols' constant fascination with the art of warfare is graphically illustrated in this late 15th-century miniature. Turbaned infantrymen join forces with cavalrymen – some mounted on camels – armed with swords, flails and bows and arrows. Even in flight the archers, steady in their stirrups, manage to fire arrows at their pursuers.*

Tower of skulls *Not content with decapitating their prisoners, the Mongols often set the heads in concrete to make a 'tower of skulls'. These gruesome pillars were built in prominent positions to show people what their plight could be if they were foolish enough to oppose the Mongols.*

army. For the military, hunting doubled as a means of keeping physically fit and alert during long days which they spent in the saddle. The most spectacular example of this was the Annual Hunt, in which leopards, tigers, boars, deer and various other game were herded into a confined area and then butchered by the armed horsemen. The terrified screams of the animals – some of which had been penned without food or water – were thought to harden the apprentice warriors to similar cries of pain heard on the battlefield. It also taught them to work in unison in demanding situations and on unfamiliar and difficult terrain.

Siege warfare was unknown to the Mongols until their horsemen poured into northern China in the early 13th century. Genghis Khan then forced Chinese prisoners to construct siege equipment for use against fortified cities. So, for the first time, the Mongols used scaling ladders, battering-rams and massive shields. They also placed prisoners as a human shield in front of the attackers, as a means of saving Mongol lives.

As well as an efficient news service, Genghis Khan set up a sophisticated signalling system, whereby orders were quickly given to his troops, and instantly obeyed. By day, black-and-white flags were the usual way of transmitting orders. By night, lanterns and burning arrows were used. Sheer force of numbers was another element in Genghis Khan's success: his army that swept into Europe may have been as many as 100,000-strong, when no European power could muster more than 30,000.

Genghis Khan's most effective tactic, however, remained terror. When the Persian market city of Nishapur, which he had spared once, dared to rise against him a second time he ordered the beheading of its citizens. Out of a population of at least 100,000, fewer than 50 survived. In addition, many prisoners were disembowelled as a means of discovering any jewellery they might have swallowed, and once Genghis Khan ordered a captured prince to be executed by having molten silver poured into his ears and eyes.

Well-dressed, well-groomed *A richly clad Mongol warrior proudly braids the tail of his sleek and mettlesome horse.*

Made to order *These ornately carved stirrups are thought to have been made for Genghis Khan and, on his death, to have been passed on to his grandson.*

A LIFE IN THE SADDLE

Stirrups, brought in from China, and cruppers – leather straps which kept the saddles in place – gave Mongol cavalrymen greater stability when using their bows and arrows. This even allowed archers to fire over their shoulders while pretending to flee from the enemy – a tactic first used by the horsemen of Parthia and giving rise to the description of 'Parthian Shot' for a final well-aimed missile or remark. In contrast to the handsome, highly strung horses of the cavalrymen the messengers, or 'arrow riders', were mounted on tough, sure-footed ponies. Standing about 4.5 ft (1.3 m) high, the ponies were raised in their thousands on the northern pastures of the realm. They were easy to look after, as they drank little and could survive on whatever grass they found in their cross-country journeys. Despite their foul tempers, the little horses were cherished by their riders and only worked for one day in four.

leader was chosen by arban leaders from among their own number. In turn, ten squadrons formed a *minghan*, or regiment; and ten regiments made a *tumen*, or division, of 10,000 men. The troops lived in an *ordu*, a Turkish word meaning 'camp'.

The cream of the soldiers formed the Imperial Guard, or *Keshik*, a personal guard for the Mongol emperor. This hand-picked body of men, 10,000-strong, consisted of 7000 lifeguards, 1000 day guards, 1000 night guards and 1000 quiver-bearers. All wore distinctive black tunics with red facing and black leather armour. In keeping,

their horses were black with red bridles and saddles. During the brief periods between wars, Mongol troops prepared for the battles to come, in which every adult member of the family had his or her role to play. The warriors had their weapons constantly at the ready, and the women kept their men well fed. In addition, the soldiers' sons had the job of sewing their fathers' sheepskin boots and cloaks.

One of Genghis Khan's favourite pastimes was hunting – in his youth he had kept himself alive by hunting and eating mice and other small creatures – and he introduced the sport to his

A SULTAN'S EMPIRE RUN BY SLAVES

Every five years without fail, specially briefed government commissioners set out from Istanbul and scoured the Ottoman Empire to find recruits to the sultan's vast network of slaves. It was against the law for Muslims to be enslaved, so the recruiting officials sought out unmarried Christian boys aged between about ten and 20. From these, they chose the fittest, the most handsome and the most intelligent. For these youngsters were not to be ordinary, sweat-and-blood slaves.

With education and special training, they were to form an aristocracy of well-paid, high-ranking soldiers, senior civil servants, chief administrators and provincial governors. Whatever their precise role, all would form part of the highly organised civil and military bureaucracy which from the mid-15th century to the early 17th century ran the empire in peace and war.

An empire at its peak

Largest and longest lasting of all the Islamic lands, the Ottoman Empire was founded around 1300 by the Turkish sultan Osman I. In 1453, under the sultan Mehmet II, the Ottomans captured Constantinople – capital of the 1000-year-old Byzantine Empire – and renamed the city Istanbul. In the next 150 years the Ottomans conquered much of eastern Europe and most of North Africa and the Arab world. Their empire reached its peak in the 16th century, under Suleiman the Magnificent – whom slave recruits could even aspire to serve in a role as exalted as that of Grand Vizier, or Chief Minister.

The recruiting drives – known as *devshirmes*, or 'collections' – were regarded with mixed feelings by the youngsters. Some had no desire to leave their provincial homes and Christian way of life and be brought up

Guests of honour *The comforts of life in 16th-century Istanbul are evident, as leading merchants and socialites mingle at a city reception. Coffee, tea and cakes are served as the guests gossip, play backgammon and listen to musicians.*

in the capital as Muslims – even if it did mean future prosperity and power. Many, however, welcomed the chance of escaping the hardships of peasant life and having the chance to rise to senior positions in imperial service.

As soon as the 'new blood' recruits arrived in Istanbul they were admitted into the Muslim faith and then they were circumcised. The brightest and most promising youths were put into the Palace Service – in which they served as pages to the sultan – and were entered in the palace schools. Their education was undertaken by the royal eunuchs, who taught them Turkish, Persian and Arabic (the language of the Koran) as well as philosophy, theology, literature and history. The youngsters were taught to ride, wrestle, sword fight and use bows and arrows. Military strategy was a main subject, and there were courses in professions such as architecture and the law.

The eunuchs kept strict discipline, and the youngsters studied, played and slept to a rigid timetable. They were allowed to talk only at certain times. They could have no dealings with the outside world, and they were encouraged to think of their parents and family as dead. Any boy who broke the rules was liable to be beaten on the soles of his feet with up to ten strokes a day from a thin cane.

This routine lasted until the young men were aged 25, when they were appointed to their selected roles in the running of the empire. One ambition for the fully trained, physically strong recruit was to join the Janissaries, or New Soldiers, an elite infantry corps whose job it was to guard the sultan in his rambling Topkapi Palace and also to police the streets of Istanbul. Most of the city's inhabitants lived in sparsely

furnished, single-storey, wooden houses, sleeping on rugs and mattresses on the floor. The walls were decorated with hand-woven Ottoman carpets, made of wool and often with a silk foundation. The carpets often had floral patterns and arrangements of small and large round medallions. Only the richer residents, who lived in spacious stone houses with gardens and courtyards overlooking the Bosporus, had carpets on the floors. However, as people took their shoes off indoors, the carpets were not subjected to much rough wear.

In the hot weather, the carpets were replaced with cool mats of fresh rushes. In the winter, the homes of rich and poor alike were heated with charcoal-burning copper braziers.

Dinner with bread and jam
The day's main meal was taken in the evening. For the well-to-do it usually consisted of soup, spiced dishes of rice and meat, white cheese, fruit, bread and jam, all washed down with glasses of tea. The poorer people frequently made do with black bread, tripe and rice, which they ate off wooden platters using three fingers. They followed this with inexpensive yoghurt, and had water to drink.

The man of the house had complete authority over his wife, children and relatives. The women were segregated from the men. When it came to divorce, all a man had to do was tell his wife they were no longer married. He was then free to take another wife. If he changed his mind later he could 're-marry' his original spouse simply by telling her that the divorce was over. A woman, however, had to go to court to dissolve an unhappy marriage. Apart from such domestic upsets, most people led orderly and quiet lives. Janissaries' patrols ensured that crime was kept to a minimum, and the streets

THE CODE OF THE JANISSARIES
The most muscular and aggressive of Turkey's boy slaves were drafted into the crack Janissary Corps, whose 15,000 troops were noted for their fanatical loyalty to the sultan – and for their even greater loyalty to themselves. Not allowed to marry, the troops swore solemn oaths of allegiance to each other, beside a tray holding a copy of the Koran and a ceremonial sword. Almost equally venerated were the massive copper soup cauldrons standing in the companies' barrack rooms. The corps' standard was a cauldron, and the officer in command of a company was called the Chief Soup-Maker. If a cauldron fell into the hands of the enemy, the company was considered to be disgraced. The Janissaries reached their peak during the reign of Suleiman the Magnificent, from 1520 to 1566. The sultan thought so highly of the corps, and all it stood for, that he joined its first regiment and, together with the rest of the troops, collected his pay from the regimental paymaster.

were almost deserted after dark, the silence was broken only by the cries of the night watchmen. Those who had to go out for any reason were obliged by law to carry a flare.

During the daytime, however, many people made their way to bargain in the spice markets, the food bazaars and the walled Great Market, with its 70 or so streets and 18 gates. Market inspectors kept a strict eye on all the transactions, and any trader who was caught giving short measure was punished on the spot, often by having the soles of his feet soundly beaten with a thick rod. The nearby hammams, or bathhouses, also did a busy trade. There the men had their beards trimmed and their hair cut, while the women had their skin scrubbed, their feet briskly massaged, and the whites and yolks of eggs were pressed around their eyes to try to erase any wrinkles.

For refreshment and gossip of the day, the men – dressed in kaftans and turbans – would then call in at one of the newly introduced and increasingly popular coffee-houses. To satisfy their taste for sweet things, the womenfolk – wearing baggy trousers and smocks – would sample the wares of the sherbet and syrup-sellers wandering through the streets and markets.

High-hatted *Janissaries wore tall headdresses, with a fold of cloth down the back. This was in memory of a revered holy man Hadji Bektash, the founder of a mystical order revered by the corps, who cut a dangling sleeve from his fur mantle and gave it to an officer, who put it on his head.*

Into battle
A crescent moon, symbol of Islam, crowns an ornate Turkish battle standard.

Whirling dervish
Among numerous orders of dervishes, or Muslim religious brotherhoods, the fanatical Mevlevi entered states of religious ecstasy by whirling, dancing and chanting to the hypnotic music of flutes, cymbals and drums. The dervishes were drawn largely from the lower classes.

Art for use *The Islamic ban on the portrayal of human beings led to the decorative use of flowers and abstract designs on household wares such as this ornate dish and jug.*

GARDEN CITY FOR A SHAH OF THE PEOPLE

When Shah Abbas the Great of Persia decided in the late 16th century to build a new capital for his growing empire, he vowed that he would not be altogether cut off from his subjects by palace walls and locked gates. Instead he sought a viewpoint from which he could observe the daily activities of his people. He also visualised a large, open, central area in which he could mingle with the public.

For a site, he picked the small town of Isfahan, set 5200 ft (1585 m) above sea level in a luscious green valley, ringed by mountains. At first he planned to enlarge the existing town, but when an uncooperative landlord refused to sell the land needed, the shah decided to create a new town centre a mile or so to the south. In 1598 began the golden age of Isfahan, the hub of the Safavid dynasty which ruled over Persia for two centuries. The task of re-creating Isfahan occupied Shah Abbas until his death 31 years later. It also gave employment to thousands of local builders and craftsmen.

The shah turned the former Ali Qapu, or 'Lofty Gate', from a high archway into a three-storey palace and grandstand. Its covered balcony overlooked a spacious park called the Naqsh-i-Jahan, or 'Plan of the World', and it was there that Abbas set the heart of his city: the Maidan-i-Shah, or 'Courtyard of the Shah'.

Coffee and chess at dawn

The daily routine began early in the Maidan, and by 7am the coffee-houses near the entrance to the Old Town were packed with men drinking black coffee, while the air was thick with tobacco smoke. The drinkers sat in a circle and cleaned their pipes in large water jars. Some men played draughts or chess, while others gossiped. By noon, the Maidan swarmed with tradesmen and customers. Tents, booths and stalls were erected, while many traders simply spread their fruit, vegetables, drugs and oils on dusty patches and squatted among their goods. Other wares included cotton and leather goods, jewellery, furs, silks, satins, trunks and boxes, locks and keys, iron tools, doors, window frames, spinning wheels, horses, mules and camels. The shrill cries of the traders mingled with the calls of vendors who slaked people's thirsts with drinks of iced water. Music played on long copper trumpets and drums poured from the upper floors of the two-storey galleries lining the square. In the midst of all the noise, friends greeted each other by bowing and laying their right hands across their chests. Weaving their colourful way through the throng were tumblers, jugglers, puppeteers, acrobats, wrestlers and dancers. Any spare spaces were soon occupied by fortunetellers and storytellers, whose clients and audiences hung on their every word.

The only clear area was in front of the Ali Qapu, where spectacles were staged in the evenings for the shah and his court. There were fierce gladiatorial contests, and fights to the death between lions, bulls, bears and rams. The shah was also keen on polo, both as a spectator and a player. Whenever Abbas hit the ball the royal trumpeters sounded a fanfare and the watching crowd dutifully cheered. When the shah was merely an onlooker, an ox-drawn polo cart was ready to take him to whichever goal was seeing the most

Carpet craft *Spinners and weavers produced the magnificent carpets of knotted wool and silk for which Persia was famous. The designs acceptable to Islam included animals, flowers and scrolls.*

PARADISE IN A CARPET

Crafts played a major part in the economy of Isfahan, and in 32 workshops in the grounds of the royal palace some 5000 craftsmen made everything from clothes to crockery, secure in the knowledge that they had jobs for life. The city became renowned for its hand-woven rugs and carpets. The designs were based on flowers, birds, beasts and trees, and often combined all these motifs of the natural world in a representation of a Persian garden; the Persian word for a walled garden, *pairidaeza*, is the origin of our word 'paradise'. Craftsmen's salaries were increased every three years, and when they retired their wages were paid to their children, many of whom started work themselves at 12. Work for the shah occupied only a quarter of a royal craftsman's day, leaving him time for lucrative private commissions.

Musical partners *Men and women musicians were a familiar sight in Isfahan. As well as entertaining the public, the players welcomed envoys to the court of the shah.*

Lovers of nature *Inspired by the countryside around them, the people of Isfahan cultivated trees, flowers, bushes and plants in their evergreen city.*

action: the marble goalposts survive today. Equally popular were archery contests, for which a melon, an apple, or on state occasions a gold cup, was placed on top of a tall pole in the middle of the Maidan. A group of mounted archers galloped past the pole, turned in the saddle and fired at the target.

The shah's nights out

When darkness fell, the Maidan was illuminated by some 50,000 lamps, which highlighted the blue-and-white tiles of the surrounding buildings. It was then that Abbas, like a prince in an Arabian Nights' tale, periodically disguised himself as a peasant and mixed with his people. He wandered freely, asking people's views of the shah and his regime. He accepted criticism of himself, but dealt ruthlessly with any court officials or state ministers guilty of cruelty or corruption. Abbas sampled the sweetmeats and fruits on sale in the bazaars, and once bought and walked away in a pair of shoes that took his fancy. If a shopkeeper tried to give him short measure, he showed no mercy. A dishonest baker was once arrested and baked in his oven, and a fraudulent butcher was roasted on his own spit.

High walls which flanked the Maidan enclosed the homes of the rich, set among gardens and plane trees. Most of Isfahan's 500,000 people, however, lived in houses made of sun-dried brick or mud, built around a central courtyard, often with a pool in the middle. They ate sparingly. Breakfast usually consisted of coffee and a hunk of bread; at midday, curds, sweetmeats and fruit were eaten. The main meal of the day, at 7pm, consisted of kebabs and egg dishes, cooked plainly and washed down with fizzy fruit drinks. The residents of Isfahan were so devoted to fruit that irrigation canals were built

to help to produce it – and the rich had fruit stored all year in ice houses. The poor, who lived in overcrowded hovels in the unpaved lanes of the Old Town, existed largely on cucumbers, roots and melons. Even so, they were well fed and well clothed, and even the poorest women bore gold or silver ornaments on their arms, feet and necks.

Shah Abbas died in 1629, but the Safavid dynasty lasted for nearly another century, until Isfahan fell to the Afghans in 1722. The city survives to the present day – still producing its traditional carpets and rugs, handprinted fabrics and metalwork.

Weapons of war *Encased in a wooden, leather-covered scabbard, this curved sword has a single-edged steel blade and a carved ivory hilt. The warrior's shield is of steel inlaid with gold.*

A shah's helmet *The helmet of steel and gold made for Shah Abbas has an adjustable nosepiece, and a mesh web to protect forehead and neck. The band around the rim has verses praising the ruler.*

Production line *Reinforced helmets of chased steel were made for the shah's warriors by the metalworkers of Isfahan.*

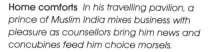
Home comforts *In his travelling pavilion, a prince of Muslim India mixes business with pleasure as counsellors bring him news and concubines feed him choice morsels.*

inner circle had a choice of anything up to 1000 rich dishes a day. Supplies of ice were brought daily by runners from the snowy northern mountains, and the emperor's drinking water came straight from the holy River Ganges.

To move the emperor's quarters alone took the combined efforts of some 500 camels, 400 wagons, and 100 elephants and their bearers. The harem ladies travelled in covered litters carried on poles on men's shoulders or in howdahs, or canopied seats, on the backs of elephants. Swelling the camp's population were thousands of followers, wandering tradesmen, and an immense host of grain merchants with more than 100,000 bullocks bearing supplies.

Escaping from the summer heat
The urge to move from place to place was typical of the unbroken line of emperors who ruled much of India from the 16th century to the middle of the 18th century, when their empire started to disintegrate. They made their journeyings for a variety of reasons. Jahangir travelled to see at first hand how his army was dealing with the rebel forces which in 1616 threatened to overrun the southern state of Deccan. Periodically emperors and their courts journeyed north to Kashmir to escape the sweltering heat of the Indian summers.

Sometimes, however, Mughal rulers travelled simply because it was in their blood to do so. For the emperors were descended from the Mongol conquerors

Crowning glory *A woman of the harem uses the idle hours to dress her long hair in the hope of winning her lord's favour.*

MUGHALS OF INDIA, RULERS ON THE MOVE

Each time the travelling camp of the Mughal emperor Jahangir stopped for the night, it covered an area some 20 miles (32 km) in circumference. It took half a day for the vast procession to pass by any one spot along the way. Even so, the entire complex could be set up in about four hours.

The streets, red and white tents and wooden buildings were laid out to an unvarying plan. Tradesmen and their bazaars were always located in the same place so that people knew exactly where to go for their shopping needs. And at the centre of the camp stood the wood-and-canvas walled fort of Emperor Jahangir, who for 22 years, from 1605 to 1627, ruled over the Muslim empire established in India by Mongol invaders a century earlier.

The emperor's fort, some 300 yds (275 m) in diameter, was entered through an elegant gatehouse. Once in the emperor's presence, officials and courtiers stayed at strictly decreed distances from him: the more senior their status, the nearer they were allowed to stand to the royal throne. All were called to prayer several times each day in a mobile wooden mosque. Courtiers lived in pavilions which were luxuriously furnished with silk-covered couches, elaborately patterned hand-woven carpets and rich tapestries.

The emperor held public and private audiences in halls equipped with glass hookah bowls and spittoons, and every morning he appeared on a balcony to show his subjects that he was alive and well. Nearby, a painted tent accommodated a selection of the 5000 members of the emperor's harem. In addition there was a studio for the court painters, who accompanied Jahangir on his travels and recorded the splendours of his reign. Hundreds of tents housed the camp's 3000 servants: these included a thousand or more swordsmen and wrestlers to provide evening entertainment, 500 torchbearers to light the scene, and hundreds of elephant minders.

Wherever the court moved, the emperor was supplied with fresh fruit from Kabul and Kashmir. He and his

178

Siege tactics *Protected by leather screens, engineers erect a sabat, or covered passage, along which their troops can advance to attack an enemy stronghold. Despite the shields, constant bombardment killed scores of workers.*

Genghis Khan and Tamerlane. Their background influenced India's culture, architecture and art. Persian became the language of government and diplomacy thoughout India: the name 'Mughal' is a Persian form of Mongol.

Wherever the emperors went, their extravagant way of living contrasted starkly with the conditions of the poor, who lived in tiny, overcrowded mud huts with thatched roofs. They had little furniture and only thin cotton sheets. On cold nights, entire families huddled for warmth round small, cow-dung fires lit outside their front doors. During periodic plagues and famines, the starving poor would even resort to cannibalism.

Meanwhile, the emperors lavished money on elaborate water gardens in which several emperors, including

Precious wares *Turbaned Mughal jewel merchants sit crosslegged on the ground, offering their rings and necklaces from plush-lined trays.*

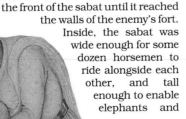

Jahangir, were buried. The emperor Akbar, who ruled from 1556 to 1605, lies in a garden tomb in the village of Sikandra, near Agra in northern India. The gateway to the mausoleum bears the inscription: 'Here are the Gardens of Eden. Enter them and dwell within forever.'

In many gardens spring water cascades from terrace to terrace, splashing its way down towards a tranquil pool, and spouting skywards from ornate marble fountains. Artificial lakes surround domed pavilions, reached by steppingstones or else by slender, stone bridges which seem to rise like mist from the surface of the water. Miniature portraits of the emperors and their courts, mainly in rich red, yellow, gold and orange, were another popular art form, as were paintings of animals and birds, including deer, zebras, wild Himalayan goats, and black bucks.

Operating as a team, the painters divided up the work between them. One artist specialised in the features of individual faces, another determined the composition, while a third did the colouring. Fine brushes made from the tail hairs of squirrels added to the delicacy of the paintings, while their brilliant, enamel-like finish was achieved by burnishing the pictures with pieces of polished agate.

A sabat at the siege

The Mughals were also renowned for their prowess in battle. One of their most successful techniques was the use of the *sabat*, a covered passage with cannon-proof walls of mud-and-rubble and a wooden roof secured with hides. Teams of workmen added to the front of the sabat until it reached the walls of the enemy's fort. Inside, the sabat was wide enough for some dozen horsemen to ride alongside each other, and tall enough to enable elephants and

riders with raised lances to pass through in comfort. Soldiers armed with muskets and cannons could fire at the enemy through loopholes in the roof and walls. The emperor Akbar used a sabat to great effect in 1568 when he captured the hill fortress of Chittor, in central India. The structure writhed its way slowly up the steep hill-side and struck serpent-like at the walls of the fort. Akbar showed no mercy to Chittor's defenders, nor to the 35,000 peasants living in the fort, all of whom were slaughtered.

The Mughal armies spent most of their time in waging war. In between actions, the soldiers kept in training by taking part in large-scale animal hunts. Following the example set by early Mongol warriors, they acted as beaters, forming a large circle up to 50 miles (80 km) in diameter. They then closed in on their prey, such as deer, forcing them into an enclosure some 3 miles (5 km) wide. The emperor and his nobles then proceeded to slaughter the animals with swords, spears and bows and arrows.

Akbar himself went hunting with cheetahs, which pinned the deer to the ground and tore out their throats. After several days the troops were allowed their turn, killing any animals still alive. Their taste for bloodshed sharpened, and their skill for manoeuvres enhanced, the soldiers were then ready to do battle again.

Weapons of war *Mughal daggers were noted for their ornamental scabbards, handles and blades, often overlaid with gold. One handsome weapon has a pommel shaped like a goat's head, with onyx eyes and a central ruby set in gold. The hilt is of enamelled jade.*

Grim warning *Like the Mongols before them, the Mughals erected 'towers of skulls' studded with the severed heads of their enemies as a warning to foes. An English traveller made this drawing of one such pillar: 'The heads of rebells and theeves', he wrote, 'are mortered and plaistered in.'*

EUROPE ON THE MOVE

A heady mixture of trade and scholarship, exploration and rebellion, artistic flowering and religious reform marked the transition in Europe from the Middle Ages to the modern world. Among the city-states of northern Italy, Venice became the centre of maritime power, while in Florence wealthy bankers became patrons for great artists, sculptors and architects. In Rome, however, the splendour of papal ceremony could not disguise the mounting corruption of the Church, which was to lead to the stormy birth of Protestantism under the influence of Martin Luther and John Calvin. The first Bible printed from movable type by Johann Gutenberg led to the spread of cheaply priced books and new opportunities in education. The new spirit of adventure inspired Columbus to set sail across the uncharted Atlantic – and accidentally to encounter the New World. Meanwhile for ordinary people, especially those trying to make a living off the land, life remained hard and money scarce.

WESTERN EUROPE AD 1400–1600

WEALTH FROM TOIL BY MINER AND TRADER

Before dawn, in the hills of Saxony, miners gathered in the little chapel at the pithead. They had already walked some distance from their cottages by the light of horn lanterns, carrying with them crude helmets, picks and shovels and the bread and ale that would sustain them in the bowels of the earth as they battled against darkness and damp, listening fearfully to the creaking timbers of the supports and the dripping water which threatened to flood the workings, alert for the first sign of any one of the disasters that could put a sudden end to their lives.

The silver-bearing lead or copper and gold ores which they extracted provided the coinage on which the expanding commerce of 15th-century Europe depended, fine statues with which rich patrons embellished their cities, and wealth to buy the weapons with which states fought to establish their supremacy. Within their defensive

Horseman for hire *The proud figure of the mounted Bartolommeo Colleoni expresses the might of the* condottieri, *the new class of professional soldiers who served the warring city-states of Italy. They hired themselves and their men out to the highest bidder by a* condotta, *or 'contract'. The bronze statue is one of the masterpieces of Andrea del Verrocchio, of Florence.*

walls, the townsfolk who flourished by trade and manufacturing were living a richer and fuller life, against the background of an ambitious programme of public building works.

With building went art, and a new prestige for the artist. Costumes, too, could be lavish – especially those of the merchants and financiers who created and circulated the wealth of the time. Some medieval financiers were so affluent that they wielded more power than the monarchs who, in order to keep or gain their thrones, borrowed vast sums of money from them.

Families such as the Medicis in Florence and the Fuggers in southern Germany dominated the European banking and mercantile world in the 15th and 16th centuries. From 1508 to 1515, Georg and Ulrich Fugger held a lease on the Roman mint and handled remittances to the papal court for the sale of indulgences – payments for the remission of punishments for sins.

Even their wealth and influence, however, was exceeded by that of their young brother Jakob the Rich. He controlled silver and copper mines in Silesia and the Tirol, and raised money to finance the election, in 1519, of Charles V as Holy Roman Emperor.

'How many towns which when we were children were built of nothing but wood, are now lately started up all of marble !'

LEONE ALBERTI, c. 1500

Knowledge was all-important, and especially information about developments happening elsewhere. The great merchants ran their own news services: the Fugger brothers circulated handwritten commercial newsletters among the far-flung branches of their banking empire, and in France, Jacques Coeur, chancellor to Charles VII and banker to the royal court, had his own private pigeon post.

New, speedier methods of communication were soon, however, to bring news not only to merchants but to ordinary people. In the 1450s, in the German town of Mainz, Johann Gutenberg produced the first books printed from movable type. By the end of the 15th century no fewer than 110 places in Europe – from Toledo to Oxford to Stockholm – had their own printing presses. As well as books, printed news sheets, circulated

City between worlds *Merchant aristocrats made Venice a link between west and east. Its shipyards turned out galleys for trade and experimented with new fighting ships. Foreign merchants crowded its harbours, and pilgrims passed to and fro on the way to Rome.*

cheaply, gave people the latest information on European and world events. One such sheet, printed in Rome in 1493, described the recent voyage of Christopher Columbus to the New World.

The rapid dissemination of ideas made possible by the invention of printing also spread dissent against the power of the Church, which came under increasing attack both by religious reformers and by secular rulers. In 1517 the Augustinian monk Martin Luther fastened to the door of Wittenberg Cathedral his Ninety-Five Theses – the original documents of the Protestant revolution. Within a month his bitter criticisms were the talk of Europe, and they led to bloody warfare as German troops butchered Catholics.

Everywhere, the power of the Church was further eroded by the challenge of secular rulers – who nevertheless invoked divine right to support their claims to rule. To consolidate their power, the new national monarchs raised ever-larger armies and navies. Increasing numbers of able-bodied men were pressed into service – and those left on the land staggered under ever-heavier tax burdens.

War and recurring plagues took their toll: by 1500 the population of Europe had fallen to some 60 million – little more than two-thirds of the total in 1300. While in some areas new and flourishing industries such as ship-

building and publishing brought about a mutually beneficial union between masters and workers, in other areas the underprivileged masses revolted against their wealthy masters in a series of peasant and urban revolts.

Meanwhile, against the background of a Europe generally on the move, the miners of Saxony and Thuringia continued the toil they started at dawn until long after dusk, crawling on their hands and knees, twisting and turning as they sought the precious veins of ore. To compensate them for their toil, some miners were granted concessions, such as exemption from military service and certain taxes. Even this failed to attract enough new recruits. Work in some mines was a punishment for criminals. Though the children of mine managers might take up well-paid careers, most miners' sons could expect nothing better than to follow the dangerous trade of their fathers.

Centres of power *All over Europe, rapidly expanding towns were centres of invention, of trade, of the arts, of religious reform and of maritime adventure.*

Leaders of fashion *Money allowed free rein to self-expression in dress. Pointed hats, long coloured hose and rich velvet cloaks created a peacock spectacle.*

MERCHANTS AND GALLEYS OF VENICE

Money at work *The gold fiorino, or florin, named after the lily flower it bore, was with the gold ducat and silver scudi one of the principal coins used in trading the goods unloaded by Venice's stevedores (left).*

From an early hour the merchants of Venice congregated on the Rialto, the bustling market of craftsmen and retailers who acted as the merchants' eyes and ears. To ban a merchant from the Rialto was to bankrupt him: for in an age without newspapers, the information arriving on the Rialto in letters from factors and commission agents throughout their trading world – shared with colleagues or jealously kept secret from rivals – was the source of knowledge and power.

Money and its use was the key to the city's prosperity, which reached its height in the early 15th century. Sheltered behind her lagoons, Venice had through the might of *condottiere* mercenaries conquered most of the surrounding territory and a seaborne empire extending from the Adriatic to Cyprus. Seaborne trade was Venice's lifeblood – and it was the merchants and bankers who kept it circulating. The bankers made their living by accepting deposits from merchants and making transfers, and by providing bills of exchange to other cities, or bills of credit to travelling merchants.

If ready cash was hard to come by, the Rialto merchants could turn to the Jews. Marked out by their yellow hats as social pariahs, and officially acceptable only as doctors, they nonetheless engaged profitably in pawnbroking.

Men of business and the law

Most of the merchants on the Rialto were taught as children to read and write, and were then sent to a master of the abacus to learn mathematics, bookkeeping and other essentials of business. They next spent some time apprenticed in a business, working behind the counter and getting experience of accounting. Some had legal training and had practised for a time in the busy commercial court.

Many merchants had personal experience of the Mediterranean ports from which the most valuable goods came, having sailed there as armed escorts on the merchant galleys. Now they operated through agents, or by entering into an agreement with a

Heart of a city *Noblemen, merchants and moneylenders rubbed shoulders in the Rialto, the financial heart of Venice. The old timber Rialto bridge – which burned down in 1514 and was later rebuilt – spanned the Grand Canal, beside a maze of arcaded streets where spices, silks and other goods were sold in wholesale shops.*

younger merchant whereby the older partner provided the capital and the younger the hard work. The business was difficult and delicate. A merchant needed an ear tuned to the nuances of domestic and overseas politics. What was the Turk planning? What were the risks to the fleets? What were the chances of space in the spice fleet to Alexandria, which was government regulated? What freight rates would be set? What would the government decree as this year's priorities? Was there demand for Florentine cloth in the East, or should gold and silver be sent?

On the answers to such questions, merchants bought spices, silks and oriental exotic goods from their agents in Alexandria, dealt in grain and wine, alum and rare dyes, and sold them to other agents in all parts of Europe.

All had an interest in the well-being of the Arsenal, the dockyard at the centre of Venetian shipbuilding and naval power and probably the largest industrial organisation in Europe. Owned by the state, the Arsenal covered 60 acres (24 ha) and produced, equipped and repaired a range of ships: light galleys for war, great galleys to carry silks and spices, smaller ships for general merchandise. Their design was standardised, so that parts to fit any ship of a particular class were readily available; the production line could make an entire galley in a week.

The Arsenal employed as many as 2000 people. Its discipline was like that of a factory, a bell being rung at dawn for half an hour to summon the workmen and again at noon. Workers who arrived late lost their day's pay. Wine was passed round the yard six times a day as part of the wages. Despite rigid discipline, constant pilfering went on.

Within the Arsenal were foundries, magazines and ropeworks. Outside, it indirectly employed many more craftsmen at ancillary tasks, as well as the thousands of sailors who manned the boats. To ensure the pre-eminence of the Arsenal, other, private shipyards in Venice were limited to building vessels of 94 tons and less.

'When the galley had reached the end of the street all the men required were on board, together with the complement of oars, and she was equipped from end to end. In this manner there came out ten galleys, fully armed, between the hours of three and nine'.

PERO TAFUR, c. 1636

The numerous craftsmen involved – carpenters, sailmakers, ropemakers, oarmakers, blacksmiths, gunfounders, caulkers – were supervised by guilds. These managed the education of the apprentices and ensured that high standards were maintained. They also provided for the elderly – ensuring, for instance, that those over 55 got a share of the work and that the sick were paid during illness. The guilds also looked after the aged, and the widows and orphans of their members.

Men whose trades were vital to Venice were prohibited from leaving the city, but their well-being, and that of their families, was ensured. The government itself made provision for the advancement of the impecunious children of deceased patricians, while the orphans of ordinary citizens were looked after in orphanages run by rich and powerful religious brotherhoods known as *scuole*, or schools. These brotherhoods also played a large role as patrons of the arts, and in particular the music which became one of the splendours of Venice.

At the head of the skilled workers in the Arsenal were the shipwrights. It was the foremen in this trade who designed the ships on whose speed, capacity, manoeuvrability and defensibility so much depended. Experiments were carried out to solve the problems which arose as guns had to be mounted on galleys, and to improve ships' design and speed – as, for example, by altering the number of oars on the galleys and by changing the number of masts and rigging. New designs for ships were commissioned, examined and amended by committee.

A wedding with the sea

A great regatta on January 10 each year was a festive occasion which included competitions for ships' beauty and decorations. It was also the occasion for races, which all Venetians from

Trade secrets *Glassworkers were confined to Venice to keep their methods secret. They excelled at adding gem-like enamels to their goblets.*

the humblest stevedore to the Doge himself watched with vital concern. Every year on Ascension Day the Doge took part in a ceremony which symbolised the marriage of the cityport – built on almost 120 islands and laced with canals – to the sea.

What they earned by trade, wealthy Venetians spent on a rich lifestyle, and particularly on food, jewellery and clothing. Public feasts for visiting dignitaries included lavish spectacles with dancing, clowns and acrobats. A law restricted to 1600 ducats the maximum dowry a woman might receive – but expenditure on wedding feasts far exceeded this. Though Venetian women had little visible power, women who had personal property were able to trade on their own account. The whores of Venice, notorious throughout Europe, were strictly regulated by the state; it forbade them from having intercourse with Jews or Muslims, defined the area in which they operated, and ordered them to display their legs and bosoms when there was a downturn in customer interest.

Visiting the sick *Free medical care for the needy was a feature of life in Venice. The hospitals that provided it commissioned paintings and friezes from the finest artists of the day. Patients were visited in their sickbeds by their relatives and friends, who brought them gifts of food and drink. Poor patients were transported to so-called 'hospitals of mercy' by teams of volunteer* stretcher-bearers, *who were ready to turn out at any time of day or night. Waifs were also given shelter.*

Binding the young *Infants were wrapped in swaddling bands, which were supposed to make the limbs grow straight.*

Fine feathers *Dress showed riches or rank, and sumptuous clothes were worn even on everyday occasions. These two young strollers wear the elaborate caps typical of Venice, and have long cloaks of brocaded velvet, without collars.*

THOUSANDS FLOCK TO A REBORN ROME

A city sacked *Rome's time of splendour created by Leo X was short-lived: in 1527 a rabble of 22,000 unpaid and leaderless mercenary imperial troops sacked the city, and some 13,000 Romans died, many after being tortured and raped. Among the attackers were supporters of the monk and religious reformer Martin Luther.*

As darkness falls, a steady stream of travellers pours towards Rome, anxious to reach the gates of the city before they shut for the night. Two out of every three travellers are on foot, many of them bearing the staff, satchel and scallop shell badge that identify them as pilgrims; every year some 50,000 pilgrims throng to the Holy City, mainly during Lent and at Easter.

Others on the road, on a typical day in the early 1500s, range from special ambassadors bound on secret missions to the papal court, to humble priests, monks and nuns on business for their parish or order. Many of those making for Rome are ordinary folk from other parts of Italy and farther afield, eager to try their fortunes in the city. Some travellers have been on the road for more than a month.

Jostling for space are herdsmen driving sheep, goats and cattle, and innumerable clumsy eight-wheeled carts laden with provisions, firewood and building timber for Rome. Suddenly all this motley throng is elbowed aside as a noisy, roistering company of 300 archers, halberdiers, gamekeepers and beaters surges down the road, guarding in its midst a plump, shortsighted man in leather boots and hunting gear. Pope Leo X and his mounted courtiers are coming home from a hunting expedition.

A new city from the ruins

Passing through the gates, pope, pilgrims and peasants enter a city in the throes of a spectacular rebuilding programme. After a century of neglect since a catastrophic earthquake in 1419, Pope Leo since his succession in 1513 had set out to make Rome a glittering metropolis of art, architecture and learning.

Under the guidance of the architect Filippo Brunelleschi, the pope re-aligned the streets and pulled down the ruins of the old Rome. In their place rose splendid new buildings in the classical style, the lime for their cement produced by burning the broken statues of an earlier age. In addition to a massive programme of new public buildings, humbler homes

Pilgrims' progress *Maps in hand, pilgrims make a penitential tour of seven of Rome's churches. The tour took them about eight hours, passing from inhabited areas around the Vatican to desolate marshes, with the pilgrims often knee-deep in mire.*

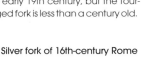

Life in the Cowfield *At the start of the 16th century much of Rome lay in ruins. Many years of neglect before the accession of Pope Leo X had turned even the once proud Forum (left) into a shambles overrun by farm animals, shepherds and squatters. The people of Rome nicknamed the area the Campo Vaccino, or the 'Cowfield', after the cattle which grazed there. It became such a popular meeting place for the poor that a cheap inn was established with benches and tables for the patrons, their children and their dogs.*

On the house *Three poor travellers to Rome receive a free meal and shelter in a monastery along the route. Travellers with money were expected to pay their way.*

for the people were built in thousands, extending the city slowly eastwards. Leo also sought to improve the city's water supply and sewerage and so reduce the risk of disease. He attempted to drain the Pontine marshes, and built hospitals and schools.

Meanwhile, no fewer than 236 inns and hostelries stood ready to cater for weary travellers entering the city. At the gates, guides and hustlers waited to lead the better-off visitors to inns near the Pantheon. Poorer travellers found shelter in the wooden houses of the crowded Trastevere district. Monks and nuns headed for the religious colleges, while diplomats went to the palace of the cardinal who looked after the interests of their country.

Servants of the Church

Rome had no industry, few crafts other than the luxury skills of goldsmiths and silversmiths, and little trade beyond catering for the needs of its constant stream of visitors. More than one in three of the city's population were employed by the Church, and most of the remainder were connected to it in one way or another.

The pope's household numbered nearly 700 people; these included his personal bodyguard, the Swiss Guard, 27 domestic prelates, 64 chamberlains, 68 gentleman of the bedchamber, 265 servants and an assortment of priests, musicians, dwarfs and buffoons. Emulating this display, cardinals, bankers and the old Roman aristocrats abandoned the fortified towers on the Capitol that had sheltered their ancestors and competed with each other to build their own magnificent palaces. Then they commissioned the finest artists of the day to embellish and furnish the interiors with statues, paintings, carpets and jewels.

In these sumptuous surroundings the Roman well-to-do indulged their taste for luxurious living, feasting and pomp on an unprecedented scale. One banking family, the Chigis, always threw their dining-room silver into the River Tiber after a banquet, boasting that no important guest would ever dine off the same plate twice. In fact, the silver was said to be caught in a specially placed net and later retrieved by the family's servants.

The expenditure of the Church, the cardinals, the bankers and the visitors also supported Rome's merchants and shopkeepers, its butchers and bakers, its prostitutes, pimps, pickpockets and cutpurses. Even the cast-off

clothing and surplus food from the great palaces, and the free entertainment in the streets, provided richer living than was available to most people in city or country life at the time. A visitor might make for the Vatican, to admire Raphael's new frescoes in the Sistine Chapel; or he could go to see the papal menagerie, with its elephants and lions. There was horse racing in the Corsa, bullfighting in the Piazza of St Peter's, and entertainment by acrobats, tumblers, fire-eaters and clowns below the papal fortress of St Angelo.

The humanist and the monk

The city's intellectuals were catered for at the villa of one of Italy's leading humanists, Jacobo Sadoleto, who might discuss with his guests the reformation of Christian life. Perhaps in Sadoleto's company visitors might hear of a little-known German monk named Martin Luther, who was shortly to stand at the forefront of the revolt against the ostentation and decadence that he saw characterised in Rome.

Many of Luther's supporters were among the forces who in 1527 reduced Rome once again to ruins. Corpses lay unburied in the streets, gnawed by starving dogs. Some 30,000 houses were destroyed, palaces and hospitals pillaged and burnt, priceless manuscripts and books lost. Plague and famine finally drove the army out. The rebuilding that followed was undertaken in a more restrained mood. Display had not vanished, but the extravagance of Renaissance Rome was gone for ever.

FROM FINGERS TO FORK

Forks were first used in Italian households in the 11th century, mainly for eating fruit that would otherwise stain the fingers. By the mid-15th century other countries began to adopt the two-pronged fork as an alternative to the sharp-pointed knife for lifting meat from the plate. But forks were still not in common use when around 1600 a traveller presented Elizabeth I of England with a fork of such elegance that she had replicas made in gold, coral and crystal. Forks with three prongs arrived in the early 19th century, but the four-pronged fork is less than a century old.

Silver fork of 16th-century Rome

Artist's method *On a plate decorated in the same style, a painter works on the distinctive pottery called maiolica, in which the decoration is painted on a white glaze containing tin oxide. It is named after Mallorca, where the style originated.*

Craftsmen's toil *Urged on by their master – who sits on a stool – a team of pottery assistants feverishly stoke the kiln.*

RIVALRY MADE ARTS BLOOM IN FLORENCE

Early in 1401 the citizens of Florence seethed with excitement. Their mood was not in anticipation of some great political change, but because the design for the new north doors of the Baptistry had been put out to competition. This venerable building, which faces the great Duomo, or Cathedral, had a history stretching back 1000 years. The Florentines of the 15th century believed that it had once been a Roman temple to Mars, so linking them with their classical past.

To emphasise the city's pride and unity, every New Year's Day, which in those days fell on March 21, all the children born in the city during the past year were brought to the Baptistry for a communal baptism – hence its name. The new north doors had been commissioned by the wool merchants, who controlled the trade on which so much of the prosperity of Florence depended. As one of the seven major Florentine guilds, they were eager to display their civic spirit by a beautiful addition to one of the city's most revered and treasured buildings.

Rivals in splendour

The competition was won by Lorenzo Ghiberti, against strong opposition from six other great sculptors. The runner-up was Filippo Brunelleschi, architect of Florence's chief glory, the cupola of the Duomo, which still dominates the city today. Begun in 1403, the huge Baptistry doors were not completed until 21 years later. Their 28 gilded bronze panels, in high relief, show scenes from the life of Christ. In spite of their outward display of unity, the Florentines were fiercely competitive, and monuments erected by each group had to

Clothing the poor *Wool was the basic material used for clothing, and one in three of Florence's citizens worked in the cloth industry. Once a year the wealthy wool manufacturers' guild gave out clothes to the city's poor, with special concern for children.*

Enriching a city *Every May, Florence paid tribute to Mercury, the Roman god of merchants. An engraving topped by the figure of Mercury shows craftsmen at work. In the street, in front of a goldsmiths' shop, a sculptor shapes a head and an astronomer holds up a sphere. Indoors are a scribe and a clockmaker, and on upper floors a musician and two house decorators. Rising above the rooftops is the dome of the city's cathedral. Each craft had its own guild; the wool guild's symbol was the lamb (right), in a medallion by Luca della Robbia.*

outdo in splendour those erected by their rivals. The wealthy patrician group had been faction-ridden since time immemorial, and rivalry spilt over into vendettas which continued from generation to generation. Internal divisions cut across the lines of economic and social interests, separating members of the same social group. Division showed itself in processions, parades – even in football games.

The power and influence of great Florentine families such as the Medici, which virtually ruled the city-state, was measured by the numbers of their hangers-on, who ranged from the richest to the poorest members of

the community. Some of them might be allowed to adopt the family name, most of them were expected to live around the principal family residence, and all of them were required to fight to the death for the family honour.

Conspicuous consumption was an integral part of that honour. By the 15th century, patrician town houses were ceasing to be the fortified towers of medieval times; instead they were being rebuilt as sumptuous palaces, to the designs of leading architects. The patrician families commissioned artists such as Masaccio and Botticelli to paint portraits to hang on their walls, and altarpieces for the churches

of which they were the patrons. Artists, like craftsmen, belonged to guilds. Sculptors usually belonged to the guild of masons, one of 14 minor artisan guilds. Painters, on the other hand, because of their use of pigments and rare elements, were members of the major guild of the doctors and apothecaries. They were seen primarily as craftsmen, and they mostly lived in the poorer districts of Florence, among the other craftsmen whose assistance was essential to their work.

In their workshops, apprentice painters learned to grind and mix pigments, and to prepare the canvas or walls ready for the paint to be applied. Eventually they would be given small areas of background or minor subjects to paint themselves. Later, as journeymen, they might be entrusted with studio works considered unworthy of their master's personal touch, though produced under his supervision. Apprentice sculptors had to learn not only the art of stone-working, but also the process of casting – making patterns and moulds, and mixing metals.

Claiming a lady's favour

Alongside painting and sculpture went demands for other luxury crafts, which boosted the status of the craft guilds. Fine furniture was needed for the new palaces. Potters produced plates decorated with family coats of arms, or scenes of notable family triumphs. Specialist workshops turned out brides' marriage chests, painted and carved with scenes from the Bible or classical legends.

Apart from their love of visual display, the aristocratic Florentines rivalled one another in poetry and oratory, holding competitions to choose the outstanding writers and speakers in both Latin and Italian. In music, they composed and sang serenades and madrigals, laying claim to a lady's favour. They developed religious drama, introducing not only new forms of dialogue but an astounding range of special effects, such as elaborate chariots and water displays.

All this splendour was not achieved without cost. The city was brutally divided between rich and poor. The workers at the bottom of the social pile were squeezed by poverty and scarcity, and physically damaged by the demands of heavy labour. They bore the brunt of any recession, yet shared only marginally in the city's glory. The pieceworkers employed by the wealthy clothmakers, in tasks from combing

and carding the wool to the higher skill of dyeing, were paid a meagre wage. The harsh conditions endured by the *ciompi*, or ordinary workmen of the city, led them to revolt several times in the late 1300s.

Then, at the end of the 15th century, the Florentines reacted against the cult of vanity and display. Under the influence of the Dominican friar and preacher Girolamo Savonarola, who incited citizens to believe that ostentation was the work of the devil, many works of art were burnt in a huge bonfire – the so-called 'Bonfire of the Vanities'. However, in 1498, Savonarola was convicted of heresy and burnt at the stake, and the citizens of Florence returned to their old flamboyant ways.

SYMBOL OF A PROUD CITY

For most of the 15th century the city of Florence was dominated by one family, the Medicis. Rising from obscure origins to found a bank in 1397, the Medicis made their money out of money itself, and with their resources they were foremost among the patrons whose flow of commissions to great artists, architects and sculptors made Florence the outstanding city of the Italian Renaissance. The artists looked beyond Italy's recent past to find their inspiration in the creations of Ancient Rome. Donatello's *David* (right) was the first nude figure to be cast in bronze since classical times. The proud youth, exultant in victory over his giant foe, was regarded as a symbol of the pride of the city of Florence itself, as well as of the magnificence of the Medici family, in whose courtyard the statue once stood. The Biblical figure of David was to inspire another masterpiece of Florentine sculpture 70 years later, by Michelangelo.

Giant killer *The severed head of Goliath lies beneath the raised foot of Donatello's bronze David.*

PRINTED WORD SPREADS NEW LEARNING

The media age began with printed books. They transformed human consciousness, making the works of the scholarly few available for the first time to the many, opening networks of communication that had never been imagined before. But the revolution did not happen overnight.

In the 15th century, when the first printed books appeared in Europe, an average edition ran to no more than some 200 copies. Books then were still thought of in medieval terms, almost as a form of treasure. The monks' handwritten works, splendidly bound and illustrated, might change hands for a vineyard, a herd of cattle or similar valuable commodities. Even with the coming of printing, when multiple copies of a work could be purchased for cash, books remained possessions of prestige and substance.

In 1522, when Martin Luther published his best-selling New Testament in German, the first edition was of 3000 copies. Each book cost half a gulden, which was roughly the weekly wage of a top craftsman, or enough to buy 30 lb (13.6 kg) of beef.

Europe did not invent printing. The first printed texts were known in the Far East as early as the 8th century; they were carved from a single block of wood, in the same way as woodcut pictures. A book printed from movable type – that is, using individual letters – was published in Korea in 1409.

A Bible 'written' in type

In the West, the advent of printed books was celebrated in the mid-1450s by a Bible published in the German city of Mainz. This great work, with 42 lines per page, was printed by Johann Gutenberg, who designed it to look like one of the superb handwritten volumes of his day. The letters were formed in Gothic script, like those of the scribes; but instead of being written with a quill they were printed from movable type, cast in metal. 'Artificial writing' was the term Gutenberg used

Colour Bible The coloured decorations in this Gutenberg Bible were added by hand. The lines were made equal in length by widening spaces between words.

for his invention, and the Bible was an astonishing achievement. It came in two hefty folio volumes together totalling 1282 pages, each requiring about 2620 characters. In total, some 3,000,000 characters are thought to have been employed.

The implications for the future were immense. Where a single copy of the Bible had once taken months for scribes to write out by hand, a multitude could now be run off. Gutenberg, like other early printers, was secretive about his art and seems deliberately to have produced a limited edition so as not to flood the market. Nonetheless, he pressed a couple of hundred copies, of which 38 survive today.

Some of Gutenberg's Bibles were printed on vellum, a fine parchment of calf or kid long used by scribes for their manuscripts. But it was an expensive

Team work Under the overseer's eye, compositors select letters from a case, and a colleague inks the type ready for the screw-press. An apprentice stacks printed sheets.

Ioan. Stradanus inuent.   Phls Galle excud.

PIONEER IN THE PRINT SHOP

Before the 15th century, books in Europe had been printed by the laborious process of carving each page as a separate woodcut. The great advantage of the movable type developed by Johann Gutenberg was that it allowed any combination of characters to be put together – and then taken apart and rearranged for the next job. The technique answered the demand for a means of rapidly disseminating knowledge and ideas. The type was set and the process operated by hand, so the process was still a slow one: it was to be another 350 years before the first powered press was introduced.

The earliest printed characters were based on the handwriting of the day, but by 1470 a clearer Roman typeface was designed specifically for printing.

Learning to write A new script with linked, slanting letters became popular in the late 15th century and was taught in books such as Ludovico Arrighi's Operina of 1539. An italic typeface based on it was devised by the Venetian printer Aldus Manutius.

Learning to read Printed books helped to broaden education – but older methods survived. This 16th-century schoolmaster is beating the alphabet into a backward pupil, while his wife teaches a girl to read. Two other pupils pore over their books.

material. Others were printed on paper which was not only cheaper, but offered a much better surface for the inked type. Papermaking quickly became an industry as important as printing in hastening the mass production of books. The paper was made from linen rags, boiled and beaten to a creamy pulp before being pressed to squeeze it dry. As demand increased, paper mills were set up using water wheels to power their huge, pounding hammers.

Lampblack for printer's ink

In the printer's workshop a lot of cooperative effort was required from several specialised craftsmen. At the foundry, for example, type was cast by men known as typecasters who poured their molten metal into tiny moulds where it cooled and hardened to form each little oblong, with the letter in relief at one end. Filed down to remove any rough edges, the pieces of type were sorted and set up by a craftsman known as the compositor.

With a manuscript before him, the compositor peered at the words, chose the letters he needed and placed them in a long tray called a composing stick. On a rough print, the text was checked line by line for mistakes, after which each line was then fitted into a page-sized framework called a forme. When the forme was filled it was passed on to the men at the press.

For ink, printers used lampblack or charcoal powder mixed with linseed oil, spreading it over the type. Paper was dampened to give a good impression, while the press itself worked on the screw principle and was manually operated. A corrector checked the first proofs, and when the pages were printed they often went directly to the bookseller, who did the binding himself.

This complex process, pioneered in a handful of German towns, swiftly spread abroad: to Venice, Rome, Paris and elsewhere. By 1500, presses had been founded in 250 European towns,

Anatomy lesson *The questioning spirit of the times led doctors to dissect human bodies to see how they worked. Among the pioneers was the Flemish anatomist Andreas Vesalius, whose influential work,* On the Form of the Human Body, *appeared in 1543.*

all serving their peoples' new hunger for printed matter. The principal demand was for religious works, which ranged from single-page woodcut images of saints, with only minimal text, to entire Bibles.

Luther's followers in Germany invented mass propaganda in their struggle towards the Reformation. Sermons, theological treatises, broadsides and even comic strips flooded from the presses, reinforced by many a woodcut illustration depicting the pope in Rome as a devil or a monster.

'Simple folk,' Luther stated, 'are more easily moved by pictures and images to recall divine history than through mere words or doctrines.' His own output was prodigious. During the first ten years of the struggle it is believed that Luther himself penned nearly one in four of all the works published in Germany.

Besides the huge body of religious material, other mainstays of the new publishing industry were Latin classics, legal books and school books. The book-buying public consisted chiefly of professional men such as doctors, lawyers and teachers, and the ancient authors were popular because all the educated classes knew Latin. A Venetian printer named Aldus Manutius became well known for his pocket-sized grammars and Greek and Latin classics which were cheap enough even for the most down-at-heel

scholar to afford. These helped to spread a reawakened respect for classical learning. Besides the ornate Gothic script, simpler and easier-to-read Roman typefaces came into widespread use, and the range of subjects covered by books gradually broadened. There appeared books of etiquette, manuals on hygiene and diet, town guides and accounts of the great voyages of discovery. Romantic and ribald tales were popular, too. In 1476 William Caxton opened the first English press at Westminster, and one of his first productions was Chaucer's *Canterbury Tales.*

Thinkers of the time, however, were often cautious about rushing too precipitately into print. The Polish astronomer Copernicus, for example, first formulated the modern theory of the solar system in 1530, concluding that the earth revolved around the sun. However, his findings were in conflict with the Church's teaching that the earth was the centre of the universe. Copernicus did not publish his great work *On the Revolutions of Heavenly Bodies* until 1543 – the year of his death, it is said that he received his first copy on his deathbed.

Printing was not the only new industry in this age of change. It came out of a manufacturing tradition well established in Germany, based on the thriving workshops of metalworkers. Nuremberg was a particular focus of activity, a major hub of European trade, supplied by silver and copper mines in Saxony. More than 140 separate crafts flourished, including those of the gunsmith, locksmith and maker of scientific instruments.

Clockmaking was developing, too. The world's earliest-surviving pocket watch was made at Nuremberg by Peter Henlein in about 1504. Almost imperceptibly at first, mechanical timepieces like this started to change the tempo of everyday life. Church time, marked by the tolling of great bells, gave way to secular time and the incessant ticking of innumerable clocks.

Dream car *The Middle Ages produced a number of inventors and visionaries – none more remarkable than Leonardo da Vinci, whose schemes included this eight-man 'armoured car'. Hand cranks would have moved the wheels, while soldiers fired from portholes. Like most of Leonardo's designs, this car stayed unbuilt in his notebooks.*

Bookkeeping *The spread of double-entry bookkeeping helped bankers such as Jakob Fugger to record their business.*

Precious light
Candles of tallow or beeswax were expensive. Lanterns were often used to guard the flame.

RUSTIC PLAY EASES TOIL ON THE LAND

The light was fading on a damp spring afternoon as Coll and Gib plodded wearily back to their village. They were returning home after a day spent wrestling with a plough behind a team of lumbering oxen, knowing they had only the few hours of darkness to ease their mud-spattered soreness before the sun rose on another day of toil.

Home to Coll and Gib was an upland hamlet of a couple of dozen families, clustered round the church – the only stone building in the parish. Each family had a two-roomed cottage, and in the garden at the back they grew their own cabbages and herbs and kept hens and a pig or two. At the end of the garden was the privy, moved from time to time as the smell from the open hole it covered became offensive. If the cottage had no well, one of the women's chores was to fill a bucket from the communal village well, or from the stream which was also used for washing clothes. These short trips were a good excuse for a gossip. The villagers rarely saw the lord of the manor, who lived in a large house, timber-framed and surrounded by a moat, some distance away. However, they

Washing vessel *Bronze water vessels known as lavers, with spouts for pouring, hung on the walls of kitchens in the better-equipped medieval homes of Britain and Europe.*

Travelling salesman *Pedlars in rural Germany in the 1500s had to walk many footsore miles each day to sell their wares. Widespread poverty among peasants of much of Europe left them little money to spend on luxuries, and their grievances led to a series of bitter revolts.*

HUMANS AND ANIMALS SHARE A HOUSE IN THE COUNTRY

Staff in hand, the head of the family returns from a hard day's work in the fields to his warm and sturdy house. The framework is formed by curved timber beams, known as crucks, placed in facing pairs, their tops meeting and lashed together with cord and their bottoms resting firmly on the ground. The crucks, and the beams placed between them, support the weight of the roof, its thatch of reeds pierced by a hole to let the smoke from the fire escape. The walls are of wattle, or intertwined twigs, reinforced with a daub of clay or mud.

As it is winter time, the family's cows and pigs live and eat indoors, in their own fenced-in quarters at one end of the ground floor of the house. Despite the cold, the window shutters are thrown open, to let light into the large single room, with its partitions made of interwoven twigs. Rushes cover the floor of beaten earth. The centre of the living quarters is dominated by a brick fireplace at which the woman of the house is preparing a meal; this household is relatively well-to-do in having a chimney rising through the house, an innovation which first appeared in continental Europe during the 15th century. Crude ladders lead to the loft, which is floored with poles. Here hay stored after the autumn harvest provides a warm 'bedroom' for the family. Storage jars stand on cross-beams alongside the chimney. Outdoors, two children in warm shawls, caps and stout clogs against the weather and muddy conditions watch over the chickens, which provide the family with meat and eggs.

were only too familiar with the bailiff or steward who came from time to time to preside over the local court and collect the rents and dues. They knew the character and foibles of the parish priest, who christened, married and buried them, and heard their confessions.

Dialect of the clan

Villagers were inward-looking and clannish, and often talked a dialect distinct even from that of their near-neighbours. They managed their own affairs, rather than relying on the law of the land which seemed unbelievably remote. They had their own social hierarchy, led by the blacksmith, the carpenter and the miller. Although some peasants had landholdings, others were dependent on wages to supplement their meagre living.

Apart from his land, the peasant owned stock and equipment, seed grain and hay, all of which could be used for barter. Where the fields were open and held in common, he would have the right to run his stock on the common. However, few farmers had the resources to provide a plough and a full plough team, and often a cow and a donkey were yoked together.

Children in country homes, from the moment they were able to walk unaided, undertook simple tasks such as feeding the hens, or scaring the birds from the crops by throwing stones. A boy who was a good shot with sling or catapult might bring home a rabbit or rook for the family pot – though he would be in trouble if he hit one of the lord of the manor's privileged doves.

Children were sometimes allowed to bring the cow to the bull, or take broken bits of iron-work to the blacksmith for repair. When they grew up, young people's marriages were usually arranged by their parents. The realities of village life did not demand mutual affection from the couple, though they were often given the opportunity before marriage to find out whether they were suited to each other. In the common practice of 'bundling', a couple were allowed to lie together on a bed to chat and get to know each other, while being rolled up separately to stop physical contact. Country people often disapproved of second marriages, or first marriages with a great difference

in age, and expressed their disapproval by banging pots and pans beneath offenders' windows. Though peasants toiled from dawn to dusk six days a week, they made the most of their Sundays and 'holy days'. The young men played football, wrestled, fought with wooden staves and practised archery. The whole village took part in the Yule Feast, the New Year celebration of Plough Monday, and Harvest Festival, with its flails, 'corn dollies' and the last sheaf of the harvest. The most popular of all celebrations was Carnival, when villagers, imitating the royal court, elected temporary kings, queens and courtiers and held their own rough-and-ready masques, dances and feasts.

As the Middle Ages drew to a close, home life for the peasant was much the same all over continental Europe, from northern Scandinavia to southern Italy. Oppressed by overlords and threatened by war, plague and famine, his primary goal was self-sufficiency for his family, achieved by independence rather than by specialisation. This attitude was to survive for three centuries longer, until advances in technology and creeping urbanisation swept it away for ever.

Grown-ups at play *A pair of strapping peasants dancing in his local market square in Nuremberg inspired the German artist Albrecht Dürer to create this engraving in 1514. Despite their loose but cumbersome clothes and skimpy shoes, the dancers have no difficulty in whirling round, arms and feet flying. From the bunch of keys at her waist, it seems the woman is in charge of the couple's treasured belongings.*

Children at play *Peasant children climb a 'ladder' of their friends' outstretched legs.*

GENEVA'S AGE OF THOUGHT CONTROL

The lakeside city of Geneva at the start of the 16th century was a boisterous, hard-working place, turbulent and undisciplined but proud of its independence. About 10,000 people lived there, mainly artisans and their families. Skilled goldsmiths worked intricate chalices for the Catholic church and goblets for prosperous merchants; woodcarvers chiselled crucifixes and decorative beam ends.

These busy craftsmen – along with the city's furriers, tanners, cauldron-makers, pastrycooks, butchers and cobblers – lived in rows of two-storey houses. There were shops and store-rooms on the ground floor, while a back stairway led up to the first-floor living room, bedroom and kitchen, which were furnished with well-built tables, stools and benches.

The leading citizens were mostly middle-class tradesmen, who lived in stone-built three-storey mansions, with courtyards and gardens, barns and stables. They married well, accumulated property and, if they were Geneva-born with full civic rights,

The way of simple worship *Followers of the French religious reformer John Calvin attend a typically austere Sunday service in a converted house at Lyons, in France. Instead of an altar, a pulpit occupies the centre position. The men, in hats and subdued clothing, sit apart from the women. The seats range from hard wooden benches for the ordinary worshippers to upholstered pews for their superiors. An hourglass to time the preacher's sermon hangs by the pulpit, and a large white dog sits attentively by.*

took an active part in the affairs of the city. Such was Geneva in 1541 when the 32-year-old John Calvin returned to the city. Born in Picardy, north France, Calvin had studied law and the humanities, but he became converted to the cause of religious reform after the breach with Rome by the German monk, Martin Luther. Calvin and his followers believed that the Bible was the only source of religious truth, and that man's innate sinfulness could only be counteracted by one of the most rigid codes of personal discipline ever devised.

Central to their creed was the doctrine of predestination, which said that the destiny of every human being was settled from the beginning of time.

Those who were members of the so-called 'Elect' were destined for eternal bliss in Heaven; the rest of mankind were predestined to be damned forever. To spread his 'true religion' among the Genevans, most of whom preferred the traditional Church practices, Calvin established the Consistory – a body of 12 ministers and laymen, modelled on the 12 Apostles, whose role was to supervise religion and morality.

Their eyes and ears were everywhere, as they carried out Calvin's rigorous instructions. The Genevans' traditional entertainments were condemned as ungodly and even obscene. The young men who had controlled the traditional

Carnival mumming and dancing were relieved of such duties and restricted to their more formal role as members of the militia for the defence of the city.

The old Catholic religious practices were gradually eliminated. People were summoned before the Consistory for failing to attend church, for praying to the Virgin, or for adorning their altars with images. Their knowledge of the Scriptures was examined, and if they fell short they were recalled for further examining. After they had confessed the error of their ways, they were kept under observation; those who still found it hard to abandon traditional religious practices were punished by whipping and bread-and-water diets. There was a ban on superstitions such as dancing round maypoles or drinking from sacred springs. Christmas and Twelfth Night were abandoned as popish practices lacking scriptural justification. Godly persons, stated Calvin, should wear sober black and eat to live, not live to eat;

consequently he frowned on the wearing of ostentatious clothes and the making of luxury foods.

From the outset, Calvin made education the means of drawing souls to God. Every Sunday at midday Genevan children had to recite their catechism, while adults unfamiliar with it were allowed to take private lessons. The first printed version, which appeared in 1545, began with the question 'What is the principal aim of human life?', to which the required answer was 'It is to know God'. Religion was drilled into the people, and ideological opposition to Calvinism faded.

By the time that Calvin died in 1564, he and his followers had made Geneva the undisputed centre of the Protestant educational world. Calvinist churches had also been established in Scotland, the Netherlands and France, and social and religious life had been irrevocably changed, not only in Geneva, but over much of northern Europe.

John Calvin, religious reformer

THE FIGHT BETWEEN SINFUL CARNIVAL AND SACRED LENT

At the same time that Calvin was preaching that man's sinfulness must be fought by a stern moral code, the Flemish artist Pieter Bruegel the Elder was taking the clash between sacred and profane as the theme for a painted pageant of medieval life. He ranged the gluttonous forces of Carnival time, on the left of the picture, against the sober observers of Lent, on the right.

Riding on a vast wine barrel, the corpulent leader of the Carnival brandishes a meat-laden spit at his opponent – a skinny, elderly woman wielding a shovel containing two

small fish, her fare for the start of Lent. Two other women pull her cart, while the wine barrel is pushed from behind by a straining figure in a red-and-white cap. Revellers – some of them masked – are cooking, taking part in theatrical displays, and playing music. A cripple crawls on the ground, and a man and woman are led off by a figure in green-and-white stripes, holding a torch.

The observers of Lent include a woman selling fish from a stall, another pulling a cart filled with the fishwife's wares, nuns leaving church, and men giving alms to beggars.

VOYAGERS TO THE EDGE OF THE EARTH

All week long the midsummer sun blazed down on the quayside of the southern Spanish fishing port of Palos as teams of dockers toiled to load three vessels – the *Santa Maria*, the *Nina* and the *Pinta* – with provisions for a voyage into the unknown.

Men trundled barrels of salted fish, salted beef and rough wine up planks and onto the vessels. Pigs and flocks of hens were herded aboard and put in pens on the decks to provide fresh eggs and meat on the voyage. Baskets of glass beads, brass rings, hawks' bells and other cheap trinkets for trading were carried on by hand. Large boxes filled with tackle, blocks, chains and plumb lines were hauled up by rope and pulley and then guided through hatches in the ships' sides. Crates containing granite balls for the guns were lifted by cranes and lowered onto the main decks.

Meanwhile, on the poop deck of the *Santa Maria*, the admiral of the expedition, Christopher Columbus, looked pensively down on the bustling, noisy scene. Preparations for the

Billowing sails *A fleet of three-masted Portuguese carracks, which were merchant ships equipped for war, sails into action. Their three masts carry square sails on the fore and main masts and a lateen, or triangular, sail on the mizzen mast.*

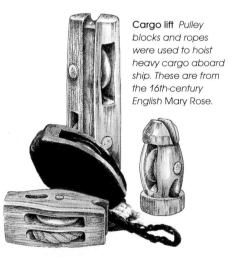

Cargo lift *Pulley blocks and ropes were used to hoist heavy cargo aboard ship. These are from the 16th-century English* Mary Rose.

NEW SHIPS TO CARRY ADVENTURERS TO NEW LANDS

The revolution in sailing-ship design which was to carry European explorers to the ends of the earth was the development of the three-masted ship. A mixture of square sails and triangular sails meant that the ship could take advantage of winds from many directions, and a hinged sternpost rudder gave additional manoeuvrability.

Compasses with magnetised iron needles were mounted on pivots set in round wooden boxes. During the 15th century, however, it was found that the needles did not point to true north but at an angle to it, which varied from place to place. This variation had to be allowed for when sailors calculated directions. Maps were based on bearings and distances between landmarks such as capes and ports, the areas between them being filled by observations.

Early map and log book

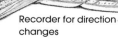

Recorder for direction changes

expedition had started three months earlier, in May 1492, when Columbus – an Italian navigator employed by Ferdinand V and Queen Isabella of Spain – arrived in Palos seeking three vessels 'well supplied with provisions and seamen', as he put it.

Columbus had no difficulty in securing three small but serviceable ships. Finding crews for them, however, was not so easy. The local seamen thought Columbus would either sail off the edge of the earth, or would enter an unknown region of perpetual darkness and storm.

Finally, by bribery and persuasion, Columbus raised about 100 men and boys to man the three ships. Most of them were experienced mariners, including some shipwright carpenters. However, about a quarter of the men were convicts, who were granted free pardons for signing on.

So, shortly before sunrise on Friday, August 3, 1492, the three vessels sailed from Palos, bound for the Canaries and whatever lay beyond them. The voyage was the culmination of 15th-century maritime exploration. And the routine and conditions aboard Columbus's flagship, the *Santa Maria*,

Under construction *Watched by a master shipwright, two carpenters trim a length of timber to size and shape in making a beam for a 15th-century, oceangoing vessel. Supported by a raft, other workers hammer out the portholes and take materials aboard the half-finished ship, while more craftsmen work on deck.*

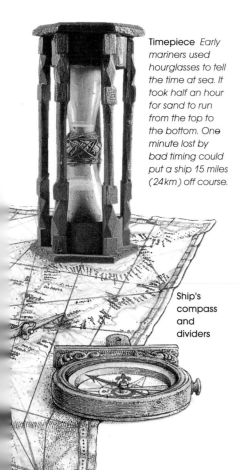

Timepiece *Early mariners used hourglasses to tell the time at sea. It took half an hour for sand to run from the top to the bottom. One minute lost by bad timing could put a ship 15 miles (24km) off course.*

Ship's compass and dividers

were typical of life at sea at that time. At dawn the first watch of the day came on duty. After breakfasting on salted sardines or anchovies, dry biscuits and wine, the men set about swabbing the decks with mops and buckets of sea water. Lookouts took their places in the rigging and at the bow of the ship. The sails were regularly trimmed to take full advantage of the prevailing winds. The cannons mounted on deck were cleaned and checked. Ropes were examined for wear and tear, and any rips in the canvas sails were stitched.

'These wondrous men who have travelled across an unknown and boundless sea have taught us that there is nothing that is impossible for man.'

PETER MARTYR, 1493

In the galley the cook prepared the midday meal – possibly of cheese, figs and almonds – and planned the one hot meal of the day. This was taken in the evening and usually consisted of beef, pork or chicken washed down with most of the wine ration of 2½ pints (1.5 litres) a day per man. A special lookout was kept for the rats, weevils and cockroaches which often infested ships' galleys, adding to the unappetising quality of the food which was often rancid and hard to chew.

The watches, meanwhile, changed every four hours. At night the boy on duty chanted prayers every half-hour. In addition, prayer meetings were

usually held three times a day – morning, noon and evening. During their spare time the men played dice or cards, and sometimes fished with a line hung from the stern.

There were few if any berths on the *Santa Maria*, and when darkness fell the off-duty seamen slept fully clothed on mats or sheets of sailcloth on or below deck. Columbus, whose own quarters were a tiny cabin in the stern, kept an overall watch on the vessel and crew. He wrote in his journal that he slept very little and supervised every detail of the welfare of the crew and the running of the ship. 'The smallest mistake can be disastrous', he wrote. 'I keep an eye on everything all the time.'

Columbus largely spurned the use of navigational aids – such as astrolabes and hand-held quadrants, used for calculating latitudes. Once the *Santa Maria* was under way he gauged the ship's speed by watching the sea as it broke along the sides.

As the magnetic compass was generally inaccurate, he steered by the Pole Star. And he calculated the ship's position by dead reckoning: that is, he estimated how many leagues had been covered each day, noted the direction

by the sun and entered the relevant information in the log, and then calculated the *Santa Maria's* approximate position.

The mariners reached the Canaries on August 9 and spent almost a month there taking on more supplies and repairing the *Pinta's* rudder, which had broken on the third day out. The voyage resumed on September 6 and ten days later the ships were the first to enter the calm seaweed-ridden water of the Sargasso Sea. The seaweed convinced Columbus that land was not too far off, and when the wind picked up he gave orders to sail.

Throughout the night of October 7 the sailors heard birds flying overhead, and in the morning welcome signs of land appeared on the water: some reeds, a flower, a broken branch and, most significant of all, a carved stick. At ten o'clock on the night of October 11 Columbus saw a 'light like a wax candle' rising and falling in the darkness ahead. Then, four hours later, the lookout on the *Pinta* gave the cry for which they had all been waiting: 'Land! Land!' The explorers had reached the Bahamas, 36 days after leaving the Canaries.

At dawn, Columbus was rowed ashore. He carried the Spanish flag, while the captains of the *Nina* and the *Pinta* held banners bearing a green cross, two royal crowns, and the letters 'F' and 'Y', for Ferdinand and Ysabel (Isabella). Watched by groups of curious natives, Columbus knelt on one knee, kissed the ground, and claimed for the king and queen of Spain the tree-covered island, which he named San Salvador. The door to the New World was open.

Under sail *Columbus himself may have drawn these sketches of the three ships in his fleet, showing their different types of rigging. They are (left to right) the square-rigged* Pinta, *the 100 ton flagship* Santa Maria, *and the triangular-rigged* Nina.

MEETING A NEW WORLD

Spanish conquistadores landing in the New World found gold and silver, and marvelled at the cities, temples, roads and canals built by the native civilisations of the Mayas, the Aztecs and the Incas. The exchange of different cultures that followed was to transform the lives of people on both sides of the Atlantic. The explorers thirsted for the precious metals and spices that would please the kings, queens and merchants backing their voyages. In their search they found new foods, medicines, customs and climates. When the invaders began to establish colonies, they shipped home boatloads of chocolate beans, sugar and tobacco. To cultivate America's wide expanses, the settlers first tried to enslave the Indians, then imported shiploads of African slaves. Europeans sought to remake the New World in the image of the Old. The attempt involved much ruthless treatment of the native inhabitants who, while quick to adopt some European innovations, reshaped others or rejected them totally.

THE AMERICAS AD 1000 – 1750

COLONIES TO WIN GOLD – AND SOULS

On their return from the New World the 16th-century Spanish conquerors regaled the younger sons of nobility and others eager to make their fortunes with tales of the limitless wealth and gold that were there for the taking. Soon waves of adventurers poured across the Atlantic, and the Caribbean islands of Hispaniola – now Haiti and the Dominican Republic – Jamaica, Puerto Rico and Cuba were swamped by fortune-seekers.

Enslaving the native Indians, the newcomers panned for gold and cultivated huge plantations of the sugar cane brought by Spaniards to the New World. When the Indians refused to co-operate, or died from Western diseases, Europeans combed the coasts of Africa to gather human labour. Eventually, the slave trade that emerged was to bring millions of Africans to the Americas.

Gold over the Andes

Often the best veins of gold ore were found in the remote mountainous regions of South America. So the Spanish learned how to carry out the metals on the backs of sturdy llamas, sure-footed over the Andean passes. In Peru, the Andeans had designed an oven that relied on the fierce mountain winds to generate the intense heat needed to smelt the silver ore; and it was Indian miners who dug the shafts and chipped away the rock.

Spanish colonisers controlled their labour through a system called the *encomienda*. Under this, the Crown and its Latin-American representatives granted their favourites the right to demand yearly labour service from conquered Indians. Led by a local chief, or *cacique*, village Indians spent a couple of months working at the distant mines. Although run by

War paint *The proud native peoples caught the imagination of the artist John White, who accompanied Sir Walter Raleigh on his 1585 expedition. The elaborate tattoos of this Florida Indian warrior denote his high rank. He wears a headdress of skins, and metal discs adorn chest, elbows and knees.*

the Spanish or Portuguese, the mining settlements generally retained their Indian character: most of the miners continued to speak their own native languages, and to maintain religious and domestic customs at home.

From the earliest years of conquest in South America, the invaders built colonial cities with gracious arcaded blocks of buildings and grand, open plazas. Often constructed amidst the remains of the great Indian cities, these colonial government centres handled the trade which linked frontiers and ports. In the market plazas, pineapples, baskets of corn, strings of peppers and lengths of handwoven cloth were exchanged for rare tools and finished goods imported from Europe.

The highly centralised governments of early colonial times transmitted the authority of the kings and queens of Iberia through the large landowners out to the countryside. The colonial government's main concern was to protect the trade in precious metals. While life in colonial cities could be elegant and orderly, out on the frontiers the central government's grip was shaky indeed.

Bandits on the rampage
In frontier areas, landowners and government troops cooperated to build *presidios*, or forts. The colonial powers relied on the manpower of local Indian allies to try to impose order. In most cases the law turned out to be whatever the largest landowners wanted – but even those powerful men did not fully control what happened far from the ports. Some warrior tribes, such as the Araucanians of Chile, resisted white settlement until the late 19th century. Bandits sometimes rampaged over entire regions and would attack the Crown's gold and silver pack trains.

The encomienda system prevailed for much of the agricultural work, as well as the mines. While the wealthiest landowners lived most of the year in the cities, their representatives looked after work on the estates and ranches. Indian hamlets supplied a work force to till the fields, build fences and tend cattle. The cowboy of Latin America was usually Indian, or of mixed Spanish

and Indian descent. Meanwhile, a struggle for the souls of the native Americans was waged by the Jesuit, Franciscan and Dominican orders, competing for converts and dominion as they founded missions from Brazil to California.

The missionaries' attempts to convert New World inhabitants limped along slowly for many generations. Within the large walled expanse of their specially built mission stations stood a church, quarters for the monks, a cloister, gardens, a granary and sometimes native dwellings. Often only Indians on the losing side of a conflict would be willing to convert – to a 'limited' religion with only one God.

Anger of the gods
Frequently, missionaries erected their new Catholic churches on top of the ruins of older temples, which led locals to imagine that the spirits of angry discarded gods lurked in the shadows of the Christian altar. Indians smuggled many pagan beliefs into their seemingly catholicised rituals. The Great Mother of Corn, for example, would receive offerings on the Feast of the Nativity of Our Lady, both of which conveniently fell on the same day in September; and a Christian wedding ceremony celebrated in a mission church might well be followed by a ceremony in the village, involving sacrifices to traditional deities.

In North America, by contrast, the encounter of native American and British and French settlers had a different outcome. When not felled by epidemics of diseases such as smallpox, measles and influenza, the northern Indians often fought to hold the line in frontier

areas. Others fled north and west away from the pressure of settlement by whites. While the groups exchanged techniques of agriculture, technology and hunting, the intermixing of European and native cultures was not as extensive in the northern areas of the New World as it had proved in Latin America. One effect of the arrival of settlers from the Old World, however, had the same impact in the North as it had in the South: the forced migration of so many Africans profoundly altered the society evolving in the new lands.

Amid the cultural upheaval in the Americas, words and concepts passed to and fro between the languages of the New World and the Spanish, French, Portuguese, English and African tongues of the newcomers. Native Americans thought European clothes hot and clumsy, and found the bearded adventurers too hairy. Compromises were made. In 400 years the European settlers, the remaining Indians and the Africans had shaped new blends of cultures from the frozen north to the tip of Argentina.

Native lands *As the colonists spread out across the Americas they encountered the lands settled by the Incas, the Aztecs and the Mayas in the centre and south, and the Indian territories farther north.*

Glitter of gold *Gold was plentiful in the New World, and craftsmen beat it and shaped it into vessels, ornaments, masks and ritual objects. The stylised human figure (left, above) has horns, and flowers sprout from its mouth. The chest disc (left) combines the angular figures of a woman and a tree frog.*

Gold slaves *Native slave workers on the Pacific coast of the South American continent wash gold before handing it over to their Spanish overseer.*

Fruits of the land *The 'pyne fruit' of the Caribbean was among the new fruit found by the colonists, while the horn plantain from South-east Asia flourished in the New World. Both became popular in Europe; the pineapple was often carved in stone on gateposts and parapets.*

SACRIFICES TO GODS THIRSTY FOR BLOOD

Life for the Aztec people of central America was dominated by the sun, which they worshipped as the source and mainstay of their world. To ensure that the sun was 'reborn' each morning, tens of thousands of men were sacrificed by priests each year at temples in the Aztecs' capital city of Tenochtitlán. In a matter of seconds a victim had his heart torn out and burnt in a stone bowl. Other victims were hacked to death and decapitated, after which their severed heads were skewered onto long poles and placed beside the skulls of thousands of other victims, stacked row upon row, on a rack for public display.

When the temple of the sun god Huitzilopochtli was dedicated, at least 20,000 victims were said to have been sacrificed over a period of four days. In 1519, when the Spaniards arrived at Tenochtitlán, one of the conquistadores counted 136,000 closely packed skulls in the storehouse.

Jesuit missionaries such as José de Acosta, recording these human sacrifices, said that on certain feast days Aztec priests sacrificed young women, cutting off their heads with sacrificial knives. Small children were drowned in Lake Texcoco to satisfy the rain god Tlaloc; others were tortured in the maize fields until their tears 'watered' the farmers' crops.

Drums at daybreak

Every day at dawn the inhabitants of Tenochtitlán were awakened by the throb of temple drums and the strident blowing of conch shells by the priests. From the emperor downwards, people slept on the floor on skin rugs or rush mats. Workers left their scantily furnished mud huts and paddled their dug-outs through the city's network of canals to the surrounding maize fields and *chinampas*, or 'floating gardens' – small man-made islands of mud and reeds on which vegetables were grown.

Most people ate breakfast at 10 am, usually *tamales* – highly seasoned maize-and-meat cakes – which they took out with them or bought from street-sellers. By then the city was seething with life. The law courts, for example, opened at first light, and by mid-morning the judges were dealing with the daily run of crimes. These might include persistent drunkenness, the penalty for which could be death. Commoners committing a first-time offence merely had their heads shaved in public. A nobleman found to be drunk, however, was invariably executed. A concession was made to ordinary people more than 60 years old, whose working lives were regarded as being at an end: they were allowed to drink as much alcohol as they liked. The staple alcoholic drink was a potent, cider-like brew called *octli*, or *pulque*, made from the fermented juice of the agave and drunk principally on ceremonial occasions. The same versatile plant provided needles for sewing, and fibres for ropes, garments and sandals.

Meanwhile, from all over the city people began to throng towards the marketplace, where they traded such foods as tomatoes, turkeys, cacao beans and avocados. On the way they

Cruel worship *Every year in March, Aztec priests flayed human victims and paraded in their skins in homage to Xipe Totec, the god of spring. A sculpture shows one priest speaking through the gaping mouth of a victim, with his flayed hand dangling at his wrist. Xipe Totec was also worshipped as a healer of eye and skin diseases.*

Temple of blood *An Aztec priest wields his knife to expertly rip open a sacrificial victim from the breastbone to the pit of the stomach. He then cuts out the man's heart and offers it to the sun god. The victim is held down on an altar stone at the top of the blood-stained temple steps. Meanwhile, the body of a previous victim is dragged roughly away by the priest's assistants.*

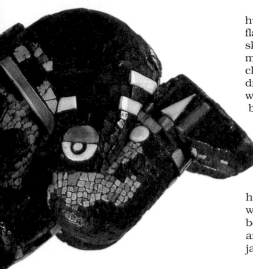

Knife of death *Though the Aztecs used metal for everyday tools, they preferred traditional materials for religious rituals. The sacrificial knife had a blade of chalcedony, and a wooden handle encrusted with turquoise and shell. The hilt shows an eagle warrior, a guardian of the sun god.*

BAD DAYS AND GOOD YEARS

The Aztec year was based on two different calendars. The first used a cycle of 365 days, founded on the rising and setting of the sun and divided into 18 periods of 20 days – with five 'unlucky' days left over. This calendar determined the times and seasons for planting and harvesting. The second had a 260 day time cycle and was used for fortunetelling. Each day was astrologically considered 'good', 'bad' or 'indifferent'. Those born on 'lucky' days would prosper in life, while others would not.

The solar years were divided into 52 year cycles. At the end of any one of these the sun was liable to 'die' – despite the sacrifices that had been made to it. The world would then end in a series of earthquakes. At the end of a 52 year period, when all was found to be well, the priests sacrificed thanksgiving victims. Their chests were cut open, and fires started in the cavities, then messengers lit torches from the flame and carried the 'New Fire' around the empire.

hurried along the straight streets flanking the canals. Short, dark skinned and black haired, the men mostly wore loincloths and colourful cloaks and sandals; the women were dressed in loose-fitting cotton shirts, white, ankle-length skirts with embroidered borders, and ornamental belts. For decoration, some women painted their teeth black or scarlet, others displayed delicate blue tattoos, while married women plaited their hair in two horn-like tufts at the front of their heads. Jewellery such as necklaces with small, tinkling bells was worn by both sexes – and some of the men's lips and noses had been pierced to hold jade rods and gold plugs.

Outdoing the finery of the ordinary citizens were the jaguar skins and eagle costumes of the warriors, whose resplendent headdresses were made from the long, blue-green tail feathers of the quetzal, the sacred bird of the Aztecs and Mayas. Almost as eye-catching were the noblemen's cloaks with their whirling designs of serpents, butterflies and multicoloured exotic flowers. Pushing their way through the throng were the porters, their backs bent with heavy loads. Wheeled transport was not used by the Aztecs.

Born to be soldiers

From the day he was born, a male child was marked for military service. His umbilical cord was buried with arrows and a shield, and at the age of ten his hair was cut so that a lock called a *piochtli* lay on the nape of his neck. He was not allowed to cut off the lock until he had captured at least one prisoner in battle and brought him back alive for future sacrifice.

The warriors believed there was a mystical bond between themselves and their captives. When a soldier took

Names for the days *The Aztecs' solar calendar was divided into 'months' of 20 days, each of which was named after an everyday object, animal or phenomenon, and had its own associated god.*

Shield of the coyote *A mosaic made up of pink and blue feathers, depicting a coyote-like animal, decorates a wooden shield. The mythical creature, picked-out in gold leaf, was a symbol of the Aztec emperors. The shield was sent back to Spain as a trophy.*

a prisoner he said to him: 'Here is my beloved son!' The prisoner, joining in the well-established ritual, dutifully responded: 'Here is my revered father!' He later went stoically to his fate, believing that once his heart had been cut out he would become one of the heavenly companions of the sun.

Every so often, evenly matched, ceremonial battles called 'Wars of Flowers' were fought between the Aztecs and rival states which also made human sacrifices to their gods. The objective was to take as many prisoners as possible without a formal declaration of war. As soon as both sides felt they had captured enough victims for sacrifice they ended hostilities and went home.

The Aztecs also believed that in the year *Ce Acatl*, or 'One Reed', their white-skinned and bearded god-king Quetzalcoatl, the 'Feathered Serpent', would return from exile in the east, heralding a period of unprecedented glory for their people. Towards the end of 1519, which happened to be the Aztecs' long-awaited year of One Reed, Montezuma and his subjects believed this had happened when a bearded, light-faced stranger arrived in the capital. In fact, the newcomer was a Spanish explorer named Hernán Cortés, and he and his followers were to conquer the Aztecs and to make the central American empire their own.

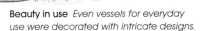

Beauty in use *Even vessels for everyday use were decorated with intricate designs.*

Toy on wheels *Looking like a Walt Disney creation, this clay animal of around AD 1000, possibly representing a dog or a deer, shows that some Middle American peoples understood the use of the wheel. But as they had no draught animals they used wheels only for toys and not for transport.*

| Crocodile | Wind | House | Lizard | Serpent | Death | Deer | Rabbit | Water | Dog |

| Monkey | Grass | Reed | Jaguar | Eagle | Vulture | Motion | Knife | Rain | Flower |

199

THE SWEAT OF THE SUN

The Incas were noted for their ornamental use of gold, which they called 'the sweat of the sun', and of silver, the 'tears of the moon'. One of their most remarkable creations was at Coricancha, the Temple of the Sun, in Cuzco. This had a garden entirely made from gold and silver, with life-sized figures of birds, llamas, and even replicas of maize with stems of silver and ears of gold.

Craftsmen made golden half-boots for women, and vases were embossed in gold with designs of fish, birds, snakes, caterpillars and spiders. Long gold knives fashioned in the shape of winged gods were made for symbolic use in religious rituals, rather than for sacrifices. As well as gold and silver, copper was mined to make the heads on the Incan army's battle-axes, spears and maces. Skilled metal craftsmen were held in high respect in the community, and their sons were trained from an early age to follow in the family tradition.

CITY OF GOLD THAT RULED THE ANDES

Gold for the dead *Many of the treasures found in Peru by the Spanish conquistadores were inherited by the Incas from earlier Peruvian peoples. Magnificent funeral masks adorned the mummies of chieftains of the north coastal people. The masks had nose and ear ornaments, and jewels for eyes. Hands and arms of hammered gold were placed on some mummies.*

Dawn breaks over the peaks of the Andes as the 'procession of the living dead' moves solemnly through the holy square of Cuzco, the highland capital of the South American Incas. Borne on litters, the mummies of former emperors are taken from their nearby palaces into the forecourt of the imposing Temple of the Sun. There they are placed on stools facing a throng of emotional worshippers.

It is June, the month of *Inti Raimi*, the Festival of the Sun, and each day the mummies – dressed in their richest robes – are the centre of the celebrations. In front of them, a hundred pure white llamas, decked in scarlet-and-gold harness, are sacrificed to the sun; young llamas are roasted and eaten, their tender flesh tasting something like lamb. Thousands of jars of freshly brewed *chicha* are consumed in

Human bellows *As the Peruvian peoples had no bellows, smithy workers smelted metal by blowing on it through long tubes of cane. The furnaces were set on hillsides, where wind increased the draught.*

the public plaza, and dancing and singing go on until dark; then the mummies are placed in niches in the temple, ready for more festivities next day.

Presiding over the celebrations is the current *Sapa Inca* – the Supreme Inca, or Emperor – who otherwise is rarely seen in public. Ordinary citizens are not allowed to look him in the face, and when visiting his palace the city's noblemen carry baskets on their backs to show their own humble status.

As each emperor dies, his body is embalmed. His mummy is then placed on a throne in the treasure-crammed palace which the emperor inhabited in his lifetime – and which he continues to occupy in death. There he is joined in time by the petrified body of his *Coya*, or Empress. This was usually his sister; for though the Inca had hundreds of wives, many of them his close relatives and many others drawn from elite families in the conquered territories, his principal wife had to be a woman of equal rank with himself, who could only be his sister. In death the Empress squats dutifully next to her Inca, as though in meditation.

Sons of the sun

The Incas were originally a small mountain tribe that emerged in the Andes in about AD 1000. Culturally, they reached their height under the Emperor Pachuti, and his son and successor Topa, who ruled the expanding empire for much of the 15th century. Between them, they welded dozens of tribes – many of whom spoke a different dialect or language – into a stable and highly organised society of some 12 million people whose ruler was worshipped as the son of the sun, a living god whose word was law.

Standing some 11,480 ft (3500 m) above sea level, Cuzco (in present-day Peru) grew from a small, riverside village of mud huts into a metropolis dominated by magnificent palaces and temples. For their main buildings the Inca masons used massive stone blocks placed together in close-fitting,

High crossing *Bridges made of stout ropes, woven twigs, vines and plant fibres spanned the deep gorges of the Andes. They formed links in a network of roads along which teams of runners could carry messages over 50 miles (80km) of mountainous terrain in a day. Writing was unknown to the Incas, so the runners memorised the messages. The bridges were regularly checked by official inspectors.*

mortarless joints, through which not even a knife blade could be forced. In the event of an earthquake, the interlocking stones jumped up slightly and then settled back in place. So the buildings stayed upright during even the most violent earth tremors. The engineering skills of the Incas were also demonstrated by the building of a network of some 15,000 miles (24,000 km) of roads which crisscrossed the rugged mountains to knit the empire together. Storehouses of food, clothes and weapons were placed a day's journey apart for a marching man, as the Incas did not possess any wheeled vehicles or horses.

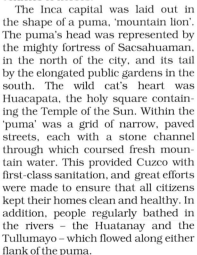

Inspector of bridges

The Inca capital was laid out in the shape of a puma, 'mountain lion'. The puma's head was represented by the mighty fortress of Sacsahuaman, in the north of the city, and its tail by the elongated public gardens in the south. The wild cat's heart was Huacapata, the holy square containing the Temple of the Sun. Within the 'puma' was a grid of narrow, paved streets, each with a stone channel through which coursed fresh mountain water. This provided Cuzco with first-class sanitation, and great efforts were made to ensure that all citizens kept their homes clean and healthy. In addition, people regularly bathed in the rivers – the Huatanay and the Tullumayo – which flowed along either flank of the puma.

The suburbs in which most of the citizens lived lay outside the puma. Their one-roomed, windowless houses were made of stone and brickwork, joined by mud and mortar and finished in mud stucco. Many of them were painted a bright red or yellow, with small, low front doors, like the doors of an oven, steeply sloping thatched roofs, and wide eaves to protect walls from mountain downpours. Cooking was done on tiny clay stoves, the smoke simply drifting out through the thatch. The two staple foods were maize, grown in the sunny lowlands, and potatoes cultivated in the frosty highlands. The main sources of meat were llamas and alpacas; roast guinea pig was popular, and most households kept numbers of the animals. Among the most popular fruits were guavas and cactus fruit.

Meals were eaten twice a day, in the morning and at night. As there was little or no furniture, people mostly sat crosslegged on the earth floor, eating from platters with fingers or spoons. They also slept on the floor at night, usually without changing their clothes.

The Inca priests – who also acted as doctors and surgeons – were skilled at amputating crushed or diseased limbs and at burning wounds to prevent infection. They also performed trepanning operations on people whose skulls had been fractured in combat or in accidents. The operations involved cutting out pieces of broken bone while the patient was anaesthetised with the drug coca, made senseless by drinking large amounts of chicha, or 'put under' by hypnosis.

The skull might be cut with a razor-sharp piece of obsidian set into a stick and rotated by a bow-string. A hole about 1 in (25 mm) across was made, enabling the broken bone to be removed, so relieving the pressure on the brain. Then the section of the scalp was carefully replaced, and the wound bandaged with fibre.

Some surgeon-priests are believed to have practised blood transfusions some 500 years before they became standard in Europe. Like all South American Indians the Incas had the same blood group: O rhesus positive. This meant that the blood of the recipient and the donor 'matched', keeping cases of bad reaction to a minimum.

Omens of doom

As well as worshipping the sun and a host of gods, the Incas were highly superstitious. They believed that everyone had a *hauqui*, or guardian spirit, which looked after his or her well-being, and they revered holy objects and places called *huacas*. These included pebbles, stones, caves, hills and springs – as well as man-made structures such as bridges and houses. In addition, it was held to be bad luck to hear an owl hoot, or to see a shooting star flash across the sky.

In 1530 a series of omens foretold the imminent end of the empire. Within three years the last emperor, Atahualpa, had been captured and strangled by the Spanish conquistador Francisco Pizarro. Almost a century of prosperity and power was over, and the empire was ruled by a new Sapa Inca from across the ocean.

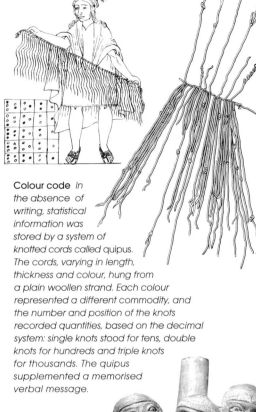

Colour code *In the absence of writing, statistical information was stored by a system of knotted cords called quipus. The cords, varying in length, thickness and colour, hung from a plain woollen strand. Each colour represented a different commodity, and the number and position of the knots recorded quantities, based on the decimal system: single knots stood for tens, double knots for hundreds and triple knots for thousands. The quipus supplemented a memorised verbal message.*

Helping hands *Two women – possibly a wife and mother-in-law – support an intoxicated man and help him home. The Incas drank a potent alcoholic beverage produced from fermented maize, and called chicha. Drunkenness was common.*

Building blocks *Irregularly shaped blocks of white granite were dressed with stone tools to make jigsaw-pattern walls for Inca buildings, which proved earthquake-proof.*

HUNTERS WHO LIVED BY THE BUFFALO

In the shadows of the pre-dawn prairie, smoke rose from a circle of painted warriors passing round their stone pipe. The head Comanche medicine man was leading an Eagle Dance to usher the young man called Breaks Something – after his notorious clumsiness – into manhood. The young dancers shook their long loose hair and their decorated rattles. Every young warrior waved his fan of eagle feathers in wide circles through the morning fog.

The dancers swooped and soared, not singing but crying in imitation of the squawks of a young eagle struggling to leave its nest. Hour upon hour they danced, as the medicine man urged on laggards with a blast from his eagle-bone whistle. The rhythmic stomping, endless drumming and fervent cries of the witnesses shook the very poles of the nearby tepees.

The Eagle Dance ended at dusk. Now Breaks Something was regarded as a man, ready to take his place on the autumn buffalo hunt. To mark this, his friends and relatives presented him with a speedy new pony and a powerful elk-horn hunting bow.

Next day scouts rode into the village bringing news of a huge herd of buffalo, and a nearby canyon that could serve as a natural trap. Immediately the Comanche women began dismantling the tepees to move the whole village closer to the kill. Because a typical Comanche family owned from 50 to 200 horses and lived with just a few light goods, these frequent group migrations were quite simple.

Removing the covering of buffalo skins from the tepees, the women attached the poles to their packhorses. Buffalo skins lashed across the poles formed a platform, or travois, to carry household goods. Even the horses sometimes grew footsore on long journeys over rough terrain, so the horse-loving Comanche carried rawhide horse 'moccasins' which were soaked in water and wrapped around tired hooves.

Like their fellow Plains Indians – the Blackfeet, the Cheyenne, the Pawnee, the Crow, the Kiowa, and the Sioux – the Comanches were excellent hunters and horsemen. When, in 1541, the conquistadores explored as far north as present-day Kansas as many as a million

PORTABLE HOME OF THE PLAINS

Kneeling in her tepee, a Plains woman places an extra stone on the pile heated by burning brushwood and used for cooking. Suspended from sticks is a cooking pot made from the paunch of a buffalo and containing the day's soup of buffalo meat, wild onions and turnips. Opposite, a man checks a hunting arrow he has just shaped. A baby plays on a rug by an embroidered sewing bag. Behind the woman is one of the family's chairs, or backrests. It stands next to a fur-wrapped cradle-board designed to hold the baby securely when the family is on the move. Also hung around the buffalo-skin walls are a pot, a bow and quiver with arrows and, on the left, a medicine bag. In cold weather, the flaps of the tepee are closed, and a small opening allows entry. The top of the tepee is secured with wooden pins; the long poles jut through smoke flaps which can be adjusted to retain heat or to ventilate.

Warrior's shirt

Family outing *An Indian woman on horseback prepares to trek across the Plains, with her children seated behind her on their sledge-like travois. The long travois poles often doubled as supports for large tepees. The doll (right) shows how such a woman might have dressed, in a colourful fringed top, skirt and pouch and matching moccasins.*

Fancy footwear *The bear-claw and buffalo-head designs on these moccasins are made of dyed porcupine quills, each individually sewn. The warrior's shirt, made of buffalo skin softened by repeated smoking and rubbing, has painted stripes, representing his fighting record. Rows of tiny hoof marks below the shoulders record the number of ponies captured.*

Moccasins

Indians inhabited the Great Plains. As they captured the horses descended from those brought by the Spanish explorers, the people of the Plains hunted over larger territories. Food, rituals, manly courage and daily existence all focused on the buffalo.

On a buffalo hunt, each hunter would set out with a string of horses. The men fanned out over a wide area downwind from the herd and gradually closed in, driving the buffalo towards a canyon. A bull buffalo could weigh anything up to a ton, and the weight of the huge animals raised a cloud of dust that could be seen for miles.

As the herd rushed into the canyon the hunters picked off the beasts one by one, usually not wasting more than a single arrow carefully aimed between the ribs. After the kill, each hunter removed his arrows for re-use: unlike war arrows, which were barbed, the smooth hunting arrows were easy to pull free without tearing the hide. While the men and boys killed the buffalo, the women and young people were busy making camp.

Native Americans of the Great Plains had as many as 90 uses for buffalo. The hides were made into clothing, tepee coverings, saddles, blankets, boats and shields. A shield made from smoke-cured buffalo hide was so tough that it could deflect a bullet. Buffalo tallow and grease could be used to clean or soften the skin or as medicine or food. Many Plains people used buffalo paunches as pots for cooking before they had metal vessels: they filled the paunch with meat and liquids and then dropped hot rocks from the fire into the mixture till it boiled. The head of the buffalo might even be used to make a cap to soothe the spirit of the fallen animal, so that future hunts would be bountiful. At the camp near the site of the canyon kill, the women made fires, as the children gathered wood to feed the roaring flames. The hunters led their burdened horses into the camp and slung great slabs of buffalo meat to the waiting women. They would then cut very long thin strips against the grain of the meat, ensuring that each strip contained some fat meat and some lean. Finally the strips were dried and smoked on racks placed over the fires. Ready-to-eat pemmican was made from strips of buffalo or deer meat, pounded with berries, fat and nuts. The mixture, stored in hide pouches, would keep for months, and fed the band while on the move. As the women smoked the meat and staked out the hides, the men got ready for a feast, painting themselves and tending their long hair.

'The pipe is us. The stem is our backbone, the bowl our head. The stone is our blood, red as our skin.'

SIOUX WARRIOR.

No self-respecting man would go to a feast with hair on his face, so one pre-party ritual was plucking any stray beard, nose or eyebrow hairs. Both men and women wore red, yellow and blue make-up.

A good hunt might supply the meat for several weeks of feasting. The Indians most loved the tongue and hump of the buffalo. Each night as the flames blazed, the entire band would gorge, often eating till they became sick. These feasts helped the band gain the strength to endure the long, hard, winters, until spring melted the snow.

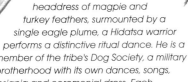

Hunters and hunted *Buffaloes fell easy prey to Comanches trained in horsemanship from childhood. Indispensable in hunting and combat, the mounts bred from the first horses introduced by the Spaniards became a form of wealth; some chiefs owned 1000 horses.*

Dog Dance, buffalo bow
Wearing a ceremonial headdress of magpie and turkey feathers, surmounted by a single eagle plume, a Hidatsa warrior performs a distinctive ritual dance. He is a member of the tribe's Dog Society, a military brotherhood with its own dances, songs, insignia and ceremonial dress. Each military society had its own way of behaving. The peculiarity of the Hidatsa Dogs was to act contrary to instructions: if, for instance, they were ordered to flee in battle, they would attack. The bow the warrior carries resembles the buffalo-hunting bow of the Crow Indians (above). This is made of orange wood and has a bowstring of twisted sinew. The handgrip consists of sewn rawhide, beadwork and a colourful cut fringe.

Pipe and pouch *Pipe-smoking played a large part in Indian life, and the pipes – such as this long-stemmed, stone-bowled pipe – were deftly carved. Decorated, buffalo-skin pouches held a mixture of tobacco, dried bark and sumac leaves.*

203

War and peace *The Indians' twin passions for war and smoking are both served by the instrument held out by this Iroquois brave: the axe has a hollow stem, and a pipe bowl opposite the axe head. The brave also holds a traditional war club. The stockings and boots are the whim of the 18th-century artist.*

Ordeal by fire *Indian hunters in Nova Scotia light fires to drive deer out into the open. They then pursue their quarry on foot and by canoe until they are near enough to loose their arrows. In the foreground of this artist's fanciful impression another hunter is gathering up the fish he has just caught.*

Beaver trap *Iron traps for catching beavers came into use in the late 1790s. They were baited with a secretion from beaver glands called castoreum, and were set on land or under the frozen surfaces of lakes.*

TRAPPING THE BEAVER – FOR A FELT HAT

The Algonquin boy crawled on his belly, making the curious chattering noises that were part of the Beaver Dance. Other boys scampered like partridge or stepped daintily like deer. They were enjoying themselves by acting like the animals they would some day hunt – but at the same time they were learning valuable lessons about the animals' habits.

Some day, their lives and the lives of their women and children might depend on their ability to know exactly how each animal behaved, and where it was likely to be on the day they needed it for food or for clothing.

The Algonquins, like the Cree, the Micmac and other Indian tribes of the forests of what is now eastern Canada,

lived by hunting. Their clothes and blankets were the furs of beaver, while deerskin made comfortable moccasins that stayed soft and supple even when wet. Meat was provided by rabbits and deer and, on special occasions, by dogs. Porcupines, overconfident in the protection of their sharp spines, were easily clubbed, providing meat and also quills that could be coloured and sewed painstakingly onto items of clothing for decoration.

The camp, like those of all woodland Indians, was small, consisting of not more than 20 people, because the wildlife of any region could support nothing more than family groups. In front of each tiny bark shelter, women chatted as they sewed skins with animal gut or spread slivers of meat to dry. One boiled water by dropping hot stones into a pot made of the paper-like bark from a birch tree. Another woman staggered from the woods carrying the huge haunch of a bear.

Women did the heavy work among woodland Indians because men had to be healthy and well-rested for the hunt.

When women became too old to work and men too old to hunt, they would voluntarily go alone into the woods to their deaths. They knew that during the long months of winter, when food was scarce, extra mouths could mean starvation for everyone.

One woman stood out from the others because she was cutting meat with a steel knife. It was faster, and held its edge far better than the bone knives used by the other women. It was cheap, too, having cost only three of the beaver skins taken by the men and traded to the European pedlars. Beaver was in demand in a Europe

A DAY IN THE LIFE OF A TRAPPER

The Algonquin trapper wakes in his shelter of spruce boughs to the cracking and groaning of lake ice in the 40-below-zero cold. He rolls out of his beaver-fur sleeping robe and puts on his parka of wolf fur on which, unlike other furs, the frost from his breath does not form an icy ring, and boots made from the hocks of a moose. Over these he straps wide, 'bear-paw' snowshoes. Picking up his axe, and swinging his pack onto his back, he heads for the last trap left to inspect at the end of his arduous three-day trek.

It is under the ice of a pond he marked out the previous summer. He cuts through the ice with the axe and grunts with satisfaction at the sight of a beaver, caught in the jaws of the trap. He forces the trap open and then, with a steel knife brought by traders from a factory in England, skins the beaver. He then rolls up the pelt, thrusts it into his pack and resets the trap – sprinkling animal oil around to cover his scent. Later that afternoon, sweating under his load of skins, he reaches his base camp. A quick glance at a platform set high on poles shows him that his winter food supply is still there, safe from foraging animals. That night, by the light of a log fire, he scrapes the skins and stretches them on circular frames made of twigs. Later, the women will chew on the stiff pelts, making the skins supple for the hands of the white traders, who will soon arrive at the camp.

that prized felt hats. Felt made from beaver fur would hold its shape for many years, even through the repeated soakings of European rains. Particularly valuable were furs that Indians had slept on for a year so that the coarse, reddish hairs wore off to reveal soft, grey fur beneath.

Not all the Indians of Canada lived in woodland style. The Iroquoians of the Great Lakes region were farmers who lived in towns of as many as 2000 or 3000 people. They had a surplus of corn and squash and tomatoes to carry them through the winter. There was no need for the elderly to commit suicide, or for the women to do so much heavy work; senior women even had the power to choose and dismiss chiefs.

Indians of the Pacific coast, such as the Haida, lived in a land rich in fish, animals and delicious wild plants. Food gathering was so easy that people had plenty of time left on their hands in which to make their richly decorated clothing, woven from the shredded bark of cedar, and to carve and colour the tall totem poles on which were told the legends of the tribe.

Like all Indians, the Haida had little use for possessions – except to give them away. Social status came from giving gifts, a practice the Haida elevated to an art with regular gift-giving ceremonies called potlatches.

Call of the kilted bagpiper

As the sun declined over the Algonquin camp, one of the men lifted his head to listen. The sound was unmistakable. He ran to the nearby stream just as two canoes swept into sight. In the bow of the first, a kilted bagpiper stood braced against the bench seats, his pipes shrieking through the forest.

The stocky paddlers – who called themselves *voyageurs* in their native French – edged to the bank to avoid damaging the birch-bark skins of the canoes. Each wore a bright sash, the distinguishing badge of

Striking a bargain *A pipe of tobacco was passed from hand to hand as beaver trappers and traders conducted their business until long into the night. In exchange for furs, trappers offered such items as tin bowls, blankets, axes and knives.*

the voyageur. As the canoes touched land, they stood, then lifted a man from the second canoe and carried him to shore. Impressively dressed in top hat and suit, this man was one of the traders from the Northwest Company. Solemnly he greeted the Indians, giving a package of tobacco to each man and a piece of brightly patterned cloth to each woman.

Traders of Hudson's Bay

There were two major fur companies in Canada. The Northwest Company, a partnership of Scots and French, sent its fleets of canoes from Montreal into the land of the trapping Indians. The Hudson's Bay Company, British and much the larger of the two, was given its charter by Charles II in 1670. It later established bases called factories on the waterways draining into the bay. There, the Hudson's Bay traders waited for Indians to bring the furs to them.

Life was pleasant in the factories, with huge meals of wild goose and ptarmigan and delicious beaver tail. Many of the Hudson's Bay men even

had wives from Britain with them or, more commonly, Indian wives who also served as interpreters. The lives of the Northwesters, however, were harsh and laborious, with long hours of paddling and a monotonous diet of the dried meat and berries called pemmican. Nor was there room in the canoes for their wives, had they wanted to go along.

The Northwester official noted the healthy appearance of the Indians with relief. Several days before, he had passed half-a-dozen tall scaffoldings by the stream. These were burial platforms, built high to keep bodies safely above scavenging animals. So many platforms meant a terrible loss of life for a single camp. Indian medicine of the 18th century was at least as advanced as European medicine; but both were powerless against the diseases that Europeans carried with them to Canada. Tuberculosis and smallpox destroyed whole tribes.

Luckily, this camp had so far been spared. Trader and trappers sat cross-legged in a circle. A long but exciting night of bargaining lay ahead.

A fortune in furs *Two adventurers, Pierre-Esprit Radisson (standing) and Médard Chouart Groseilliers (seated), set out by canoe, in 1659, in search of the uncharted 'Bay of the North', said by Indians to border a land in which vast quantities of furs awaited the trapper. The Frenchmen did not find the bay, but they did return with 60 canoes laden with pelts. They were rewarded with jail sentences by the authorities of New France, but later gained their revenge by helping to found the British-run Hudson's Bay Company.*

HARD LIVING ON THE SLAVE PLANTATIONS

Battered by a tropical hurricane on the long voyage from the west coast of Africa, a slave trading ship limped into the harbour at the Brazilian port of Pernambuco (present-day Recife). In the early 16th century the local sugar industry was booming, and planters eagerly spent their gold doubloons to purchase captured African slaves.

Even as the Dutch sea captain figured his profits on the voyage, which would add up to a fortune for the expedition's merchant shareholders back in Amsterdam, he also reckoned his losses. One out of six of his cargo of slaves had perished from sickness or starvation during the voyage across the Atlantic. Some slaves lodged on deck jumped overboard rather than face a lifetime of servitude.

The 'sweet gold' of the sugar industry kept the whole system running. Richly dressed planters and millowners who strolled through the elegant quarter of the seaport's Portuguese colony were proof that New World treasure could finance a life of luxury and ease.

Meanwhile, the plantation slaves worked day and night during the harvest season, cutting sugar cane and loading wood into oxcarts that lumbered over mud tracks to the mills. There the fires roared through the night, their flames blazing furiously

as slaves worked to purify the cane. Thousands of acres of trees fed the fires, as the slaves toiled day and night in the September to April season.

In their few hours spared from gruelling plantation labour, slaves grew crops they had encountered for the first time in the New World, such as cassava, corn and herbs. The herbs often found their way into the pouches of healers and shamans who practised a mixture of medicine, magic and religion that grew in the slave quarters. Their charmed ointments could ease the wounds made by the overseers' whips. Some of these 'magicians' gained such great reputations for arranging affairs of the heart that veiled ladies from the Big House would visit them in secrecy, seeking their love potions and vengeance charms.

Where tobacco was king

Farther north, in the British colony in Virginia, tobacco was king. As planters expanded their acreage and built mansions with pillared terraces, the slaves cleared fields, built zigzag fences and harvested the scented weed. Slaves on the tobacco plantations of Virginia lived longer than slaves in the tropics, and so might find time to make comforts and furniture for themselves, such as beds of cord strung through pine poles.

On the larger plantations, teams of cooks prepared meals for the whole slave community. The little children would eagerly eat their 'potlicker' and cornbread straight from a trough, before the other slaves returned from the fields. A few times a year the work rhythm eased and the slaves gathered

Tobacco town *Founded in 1729 as an outlet for tobacco, the port of Baltimore flourished; when an artist painted it 13 years later it had 100 residents, 30 houses, two inns and a church. Local Indians were addicted to nicotine, which they believed was good for the health. They chewed the leaves of the tobacco plant, or rolled the dried leaves into tube-like tabacos (right) to smoke like cigarettes. The smoke made them light-headed.*

Sugar slaves *Indians forced into slavery on a Spanish plantation grind cane to release the sugar-bearing juice, then purify the juice by heating it in copper cauldrons.*

to celebrate a harvest, Christmas or a wedding. At a slave marriage ceremony the couple jumped backwards over a broomstick held in the air. Whoever jumped higher would be the boss in the family. A whole hog might be roasted, and plentiful cider and whiskey kept the dancing and singing going all night. Much African musical culture survived and evolved in the New World: homemade percussion instruments echoed the drumming heard along Africa's west coast. African-Americans gradually blended their own heritage with the Christianity that they came in time to adopt. Staid Methodist hymns sounded very different after they had been transformed on the plantation into spirituals that incorporated communal chants, with alternating calls and responses.

Many of the work songs swelled with long sighs for freedom. Even more explicit were the other tunes hummed when masters were not around. 'Massa sleeps in de feather bed, Nigger sleeps on de floor; When we'uns gits to Heaven, Dey'll be no slaves no mo'.'

Plantation labour forces usually consisted of slaves drawn from different tribes, so dialects developed, mixing English and African terms. On the islands off the Carolinas and Georgia, slaves worked on the task system. This assigned a certain job as a day's work, after which the slave was allowed to cultivate his or her own plot. Practised mostly on rice and long-staple cotton plantations, the task system needed less supervision, which meant that its workers had little contact with English speakers. Thus a rich dialect called 'Gullah'

emerged, which crossed translated Africanisms and syntax with an accented New World English. Colourful expressions such as 'sweet mouth', for flatter, and 'day clean', for dawn, have survived – and to this day southerners call peanuts 'goobers' and bags 'totes'.

A bet on the cockfight

In the Big House, as legions of house slaves scurried around polishing plate and thumping cushions, the ladies upstairs would be adjusting their layers of petticoats for a ball. Virginia gentlemen prided themselves on their dancing, and a lady must tie her skirts just so in order to survive the energetic quadrilles at the colonial festivities so prominent in their social calendar.

When they were not exchanging sweet nothings with the belles of the county, young gentlemen might be out betting their next tobacco crop on horses or on a cockfight. Although the elite among the plantation societies amassed great fortunes, there sometimes appeared a generation of heirs ready to gamble away the family treasures. Many a Saturday night debt in Virginia was discharged in tobacco rather than cash.

For the tobacco kings, the sugar barons and the cotton royalty, plantation life comprised a round of sophisticated, aristocratic pleasures combined with agreeable rural settings. But for their indentured servants and slaves, the New World was a bitter row to hoe.

A LONG DAY OF LONELY TOIL

Before dawn, the long line of slave workers, male and female, chanted on their way to the sugar or tobacco plantations. After a day of backbreaking work, which could last as long as 12 hours, the slave gang padded wearily home to their cabins, past the Big House of the masters, with its comforts paid for by the slaves' unrewarded labour. For male slaves, life was lonely as well as hard, for slavers shipped more men than women.

Women slaves, after a day in the fields, still had to tend their children and prepare food. On Sundays they plodded to market to sell the produce of their garden patches. Often wretched slaves would run away. In the Caribbean, some of these escapees – called maroons from the Spanish-American *cimarron*, 'living on the mountain tops' – founded villages. One lasted for 60 years.

Homes apart *Home for the slave was a cramped space in a flimsy thatched cabin, shared with other families and set well apart from the Big House of the plantation owner. The social divide between them was even greater.*

Exporting the weed *The demand for tobacco was so great in Europe that leaves of the plant* Nicotiana tabacum *were cured by smoke from wood fires to withstand the rigours of the long voyage from the Americas.*

Captains carousing *The finely dressed captains of the ships that brought slaves to the New World, and sailed back to the Old World bearing sugar and tobacco, celebrated a successful voyage with drunken parties. Pipes were smoked and grog – a potent mixture of spirits and water – was drunk from a glass or bowl until the merrymakers were sick or unconscious.*

OLD EUROPE IN THE NEW WORLD

Three ships arrived off the coast of Virginia in 1607 after crossing the Atlantic, crowded with 104 adventurers eager to make their fortune but badly equipped to do so. Several previous English expeditions had failed, and this latest commercial voyage of the Virginia Company of London looked uncertain, too. The voyagers crossed Chesapeake Bay to the mouth of the James River, where they founded Jamestown, the first permanent English settlement in the New World.

Other settlements followed, both in Virginia and, farther north, along the coast of what came to be called New England. By the end of the century many had become stable communities, with a way of life as different from that of the England the colonists had left behind as it was from that of the native

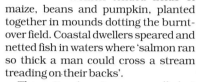

America's first coin, of 1652

Americans around them. Farming and commerce flourished, and in an early act of rebellion against Britain the colonists minted their own currency. One of the first Jamestown settlers, Captain John Smith, both admired and feared the Indians he met. 'Such great and well-proportioned men are seldom seen,' he said 'for they seemed like giants to the English...their attire is the skins of bears and wolves.' Their homes were barrel-roofed, made of branches lashed together and topped with mats. Women tended fields of maize, beans and pumpkin, planted together in mounds dotting the burnt-over field. Coastal dwellers speared and netted fish in waters where 'salmon ran so thick a man could cross a stream treading on their backs'.

The native Americans marvelled at the clumsiness of the Europeans, who could scarcely use their swords to spear the 9 ft (2.7 m) long sturgeon trapped in tidal pools, and who let entire schools of fish swim through the holes in their nets and weirs. Even as the Europeans begged their Indian neighbours to trade them maize, game birds and deer, the Indians lived well on the riches of the bay and forest. They set fire to the woods to clear under-bush. These fires created forests favourable for berries, tall hickory and oak trees bearing nuts, and open glades to attract and fatten deer. When the locals could spare no more food to trade to the hungry settlers, the English seized supplies. As a result, they soon had to spend more time in fortifying Jamestown with a strong palisade than in planting of crops with which to feed themselves.

The water the settlers drank from the river was so salty and polluted from their own wastes that the English soon fell ill. The first arrivals looked down on manual labour. Amid fevers, famine, war and hardships during the first years in Jamestown, many settlers spent their time doing no more than bowling in the muddy streets and arguing about what to do next.

Deciding the settlers had grown too numerous, the Indians launched a surprise attack in 1622. This might have discouraged the colonists if the profitable tobacco had not already become a boom crop. The Virginia Company grumbled when the first ships returning from the New World carried sassafras (said to cure syphilis) and lumber, instead of gold. But once the hogsheads of tobacco landed on British wharves, the weak little colony no longer risked abandonment. English vessels sailed back to the New World loaded with luxuries, cloth, finely worked plate and casks of the sack that the emerging planter-class loved to drink. With land in plentiful supply, planters just cleared new land when the old wore out. Fields were cleared by stripping a band of bark right around each tree, which killed it. A tobacco field presented a landscape of plants sprouting amidst bare trunks and burnt stumps.

In the early years of the colony, very few women crossed the Atlantic. Most arrived as indentured servants, bound to serve up to seven years. Chances for

Death on the farm *Friendly at first, many Indian tribes soon became hostile to the settlers. A woodcut of 1622 shows warriors slaughtering coastal farmers with clubs and knives, while canoe parties attack Jamestown.*

success were good, provided a servant survived disease until his or her service term ended. Animals gave lessons in survival as cattle and pigs feasted on hickory nuts, acorns, grasses and berries – all easy to forage without human help.

To New England with the Bible

To the north, settlers arrived in Massachusetts armed with Bibles and strong convictions, but ill prepared for anything but prayer. Lacking fish hooks, the settlers had to rely upon netting or spearing. Although some of the original English refugees from Holland had been weavers, no one brought over a loom or spinning wheel until the 1670s. Bearskins traded from Indians supplemented quilts brought from the home country.

Children rode down snow-clad slopes on toboggans made of curved pine planks, though staunch Puritans raged against many other recreations. Massachusetts Bay in 1646 banned shuffleboard and bowling – though it said nothing against alcohol. Dancing was a practice it proved impossible to ban, though music in general was regarded as useless frivolity.

To save powder and shot, boys as young as eight years old went out with slingshots to hunt partridge and quail for the family table. Gradually, as the settlers adapted Old World tastes to New World products and ways, they began to feel at home among the natives of North America.

HOW THE INDIANS TAUGHT THE SETTLERS A NEW DIET

Many of the first settlers from England who arrived in the New World died from scurvy contracted on the long voyage across the Atlantic, caused by the lack of the vitamin C contained in fresh fruit. Many of the deaths might have been avoided if the newcomers had more speedily adopted the Indians' diet. This included beverages of berries and herbs, and pemmican – a paste made from dried meat, ground up and mixed with berries, and eaten in winter and on journeys.

Gradually the colonists came to appreciate native foods such as turkey, popcorn, roasted squash, and cornbread with acorn oil. The colonists preferred brewed drinks to water, especially potions such as flip, made of beer sweetened with molasses or pumpkin and laced with rum, then stirred with a hot iron rod. They also adopted Indian remedies: parts of the rattlesnake cured fevers and stomachache.

Table bird *The North American turkey became a popular food of the colonists, adopted as part of their autumn harvest thanksgiving feasts, and finding its way onto Old World menus.*

Indian corn *Kernels of maize, when heated, burst to make popcorn.*

SETTLING DOWN TO LIFE IN THE NEW WORLD

The distinctive high-crowned, wide-brimmed beaver hat of the Puritan shields the thatcher from the sun as he adds a covering of reeds to a house in one of the early American colonists' fortified settlements. Other homes are covered with shingles of wood which, like walls, floors and ceilings, come from the trees which grow in profusion around the stockade and have to be cleared before the settlers can start to farm. The stumps of some trees are so large and deep-rooted that they defy the attempts of the settlers to remove them – the origin of the description of one as being 'stumped', or beaten, by a problem. In the centre of the settlement sawyers use a trestle and a large, two-man saw to cut a tree trunk into planks.

Pointed stakes encircle the settlement to protect it against attack by Indians. Soldiers armed with muskets guard the governor's residence, surrounded by neat gardens and topped by the cross of St George fluttering in the breeze. The chimney is set in the centre of the roof, to radiate most warmth in winter, though it presents a fire hazard in wood-built homes. At the far end of the sloping main street, more soldiers man the cannons on the top floor of the fort which overlooks the mouth of the river. The fort's lower storey is used as a meeting house where the Pilgrim settlers hold their traditional services every Sunday.

On the far side of the river, farmers work on a hillside cleared for agriculture. A law passed by the governor to help make the colony self-sufficient demands that every able man grows a year's supply of corn. Part of the farmer's day may also be spent feeding hens, putting sheep out to graze, and checking on the community's cattle and pigs which feast on hickory nuts, acorns, grasses and berries, or on hogs which root for clams at the water's edge at low tide. Most early settlements are located near water, where supplies from England can be unloaded and barrels of tobacco and other goods rolled down to the ships for the return journey. As metals and manufactured goods have to be imported, the settlers copy Indian customs and use wooden pegs to hold tables and bedsteads together, instead of wasting scarce nails.

On winter nights men carve wooden plates, spoons and other utensils.

Hand brush *This wooden brush, 8in (203mm) long, was shaved from one piece of wood.*

Hair care *This 17th-century tortoiseshell case and two combs comes from Jamaica.*

Milk pot *Posset, a drink of hot milk curdled with ale or wine, was kept in this Delft pot.*

Wine bottle *Made in England, this jug was used to keep sack – a strong white wine.*

Designer bowl *This red earthenware bowl, with lattice design, is English-made.*

GIANTS OF EAST ASIA

The more that China increased her links with the outside world, the more she was envied by others. Time and again, fierce and hungry nomads from the north fought their way into the homeland of the world's most civilised nation. Some came only for spoil, while others ruled all or substantial parts of the country for decades or even centuries. None of them left a lasting impression, largely because they were seduced into adopting China's superior values – the cause of their incursion in the first place.

China's neighbours, too, usually recognised her superiority and adopted her ways. The Japanese learned about Buddhism from China, and they imported her systems of writing and money. But while they welcomed Chinese civilisation, the Japanese guarded their independence fiercely. Under the rule of shoguns, a distinctive culture blossomed, and its unique ways, such as Zen Buddhism, the tea ceremony and Noh drama, came to maturity.

CHINA AND JAPAN AD 1150–1650

LANDOWNERS WITH A SACRED DUTY

Seen from a high vantage point, the Chinese landscape looked like a patchwork quilt, with tiny plots of land and larger ones interlocking. No land was wasted. Every fragment of it that could be used to grow food had been tamed by AD 1000, and even the hillsides, hollowed and flattened to form terraces, were cultivated. Land was thought to be the best investment of all for both rich and poor. Most men had some stake in it, and there was almost a sacred obligation for a father to pass on land to his sons. When a man died, his fields were divided between his sons, so that even more patches of land were created, some of which were not really economic to farm, and not big enough to support the owner's family.

The small size of many families' land meant that there was no incentive to introduce mechanised equipment to lighten the farmer's burden. So the main source of power in Chinese farming was backbreaking human labour, and even where ploughs were used they were often drawn by men, for want of money to buy and feed a buffalo or other draught animal.

The vast majority of the Chinese people lived in the country, and their lives revolved around the village where they lived and the annual cycle of sowing, weeding and harvesting. Grain, which fed the nation, was the most important crop.

Chinese governments were always well aware of the vital importance of grain to the economy. Even as late as 1727 an emperor took to task the people of two southern provinces for planting their land 'with such things as lungan, sugar cane, tobacco and indigo', and went on: 'They must not neglect agriculture for the sake of making profit...As for things like plantations

Teeming with life *A mother with her lively trio symbolises the booming population which gave China several cities of more than a million people, at a time when few towns in Europe were even a tenth of that size.*

RULERS OVER THE CHINESE

A long period during which rival dynasties battled for ascendancy gave way finally to more peaceful times. The Song and Ming dynasties brought a blossoming of the arts.

'Six dynasties' period (AD 222 – 589) Short-lived dynasties ruled a divided empire.

Sui dynasty (AD 589 – 618) China was reunited, and many canals built.

Tang dynasty (AD 619 – 906) During a time of contact with many cultures, art flourished.

Song dynasty (AD 960 – 1279) Rulers were based in north China, until invading nomads pushed the government south in 1126.

Yuan dynasty (AD 1280 – 1367) Mongols conquered and ruled China.

Ming dynasty (AD 1368 – 1643) The empire was reunited and its culture restored.

Manchu dynasty (AD 1644 – 1912) Invaders from the north seized Peking and set up the last imperial dynasty.

and orchards, they should only be worked when there is surplus land and labour. How can it be right to look for short-term profit at the expense of neglecting the vital source of life?'

In the north of the country farmers grew vast quantities of wheat, barley and millet. In the southern half of China rice was more common, and the paddy fields created vivid patches of green in the landscape. Rice plants need fertile soil, and varying amounts of water through the growing season. Farmers regulated the level of water standing in fields with sluices and embankments which they opened or blocked off as needed. Some also built water wheels to lift water from rivers into irrigation channels. In some areas two crops of rice could be grown each year, and farmers there had two series of exceptionally busy weeks when the grain was planted and harvested.

Throughout history, the peasants of China seem to have been on the dividing line between survival and starvation, and nothing was wasted. The village drains, which were open channels, flowed into the fields. Pigs and chickens foraged in villages, and their droppings, and nightsoil, were spread on the fields to enrich the soil.

No entry for evil spirits

Villages were usually built on outcrops of poorer land, and the mud brick or wattle-and-daub houses were packed as close together as possible so that any land that might be useful for crops

Inside city walls The main gates of Kai Feng, one of which is shown here in a 12th-century scroll painting, were built on a scale in keeping with the size of the city. A caravan of camels passes through the gate on its way out of the city; a heavily loaded wheelbarrow, drawn by donkeys, has just arrived, and has come to a halt outside a shop selling bows and arrows. To the right of the shop is a letter-writer's stall.

Well caught A bearded fisherman, exquisitely fashioned in jade, inspects a plump fish. Between his feet he holds a wicker creel.

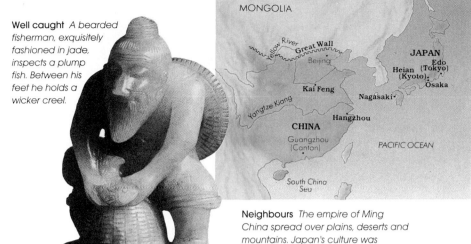

Neighbours The empire of Ming China spread over plains, deserts and mountains. Japan's culture was confined to four main islands.

was not misused. Few of the houses had windows, because that would have allowed evil spirits – not to mention the cold – easy access.

For most people the village was the limit of their world. They worked in fields nearby, found their amusements there and worshipped there. A man might die in the house where he was born and brought up, and where his wife joined him on marriage.

Almost the only occasion for leaving the village was to go to market, and that might mean a walk of an hour or more. There were markets of varying degrees of importance, and the dates of lesser ones were arranged so that they did not coincide with more important markets in the same area. Pedlars travelled from market to market, constantly buying new stock and disposing of what they had bought elsewhere.

While most Chinese lived in villages and worked on the land, others led very different ways of life. China had a large population of boat people who lived in flat-bottomed sampans and junks. Some of them earned a living on the rivers, lakes and canals by fishing or providing transport; others plied the coastline, fishing and trading.

To the land-based government, the idea of wanting to live on the water was suspicious in itself, and boat people were discriminated against – they were not, for example, allowed to sit the examinations for entry to the Civil Service. Some were forced at spear point into the dangerous task of pearl fishing; attached to a weighted rope, they descended into the water and, if they were lucky, they were hauled up before their breath gave out.

Walled cities, and the throng within

As early as the 12th century China had several large cities. Kai Feng was home to about a million people. Hangzhou had a population of well over a million, and was probably the world's largest and most prosperous city at the time.

Cities were surrounded by walls with gates that were closed at night for security. Inside the walls, city life was cramped, with people crowded into insanitary shacks and tenements approached by narrow alleys. Most of the buildings had one storey, and were arranged round a courtyard. There were also multistorey blocks, and Kai Feng had inns that could sleep more than 1000 people at a time.

211

BOUND FEET AND TROUBLE WITH IN-LAWS

Within the Chinese family, there was a strict pecking order. The younger generation was expected to serve and obey the older generation, while even among members of the same generation, the younger members deferred to those who were slightly older. Everyone had a place in relation to everyone else, and, in theory at least, was content with his or her position, which slowly improved as the years went by.

Age was not the only way of allotting status; sex mattered too, and women were denied some of the rights enjoyed by their menfolk. Sons inherited their fathers' property, but daughters only received small gifts as dowry when they married. A man could have more than one wife, but a woman was not supposed to remarry if her husband died. Only men could sue for divorce. A woman was confined first to her father's house, and then to that of her husband. Few women could make up for their ignorance of life outside the home by education, because women rarely learned to read and write.

One way of underlining women's lowly position was the custom of foot-binding. From the age of about five, a girl's feet were bound up with cloths which were tightened until the instep broke and the foot doubled up on itself. The painful process made the feet look very small – at its most severe, binding could produce feet only 3 in (75 mm) long – and small feet were thought to be beautiful. Women with bound feet found walking painful, which deterred them from straying far from home.

Marriage rarely came about through the mutual attraction of boy and girl; parents usually arranged the match. It was usual for a boy to marry a girl from a different village – and with a different surname – and for the girl to join her new husband in his family home. The families exchanged gifts, with the help of a matchmaker, and on the day of the marriage a sedan chair collected the bride from her parents' home. When she arrived at her new home, she took part in a ceremony involving worship of her new husband's ancestors and of his family's household gods, then offered tea in the humblest fashion to her new in-laws.

The position of a daughter-in-law was often unenviable; because she was both young and a woman, she had the lowest status in the household. She came under the direct authority of her mother-in-law, who, if the new bride was unlucky, abused her power and dealt out beatings, torture, hard words and deprivation.

The young wife immediately played her part in running the home, and in preparing the family's two main meals a day, which were cooked in a wok. Those who could afford it drank tea, which was thought to have hygienic qualities because it was made with boiling water. Poor people might drink boiled water and call it 'tea'.

Eating for health

Food was thought to have healing effects. Chinese medicine assumed that disease was due to an imbalance in the body between yin and yang forces. Food was either yin, like fruit, or yang, like grains, and the body's balance could be maintained by eating appropriate food.

Chinese medicine had reached a sophisticated level by the 2nd century; treatments included acupuncture, herbs and moxibustion. In moxibustion, doctors applied powdered leaves to the appropriate part of the body, ignited them and crushed them into the blister that formed. Modest ladies used a doll to indicate to the doctor the

Before the shrine *A mother and daughter look on, as their male relatives worship at the family shrine. The youngest looks aside for guidance from his elders on the next stage in the ritual.*

RITUALS THAT LINKED THE LIVING AND THE DEAD

The worship of ancestors as gods meant that every Chinese family had its own religious system. The dead needed the worship of the living to keep their souls nourished in the after-world, while the living needed the spiritual help of the dead to enable them to flourish in this world. Sons were essential to ancestor worship, for only people with sons could become gods after their death. Those who had no sons could not be worshipped as ancestors, and therefore had no support in the next life. So the arrival of a baby boy was greeted with relief, both for the benefits he brought in this world and in the next.

Because ancestors were worshipped, death marked the beginning of a relationship between people, and not the end. Funerals and other rituals surrounding death were elaborate and costly ceremonies, and mourning dress, which was white, was graded according to the closeness of the relationship with the deceased.

For the sons and daughters of the dead, mourning was a testing time. For 27 months after a parent's death, they had to wear clothes made from the heaviest and most uncomfortable sackcloth, and they were forbidden to eat meat, to use porcelain, to have sexual relationships, or to shave.

Mourners who were very strict in their observances were supposed to build a crude shelter on top of the new grave, and to live there for the mourning period, watering the ground with their tears. State law even laid down punishments to be meted out for failure to observe mourning in the correct manner – but it was almost unheard of for anyone to be brought to court.

In spring and autumn there were grave-sweeping festivals, when Chinese families went to the graves of their ancestors to clean away encroaching vegetation, to repaint the gravestone, and to worship the soul of the dead person. Afterwards they ate beside the grave, consuming the offerings of food which the dead were supposed already to have enjoyed; in this way the meal was shared among the family, past and present.

Extended family *Close family ties brought relatives together in large gatherings. The hosts shown in this Ming dynasty scroll have their pet dog with them as they say their goodbyes to guests of all ages, including an elderly man who supports himself with a stick. Two leave mounted on donkeys.*

site of their ailment for his diagnosis. There were festivities, both within the home and for the whole community, throughout the year. At home, the birth of a baby son was particularly welcome, and was celebrated with feasting. Weddings were occasions for banquets, when even poor families enjoyed lavish spreads of pork, fish, chicken and foods rarely tasted at other times.

The greatest festival, for which everyone tried to be at home, was New Year. Before the old year was quite finished, the god of the household's stove had a part to play in the rituals. He had sat spying on the family all year, and went up to heaven at the end of the year to report on what he had observed. Since almost everyone would have been detected in some misdeed, before the god left people offered him sweet sticky cakes. They hoped that these would make the god unable to open his mouth to report on them – or that, if he could open his mouth, he would say only sweet things.

On the first day of the new year younger members of the family lined up in order of seniority to pay their formal respects to the head of the family. Those who were not married received small gifts of money in red envelopes – red was the lucky colour. Everyone worshipped all the gods in the home – ancestors, the stove god,

Diagnostic doll

the door gods, the god of the land on which the house was built, the well god outside, and a host of other deities. Offerings were put out for ghosts, so that they would not make mischief and spoil the new year's luck. Then, on New Year's Day itself, all scissors, knives, brooms and swearwords were banned, as they could damage good luck. As it was also forbidden to take life, people ate only vegetarian food. On New Year's Day everybody added a year to their age; since at birth a child was regarded as aged one, this meant that a baby born just before the new year would be two years old shortly after coming into the world.

The birthdays of the temple gods were also cause for celebrations. Village temples often accommodated Taoist, Buddhist and Nature gods under the same roof, for Chinese people observed several religions and worshipped many gods at the same time. On the god's birthday, people offered him fruit, incense and imitation money. In spring, some areas had fertility rituals, when people threw rice over the gods of the soil, and over women. People in many parts of China celebrated the fifth day of the fifth month of the lunar year with dragon-boat races. In late summer, hungry ghosts roamed the earth, and nuns and spirit mediums were in demand to protect the living from them.

Bathing baby *In a domestic scene painted on silk, ladies of the royal palace are bathing their children. The boys have their heads shaved in the traditional manner.*

Porcelain head-rest

FOR USE AND ORNAMENT

As early as the 9th century, Chinese craftsmen were making porcelain by firing a mixture of china clay and felspar – though it was another 800 years before the secret was known in Europe. By the 12th century a huge variety of wares, functional and decorative, were being produced. Head-rests, used with no padding, were carefully shaped but left undecorated. Tea-bowls for everyday use, although not decorated, were finely glazed. Dishes bore colourful figures of dragons, clouds and flowers standing out in relief.

Dish and tea bowl

Flow of words *The character (left) shows how the Chinese calligrapher's brush can make strokes of varying thickness. The left-hand part means 'rice', or 'grain of rice', and the right-hand part means 'green' or 'young'. Put together as one character they mean 'essence' or 'refined'.*

ARTISTS OF THE WRITTEN WORD

As the Chinese Empire grew, problems arose when people in different parts of the country wanted to speak to each other. Local variations of the language drifted so far from each other that they became, in effect, different languages. But the Chinese had a way of writing that allowed literate people anywhere to communicate with each other.

The characters used in Chinese writing represent ideas – in contrast with the Roman alphabet, in which symbols represent sounds. This meant that ideas could be written down in the same way everywhere, regardless of the words used locally to express the ideas or the way they were pronounced. Similarly, the word 'five' can only be understood by someone who knows English, but the symbol '5' is understood by anyone who has learnt numbers, whatever word they use for it. The earliest examples of written characters date back

to about 1700 BC. At first, they were pictures of simple objects and activities, but as time went on they developed from pictures into abstract symbols, as more were invented to represent increasingly sophisticated ideas. By the end of the Han dynasty, in AD 220, there were more than 9000 standardised characters; there are now about 50,000 of them.

Calligraphers wrote the characters with brushes made from the hairs of animals such as horses, wolves and

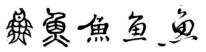

Fishy tale *The symbol for a fish evolved from a simple picture, complete with head, tail and fins, to an abstract character.*

hares, arranged so that they tapered to a fine point. They used ink made from carbon mixed with animal glue; it came in the form of a cake or stick which was ground in water on a hard stone to produce a thick ink. People began to see the characters as objects of beauty in themselves; calligraphy was raised to an art form, and calligraphers became respected artists.

Early calligraphers wrote on strips of wood or bamboo which could be tied together so that they

Pen and ink *Calligraphers' tools were themselves works of art. Brush handles could be made from jade or, like this one, from porcelain. A celestial horse decorates the cake of ink.*

Waterfowl *Calligraphers and artists used a dropper to shake water onto the stone where they mixed ink. A pottery dropper in the shape of a duck has a hole for the water above its left wing.*

Brush strokes *A calligrapher works on a scroll which she has started to decorate with flowers. She holds the brush upright so that only the tip of it is in contact with the paper, and moves her arm freely to create the flowing characters. To her right are ink and an inkstone.*

formed 'books', or on lengths of silk which they rolled into scrolls for easy storage. Then early in the 2nd century the Chinese started making paper from bamboo, hemp or bark.

To make paper from bamboo, the shoots were first soaked and then went through several stages of boiling, pounding and washing until the fibres formed a pulp. Paper-makers used a press to squeeze the excess moisture out of the pulp, and placed sheets of paper on heated walls to dry them.

For many centuries, only useful documents were written: government records, dictionaries, and books on medicine, astronomy, mathematics, agriculture and Chinese history. But poetry was an exception to the rule.

Natural world *Chinese landscape artists sought to create a harmonious impression of nature by the careful placing of stylised water, mountains, rocks and trees. In this Ming dynasty painting by Ch'iu Ying, the tiny human figures make no ripple in the serenity of the scene.*

'The moonlight shines on
*   my bed;*
It's like frost on the ground.
I lift my head to look at it;
Lie back again and think of
*   my old home.'*

LI PO, AD 701-762

Poetry was considered respectable; the philosopher Confucius is thought to have played a part in compiling and editing a collection of poems and songs. Many styles of poetry developed. Some were hundreds of lines long, with exotic words and colourful images; others, like the four-line poem above, were deceptively simple short verses. Unlike poetry, novels were for a long time considered improper, but they still flourished under cover. Short tales – about the supernatural, romantic love and heroes real and imaginary – began to appear during the Tang dynasty.

But the real germ of China's popular fiction was the tradition of storytelling in local marketplaces. Book publishers started to sell the promptbooks that storytellers used, and later on fuller versions of the promptbooks were published as novels. Books could be produced in large numbers – the Chinese invented printing as early as the 8th or 9th century, and developed movable type in the 11th century.

Storytelling was one form of Chinese entertainment; drama was another, and it always took the form of opera with a full orchestra. Scenery was seldom more than a plain backcloth and stage props were rarely used; actors indicated the existence of a hill by gestures, and of a horserider by the actor carrying a whip. Costumes were lavish and brightly coloured, and in some forms of opera the actors' faces were painted in coded colours to show the nature of the character they played.

Specialists in the art of nature

Painting and pottery flourished, as well as writing and drama. Calligraphy influenced painting – artists placed great emphasis on balance in their compositions, and hardly ever used perspective because overall balance counted for more than correct size relationships. Many artists worked like calligraphers, in black and white.

Some paintings showed daily life realistically; others were highly stylised 'expressionist' works. Artists tended to specialise – in birds, flowers, bamboos, or imaginary mountain scenes – and students practised for decades to master just one of these features.

Chinese porcelain reached the peak of its development in the Song dynasty. Factories all over the country made elegantly shaped yet austere bowls, jars and vases whose glazes have a purity and depth unmatched by later potters. Some had raised or incised decorations.

Masterpiece in china *The flowing scarves of this porcelain Buddhist figure, which is associated with compassion, show the skill of Chinese potters. The hands and fish basket are meticulously detailed, in a figure only 5½in (140mm) high.*

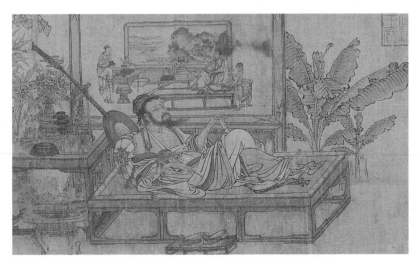

Awaiting the muse *His shoes laid neatly beside him, and a musical instrument behind his head, a scholar reclines in his comfortable home. On the table behind him lies a bundle of scrolls; he is holding a scroll in his left hand, and a fly whisk in the other.*

Tea set *The 18th-century porcelain teapot and cup are both delicately painted with leaves and lotus blossoms. The pot is a little over 4in (100mm) high. On the 14th-century plate a dragon chases a pearl.*

Great Wall *Mongol invaders ended the prosperous Song dynasty, and ruled China for nearly 100 years. To keep them out in future, the Ming emperors, who reunited China, built a new brick and stone wall following the line of that of the Qin emperor of the 3rd century BC. The Ming wall stretched for about 2000 miles (3200 km), with towers and platforms for warning fires at intervals.*

PUPPETS AND PUNISHMENTS IN THE CITY

When Marco Polo visited Hangzhou in the late 13th century, he found a 'noble and magnificent' city. Its residents, he said, were handsome people who were cordial to strangers and very partial to cold baths. The owners of the city's thousands of craft workshops lived in style – their houses were richly adorned with carvings, and their wives dressed in fine silks and adorned themselves with costly jewellery.

City life, however, contrasted sharply with life in the country and in the small market towns where most people lived. Cities had an underworld of beggars and criminals, but they also attracted wealthy people because they offered security from attack, and opportunities for trade and investment. They also offered plenty of scope for easy living.

The well-to-do people of Hangzhou, for example, could visit public gardens and tea houses, or wander through amusement grounds where they could listen to music, join in dancing, and watch performances of puppetry, tight-rope walking, acrobatics, conjuring and snake charming. The amusement grounds also housed wine shops and brothels. The poor could join in the fun too – though they were more likely to provide the services than enjoy them.

City folk not only had a choice of amusements; they also had access to a vast assortment of food and other goods. The city of Hangzhou had many large specialist markets, frequented, according to Marco Polo, 'by 40,000 or 50,000 persons, who bring thither for sale every possible necessary of life'. There were markets for vegetables, medicines, cloth and fresh fish, for flowers and books, and for jewels. Scattered throughout the city there were also hundreds of shops selling goods that included spices, oil, soy sauce and noodles as well as the pearls that boat dwellers risked their lives collecting.

The variety of food on sale impressed Marco Polo. In Hangzhou's markets, he said, 'there is always ample supply of every kind of meat and game, as of roebuck, red deer, fallow deer, hares, rabbits, partridges, pheasants, francolins, quails, fowls, capons, and of ducks and geese an infinite quantity'. In the well-watered areas of south China, fresh and pre-served fish were particularly popular, and people everywhere could buy grain, pork and vegetables.

Guilds for each trade looked after the interests of their members and helped to regulate business practice. In one small city alone there were guilds of boatmen, tanners, barbers and cooks. Dealers in incense and silver, candles and priests' fly whisks also had their own guilds, as did traders in the imitation paper money used during the worship of gods and ancestors.

Cities were centres of government, as well as of business. China was ruled by an emperor who was an absolute monarch, though the day-to-day running of the country was left in the hands of officials. Some officials worked in China's capital city, which moved over the centuries – Hangzhou was the capital from 1128 to 1276. Other officials held posts in local centres. The country was divided into provinces, each of which had a governor. Provinces were divided into prefectures with prefects in charge, and the prefectures were divided into counties.

The officials at county level were the county magistrates, and there were sometimes assistant magistrates as well. These lowest-level officials were known as 'father and mother officials', because they had full responsibility for the lives of the 20,000 or so people under their care. They combined the roles of chief of police, magistrate, tax collector, coroner, detective, hydraulic engineer, relief worker, agricultural adviser, examiner and religious leader.

Officials in posts at all levels were selected by examination.

The passing show *Chinese city streets teemed with all manner of entertainers – in this 14th-century scroll, a portable puppet theatre has attracted a large audience of all ages. A drummer draws a crowd and accompanies the actions of the two puppets, whose manipulators are behind the curtains. On the far left, a man strides purposefully towards two men who think that they will get a better view if they stand on the wooden containers they carry on a yoke. To their right, women encourage the interest of a very young child whose trousers, open at the back, show that he is not yet toilet-trained. Both this child, and the one who points towards the puppets, have shaved heads. Behind the women, an old man hobbles away with the help of a stick; a boy carrying a musical instrument follows him.*

Candidates for the Civil Service examinations were tested on their knowledge of Confucian literature, which they had to learn by heart. The examinations were held every three years in prefectures. Those who were successful went on to the next stage at the provincial capital, and the candidates who passed at that level sat a final examination in the capital city.

Crime and punishment

Very few candidates for the Civil Service survived to the last level of examination – and even those who did had no guarantee of a job to reward their perseverance. For jobs were awarded at the whim of superior officers and the fickle moods of the emperor, and scheming and party politics made life in the Civil Service perpetually insecure.

A candidate whose knowledge of Confucius had satisfied the examiners might find himself administering China's criminal laws. Punishments for crimes of all levels of severity were laid down in

minute detail and the aim was to make the punishment fit the crime as closely as possible. There were several grades of each category of punishment.

For miscreants for whom corporal punishment was decreed, there were different numbers of strokes ordained with different weights of rods. There were also several different kinds of capital punishment, ranging from strangulation, the least severe, to the 'lingering death' by multiple slicing.

Waiting in the condemned cell

All death warrants had to be signed by the emperor. In practice he frequently issued amnesties and reduced the death sentence to lesser punishments. Condemned criminals also benefited from the fact that there were few days in the year when capital punishment could be carried out.

The whole of spring and summer were inauspicious times for carrying out the death sentence. Neither could it be carried out on any of the Buddhist festivals, which included the whole of the first, fifth and ninth lunar months, and the ten Buddhist fast days of each of the other months. Capital punishment was also taboo on rainy days and at night-time. Even if a suitable dry day could be found, there were other reasons why criminals might escape execution. Their sentences were usually reduced if they were infirm, had aged parents to support, or were over 70 or under 15.

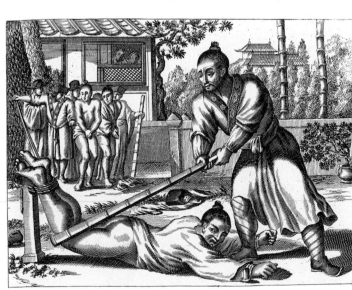

Just deserts *A 17th-century Dutch engraving shows an offender being beaten, while other sentenced criminals await their fate. Magistrates could use torture to extract the confessions which were required by law; one method was finger-squeezing, using wooden compressors made in a legally defined way.*

WARRIORS OF THE SWORD AND TEA BOWL

In medieval Japan, ordinary people faced the ever-present danger of having their heads lopped off. A samurai warrior could approach and with one warning whoop do the deed with the sharpest of swords – merely for 'killing practice'. He ran no risk of prosecution, and in the 16th century the samurai's 'licence to kill' even became enshrined in law, in a slightly modified form: the warrior had to have been provoked on a point of honour, and was required to notify the authorities afterwards.

Samurai were warriors who served local lords. Military families dominated Japan from the 12th century onwards, after rule by an emperor had been all but replaced by the rule of a military overlord, the shogun. The next few centuries were years of turmoil, with incessant outbreaks of fierce fighting between rival lords, and struggles by emperors to reassert their authority. Later, in the more settled 17th and

18th centuries, a samurai was more likely to serve his lord as an administrator rather than as a warrior. And he might spend longer in Zen meditation and the formal etiquette of tea drinking than in fighting his master's enemies. But in the years of chaos and unrest the samurai's way of life revolved around war, and the principle that guided him was *bushido*, 'the way of the warrior'.

Loyal devotion to one's lord was the basis of the warrior code. No samurai was supposed to question or even pause to consider an order, and warriors often sacrificed themselves in battle to shield their lord from danger. So strong was the bond of service that when a lord died, his followers might commit mass suicide rather than go on living without a lawful leader.

A samurai was supposed to hold death in contempt, and warriors killed themselves on the battlefield in order to avoid the shame of surrender. One traditional method of suicide was *hara-kiri* – literally 'abdomen-cutting'. The grisly procedure was carried out according to strict etiquette: a horizontal cut was made across the abdomen from left to right, with a sharp upward

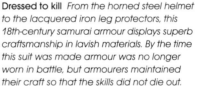

Bowl for the tea ceremony

tug of the knife afterwards. This form of suicide was an excruciating business, and an assistant sometimes ended the agony by cutting off the samurai's head with a sword.

Not all warriors followed bushido to the letter. The ideals of the warrior code weakened amid the betrayals and coups of peasant uprisings and civil wars. In peacetime, too, loutish and quarrelsome warriors abused their training and bullied the local population. The way of the warrior was always there, however, and it promoted indifference to hardship, self denial, and also a spirit of generosity towards the defenceless.

Fighting was the samurai's main business, and a warrior in full battle dress was an awesome sight. A suit of armour had six main pieces: helmet, mask, body armour, thigh pieces, gauntlets and leg guards. Body armour, made from tough leather strips or lacquered iron scales, was colourfully

Dressed to kill *From the horned steel helmet to the lacquered iron leg protectors, this 18th-century samurai armour displays superb craftsmanship in lavish materials. By the time this suit was made armour was no longer worn in battle, but armourers maintained their craft so that the skills did not die out.*

Formidable foe *The samurai wore a fiercely grimacing face mask to deter the faint-hearted opponent. If that failed, the warrior deployed his bristling armoury of lance and swords.*

MASTER OF THE ART OF KILLING

Of all Japan's craftsmen, swordsmiths were the most highly regarded. The secrets of their art were never written down, but passed from master to pupil. The smiths worked in an atmosphere that was almost religious, and wore priest-like clothing and purified themselves with daily ablutions. The steel for the blade was hammered out, folded and forged many times over; the layers of steel produced at each folding, when welded together, gave the blade its enormous strength. This smith is giving a blade its final polish.

Fatal beauty *The care taken in creating the blade of a samurai sword was matched by the skill applied to the decoration of its hilt and scabbard. The sword below, which was worn hung from the waist, has a lacquered scabbard decorated with family crests, and bound with silk to save it from being scratched by the armour. The hilt is also covered in silk. At the base of the hilt is a guard to protect the hand: early sword guards were simply circular iron plates with a slot for the blade, but they became increasingly ornate, with their own decorative inlaid designs..*

laced and quite flexible. The helmet, or *kabuto*, was particularly impressive: with horns or antlers sprouting from the sides it made the samurai warrior look like a giant stag beetle and was intended to intimidate the enemy.

A head bag was an optional extra for the samurai warrior. This was used to carry the severed head of an enemy, and readers of a guidebook written for warriors were advised: 'When walking, carry it hung to your waist; when mounted, fasten it to the saddle.'

Swords and a recitation

Bows and arrows, fired from horseback at full gallop, formed part of a warrior's armoury, but his most prized possessions were his swords. Their hilts and scabbards were exquisitely decorated, and the single-edged, slightly curving blades were razor-sharp and extremely strong.

Samurai fought one-to-one, and wielded their swords with the utmost skill – the result of years of training. Many samurai practised with wooden swords, and martial arts such as kendo have their origins in sword practice. Before an onslaught, each warrior called out his name and recited at length the brave feats of his ancestors, in order to strike terror into the hearts of ill-bred adversaries.

Until the 16th century, samurai came from a wide range of backgrounds, and illustrious knights fought alongside quite lowly commoners. But

from then onwards Japan's class system became more rigid, and commoners were no longer allowed to carry swords. As the country became more settled, samurai spent less time in battle, and more time farming their own land or managing the farms of their lords.

Samurai families made up about six per cent of the population and intermarried to maintain the cherished samurai stock. Warriors' wives were supposed to instil in their young the ideals of bushido, but the code's rigours and disciplines were such that a samurai mother's lot cannot have been an easy one. Laments show how arduous life was for some women:

'I spend my days bewailing
Wearily, so wearily
The sorrows of this life.
The longer it lasts
The more grievous they become.'

From the 16th century, the warriors often lived apart from their wives in the castles and mansions of their lords. They were paid with rice, and wartime rations were 1½ pints (nearly 1 litre) of uncooked rice a day. The warriors' habit of eating rice, and of having three meals a day instead of two, spread to the farmers who had previously eaten cereals such as millet and wheat.

A peaceful retirement

In old age, some warriors gave up their swords and entered Buddhist monasteries. From the 14th century, a new form of Buddhism called Zen gained a widespread following among samurai. Its austerity and indifference to death appealed to warriors who found in Zen

Divine wind *Mongols led by Kublai Khan tried to invade Japan in 1281, but their fleet of ships was destroyed by violent winds. The grateful Japanese called the storm kamikaze, 'divine wind'. A painted screen made in the 17th century shows an artist's impression of the event.*

the rigorousness of the samurai way of life but none of the violence. Zen taught that enlightenment could come through intuition and contemplation, and warriors who had once fought in savage battles sat crosslegged for long periods in meditation.

Japanese gardens, with their careful arrangements of stones, shrubs and bridges, owe much to Zen tradition. And a tea ceremony which began as a Zen ritual spread throughout Japan in the 15th century. It took place in sparsely furnished rustic pavilions designed to induce calmness, and an elaborate etiquette governed the way in which the utensils, powdered green tea and hot water were handled.

A samurai left his swords outside the pavilion, entered through a low door and sat in quiet conversation with the other guests. When the tea bowl was brought to him, he took it in both hands, admired its texture and simple form, and drank from it in three sips.

Gables and gilding *The moated hilltop castles from which samurai operated, such as the gabled Himeji Castle, were built by the local lords who employed them. Within the thick walls of such castles were gardens, rooms for warriors, guests and horses, and sometimes a Buddhist temple. Some castles, including Himeji, were very ornate, with gilded and painted staterooms.*

LIGHTWEIGHT HOUSES AND HEAVY TRAFFIC

During the hot, sticky summer season, Japanese homes were a delight to live in. The mansions of the nobility, set in spacious gardens and often overlooking an ornamental lake, had a stream running under the raised floorboards to keep cool air circulating. Enormous roofs, clad with shingles of cypress or pine bark, offered plenty of shade.

Everything possible was done to counter the oppressive humidity. Those who could afford it even enjoyed iced drinks, and sorbets of crushed ice flavoured with herbs, for blocks of ice were collected in winter, wrapped and stored in huts sunk into the earth, and then sold in summer.

In cold weather, however, all houses, even those of the most wealthy, were desperately uncomfortable. Biting winds easily penetrated the flimsy walls, which were often made from removable shutters or bamboo blinds. Inside, the curtains and movable screens that took the place of partition walls did little to block out draughts.

Small charcoal braziers provided the only heating even in the homes of the wealthy, so that people shivered in spite of the thick layers of clothing that they wore indoors. Poorer people could at least huddle round the hearth sunk into the earth floor of their box-like huts, which resembled makeshift shelters more than permanent homes.

Menace from fire and tempest

The temporary character of many buildings reflected the ever-present risk of sudden catastrophe. Natural disasters could strike at any moment, for Japan is plagued by storms, earthquakes and *tsunamis* – violent sea waves triggered off by underwater earthquakes or volcanic eruptions. Disastrous fires were common too, caused by sparks from braziers or by accidents with lights. So noblemen had a storehouse, built of stone or clay and set apart from the mansion, where they stored documents and works of art.

Town dwellers were also prepared for fires. Commodore Matthew C. Perry, who led an American delegation to Japan in the 1850s, described watch houses in almost every street, fireproof warehouses to store valuable goods and merchandise, tubs of water in the streets and numerous fire engines.

Perry's visit marked the end of 200 years of deliberate isolation by Japan from the rest of the world. In 1603 a military family, the Tokugawa, seized power, and its members presided over Japan for the next two and a half centuries. They moved the capital city to Edo – modern Tokyo – and placed strict limits on foreign contact. The so-called Edo period was an age of relative peace and stable government, and life in Japan went on undisturbed by events elsewhere in the world.

A ban on drinking tea

During the Edo years, an increasing number of people lived in towns, but the great mass of the people were farmers and peasants. They lived a regimented life, heavily taxed and frequently the victims of flood and famine. Festivals such as New Year, however, provided some relief and occasions for drinking and dancing.

A number of prohibitions governed the peasants' life. They could not leave the village or sell their land, and they were forbidden to wear the silk worn by nobles and samurai, or drink tea or *sake*, the rice wine – although that law was broken at festival time. Dressed in cotton or hemp clothes, they grew rice to sell to samurai, priests and craftsmen, and barley, millet and wheat to make noodles for their own food.

Grain and goods made by craftsmen were carried from place to place on a network of roads which included the Eastern Sea Road. This highway, 300 miles (480 km) long, connected Kyoto and Edo, and at the time it was probably the world's busiest road. A constant traffic of merchants, government officials, pilgrims, priests and doctors travelled along it.

Most people travelled by horse or on foot, and it took 20 to 30 days for pedestrians to complete the journey. The few wheeled vehicles were used to carry very heavy loads. There were incessant stops at checkpoints where agents of the shogun kept a watchful eye on

Gold weight *Taxes could be paid in rice, but traders needed money to carry out business efficiently. The idea of money, and the first coins, came from China. In an 18th-century painting, gold coins are being weighed, and recorded by an official.*

Daily grind *Bamboo and wood machinery removed some of the drudgery from Japanese peasants' lives. In this ink painting, peasants bowed under a bale of grain approach threshers using flails. In the building on the right, men operate a hulling mill to remove the outer husks from rice; the water-driven pounding mill in the stream removes the bran.*

Coins from China, holed for stringing together

Kitchen scene *Japanese women of the 18th century, their hair carefully arranged with combs, are busy with domestic tasks. One peels vegetables with a substantial knife; for her companion, housework goes on just the same with the extra responsibility of a baby.*

BEHIND THE BAMBOO BLINDS

The homes of all Japanese, rich or poor, were sparsely furnished. People kept their possessions in chests, some of which were varnished with lacquer – the sap of the lacquer tree – which gives a glossy but hard-wearing surface. They slept on rectangular straw mats called *tatami*, sat on circular straw cushions, and sometimes used freestanding concave elbow rests. Low, lightweight tables completed the furniture. Lighting, even in wealthy homes, was very simple and consisted of resin tapers which gave a poor light, or lamps that were little more than shallow bowls of sesame oil with a floating cotton wick. The poorest people had no lighting at all, and very little furniture.

Most Japanese food was equally simple, even for wealthy citizens. Little meat was eaten, because of the Buddhist prohibition on taking life, and many dishes were based on rice, vegetables and fruit. Seafood provided the most important source of protein. The Japanese attached great value to the taste of food, however, so ingredients were lightly cooked to preserve their flavour. The appearance of food was considered important as well, and much care was lavished on carving vegetables into elegant shapes. Seaweeds were used both for flavour and as garnish.

Use and ornament *Decoration on a wooden rice bucket shows the unrivalled skill of Japanese craftsmen in applying lacquer to wood and metal objects.*

travellers. Their main concern was to give the shogun advance warning of powerful local lords on the move with large bodies of armed men.

Crafts of all kinds flourished in Edo Japan. In the towns, guilds of crafts-men trained apprentices and regulated trade as in Europe. Potters, dyers, woodworkers and paper-makers, and craftsmen in lacquer and metal all produced finely made goods, and weavers opened huge drapery stores.

There were also specialists in bamboo who made anything from baskets to water pipes, umbrellas and fans. The folding fan is said to have been invented in Japan round about AD 670. There were fans for dancers, for tea ceremonies, for court ladies and even fans used for signalling in battle.

Craftsmen, like everyone else in Edo Japan, had their own particular status in the official ranking of citizens. At the top of the social order stood the sword-wielding samurai. Farmers, including the most humble peasants, came next because they produced food, although high rank did not necessarily result in an income to match. Farmers were followed by the craftsmen, although

leather workers were treated as out-casts because they handled carcasses. The lowest rank was that of merchant, whose profession was considered worthless – it produced nothing, but only profited by other men's efforts.

The position allotted to merchants reflected the teachings of Confucius, whose philosophy came to Japan from China. Confucianism stressed personal virtue, devotion to the family, social obligation and acceptance of one's place. Confucianism offered a third set of beliefs to the Japanese, who already lived comfortably with two religions.

Shinto, the native religion, was based on the worship of ancestors and nature spirits. The emperor claimed descent from the Shinto Sun Goddess, and was held in awe even when he had no power. Another religion was Buddhism, which also came from China; its Zen sect had many adherents among the samurai.

Made in Japan *Oriental goods such as this ornate decanter were in great demand in the West. The painted porcelain is embellished with Dutch brass.*

Tea set *Tea drinking, an art in itself, called for unpretentious china like this tea caddy and plate.*

PLEASURES OF THE 'FLOATING WORLD'

The instruction 'No smoking' is not a 20th-century innovation. Tobacco was brought to Japan by European traders in the late 16th century and it quickly caught on. It was especially popular, smoked in long pipes, among the *kabukimono* – the wild and reckless youth of noble and merchant families, and of samurai who had lost their status and purpose in life.

The authorities officially banned the growing, selling and smoking of tobacco because of the risk of fire in Japan's wood and bamboo buildings. But the ban was to no avail: tobacco continued to be grown illegally, and smoking spread to all levels of society.

Regimented as it was, Edo Japan had its outlets for pleasure-lovers and nonconformists, especially among the privileged classes. In each of the great cities of Kyoto, Edo and Osaka there were licensed districts devoted to leisure and entertainment, and there all manner of frivolities, including smoking, were tolerated.

> *'All over the city there is an enormous number of inns and taverns and there are also many public baths, for the Japanese are very fond of having a bath.'*
>
> FATHER JOAO RODRIGUES, *c.* 1600

Here were theatres, taverns, public baths and geisha houses, where all the thrifty and orderly values of Confucian teaching were overthrown. The ways of the luxury-loving merchants prevailed over the austere samurai code, and styles were set by courtesans, actors and the swaggering kabukimono. The pleasure quarter was a dreamland: colourful, exotic and unreal. People called it the 'floating world'.

In the leisure districts, hardworking townsmen and visitors from the country could relax in the company of women known as *geisha*, who were schooled in the arts of singing, dancing and witty conversation. Their training often began as early as the age of seven, and accomplished geisha were celebrated figures in society. Not all of them were courtesans: men paid for their company but did not necessarily sleep with them. It was pleasure enough, often, to hear a talented geisha playing the *shamisen*, a three-stringed musical instrument which became popular around the same time as tobacco.

In the geisha house, men might also relax at cards, backgammon or at *go*, a board game played with pebble-like counters. Like the court ladies of the time, women of the floating world wore the kimono – a loose, long-sleeved gown, often made from sumptuous silk.

In Japanese society at large, strict rules governed the various colours, cloths, patterns and hairstyles that people of different rank were allowed to wear; silk, for example, was strictly for the nobility. But in the floating world people wore just about anything. The kabukimono were particularly known for their kaleidoscopic clothes with colourful emblems, and they added to an already startling appearance by wearing their hair in long sidelocks.

In the late 16th century, the word *kabuka* was all the rage. It meant rakish, bizarre, or even 'kinky' in an erotic sense. It had echoes not only in the term kabukimono but in the famous *kabuki* theatre which emerged at around the same time as the most popular form of Japanese drama.

Drama on and off the stage

Kabuki theatre is said to have begun in 1586, when an actress called O Kuni performed parodies of Buddhist prayers with a troupe of men dancing as women and women posing as men. From O Kuni's first sensuous and strangely exciting routines, kabuki developed into a spectacular theatre of music, dance, mime and melodrama. Actors in gaudy costume performed amid splendid

Quiet interlude *Board games and the music of the shamisen were two of the less clamorous ways of satisfying townspeople's appetite for entertainment. On a painted screen a board game called* sugoroku *is in progress, to a background of shamisen music. A tea tray lies beside the musician.*

A picnic in style *The lacquered wooden case of this picnic set contains bottles for sake, the rice wine, and tiered boxes for food.*

Battle song *Tales of ancient family rivalries were told by blind priests to the accompaniment of the heike biwa (left). The back of this biwa, carved from a single piece of wood, is chestnut, and the front is quince. It has ebony pegs and silk strings.*

sets: stages revolved, and performers burst suddenly from trap doors. A passageway ran from the stage to the back of the theatre, through the heart of the audience, and gave the action special immediacy.

The actors themselves delighted in exaggerated posturing and flamboyant style. They were superstars, their features known to thousands through the coloured woodblock prints which were popular at the time. Their private lives were surrounded by gossip and scandal, and murderous quarrels broke out over much-adored actresses. As a result women were banned from the kabuki stage, only to be replaced by suave, boyish female impersonators who in a short time proved to be even more scandal-prone. Eventually all parts were played by adult men.

Noh mask of a young girl

Two other forms of drama that were popular in Japan at this time were *bunraku* and *Noh*. Bunraku was a puppet theatre which reached its peak of popularity in the 18th century; its half life-size puppets were accompanied by the shamisen.

Noh theatre was the preserve of the nobility and samurai, and was a more highbrow form of drama, set apart from the fun-loving floating world. It combined chanted verse, the music of flutes and drums, and stylised movements, and the performers, who were all men, wore richly embroidered kimonos and wooden masks to show the character being played.

A love of romantic novels

As sober citizens succumbed to the seductions of the floating world, storytellers explored the continual tension that existed between the paths of duty and of love. Romance had for a long time fascinated Japanese writers. A novel written in about 1015, *The Tale of Genji*, was already a classic by the Edo period. The work of a woman called Murasaki Shikibu, this masterpiece described in 54 chapters the amorous adventures of the handsome Prince Genji. As books and literacy became more widespread, the reading public was avid for everything from Buddhist texts to steamy novelettes.

Another favourite form of entertainment at this time was watching sumo wrestling, an ancient sport that originally took place in shrines and temples. Contests later became important features of the yearly harvest festivals, and had a strong ritual element. This included a preliminary sprinkling of salt on the ground as a symbol of purification; it also helped the wrestlers' feet grip the ground.

Then, as now, sumo fighters were immensely heavy, but they were also very light on their feet. Tournaments were held several times a year in great stadiums, and began with a parade of wrestlers wearing long 'aprons'. The wrestling took place in a raised circular ring, and the contest was over when a wrestler was forced outside the ring or touched the ground with his feet.

The Japanese love of entertainment impressed the Europeans who started to visit Japan from the 1540s onwards. 'The people of Kyoto,' wrote one early traveller from Portugal, 'are well dressed, prosperous and are much given to continual recreations, amusements and pastimes, such as going on picnics to enjoy the sight of the flowers

Licensed to trade *For more than two centuries there were severe restrictions on trade with Japan, and both native and foreign ships had to carry a 'red seal' – a licence to trade issued by the shogun. On the deck of this ship, people pass the time by listening to music.*

and gardens. They invite each other to banquets, comedies, plays, farces and their type of concert.'

Early Europeans were fascinated by the refined manners of the Japanese. An English writer recorded that they used little forks when they ate, as they considered it rude to touch food with their fingers. He went on to describe how they kept the straw matting of their homes clean: they went barefoot indoors or they used outdoor 'overshoes' to keep their indoor shoes clean.

The Japanese, by contrast, found their foreign visitors' manners crude and uncouth, and branded them as 'barbarians'. They were also quick to ridicule their long spindly legs and prominent noses, and their pale faces with pointed beards and moustaches.

Foreign influence *A Japanese helmet of 1600 has a distinctly European look. The Japanese copied their foreign visitors' body armour as well; the iron sheets gave protection against gunfire.*

TRADERS AND MARTYRS

The Portuguese were the first Europeans to visit Japan. They were followed by Spanish, Dutch and British adventurers, who all set up trading posts exporting goods such as gold, silver, lacquerware and fans. Christian missionaries, chiefly Jesuits, came with the first traders and they built churches and founded seminaries to train priests. By 1580 they could claim 200,000 converts.

Gradually, the fear that Christian culture would unsettle Japanese society led the shoguns to close ports to foreigners, and to persecute Christians. Some were tortured by branding or having their limbs sawn off, and in one incident, 25 Christians were burned at the stake and 30 were beheaded. In 1637-8 more than 30,000 Christians rose in a rebellion that ended in appalling massacre, and after that only a few Christians worshipped in secret. In 1641 Japan was closed to foreigners, except for a group of Dutch traders at Nagasaki.

Large following *Sumo wrestling matches attracted audiences of a size that matched the performers' bulk, and leading wrestlers were worshipped by their fans in much the same way as geisha and kabuki actors were admired. In this 18th-century scene, a group of wrestlers, their long hair arranged in 'buns', follow closely the performance of their colleagues who wear deeply fringed belts for wrestling in the ring.*

EUROPE TAKES SHAPE

As the ferment of ideas liberated in the city-states of 15th-century Italy spread north, other countries entered upon their own times of high adventure. Overseas trade brought economic growth and a 'golden age' to Spain, England and the Netherlands, with an outpouring of talent in the arts that enriched the world's culture. Not everything, however, was 'golden' in the everyday life of ordinary people. There were famines and plagues, and fierce religious wars which culminated in the Thirty Years' War, the bloodiest war ever fought until that time on European soil. In an 'Age of Enlightenment' in the 18th century, science and medicine made giant strides, while the Grand Tour introduced privileged young Englishmen to the Mediterranean roots of their own culture.

WESTERN EUROPE AD 1550–1775

GOLDEN AGES BRING RICHES – AND RUIN

Lavish displays of high living and big spending – on country houses, palaces, cities and the growth of nations themselves – were a feature of life in northern Europe as the evolving states, proud of their nationhood, showed off their wealth and jostled their neighbours for power and pre-eminence.

England and the Netherlands both had 'golden ages'. Under Elizabeth I, who came to the throne of England in 1558, there were great contrasts in ways of everyday life in town and country, but there existed a common feeling of 'Englishness', expressed in particular at the time of the Spanish Armada in 1588, when beacons were lit from hilltop to hilltop. It was expressed, too, in Shakespeare's plays and the audiences they attracted; for this was the great age of the stage and of 'players', of music and of costume.

By comparison with other European states, England was small. It had fewer than 5 million people when Elizabeth died, as against 16 million in France, 13 million in Italy and 11 million in Spain and Portugal.

The Netherlands, which had about 3 million people, had a golden age in the 17th century, after securing its independence from Spain in 1609. Here everyday life was recorded not on the stage, but in paintings of towns and villages, of the interiors of houses and their occupants and possessions. The Dutch enjoyed a high standard of living, and despite their austere Protestant religion they developed new tastes in food and drink, including spirits as well as wine – and beer.

The Puritan influence had a wider effect on attitudes to marriage all over Europe. In medieval times many young brides were the victims of arranged marriages. Puritans, however, believed in the importance of spiritual relationships between husband and wife. One

One-man business *The growing spirit of free enterprise saw the spread of street pedlars, such as this itinerant salesman who proffers a pair of eyeglasses, and whose other wares include brushes, combs, rings, knives and inkhorns.*

Puritan writer warned: 'It is to be feared that they that marry where they do not love, will love where they do not marry.'

Europe was still divided by religion, as well as by government, for after Luther's revolt against the papacy and the breakup of Christendom, people no longer shared common religious beliefs. The fierce religious wars of the 16th and early 17th centuries culminated in the Thirty Years' War which, triggered by hostility between Protestants and Catholics, came to involve much of Europe. As armies trampled over cornfields and destroyed cities, a third of all Germans were killed.

The war ended in exhaustion in 1648 with the Peace of Westphalia, which acknowledged the emergence of the new nation-states and rearranged the map of Europe. France, under the 'Sun King', Louis XIV, replaced Spain as Europe's dominant power – and economic strength moved north from the Mediterranean. Unlike Elizabeth, who went on annual progresses, Louis in his later years rarely went far from his favourite palaces. There, until his death in 1715, he met only courtiers, mistresses and sycophants – and was as remote from the ordinary citizens as money and power could make him.

Frederick, 'servant' with an army

The Germans were not for long to be left behind, and in 1701 the powerful new state of Brandenburg-Prussia was born. While Louis was still improving Versailles, the Prussians were building a capital city fit for a king. In 1740, Berlin became the headquarters of Frederick the Great, who described himself as 'first servant of the state'. Frederick maintained a huge and highly disciplined army to protect his kingdom and his subjects. Priding himself on his 'enlightened' ideas, he abolished the torture of criminals, did away with the bribing of judges, and encouraged forestry and farming.

Nation-states fought over their boundaries, and did not hesitate to absorb areas embracing quite distinct people and languages. The struggle to centralise and extend direct control over distant and sometimes scattered territories led to uprisings; the years 1648 and 1649 brought six revolutions in different parts of Europe.

In all European countries, however, people felt the same pressures as state-building proceeded – pressures on their pockets through taxation, on their stomachs through hunger, and on their very lives through war. In all

countries peasants were in the majority, living precariously from their own patch of land. Their lives were short as well as hard. No more than one in four of their babies reached the age of one, and no more than half reached the age of 20. Meanwhile, as wealth increased and as education began to be more highly prized, new contrasts developed in everyday life. City-based merchants became an influential minority, lending money as well as making it through trade or in some cases manufacturing.

Crime by land and sea

Aristocrats, on the other hand, were socially and legally privileged people. Merchant families rose by marriage and the purchase of noble estates. Spain had a relatively large number of people with noble titles, many of them impoverished. Codes of honour were strong, insults being avenged in duels. Despite harsh punishments, lawlessness was rife, from the pirates and Barbary corsairs who raided the coasts of Europe seeking slaves and booty, to highwaymen and smugglers, burglars and footpads.

Educated people in all countries were increasingly drawn to the arts and to the sciences, both of which were transformed in the 17th and 18th centuries, the latter held up as the Age of Enlightenment. Yet the members of the educated minority were usually contemptuous of the superstitious poor in the countryside and afraid of the 'mob' in the cities. Their aim was to achieve contented 'civilisation'. For such people life was not localised. They corresponded and travelled. The 18th century was the age of the Grand Tour. Divided though it was, Europe was conscious of a basic unity.

Improvements in the standard of living particularly affected people in the 'middle ranks' of society, as they came to be called. There was a growing demand for sugar, coffee and tea, for linen and cotton cloth, for furniture – and for books. Hand in hand with the creation of a stronger state went the rise of a more varied consumer society.

Two-class society *The social gap between the traditional peasantry and the newly rich landowners and their wives is graphically shown at this village fair in Holland. The boisterous peasants in their everyday clothing carouse in their time-honoured way with eating, drinking and dancing, while the elegantly dressed gentry saunter by with their heads averted.*

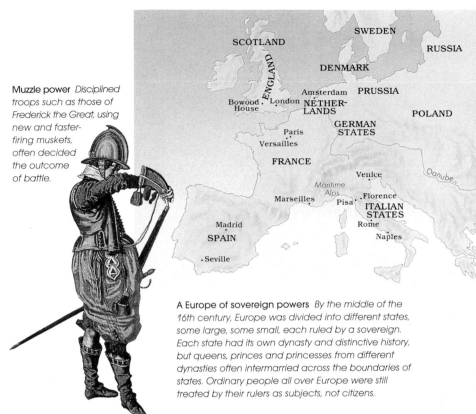

Muzzle power *Disciplined troops such as those of Frederick the Great, using new and faster-firing muskets, often decided the outcome of battle.*

A Europe of sovereign powers *By the middle of the 16th century, Europe was divided into different states, some large, some small, each ruled by a sovereign. Each state had its own dynasty and distinctive history, but queens, princes and princesses from different dynasties often intermarried across the boundaries of states. Ordinary people all over Europe were still treated by their rulers as subjects, not citizens.*

225

TULIPS AND TRADE ENRICH HOLLAND

Two loads of wheat, four loads of rye, 12 fat sheep, two hogsheads of wine, one complete bed, one suit of clothes, four fat oxen, eight fat swine, four casks of beer, two casks of butter, one silver drinking horn and 1000 lb (454 kg) of cheese: all this, in the Holland of the 1630s, was considered a reasonable exchange for a tulip bulb called 'Viceroy'.

Tulipomania – a craze for the bulbs, which had first reached European gardens in the 16th century – was near its height. In the end, the Dutch government was forced to intervene to check the wild speculation, and the bubble burst. Nevertheless, the Dutch had discovered a new and profitable business – the production of quality seed for sale abroad. Their soil was so suited to the tulip that Holland remains to this day the bulb nursery of Europe.

The United Provinces in the northern Netherlands were entering their golden age. Decades of war in the Low Countries in the late 16th century had ended with the area divided – the southern provinces were in Spanish and Roman Catholic hands, the seven northern provinces were 'united', self-governing and formally Protestant. The end of the struggle for the trading hub of northern Europe opened up an apparently limitless vista for the Dutch. The demands of a large population crammed into a small area turned them into scientific farmers and engineers as they built dykes and drains to increase their growing space and to control the threat from sea and river. Continuous bucket chains, powered by windmills taking advantage of the westerly winds, moved the water from the dykes and poured it into canals so that it ran safely out to sea.

A haven for refugees

The population also sought an outlet in trade and manufacturing. Profiting from the sack of Antwerp by the Spanish and the end of its free market, the more northerly city of Amsterdam took over its role as the key trading city of northern Europe. Its population soared from 50,000 in 1612 to 200,000 by 1660. Refugees from the southern provinces fleeing from retribution by Spain, French Huguenots and others attracted by Dutch religious tolerance brought much needed capital and skills, opening up various trades including a thriving textile industry.

Jews, cast adrift after the Spanish government expelled them, gradually found shelter in the Amsterdam ghetto and contributed enormously to the city's rise as the world's money market. The Exchange Bank, opened in 1609, rapidly became the nerve centre where noisy crowds of merchants haggled incessantly over bills of exchange, bought and sold shares and went in for commodity broking. Goods brought back from the ends of the earth were sold in what became known as the Dutch auction, while the returning mariners were hailed as heroes of exploration and trade.

Because no single merchant was rich enough or influential enough to trade independently in distant parts, chartered companies were created to pool resources. The most powerful of these groups, the Dutch East India Company, founded an empire, destroying local rulers in what are now parts of Indonesia in order to ensure a monopoly of spices – especially cloves. Amsterdam's harbour teemed with ships, many of them the slow, clumsy hulks which required few sailors but which carried bulk cargoes from one end of Europe to the other at lower cost than any rival, making the United Provinces the shippers of the world.

Cargo brought ashore by small, flat-bottomed boats known as lighters was off-loaded at Dam Square, where all cargoes weighing more than 50 lb (23 kg) had to be recorded and tested for quality at the weigh-house. Goods were trundled along in wheelbarrows or sledges, through cosmopolitan crowds in which sober Dutch burghers and their wives might rub shoulders with eastern merchants in turbans.

The character of Dutch society was set not by the handful of privileged elite known as the regents, who dominated the city councils, but by the large middle class of citizens noted for their hard work, thrift and sobriety. They built themselves tall, narrow-fronted

Home with the spoils *Heavily armed Dutch merchant ships were prepared to turn their guns on trading rivals to safeguard Holland's position as the leading shipping and trading nation of the world. From Europe they took grain, cloth and naval stores, exchanging them for spices and porcelain from the East, fruits and silks from the Mediterranean, tobacco, sugar, cotton and quinine from the New World.*

Art of the people *The life of ordinary men and women came into its own as a subject for great art in the paintings of the 17th-century Dutch masters. Here Jan Bruegel shows a Flemish peasant family receiving three well-to-do visitors. Surrounded by her children, the mother of the house warms herself by the hearth, over which hangs a huge cauldron cooking the family meal.*

THE
DESCRIPTION
of a voyage made by certaine Ships
of Holland into the East
INDIES.

With their aduentures and succeße:

Together
With the description of the Countries,
Townes, and inhabitantes of the
same:

Who set forth on the second of Aprill 1595. and
returned on the 14. of August,
1597.

Translated out of Dutch into English by W. P.

LONDON
Imprinted by Iohn Wolfe. 1598.

SCENTS FROM THE EAST

Europeans developed a taste for the various spices, such as nutmegs and cloves, brought by Dutch merchants from the East Indies towards the end of the 16th century. The fragrant aroma and slightly warm taste of nutmegs (left) made them a popular choice for flavouring meats, puddings, sauces, vegetables and baked foods. Dutch merchants conspired to keep prices high, while French and English merchants strove to import fertile seeds from the Indies to try to grow the spices at home.

Clove tree and seeds

Nutmeg

gabled houses along the canals, with many windows and beams by which they hoisted goods into upper storeys. Families lived on the middle floors, while the ground floor served as a workshop and the attics as a storeplace.

Inside, in contrast with the bustling chaos of the markets, all was peace and tranquillity. Rooms were clean, spacious and orderly – sometimes with floors tiled in black and white squares of cool marble. The wealthier liked heavy wood furniture, richly carved, and graced their walls with paintings in which the whole nation took delight. An English visitor in 1640 was astonished to find paintings hanging in the shops of butchers, bakers and cobblers. A blacksmith might even have a picture by his forge. The Dutch liked 'realistic' paintings

Travel guide *The Dutch were the first to break the Portuguese hold on the highly profitable trade in spices from the East. This account of the first Dutch voyage to the East Indies in 1595 inspired the merchants of London, in their turn, to establish a British East India Company to challenge the Dutch.*

which idealised their daily lives: quiet domestic interiors, labourers relaxing at the alehouse, skaters on the canal. Pictures of domestic music-making with harpsichords, lutes and violins were often seen. Books of love songs were included in the home library.

Wedding feasts and public festivals could be boisterous affairs, as could the annual *kermis*, or fair, which celebrated the founding of the parish church. Food was an important part of all public rejoicing. At home, people ate barley or rye bread, beans, turnips and fried onions. Herrings, cured or pickled, were a staple, and some salt meat and bacon were enjoyed. The national dish was the *hutsepot*, a stew of minced beef or mutton.

Dutch women held considerable rights by the standards of 17th-century Europe. Girls were educated to a level which allowed them to manage a business if their husband was away or dead, and widows might take their spouses' places in the craft guilds. Teenage girls were allowed a freedom which surprised many foreigners.

Religious feeling ran deep. The day began with prayer and Bible readings, and the pious family unit formed the core of every local congregation. The home was in fact a shrine of Dutch Protestant culture, so that keeping it clean and tidy was almost a religious duty. Foreign observers noted how Dutch housewives scrubbed and cleaned incessantly. Visitors had to remove their shoes before entering homes – and woe betide the man who spat on the floor.

Men of commerce *Amsterdam merchants and city elders, such as the cloth drapers painted by Rembrandt, acted as patrons to artists. Only white lawn collars and cuffs relieve the sober black garb of these down-to-earth, middle-class burghers.*

TERRORS OF THE SPANISH INQUISITION

Church bells tolled and masses were said for the souls of those about to die in an *auto-da-fé*. The term, Portuguese in origin, means 'act of the faith', and the ceremony amounted to much more than a ritual of cruelty. It was conceived as a celebration – an exaltation of the true Church that would instruct the faithful and terrify the ungodly.

From their prisons, the condemned men and women were led in weird procession, the Inquisition's standard-bearer at their head, followed by drummers, trumpeters, men bearing crosses, banners and lighted candles, with priests from differing religious orders among them.

Then came the grim procession of doomed prisoners. The accused wore a penitential garment known as a sanbenito, a tunic blazoned with a red cross. Some of the men had shaved heads, while others, in a touch of grim comedy, wore the coroza, a pointed dunce's cap, a symbol of the Jew. At the back of the procession walked the judges and officials, and last of all came the local inquisitor with the bishop of the town.

Facing the final act

The officials repeated the Creed – the statement of the key articles of Christian faith – as they walked. Lining the streets, peering from windows or gazing from the doorways of closed shops, the crowds watched in awe. Some knelt in silence, others yelled insults at the condemned and many followed to the place appointed for the final act. A huge platform held tiers of benches for the condemned, and an altar and dais for the functionaries.

Oaths were taken and a sermon preached. Then followed the public reading of the names of the condemned and the crimes with which they stood charged. Finally, sentence was pronounced. Some faced only the disgrace of having to wear the sanbenito for a given period; some faced floggings, others imprisonment. Others were 'released' for execution to the secular courts, for the Church did not take life. It was the officials of the state who led their victims to stakes piled with

Decisions of life and death *In a long ritual combining religious ceremony with a spectacle to entertain and chasten the masses, prisoners found guilty by the Inquisition of crimes against the Church are publicly sentenced in a theatre built in Madrid's main plaza, under the eye of King Carlos in the royal box. The prisoners, in dunce-like hats, descend steps on the right and monks drag them round to take their places, two at a time, in the central dock.*

faggots on the outskirts of the town. Those who recanted their errors at the last moment might be strangled before the flames were lit. The remainder were burned alive.

The Spanish Inquisition was founded in the 15th century to defend the purity of the faith. By this time the Christian reconquest of Spain had reduced the extent of Moorish power in the Iberian peninsula to the stronghold of Granada alone. The Inquisition's main targets were the many *conversos* – Jews and Muslims who had been persuaded to adopt Christianity but were believed guilty of practising their previous faiths in private.

Throughout the period of Spanish greatness, as treasure fleets returned from the New World laden with silver, the Church inquisitors, usually Dominican friars, went about defending the Church; censoring books and examining accusations of deviation from Catholic orthodoxy. These accusations were levelled in secret, sometimes by neighbours who were settling old scores. The charges usually identified Muslim or Jewish ritual practises – a refusal to eat pork or drink alcohol, or the alleged taking of baths of purification. Sometimes they were as slight as smiling at the name of the Virgin.

Imprisonment could be prolonged for an indefinite period, as the inquisitors often preferred the effects of long uncertainty and solitude, and questioning at irregular intervals, to produce a confession. Torture was not a method employed only by the Inquisition. At this time it was legally authorised throughout most of Europe, and burning was a punishment widely used in secular courts.

Spain in the 16th century was a land of immense prestige and power. By inheritance the Hapsburg monarchs

Chamber of tortures *To strengthen their hold on the populace, and to gain converts to Catholicism, the inquisitors condoned torture. A contemporary artist assembles methods of torture used on different occasions, including hanging upside down or from the ceiling, burning, stretching and filling victims with water.*

Wages of sin *Some prisoners of the Inquisition wore tunics by which onlookers distinguished the unrepentant from the repentant. The heretic (left), whose tunic shows a figure burning in Hell, is bound for the stake. The penitent (below), who holds a rosary and bears a staff, is spared.*

not only held all the different kingdoms in Spain but also the Low Countries, Naples, Austria and areas of the Holy Roman Empire. A family arrangement made on the death of the Holy Roman Emperor Charles V left his son Philip II with Spain, the Low Countries and Naples, and the empire outside Europe – which he expanded until Spanish rule extended from the Indies as far as the Philippines.

The wealth acquired in this way helped to cause inflation throughout 16th-century Europe, and at the same time obscured the decline of Spain's domestic economy as Philip poured his share of the silver mines into fighting on two fronts – to retain the Low Countries and to repel the Ottoman Turks. Philip's campaigns produced major victories such as Lepanto, as well as failures such as the Armada. Armies and navies alike were led by the highest-ranking Spanish nobles. Such aristocrats, to whom *liempienza di sangre*, purity of blood, was an obsession, were reputed to be the proudest in the world, from the grandees who dominated at court to the hidalgos, or minor nobility, whose sense of honour, whatever their poverty, was reinforced by their swordsmanship. Spanish court etiquette was the most rigid in Europe, carrying hierarchy to the point of absurdity.

Riches squandered *Much of Spain's wealth from the New World went to pay for wars in Europe. A bespectacled tax-gatherer records sums paid or owed, while a grandee keeps check. In 1599 the currency was debased by using Europe's first copper coinage (right).*

Partly inherited from the southern states so recently liberated from the Turkish Empire, it in turn influenced the whole of Europe.

Although Philip in 1561 made Madrid his capital, the largest city in Spain was Seville in Andalusia, with its teeming population of 150,000. This great inland port handled much of Spain's trade with the New World and grew rich from the cargoes brought in the fleets that berthed downstream – fabulous cargoes which included the spoils of the Indies and exotic new addictions such as tobacco from Haiti.

Orange juice and gossip

The people of Seville lived in villas opening onto a separate patio. The wealthiest had salons for entertaining. Men sat on stools and chairs, while the women, separated from the men by a wooden screen, squatted Moorish fashion on rugs and cushions and gossiped over iced orange juice or the immensely popular chocolate newly imported from America.

Women rarely drank wine, and men only in moderation, although the nearby vineyard of Jerez provided the fortified wine called *sherris* which was to become one of Spain's successful exports. Women had few rights and led restricted lives. Fashionable ladies, if they went out, often had a pair of slaves in Turkish style following behind.

Much of Spain's noble wealth was the product of the Mesta – the great corporate sheep farms whose flocks were constantly driven from the north of Spain to the south along routes with grazing rights which overrode any rights the peasant farmer might claim. The flocks drove the peasant from his fields, leaving the countryside depopulated except for the drovers – men and women whose lifestyle and skills were transferred to the New World and its gauchos and cowboys. Life on the roads became more and more difficult and dangerous. Goods were usually transported on mule trains, and common inns were bug-ridden fleapits. Visitors ate at long wooden tables, using a single shared knife anchored to the middle by a chain, and slept on straw mats in common dormitories. A great gulf separated rich and poor, but common amusements might draw them together – such as attending bullfights and indulging their passion for dancing to the frenzied strumming of guitars and snapping of fingers.

Two-tone tower *On the site of a 12th-century mosque in Seville, the Christians built one of the largest churches in the world. They turned the original minaret into a bell tower.*

THE MARK OF THE MOORS

The Moors who conquered Spain by AD 720 and stayed for seven centuries left a lasting mark on the country's architecture. In their palaces and mosques, intricate mazes of chambers fanned outwards through interlocking arches resembling the branches of a palm tree, supported on rows of trunk-like columns. Floors and interiors were tiled with mosaics in a multitude of colours, and the ceilings were panelled with cedar wood. The buildings were surrounded by gardens with pools, artificial cascades, and orchards of peaches and pomegranates.

When Christianity regained control of Spain, cathedrals replaced the mosques or were added alongside them – or even, in the case of Cordoba, in their midst. But even new palaces for the Christian rulers were built and decorated by craftsmen trained in the Islamic tradition, blending Western and Moorish influences in a style known as Mudéjar. The style is characterised by the richly decorated stonework and tiling which covers their walls, arches and door frames with a maze of abstract and geometrical designs. In the south, the Moorish influence affected ordinary people's houses, which were built facing inwards onto a patio.

MERRYMAKING IN ELIZABETH'S ENGLAND

The Elizabethans loved display. Their appearance must be splendid, even if they were wearing their fortune on their backs. They went deeply into debt to pay for their attire. Their dress proclaimed their station, their prominence, and their dominance.

The successful of all ranks sought to flaunt their wealth by adopting the clothing of the rank above them. They poured their money into fashionable plate, tapestries, carpets and furniture, into new-fangled coaches, fine horses and elaborate equipment. To have influence, the right to appear at court was essential, for the court was the place which controlled government.

At court, the queen and ladies of fashion wore dresses stiff with jewels and embroidery over a contraption known as a farthingale. This was a circular whalebone frame which was fixed around the hips to extend the petticoat and skirt – wide enough, moralists complained, to hide lovers underneath. The farthingale was a foreign import, coming from Spain – like much else that was considered chic – and was worn with a tight, breast-flattening corset to exaggerate its width. High collars on wire supports completed the fantastic effect. Men, too, were extravagantly dressed. Stockings with fancy garters were topped by hugely padded trunks and doublets, sometimes slashed to display the gaudy colours of material underneath. The padding was done with a stuffing known as 'bombast', from which comes the word 'bombastic', meaning loud and showy. A ruff around the neck, sword, dagger, cloak and hat added further swagger. Shoes for both men and women were lovingly crafted from soft leather, silk or velvet, with cork soles and heels. The heel itself was a new device to make the wearer seem taller.

Clothing alone, however, was not enough. Manners maketh man, said the old saw, and courtiers had to have

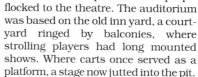

Fiddler at the feast

many skills. The men needed to be able jousters, while both sexes should be good dancers, able to play the lute and sing, and make witty conversation. Books advised the courtier on the niceties of etiquette and how to frame witty and elaborate compliments. In the social hierarchy, inferiors imitated their betters. Country girls, for example, made 'bum rolls' of cloth fastened around the waist to serve as farthingales. It was, too, an Age of Entertainment, when itinerant musicians such as fiddlers played for the public, and people flocked to the theatre. The auditorium was based on the old inn yard, a courtyard ringed by balconies, where strolling players had long mounted shows. Where carts once served as a platform, a stage now jutted into the pit.

The playgoers were a mixed crowd, with rough-hewn tradesmen and apprentices rubbing shoulders with gentry and noble patrons. Entrance fees were collected in a lock-up box placed in a small office – hence our 'box office'. The common people paid a penny and stood in the pit, while the threepenny patrons had stools in the balconies rising in tiers around, and the wealthiest paid a shilling to sit on the stage itself.

All shows were staged in the afternoon: Elizabethan playhouses were open-air affairs, with no lighting for the evening performances. Pressing on three sides around the stage, the rowdy onlookers gossiped, joked and cracked nuts through the performances, and actors had to utter their lines in loud, declamatory style simply to be heard. Above all, it was Shakespeare's theatre, where the great glories of *Hamlet*, *Romeo and Juliet*, and *King Lear* were first produced.

Jugglers and fighting cocks

When the show was over, the audience continued to mill around purchasing pamphlets, herbal remedies, Seville oranges and pies, while jugglers and acrobats occupied the stage. Civic authorities regarded playhouses as disreputable, not only as meeting places for underworld characters but as breeding grounds for disease. The theatres were closed in summer, when wealthier patrons left the city and the players went on tour.

There were no permanent theatres outside London, but inns, village greens and market squares offered all that was needed for vagabond troupes who, since medieval times, had gone about the country acting out folk tales. Inside the inns and alehouses, labouring men played shove-ha'penny, backgammon and draughts, and there were alleys outside for bowls and skittles.

> *The ploughman must nowadays have his doublet of the fashion with wide cuts, his garter of fine silk of Granada, to meet his Sis on Sunday.*
>
> ANON, c. 1590

Rougher entertainments included bull-baiting, bear-baiting and cock-fighting. Bloody contests between specially bred gamecocks, with metal spurs and sharpened beaks, were very cheap to set up in a small, enclosed arena known as a cockpit. On Shrove Tuesday each year, schoolboys were allowed to bring their own game-cocks to school where they did battle in the school cockpit. In bull and bear-baiting, the tethered beasts were set

SPORT IN THE STREET

With a rough leather-cased ball, a bunch of youths lay about each other in a no-holds-barred game of street football. They have the close-cut hair and flat woollen caps of apprentices, enjoying time on their Shrove Tuesday 'Holy Day'. There are no fixed goals – the object is simply to keep the ball out of the smelly gutter and propel it from one point in the town to another. For many players, the game soon becomes a chance to settle old scores, degenerating into a free fight in which noses are bloodied and limbs broken. Owners of the surrounding inns and shops, worried for the safety of their goods and hanging signs, barricade their premises and pelt the players with apples, stones, sticks and beer mugs. Some seek safety on the rooftops, shaking their fists at the hooligans. Contemporary writers inveighed against football – one called it 'a devilish pastime, a bloody and murderous practice'. Queen Elizabeth even tried to ban the game, but without success.

upon by mastiffs. Several dogs were killed at each session, and the roaring spectators bet feverishly on how long a particular dog would last. The most successful bear killers became household names: Harry Hunks, Tom of Lincoln, the Great Sackerson, and so on. Crowds at the bear-baiting were so rowdy that 'bear garden' survives as a term for a place of noisy disorder.

Blood also flowed freely in human contests between sporting opponents who thumped each other with cudgels and quarterstaffs, while public executions drew huge, enthusiastic crowds. Pain and bloodshed found easy acceptance among the Elizabethans.

Music at the barber's shop

For cheerier entertainment there was music and dance. The English at this time were thought an exceptionally musical nation, and singing in four, six or eight parts was an accomplishment in many a family. People sang after dinner, sometimes with their servants, and the ability to read music and play an instrument was expected of anyone with pretensions to an education. The virginal – a precursor of the piano – was a popular instrument for girls. The lute, the viol and the recorder were more widespread still, especially to

accompany madrigals. The court enjoyed stately dances such as the pavane and the coranto, while lowlier folk had jigs, hornpipes and morris dances.

The Elizabethans had such a keen interest in music that some barbers kept lutes in their shops, so that customers could play on them while they waited their turn for a trim. Elizabethans also devoted many of their idle hours to cards. The deck of 52 cards, in suits of spades, diamonds, hearts and clubs, was a French invention which came to England late in the Middle Ages. The court cards of the modern pack still depict the elaborate garb worn by Tudor royalty.

Another game originating in France was tennis, played with rackets in a walled and roofed court. Tennis was taken up by Henry VIII, who built courts at all his major palaces, including one at Hampton Court Palace which is still used today.

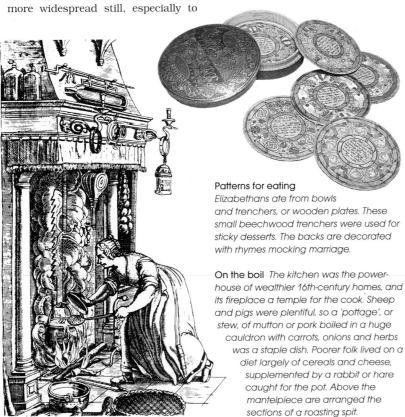

Patterns for eating
Elizabethans ate from bowls and trenchers, or wooden plates. These small beechwood trenchers were used for sticky desserts. The backs are decorated with rhymes mocking marriage.

On the boil *The kitchen was the powerhouse of wealthier 16th-century homes, and its fireplace a temple for the cook. Sheep and pigs were plentiful, so a 'pottage', or stew, of mutton or pork boiled in a huge cauldron with carrots, onions and herbs was a staple dish. Poorer folk lived on a diet largely of cereals and cheese, supplemented by a rabbit or hare caught for the pot. Above the mantelpiece are arranged the sections of a roasting spit.*

COMFORT IN THE HOME

Apprentice cobblers practise their craft in the ground-floor workshop of a shoemaker's timber-framed home. Beyond, in the kitchen, the woman of the house is preparing food; a door beside her leads into a brick-walled yard, with an outside privy. A drinking trough for the animals is filled with water drawn from a cistern in the street.

A twisting wooden staircase leads to the main bedroom, where mullioned windows let in the light and shut out draught. Across from the bedroom is the dining room, whose fine oak panelling gives protection against cold and damp. The shoemaker and a friend sit eating boiled meat, bread and vegetables from a cloth-covered table. In the corner is an aumbry, or ventilated food cabinet, the forerunner of our cupboard. Some of the household's best pewter plates and blue-and-white pottery are set out on the aumbry and over the stone fireplace. More stairs lead to the attic, in which the cobbler's apprentice sleeps in a truckle bed.

The coming of brick chimneys in the 1500s had revolutionised house building. Fires no longer smouldered in the centre of the great hall, with smoke billowing out through a hole in the roof. Instead, fireplaces were let into the walls of individual chambers, each of

Furnished in oak
Bed linen was stored in chests, often inlaid with oak. People usually sat on oak stools, as chairs were few.

which now had a specialised purpose: parlour, withdrawing room, dining room and so on. With fire risks lessened by the use of chimneys, and by the banning in many areas of wooden roofs in favour of lead or tiles, kitchens came increasingly to be built inside the main house. Altogether, something like a modern house plan was evolving. However, corridors giving privacy to individual rooms were not yet common. Many rooms opened directly into one another, so that curtained beds – often great four-posters – were still important items in the bedroom.

LONDON RISES AFTER PLAGUE AND FIRE

London's Great Fire started around midnight on Saturday, September 1, 1666, sparked from the oven of the king's baker, Thomas Farriner, in Pudding Lane. Picked up by a dry east wind, the flames rushed through neighbouring warehouses which were packed with pitch, tar and cordage, and within a few hours some 300 houses had been gutted.

The diarist Samuel Pepys hastened to the waterside and saw 'everybody endeavouring to remove their goods, and flinging them into the river or bringing them into lighters that lay off. Poor people staying in their houses as long as till the very fire touched them, and then running into boats or clambering from one pair of stairs by the waterside to another. And the poor pigeons were loath to leave

their houses, but hovered about the windows and balconies till they were burned and fell down'.

For three days the fire raged on, carried northwards and westwards, 'a most horrid, malicious, bloody flame', in Pepys's words. Timber-framed houses vanished in the inferno; brickwork exploded and the stones of old St Paul's flew like grenades, the cathedral bells melting and cascading down with lead from the roof so that, it was said, the very pavements glowed fiery red.

Bucket chains and crude fire engines proved totally inadequate to quench the flames. It was only on the following Tuesday night, when seamen began to blow up houses around the edge, that the conflagration was checked. Then, on the Wednesday, the wind dropped and the fire began to peter out, allowing more than 100,000 homeless people to drift back and survey the smoking ruins of their dwellings.

Catastrophic though it was, the great fire had some beneficial side effects. The flames destroyed a host of rat-infested medieval buildings, and also wiped out the last major visitation of the bubonic plague, which in 1665 had claimed the lives of almost one in three Londoners. A cleaner and more open city was built, graced by handsome

Bell, book and 'treacle' *During the Great Plague of 1665 in London a plague bell was rung to announce the arrival of the collector of corpses. Citizens fought the disease with a supposed antidote, a so-called 'treacle' made of gunpowder, oil and sack (sherry). Deaths were recorded by parish clerks in 'mortality books'.*

new stone buildings – though more ambitious plans for a city with broad main thoroughfares failed because there was no money to buy out those who clung to their own plots.

The first modern fire brigades also emerged after the disaster. Several fire insurance companies were founded in London, each maintaining their own colourfully costumed fire-fighting forces equipped with axes and hand-pumped engines. Should a fire break out, the brigades would race to it and (if the property belonged to one of their clients) start pumping. The firemen often offered free beer to anyone who lent a hand at the pumps, which meant that the work was done to a deep-throated chorus of 'Beer-oh! Beer-oh!'

Paper for the walls

London before the fire had been typical of medieval cities throughout Europe which were bursting at the seams, with continually worsening congestion and squalor in their haphazard mazes of narrow, dark alleys. Inside their homes, however, the wealthier citizens lived more comfortably than ever before. Where new houses were built, the communal hall of earlier days had now shrunk to a small entrance hall, with a handsome staircase leading to the upper floors. Flock wallpaper from Holland had

Rome on the Thames *The rebuilt London that emerged after the fire, as portrayed by the Italian artist Canaletto, was considered among the finest cities in Europe. It was punctuated by the steeples, spires and towers of the architect Sir Christopher Wren – whose mighty dome of St Paul's rivalled Michelangelo's dome of St Peter's in Rome.*

Down and out *As more and more people crowded into the towns in search of work, the Great Fire aggravated the problem of London's homeless. Mothers and their starving children were reduced to living and begging on the streets.*

started to replace dark wood panelling, while mats and carpets now more often covered floors which were formerly strewn with loose rushes.

Something resembling the compact, modern town house had arrived – and there were new items of furniture to go into it. In place of heavy wooden benches and stools, lightweight chairs became popular, and the upholstered armchair appeared. For centuries, people had kept their clothes and other belongings in simple wooden chests,

perhaps with a drawer at the bottom. Now, whole 'chests of drawers' came into widespread use. Wardrobes, desks and glass-fronted bookcases were other innovations, and cabinetmakers even crafted baby-walkers for pre-toddlers.

Sets of knives and forks were now being made for the table, and the first toothbrushes appeared in about 1650. Sugar began to be imported in bulk from the West Indies, in 10 lb (4.5 kg) loaves that had to be broken with special cutters. The availability of this

new sweetener led to a great increase in the making and consumption of preserves and confectionery. The habit of tea-drinking, destined to become typically English, began in the mid-century too, though tea was far too expensive yet for ordinary people, costing as much as 50 shillings a pound.

The great venue for fashionable society was the playhouse – which had changed much since Shakespeare's day. Roofed over, with colourful scenery and the glimmer of wax candles all about, the theatres had become magical places where royalty and high society paraded in style. Plays by authors such as William Congreve and William Wycherley were barbed with worldly wit and often based on the amorous adventures of stock characters such as fops, duped husbands, stout squires, gay blades and wealthy heiresses.

In Shakespeare's time the women's roles had always been played by young men and boys. Now women appeared for the first time on the public stage. Playgoers might be brought to the theatre in sedan chairs, introduced from France in 1634, and

French fashions were all the rage. One of the most popular of fashion accessories for women was the black beauty patch, made from silk or taffeta. Cut into the shapes of crescent moons, stars, or even an entire coach-and-horses, they were worn coquettishly on cheek or breast. Meanwhile, men wore outrageously feminine attire such as lacy 'petticoat' breeches, ribboned at the waist, with the shirt hanging out. In 1666, the ensemble of doublet, cloak and breeches was challenged by what was called the 'Persian mode' of a long coat and vest, introduced at court by Charles II. Sometimes worn with breeches of the same cloth, this was the precursor of the three-piece suit.

The moralists railed against such vanities as artificial ringlets and beauty patches. And religious devotion retained its important place in most households. The day began, for many families, at around 6am, with prayers and Bible readings. Father usually led the prayers – he was still very much the head of the household, with the legal right to chastise his wife and children, within limits. Punishments for nagging wives included the scold's bridle, a contraption with iron hoops to frame the head, and an iron piece jutting into the mouth to hold the tongue down. The ducking stool was in use too; this was a wooden chair into which the scold was clamped by an iron band, then see-sawed into the water. Many offenders were flogged at a whipping post, and every parish had its stocks where culprits sat for hours, with their wrists or ankles thrust through holes in the boards, to be pelted by their fellow citizens with rotten eggs or vegetables.

The SPECTATOR.

*Non fumum ex fulgore, sed ex fumo dare lucem
Cogitat, ut speciosa dehinc miracula promat.* Hor.

To be Continued every Day.

Thursday, March 1. 1711.

Type and talk The spreading of literacy gave rise to publications such as The Spectator, whose opinionated articles were eagerly discussed in the new coffee houses. Charles II tried to suppress the coffee houses as breeding grounds for conspiracies. He failed – and the houses became the forerunners of the men's clubs of later times.

'Come and buy' Day and night London rang with the cries of pedlars selling their wares from baskets and barrows.

'Oysters, twelve pence a peck'

'Fresh, ripe asparagus'

'Fresh milk to sell'

'New songs, one penny a sheet'

WITS AND WIGS IN THE LONDON COFFEE HOUSE

Chocolate and coffee houses opened in London in the 1650s, soon after the arrival of these new drinks in England. They became great centres of gossip, where men drank steaming black coffee out of bowls, puffing at their clay pipes as they argued about politics, displayed their wit, swapped news, gambled and conducted their business.

From the 1660s, few self-respecting men would be seen in a coffee house without a wig – a new fashion introduced from France. The wig was worn in mountains of ringlets and curls that required heads to be cropped or shaved bald to achieve a fit. The diarist Samuel Pepys took the momentous step of adopting the fashion in 1664. In his entry for

November 8 that year there is a note of surprise that his first appearance at church wearing a wig 'did not prove so strange to the world as I was afeard it would'.

With the wig came many trials. Pepys complained of catching a cold through removing his wig too often. He had one wig catch fire – and rebuked his wig-maker for delivering a wig full of nits. When the plague struck London, nobody dared buy any hair for fear it had been cut from the heads of disease victims. Still, the fashion endured. Wig-snatching became common, and the demand for hair was so great that children were forbidden to go out alone in case thieves cut off their locks to sell to wig-makers.

SONS AND DAUGHTERS OF THE SOIL

Life was hard for countryfolk in 18th-century Europe. In the early part of the century most people still lived in villages, hamlets and scattered farms, earning their living directly or indirectly from the land. Villagers were prey to diseases such as smallpox, influenza and tuberculosis, to say nothing of accidents and – for women – the high risk of dying in childbirth. The rural poor were pinched by hunger, shivering through the winter in their threadbare clothes, sleeping on pallets on the floors of their cramped and dirty hovels.

Justice could be brutal: an English peasant convicted of stealing potatoes was whipped through the streets of his village at a cart's tail – and the public subscribed 17s 6d to encourage the public hangman, who administered the whipping, to lay it on thick.

In some ways, little had changed since medieval times: life was still lived according to the rhythm of the seasons, and marked by an ancient calendar of fairs and festivals. Folk cures served for medicine, and superstition was rife. At night by the fireside, traditional tales were told of ghosts, hobgoblins and fairies. But in other respects things were changing.

At the beginning of the 18th century the landscape was firmly stamped with medieval farming patterns, consisting in many areas of large open fields in which each farmer worked a given number of strips. The great lord might own hundreds of strips and the poor farmer only a couple, but they were all involved in the same kind of enterprise, with no hedge or wall to separate their holdings.

In the course of the 18th century, however, new and profitable forms of crop rotation encouraged landowners to enclose the remaining open fields, with the help of their powerful stewards or land agents. Many small farmers lost their holdings in the process. They became tenant farmers on the big estates, farm labourers working for wages, or even vagabonds. There were fewer common pasturelands where once a humble cottager might graze a single cow for cheese and butter. Ancient rights to collect wood for fuel and fencing went too. Hedges sprang up as barriers around farmers' fields. The self-sufficient peasant supporting his family by traditional practices was disappearing. Farming now required capital, resources and a good head for business. Despite the

drawbacks, the 'new farming' meant that society as a whole benefited from the greatly improved quality and quantity of food available. Among the innovations which boosted yields were more efficient ploughs, and the seed drill invented in 1701 by the English farmer Jethro Tull. His apparatus planted seeds in straight lines, making weeding easier, and covered them with soil to protect them from birds.

The big landowners made enormous profits from such innovations as these – although wages in the country remained pitifully low. To show off their wealth, landlords commissioned architects to build them splendid houses in the classical manner. Landscape designers were brought in too, to sculpt the surrounding park-land in a manner pleasing to the eye.

In Britain, the most famous of these designers was Lancelot Brown, nick-named 'Capability' because he often told his patrons that their grounds had

Cottage industry *A Jersey spinning wheel (above) has a horizontal spindle on which spun yarn is wound. Such wheels were often used in farmhouses (right), where families lived in simple surroundings. One woman sits cooking over an evilly smoking kitchen fire, heat from which warms the adjoining bread oven. Beside her, a child uses a baby-walker, while the mother of the house sorts out her washing on a table. Food and house-hold goods hang from hooks on the wall.*

a 'capability' for landscaping. He liked naturalistic effects, with smooth lawns rolling down to serpentine lakes, and noble groups of trees shading deer. Rivers were dammed and mountains of earth moved to achieve his aims. Sometimes, indeed, an entire village might be razed if it interfered with a view, and rebuilt some miles away. This was not necessarily a calamity for the villagers, though. Their new 'model' cottages were often cleaner and more spacious than their old hovels had been, having a sensibly planned arrangement of bedrooms, parlour and a kitchen – some of which even had an oven for baking bread.

The key figure in country life was the area's chief landowner – in England usually known as the squire. Much of his day was spent in managing his estate, riding round to talk to the tenants, discussing breeds of farm animals, crops and new farming techniques. The squire was not only lord of the manor, but also acted as the principal local magistrate, before whom any villagers who were caught poaching or breaking the law in any other way were taken. Poaching was an illicit sport in which many a countryman indulged after the enclosures deprived him of the woodcock or trout which he once took in the unfenced woods and streams. For his part, the squire often went hunting, and his hard days in the saddle were usually

Family for hire *It is haymaking time, and an entire family of farm labourers sets out to look for work. They carry their own implements and simple possessions – and the father has a tub of ale tied to his scythe.*

Tightening the load *Using a pole tied to a rope, a wagoner and his team make fast a load of woolpacks, while his wife stows barrels of beer. The broad wheels cope with rough country tracks.*

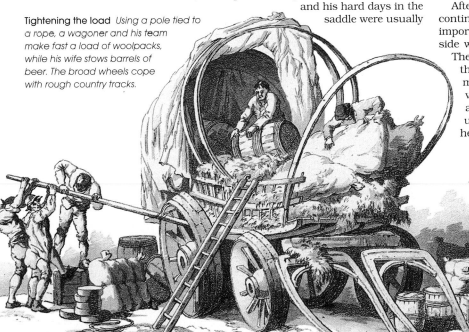

Thrill of the hunt *For recreation, country squires hunted foxes and hares, using packs of dogs. Some used spears like battlefield warriors of an earlier age.*

followed by equally hard drinking bouts, and sometimes, too, by wild escapades. 'Drunk as a lord', is a phrase dating back to this time, when the fox-hunting squire and his cronies would gorge themselves at dinner, the ladies retiring afterwards so that the gentlemen could indulge in long rounds of toasts – from time to time relieving themselves in a chamber pot from the sideboard drawer.

'Fox-hunting, drinking, bawling out obscene songs and whoring was the common delight of these people', wrote the Reverend Robert Knipe, recalling the dissolute gentry of his childhood in northern England.

After the English squire and the continental landowner, the most important personages in the countryside were the parson and the priest. They had charge over the souls in their parishes, and it was to the men of the cloth that many villagers took their difficulties and problems, expecting – and usually receiving – a sympathetic hearing and practical advice.

A DAY IN THE LIFE OF A COUNTRY PARSON

Like many well-to-do country gentlemen of his time, the Reverend James Woodforde has a voracious appetite, and his day is measured by its four main mealtimes. He breakfasts on oysters or cold tongue, with bread, butter and tea. A tasty snack of, say, pork is taken at noon, followed by the big meal – dinner, eaten at about 2 pm.

In his diary he records a typical dinner given on January 20, 1777, when he serves his guests 'a couple of Rabbits smothered with onions, a Neck of Mutton boiled and a Goose roasted with a Currant Pudding and a plain one'. Coarse fish are staples too, especially tench, and also pike which Woodforde eats stuffed 'with a pudding in its belly'. This is followed by more tea drinking, perhaps with cake.

Parson Woodforde's living is at Weston Longville, in Norfolk, and like many other respectable citizens, he gets his tea from the local smuggler. Customs duties in the 18th century are so heavy, and so generally resented that smuggling is dismissed by all with a nod and a wink. As well as seeing his parishioners, the parson is in regular touch with the local squire, whose prowess at the hunt and on the cricket green are the pride of the village. Cricket had begun as a game of the lower classes. By the mid-18th century, however, its status had risen and the squire plays it on the village green alongside blacksmith, cobbler, innkeeper and farmhand. Their families watch and applaud, while the parson beams approval – and looks forward to his supper.

FROM RABBLE TO REGULAR ARMY

With the raising of a regular national army by King Gustavus Adolphus of Sweden around 1615, warfare entered the modern age. But it brought little improvement to the lot of the ordinary soldier, who fought much the same type of bloody campaigns in gruelling conditions as his predecessors.

Gustavus deployed his army in the Thirty Years' War (1618-48), which began as a conflict between Catholics and Protestants and developed into a struggle for European supremacy. Although limited manpower compelled Gustavus to employ mercenaries, most of them Scots, Irish and Germans, they were organised, trained and equipped along Swedish lines, rather than in the haphazard way common among other mercenaries. They were drilled, and given uniforms and regimental insignia, to boost morale and to make them recognisable on the battlefield. The introduction of a lighter and shorter

Arms and the man *Even in the age of the musket, the pike kept its place on the battlefield. An opening salvo by musketeers was often followed by an onslaught by*

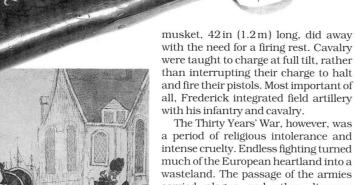

musket, 42 in (1.2 m) long, did away with the need for a firing rest. Cavalry were taught to charge at full tilt, rather than interrupting their charge to halt and fire their pistols. Most important of all, Frederick integrated field artillery with his infantry and cavalry.

The Thirty Years' War, however, was a period of religious intolerance and intense cruelty. Endless fighting turned much of the European heartland into a wasteland. The passage of the armies carried plague and other diseases often more devastating than the battle, while the exceptionally cold winters of the 'Little Ice Age' reduced civilians to eating cats, dogs and rats.

Swordsmen at the gallop

As the Thirty Years' War entered its closing stages, the Civil War started in England. In this struggle, which lasted from 1642 to 1648, allegiance to Charles I or to Parliament cut across social and economic divisions, and even divided families.

At the beginning, Charles had the military edge, as aristocrats who had been serving as mercenaries abroad rallied to his cause. But Parliament had better financial resources. England had no significant professional army, since hitherto forces had been raised and disbanded as occasion demanded.

Both sides were lax in discipline, as most of the lower ranks had enlisted for pay and booty. But pay was often in arrears, and there was widespread pillaging after a victory. Troops were

Joining the ranks *Volunteers for the army were thin on the ground in 17th-century Europe, and recruiting officers often took men by force. They were not too particular in their choice of 'recruits', and rounded up pickpockets and petty thieves, as well as the unemployed, drunks and idlers.*

Rapid fire *Around 1610 the flintlock musket replaced the slower matchlock mechanism, in which a slow-burning match cord ignited the priming. When the trigger of a flintlock was pulled, a flint was released to hit a steel plate attached to the pan cover. This struck sparks into the priming pan, igniting gunpowder which fired the charge in the bore, propelling the ball out of the barrel. The flintlock musket remained the standard infantry weapon until the adoption of the percussion rifle more than 200 years later.*

billeted on local householders, who feared them because of their often licentious and drunken behaviour. The Parliamentary commander Oliver Cromwell resolved these problems by turning the Parliamentary forces into the 'New Model Army'. This consisted of 12 infantry regiments each of 1000 men, 11 cavalry regiments each of 600 men, and 1000 dragoons or mounted infantry, equipped with musket and sword, who generally fought on foot.

Cromwell armed his infantry with flintlock muskets, which were lighter and safer than the matchlock, and provided them with regular uniforms. These were coloured red, which made it easy to distinguish friend from foe and also concealed the blood flowing from wounds, so avoiding damage to morale. Red remained the standard colour for the British army until it was superseded in 1902 by khaki, which provided better camouflage.

The New Model Army was welded into a highly efficient fighting force, cemented by a common religious zeal.

Cromwell described his troops as 'honest, sober Christians', and none was a mercenary. After Cromwell's triumph and the setting up of the Commonwealth, the army became a powerful force, and the fear of such a standing army remained a constant thread in British politics. France, however, did not share the mistrust of a standing army felt in Britain. Louis XIV's army, raised by conscription by ballot and led by trained aristocrats, served his expansionist aims and forced England to raise and maintain a powerful armed force. Under John Churchill, 1st Duke of Marlborough, the allied armies of England, Holland and the German states won a string of victories over the French, from the siege of Liege in 1702 to the battle of Malplaquet in 1709.

'If a soldier during an action looks about as if to flee, or so much as sets foot outside the line, the NCO standing behind him will run him through with his bayonet and kill him on the spot.'

FREDERICK THE GREAT (1712-86)

Marlborough was not only one of history's greatest commanders; he also had a genuine concern for his men's welfare, rare in an age indifferent to the hardships of the underprivileged. He devised march timetables to save them from the noon heat, and allowed them to march at their own pace, rather than to a regular drumbeat, provided

massed pikemen, with banners waving and horns blaring. Pikemen needed rigid discipline to use weapons which were sometimes 18 ft (5.5 m) long, and instruction books appeared.

they remained in formation. He made sure that they got their pay, and were provided with rations and uniforms. He was a firm disciplinarian, however, stipulating that if any of his soldiers stole so much as an egg from a peasant bringing provisions to the camp, he would be hanged. Plundering and marauding were also hanging offences. Women camp followers, whether married or whores, were whipped for offences such as looting dead bodies.

Punishment in Marlborough's army, though harsh, was more lenient and more justly applied than in the army of Frederick the Great. On his accession to the Prussian throne in 1740, Frederick set about perfecting the 83,000 strong army he inherited, half being Prussian citizens and half foreign mercenaries. His attitude to his army was summed up by the remark: 'If my men ever begin to think, not one would remain in the ranks.'

Frederick's troops were drilled in manoeuvres carried out while they marched at up to 120 steps a minute. Bayonets were fixed on their flintlock muskets, and each man carried 60 rounds of ammunition. The battle priority was rapid fire rather than accurate marksmanship. Along with this rigorous training went severe punishments for deviating from their orders. A soldier could be flogged by up to 1500 lashes over a period; his hands and feet might be tied to induce cramp; or he could be made to 'run the gauntlet' between two ranks of his fellows, who beat him

with sticks, while his speed was kept down by an NCO who walked slowly in front of him, with his pike pointed at the victim's chest. Such punishment often resulted in death. Desertion was a problem, and Frederick turned his barracks into near prisons. With this army, terrorised but uniquely professional, Frederick paved the way for a later united Germany, to emerge in the 19th century as the strongest military power on the Continent of Europe.

Charging into battle *Severe discipline, new weapons and methodical drilling ensured that there was no letup in the savageness of warfare in the 17th century. A contemporary artist captures the massive slaughter that occurred when infantry and cavalry met in hand-to-hand fighting with swords, muskets, pistols and pikes.*

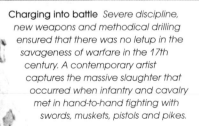

Returning from the wars
Discharged soldiers, often mutilated in the wars, were reduced to begging in the streets of their home towns. Diseased veterans were sometimes even shunned by their own families.

AT THE COURT OF FRANCE'S SUN KING

Dawn came respectfully to Versailles. It touched upon the Grand Canal and Fountain of Apollo, and tentatively lit the endless vistas of formal gardens. It warmed the pale stone and red brick of the chateau's 1361 ft (414 m) façade, struck fire from the gold leaf that covered the roof, then, with growing confidence, flared in the glass of the 240 ft (73 m) long Hall of Mirrors.

At 7am in the Royal Bedchamber, punctual as the sunrise, the First Valet arose, tidied away the couch on which he had slept, and addressed the gold-embroidered hangings closed about the royal bed: 'Sire, it is time.'

He then admitted the king's First Physician and First Surgeon who disappeared within the hangings, consulted and perhaps prescribed. Only when they had concluded was the door opened to admit the First Gentleman of the Bedchamber, who drew back the curtains and presented the morning to His Most Christian Majesty, King Louis XIV of France.

This was the moment of the *petit levée* – the little, or informal rising – to which were admitted only the king's closest intimates and officers of the court. After it, Princes of the Blood, and a highly favoured crony or two, accompanied His Majesty to the commode, on which he sat and chatted affably of affairs, or lent an attentive ear to petitions.

An hour or two snatched with a mistress apart, this was the last relatively private moment of the king's day, for there followed the *grand levée*, during which lesser nobility crowded the doors of the Royal Apartments while the king was shaved, ate his breakfast and put on his shirt, aided by two dukes. Valets helped him into his breeches, stockings, shoes and coat, his sword and sash were presented on bended knee, and the Royal Clockmaker wound his watch and gave it to him.

'The state is myself.'

LOUIS XIV

All was now ready for the grand promenade to the Chapel. Through the seemingly endless corridors and salons, with their painted ceilings, the king's approach was signalled by the tap of his cane, and the cry of 'Gentlemen, the King!' The silence that followed was broken only by the silken rustling of deep bows and curtseys as he passed.

Thus was created the legend of Versailles – the most dazzling court in the most beautiful palace in the world – and of Louis himself as the Sun King, about whom all that mattered revolved. From within this charmed circle, Louis managed a kingdom of 20 million people, meeting with his councillors and ministers, receiving reports, entertaining ambassadors and making decisions which affected the lives of people throughout Europe. Much of his power depended on the use of patronage, diverting the nobility from the serious uprisings in the country that had threatened his childhood into the no less vicious but far less dangerous paths of palace intrigue.

Entry to Louis' world was gained primarily by noble descent; but beauty, boldness and talent could also open doors. Presentation to His Majesty gained invitations to banquets and balls, access to one or more of the numerous cliques and, with luck, an appointment to some office or other.

There were some 7000 court officials struggling for living space with about the same number of Household troops, not to mention the vast army of servants, priests, gardeners, playwrights, musicians, savants, doctors of medicine and seekers after place and favour who gazed upon this glittering world with awe.

Versailles was therefore desperately overcrowded. Even niches in kitchens and storerooms were at a premium, and while the palace was crammed with art treasures, it was woefully lacking in sanitary arrangements. Perfumes frequently substituted for washing, and though there were privies in the courtyards and commodes in the salons, they were quite insufficient for

An outing for a king *On golden summer afternoons it was Louis XIV's pleasure to be wheeled through the gardens of Versailles in the company of his gorgeously dressed courtiers, friends and, in some cases, their wives and children. The king wears a stylish hat, but those attending upon him are respectfully bareheaded.*

Building a dream palace *Louis XIV's dream of a grandiose palace to house him and his court took more than 30 years to realise. Originally a modest hunting lodge some 20 miles (32 km) outside Paris, Versailles was transformed by thousands of workmen and craftsmen who swarmed over rubble-strewn meadows to create suites of public rooms and private apartments, and a maze of courtyards, stables, orangeries, statues and ponds.*

such a household. Occasionally even the haughtiest of aristocrats had to disappear behind the stair curtains. Louis dressed in extravagant style and expected the court to follow suit. Jewels, ribbons and wigs cost a fortune, and so did entertaining. Food at court was extremely elaborate and highly spiced – venison stuffed with truffled partridges is a fair example – while the poor soil of the kitchen garden was called on to produce luxury foods all the year round – including, it was said, asparagus in December and melons in March. However, there was no shortage of manure, which was just as well, for the king demanded petits pois almost daily, and was fond also of potatoes, still a novelty as human fare. He hated forks, and ate with a knife and his fingers, as of course did all the courtiers. They dined later than the king, and swiftly, for they had to return within the hour to attend him. Nevertheless, to keep an open table for the benefit of passers-by was obligatory, and yet another contributor to ruin. To maintain carriages, servants and a satisfactory appearance at court was immensely costly, and paid for by any means available. Courtiers besought the king for gifts and for pensions which, if granted, bound them ever more closely to him. Others sold their influence in obtaining positions at court, military and naval posts, and invitations to attend important functions, while the women dealt in arranging profitable marriages. But the basis

of all incomes came from long-neglected estates, whose agents often sent only a fraction of the rents due to the absentee landlords and pocketed the remainder.

It was upon the peasant that the burden of payment fell, together with the lion's share of tithes for the support of the Church, taxes, and the myriad perks that custom decreed were the seigneur's due. These varied from one part of France to another, but would certainly include payment for the use of his mill or winepress, and probably a levy on such changes of tenure as marriage or a son's inheritance. His wife was often pregnant, but few of his children were likely to survive beyond infancy; like his livestock they died of diseases that no one in those days knew how to fight. He would never have possessed a horse, nor probably a cow or a pig; a few sheep and hens pecking and grazing on the common land were the limit of his resources. His home was a hut, earthen-floored and roughly thatched, his plates and bowls of wood, his only furniture a few sticks. For most peasants the height of optimism was to survive until the next harvest came round, suffering as best they might the bitter contrast between their own poverty and the extravagant fripperies of Versailles.

Baker's lot *The streets of Paris were filled with vendors hawking their wares. This baker has many mouths to feed on the money he earns from his freshly baked loaves.*

Rise of the Sun King *The keynote of Louis XIV's court was one of flamboyance and ostentation. As early as 1653, at the age of 15 and already king for ten years, Louis had set the style for the age and found the title by which he was to be popularly known by appearing as Sun King in the ballet La Nuit, 'The Night'.*

Paying for war *It was the people who financed France's wars, and in 1709 a much-hated poll tax was imposed to pay for the upkeep of the armed forces. Men and women had to pay the tax in person, and the tax offices were crammed with citizens, officials and chinking bags of coins.*

PAYING FOR PLEASURE

To create the splendour of Versailles, peasants all over France were subjected to royal taxes to pay the many architects, craftsmen and builders who worked on the palace. Together with tithes, rent and taxes to pay for wars, exactions sometimes totalled about half the average peasant's income. Some peasants were relatively well-to-do, enjoying the status of tenant farmers, and able to pay their dues in cash. The majority, however, were not, and had to pay by day labouring or in goods. Those who paid in goods were not allowed to harvest their own meagre crops until the royal wagons had removed the seigneur's share.

It was life on the knife edge. One or two bad harvests, and the peasant entered into a spiral of debt and poverty from which it was almost impossible to escape. Unable to read, what news he received from the world outside – usually of fresh tax demands – was dispensed by the priest on Sunday.

THINKERS PUT ALL LIFE TO THE TEST

Science in the 18th century enjoyed an ever-growing prestige. The scholars of the age, no longer content to follow superstitions, instead weighed, tested and classified according to rational principles. The trend was part of the Enlightenment, a broad movement among educated people keen to shrug off all authoritarian beliefs and to release the free, questioning spirit.

France was a major centre of debate, and here the publication of a great encyclopedia of human knowledge caused a sensation. Edited by Denis Diderot and issued in 35 volumes from 1751 to 1772, the *Encyclopédie* had some 200 contributors, among them outstanding intellectual figures of the time such as Voltaire and Jean-Jacques Rousseau. Among the Encyclopedists, as they came to be known, knowledge was seen as a liberating force which would promote human virtue and happiness. Their radical philosophy made them many enemies in Church and state, helping to trigger the French

Gasping for air *Chemists of the 18th century were obsessed with experiment: no theory was accepted unless it could be backed by practical tests. Absorbed onlookers watch as French chemist Antoine Lavoisier shows that a living thing will collapse and eventually die if denied oxygen. The lark in the glass bell loses consciousness as air is sucked out by a pump.*

Sir Isaac Newton's reflecting telescope

Water synthesiser

Fashion's slaves *Interest in science became an upper-class fashion. An artist satirises the gentry who peer through reversed telescopes and stare uncomprehendingly at globes.*

DARING SCIENTISTS AND STINKING DRAINS

The tastes and interests of an educated gentleman of the 18th century are summed up in the story of a house set in the rolling downlands of southern England: Bowood House in Wiltshire. The grounds include an artificial lake, with a man-made Cascade at one end, and a purpose-built Hermit's Cave. Beyond the fine Orangery, where servants tended orange and lemon trees in tubs. is a small room called the Laboratory.

It was here, on August 1, 1774, that Dr Joseph Priestley discovered oxygen gas. Priestley was librarian and tutor to the two sons of the 1st Lord Lansdowne – a keen patron of science – and made his discovery by heating mercuric oxide. His findings, developed by the French chemist Antoine Lavoisier, proved that the air all around us is not just an insubstantial nothingness but a mixture of two complementary gases – oxygen and nitrogen – which can be measured and quantified. Lavoisier also built a water synthesiser to show that oxygen combines with hydrogen to form water.

It was a great age for discoveries and inventions – serious and frivolous – that would bear their fullest fruits in the century that followed. Sir Isaac Newton used his reflecting telescope for astronomical studies which guided him to new laws of gravity and mechanics, while steam engines pioneered by Thomas Savery, Thomas Newcomen and James Watt provided a new source of energy to power the Industrial Revolution. Innovations for the family included the perambulator of 1733, mayonnaise (first mixed by the chef to the Duc de Richelieu in 1756), and the roller skate of 1760. From 1780, Londoners could brush their teeth with the first factory-made toothbrushes.

In 1778 a London cabinet-maker, Joseph Bramah, patented his superior ballcock WC; he had sold 6000 by the end of the century. Unfortunately, drainage was still bad, so that many a WC, installed under the stairs in an ill-ventilated cubbyhole, led straight down to a private cesspool from which foul gases spread throughout the house.

For all the elegant furniture which now graced their homes, standards of personal hygiene among people at every level of society were as low as ever. Even so, some 'gentlemen scientists' were reluctant to soil their own hands, and left the dirty work of actual experimentation to humbler folk such as mechanics and laboratory assistants.

Revolution. In England, tempers were cooler, but a new curiosity about the natural world was reflected in the publishing of encyclopedias and in the founding of learned societies. The Royal Society founded in London by Charles II in 1660 took the whole field of knowledge as its province, and was a spur to research both practical and theoretical throughout the 18th century. The British Museum and the Royal Botanic Gardens at Kew were both established in 1759, while in Paris the world's first public zoo was opened at the Jardin de Plantes in 1793.

Throughout Europe the same scientific impulse was felt. Gabriel Fahrenheit, who devised the famous temperature scale, was a German; Anders Celsius, who created the centigrade scale, was a Swede – as was the biologist Linnaeus, who invented the first systematic system for classifying plants and animals.

> *'Dare to know! Have the courage to use your own intelligence!'*
>
> IMMANUEL KANT (1724-1804)

Scientists discussed earlier breakthroughs, and were as fascinated by small discoveries in everyday life as by their more rarefied researches. When the English chemist Dr Joseph Priestley published his *Introduction to the Theory and Practice of Perspective* he could not resist adding a last-minute note which makes the first mention in English of a pencil eraser, or India rubber. This novelty would, he wrote, be of singular use to those who practise drawing: 'Mr Nairne sells a cubical piece of about half an inch for three shillings, and he says it will last several years.' In England, the coffee-house had now become a great centre for the exchange of ideas, where men of science, philosophers and wits mingled with the nobility on equal terms. One habitué was the formidable Dr Samuel Johnson, whose *Dictionary of the English Language* of 1755 had an enormous influence in standardising English spelling. In France the

focus was the salon, a reception held by noble patrons – often ladies – in the chandelier-hung drawing rooms of their mansions for writers, artists and intellectuals.

Men of the Enlightenment wore powdered wigs which were generally smaller and more compact than the mountainous examples of earlier times. Though wigs went out of fashion towards the end of the period, their present-day equivalents are worn by British judges and barristers. Gentlemen also sported knee breeches, trousers being the garb of the lowest classes: in Paris during the French Revolution the insurgent poor were known as the *sans-culottes* – 'without knee breeches'.

For headgear, the tricorn, or three-cornered hat, was widely worn, while in 1715 a manufacturer in Paris produced a new piece of fashion gadgetry: the folding umbrella. In London the mob jeered at men who carried umbrellas in the street – and Dr Johnson came out strongly against the new devices, too.

The Enlightenment woman, familiar with microscopes and new chemical theories, nonetheless submitted to tight corsets and new kinds of hooped skirts known as panniers. They were flat at front and back, but so wide that staircases had to be redesigned with a widening curve at the bottom steps to allow wearers to sweep down in style.

Fashionable ladies wore their hair in colossal coiffures, 3 ft (1 m) or more high, with horsehair padding and wire foundations, ribboned with ostrich feathers and sometimes decorated with models of farms, battles or ships at sea. Doors had to be heightened to allow them through.

Happiness and Haydn

The pursuit of happiness was one of mankind's great goals promoted by Enlightenment thinkers, and for their musical delight audiences could now enjoy orchestral works. The sound was built around enlarged string sections and new instruments such as the oboe, clarinet and piano, whose overall effect was to blend sounds into a single symphonic voice.

Orchestral music was perfected by composers such as Mozart and Haydn, and the earliest ballets were performed around this time. Amusements of a more perilous nature derived from electricity. While physicists learned by experiments

using generators, and by close study of lightning, the less serious used electrical apparatus for party games. One such was a German scholar who would charge a pretty woman with static electricity and invite men to kiss her. The shock, it was reported, almost broke their teeth. In medicine, improvements came through the detailed study of anatomy, the use of post-mortems in training, and of forceps in childbirth. An important breakthrough in the control of smallpox occurred towards the end of the century. Inoculation against the disease had been practised with live smallpox vaccine for half a century, but in 1796 an English country doctor

Ideal form *This elegant violin, made in Italy in 1716 by Antonio Stradivarius, set a form and size for the instrument which survive today.*

named Edward Jenner introduced the use of cowpox vaccine for the same purpose. He had heard a dairy-maid comment of smallpox 'I cannot take that disease, for I have had cowpox'. Taking as his subject an eight-year-old country boy, Jenner scratched some fluid from a diseased cow into his skin. The boy contracted cowpox, but when he was later infected with smallpox he was found to be immune. Jenner's success would wipe smallpox from the face of England and, in due course, from the world.

Side show *The popularity of the theatre introduced actresses of humble birth into high society. There they found patrons whose love of the theatre extended beyond the fare on the stage.*

Fancy figure *Devotees of the new Italian art of the opera expected not only fine singing and acting but also colourful finery with silks, laces, frills, feathers, tassels and bows.*

Coke's tour *Thomas Coke, the future Earl of Leicester, was 18 when he set out on his Grand Tour of Europe. Dressed for a fancy-dress ball, he posed for this portrait in Rome in the early 1770s. The pillars, landscape and statue are typical of the 'classical' backgrounds favoured at the time.*

Words of warning *Guidebooks warned tourists against beggars, cheats, thieves and whores.*

Bottles of healing *Fear of foreign doctors led tourists to take their own medicine chests, complete with bottles of smelling salts and painkilling solutions of alcohol and opium.*

ADVENTURES ON THE GRAND TOUR

Tired and aching, three travellers stepped from their coach and gazed apprehensively at Mont Cenis, the last and most daunting obstacle on their journey across France to Italy. Almost 7000 ft (2130 m) high, it was one of the most dangerous and dreaded passes in the Maritime Alps. A steep, narrow path started above the snow-covered village of Lanslebourg and ran dizzily for about 45 miles (72 km) along the mountain and down into the plain leading to Turin.

It was winter in the late 18th century and the three travellers – a teenage English nobleman, his tutor, and a servant – were making a Grand Tour of Europe as a vital part of the youngster's general education. At this time such tours were at their peak, and many thousands of Britons between 15 and 21 were exploring the Continent to learn languages, to observe the manners and habits of foreigners, to view and appreciate works of art, and to bring

home with them after two or three years the fruits of their experience and so take their place as fully fledged members of their class in society.

As the tourists booked into the village inn, their coach was driven to a nearby shed, where it was dismantled ready for the crossing of the pass. Next morning the sections of the coach were strapped onto the backs of a string of mountain mules, whose muleteers led them, stumbling and slipping, along precipitous, rocky paths, down icy slopes, and over treacherous, wind-buffeted bridges spanning turbulent mountain streams.

The tourists, wrapped from head to toe in hooded bearskins, fur muffs, fur-lined boots and beaverskin masks, were carried in sedan-like wicker chairs, borne on long poles by teams of agile porters. These porters were often likened by the tourists to mountain goats. 'The dexterity and nimbleness of the mountaineers are inconceivable',

said Horace Walpole, the 18th-century English author, who crossed Mont Cenis during his own Grand Tour. 'They run with you down steeps and frozen precipices, where no men, as men are now, could possibly walk.'

Conditions were even grimmer on the notorious St Gothard Pass, where travellers were forced to quit their chairs and crawl on all fours over a high, slippery bridge, where the force of the wind threatened to blow them down into the rushing, rock-strewn water. But whichever way they went, it took them up to two days to reach the

peace and safety of the Italian lakes. Despite its hardships and hazards, however, the Alpine route was considered safer than going by water, where travellers faced the risk of being murdered by Barbary pirates.

The Grand Tour invariably began in London, where the travellers boarded a stage-coach to Dover. Among the equipment they collected for the journey were pistols, telescopes, a well-equipped medicine cabinet, 'lice-proof

linen nightshirts, inflatable baths complete with bellows, and useful guidebooks such as *The Grand Tour containing an Exact Description of most of the Cities, Towns and Remarkable Places of Europe by Mr Nugent*, which was published in four volumes in 1743. The books advised travellers to disguise themselves when necessary in old, dirty clothes – and to hide their gold coins in their shoes.

The crossing from Dover to Boulogne took up to six hours, and once on French soil the tourists lost no time in hiring a coach for the week-long journey to Paris, more than 180 miles (288 km) away. There the tutors, who were called 'bear-leaders', urged their charges to make sketches of the major landmarks, such as the Louvre and the Palace of Versailles, and to ask as many questions as possible about the capital's culture,

Tourist attraction *A group of Grand Tourists gazes awestruck at the remains of the Temple of Castor and Pollux in the ruins of the Forum in Rome. Sights like these repaid the travellers for their long, arduous journey.*

Souvenir
A fan records sights of the Grand Tour which were to influence English architecture.

A collector and his haul *With his dog at his feet, an English art collector sits in his gallery surrounded by classical statues, busts, friezes and vases. They are typical of the vast number of works brought back by the Grand Tourists from Italy and France.*

inhabitants and way of life. Many young tourists, however, were much keener to consult valets, fashionable tailors and wig-makers, and to start turning themselves into posturing fops. The vainer among the tourists donned scarlet-and-yellow velvet suits with white satin linings, shirts of frothy Brussels lace, silk ruffs, white silk stockings, and pumps with buckles and red heels. At their sides they carried gold-handled swords.

> *'A man who has not been in Italy is always conscious of an inferiority...the grand object of travelling is to see the shores of the Mediterranean.'*
>
> DR SAMUEL JOHNSON, 1750

As well as visiting art galleries and concerts, many of the richly attired youngsters frequented brothels and gambling houses, took lessons in fencing, riding and dancing, and still found time to learn the art of flirtatious conversation. Many of the travellers, according to a contemporary observer, returned home with 'the manners of a dancing master and the morals of a whore'. From Paris, the tourists went south to Marseilles, where the main 'attraction' in the harbour was the almost naked, shaven-headed galley slaves chained to their benches in the king's ships. Then followed the crossing of the Alps, after which the travellers headed for Pisa, Florence and Venice. Most of the Grand Tourists contrived to reach Venice at carnival time, the week before Lent. There they watched the gondola races and bull hunts through the streets and squares. Their principal goal, however, was Rome, where they might meet the sculptor Antonio Canova, whose neoclassical style emulated the style of Ancient Greece, and the architect Giovanni Piranesi, who sketched hundreds of Roman antiquities.

Many of the inexperienced young Englishmen gravitated to the Piazza da Spagna, the haunt of unscrupulous art fakers and dealers. More reliable antiquarians were employed to show tourists the sights of the Eternal City, such as the catacombs, and to arrange for their portraits

to be painted by the society artist Pompeo Batoni against historical backgrounds such as the Baths of Caracalla and the Forum. Tourists' education, however, was not complete until they had visited the ancient cities of Herculaneum and Pompeii in the Bay of Naples. The remains impressed the tourists more than anything else on their travels, and the sketches and souvenirs they took home with them had a profound influence on houses and pottery. Architects such as the two brothers Robert and James Adam transformed rambling English country houses into models of classical order, complete with slender pillars, gabled porches and central domes. The potter Josiah Wedgwood produced delicate vases with Grecian figures in white cameo relief on unglazed blue backgrounds.

Inspired by the Italianate paintings of Poussin and Claude, the gardener 'Capability' Brown created parks and gardens in imitation of natural landscapes, such as those at Blenheim and Chatsworth. Usually, tourists chose to journey home through Germany – where, at Yuletide, they delighted in the candlelit Christmas trees, then unknown in English homes.

By the end of the century, however, the days of the Grand Tour were numbered. The Napoleonic Wars, and the coming of the railway, put an end to leisurely and protracted journeys throughout Europe. Instead, the age of Cook's tours was about to begin.

Tricking the tourists *Italian picture dealers were skilled at selling fake masterpieces to naive and impressionable tourists. Copies of works by painters such as Titian, Raphael and Botticelli were passed off as originals at ridiculously high prices.*

SERFS OF THE TSAR'S EMPIRE

Viking warrior-traders who penetrated deep into Europe established the first Russian state around AD 850, with its centre at Kiev. At the end of the following century the people of its growing towns started their fervent embrace of Christianity, recently introduced from Byzantium. Centuries of Mongol invasions followed before the Russian state emerged anew under powerful rulers who, from their base in Moscow, built up a huge state. In 1547, Ivan IV became the first ruler of this state to be called Tsar.

Tsar Ivan, known as the Terrible, set a pattern of absolute rule that imposed great hardships on the Russian people, and denied peasants their freedom by introducing serfdom. They suffered the same harsh control even under the forward-looking Peter the Great, who struggled to remodel his realm on Western lines. As well as state-imposed hardships, Russians have always suffered from extremes of climate and scarcity of fertile soil. Rising to the challenge, however, people hewed splendid churches and comfortable homes out of the wood of the forests, and found relief from their arduous lives in fairs and extravagant feasting, music and merrymaking.

RUSSIA AD 1550–1750

VILLAGES OF WOOD IN A HARSH LAND

Across the vast and varied land of Russia, log-built houses huddled together in clusters. Villages of anything from a dozen to a hundred homes stood in forest clearings and on the banks of rivers, and there Russian peasants found their basic needs met.

Trees provided them with firewood, timber to build homes, and bark to make shoes. They could hunt animals for meat and fur, catch freshwater fish, and gather berries and mushrooms. Wagonloads of mushrooms of many different sizes and colours were taken to sell in the towns, and some were turned into preserves and pickles for the cold winter days. People grew vegetables, including cabbages for the soup which was a staple part of their diet, and asparagus and cucumbers.

The peasant's life was a hard one, however. Though Russia had huge areas of arable land, the rainfall was unreliable and roughly every third harvest failed disastrously. The soil was poor, except for the 'black earth' of the steppe – the grassy plains of southern Russia. The farming season was short, lasting only four or five months, compared with eight or nine months in Western Europe.

The harsh conditions made it hard to produce a good yield of crops, so farmers had little money to spend and could not buy other people's produce. The lack of buyers in turn discouraged any efforts to improve the crop yields.

From freedom to serfdom

Except in the steppe, individual farming was almost impossible. Peasants farmed collectively, either as extended families – father, mother, children, and married sons with their wives and children – or else as several families working together. The head of an

From fur and bark *The Russian peasant's coarse tunic was belted at the waist over baggy trousers, and his leggings were rags bound with twine above shoes made of bark. A Western visitor observed: 'Their hair is cropt to their ears and their heads covered winter and summer with a fur cap. Their beards remain yet untouched…'*

extended family, usually the father, was called the *bol'shak,* or 'Big One'. He had the final say in family matters and organised the farming work. When he died, the family elected a replacement, usually the eldest son, to succeed him.

Until the 16th century, tenant farmers had been free to move from place to place. They worked the land until the harvests failed too often, and then moved on to start again elsewhere. The peasants' lot changed, however, under Ivan the Terrible. Ivan ruled through an elite of nobles who in return for their obedience were given land – and the services of the peasants who lived on it.

More and more peasants became enslaved to a single plot of land. In 1649 serfdom was confirmed by law – at a time when it had virtually disappeared from Western Europe. By that time, well over 90 per cent of the population – some 12 million people – were serfs.

The difficulties of making a living from farming alone meant that many peasants had a second source of income – a craft or industrial enterprise known as a *promysly.* Earning extra money in this way was common in all ranks of society: a Western merchant in the 1650s wrote: 'Everyone, from the highest to the lowest, practised trade.'

Fruits of the forest and rivers

There was no shortage of goods to be traded. The forests abounded in deer, elk, bears and fur-bearing rodents whose skins or furs could be sold. Honey was plentiful, deposited by bees in cracks in dead tree trunks. The waters were full of fish, especially sturgeon, which came up the great rivers from the Caspian Sea. Other ways in which peasants could add to their income included tanning, salt-distilling and weaving.

Trading fairs were an important part of life in Russia, and merchants set up booths to sell their wares among the hosts of entertainers who were always at fairs. They took their goods there by sledge and caravan, and also by barge.

Travel in Russia at this time was both slow and difficult. The huge distances, and the long, severe winters followed by extensive spring flooding, hindered the building of a proper network of roads. Instead, people and goods moved from place to place in boats and barges on the rivers.

In the cities and towns, Russians travelled in horse-drawn carriages of many different styles. Most carriages were decorated with elaborate carvings

and gaily coloured. Equally ornate were the sleighs, some of them shaped like swans or deer, that were necessary in the frozen winter months. One of the most widely used vehicles was the *drozhki,* a light, open, four-wheeled carriage designed for fast travel. In winter, it could be converted into a sleigh by substituting runners for the wheels. The larger *troika,* pulled by three horses, demanded great skill on the part of the driver.

Winter travel *Wealthy people travelled in closed satin-lined carriages, some of which could be converted into sleighs for the long, snowbound winters.*

Frozen food *Outdoor winter markets such as this one in St Petersburg were held in every major town throughout Russia, and nobles, merchants and peasants flocked to them. In the sub-zero temperatures traders sold frozen raw meat. An English visitor wrote: 'Your astonished sight is arrested by a vast open square, containing the bodies of many thousand animals piled in pyramidal heaps on all sides. Cows, sheep, pigs, fowls, butter, eggs, fish are all stiffened into granite.' Visitors noted that the frozen meat could be thawed and cooked with little loss in flavour. Food was taken to market from all over the country, and hand-pulled sledges were used to carry carcasses home.*

Rugged residences *Peasants' homes were built of logs, the gaps between them being sealed with moss to keep out the cold. The inhabitants of these houses in a north Russian village are sufficiently well off to have chimneys; in many homes, however, smoke from the wood-burning stove escaped through unsealed cracks in the logs or through shutters over the windows. A woman uses a weighted beam to raise water from a log-built well. Amid all the harshness of rural life, Russians found consolation in religion, and each home had a 'beautiful corner' reserved for icons, or Christian images. They also attached great importance to cleanliness, and there were public baths in all villages. While many people in Western Europe often went weeks or even months without taking a bath. Russian peasants bathed at least once a week.*

Giant empire *In 1700 the people of Russia were thinly dispersed over the plains and forests of their vast country. Peter the Great extended the empire as far as the Baltic Sea in the west.*

TOWNS THAT ROSE BY THE AXEMAN'S ART

Russians of the 1600s did not talk of 'building' a new town. Instead, they 'cut' it. Wood was the most important construction material, and the axe was virtually the only instrument used. Churches, shops, houses, palaces and public baths were built of timber, and wood was even used in road-building.

Most people bought their houses ready-made, or in prefabricated units that could be quickly put together on the chosen site. To cater for these early do-it-yourself practitioners, carpenters sold building parts at local markets in towns and villages. Logs in a huge range of lengths and widths were marked and numbered for easy assembly; a buyer simply specified the number of rooms and the sizes he needed and ordered the parts.

In wood-built cities and towns such as Kiev, Novgorod and Moscow, fire was a permanent hazard. Watchmen kept a lookout from towers, ready to raise black leather flags to warn of fire by day; at night they held up torches. Despite these precautions fire occurred all too often – Moscow alone suffered as many as 30 major outbreaks in the 16th and 17th centuries. To help the victims repair their homes quickly, carpenters set up smaller depots at the end of major streets where spare wooden parts for houses were stored in racks. People whose property was damaged could simply go to a depot and buy replacement parts such as beams, roof shingles, doors or window frames.

The ease with which houses could be replaced impressed the German diplomat Adam Olearius, who visited Moscow in the mid-17th century. 'Those who have had their houses burned may buy houses ready-built at a market, and in a short time set up where the former stood', he reported.

Carving a spoon with an axe

Russia west of the Urals is short of stone. Timber, however, is abundant, and from the time of their earliest settlements the Russians developed carpentry skills that enabled them to

Bustling 'Basket Town' *Most of 17th-century Moscow was a city of timber, in which logs of pine and other woods were used for buildings of all kinds. The main roads were constructed of oak planks laid down on timber foundations, through which underground wooden pipes, sewn tightly together with birch bark, drained off the water from melting snow or rain. The painting (right) shows wooden streets in the heart of Moscow's commercial quarter, the Kitai Gorod or Basket Town so called because the district was once fortified with baskets of earth. One of the district's richly dressed merchants is followed by his wife, who carries a casket. A huge inn dominates the scene, a symbolic wine pitcher hanging over its entrance staircase. On the right, prisoners sit in the stocks, pleading for food, while on the left bodies lie in their coffins. Bells are being rung to summon relatives to identify them and collect them for burial.*

Workers in wood *There were more wood-workers than any other type of craftsman in 17th-century Russia. Nearly all peasants were carpenters by necessity and, as well as building and repairing their homes, they made everyday utensils which were works of folk art. The design of the drinking bowl dates back to 2000 BC; the painted mug, for honey or beer, has a hinged cover.*

Drinking bowl and mug

Home comfort *Within the izba, or peasant's log-built house, warmth was provided by a log-burning stove made of earthenware or brick. The stove also served for cooking and baking, and people slept on its platform or on benches around it. In this household, two boys lie on top of the oven, as their young mother puts her baby to sleep in a blanket suspended by the fire. Most homes were divided into two or three rooms, although some were larger; the layout was determined by the position of the stove. During the long Russian winter, the main stove would be kept going day and night, and larger houses had secondary stoves to heat the smaller rooms. To keep the interior as warm as possible, most homes were built with low ceilings and double-glazed windows. The earliest windows, dating from the 10th century, were glazed with sheets of mica, but later homes had glass windows.*

build almost anything. With equal ease they built the *izba*, the basic house with two or three rooms – and complex structures such as the Kolomenskoe Palace near Moscow, a series of more than 250 interlinked dwellings, with 3000 mica-filled windows gleaming in the sun. They also built a wealth of fine churches, many of which survive to the present day.

Wooden buildings such as these were invariably constructed without using a single nail, peg or screw. The axe was the principal tool used, although intricate decoration was done with a chisel. Carpenters were so skilful that, as Tolstoy once remarked, they could carve a spoon with an axe.

Because the building season was so short – and through their natural impatience – Russians also worked with amazing speed. An izba could be ready for occupation in a day.

> '*The common houses of the country are everywhere built of beams of fir tree...and where the timber is joined together, there they stop the chinks with moss.*'
>
> RICHARD CHANCELLOR, *c.* 1550

The principal wood used for building was pine, though other conifers and chestnut, oak and beech were also employed. Logs for an izba were up to 30 ft (9 m) long and 12 in (300 mm) in diameter; they were laid horizontally and interlocked at the ends and corners by one of several types of joints.

Roofs were very steep, so that the snow would slide off. In some buildings the floor level was raised clear of the ground on stilts or on wood, brick or stone foundations; a covered stairway then gave access to the building.

Added to their flair for building in timber was the Russians' love for decorating their homes. They thought nothing of removing doors, windows or even party walls to improve their homes, and sometimes doors and walls disappeared simply to accommodate guests for a night-long party.

Every cottage had its ornamental carving, or 'wooden embroidery'. The ends of the horizontal beams, roof rafters and ridgepoles were skilfully and individually carved. Decorations on porches, bargeboards and window-frames often reflected the current building style in the cities, and imitated the stone ornaments on city

Do-it-yourself houses *Cooperative endeavour, and the use of logs already cut to the right lengths at carpenters' depots, made quick work of building the typical Russian izba, or peasant's hut.*

A CITY BUILT ON HUMAN BONES

To build St Petersburg, his great new capital on the banks of the River Neva, Peter the Great exacted sacrifice on a colossal scale. Peasants from the fields, soldiers taken out of the army and prisoners were among the million or more men gathered from all parts of Russia and forcibly taken to St Petersburg. Between 100,000 and 200,000 of them died there, and the new city was said to have risen upon a charnel house of human bones.

Thousands of masons, engineers, blacksmiths and carpenters, and countless more thousands of unskilled labourers, worked from dawn to dusk on a bare subsistence diet every day for six months. They were then, in theory, allowed to go home, although thousands were kept behind for months or even years longer. Punishments for desertion included cutting the nostrils to the bone. The men were housed in damp, filthy huts, or else slept in the open under blankets or overcoats. They had to drink foul water and were grossly underfed, and scurvy, dysentery and malaria were rife. They were given few tools and no wheelbarrows, and had to carry the mud that they scooped up with their bare hands in the skirts of their clothing, or in sacks made of old matting.

Stone city *Builders of the 19th-century St Isaac's Cathedral in St Petersburg, which replaced Peter the Great's original building, used similar wooden ramps and poles to their predecessors.*

buildings: there were balusters and pediments, and carved panels inset in walls. Bigger houses often had fine parquet floors, made from many varieties of wood.

A new capital built on a swamp

Russia's traditional building materials, however, meant nothing to Peter the Great, who became Tsar of Russia in 1689. He loathed Moscow, its wooden buildings and its Asiatic outlook. Peter the Great wanted a new capital city which faced the West, whose influences he was determined to graft upon what he regarded as a backward Russia.

The site the tsar chose for his new capital, to be called St Petersburg, was unpromising – a patch of soggy ground in the marshy delta where the River Neva flows into the Gulf of Finland. The river was frozen for half the year,

afflicted with dank mists, and prone to flooding when the ice thawed: while the new city was being built it was often under several feet of water. To create foundation platforms for the buildings, thousands of wooden piles were sunk into the swamp. In winter, wolves roamed the streets, and in 1715 they ate a woman alive.

Yet despite the difficult conditions and the herculean scale of the project, a splendid new city of stone buildings arose. Work started in 1703, and by 1710 the first stage of construction was complete and work had begun on the tsar's Summer Palace. Some 34,000 people already lived there when the tsar declared St Petersburg the new capital of Russia. The city was not completed when Peter the Great died in 1725, but enough had been done to impress Europe.

Worship in wood *Cathedrals and churches were set in commanding positions on hilltops or, as in the case of the Church of the Intercession at Kizhi, on an island in Lake Onega, in northern Russia. The church, built in 1764, is made entirely of wood, and its nine shingled domes represent the nine choirs, or orders, of angels.*

Symbol of faith *The crucifixion scene embossed on this 18th-century crucifix shows Christ's feet nailed to the slanting cross bar, which is a feature of the crucifix itself. The lower figure wears the garb of a bishop.*

TREASURED IMAGES

Among the Russian Christian's most important possessions were icons – portraits and pictures of religious scenes painted on wood. The most familiar figure in icon painting was the Virgin. Much more than simply a painting, an icon was regarded as a sacred object, close to a living being, whose presence helped the faithful to gain access to the spiritual world. Icons were sold in marketplaces, shops and stalls, and were hung in every peasant's home, in stables and offices, and near springs. No event was complete without the blessing of an icon; an English visitor recorded that 'he who comes to his neighbour's house doth first salute his saints'.

Madonna and child *Icons of the Madonna were believed to have the power to work miracles.*

Revered hero *St George, dragon slayer and patron saint of England, is also honoured on Russian icons.*

DOMES AND ICONS OF A SHINING FAITH

A tolerant attitude to drinking and the stunning beauty of its cathedrals finally persuaded Vladimir, Prince of Kiev, to accept Byzantine Christian baptism in AD 988. A pagan ruler who enjoyed wining, dining and wenching to the full, Vladimir had several faiths examined so that he could decide which one to choose.

Vladimir was following the lead of his powerful neighbours, who by the 10th century had abandoned paganism and converted to a faith with one god – Judaism, Islam, or one of the forms of Christianity. He concluded, it is said, that 'We Russians cannot live without drinking', and adopted Eastern Orthodox Christianity as the official religion of Russia.

Russians embraced the new faith with enthusiasm. They brought to it their folk art and music, and also their building skills – within half a century nearly 400 wooden, brick and stone churches had been erected in Kiev. Cathedrals and churches became landmarks in towns and villages, and were instantly recognisable when the sun flashed upon the shining domes that topped every one of them.

Domes had great symbolic value. One dome stood for God as the head of the Church. Three domes represented the Trinity, and five of them stood for Christ and the four evangelists. Nine domes represented the nine choirs of angels, and 12 domes clustered around a larger one represented Christ and his 12 apostles.

Onion domes to catch prayers

Every dome carried a cross. At first domes were hemispherical, following the style of Byzantine ones, but before long native Russian onion-top shapes began to appear. This design was said to catch the prayers of the worshippers and direct them towards heaven – though more prosaically the shape helped to deflect heavy snowfalls.

Churches were the most important buildings in Russia, and leading events took place in or outside them. People often gathered outside for open-air services and watched the holiest parts through open doors. Churches were square or rectangular, with a large central space under the main dome. There were no seats: Russians believed in standing in God's presence, although it was permissible to mill about and even chatter during services. 'They gaggle and cackle like geese', wrote one shocked English observer in the late 18th century.

Ringing out the news

In Russia, bells 'shook the earth with their vibrations', according to a 17th-century visitor to Moscow. They were rung in church belfries before and during services, and every day at, or even before, dawn. Bells were rung to warn travellers about snowstorms, to summon people to funerals, weddings or festivals, and to announce holidays, disasters and victories in war.

> 'Nothing affected me so much as the united clang of all the bells on the eves of Sundays and great festivals.'
>
> VISITOR TO MOSCOW, c.1660

Russian bells were made of iron, copper, bronze and silver, and some were huge – it was said that the bell in the church belfry of Rostov church could be heard 20 miles away. The Tower of Ivan the Great in Moscow, which was nearly 320 ft (97.5 m) tall, housed a collection of bells positioned one above the other, the biggest weighing 64 tons. A niece of Peter the Great had a 200 ton bell made.

The Church affected every aspect of daily life in 17th and 18th-century Russia. Ecclesiastical laws were binding on every devout citizen, while each profession, trade and craft had its patron saint. In the mid-17th century a German diplomat wrote that there were more than 2000 monasteries, churches and private chapels in Moscow alone, and that anyone of wealth built a chapel and maintained its priest at his own expense.

A week of carousing in winter

Christmas and Easter were celebrated with weeks of festivities interspersed with long periods of fasting. Easter celebrations were especially prolonged, and preparations began as early as February or even late January, in the depths of the Russian winter with its deep snow. Eight weeks before Easter Sunday a week of carnival known as Butter Week began, when everybody ate huge amounts of food.

Special foods for the week included *blini*, which were small pancakes soaked in butter. Blini were symbolic of the sun, and lovely days and happy marriages, and were accompanied by Latvian vodka and lemon. There were also hosts of little cakes, some made in the shape of birds with currants for eyes.

During the carnival week masked figures ran through streets where actors and dancing bears entertained the crowd. In larger towns ice slides were put up for sledging, and swings – some with windmill-like sails – were built. Stalls and bars were set up to sell tea from samovars or from small teapots, and temporary restaurants served food of many different kinds.

Larger towns held processions of sleighs along the main streets; one observer noted that about 7000 sleighs filed around Moscow during Butter Week. Theatres were open all day and evening, and plays and shows were performed in Russian, French, German and Italian.

Towards the weekend public offices and schools were closed. On the last day of the week the Great Fast began – a seven-week penance when people ate only fish, vegetables, mushrooms and coffee. Meat, milk, butter, sugar and eggs were forbidden. In Easter Week the fast ended, and people celebrated with more feasting, dominated by the decorating, giving and eating of eggs.

Comfort from Mother Earth

Although Christianity played such a large part in their lives, Russians clung to many of their old pagan beliefs and superstitions, and even developed some new ones. The lives of the peasants, in particular, were often dominated by the old ways. Pagan gods of the Wind, Sun, Frost and, above all, Mother Earth helped them to cope with a world where Christianity did not provide all the answers. Many Russians believed in several different spirits, including *rusalki*, the female water spirits that were said to lure men to them to be tickled to death. They also worshipped their ancestors, whom they believed inhabited birch trees.

Beard tax *Peter the Great tried to break the power of the boyars – aristocrats who wore long spade-shaped beards as a sign of their class. He ordered them to shave off their beards, but later relented, provided that unshaven ones paid a tax and wore a medallion (below) to prove it.*

STATE SECRETS AND SECRET POLICE

Religion governed many aspects of people's lives; another code of law came from the tsar. The tsars were despots who believed in tight censorship, heavy surveillance and policing, and ruthless penalties for those who broke the law. Russians were paid to inform on offenders such as shopkeepers who failed to declare their profits. Printing presses, except those of the Church, were state owned and all news was a state secret. The police force of Ivan IV dressed in black, rode black horses and had saddle bags with an emblem which included a broom, symbolising treason being swept from the land. People of all ranks could be sentenced to torture and execution; a common punishment was a beating with the knout, a whip of leather strips attached to a short wooden handle.

Beating with birches *Corporal punishment was common, and peasants were given the choice of a fine or a beating for certain offences. Most chose the beating.*

Man-made heights *Russians built 'ice hills' up to 35 ft (10.5m) high, for sledging in the snowy winter months. The passenger sat in front and a driver steered from behind.*

HIGH SPIRITS AND A TASTE FOR VODKA

The public square is a kaleidoscope of colour as Armenians, Balts, Bulgars, Cossacks, Tatars and all manner of foreign visitors, each wearing their national costumes, throng and jostle in the search for entertainment. Giant wooden wheels whirl and swingboat gondolas swish to and fro, as clowns and conjurors, jugglers and tumblers, mountebanks and merchants ply their wares at side booths. Milling among them, serfs, in their belted tunics and baggy trousers, rub shoulders with the gold-brocaded gentry. Outside the inns, street musicians strum, and men who have sold their last item of clothing for a drink lie naked in the street.

Enormous, elaborate open-air fairs that went on for months had died out in the West before the 16th century, but remained a dazzling feature of Russian life until the present century. There were fairs in their thousands, from the smallest street party to sprawling extravaganzas embracing whole cities. From the 16th century the Russian state expanded to include many different peoples, each of whom retained their own distinctive national dress, music and customs. So fairs provided kaleidoscopic spectacles that were unmatched elsewhere.

The greatest fair of all was the Summer Fair held at Nizhni-Novgorod (modern Gorky), which for decades was the biggest fair in the world. During the fair the city's population swelled from fewer than 50,000 to more than 250,000. Millions of merchants from all over Europe and Asia congregated there, some taking the best part of a year to get there and back. And they

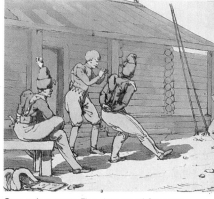

Cossack capers *The dances of Cossack horsemen from southern Russia involved strenuous knee bends, spectacular leaps in the air and crouching, forward kicks.*

Ringing strings *Two horses' heads decorate this balalaika, an instrument long familiar to the Russians. Its three strings are plucked with a plectrum.*

Spring fair *Every town in Russia loved to hold a fair, especially during festivals such as Easter, and the 18th-century English painter John Atkinson has captured the lively scene at this Easter fair. Flying boats soar through the air and, in the background, young and old dip and bob on seesaws and sail to and fro on swings. On the right of the picture, clowns mounted on a platform receive the praise of a crowd, one of whom applauds the performers by throwing his hat in the air.*

were always greeted with the hospitality which Russians gave to family, friends and strangers alike.

For centuries the Russians have had an unbridled enthusiasm for enjoyment – for hospitality, feasting and drinking on a gargantuan scale. The most extravagant tsars and the humblest peasants alike delighted in music-making, dancing, theatre, fairs, street parties, sports and bazaars.

'Open house' to the serfs

The Russians' love of food and drink is shown in their richly varied and long-drawn-out meals. Some landowners regularly organised feasts for 100 or 150 guests of all classes. Nobles threw open to the public the grounds of town and country houses and provided lavish refreshment, dancing, fishing in natural and artificial lakes, music, and entertainment of all kinds. Count Grigori Orlov, one of Catherine the Great's lovers, opened his town house to everyone, including serfs, every day; most other big houses were open at least once a week.

Guests sat down at long tables to enjoy cakes and sweetmeats, walnuts, almonds and pistachio nuts, raisins, figs, dried apricots, mushrooms and caviar. The food was washed down with rivers of drink, especially vodkas of many kinds and colours.

The Reverend William Coxe, an 18th-century English clergyman who made several visits to Russia, described 'a very singular entertainment' – a huge outdoor party thrown by a Russian businessman. 'At the extremity of the grounds,' he wrote, 'was a large square of ice well swept for the skaters, near which were two machines like the swinging vehicles at Bartholomew Fair.'

The 'machines' Coxe saw provided exhilarating rides. One of them had 'four sledges in which the people seated themselves, and were turned round with great velocity; the other had four wooden horses, and the riders were whirled around in the like manner'.

The hosts provided a challenge for more daring partygoers. Two poles were erected, each more than 20 ft (6 m) high, and, Coxe reported, 'at the top of each was placed a piece of money, as a prize for those who could swarm up and seize it. The poles, being rubbed with oil, soon froze in this severe climate'.

The climate – and the vast quantities of drink consumed – took its toll. The party witnessed by Coxe was attended by 40,000 guests, but some 400 of

them never saw the dawn. They had died from exposure where they lay, drunk, in subzero temperatures.

Russians did not drink in small, regular amounts, but instead drank sporadically, and in huge quantities. They made a three-day event of it: one day to drink, a second to get drunk and a third to sober up.

A secretary at the British Embassy in St Petersburg described how, in 1714, after 'a dozen bumpers of Hungary wine' and a quart of brandy which he was forced to finish in two draughts, 'I soon lost my senses...'. No one would have noticed this embarrassing lapse, for 'the rest of the guests lying already asleep on the floor were in no condition to make reflections on my little skill in drinking'.

By the mid-17th century there was a state monopoly of liquor production. People went to state taverns, which did not sell food, and drank vodkas until they reached *zapoi* – alcoholic stupor.

> **'There is no place in the world where drunkenness is more common than in Muscovy.'**
>
> ADAM OLEARIUS, *c.* 1630

Drunkenness became a national problem, but the Church's attempt to control it threatened one of the state's biggest sources of revenue, so drinking went on. When Peter the Great threw parties, his guests were not allowed to plead that they had had enough, an argument in line with the old Russian proverb which said that 'a feast is only happy when everyone is drunk'.

Music and dancing abounded too. In the early years of the reign of Tsar Alexis, who came to the throne in 1645, an edict had been issued forbidding people to play and watch games, and banning dancing, singing and the playing of musical instruments.

But when Tsar Alexis married for the second time in 1670, an orchestra played and a Russian choir chanted. Royal patronage of the theatre quickly followed – and soon all Russia rang to music once again.

Travellers' accounts of Russia from the 16th century onwards describe the people's love of music and their enthusiasm for singing. They sang to their horses, sang while rowing boats, and sang even while selling goods in the street. Coachmen sang part songs when driving coaches, and soldiers

sang in harmony as they marched. Tsar Ivan the Terrible was devoted to music, and in the 1550s ordered that it should be taught in all schools.

The 18th-century Tsarina Elizabeth played a large part in introducing opera and ballet to the Russian people. She collected and published traditional folk songs, and also encouraged singers from the Ukraine and foreign lands.

For the wealthy, there was an endless succession of balls, especially in the winter months. An Irish lady who toured Russia in the 18th century said of the nightly balls: 'You danced until you dropped.' And a German traveller noted 'the lightness and physical grace of the Great Russian Peasant which made him delight in dancing: the men dancing on their own, especially the Cossacks, give themselves up to the dance with a passion'.

Russians also felt great enthusiasm for steam baths. Every village had its public bathhouse, which people visited at least once a week; many went every day. Large private houses had their own bathhouse, and the wealthy often scented the steam with herbs.

In Moscow, government ministers met at one another's bathhouses to discuss state affairs while they steamed themselves to near exhaustion and beat themselves with birch twigs. They then plunged into a cold bath.

Russians who went to public baths finished by jumping into a nearby river or stream. The 16th-century English visitor Anthony Jenkinson described the abrupt transition from heat to cold: 'You shall see them come out of their bathhouses all of a froth and fuming and presently leap into the river stark naked in the coldest of wintertime.'

Tavern tipple *Peasants traditionally drank kvas, a brew made from fermented black rye bread. In the 16th century Russians began to distil spirits and drink Polish vodka.*

The Modern World

From the time of the great voyages of the 15th and 16th centuries, it had been possible to talk of one world. Yet getting to know more of this world took time. In the name of religion and trade the European powers acquired colonies in distant parts of the world, carrying with them their own ways of life and often clashing violently with local inhabitants who had their own distinctive customs. China and Japan long remained isolated, and Australia and New Zealand, reached by travellers in the 18th century, were at first sparsely settled.

In North America, modern times were ushered in when 13 British colonies broke away from rule by Westminster and fought for independence, pledged to goals of freedom and the pursuit of human happiness that were to attract immigrants from many lands during the 19th century.

The French Revolution, also proclaimed in the name of 'the people', was a more violent revolution, culminating in the march of Napoleon's armies through Europe. Aristocrats lost their privileges and many of the long-standing grievances of the peasants were met, as the ideals of liberty, equality and fraternity were proclaimed.

The third revolution, the Industrial Revolution, which began in Britain, was to have far-reaching economic, social and political consequences. As machines were devised to supplement or replace human skills, and as new forms of power were developed to augment human and animal strength, ways of work were transformed. Behind the transformation was a huge increase in population. The numbers of Europeans more than doubled in the 19th century as industrialisation proceeded, from around 200 million to 430 million.

These were still, however, a minority in terms of the total world population, which also doubled during the century.

All three revolutions brought permanent changes to human prosperity, expectations and daily life, but none was without its human costs. In its first stages, the Industrial Revolution depended on the labour of women and children, and in many centres of industry it created class conflicts between employers, living on profits, and employees, living on wages. It thereby stimulated revolutionary ideas and movements. There were sharp contrasts between the everyday lives of rich and poor, the latter creating trade unions and, in time, political parties. The industrialising process also damaged the environment, darkening the skies and polluting the rivers. Old values, particularly religious values, were challenged.

In the long run, however, material standards of living were raised, along with human expectations. Over large parts of the world there was a movement, too, towards democracy – the granting of the vote to all men, although in most countries still not to women, who were beginning at last to fight for their rights.

Even in autocratic Russia, which in 1900 was still ruled by a tsar, the serfs had been liberated and industrial growth had begun. It was Russia, which had escaped revolution during the 19th century, that was to become the first nation to experience revolution in the 20th century. The repercussions were to be felt throughout the world, as the new century progressed. So, too, were the repercussions of growing American wealth and power.

REBELS WITH A CAUSE

The American Revolution drew together the people of 13 different American colonies to draft a Declaration of Independence which in 1776 launched them into war against the British. A new nation with a new flag was forged, but only through struggle. French soldiers fought alongside American rebels while France was still ruled by an autocratic monarch. Yet France's turn was soon to come. The French Revolution, even more violent and explosive, came to a head on July 14, 1789, with the storming of the Bastille by enraged Parisians. The sequence of revolutions continued with a military coup in 1799 that handed over power to one of revolutionary France's most successful new generals. As Napoleon's armies marched across Europe they carried revolutionary ideas with them. But they also, like the revolution itself, carried with them death. By the time Napoleon's armies had retreated from Russia and Spain, some 750,000 French soldiers had died.

NORTH AMERICA AND WESTERN EUROPE AD 1776–1815

FROM SUBJECT TO CITIZEN BY REVOLUTION

Modern times began with revolutions, movements from below that were inspired both by grievances and by ideas. Once started, they developed a life of their own which inevitably affected the everyday lives of ordinary people, changing human relations and human hopes, although not always as permanently as the revolutionaries themselves had wished.

The first two revolutions, in North America and in France, proclaimed the rights of man – of every man, though not yet of every woman. One revolution was the prelude to the other, for France's old regime supported the Americans against the British. Yet the previous history of the two countries and their ways of life were so different before the revolutions began that both the experience and the outcome of the two revolutions were bound to be strikingly different.

The American Revolution united colonists as widely different as Boston merchants and Virginian plantation owners against the British Redcoat army. They established a new national identity in the process, although they fell back on ideas that had their origins in Britain and which a minority of people in Britain shared.

New ranks for old

In the case of France, there was no great empire from which to break away, although in the aftermath of revolution there arose a Napoleonic empire with Paris as its centre. At first old distinctions of status crumbled, as revolutionary clubs called on the people of France and outside to cast off their chains. Later, new distinctions of status were introduced as Napoleon promoted his own court.

Both the Americans and the French had their new marching songs and their new flags, symbols of revolution. The Americans did not have to kill a

Woman of action *A French girl, fine clothes laid aside and armed with a sabre, symbolises the way in which women were drawn into the revolutionary movement, and fought alongside men in the streets.*

king, for George III remained on the British throne. The French, however, guillotined their king and his wife and began a Reign of Terror, when the revolution devoured its own children.

Even before the execution of the king and queen and the proclamation of a republic – the same form of government as that chosen by the Americans – a British observer had noticed how servants no longer wore livery, a badge of slavery, how all coats of arms in stone had disappeared over the large town houses of the aristocracy, and how one could buy in the streets a *Private Life of the Queen* which might have been entitled *The Woman of Pleasure*. Yet the same observer noted, too, how 'the common people are in general much better clothed than they were before the revolution, which may be ascribed to their not being so grievously taxed as before'.

Cheap bread and price control

In fact, the revolution, a new experience for men and women, who now became citizens, not subjects, was far from complete. By 1792 the peasants, half the population of France, had

Instant army *At the outset of the American Revolution, a group of citizen volunteers known as Minutemen was formed ready 'to stand at a minute's warning' to block the advance of the British Redcoats.*

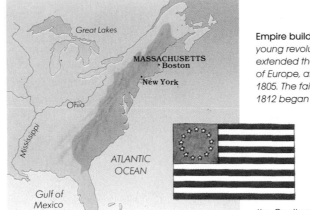

found satisfaction for their grievances against the nobility – who themselves had, on the eve of the revolution, played a key part in forcing change. There was, however, still considerable discontent in Paris and other cities, where revolutionaries asked questions about rights and justice, some of which had been raised earlier by pamphleteers. One petition of 1793 demanded what freedom meant 'when one class of men can starve another?'

Some revolutionaries attempted to respond to these demands, and in the second year of the revolution they at last succeeded in providing a daily bread ration to every citizen at a low price. Another achievement was the fixing of maximum prices; they had previously been continually rising, through the issue of paper money and heavy inflation.

Among many consequences of the revolution, one of the most remarkable was the forging, before Napoleon, of a citizen army based on conscription. 'Until the enemies of France have been chased off the territory of the Republic,' proclaimed a manifesto of 1793, 'every French person must stand ready to serve and support our armed forces. Young men will go to fight, husbands will forge weapons and manage the transport services; wives and daughters will make tents and uniforms and serve in the hospitals.'

In spite of the enthusiasm felt by the French, however, when Napoleon led his great army across Europe, carrying with it the idea of revolution, the results were

Flag of freedom *The original Stars and Stripes, unfurled in 1777, bore a stripe and star for each of the 13 eastern states of North America which had freed themselves from British rule. The 13 stars were said by the Continental Congress to represent the 'new constellation' of the United States.*

Words that led to deeds *In pre-revolutionary France, the subversive doctrine of liberty for all was the main talking point in fashionable coffee houses, where people from all walks of life met to discuss the political writings of the Englishman Tom Paine and other freethinkers.*

ambivalent. Some peoples responded readily to a revolutionary appeal that transcended frontiers. Other peoples, however, offered a sharp popular resistance. In Spain, for example, where Napoleon had many admirers even after he was overthrown, guerrillas made life extremely hard for uniformed French soldiers. One of the guerrilla bands was led by a peasant, another by a doctor.

After the fall of Napoleon and his exile to St Helena, the old order was restored. Nonetheless, ideas of revolution were not eliminated. There were revolutions in France in 1830, 1848 and 1870, and on each occasion they inspired revolutions elsewhere. In the 19th century the range of revolutionary ideas was widened to attract industrial workers and students. So also was the range of revolutionary experience. Though all revolutions had something in common, no two of them were completely alike.

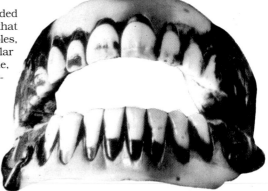

DENTURES FROM THE DEAD

Tooth-drawers descended like vultures on the battlefields of the 19th century to remove teeth from dead soldiers. They sold them to dentists who made them into sets of false teeth. Barrels of teeth were shipped to Europe during the American Civil War, and 'Waterloo teeth' such as this set were much sought after by Regency bucks in England.

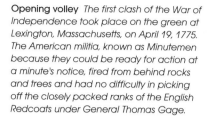

Symbols of war *The helmet of toughened leather, with a badge of St George, was worn by an English infantryman at Lexington and later battles. The powder horn, bearing a plan of defences at Charles Town, South Carolina, was carried by his American foe.*

REVOLUTION THAT BEGAN IN THE HOME

The American Revolution started at the table. British duties on sugar, Madeira and tea so annoyed the settlers in the 13 colonies along North America's Atlantic coastline that in the 1760s they began boycotts that converted a nation of tea drinkers into coffee addicts. Loyal Sons and Daughters of Liberty sipped chicory coffee, herbal brews and Dutch chocolate – laced with molasses, honey or maple syrup instead of taxable sugar. One New Jersey debutante, invited to tea at the Royal Governor's mansion, tossed her cup out of the window to signal her disdain for the enemy brew.

The Boston patriots who dressed as Indians and hurled a shipload of Far Eastern tea into the harbour went down in history as the leaders of the world's most famous tax revolt. Ladies and housewives, forbidden prominent roles in public politics of the time, enforced the boycotts in other ways. Daughters of Liberty sacked the warehouses of merchants suspected of stocking dutiable British goods, then

burned the imported products in huge bonfires that attracted throngs of new supporters to the cause. Refined ladies gave up their imported silks and lace in favour of homespun cloth, while towns sponsored spinning contests to supply thread for homemade textiles. As many as 70 local women might race their spinning wheels together in a central meeting house. Meanwhile, patriotic men wore sprigs of evergreen or cockades in their tricorn hats, lest anti-loyalist apprentices in the street knock them off with rocks or snowballs.

Breakdown of authority

Masters were supposed to keep their apprentices in line, but in these revolutionary times many forms of authority broke down. Parents initially complained that children no longer obeyed, then they began to try raising their children to become citizens capable of exercising their hard-won liberties. Adult offspring demanded a voice in their own marriages, and the rate of premarital conceptions rose. Laws passed during and after the revolution made divorce easier, too.

The schools echoed these shifts in family authority. Literacy spread, and the Greek and Roman classics were

given less emphasis, except for their teachings on Republican ideas of freedom and justice. A new corps of young teachers, many of them women, rewrote grammar school books to eliminate tributes to the king. Whole schools joined in re-enactments of battles and the heroic deeds of revolutionary leaders.

American religion, too, had been questioning regular clerical authority, favouring instead the law of individual conscience. Many patriotic preachers mounted their pulpits to decry the unholy actions of George III and to justify the rebellion. Every sabbath, ministers would 'thunder and lighten' against British oppression. Travelling music masters, who trained choirs for churches, began to write their own hymnals, newly garnished with local references and patriotic anthems. One such widely used book, *Billings*

New England Psalm Singer, had its publication delayed for more than a year so that it could be printed on homemade American paper, while its frontispiece noted that it could be bought 'under the Liberty Tree'.

In Boston, a mob pulled down the house of the Royal Stamp Collector and proceeded to use the wood to burn him in effigy. In the port of New York, a maddened crowd broke into the Lieutenant Governor's coach house to steal his carriage in which they paraded him in effigy to meet another crowd armed with a gallows. Then they hung, stoned and burned the figure in front of the governor's own windows in Fort George.

Hordes of apprentices, mechanics and seamen joined these rebellious festivities. Seamen had a particular

COLONIAL PRINTERS GO TO WAR

Shipping news and three-month-old reports from England filled the narrow columns of colonial America's early newspapers. In the 1760s, however, these were swept aside by spirited articles of revolutionary comment, and heated letters to the editor. The colonists attacked those who 'conspired against the liberty of the colonies', calling royal officials 'dirty, drinking, drabbing contaminated knots of thieves and beggars'.

The Pennsylvania newspaper of July 8, 1776, shown on the right, opens with the words of the Declaration of Independence adopted four days earlier. Printers ran their wooden presses day and night to feed the colonists' appetite for news. Each paper was passed from hand to hand, reaching as many as 15 or 20 people. Post riders took bundles of rebel publications to towns across the colonies. Pamphlets and broadsheets could be found on the trestle tables of taverns, and pasted to the walls of buildings. Handbills were read aloud to apprentices hunched over their cobbling benches, idlers on the village green, and labouring men drinking their cider. One pamphlet, Tom Paine's *Common Sense*, became America's first best-seller, selling 500,000 copies in 1776.

VOL. V.

DUNLAP's

Pennsylvania

OR

GENERAL

DUNLAP's
Pac

TH
ADVERT

MONDAY, JULY 8th, 1776.

grudge against the mother country in those years, since the Royal Navy had impressed them into forced service. Even worse, off-duty British sailors competed for work in colonial port towns, labouring for as little as half the wages local people demanded. The revolutionary practice of tarring and feathering loyalists and royal officials sprang from ritual punishments sailors used to apply to miscreants at sea. Patriots also took to riding unpopular Britons out of town on a fence rail.

Some of these ritual punishments meted out to supporters of the crown were taken over by militias as the war dragged on. Local militias patrolled the large parts of the colonies that had no garrisons of the regular army to protect them. These militias, like the ragged colonial troops, usually had to muster all their own supplies and arms. To fit himself out with flintlock, powder, shot and provisions a man could spend two weeks of his pay.

Meanwhile, metals ran out throughout North America, which had few foundries. Housewives contributed to the war effort by melting down their pitchers, mugs and window weights for bullets. Statues of King George and other symbols of crown authority were pulled down and promptly turned into ammunition, too. Daughters of Liberty saved rags for bandages and canvassed houses to collect blankets for troops and militia patrols. Soldiers who came from seaport towns could get sailcloth for tents, but other bands of rebels sat shivering through the cold nights clad in their buckskin shirts, with no shelter from wind and rain apart from the protection of a cave or rocky overhang.

As men disappeared for months of war, women and children took over their tasks. Women made and collected edibles and other supplies that could enable the Continental Army to survive. All these little changes in daily life added up to a new way of seeing themselves and the world for the rebels who were soon to become Americans.

During the seven years which passed between the drawing up of the Declaration of Independence in 1776 and the signing of the peace in 1783, the world of the American colonists changed enormously. The struggle for independence overturned old habits of eating, drinking, dressing, singing, praying, reading and politicking. At the time of the revolution, fewer than half of the colonial population had reached their sixteenth birthdays, so it was the energy and exuberance of young people, not the caution of their elders, that fed the flames of revolt.

Living death *Captured American troops were kept prisoner by the British on old ships, like the Jersey (below), anchored off Brooklyn. Some 11,000 prisoners died in this hulk from malnutrition and disease.*

Rebels' money *Even before the outbreak of the war, American colonies began to issue their own paper money, defying a British ban. The Massachusetts shilling note was issued in 1776. War costs, and widespread forgery, debased the currency.*

Rebels' tree *Elms, oaks and even poles in towns and villages became 'Liberty Trees', or meeting places for revolutionary crowds. The mobs often rushed off to punish loyalists, and royal officials enforcing the hated British taxation acts.*

SHARP EDGE OF TERROR IN FRANCE

It was upon the ruins of the old prison of the Bastille that thousands of National Guardsmen and citizens danced on the night of July 14, 1790. Fireworks soared, illuminations blazed, and from huge pavilions floated the new symbol of the Tricolour. Paris gave itself up to an access of joy, for in the year since the hated Bastille had been torn down, what had the city, and the French people, not achieved?

Ancient seigneurial perquisites had been abolished and Church lands nationalised. A citizen's army had been founded, and the Constituent Assembly had made a solemn Declaration of the Rights of Man. No longer was Louis XVI permitted to remain aloof at Versailles. Now he was installed in the Tuileries, in the heart of the city where, without much enthusiasm, he undertook to wear the red and blue cockade of Paris, asking only that the royal white should be added as a third element in the new colours of France.

True, not much seemed to have been done about the food shortages, but nothing could stop the electrifying sense of new beginnings that spread through the districts. In many ways, Paris was still a medieval city, in whose various quarters the same crafts had been practised for centuries. Masons worked in Saint-Paul, for example, and furniture makers in Croix-Rouge, while the faubourgs, or suburbs, of Montmartre and Saint-Marcel were renowned for cloth, breweries and the Gobelins tapestry works.

The various districts tended to be self-contained, and as communication was by word of mouth only, great events might be taking place in one area, while the rest of the city went about

Memento *This plate marked the storming of the Bastille – which was found to hold no more than seven prisoners.*

its daily affairs. A riot might occur in one part of the city without another hearing of it until days later. Those who wished to be in the know therefore took themselves to traditional assembly points such as the Jardin des Tuileries, which since the revolution's earliest days had become almost an outdoor extension of parliament. Between the bookshops and scribbling pamphleteers the crowds strolled, pausing now and then to be exhorted by politicians, entertained by buskers and titillated by scandalmongers.

Many chose to visit the Palais Royal with its numerous cafés which offered infinite shades of political opinion and attracted women, as well as men, into political discussion and action. There were cafés for revolutionaries, for lawyers, for National Guardsmen and extremists, just as there were cafés famous for their beer, for their decor or for their novelty – such as the Café Mécanique, where the coffee was pumped up through the central legs of the tables. In the brave new world, all relics of the past were abandoned, few of them with greater enthusiasm than the *culottes*, or knee breeches, and the wigs and stockings of the old régime. The well-dressed revolutionary appeared wearing tricolour trousers – hence his nickname of *sans-culottes* – a short woollen jacket, egalitarian clogs and a red Cap of Liberty. This was the correct dress for manning the barricades, at least. The dandies of the period, the *Incroyables*, or 'Incredibles', wore pantaloons, tight-fitting, long-skirted, coloured coats and cravats that rose in six folds to meet the shaggy locks that covered the ears. Their female companions, the *Merveilleuses*, or 'Marvellous Ones', wore body-revealing Grecian tunics.

Fashion was only the froth on the surface of change. More confusing were the changes in language, in the calendar and in forms of address. *Monsieur* and *Madame* smacked too much of deference, and were altered by law to 'Citizen' and 'Citizeness'. The formal *vous* for 'you' was also dropped, since it was the manner in which servants addressed masters. Everyone was to be addressed by the informal *tu*; anyone who continued to use the old form might incur suspicion of aristocratic sympathies. Place names which incorporated names of royal

Bread crisis *Revolution failed to feed the people. The bitter winter of 1794-5 made roads impassable and brought famine to the cities. In Paris, crowds waited all night for a bread ration of 8 oz (225 g) a day.*

The Tricolour, symbol of the new republic

persons or saints were expunged, while earnest patriots gave their children classical or revolutionary names such as Brutus, Fructidor and République. God was officially abolished and given the new name of 'Supreme Being', while Notre Dame Cathedral was renamed the Temple of Reason. The calendar of the Christian era was dropped, and 1793 became Year I of the new age. It was divided into 12 months, each of 30 days, with names such as Brumaire, the misty month, Florial, the month of flowers, and so on. Each month was subdivided into three units of ten days. More enduring was the institution of a new system of weights and measures, based on the metre. Though resisted by the French at first, it was to gain worldwide recognition.

Even as Parisians laughed at the extravagances of the city's festivals, the revolutionary madness of the Terror was fast gaining momentum. Inspired by Maximilien Robespierre and other extremists, earlier purgings of counter-revolutionary elements had grown into a juggernaut that almost of its own volition crushed anyone who failed in the slightest way to conform.

From the grim cells of the Conciergerie and other anterooms of death up to 70 people a day were trundled down the Rue Saint-Honoré

Kindly cut *In 1789, Dr Joseph Guillotin suggested that France should adopt the humane form of execution machine already in use in Italy. The Assembly was impressed by its swift, slicing action – as demonstrated in the tests performed on 15 bodies provided by a hospital – and in April 1792 it decapitated its first French victim, a highwayman. By the end of the Terror the king and queen and some 17,000 others had died beneath the guillotine's blade.*

WATCHERS BY THE SCAFFOLD

To speed the dispatch of his enemies, on June 10, 1794 Robespierre withdrew the right of prisoners to defend themselves, and limited the choice of juries to acquittal or death. Consequently, the number of victims bound for the guillotine grew to a flood. Most Parisians, sickened by death, avoided the square where the guillotine stood. Prominent among regular spectators were the *tricoteuses*, or 'knitters' – women who stood or sat daily by the scaffold with knitting in hand to watch the heads roll. With their jeering for aristocrats who showed signs of fear, these harpies became a symbol of the Terror, and were dubbed 'The Furies of the Guillotine'.

> *'Make sure you show my head to the people, it's well worth it!'*
>
> GEORGES DANTON, 1794

to the guillotine. Large sections of the populace remained indifferent, hardly bothering to look up as the tumbrels went by. Only the highlights impressed – the trial of King Louis XVI at which women of fashion drank liqueurs and ate ices; his subsequent execution; and the execution of his queen, Marie Antoinette, whose reported escapades with her attendants dressed as milkmaids in the grounds of Versailles had outraged the public.

Other deaths caused comment: that of the leading revolutionary Danton, cursing to the last breath, Robespierre's agonised scream as the executioner tore the bandage from his shattered jaw, and the terror of Mme du Barry, the aged mistress of Louis XV.

Otherwise Parisians went about their business as normally as possible, thronging the cafés and strolling in the Champs Elysées. Perhaps they did not fully comprehend the horror. The guillotine seemed so swift – Sanson, the executioner, spoke of removing 22 heads in 36 minutes – and painless, so far as anyone knew, and the victims generally put on a show of courage. Had more of them exhibited the fear of Mme du Barry, the populace might have sickened sooner of the terror.

Of more immediate concern were food shortages. Bad harvests reduced the poor to near starvation; even the better-off were paying high prices for ox heads and hooves. The execution of the king had united Europe against France, and armies were massing on her borders to support the Royalist uprisings in the provinces. War on a massive scale was now inevitable.

Vintage award *A certificate of patriotism was awarded to a winegrower for selling his product in revolutionary pitchers.*

Tyrants' downfall *Finally the revolution devoured its own, as the Paris mob turned against the leaders of the Terror and sent them, in their turn, to the guillotine. Maximilien Robespierre was the last to perish, in July 1794.*

The die is cast *On October 6, 1789, the Paris mob marched on Versailles to demand bread and to force the king to return to the city. The same evening, the royal family was brought to the Tuileries Palace by the triumphant crowd who waved the severed heads of the guards who tried to stop them. The path of revolution was set.*

New gods *One of the feasts decreed by the revolution was that of the 'Supreme Being'. In the Champ de Mars, the artist Jacques-Louis David built a mountain topped by a 'Tree of Liberty' and a statue of Hercules. In front of a huge crowd, the National Assembly marched in procession, preceded by orchestras and choirs.*

FIGHTING AND DYING WITH NAPOLEON

Soldiers' farewell *Napoleon's infantry are cheered on their way by the people of Frankfurt as they march against Austria. Many German states welcomed the French forces and gave lodgings to their officers.*

Irons for the Duke *In the field, the Duke of Wellington ate and drank from solid-silver plates and beakers. He carried his personal cutlery in a bottle-shaped case.*

To stand in line, even a line thousands strong, awaiting the onslaught of Napoleon's legions was a fearsome experience. Artillery, firing from no more than half a mile (1 km) away, slaughtered entire ranks with a single salvo. The guns of the defenders replied, but their infantry, armed with muskets that were hardly effective at much over 100 yds (91 m), could do nothing but wait and watch the advance of the massive dark columns, whose menace was emphasised by the slow drumbeats that kept the step.

Always in the van were the burly, moustachioed veterans of the Imperial Guard, each one of whom was a senior NCO who had learned his trade in a dozen battles. As the lines closed, the firing of the lightly armed skirmishers of both sides redoubled and the cavalry prowled, seeking a gap through which a wedge could be driven. At last, when columns and line were about 70 yds (64 m) apart, the first volleys were fired into the tightly packed masses opposite. Loading, priming, aiming, firing, a good soldier could get off three rounds a minute, which was about all the time he had before the bayonets of the attackers crossed those of the defence.

What followed was bludgeon work, stabbing and firing amid the screams of the wounded and the throat-catching reek of powder smoke. Then the sheer weight of the battalions in column carried them through to deploy in the rear of the enemy line and roll it up piecemeal. Shock tactics and speed of manoeuvre carried the Napoleonic armies to victory at Marengo and Austerlitz, Jena and Wagram.

In August 1799, General Bonaparte, as Napoleon then was, had abandoned his army, trapped in Egypt, and sailed secretly for France. In November, at the age of 30, he ousted the French

THE CHAOS OF A NAPOLEONIC BATTLE

On the battlefield of the early 19th century, the commanders' carefully planned troop movements often ended in a hand-to-hand melee of confusion, noise and carnage, in which even the generals were hard put to distinguish their own troops from the enemy. Infantry and cavalry struggled to rally round their standard, flourished bravely (above) amid the thickest of the fighting at the Battle of Borodino, fought near Moscow on September 7, 1812, and spelling doom for

Napoleon's plans to conquer Russia. After devastating artillery fire from both sides came the savagery of close combat, as Napoleon directed wave upon wave of troops against the Russian defenders from a nearby hilltop. Each assault found its way more impeded than the last by the litter of bodies and discarded equipment. At the end of the day Napoleon had lost some 30,000 troops – one in three of his entire Grande Armée.

Lethal fruit *Hand grenades, named for their pomegranate shape, consisted of an iron case filled with gunpowder and fired by a fuse.*

parliament and appointed himself First Consul. With all Europe in arms against him, the first task he set himself was the reorganisation of the French military machine. To supplement the volunteers of the National Guard and new conscripts he recruited veterans, emigrés and even officers of the old regime. It was a new kind of army, depending less upon brutal discipline than upon patriotism, revolutionary élan, some profit and the personal magnetism of the First Consul.

There was nothing particularly novel about the Republican Army, or the Imperial Army as it became after Bonaparte had assumed the title of Emperor in 1804. Its weapons were much the same as those of a century earlier. Cavalry were armed with sabre or lance, the infantry with smoothbore muskets and the artillery with smoothbore cannon firing solid shot. The strength of Bonaparte's armies lay in their manoeuvrability and in their single-minded insistence on destroying the main body of the enemy before occupying terrain or bothering with his lines of communication. Even before battle was joined, Bonaparte the ex-artilleryman made sure that half his infantry's work was done by light field guns galloped up to the front.

These very strengths, however, also contained the seeds of eventual ruin. In his hard-hitting, fast-moving armies, slow-moving supply columns had no place, and for reasons both economic and strategic it was always Bonaparte's

policy that his troops should live off the land. It was not a policy that endeared itself to the invaded populace, whose objections led to reprisals, hangings and burned villages. Neither, except in the early days of an invasion, was it practical. When the army had eaten all the produce of the area, the people starved – but so too did the army.

> *'A village should feed a battalion for a week, or a division for a day.'*
>
> NAPOLEON BONAPARTE, c. 1800

Napoleon could have learned wisdom from the humblest soldier on his Portuguese campaign. He would have found him, with other conscripts, on a rocky, rain-lashed hillside above the River Tagus in its winter guise of tumbling, brown-green water. Like his comrades in the 3rd Battalion of the 21st Infantry, he was dressed in the tattered remains of a faded blue uniform, but was more fortunate than some in that he had a pair of boots taken from the corpse of a hussar. Like his companions, he was buoyed up by the hope that after Marshal Massena

had driven Wellington and the British and Portuguese armies into the sea at Lisbon, the city and its riches would be theirs for the taking. But even before the weary French troops reached the Tagus they were aware that something was wrong. For a mile back from the river there was not even an olive tree to give cover. The entire clifftop along the far bank had been turned into a fortress, bristling with guns. Based upon the Tagus and the old citadel of Torres Vedras, Wellington had built towering redoubts and more than 150 hilltop forts, using peasant labour over the past six months.

Sickness soon entered the French ranks. They seldom saw food, and in their misery were only too aware that the enemy's armies behind the lines were growing sleek and fit on rations brought in by sea. They huddled round their smoking fires and wondered when they were going to retreat.

So too did Wellington. But Massena hung on until March, and when at last he began to fall back, two-thirds of his soldiers had died from sickness or starvation. The British, in hot pursuit, were horrified to find houses, chapels and pits filled with skeletons and corpses, many mutilated. Whether they included any conscripts of the 3rd Battalion, history does not relate.

LIVING OFF THE LAND

Generous in issuing his army with flags, and mottoes with which to embellish them, Napoleon paid less attention to food supplies, expecting his men to forage in the lands they overran. An infantryman (above) serving in the Russian campaign of 1812 has stolen a half-starved nag, together with the livestock hanging from the saddle, from a farmyard. Within a fortnight of crossing the Russian border the French army had eaten all its rations, and had to advance through a countryside cleared of crops and animals.

In Portugal two years earlier the French army were reduced to living on maize porridge, and the only meat they ate came from dogs and cats. In desperation, they tortured the local peasants to make them reveal the whereabouts of their caches of food. Such behaviour made Napoleon's armies the most feared and hated in Europe.

Battle's aftermath *The dead and the dying lie among shattered gun carriages and broken weapons on the battlefield of Austerlitz, scene of Napoleon's victory in 1805 over the forces of Austria and Russia.*

Rough surgery *Field medicine in Napoleonic times was mainly a matter of stitching wounds and amputating limbs as fast as possible. Conditions did not improve until the Crimean War (left), with the reforms of Florence Nightingale.*

Balancing act *One of the most dangerous tasks at sea was struggling to furl a sail in rain and wind. One slip meant death, for a ship under sail could not be stopped or turned to rescue a man fallen overboard.*

BRITAIN'S WOODEN BULWARKS

Superlative seamanship and gunnery made the British navy everywhere master of the oceans. Such skills were acquired in a hard and often brutal school. Naval communications were in their infancy, and each ship, large or small, was virtually a world on its own. Each too was a finely tuned machine, whose crew were the cogs and levers that, by hauling and heaving in their allotted places, made the machine work.

The will that controlled the machine was that of the captain, whose authority over the crew was near-absolute. There were mad captains and sadistic captains whose joy it was to have men roped up to a grating and flogged into insensibility with a cat-o'-nine-tails. But there were decent men, too, who believed that a spell of cleaning out the heads–the ship's two lavatories, high in the bows–acted as a more effective punishment than the lash. Others had dazzling prize money to offer.

Salt pork and paltry pay

The call of adventure needed to be strong to make a man volunteer for the navy. The pay was abysmal; the able seaman's 26 shillings a month had not been raised since Cromwell's day. The food consisted of salt beef or pork, pease pudding and biscuits and was not particularly appetising, though a good messman could mix these unpromising ingredients into quite a palatable dish known as lobscouse. The food was washed down by alarming amounts of beer and rum, or wine on tropical stations, always supplied with a ration of fruit juice to prevent an attack of scurvy. The navy was also a high-risk career, though generally the enemy was the least of the sailor's problems. The hymn by the Victorian poet William Whiting that asks the Eternal Father to save those in peril on the sea 'from rock and tempest, fire and foe', listed them in the right order of danger. In the 23 years of the French wars, during which the navy constantly patrolled the oceans of the world, 344 ships were wrecked in storms, accidentally burned or blew up, or simply vanished without trace, while only ten were lost through enemy action.

Human casualties through accident were also high – hardly surprising when men on the upper yards were called upon to perform tasks that would daunt a trapeze artist, not only in good weather but on black nights and in howling gales.

Then, too, a gun might break loose, to trundle its 2 tons of weight about the deck, crushing everything in its path. Few sailors could swim, since once a sailor had fallen overboard the ship could not stop to pick him up, and a knowledge of how to swim would only have prolonged his suffering. Fractures and rheumatism were common, and ruptures almost an epidemic. Yellow fever decimated crews in the tropics, and typhus came aboard with men brought from the prisons. All the same, casualties in battle were relatively light, at least in contrast with

Reluctant service *During wartime, the navy resorted to a 'press gang' to drag unwilling rustics, idlers and former seamen off to sea.*

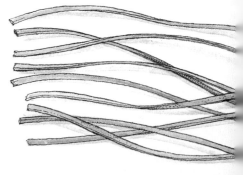

Slaughter at sea *Splintered masts, sails ripped by gunshot, and seamen struggling in the water symbolise the horrors of naval warfare. A painting by De Loutherbourg depicts the Battle of the Glorious First of June in 1794, when the British beat the French off Ushant, Brittany.*

those of the French. This was due in part to the French practice of firing at masts and sails to cripple ships, while the British fired on the down roll into the enemy's hull, turning the 'tween-decks into a hell of flying iron and wooden splinters.

The Royal Navy spent much of its time escorting convoys, or blockading French ports – sometimes for as long as two years at a stretch, which could demoralise ships' crews thirsting for action. But battle was the navy's reason for being, and it was something it did extremely well. In those last years of sailing warships there was a terrible beauty in the sun-filled, cloud-like sails and ponderous hulls of the opposing fleets as they manoeuvred for position and wind advantage.

> *'My wandering habitation, the* Alceste: *the happiest home I ever knew.'*
> MEMORIES OF AN OLD FRIGATE HAND

Probably the first intimation that most of the crews had of the forthcoming fight was the order 'Clear ship for action!' Frantic activity followed as the partitions of officers' cabins were knocked down, benches and mess tables were stowed and all inessential gear was carried to the hold or thrown overboard. The long gun decks were cleared and sanded to give bare feet a grip, powder monkeys ran with charges, sharpshooters climbed to the fighting tops and marine marksmen lined the rails.

Gun crews closed up, stripped to the waist and wearing bandannas about their ears. There was the deep rumble and thud of the guns being run out, then a disciplined silence fell as the fleets entered the last slow movement of the long approach. Gun captains looked along the lengths of their guns to the empty square of ocean visible through the ports.

Suddenly, and shockingly close, the square was filled with the dark red hull of a French warship, wet and glistening as it heaved itself up from a roll, and every few feet sprouting the gaping mouth of a gun. An officer's whistle shrilled, and symmetry dissolved in

the iron punch of a broadside, the reek of powder smoke and the screams of men. To build the hull of a 74-gun ship, a so-called 'third-rater', one of the navy's workhorses, took 2000 oak trees, each at least a century old. The lower sections of her masts were composed of several fir trees, bound together by iron and bedded in the

keel, and her upper masts and yards were generally single firs. Her reason for existence was to carry her guns to the enemy, and to do this she required a crew of about 590. Some – the sail-makers, the carpenters, the gunners – were specialists; others, such as the topmen who worked high on the yards, and the forecastle men, were skilled seamen. The rest were unskilled hands, employed to haul on ropes and scrub the decks. There was also a detachment of Royal Marines, and one or two oddly named categories like the 'lady of the gunroom', an elderly seaman who looked after the midshipmen, and the 'widows' men' – actually fictional names on the ship's roll whose wages

Time off *A sailor's life was not all hardship and privation. At sea in the tropics (right) officers stroll at ease beneath awnings. Back in harbour (below), prostitutes swarm aboard, while a sailor scrapes out a hornpipe on his fiddle.*

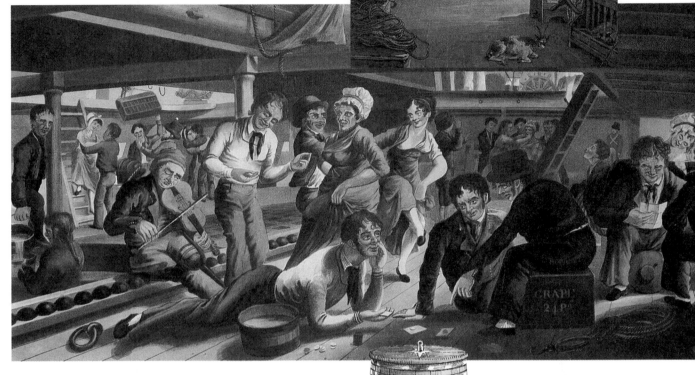

would pay a pension to dependants of officers killed in action. Most ships had a number of women on board, who were nominally at least wives of crew members. In action, they carried powder to the guns and nursed the wounded.

Officers apart, all lived on the gun decks; each man was allotted a space 14 in (360 mm) wide for his hammock, and a place at the table between the guns where he ate his ship's biscuit, drank his

The rum barrel

grog and spent his time off watch. The life was without privacy of any kind, and in rough weather, with the ship rolling and pitching and men with inexperienced stomachs vomiting, it could be pure hell. Yet the wonder of it was that many seamen, recalling old friends, the hours spent yarning off watch, and the tot of rum doled out every morning and evening, looked back to the years spent aboard their ships with nostalgia and affection.

Swinging the cat *Most feared punishment, the cat-o'-nine-tails had nine thongs that left marks like the scratches of a cat. Offenders often had to make their own 'cat' before being flogged.*

INTO THE AGE OF MACHINES

Almost parallel in time with the French and American Revolutions there occurred another revolution whose effect upon the human condition was to be even more far-reaching. It began in Britain, and became known as the Industrial Revolution. Hitherto, the term 'industry' had been used to describe a human virtue – hard work, or application to a task. Now it acquired a wider meaning, to describe a whole sector of the economy that was to contribute far more to wealth than agriculture had ever done – though often exacting a high price in individual misery.

Machines in themselves were not new to the age. The true innovation was the harnessing of steam, which enabled more powerful and efficient machines to be applied to the production of coal and minerals and the manufacture of goods such as textiles. Most startling innovations were the railways and the steamships that seemed to shrink Time itself. Britain's lead was real but short-lived. Soon other countries began to progress, each in its own way, along the road of advancing technology.

WESTERN EUROPE
AD 1775–1900

STEAM POWER AS SLAVE – AND MASTER

The story of the steam engine begins with the Ancient Greeks. Around AD 60, Hero of Alexandria described how 'vapours of water' could be used to open temple doors and blow horns without any apparent human agency, and to create other special effects with which priests could awe congregations.

There followed an interval of some 1650 years before an English iron-monger and brassfounder, Thomas Newcomen of Dartmouth in Devon, devised the first practical piston and cylinder engine. In 1712 he put the engine to work pumping water from a flooded mine in Staffordshire. By 1775 about 100 Newcomen engines were being used in the coal mines along the Tyne alone, and a further 60 in the Cornish metal mines.

The possibility of harnessing steam engines to drive machinery was now nearing reality. The greatest of the pioneers was an instrument maker from Glasgow named James Watt, who arrived in Birmingham in 1775 and improved the Newcomen engine by attaching a condenser and steam jacket. The greater energy which these additions provided impressed the manufacturer Matthew Boulton, who took Watt into partnership.

Boulton and Watt applied for patents and built a number of pumping engines for mines and breweries; both knew, however, that the real money lay in providing engines for the burgeoning textile industries, whose machinery so far had been operated by water or animal power. It was a demand of which many other engineers were equally aware, but again Watt led the way with his rotative engine – an engine that would turn wheels. By this means, not only textile machinery but a myriad other manufacturing

Life at the mill *By the middle of the 19th century, more than a million workers were employed in Britain's textile industry. Many of the loom operatives were women, who worked long hours in unhealthy conditions.*

Triumph of steam *The line from Liverpool to Manchester opened in 1830 was the first to rely entirely on steam locomotives and to carry a high proportion of passenger traffic.*

processes were to be harnessed to steam. In the midst of his innovations, Watt even took time to find a way to measure the new energy. After experiments with a strong dray horse, he established it in units of horsepower, a single one of which he defined as 33,000 foot-pounds of work per minute – a foot-pound being the force of a one pound weight acting through a distance of one foot.

The quest for a self-propelling steam engine was at least as old as the demand for one that drove machinery. The credit for the first successful steam car justly belongs to the French army officer Nicholas Cugnot, who was imprisoned for driving one along a road at a slow walking pace in 1769. It was Frenchmen, too, crowding the banks of the Seine, who in 1803 witnessed the first successful operation of a steamboat, though in this case the inventor was an American, Robert Fulton. From these small beginnings, well within the span of a single lifetime, there grew the railways and the steamship lines that between them girdled the earth.

> *'Nature can be conquered, if we can but find her weak side.'*
>
> JAMES WATT, 1765

Cheap goods manufactured by steam-driven machines and cheaply delivered by steam-driven transport would, it was envisaged, create a new Utopia from which drudgery was banished. But there was a snag: Alexander Ure (1778-1857), the Scottish author of the *Philosophy of Manufactures*, pointed out that 'it is the constant aim and tendency of every improvement in machinery to supersede human labour or to diminish its cost'. This was to be achieved, added Ure, 'by substituting the industry of women and children for that of men; or that of ordinary labourers for trained artisans'. In the

earliest stages of industrialisation this was a philosophy that held great appeal for many factory owners, who staffed their factories with cheap labour working long, monotonous hours, often in conditions that were hazardous, or injurious to health. For many working people, steam was not a benefactor but a slave master. Karl Marx, who was exiled in Britain and saw the industrialisation of Europe, with the discontent it fostered among the workers, regarded social and political revolution as inevitable: the old order would be swept away and a workers' state take its place. Gradually change did come, but not by revolution. It was achieved as the working classes won the vote, and as hours and conditions of work were brought under control by trade-union pressure and state intervention.

As machines became more complex they required more highly organised training, including an element of theory. In the last decades of the 19th century, technical education was more highly developed in Germany than in Britain. The Germans, it has been said, developed their schools in advance of industrialisation, while the British by contrast developed them only in response to the changing times. It was Germany which in Europe led the way in applying science to industry.

Industrialisation opened up new opportunities for skilled men and raised expectations for all workers. Life need never be the same again.

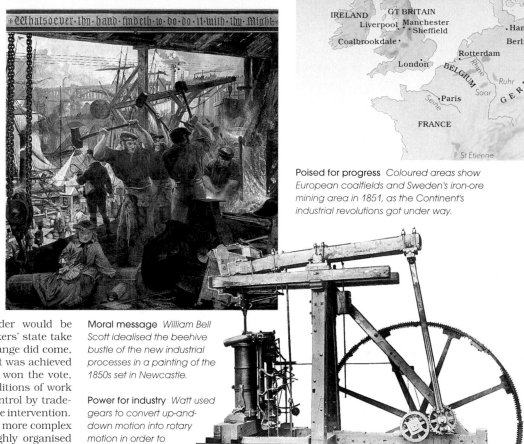

Moral message *William Bell Scott idealised the beehive bustle of the new industrial processes in a painting of the 1850s set in Newcastle.*

Power for industry *Watt used gears to convert up-and-down motion into rotary motion in order to drive machines.*

Poised for progress *Coloured areas show European coalfields and Sweden's iron-ore mining area in 1851, as the Continent's industrial revolutions got under way.*

Things to come *In an 1830 artist's view of future traffic problems, steam planes soar over an exploding steam car and a man on steam-driven stilts, while ladies in a coach choke on smoke from another's chimney.*

MACHINES TO BRING HOME THE HARVEST

The Mop Fair was a great event of the country calendar. It was a hiring fair, at which farm hands and servants were engaged for a year to work for a fixed wage, plus board and lodging. Labourers stood in the streets wearing a token in their lapel or hatband to indicate their trade: shepherd, horseman, stockman, dairymaid. The girls were gaily ribboned and the men sported gaudy silk neckties.

By the later part of the 18th century, new machinery and scientific techniques of crop rotation and selection were beginning to make agriculture more efficient and productive. Hand in hand with the Industrial Revolution proceeded an agricultural revolution. Still, however, much of farming life went on following traditional ways. Some people considered the Mop Fair demeaning, but in reality it enabled the farm hands to size up their

Victory celebration *Farming folk depended on winning their annual struggle against time and the weather. A harvest supper, sometimes preceded by a roistering procession, such as the one captured by Thomas Rowlandson in 1823, marked a bumper harvest gathered in.*

prospective masters. Not every deal worked out: in some market towns the hiring fair was followed a fortnight later by a Runaway Fair at which unhappy servants could seek fresh employment. On the farm itself, the men often lived in separate rooms over the stables while the women lodged in the house. Migrant workers also helped out when seasonal demand required. At harvest time the men, women and children of entire villages – even of whole country towns – would be out in the fields, often working 16 hour days, and by moonlight if

necessary, to get the crops in. The corn was cut, using a sickle or scythe, by men advancing in a staggered line. It was painful work, for the straw scratched in the hot sun, and tempers often flared, especially if one reaper strayed into the path of another, breaking the working rhythm. Richard Jefferies, son of a Wiltshire farmer, recorded that 'no one could stand the harvest-field as a reaper except he had been born to it. Their necks grew black. Their open chests were always bare, and flat, and stark. The breast bone was burned black, and their arms, tough as ash, seemed cased in leather'.

Behind the men came the women and children who scooped up the corn and bound it into sheaves. This was a task with its own rhythm. The sheaves were stacked and left to dry in the sun and wind before being carted back to the farm. Here the corn was built into ricks to finish drying under thatch or tarpaulin, and raised on brushwood or iron stands to assist airing and give protection against rats. A year's work depended on good weather and an efficient harvest, and wet weather,

carrying risks of rot and mildew, might spell disaster. Steam engines came into use on the farm by the middle of the century, although steam-powered machinery never supplanted the heavy horse, which provided all the motive power needed on many farms. Great breeds that reached maturity during the 19th century included the Suffolk, Clydesdale, and British Shire, and the continental Percheron, Ardennes and Belgian. Weighing a ton each, these giants ploughed, raked and carried mountainous loads.

Enclosure of common grazing land had forced country folk to abandon the family cow, so that farmers came to monopolise production of cheese, butter and milk. The dairy was always an important installation, and some farms also had a cheese room, partly sunken into the ground to maintain an even temperature for the maturing process. The Cheddar caves had for centuries been used for this purpose, but it was only in 1856 that Joseph Harding established a procedure for making farmhouse Cheddar.

Milking of dairy herds was done in the early morning and late afternoon. As often as not the milkmaid worked in the open field or cow yard, sitting on a

Paint your wagon *Each part of Britain had a distinctive style of wagon for hauling heavy loads. This West Midlands version had broad wheels for rough tracks, and a deep body. Detachable poles supported hay or corn.*

Modern marvels *Rows of top-hatted gentlemen farmers admire a display of the latest machinery. Steam ploughs, turnip slicers, rotary diggers and other implements helped to make farming more efficient.*

Keeping cool *The stone-floored dairy, sometimes beautifully tiled, was sited on a north wall and often shaded with trees.*

Dairy bygones *Beside the well-worn milking stool is a table used for storing cheeses.*

IMPROVING THE LIVESTOCK

People began selective stock breeding as early as the Stone Age, by domesticating the fittest wild animals and breeding only from them. Robert Bakewell, a Leicestershire farmer's son born in 1725, introduced more scientific methods. He selected breeding stock from animals which already displayed the qualities he wished to develop, such as better wool or higher milk yields. Careful in-breeding and the eradication of unsuitable beasts helped him to achieve his goal, especially with Longhorn cattle, Leicester sheep and Large White pigs.

Proud owner *A farmer shares the portrait artist's canvas with a sheep carefully bred to produce a highly profitable fleece.*

stool. Her head buried deeply in the cow's haunches, she gently stroked the creature to direct a frothing jet of warm milk into her pail. Metal buckets, mass produced in factories, contributed to improved hygiene, but it was still a job to prevent the cow from ruining a successful session by sticking a hind foot or dropping a cow pat into the pail. There was no bottled milk. From the dairy, milk was taken around the towns and villages by pony and trap in 50 gallon churns, and housewives brought their own jugs to the churn. From 1850 milk was carried by rail to the cities, using cold-water cooling apparatus. Apart from dairying, women did much of the physical work. Stone-picking gangs, chiefly women and girls, cleared the land after it had been ploughed and harrowed. They pulled weeds and thistles and picked fruit in the orchards; in winter, with fingers numbed by the cold, they cleaned turnips and beet for cattle. 'They would come home up to their knees in mud and wet,' wrote a contemporary, 'and then they would have the household work to do, the washing, cooking, mending, and all the other jobs which come along when there is a big family to do for.' British farming underwent cycles of

prosperity and depression. The Golden Age lasted from about 1850 to 1870, when the use of modern techniques and fertilisers, with better drainage and mechanisation, contributed to bumper yields. A series of wet summers followed, but what triggered a crisis was transatlantic competition. Wheat grown on the great prairies of the United States was shipped across and sold at prices that proved disastrous for British farmers.

Farming throughout Europe was affected by the American challenge. French and German governments raised tariffs to keep out American wheat. In the 1880s, frozen meat began to arrive from Australia and New Zealand, and by the end of the century tinned food was being imported. Cottage industries had largely been eradicated, so that jobless country folk had to drift to the towns – or emigrate.

Holland and Denmark had led the way in introducing machinery into agriculture, but elsewhere on the Continent farming changed more slowly than in Britain. The French peasant, for example, remained more independent than his British counter-part. There was plenty of common grazing land and he had little use for machinery, so that at the end of the century French farming remained largely unmechanised. Fertilisers were available, but older practices endured. Men crisscrossed French towns with barrels buying human excrement and selling it to farmers as fertiliser.

Milk bar *Stone bottles of cow's milk helped to feed hungry piglets.*

Protection *Workers cast seed using large gloves. Horses drawing lawn-cutters on estates wore boots to prevent hoof marks on the grass.*

Mixed blessing *Steam-powered threshing machines began from the 1840s to take the drudgery out of separating the grain from the chaff. Now that the hand-operated flail was obsolete, many farmers cut costs by getting rid of redundant labourers.*

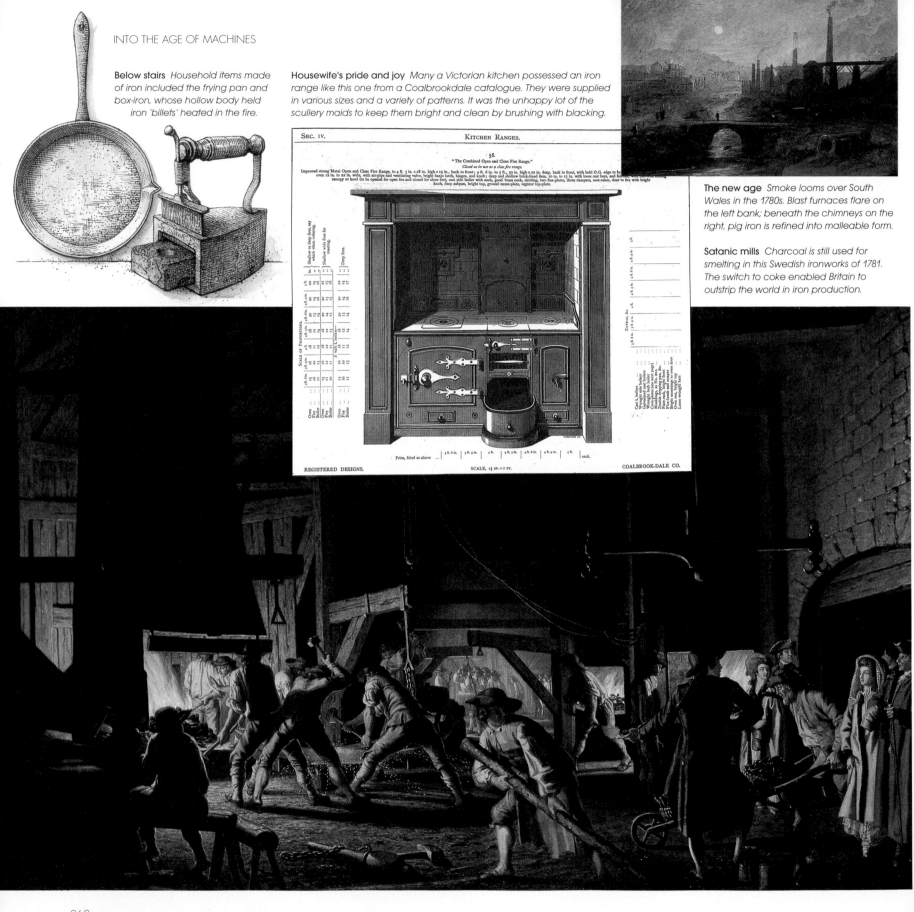

Below stairs *Household items made of iron included the frying pan and box-iron, whose hollow body held iron 'billets' heated in the fire.*

Housewife's pride and joy *Many a Victorian kitchen possessed an iron range like this one from a Coalbrookdale catalogue. They were supplied in various sizes and a variety of patterns. It was the unhappy lot of the scullery maids to keep them bright and clean by brushing with blacking.*

The new age *Smoke looms over South Wales in the 1780s. Blast furnaces flare on the left bank; beneath the chimneys on the right, pig iron is refined into malleable form.*

Satanic mills *Charcoal is still used for smelting in this Swedish ironworks of 1781. The switch to coke enabled Britain to outstrip the world in iron production.*

SEC. IV.   KITCHEN RANGES.

. 58.
"The Combined Open and Close Fire Range."
Closed as in use as a close fire range.

Improved strong Metal Open and Close Fire Range, to 4 ft. 3 in. x 28 in. high x 19 in., back to front; 4 ft. 6 in. to 5 ft., 30 in. high x 22 in. deep, back to front, with bold O.G. edge to hob; oven 12 in. to 22 in. wide, with air-pipe and ventilating valve, bright banjo latch, hinges, and knob; deep and shallow brick-lined fires, 10 in. to 15 in. wide, with loose cast bars, and falling, with cast-iron boiling canopy or hood (to be opened for open fire and closed for close fire); cast side boiler with neck, good brass cock, skirting, two flue-plates, three dampers, soot-raker, door to fire with bright knob, deep ashpan, bright top, ground name-plate, register top-plate.

Price, fitted as above ...   3 ft. 6 in.   3 ft. 9 in.   4 ft.   4 ft. 3 in.   4 ft. 6 in.   4 ft. 9 in.   5 ft.   each.

REGISTERED DESIGNS.   SCALE, 1¼ IN. = 1 FT.   COALBROOK-DALE CO.

KING COAL'S SUBJECTS, AND MEN OF IRON

On June 7, 1842, Lord Ashley, later to become Earl of Shaftesbury, proposed a new Bill to the House of Commons. The House listened in horrified silence as he recounted how women and children were working in Britain's mines for 13 hours a day, how recruitment began at seven years of age and in parts of Lancashire as early as four.

Beginning with lighter tasks, such as trapping – opening and closing of ventilator doors – as soon as they were able, children were chained to wheeled tubs laden with coal which they towed through seams 22 in (560 mm) high and 200 yds (183 m) long. Ashley told of Sarah Gooder, an eight-year-old trapper in the Gawber pit. 'It does not tire me, but I have to trap without a light. It scares me. I don't like being in the pit.' Isobel Wilson, aged 38: 'I was a carrier of coals, which caused me to miscarry five times from the strains. My last child was born on Saturday morning, and I was at work on Friday night.'

Despite spirited rearguard action on the part of mine owners in the House of Lords, the Bill excluding women and children from underground work was passed, and became law in August.

Coal commands

Such a heartless extension of the workforce had been brought about by the demands of the Industrial Revolution. Coal was the material that fed the new technology. 'Coal commands the Age', pointed out an economist of the period. European coal production multiplied 30-fold between 1770 and 1870, and in Britain alone the workforce in the pits increased from 216,000 in 1851 to 495,000 by 1881.

By the middle of this period, the 1860s, women and children working in the pits were no more than a memory, but even then the mines were far from idyllic. True, the lifts that descended the shafts had been made safer at least to the extent that now 'only a carelessly protruding arm or finger may be lopped off', but brutal challenges waited at the bottom. In the shallow mines of the Black Country, men were lowered to the face by a chain with loops through which they stuck their legs. Fatal accidents in these small pits averaged 800 a year. By far the greatest killers were roof falls, whose only warning was the crack of supporting timbers before there came a rumble of falling rock, and then oblivion. Explosions came when the natural gas known as firedamp was ignited by a spark. Choke damp, or carbonic acid gas, would then smother any survivors. There was kinship in mining districts: orphans were raised by neighbours; men unable to work through injury were supported. The miners were tough and independent, proud of their dangerous calling. If there was a horse race or a prize fight, they took the day off.

Close by the miners of the West Midlands Black Country were the neighbouring iron workers. Together they created a landscape that struck awe into visitors. Everywhere were sterile hills of waste from the ironworks, growing too fast even for the railways to clear them for ballast. Among them were the coke ovens, pouring black smoke and flame as though the earth itself were on fire.

Stretching to the distance were the chimneys and engine houses of the mines, but the smelting furnaces, served by endless strings of trucks on railways, were the centre of activity. Day and night, men broke limestone for flux, which was carted up a slope and jettisoned through holes into the

Grave slab in cast iron

furnaces below to help the process. A careless slip would lead to a horrible death. Sand moulds for the pigs of iron were prepared by keepers, who tapped the furnaces, removed cinders and guided the molten metal into the moulds with no more concern than if the deadly stuff were water.

First pride of Britain's iron industry was Coalbrookdale in Shropshire where, in 1709, Abraham Darby abandoned charcoal as fuel for his furnaces and fed them with coke. In 1789, Abraham Darby III built the world's first iron bridge across the River Severn, where it still stands. The Darbys provided a model village for their work force; it had an iron clock tower and the cottages were built with iron window frames and chimney pots. And when at last people were borne to the cemetery, they lay beneath slabs of cast iron. Workshops and black landscapes also scarred parts of northern Europe, especially Belgium and the Ruhr. Lorraine had rich ironfields and produced fine steel, but its land-owning peasants did not have the need to flock to cities as the Britons and Germans had. So France sent much of its iron over the border to be married to the coal of Germany.

Safety lamp *In 1815 Sir Humphry Davy invented a miner's oil lamp surrounded by metal gauze which prevented it igniting gas.*

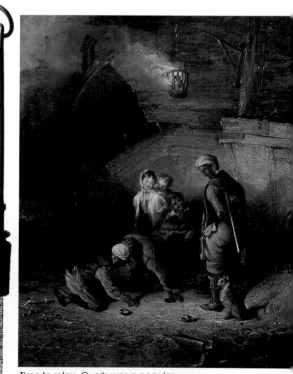

Time to relax *Quoits was a popular pastime among miners. They would also spend Sundays poaching animals for food, growing vegetables or pigeon racing.*

Depths of despair *Children chained to tubs laden with coal dragged and pushed them through the seams.*

SLAVING IN STEEL AND COTTON MILL

A man known as a 'knocker up' tapped before dawn on the windows of workers' terrace houses in Britain's mill towns. Thin, pale-faced children were dragged from their beds to hasten out, with the women and menfolk, into the cold streets. Many of the children went barefoot. All made their way between soot-blackened rows of brick-built houses to the multistorey mill.

A bell or hooter signalled the start and finish of work which, in the early 19th century, lasted for 12 to 16 hours a day. People worked in cramped and airless conditions, so deafened by machinery that they had to lip-read. Lungs became clogged with cotton dust which made people ill.

In Manchester, heart of the textile industry, the mills produced what one doctor called 'a degenerate race of human beings, stunted, enfeebled and depraved – men and women that were not to be aged – children that were never to be adults'. Now and again a wearying mill worker, losing his

concentration, would be mutilated by unfenced machinery, losing the tip of a finger – or even a whole arm. Friedrich Engels, Karl Marx's collaborator, who knew the factory system from working for his family's firm, wrote that 'a great number of maimed persons may be seen going about Manchester; this one has lost an arm or part of one, that one a foot, the third half a leg; it is like living in the midst of an army just returned from a campaign'.

The plight of the factory children aroused outrage. In the early days of the Industrial Revolution they were employed in the mills from the age of six or seven. Mill owners would get children in batches from parish workhouses. They were sometimes treated as little more than slaves and kept on starvation diets at the mercy of overseers armed with whips and straps.

One apprentice, Robert Blincoe, left an account of his time at the mill owned by Ellis Needham at Litton in Derbyshire. Famished children were given a dinner of 'rusty, half-putrid, fish-fed bacon and unpared turnips', and for supper a greasy broth made from the leftovers. Worked 16 hours a day without breaks, they raided refuse dumps for food. Punishments included being suspended by their arms above the pounding machinery. Such cruelty, however,

was exceptional. Normal punishments were dismissal or fines for neglect, swearing, horseplay and so on. Pay was docked for bad timekeeping. A mill worker who turned up five minutes late might lose as much as a quarter of his day's wages.

Reformers struggled to end the worst evils of toil in the mills. In 1833 children under nine were banned from work in textile mills, while maximum hours for children from nine to 13 were set at nine hours a day, or a 48 hour week. The Factory Act of 1847 limited children to half-day working.

Not all mill owners were ogres. The reformer Robert Owen made his cotton-spinning factory at New Lanark in Scotland famous for good labour relations. Owen became a partner in the mills in 1800 and reduced the working day to $10\frac{1}{2}$ hours. He did away with corporal punishment, instead introducing a 'silent monitor', a small, four-sided block of wood hung next to each machine. The colour facing outwards revealed the conduct of the worker: white meant excellent, yellow stood for moderately good, blue was neutral and black revealed 'excessive naughtiness'. Owen started a shop where workers could buy low-priced goods for cash tokens, and a school. Other owners also provided decent cottages for their operatives, helped to build chapels and provided excursion trips on Fair days.

Some saw advantages in this new mode of work – especially for the women and girls who made up more than half the work force in cotton. Though hours were long, wages were high by comparison with domestic service, and this was one field in which women could earn just as much as their menfolk. A report of 1840 noted: 'A young woman, prudent and careful, and living with her parents, from the age of 16 to 25, may, in that time, by factory employment save £100 as a wedding portion. She is not then driven into an early marriage by the necessity of

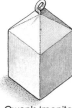

Owen's 'monitor'

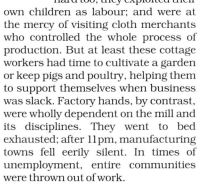

seeking a home.' What labourers found most irksome, however, was the strict regimentation of factory life. The pace demanded was a ruthless one, set by the power-driven machinery and their clock-watching overseers. This was a new experience, totally different from earlier times when cotton thread had been spun on the wheel by 'spinsters' and woven on hand looms by weavers working in their own cottages. Their lives were hard too; they exploited their own children as labour; and were at the mercy of visiting cloth merchants who controlled the whole process of production. But at least these cottage workers had time to cultivate a garden or keep pigs and poultry, helping them to support themselves when business was slack. Factory hands, by contrast, were wholly dependent on the mill and its disciplines. They went to bed exhausted; after 11pm, manufacturing towns fell eerily silent. In times of unemployment, entire communities were thrown out of work.

Factory production began in the 18th century, with the coming of spinning machines devised by such inventors as Richard Arkwright, James Hargreaves and Samuel Crompton. Running water was the main source of power in the early mills, which were sited by fast-moving streams. In 1785 a Boulton and Watt engine for the first time employed steam to power a spinning factory, and coal-fed steam engines played an increasing role. They needed a steady supply of water, so stream-side sites in the hills were still favourites, and many a mill was built miles from the

Mill money *Factory workers used tokens to buy food.*

Taking it easy *The Victorian artist Eyre Crowe painted this idealised view of a group of Wigan millworkers relaxing during their dinner hour. One girl is reading a letter, watched by an inquisitive friend. Others talk or stroll together, savouring their brief freedom before the hooter sounds for the remainder of their shift.*

Country into town *Fast-flowing water and abundant coal and iron ore turned the rural landscape around Sheffield into a booming 'city of steel'. Skilled workers in factories and small workshops made a range of goods from penny-farthing bicycles to steam engines.*

Struggle for survival *By the 1850s many of Europe's existing towns were bursting at the seams as people flocked to work in the new industries. A tailoring 'sweat shop' in London's East End, where cheap clothes were made for export, shows the squalor which resulted.*

nearest village. The mill hands lost many hours of pay through having to walk long distances to and from work.

Raw cotton from the United States slave plantations supplied the British textile industry. Cargoes arrived at Liverpool, helping to make Lancashire the birthplace of the factory system. A French writer in 1844 complained that 'overwork is a disease which Lancashire has inflicted upon England and which England in turn has inflicted upon Europe'. But benefits came too. Cotton provided ordinary people with cheap attractive clothes, such as women's print dresses. Cotton sheets, drapery and sewing thread were other products, and by the 1830s cotton goods made up half of Britain's exports. Since the new cotton clothes were far easier to wash and dry than the woollen clothes worn hitherto, hygiene was greatly improved. A huge increase was soon noticed in the demand for soap.

BEDS OF STRAW AND A DIET OF NETTLES

Hardship and poverty were widespread side effects of the Industrial Revolution. But human dignity often survived in the most squalid conditions, as an observer found when he visited the hand-loom weavers of Lancashire in 1842. In one small town he found 88 dwellings empty of furniture except for old boxes for tables or stools. Beds were made of straw and shavings. The food was oatmeal and water for breakfast, and flour and water with a little skimmed milk for dinner. Children grubbed for discarded roots in the markets. And yet, he recorded, 'all the places and persons I visited were scrupulously clean. The children were in rags, but they were not in filth. In no instance was I asked for relief... I never before saw poverty which inspired respect, and misery which demanded involuntary homage'. Elsewhere, however, weavers were reported as haggard with famine, their eyes fiercely rolling. 'We do not want charity,' they said, 'but employment.' Only 100 of the 9000 inhabitants of one town were fully employed. Many fasted every other day, or survived on boiled nettles. The weavers were kept alive by the earnings of their weary children in the cotton mills.

Child slaves *A top-hatted mill owner supervises young workers at the spinning frame. Children's nimble fingers and sharp eyes were ideally suited to tying broken threads, while their small size enabled them to crawl under the machines to oil and clean them.*

Chance find *A young British chemist, William Henry Perkin, discovered synthetic dyes while experimenting in 1856. The bottles contain his original dyes, alizarin and mauveine. Dyed fabric was woven on an automatic loom invented by the Frenchman Joseph Jacquard in 1805.*

ALL ABOARD TO 'FLY' THE IRON HORSE

In her later days the English actress Fanny Kemble recalled her first railway journey in 1830, accompanied by the engineer George Stephenson. 'When I closed my eyes,' she said, 'the sensation of flying was quite delightful.' The Iron Horse that conveyed her caused no alarm. It was 'a snorting little animal that I felt rather inclined to pat'.

Not everyone shared her opinion. Landowners warned that foxes and pheasants would be wiped out by fumes from the engines, as would be the passengers when the train entered a tunnel. By and large, however, the populace were enthusiastic about the new mode of travel.

The growth of the railways was phenomenal, from 500 miles of track in England in 1838 to 5000 miles in 1848, and increasing every year for the rest of the century. On the Continent, railways appeared a little later but soon grew apace, unrestricted by a surrounding sea. By 1914 the Germans had twice as much track as the British, and the French had a quarter more. Bradshaw published his first timetable in 1839, with a continental version in 1847; they lasted for over a century.

Clocking on to 'railway time'

If railways were to run on time, then time had to be the same nationwide. Hitherto it had varied as one moved east or west – differing by half an hour between Kent and Cornwall. Now clocks bearing 'railway time' were placed at stations, so imposing uniformity on commerce, industry and the public. For very many people, railways provided the first chance to see what other parts of the country looked like. Village people visited cities, townsfolk went to the seaside or distant hills. Cheap market-day tickets also

Helping hand Stations sprang up all over Britain during the railway age, providing jobs of all kinds for thousands, such as this porter of around 1870.

Guard's whistle

opened new vistas. In 1841, a lay preacher named Thomas Cook chartered a train to carry 570 friends of the Leicester Temperance Society to a meeting in Loughborough. By 1845 he was offering Midlands workers trips on the Clyde, and in 1851 he transported thousands of people from the North and Midlands to London to see the Great Exhibition, the success of which was assured by the railways.

Few aspects of life were unaffected. Newspapers were distributed far more widely than before. The penny post of 1840 would not have been possible had railways not been licensed to carry the mail two years earlier. Railway stations offered new attractions in their cavernous interiors. Not least of these was the station bookstall. 'The railway has been the means of at least doubling the number of books printed and published', wrote one early Victorian passenger. Thousands of gallons of milk that would have been turned into butter and cheese now arrived fresh every morning in the cities. Market gardening and fruit growing no longer needed to be on the cities' doorsteps. They moved farther away, leaving their old, expensive sites ripe for development. One of the greatest changes was the spread of the suburb. Also astonishing was the rash of new towns, or old ones that changed their character at the railway's behest. Small towns such as Crewe, Reading and Swindon quickly expanded as junctions on the national network. Manchester's trade soon quadrupled and Liverpool, the chief Atlantic seaport, was in communication with the entire country.

Factories grew up along the line, and the first commuters appeared as soon as the London to Brighton line opened in 1841. 'Suburbia was a railway state,' an early commuter recalled, 'a state of existence within a few minutes' walk of the railway stations.' On the debit side, the rawness of the cuttings and the spoil from tunnels scarred the landscape. Hundreds of houses were destroyed where tracks entered cities, and thousands of poor tenants were thrown out of their homes without compensation. There was no denying

MEETINGS AND PARTINGS

The novelty and excitement of travel by train are captured in W.P. Frith's 1862 painting of the bustle of departure time at Paddington Station. A mother kisses her schoolboy son goodbye, young ladies gossip, detectives arrest a suspect, and a bearded man – a self-portrait of the artist – argues the fare with a cab-driver. Frith spent a year painting the picture – and when it was placed on exhibition, 80,000 people paid to see it.

Pride in the railways was undimmed even by the discomforts of the journey. In the early years, third-class passengers travelled in open wagons without seating or covering from the weather, and in danger from flying sparks. Second and first classes rode in draughty, unlit carriages, not unlike the old stage coaches, though mounted on flanged wheels. As Frith shows, luggage went where it had always gone – on the roof.

Outside the towns, intending passengers huddled by a linesman's hut, with no raised platform to help them on and off. In towns, by contrast, architects built railway stations in all kinds of styles, including the fairy-tale Gothic palace of St Pancras Station in London, to honour this new marvel of the industrial age. Through their great halls soon flooded a tide of commuters, long-distance travellers and holidaymakers.

Domestic chores
The housewife's chores continue afloat, on a French canal at the turn of the century. Canal boatmen all over Europe brought their families on board as crew to save money in the face of growing competition from the railways. A distinct way of life grew up among canal folk.

WHEN INDUSTRIES WERE CONNECTED BY WATERWAYS

Before the coming of the railway, it was easier to move goods by water than by land. Great rivers such as the Thames and Severn were used by trading vessels which were sailed or pulled along by gangs of men or horses using a towpath. Winter floods and summer droughts made river navigation difficult, however: canals were preferred because of their more reliable water levels, and they became the mainstay of trade during the Industrial Revolution.

A packhorse could carry one-eighth of a ton on its back, but could pull a 50 ton load on a canal barge. So the 3rd Duke of Bridgewater decided to build the first major canal in Britain to reduce the cost of moving coal from his mines at Worsley, Lancashire, to Manchester. The Bridgewater Canal was opened in 1761. Canal boats were decorated with paint and ropework. In the intervals between working

the boat, canal women spent much of their time crocheting, making lace decorations for their bonnets and blouses, and even caps to keep flies of their horses' heads. In England, where in 1792 the enthusiasm for canals was described as a 'mania', the Canal Age was brief. It lasted longer on the Continent, where an extensive canal system linked France, Germany and Belgium, making use of the Seine, Rhone and Rhine. There were links with high seas trade, too, by Hamburg and Rotterdam. In Holland, canals were used extensively for drainage as well as for navigation.

Boat wife's lace bonnet

Ocean link *Sophisticated engineering skills created the locks and railway viaduct at Earlham on the Manchester Ship Canal, opened to traffic in 1894. The canal joined the industries of Lancashire with the River Mersey and the sea, giving rise to Manchester's prosperity.*

N.B.R. LOOK-OUT

On the alert
As 200,000 'navvies' – the same 'navigators' who built the canals – laid lines such as the North British Railway, foremen wearing armbands guarded against accidents.

Tickets, please! *A little pasteboard slip brought commuters to their offices from the suburbs, and took them away for exercise.*

the disruptive effect of the railway, on the Continent as well as in Britain. When the Berlin to Leipzig line was completed, there were complaints of 'a constant stream of pedestrians, coaches, cabs and other vehicles in the beautiful old Leipziger Strasse', and forebodings that it would become 'a thoroughfare of factories'.

Generally, however, the railways on the Continent learnt from Britain's mistakes. When Germany became an empire in 1871 all railways were owned by the state, and though in France companies were privately owned as in Britain, they were entirely under state control. Centralisation led to some sensible decisions. Many continental cities had one great station into which

all lines were fed; less upsetting to the city's life than London's 15 termini. British travellers, however, felt that such state intervention led to an excess of authority. 'The difference between the English and continental railway official,' ran one complaint, 'is that the one is the servant of the public, while the other is the master. Railway officials are like policemen... you are not allowed on the platform on peril of your life without a ticket.'

BY IRON SHIP ACROSS THE OCEANS

Inside 'Leviathan' *Brunel's Great Eastern, completed in 1859, was 700ft (213m) long, and for more than 40 years the largest ship afloat. It had both paddle wheels and screw propellers. Intended for the Australia route, the so-called Leviathan ended up laying Atlantic telegraph cables.*

Between the mid-19th century and 1914, about one European in ten left the home continent to find a new life elsewhere. It was the biggest population movement of all time: 50 million people flooded across the world. A fair number ended up in Australia, New Zealand and other territories, but most were destined for the Americas.

The earlier emigrants went under sail and could expect to spend 35 days or more crossing the Atlantic, but the coming of steamships reduced this to less than 12 days. Steamships were bigger, capable of carrying a thousand cheap-rate passengers and hundreds more in the better accommodation.

Many of the earlier emigrants were Irish, fleeing a land ravaged by the 1840s potato famine. Its victims were mainly poor peasants, and America offered escape – and opportunity – for those who could raise the £8.16s for the passage from Liverpool to New York. In the eight years following the famine almost a million Irish sailed

across the Atlantic, accounting for one in four of all European emigrants to the United States at that time. Among them were the ancestors of the Kennedy family and of Henry Ford, the motor-car manufacturer. The potato blight brought suffering elsewhere, too; German peasants were badly hit, and thousands emigrated.

Steamships supplanted wooden sailing ships in the late 1860s and 1870s, though they had been in use for decades. The first steamers were paddle boats on which everyone travelled in dread of a boiler explosion. It was the engineer Isambard Kingdom Brunel who revolutionised steam travel at sea. In 1837 his paddle steamer *Great Western*, at 236ft (72m) long the largest steamship built up to that time, left Bristol to become the world's first transatlantic liner.

Six years later the *Great Western* was joined by the SS *Great Britain*, the world's first ocean-going ship to be built of iron and the first large ship to be driven by a screw propeller. Soon steamships were offering luxury travel for first-class passengers to distant destinations, as well as taking supplies to the far-flung communities of the European empires – and also providing a cheap passage below decks for refugees

from persecution or famine. Emigrants bound for America often passed through Liverpool, where they had first to run a gamut of crooked boarding housekeepers, fraudulent shipbrokers, and cheating merchants who sold them bad food and equipment that was unnecessary for the voyage. Before an emigrant could board ship he or she was given a perfunctory medical inspection. A contemporary reported that the government doctors stood behind a little window and said as the people filed past: 'Are you quite well? Show your tongue', and in the meantime their ticket was stamped. The result was that victims of smallpox, typhus and many other diseases were processed along with the remainder. Hundreds died every year at sea.

Farewells were said at the dockside, as blocks and ropes were hauled and masses of canvas unfurled. Vendors of toffee, oranges, mirrors, ribbons and gingerbread cried their wares among the bewildered emigrant families, to fleece them of whatever could be got.

Some captains of emigrant ships ruled their vessels like tsars. They took more care of their cargo than of their human freight and would make sure it was safely stored in the hold before allowing the passengers on. There were cases of vessels moving out of dock while men, women and children were still scrambling aboard.

On board, most passengers were crammed into bunks knocked together with coarse planks, with a narrow gangway between their cramped berths and the piles of boxes containing their possessions. As often as not they slept four to a berth 6ft (1.8m) by 6ft.

Complete strangers could end up lying side by side. Rations of food and water were supposed to be doled out daily, but corruption and inefficiency could mean that supplies were often cut off for days on end. Hapless passengers who had brought no provisions of their own endured agonies of hunger and thirst, unless they managed to beg sustenance from their better-off companions who might have packed salt meat, bacon, herrings or cheese.

On many vessels crewmen cursed, cuffed and kicked passengers queuing for their rations, or for the use of the galleys which held stoves for cooking. Everyone was filthy, for washing meant sacrificing vital drinking water. Rampant seasickness contributed to a permanent stench in the airless sleeping quarters, worsened by spillage from chamber pots. Not all the peasant folk knew how to make proper use of

Daring experiment *The size of the Great Eastern called for new technological skills. The men who worked on it protected their interests by banding together in unions such as the Associated Shipwrights' Society.*

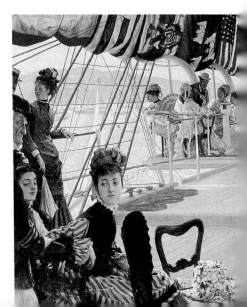

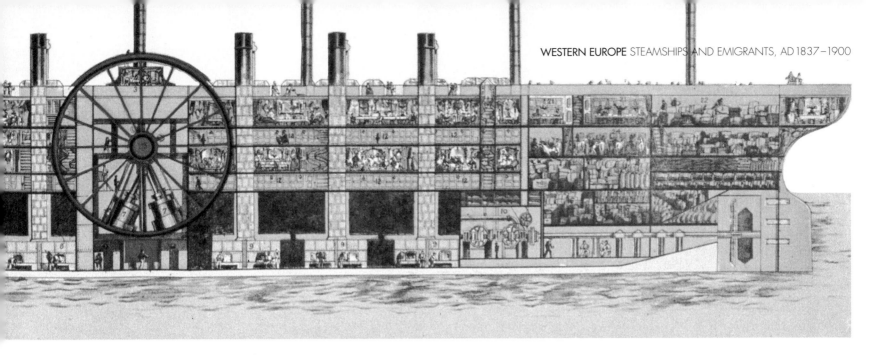

the few toilets. Complaints were not well received. An Irishman who sailed for New York in October 1850 left an account of one grim passage, during which five days passed without the food ration being served. He started to write a complaint to the captain, in courteous terms – whereupon the first mate knocked him flat with a blow to the face. Such conditions led governments to pass laws to improve the lot of emigrants. An 1855 Act ruled that a ship with more than 300 passengers should carry a surgeon. Inspectors ensured there was no overcrowding and that passengers had enough food for the voyage. Statutes regulated the height between decks and the size of berths. Reports of bad food and over-crowding were still made, but crossings were to claim far fewer lives.

Faraway places *A family of British migrants arrives at its new home in South Australia, the first state in the country to be colonised by free men. Behind them lies a long and uncomfortable sea voyage. The father gazes pensively out of the window, wondering what the future will hold.*

Floating ballroom *Steamships running to fixed schedules little affected by contrary winds became fashionable for holiday cruising as well as cross-Channel and transatlantic voyages. The French artist James Tissot, who specialised in paintings of elegant Victorian society, captured the glamour of a high-society ball on a ship, held beneath the flags of the many nations that steam-powered travel was bringing together.*

Hearty helpings *By 1891, shipping lines such as Norddeutscher Lloyd were offering high-class cuisine to attract passengers onto the booming steamship services.*

A STORMY NIGHT ON BOARD AN EMIGRANT SHIP

A wail from the berth below woke Michael from a fitful sleep. The ship was rolling hard in a storm. Baggage was sliding to and fro across the passenger deck; somewhere pots and pans crashed, and a baby shrieked. A woman muttered prayers to the Virgin Mary. Michael felt Bridie and their three children clutch at him for reassurance, but he could see little because no lantern was alight and the hatches were battened down, sealing everyone into the fetid hell between decks.

Michael was a Wicklow farmer, evicted from his smallholding after the potato failure. The sale of his pigs and poultry covered the cost of the passage for the family on a packet ship from Liverpool to New York. An uncle had lent him a further £10 in coins which he had stitched into the lining of his jacket. There were 500 others on board, and many head of cattle. It was the tenth day at sea. By midday the storm had abated and the family queued to cook some food on a stove in the galley. There they learned that a child had died of fever during the night, and Michael went on deck to watch as the small body, wrapped in weighted sailcloth, was put on a plank and tilted overboard, as the captain said a short burial service.

That night, the sea was calmer. Michael played dominoes with the children and Bridie served them an oatmeal porridge which they ate with some morsels of salt pork. Down the deck a fiddler started playing, and a couple danced in a cramped space between the luggage boxes. Bridie and the children fell asleep lulled by the tunes, but Michael lay awake long after the fiddler had ceased, listening to the creaking timbers and the lapping of water against the hull.

PROGRESS ON DISPLAY IN A GLASS PALACE

In the 50 years since 1800, Britain's commercial growth, based on coal, iron and the steam engine, had been phenomenal, while gazing down the decades to come, not even the wisest could foresee anything but the advance of peaceful prosperity. Something, it was felt, should be done to mark this moment, and what better than to present a great exhibition at which the country would proclaim to the world its achievements? The chief exponent of this idea was Henry Cole, an energetic senior civil servant, who had enthusiastic support from Prince Albert, Queen Victoria's Consort. It was the prince who proposed that the exhibition should not be confined to Britain, but thrown open to all nations. This, he explained, would 'present a living picture of the point of development at which the whole of Mankind has arrived…and a new starting point from which all nations will be able to direct their future exertions'.

Thus inspired, a committee was quickly formed, financial contributions and exhibits invited, and a site for the exhibition chosen on the south side

New home *After the Great Exhibition, the building was dismantled and rebuilt at Sydenham.*

of London's Hyde Park. The plan had its critics. One MP, alarmed at the prospect of crowds invading the capital, warned the House of Commons of the dangers to wives, daughters and property, of plague and financial failure, of foreigners stealing the nation's honour and of the wrath of the Almighty. But of more immediate concern to the committee was the fact that, with less than a year to go until the projected opening day, they still had no building to house the exhibition. Some 250 designs had already been submitted – and rejected.

Fortunately, the hour produced the man. Joseph Paxton, head gardener, close friend and business partner of the Duke of Devonshire, proposed a design based on that of the duke's conservatory at Chatsworth, envisaging the exhibition hall as an ethereal creation in cast iron and glass. The building would be prefabricated and therefore easy to construct and take down, and a tremendous eye-catcher.

A DAY AT THE GREAT EXHIBITION

Along the Crystal Palace's West Nave (below) passes a stream of parents with their children, gazing wide-eyed at the latest achievements of British industry and craftsmanship, on show for all the world to see. Above a wall panel of gleaming stucco scrollwork hang banners which bear the arms of Britain's towns, and models of dragons and birds that appeal to the contemporary taste for elaborate decoration. Objects enamelled in the new japanned style, in the Spiers and Son cabinet, draw an interested audience among visitors newly familiar with the Far East, while a massive Celtic cross asserts the key role of Christianity in society. Exhibits in the Bookbinding and Printing section include Braille books for the blind, a machine that can turn out 2700 folded envelopes an hour, and a roll of paper 1½ miles (2.4km) long made by Spicers. Among the Fine Arts exhibits are a variety of statuettes and models, of the type that mass production techniques are making available in every Victorian home. Beyond the West Nave, another 100,000 exhibits from all over the world await the foot-weary.

Into a new age *The price of a short cab ride bought Parisians a glimpse of the latest technology, and a vision of nations in harmony.*

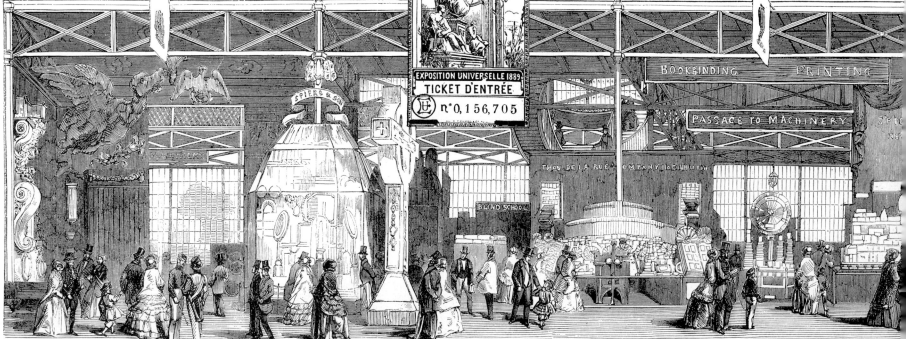

Palace of steel *The French took the lead in later exhibitions. Eiffel's 984 ft (300 m) tower startled the world in 1889, and still dominates the skyline of Paris. This exhibition marked the centenary of the French Revolution, and was boycotted by Europe's royalty. Visitors to the Paris exhibition of 1900 could ascend in a balloon, be astonished at the cinema, or admire the floodlit Electricity Fairy, riding her chariot 120 ft (36 m) above the Palace of Electricity. There was also the chance they might encounter the 'lions' of the period – Toulouse-Lautrec, Debussy, André Gide, Sarah Bernhardt, the young Picasso. Like the exhibition itself, they personified memories of the old century and the promise of the new.*

Long before it was completed, *Punch* magazine named it the 'Crystal Palace', consigning to oblivion the full title of 'The Great Exhibition of the Works of Industry of All Nations'. The finished construction was 1848 ft (563 m) long – more than three times the length of St Paul's Cathedral. Tier upon tier of slender iron columns supporting 900,000 sq ft (83,700 sq m) of glass contained some 19 acres (7.6 ha) of Hyde Park. The transept soared 108 ft (33 m) to enclose three ancient elms.

At last all was ready, and on May Day, 1851, the Queen opened the Great Exhibition in the presence of many visitors from overseas and tens of thousands of her subjects. From May to October, awestruck multitudes gazed at the exhibits gathered together from many lands and grouped under the titles of raw materials, machinery, manufactures and the fine arts.

Thousands came to the Crystal Palace daily. The South East Railway and the Northern Railway of France united to create a ferry service that brought Paris within 11 hours of London. Excursion trains brought farm labourers and factory workers who had never before left their native shires. An 84-year-old Cornish woman walked 300 miles from Penzance, although the Lord Mayor of London insisted on paying her fare home. Queen Victoria noted that this 'most hale old woman was almost crying from emotion when I looked at her'.

Among the most popular exhibits were the Koh-i-noor diamond from India, housed in a sort of birdcage, a crystal fountain at the centre of the exhibition, an astronomical telescope, and two striking sculptures – *The Amazon*, by Professor Kiss from Berlin, and *The Greek Slave*, by an American, Hiram Powers.

Less glamorous, but still impressive, were the locomotives, marine engines and steam-powered farm machinery that represented the advances made in technology. Other industrial marvels on show included Nasmyth's steam hammer, which could be adjusted to deliver a blow of 500 tons or lightly to crack an eggshell; a vertical printing press that had an output of 10,000 pages an hour; a cigarette machine which could turn out 80 cigarettes a minute; and a copying telegraph which delivered facsimiles at the other end of the line. Goodyear displayed a variety of goods in the new vulcanised India rubber, and Mr Macintosh exhibited garments waterproofed with the same material. Much interest was sparked among military men by Krupp's large steel cannon, and the American-made Colt revolver. Families were dazzled by furniture, sometimes so elaborately decorated that its function became obscure. The love of display extended to richly decorated wrought-iron beds, fireplaces and stoves, carved tables and chairs, and clocks. There was even an alarm bed that slid its occupant into a cold bath at the required hour.

By the time the exhibition closed on October 15, more than 6 million people had visited it – one in three of the population of Britain. To the delight of the organisers, they had purchased 1,092,337 soft drinks, 934,691 Bath buns, 14,299 lb (6486 kg) of pickles, jellies and hams and 870,027 plain buns. The exhibition had been a huge international success – and it even managed to make a 50 per cent profit.

Time for a break *Labourers enjoy a snack beside the almost-completed Crystal Palace. The building's foundations were laid in August 1850, and it was ready within nine months. As many as 2260 men were employed on the construction of the building at the same time.*

Science aid *This microscope set was displayed at the Paris exhibition of 1889.*

Tool set *This sports knife has a host of useful gadgets.*

SOCIETY, SUBURB AND SLUM

In the wake of railways and machines came great changes to the way in which people lived. Never before had so many people lived in towns, and with their rapid expansion came problems of inadequate and overcrowded housing, disease and unsurpassed opportunities for crime. The squalor of the slums of industrial towns stood in sharp contrast to the life of the very rich, with their splendid houses and carriages.

A new lifestyle came too, for railways and omnibuses meant that people could combine work in the towns with a home life in the new suburbs. To a middle class far more extensive and influential than before, home was very precious – a haven from the stormy world. The advent of the railways also meant that people could buy food and manufactured goods produced far from their homes, and that they in turn could travel with ease and for pleasure to see what lay beyond their own district. Railways and the telegraph brought to an increasingly literate public news of events in distant lands. On home ground, piano music filled parlours, and in churches and chapels, music halls and pubs, people found relief from the upheavals of a changing world.

WESTERN EUROPE AD 1830–1900

BETWEEN RICH AND POOR, A NEW CLASS

When Queen Victoria came to the throne of Britain in 1837 most of her subjects lived in the countryside. The words of a 19th-century hymn – 'The rich man in his castle, the poor man at his gate, God made them, high or lowly, and ordered their estate' – spoke of the inherited sense of order that people felt during the first half of the 19th century. Long before the end of Victoria's reign, however, it became apparent that new forces were taking a hand in shaping people's lives.

Chief among these were the steam engine and the new machines that were creating new industries centred in towns and cities. The prospect of work in the factories drew people to the towns and swelled their numbers at a time when the population was rising at an astonishing rate in all advanced countries. In 1837, Britain's population was 15 million; before the end of the century it had jumped to 37 million.

Just as sweeping were the changes that occurred in the structure of society during the second half of the century. The man inhabiting the castle was still rich, but there were other men, even richer, in mansions which they built overlooking the factories and mills they had founded. Meanwhile the poor man – or the poorest at any rate – was more likely to be seen dragging out a meagre existence in a city slum, than at the rich man's gate. By far the most noticeable change in society, however, was the burgeoning of a new middle class.

Beyond saying that its numerous members were neither aristocrats nor manual workers, the middle class was not a group that was easy to define. It included mill owners with incomes of £10,000 a year, and curates struggling on £200. Among its number were Wordsworth, lover of the clouded fell, and the Birmingham manufacturer

Man of substance *The paterfamilias, father of the family and pillar of society, ruled supreme in his home. A grateful wife, supported by the labour of servants, made sure that ample dinners, a well-brushed hat and starched shirts were always to hand.*

who knew of no fairer sight on earth than the pall of profitable smoke that hung over one of Europe's first industrial cities.

It was generally held that a basic qualification for entry to the middle class was at least one live-in servant. But the governess who earned £30 a year regarded herself as much a member of that class as the physician who employed her. Shopkeepers, and the growing army of clerks who manned banks, counting houses and law offices were yet another part of this diverse group. It was not so much income that distinguished the Victorian middle classes as attitudes and aspirations.

Immensely energetic and property-conscious, the middle classes placed great emphasis on individual self-help, work, thrift, punctuality and duty. Nowhere were their achievements and values better demonstrated than at London's Great Exhibition of 1851, where scientific discoveries and great inventions declared not only present gains, but an uplifting future.

Material progress, the middle classes believed, was bound up with moral improvement. Both qualities were expressed in abundance in their rather overfurnished houses, whether they were the villas that were home to upper management or the endless suburban terraces occupied by clerks.

In villas and terraces, *paterfamilias* – the authoritarian father figure – was the lodestar of existence, while his wife's 'highest pride', so the magazines told her, was her 'sweetest humility'. The dictates of Paris emphasised a

Change of clothes *In the early years of the 19th century the fashionable line was that of the Greek goddess, shown here in an illustration of 1814. By the time the design below appeared in 1861, the crinoline was in full swing, the wire cage giving its wearer a bell-shaped profile.*

wife's decorativeness and her helplessness, while the crinoline and bustle made work of any kind difficult.

Though the middle classes achieved a great deal, the paradise that they saw just around the corner was still a long way off. Indeed, around the corner from the more prosperous districts of mid-Victorian cities were the slums where as many as 30 per cent of the population lived. Slums were the legacy of the earlier years of the Industrial Revolution when little thought was given to the housing needs of the growing work force and of immigrants to the towns. As many as five families might share a single room whose only source of drinking water was contaminated by sewage. Cholera, dysentery and typhus were rife, and just over a hundred people died of starvation in central London alone in 1881. Slum clearance, when it at last

took place, was of little help to the very poor who simply drifted on to crowd other slums. A few paternalistic employers, such as the mill owners of Mulhouse in the Alsace region of France, built good-quality homes for their workers, and the housing built for skilled workers and for those in steady employment gradually improved. The living conditions of very poor people, however, remained dire.

Conditions in European cities were not on the whole so bad as in Britain, where industrialisation took place earlier and with greater intensity. But they were harsh enough: in the prosperous city of Hamburg, 10,000 people died of cholera in a six-week epidemic in 1892. A typical family in a rural suburb of Hamburg, whose lifestyle would have been echoed all over Europe, was that

Homelands *By 1870, the political map of Europe had begun to take on a familiar shape. Of the newly united German states, Prussia was by far the largest, extending well into modern Poland. Italy, too, had just achieved nationhood.*

of a building worker who also worked in a slaughterhouse in the winter. They rented a house with a small garden where they kept a pig and two goats, yet they seldom ate meat or fruit. The mother was a servant in a middle-class family; her wages paid half the rent but all five children had to contribute to the family income.

Victorian scene *The artist G.W. Joy in 1895 brought a mixed group of Londoners together on an omnibus. He described the 'poor anxious mother; beside her, full of kindly thoughts, a fashionable young woman; the City man absorbed in his paper; a wholesome-looking nurse, and a milliner, hat-box in hand'.*

Social round *Ladies had visiting cards to present at friends' homes when making calls. If the lady of the house was not at home, a card was left with its corner turned down.*

THE FAMILY HAVEN – HOME SWEET HOME

Whatever their differences in other ways, the middle classes of Europe's industrialised nations were united in their belief in the sanctity of the home. The home was a temple of peace – a resting place where the rough and tumble of the world could be shut out.

One contemporary observer, Sarah Ellis, wrote: 'When the father returns, it ought to be to a scene of order, harmony and comfort.' In the view of French philosopher Maximilien Littré: 'Private life should be lived behind walls; no one is allowed to peer into a private home, or to reveal what goes on inside.' And in Germany, a writer on the home lamented their large windows which, he said, 'deprive the space of its inner calm, relate it too closely to the outside world'.

The interior of the middle-class home was heavy with embossed wallpaper, dark furniture and patterned carpets that formed the backcloth to the family's portraits and clutter of possessions that covered every surface. Drapes shrouded mantelpieces, tables and pianos, and lace curtains and dark plants obscured both the light and the world outside. Professional 'taste-makers' were on call to guide new people of property as to what to buy and how to live. Even so, there were still wide variations between different homes and the behaviour within them; and by the end of the Victorian era there was a reaction against the cluttered interiors favoured in earlier years.

The middle classes had money to spend, and they often spent it on the new, highly ornamented products of industry. The style of suburban-villa interiors spread to ducal mansions, and even to Osborne House in the Isle of Wight where Britain's Queen Victoria and the Prince Consort lived in cosy domesticity. Aristocrats might still hold the reins of government, but it was successful, self-made men who were the strongest influence on the era. At once materialistic and moral – at least on the surface – it was these men who revolutionised European society during the 19th century. They reigned absolutely in the home, their own little kingdoms. Their wives, if they followed the advice heaped upon them by the journals of the day, subordinated

Family games *Birthdays in middle-class homes were the occasion for parties to celebrate the sanctity of the family, where children basked in an indulged and protracted childhood. The rooms were often crammed with heavy furniture and paintings in richly carved frames.*

all their own problems to the privilege and duty of helping the breadwinner with their tenderness and love. There was a strong religious flavour in these attitudes, particularly in Britain where nonconformism had been gaining ground since the start of the century. It increasingly came to appear not only desirable, but also morally right, that the home should be separated from the place of business.

One of the pioneers in this field was the evangelical Lord Calthorpe. On the outskirts of Birmingham he created the select suburb of Edgbaston where the city's merchants might enjoy 'the sweet caresses and endearments of wife and children' away from 'the cares and anxieties of business'.

Instead of playing an active role in the family mill or shop, the women of Edgbaston, and similar suburbs about the country, would henceforward be relegated to the kitchen and nursery,

Chez nous *Mock Gothic architecture was the fashion when this French house design appeared in 1864. The villa's exterior, from its turret and patterned roof downwards, is as laden with ornament as the salon behind the bay window would doubtless be.*

there to exert 'a pure and religious influence'. As if in official recognition of their status, the government included in its census of 1851 for the first time the occupation of 'Housewife'.

Most sacred of woman's missions, however, was that of being a mother. Large families were desirable, for the Scriptures so dictated; contraception was in its infancy, and many brides went to the marriage bed with only the slightest notion of what occurred there. The result was that in 1861 the average English family consisted of six children; some had ten or even more.

Obedience to father

Though mother oversaw the children's upbringing, at least when they were young, the symbol of authority was father. It was impressed on offspring from an early age that their chief duty was to please their parents; like God, parents were to be loved and feared – emotions that were reinforced with the birch when necessary.

There were no doubt many parents whose keenest happiness it was to take part in their children's play with dolls' houses, shops, model soldiers and toy steam engines. But even so, many nursery toys were instructional, and a that separated them from the French was the yawning gulf that separated them from the working class. The gap remained, even as the working class developed their own culture. Poor parents saw their children as potential wage earners, and as a prop in their old age.

From the middle of the century education became widely available, but many families could not take advantage of it, for young children's wages were an essential part of the family income. Nevertheless, in some parts of the country, particularly in Scotland, working families made considerable sacrifices to ensure that a clever child was properly educated.

Adults furthered their education at Sunday Schools, self-improvement and temperance societies and at Mechanics' Institutes. The middle-class men and women who taught there impressed their own domestic values on the 'industrial classes'.

The place of the workman's wife, they stressed, should be in the home – as manager and moral inspirer, skilled in raising children, dressmaking and cooking and cleaning. Artisans' cottages were often cosy and burnished places, filled with healthy looking children and with china commemorating royal occasions. The well-meaning business man, and the better-off worker bent on self-improvement, both found it convenient to

Fashion model *The rich fabric and elaborate style of a French doll's clothes reflect the adult fashions of the day. Made in 1875, the clockwork doll moves on wheels and says 'Mama'; the face and hands are china.*

preparation for future roles; there were 'dissected puzzles' of maps and of sovereigns of England, and for girls there were paper patterns for making dolls' clothes.

On the other side of the Channel, however, it was the custom for young fathers of the middle classes to exhibit their newborn to their friends at the earliest possible moment, and to invite the children to romp on their parents' bed in the mornings. The children's company was sought by aunts, uncles and grandparents at family suppers on Sunday evenings. Their birthdays and Confirmation days were major family celebrations, made all the more significant by grandparents usually doubling as godparents.

For the middle-class British, however, far more divisive than the strait

Exercises *Young children first wrote on slates, later graduating to paper.*

Home from home *Until education became widespread, many children learned to read and write from a woman who ran a small school in her home. In this 'dame school' of 1856, the girls also learned to sew.*

Family pursuits *By the light of a candle, a poor but industrious family passes an evening in ways designed to better its lot: reading, mending and instructive play. In this simple home, the table stands on bare boards, and outdoor clothes hang on the living-room door.*

ignore the very poor. However, there was increasing social compassion and action from the 1850s onwards, when Charles Booth estimated that a third of London's population lived in poverty. Hardly able to believe it, the Quaker Seebohm Rowntree began in 1897 to make his own survey among the inhabitants of his home town of York.

Rowntree's revelations had considerable political impact. 'When a family is housed in one small room, home life is impossible. Here the family rises, and makes its toilet, father, mother, sons and daughters, in the same room. Here in the evening, among the manifold smells of the day, the family goes to bed. That is to say, as many as possible pile into one bed and the surplus turns in on the floor. Such a room is not home, but horror.'

This was a far cry from the advice given by the household-management pundits: 'A comfortable fireside, well-cooked food, no disorder, no litter of any kind. Let no smell of washing or ironing pervade the home. Baby should be in bed when father comes home.'

AN ARMY CLAD IN CAPS AND APRONS

In service *Rigid divisions of rank were observed in the servants' hall. Every rank – from exalted house steward to humblest scullery maid – had its own distinctive uniform, carefully pressed and starched for the formal portrait which stood on every Victorian mantelpiece.*

ON DUTY FROM CELLAR TO ATTIC

Dawn light in the mid-Victorian home of a well-off professional man – a merchant or banker, for example – might find 20 or more servants already awake. The scullery maid was often first from her bed, rising at 5am or 6am to clean and light the kitchen range to boil the first kettles; housemaids also made an early start to dust and tidy the living rooms, and to light fires in them in winter.

A maid wakened the mistress with a cup of tea, while a valet roused his master and brought him hot water for shaving, together with the morning newspapers – which some masters expected the valet to iron first. Nurses roused the children and gave them breakfast in the nursery, after which adults, children and staff might gather for prayers before the family sat down to the first of its huge meals. Now it is mid-morning, and the servants have been hard at work for several hours. They fight an endless, hour-by-hour war against dirt – one source of which is the coal which a scullery maid is just preparing to carry up from the cellar to the kitchen range on the floor above. In front of the range the cook makes pastry, with a maid to pass her the utensils and the ingredients. Other maids wash crockery, a footman cleans the silver, and a boot boy polishes the shoes. A gardener's boy is bringing vegetables to the door. Servants spent much of the day on their feet, toiling, fetching and carrying. A tweeny, or 'between maid' who helped the cook and the housemaids, is hurrying up the stairs from the kitchen, while a parlourmaid is answering a call to the morning room, where a daughter of the house plays the piano. The master and mistress are going out in their carriage, seen off by a lady's maid. In an office next to the porch the house steward and the housekeeper are interviewing a new maid, while in the laundry room beyond maids are putting clothes through a mangle.

Upstairs, the governess conducts a lesson in the comfortably furnished schoolroom; the governess occupies an uneasy position in the household – not 'family', yet not quite a servant. Her lesson is about to be interrupted by a nurserymaid bringing mid-morning milk for the children. Along the blue-carpeted corridor, a butler makes his dignified way, while a lady's maid brings a late breakfast to a young lady still in bed. The servants have their rooms in the attics. Outdoor staff, some of whom sleep above the stables, include gardeners and the driver, coachman and groom who attend by the carriage.

Upstairs ways *The local policeman, his helmet and truncheon on the floor beside him, has dropped into the servants' hall for a large cup of tea. The room fills with laughter as one of the maids mimics the affected manners of a lady of the house. Even the cat seems amused.*

So far as housework was concerned, well-to-do families in mid-Victorian Britain had an easy time of it. Never before had there been such enormous numbers of servants to do the household chores and free their employers for other pursuits. The master could give his full attention to his business affairs, while the mistress could devote many hours to her social life, with its visits and dinner parties, and to any good works she might engage in.

In any home with pretensions to genteel living, a trio of cook, parlourmaid and housemaid was the norm. The number of servants employed was a declaration of status, so the more a family earned, the more servants it would employ. The greatest houses employed a staff of 40 or 50. As well as the maids for the house, kitchen and nursery found in less-exalted homes, there would be the top-ranking house steward, a chef, a housekeeper, liveried menservants or 'flunkies', stable boys, grooms and many more.

> *'After breakfast is over, the mistress should make a round of the kitchen and other offices, to see that all is in order... The orders for the day should then be given.'*
>
> ISABELLA BEETON: *BOOK OF HOUSEHOLD MANAGEMENT*, 1861

The most senior female servant was the housekeeper. Often a formidable figure, she engaged female staff, held the keys to storecupboards, and had her own room where she took her meals and a bedtime drink with the other senior servants. Footmen went about in pairs, and were often over 6 ft

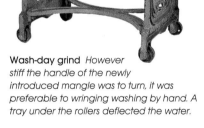

Wash-day grind *However stiff the handle of the newly introduced mangle was to turn, it was preferable to wringing washing by hand. A tray under the rollers deflected the water.*

(1.8 m) tall and carefully matched for height. As well as exquisitely tailored suits, white gloves and cockaded hats, they might wear white stockings padded with false calves to make their legs look more shapely.

A manservant, even if he were not in livery, added prestige to a household. Most servants, however, were young girls and women; their numbers increased until in 1891 nearly one-third of all women between the ages of 15 and 20 were in domestic service.

With strong leadership from the lady of the house and the senior staff, servants worked together like a well-drilled army. Even breakfast required an immaculate linen cloth and cooked dishes such as mutton chops and broiled mackerel, but organising skills

were put to their most stringent test at large and elaborate dinner parties. Glasses, china and candelabra had to be gleaming, aprons spotless, and the ladies' coiffures faultless by the time the guests arrived. All the food for at least five courses was prepared from raw ingredients, and hot dishes had to be kept hot until they were taken to the dining room at just the right moment.

There were clear demarcation lines between the various servants' tasks. The housemaid did most of the dirty work; larger homes might have upper and under housemaids, with the under housemaid doing the heaviest work. Parlourmaids, chosen for their good manners and pleasant appearance, received visitors at the front door, and brought in teacakes and thinly sliced sandwiches for afternoon tea.

Just as clear as servants' roles were their ranks in the troops below stairs. In church, servants often sat in order of precedence; at home, under servants woke senior staff, such as the head nurse and lady's maid, with a cup of tea. 'Going into service' was the usual destiny of a teenage girl who had to earn a living. At the age of 12 or 13 she might start by working in a local shopkeeper's home. After a year or two she would progress to a job in a gentleman's household, and usually had to provide her own

dresses, caps and aprons. The young maidservant received plenty of advice on how she should conduct herself and perform her duties. Magazines and pamphlets, some published by religious groups, impressed on her the need to be content with her lot, and not to gossip with the tradesmen or think too much about wages.

Although servants' wages seemed low compared with those in factories, a servant was housed and fed, sometimes better than she would have been elsewhere. In the 1880s, for instance, an under servant in her first job might earn £7 a year and a head housemaid £30; a good cook could ask for £50 a year; when there were visitors, there was always the possibility of tips as well. A girl might start as a scullery maid and, by moving from one household to another, make her way up to a position as kitchen maid, cook, or even housekeeper. Among the outdoor staff, a boy could work his way up from gardener's boy to head gardener.

Free time might be only two weeks annual holiday, but some employers gave also a free day each month, a half day on Sundays, and an evening off in the week. Even the lowliest middle-class households kept at least one serving girl, and it was in one-servant homes that girls fared worst. Maids-of-all-work, often recruited from the workhouse, were overworked and at the mercy of employers who enforced their authority with stern discipline.

Pressing problems *A flat iron was heated on top of a hot oven, or by the fire. Maids and housewives worked with two irons; one was heating up while the other was in use.*

Change of clothes *Two young maidservants pause for a chat. One wears her work clothes, her rolled-up sleeves revealing arms made muscular by heavy toil. Her companion has changed into the dress she wears to go out on errands for the household, such as collecting the morning milk.*

HIGH LIFE IN A REBORN CITY BY THE SEINE

Paths wound enchantingly among grottoes, lakes and waterfalls, and by exquisitely manicured lawns. Though in the late 1860s the Bois de Boulogne was little more than a decade old, this popular park at the heart of Paris was already well established. It was the gift to Paris of the Emperor Napoleon III, who in his years of exile in England had much admired London's Hyde Park. He vowed that if ever he gained the French throne he would give the people of Paris a similar amenity.

It was not the only change that Napoleon III wrought to Paris during the Second Empire, as the 18 years of his rule were called. With his Prefect of the Seine, Baron Haussmann, he demolished some 20,000 of the city's houses – mostly in the poorer districts that had fomented the revolutions of the past century – and replaced them with great boulevards and avenues radiating from the Arc de Triomphe and linking squares.

Alongside the new roads appeared richly ornamented public buildings: railway stations, the Louvre extension, the Opéra with its marble columns three storeys high. They dominated the numerous town houses, and even the new apartment buildings of seven or eight storeys with shops at their feet. In the late 1860s the Paris shops were the wonder of Europe – veritable treasure houses that at night spilled their light across the streets to enmesh the crowds in a golden net.

Glitter and gaiety in café and palace

No less colourful than the shops were the many cafés and restaurants where gaslight flared onto cream walls and decorated mirrors, on painted cherubs holding forth little bowls of cream, and on gilded nymphs bearing baskets of fruit. From the cafés' private rooms, giggles and squeals announced that

Life in the city *Parisians who thronged the upper-floor balconies of apartment blocks had a bird's-eye view of the busy streets of Napoleon III's rebuilt city. The vitality and colour of the city drew artists from all over the world to capture it on canvas.*

Fashion plates *All Europe turned to Paris for guidance on fashion. In 1875 bustles made from foxes' tails, kitchen dusters, wire cages or down cushions were part of fashionable women's dress.*

the *cocottes* and *demi-mondaines* were entertaining their clients with verve and enthusiasm.

Wealthy Parisians of the late 1860s devoted themselves to pleasure with unbridled self-indulgence and an orgy of ostentation, expressed in a glittering succession of banquets and balls. If inspiration were needed, it came from the Emperor himself, whose fondness for masked and costumed balls turned life in the Palace of the Tuileries into an almost continuous cabaret.

Away from court, too, exaggeration and extravagance reigned. Magnates vied with each other in the splendour of their homes: Menier, the chocolate king, had a mansion built in Baroque style. Boni de Castellane, a member of an ancient family who married an American heiress, had a staircase based on that of Versailles in his new Rose Palace. However, not even great town houses could detain fashionable Parisians for the entire year. In July, those who owned chateaux packed the silver and porcelain, the children's toys, the tweeds and other essentials, and took themselves to the country, where they hunted and shot until Christmas. A further break was frequently taken in January or February – on the Riviera, recently made accessible to wealthy Parisians by the railways.

These patterns of migration had been learned from the British, who had 'discovered' the Riviera before either the French or the railways. The great difference was that while the cream of French society had its heart in its beloved Paris, the British upper class was reluctant to leave the country. Only between April and July were the great town houses in Belgravia and Mayfair opened up for the London Season. It was during this time that daughters were presented at Court.

The round of garden parties and balls at which London's young ladies met selected young men were, however, staid affairs compared with those of Napoleon III. Wives spent the Season on shopping expeditions or paying and receiving calls. Their menfolk spent much time at their clubs; with the faded portraits, deep armchairs and aroma of cigars and leather, clubs were the nearest thing men could find to their longed-for house in the shires.

In the park *Elaborate dresses and frilly pantaloons did not prevent Parisian girls of 1856 from enjoying themselves, and even skipping. Their brothers show off their skills with hoops, while older generations of rich families take things at a more sedate pace, greeting acquaintances as they stroll, or exchanging news under a tree. One gentleman stops to read a newspaper, undisturbed by childish merriment.*

Closer look *Opera-goers used their ivory opera glasses as much to spy on other members of the audience as to watch the singers.*

Finishing touch *Ladies taken to the opera carried fans; they made attractive accessories, and also combatted the heat from gaslights.*

Race meeting *One attraction of Paris's Bois de Boulogne was the racecourse where top-hatted gentlemen lined the perimeter fence with their ladies. The well-turned-out man wearing a fashionable spiked beard seems to find the social attractions of the course more interesting than the race.*

HOURS OF AMUSEMENT

The young man of means in the Paris of the Second Empire rises at a reasonable hour, say 10 o'clock, and dresses – a serious business, for the cravat has to be just so, the black gleam on the silk hat and the boots unfathomable. After a light breakfast in a favourite café, he strolls along the shady paths of the Bois de Boulogne to the Longchamp racecourse by the River Seine, a favourite haunt of men of fashion. It is not exercise he seeks in the park, but agreeable ritual, for in his circle it is important to see and be seen, and to greet acquaintances with just the right degree of acknowledgment due to each one's social status. He takes luncheon at his club, spends a pleasant hour or two with an actress friend, and then, as the shadows lengthen across the grass, he returns to the Bois. This time he comes by the Avenue de l'Impératrice, for it is the hour when the great and famous parade there in glittering carriages, moving four or five abreast along the broad and imposing avenue. From time to time he pauses to savour the sight of high-life ladies who, descending from their carriages, sweep the ground with their trailing frou-frous. Among them may appear such legendary courtesans as the beautiful Cora Pearl who, it is rumoured, has demanded a million francs for a single night of her company. As dusk falls and lights start to blaze in the boulevards, he begins to contemplate an evening at the theatre – Offenbach's latest operetta perhaps. He remembers with a smile the composer's *Orpheus in the Underworld*, with its boisterous cancan which had electrified the city a year or so earlier, and gradually quickens his pace.

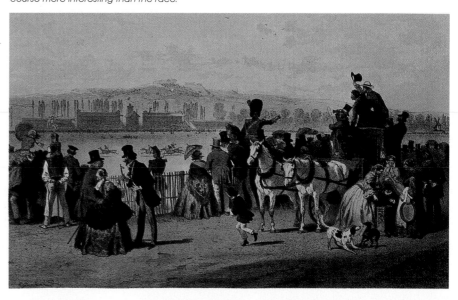

BLOOD AND IRON UNITE GERMANY

Students in a Heidelberg café in the 1860s laugh as one of them daringly tells a joke about a professor. Another calls out 'Let's sing!' They begin a melody harking back to an older and more simple existence. Suddenly the mood changes. A youth in a jaunty cap starts a nationalist chant as beer mugs thump on the table. Nostalgia has been swamped by the longing for a new way of life.

At that time Germany was a welter of little states lurching towards an uncertain future. The voice of the nation had made an impassioned plea for unity in 1848. Revolutionary civil servants, professors, businessmen and lawyers from all over Germany gathered at Frankfurt and offered the crown of a united Germany to the King of Prussia. But it was not theirs to offer: they had no army and no authority. The king contemptuously refused to 'pick up a crown from the gutter', and sent his troops to crush the revolution.

Where the intellectuals failed, force was to succeed. In 1866 Bismarck's Prussia beat Austria, its rival in the struggle for power in Germany, in a lightning war to take over the leadership of the country which he went on to unite by a policy of 'blood and iron'. He had all Germany behind him in a victorious war against France in the early 1870s. While Prussian guns blasted Paris, the King of Prussia was declared Kaiser (Emperor) Wilhelm I of Germany in the Hall of Mirrors at Versailles. The army had delivered a triumph that for years many Germans had only dreamt about.

'Better pointed bullets than pointed speeches.'

OTTO VON BISMARCK

With the unification of 1871, Prussia gained military and economic supremacy in Germany. Enlightened officials lent money to enterprising firms, while Prussia's goose-stepping might was admired and its military tradition spread throughout the nation. After 1871, admiration turned into adulation. Order became the first duty of a citizen. Discipline and drill were paramount at school – and at home the father's word was law. Militarism had an influence on civilian life: a man was of little worth unless he held the rank of reserve officer. A sergeant was more esteemed than a minister of state who had not done military service. In 1871 fewer than one in 100 Berliners were aristocrats, yet they dominated the imperial guards; one regiment had 13 princes and ten counts among its officers. The middle class could aspire only to posts in the more mundane regiments of the line.

An industrialist felt pleased with himself if a few pompous lieutenants went to a ball at his home. Police officers demanded obedience as if they were army officers. Ordinary public officials dressed in militaristic style. In their grim apartment blocks, the working class fought to educate their sons for jobs in the customs service or post office, or any other position in the civil service that carried a uniform with it.

Life was changing rapidly. Earlier *Biedermeier* homes, with their air of simple comfort, were now filled with ornate furniture in keeping with the triumphal architecture appearing in Berlin. Richard Wagner's operas on Germanic legends were a siren song to a people trying to confirm its racial

Local colour *Loyal to their roots, the peoples of the united Germany still took pride in their national costumes.*

Victors take their ease *Prussians in muddy jackboots relax in a French house on their way to occupy Paris in 1870. France soon had to come to terms with the powerful new united Germany across her border.*

identity. Kaiser Wilhelm II, in brilliant uniform, became the leading player in what many people saw as an empty show. The poet Ludwig Thoma, jailed for offending royal dignity, described Wilhelm's speeches as bombast. A court official noted that in the 16 years since the Kaiser's accession there had been 37 changes of uniforms.

A great industrial state and its people, renowned for learning and ingenuity, were portrayed to the world by officers qualified not by military ability but by birth. This veneration for uniforms was to reach an absurd level when in 1906 a penniless drifter and petty criminal called Wilhelm Voigt donned a captain's uniform and ordered soldiers to occupy Köpenick town hall in the suburbs of Berlin. He arrested the mayor and stole 4000 marks. No one thought of questioning the orders of the so-called 'Captain of Köpenick'. He was caught, but he had

A MATTER OF HONOUR

Duelling was popular among the university students. Its purpose was to overcome what they called 'der innere Schweinehund', or cowardice, by facing the slashing sabre without flinching. The eyes and body were protected: only the face was left bare.

Duellists were positioned by the seconds. Sabres were raised head-high and the bout began. If a man was hurt, the seconds stepped in and a doctor or medical student treated the wound. Unless it was serious, the fight went on. If possible, a downward stroke of the sabre would leave the flesh of the cheek hanging onto the jaw. Wounds were swabbed with alcohol and stitched up none too elegantly, so that the scar would be a focus of admiration for fellow-students and adoring females. Membership of duelling clubs was for life: scarred old gentlemen in club caps turned up for festive evenings to roar out their favourite songs, regale the young with tales of the old days and be plied with beer.

Objective achieved *'I think I have almost finished my studies. I won't get drunk any more.' – From* Simplicissimus *magazine, 1901.*

Sedate pleasures *Seaside trips were mostly enjoyed by the middle class. Parasols and voluminous clothes prevented unladylike sunburn. Berlin's working class picnicked on beer and sausage in the park, or went swimming or fishing in one of the city's lakes. Otherwise there was drinking – Berlin rated one Bierstube for every 148 inhabitants.*

Manly symbols *Student duellists switched to sabres after a spate of deaths at Jena in 1839 led to the banning of foil fencing.*

made his country and its love of all things military a laughing stock. Yet its social legislation was progressive. Already in 1853 Prussia had banned factory labour for children under 12. Bismarck introduced workers' health insurance and old age and disability pensions in the 1880s to counter the appeal of socialism.

Alongside the idealism there lay a set of rigid moral codes. Each group had its ethical values: there was family honour, officer's honour and professional honour. In Theodor Fontane's novel *Effi Briest* (1895) a husband is forced to kill his wife's lover in a duel, and then to expel his wife. He destroys family and happiness for the sake of an absurd 'honour'. Yet *Mensurfechten*, or student duelling under strict rules, was an accepted way of life for less-sensitive spirits who proudly wore their *Schmisse*, or scars.

Jumping Jack *Children loved Hampelmänner, or wooden puppets. Even these were often given a Prussian-style uniform with plenty of bright buttons.*

Cult of nature *Progress was accompanied by nostalgia for a pre-industrial past, as idealised in this woodcut of medieval travellers. Yet progress in the shape of the railway was to help people reach those beloved forests and mountains. Romantic poets set the tone; then in 1897 the youth movement was launched among schoolboys and teachers. They hiked and climbed, shunning tobacco and alcohol in favour of folk singing, in their search for a lost time of innocence.*

ROOKERIES, RATS AND GIN PALACES

In 1841 a Liverpool doctor, called to an ailing woman, found her lying on straw with her infant in a cellar. The cellar, he said, had 'no light or ventilation and the air was dreadful. I had to walk on bricks across the floor to reach her bedside, as the floor itself was flooded with stagnant water'.

City people at the lowest levels of 19th-century society lived in appalling squalor. The influx of people to jobs in the new factories put great pressure on housing, and the poorest of them colonised dark, wet and airless cellars of houses whose underground cesspools could leak their contents into the cellars. In Liverpool 20,000 people lived in cellars, and the floors were sometimes so wet that the dwellers took doors off their hinges and raised them on bricks to serve as beds.

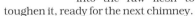

Workhouse money

In London the Earl of Shaftesbury, who did much to help the poor, found a woman keeping grim watch over her one-room home. 'Look at that great hole,' she said to him, 'the landlord will not mend it. I have every night to sit up and watch because that hole is over a common cesspool, and the rats come up, sometimes twenty at a time, and if we did not watch them they would eat the baby up.'

To meet the demand for housing, city tenements were subdivided into ever more cramped units. In Britain these were known as 'rookeries', because the tall, narrow buildings were so packed with families that they came to resemble nests of rooks. The dilapidated buildings suffered from leaking roofs, rotten timbers, and broken windows mended with oilskins, torn sacking or brown paper. Two or three – or even more – families frequently shared a single room.

Other European cities had the same problems of overcrowding. As late as 1882 a Paris physician reported: 'Of one room they have made two. They have placed twenty beds in rooms which formerly only had ten. They have built sheds in courts already too narrow, resulting in the most dangerous clutter and congestion.'

From the foul cellars and festering rookeries came suffocating stenches that made more than one middle-class visitor promptly come out into the streets to be sick. The streets themselves were littered with animal dung and vegetable refuse that decomposed to trickle and congeal among the cobblestones. So the ragged crossing sweeper was a familiar – and necessary – sight on Victorian thoroughfares.

Bloody knees for the 'chummy'

Another familiar sight in city streets was the chimney sweep, who plied his trade from door to door. Climbing boys, or 'chummies' as they were known, started work at the age of four or five and carried on until they grew too big to climb a chimney. The poor districts furnished an unending supply of boys with no one to care for them, who might otherwise be destined for the workhouse. They were taken by master sweeps and forced up narrow flues, and came down with blood streaming from their arms and knees. The master sweep then rubbed strong brine into the raw flesh to toughen it, ready for the next chimney.

When, and if, London chummies grew up, they might earn a living of sorts from one of the diverse trades practised by the denizens of the city's lower depths. According to Henry Mayhew, a journalist who made a detailed study of the very poor, there were bone-grubbers, costermongers, rat catchers, rag gatherers, beggars, street piemen and such extraordinary specialists as the 'pure' finders who scoured the city's pavements for dogs' droppings. They sold the droppings, which had alkaline, cleansing and purifying properties, by the bucketful to local tanneries.

But it was a precarious way of life, and one where ill-health or accident could lead to destitution, and the workhouse. A 60-year-old woman 'pure' finder told Mayhew 'I have earned no money today; but pray, sir, don't tell anybody of it. I could never bear the thought of going into the workhouse'.

As well as those who had a home and work, albeit at the lowest level, there were the vagrants and homeless people who slept under railway arches or in parks, and whose number swelled in times of economic depression. When – and only when – the temperature dropped to freezing might the destitute get a pound of dry bread and shelter at a night refuge.

The horrifically insanitary conditions of the poor quarters meant that they were breeding grounds for diseases such as typhoid and cholera. However, more lives still were claimed by such common ailments as malnutrition, pneumonia and tuberculosis.

> *'I attended a family of 13, 12 of whom had typhus fever. They lay on the floor, and so crowded that I could scarcely pass between them.'*
>
> LIVERPOOL MEDICAL OFFICER, c.1830

In the mid-19th century, more than half of all British children died before they reached their fifth birthday, and the average life expectancy among the working classes was only 17 years. For the middle classes, the norm was 25

Life on the streets *Behind the idealised painting of a rosy-cheeked flower girl in well-swept London streets lies the harsh reality of a childhood finished almost before it has begun. By contrast, the girl by her mother's side has years of protection ahead within a loving family.*

Wash day *One-room living was the lot of countless families. To the problem of damp walls and floors were added practical problems such as washing clothes for six people, the chore under way here. Water had to be carried in, heated and carried out again; the washing then dripped from the clothes line, often onto the bed.*

years. Hospitals were frequently unfit to tend their patients; as the great nursing reformer Florence Nightingale pointed out, mortality rates in them were higher than they were for the same class of patients treated outside.

In the rabbit warrens of dingy alleys, some comfort for the urban poor was to be found in beer shops and gaudy gin palaces. There was no minimum age for drinking in Victorian London, and until 1839 there were no restrictions on opening hours, so drunkenness was rife. 'Drunk for a penny – dead drunk for twopence' was the common saying.

Equally rife was prostitution. In Victorian London the more desirable girls promenaded in the West End, rustling their crinoline skirts. They worked singly or in pairs, and charged fees of half a guinea to a guinea. Back alleys and dark entrances, however, were haunted by those grown old and hideous, who, the younger girls felt, frightened away potential customers. One 'shameless hag' described by Mayhew had 'thick lips, sable black skin, leering countenance and obscene disgusting tongue', and resembled 'a lewd spirit from another world'.

Mayhew and critical writers such as Charles Dickens made the plight of Britain's poor widely known. In an age that promoted the benefits of self-help, improvements were often effected by individuals: Dr Barnardo established homes for destitute boys and girls, William Booth's Salvation Army helped to fight the evils of drunkenness, and Octavia Hill tackled slum housing. But government action was needed to deal with the basic problems; a step forward came when Public Health Acts made towns appoint medical officers and improve water supply and drainage.

Life at the bottom *Narrow, sunless streets wound through the poorest districts of Paris and other cities. Closely packed buildings gave little privacy, and rubbish rotting in the gutter attracted rats and caused disease.*

Demon drink *Alcohol was to blame for many a family's downfall, and the slide into degradation that it could cause was emphasised in cautionary illustrations, such as this sequence by George Cruikshank. In a modest but respectable home, father enjoys a Christmas drink and presses mother to join him. Later, his love of drink has cost him his job; his child has to visit the pawnshop; the fireplace and table are empty, and the cat is emaciated. Violence and destitution lie ahead.*

THE SLIPPERY SLOPE TO THE WORKHOUSE

Families reduced to the depths of poverty were driven to the workhouse – though they tried hard to avoid it. Here the destitute were given work and shelter in conditions that were intentionally inferior to those of the poorest labourer – in the words of a Poor Law official, 'so repulsive as to prevent them from entering'. Men and women were segregated, and families were broken up; inmates slept in comfortless dormitories, often on the floor and sometimes in coffin-like troughs; prayers were compulsory. The grindingly boring work included turning cranks to mill corn, stone breaking and picking oakum – unravelling old ropes to make caulking for ships. For a time workers were paid in tokens, which could only be spent in the workhouse. Meals were often mainly of gruel, and were eaten in silence.

To the workhouse came destitute people of all kinds – families reduced to poverty by ill-health, unemployment or drink, pregnant single women, widows unable to support their children, the sick, the simple-minded, and wives deserted by their husbands. The most pitiful were the many children: orphans, foundlings abandoned in the streets, and children of loving but sick or starving parents who could not support them. Sometimes a family with many children had to make the agonising choice of abandoning one child to ease the burden on the family.

PICKPOCKETS AND PICKING OAKUM

When Owen Haggerty and John Holloway were hanged for murder outside London's Newgate prison in 1807, a mob of more than 40,000 crammed into the area around the gallows to watch. The crush was appalling, and panic broke out. By the time the crowd dispersed 28 people lay dead, many of them crushed or trampled to death. Nearly 70 more were seriously injured.

A public hanging was one of the great spectacles of the early 19th century. The rich paid highly for rooms overlooking the gallows; lesser citizens found cheaper vantage points on roofs, while pickpockets moved through the laughing, swearing, fighting mob who looked on. Charles Dickens watched an execution in 1849 and wrote to a friend: 'The conduct of the people was so indescribably frightful, that I felt for some time afterwards almost as if I were living in a city of devils.'

At the start of the 19th century even pickpockets and sheep stealers were liable to be hanged, but as the century progressed hanging was increasingly reserved for the most serious crimes.

Perpetrators of lesser crimes, such as theft, could be transported to the colonies, or imprisoned.

Conditions in early 19th-century jails were dire. Packed inside them were prisoners of all kinds – people awaiting trial, convicted criminals, debtors, lunatics, and women with their children. Debtors were worthy of special sympathy. The country was short of minted coins, and businesses depended on elaborate chains of credit. If a link in a chain broke, just about anyone might fall into debt.

Prisoners were kept in filthy cells with rotten straw for bedding, and with rats, lice and jail fever – a form of typhus – as extra torments. Jailers ran prisons as businesses, charging the inmates for food and drink, and such privileges as clean straw and the removal of leg irons; the impoverished were plagued by hunger and thirst. Overcrowding meant that the young and innocent were swiftly corrupted by hardened offenders.

Sentenced to silence

From the 1820s laws were passed to overcome some of these evils: hygiene was improved, leg irons were banned, and every prisoner was supposed to have a separate bed in, if possible, a separate cell. But new torments were inflicted in the name of reform.

Experts in prison reform believed firmly in preventing the inmates from fraternising. Two systems of isolation, originating in the United States, were used widely in European prisons. Under the 'separate' system, each prisoner had no contact with fellow inmates during the entire term of his or her sentence. Under the less severe 'silent' system, prisoners were locked up alone at night but were allowed to work alongside each other by day, albeit in rigidly enforced silence. Monotony and loneliness, particularly under the 'separate' system, led to unnaturally high rates of madness and suicide. One

jail in which the 'separate' system of isolation operated was London's Pentonville prison, which was typical of many of the new British jails built in the 1840s. Its 520 cells were each 13 ft (4 m) long and 7 ft (2 m) wide, with a small window in the outside wall. Each cell contained a shaded gas burner, table, stool and hammock with mattress and blankets.

Prisoners worked from 6 am to 7 pm, with breaks for meals and for limited exercise in the prison yard, during which they were masked so that they could not recognise one another. At the daily service in the chapel each prisoner sat in a pigeonhole pew, walled off from neighbours.

Work in Victorian prisons often took the form of exhausting, often pointless, tasks such as working the treadmill – a huge, revolving drum of slatted steps which the men trod. Each man stood in a separate compartment, steadying himself by a handrail on either side. In an average day, each prisoner climbed an estimated 8600 ft (2600 m). More profitable toil included breaking stone, making mats and picking oakum. Oakum was a loose hemp fibre, picked from old tarred ropes and used to caulk seams in wooden ships. The practice of picking oakum went on long after iron ships had made the oakum useless.

In prisons, flogging was still a common form of punishment. There were also special cells, often soundproof and pitch dark, where prisoners

Law in action *Under reformed legal systems the accused had a hearing, even if the defending lawyer, as in this French case, did not always plead successfully.*

Police armoury
The plain wooden truncheon of the British 'bobby' was inscribed to mark his retirement.

DETECTIVE STORY

To outwit criminals, police forces started to take a methodical approach to solving crime. France led the field with a detective bureau set up in 1817 under the charge of Eugène Vidocq, a reformed thief whose staff were also largely ex-criminals. Another Frenchman, Alphonse Bertillon, pioneered a method of identifying criminals by taking detailed body measurements that together would uniquely identify the person. It was Bertillon's idea, too, that prisoners should be photographed, from a standard distance, in full face and in profile. From the 1890s fingerprints brought more science to policing.

Street school *Outside a London shop Oliver Twist, the creation of Charles Dickens, is taught the tricks of a gang of child pickpockets. Leipzig, in Germany, was notorious for its gangs of child beggars.*

Vital statistics *Alphonse Bertillon (below) took precise measurements of offenders' heads, and of limbs, feet, fingers and even ears to compile a dossier of known criminals.*

Signature *Finger-prints could uniquely identify suspects, and link them with the scene of crime.*

Detained at sea *Until 1858, overcrowding in prisons was relieved by housing prisoners, in dreadful conditions, in old and unseaworthy ships moored in the Thames and other rivers. The Warrior, moored at Woolwich, accommodated up to 500 prisoners.*

Criminal type *According to some theorists, criminals were born with evil instincts and distinctive features. The supposed 'criminal type' is sketched against a 'reward' poster.*

Boys in blue *A ragged youngster falls foul of an early Peeler, whose uniform of chimney-pot hat and blue tailcoat was designed to avoid a military appearance.*

might be sent for offences such as insolence to prison guards, irreverence in chapel, or speaking in the exercise yard. The punishment could be as short as an hour, or as long as several days.

Catching criminals and maintaining order on the streets was the job of the uniformed police forces that began to be set up in many countries in the 19th century. Berlin had police-men, who wore spiked helmets, as early as the 1740s, but in Britain policing had for centuries been the job of local magistrates who called on parish constables, night watchmen or even the army to keep the peace. With the booming urban populations a more organised body of men was needed. From 1829 Britain's towns set up forces of 'bobbies', or 'peelers', named after Sir Robert Peel, the founder of London's first police force. The original forces were not popular, partly because they were paid out of the rates, but also because there were fears that they would act like a paramilitary force. To lessen these worries, Peel armed the

tall-hatted police with no more than a truncheon, and a rattle – later replaced by a whistle – to summon help.

Well-to-do citizens came to see the police as a vital bulwark against the underworld of burglars, pickpockets and other criminals whose operations were highly organised. The sprawling cities, in particular, gave unrivalled opportunities for crime.

'Pickpockets help their comrades in difficulty. They frequently meet with many of the burglars. A great number of the women of pickpockets and burglars are shoplifters, as they require to support themselves when their men are in prison.'

LONDON EX-PICKPOCKET, c. 1850

Crime and punishment exerted an intense fascination over the public, whose appetites were fed by cheap illustrated publications describing in lurid detail the latest murder cases and other real-life horrors. Fictional crime was just as popular, especially Sir Arthur Conan Doyle's stories in *Strand Magazine* about the detective Sherlock Holmes. The short tales were written for commuters travelling by train between the crime-ridden capital they worked in and their comfortable homes in leafy developing suburbs.

SPEEDING THE NEWS ACROSS LAND AND SEA

Just a month after Britain's Queen Victoria came to the throne, directors of the London and Birmingham Railway watched a demonstration of a new electric telegraph system. They were told that the four-needle instrument could transmit five words a minute, provided the words were short.

The distance the telegraphed words were to travel was modest – less than a mile – although the inventors, Charles Wheatstone and W.F. Cooke, needed to lay 19 miles (30 km) of line to carry them to their destination. The railway engineer Robert Stephenson sent the first, suitably terse, telegram: 'Bravo!'

The idea of an electric telegraphic system had occurred to a number of people in both Europe and the United States at about the same time, and it was one of several ways in which communications were revolutionised in the 19th century. Its development more or less paralleled that of the railways, especially so in the early years when the telegraph poles carrying the wires were erected almost exclusively alongside railway lines.

It was the railway companies that were the first to grasp the significance of this new means of communication, and make practical use of it. It allowed them to establish uniform time, or 'railway time' throughout the network, and to create a system of signalling that kept the trains at a safe distance apart. Railway officials could also use the telegraph to summon help.

In these early years of telegraphy, telegraph wires ran above the ground. Then in 1847 the chemist and physicist Michael Faraday suggested insulating them with gutta-percha so that they could be laid underground or on the seabed. The first London to

The Penny Black

Paris cable was in use in 1851 and, after several attempts, a transatlantic telegraph cable was laid in 1865. By this time the telegraph was firmly established; at the end of the 1860s 111,000 miles (180,000 km) of telegraph wires crisscrossed continental Europe.

One of the great advantages of the telegraph was the speed with which news could now be collected and distributed. London's *The Times* likened the transatlantic cable to the arrival of Columbus in the New World, though at the same time the editor warned his reporters that 'telegrams are for facts; background and comment must come by post'. The telegraph service quickly revolutionised journalism. By the end of the 1850s, as many as 120 provincial newspapers in Great Britain received news by wire from Parliament daily, and the London-based news agency that Julius Reuter had first started in Germany sent foreign news to editors in every town in the country. Another innovation that

the telegraph brought was the foreign correspondent or war correspondent – the man on the spot at momentous events who could send news as soon as it happened, instead of weeks or months later. The first and greatest was W.H. Russell of *The Times*. He was his paper's special correspondent covering several wars, including the Crimean War of the 1850s from which he sent vivid accounts of the charges of the Light and Heavy Brigades.

Just as powerful were Russell's savage indictments of the inadequacies and inefficiencies of the British Headquarters Staff in the Crimea, and of the horrors of the hospital conditions. The influence of newspapers was now great enough for his reports to contribute to the fall of the government.

A development of the telegraph, and one destined to have just as great an influence, was the telephone. Patented in the United States in 1876 by the Scottish-born Alexander Graham Bell, then further refined by the American inventor Thomas Alva Edison, the telephone soon established itself. In

Post haste *Anxious letter writers rush to catch the 6 pm post, in a scene by G.E. Hicks painted 20 years after the coming of the Penny Post had introduced a new age of pre-paid letter delivery. On the left, a policeman in top hat controls the crowd, which includes newspaper boys struggling to get their editions onto the mail train, in time for morning delivery round the country.*

1884 Bell's company set in action the world's first long-distance telephone line, between Boston and New York. Networks, an increasingly vital part of communications, were developed in many countries, dialling speeded up the process of telephoning, and before long most major cities had their own telephone exchanges.

In this great age of the printed word, Britain alone had 12 national daily newspapers by the middle of the 1850s, along with eight weekly newspapers and hundreds of provincial ones. Some of them catered for the ghoulish. In 1840, a Sunday newspaper called *The Death Warrant* offered a 'Reprinted Record of Facts – compiled from authentic sources – of the most dreadful battles by Sea and Land; Horrible and Mysterious Murders and Suicides, Plagues, Storms, Famines, Earthquakes, Deathbeds, Shipwrecks and every other Appalling Calamity incidental to the life of Man, exceeding in Intensity and Agonising Interest any work ever published!'

Readers who were not interested in stories of 'agonising interest' could buy periodicals devoted to religion, temperance, fashion and pet hobbies. There were also specialist journals such as *The Lancet* for doctors, and *The Female Domestic's Instructor* for servants. Many people read

family magazines which offered a combination of true-life and fictional adventure stories, articles on bringing up children, and uplifting verse; the German family magazine *Gartenlaube*, 'Summerhouse', was so popular that its circulation reached 400,000 by 1875. Some magazines were illustrated; the *Illustrated London News*, for instance, had fashions, archaeological discoveries, and woodcuts of cities.

Of all the aids to communication, the postage stamp was the simplest. Britain's 'Penny Black' first appeared in 1840. Its begetter, Rowland Hill, foresaw the day when 'every house might be provided with a box into which the carrier would drop the letters'. Other nations quickly followed suit – France introduced a stamp depicting Ceres, goddess of the harvest, in 1849. The increase in mail was such that by the end of the 19th century Londoners received 12 postal deliveries a day.

The vast number of letters sent, and newspapers and magazines read, was a reflection of the rising standards of literacy. In Britain and France more than 60 per cent of people were literate in 1870. From then on, education in both countries expanded, and by the end of the century more than 95 per cent of people could read and write.

Ordinary lives *The invention of the camera in the 1840s meant that the lives of ordinary people could be recorded on film. The first cameras were complex devices (right) needing skilled handling; the photographer on London's Clapham Common in 1877 (above) needed a handcart for his equipment. The Kodak camera invented by George Eastman in 1888 put photography within everyone's reach. In the 1890s in Paris, the Lumière brothers showed moving pictures of everyday scenes in the first public cinema, ushering in the cinema age.*

THE ART OF PERSUASION

As news spread more quickly, and as new forms of journalism began successfully to appeal to a mass readership, the public also became a target for the advertiser. Some newspapers depended for much of their revenue on giving their front pages to long columns announcing goods for sale, places for servants and cures for illnesses.

Blank walls carried posters for anything from patent medicines to music halls. The soap company, Pears, challenged British passers-by with the question 'Good Morning. Have you used Pears Soap?' Towards the end of the century the introduction of cheap lithography allowed artists to make freehand drawings on the stone blocks from which posters advertising such attractions as the Moulin Rouge were printed.

Men and boys carried placards on poles – or wore them as 'sandwich boards' – to advertise products for sale, give news of exhibitions to visit, and to announce the results of elections. Political argument took a prominent place on the front page of some newspapers.

IN THE PUB, ON THE PITCH, AT THE SEASIDE

The 1880s and 1890s were the golden age of the British public house – a place to enjoy a full evening's entertainment, or simply to shelter from the weather and the tangled traffic of the city streets. No institution in continental Europe quite resembled it, although in Paris the café did provide people with a place to meet friends and to eat and drink in convivial surroundings.

The relaxing atmosphere of the pub made it a favourite place for people from all walks of life to meet and chat over a drink. Here they could enjoy porter for four pence a quart, or sip cheap tots of gin, while the hungry could feed themselves on the simple, but ample, fare offered.

Interiors of pubs were often ornate: mahogany furnishings and polished brass were part of their attraction, as were the charms of the barmaids. Not all pubs were equally well looked after, however, and some of the rowdier ones were frowned upon by the authorities.

Teaming up for exercise

Those whose taste was for more active amusements than the pub had plenty of choice. During Victorian times, interest in sport, both for participants and spectators, increased rapidly. Among the most popular activities was soccer. Ever since the first Football Association Cup competition in 1872, when Royal Engineers beat Crystal Palace 1–0, new clubs had been springing up everywhere.

Usually the clubs began with teams of workmates or friends; Blackburn Rovers was initially made up of old boys from Blackburn Grammar School, while Sheffield Wednesday originated with friends who played on their half-day holiday. New clubs formed in other countries – the first German club was founded in Hanover in 1878.

Cricket had become more and more popular, and at a Test Match played at the Oval in 1880 a crowd of 20,000 watched W.G. Grace score a century to help England beat Australia by five wickets. A smooth pitch could now be achieved with the lawn mower and heavy roller developed in the 1830s, and there was more scope than before

for matches, now that teams could travel to 'away' games by train. A sport that had a brief vogue around this time was 'pedding' – a nonstop walking marathon of six days and more. The winner was the last person standing. But as a public attraction, pedding was a non-starter beside the national preoccupation with horse racing.

Form was followed with equal fervour in clubland and back street, and all classes were agreed that the highlight of the racing year was Derby Day. Then, it seemed, all England was on the road to Epsom Downs, in landau or donkey cart, charabanc or coach and four. Everyone was there in their finest clothes, to see and be seen, whether they paraded the button patterns of London's cockney costermongers, the bright colours of the gypsies, or the

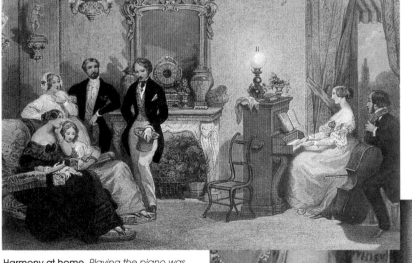

Harmony at home *Playing the piano was an essential accomplishment for a young lady from a middle-class home. It shone brightly at musical evenings – informal family gatherings at which father sang ballads to mother's accompaniment at the piano, or at musical 'At Homes' to which the ambitious hostess might invite professional singers or instrumentalists.*

Counter attraction *The bright lights, warmth and opulence of the pub made it a welcome refuge for the poor of the town. Customers crowding the bar of a London pub in 1882 include a young mother who is perhaps trying to soothe her baby's teething pains with alcohol, and a child sent to collect drinks. The Temperance lobby tried to tempt people away from pubs by setting up rival 'coffee public houses' where people could pass a few sociable but sober hours in pub-like surroundings.*

latest Paris creation by Worth, worn by the very rich. In France, racing events at Longchamp and Chantilly were as much fashion events as sporting ones.

Some of the country-based sports that had been popular in the earlier decades of the 19th century were now illegal. Cock fights had been held in inns, sometimes with spurs attached to the birds' legs, and large audiences had flocked to see terriers killing rats – and placed bets on the outcome. Blood sports had not died out, however; in Spain, bull fighting became increasingly popular, and in northern Europe ever greater numbers of birds and animals were shot for sport.

Animal performances of a different sort could be seen at circuses where horses performed along with acrobats and clowns. As circuses travelled the

country they might be joined by 'freak shows' exhibiting bearded women and the 'fattest man in the world'.

From the 1870s many people had more time to devote to leisure, due to reductions in working hours and the granting of weekly half-holidays. Bank Holidays, introduced in Britain in 1871, provided the opportunity for a trip to the seaside. To make the very most of their day off, families would set off at 4 am or 5 am on excursion trains to their favourite resort – Blackpool, Brighton, Dunoon, Great Yarmouth and many others.

At the seaside they promenaded on the pier, rode on donkeys, and changed for a dip in the sea in horse-drawn bathing machines or the newer bathing huts. They ate ice cream, fried fish and shellfish, listened to German bands and watched white-faced Pierrots act the fool in their spotted outfits and skull caps. Better-off families might spend a week or more at the seaside, staying in hotels, boarding houses, furnished villas or rooms, according to their budget.

In the 1850s, the more adventurous travellers started to go abroad – until now a luxury accessible only to the very wealthy. They went on tours run by Thomas Cook to an exhibition in Paris in 1855, and even farther afield in the 1860s to Switzerland, firmly establishing that country's landscape as a tourist image. Many would go

Art gallery Books and prints poured from the presses to adorn the walls and shelves of middle-class houses. Browsing became a popular pastime, itself the subject of a study by the French artist Honoré Daumier.

armed with the guidebooks which were researched and written by the German bookseller Karl Baedeker.

Those who could not afford to travel could, from the late 1880s, explore the countryside on a safety bicycle. With its chain drive and pneumatic tyres, it was more efficient than the *vélocipède*, or 'boneshaker', of the 1860s, or the penny-farthing of the 1870s.

City dwellers could go to one of the new public parks and listen to the band playing on the bandstand. Brass

bands were particularly popular in the north of England, where they were often attached to collieries or factories.

A variety of indoor entertainment was available. Theatre, for those who could afford the expense, ranged from Shakespeare to the latest sentimental melodramas. Scenery was spectacular and often included realistic portrayals of storms, battles or shipwrecks. Popular alternatives to theatre were music halls and magic-lantern shows – images from painted slides projected onto a screen. Parisians favoured the variety shows of the Folies-Bergère, which comprised musical numbers, acrobatics, ballets, magicians, trained animal acts and, towards the end of the century, the striptease shows for which it became renowned.

Card games and Christmas carols

At home, middle-class families created their own amusements. Reading aloud was a popular entertainment – be it from the Bible and improving books, or the works of Charles Dickens, Mrs Gaskell and George Eliot. Whist was a popular family card game, as was the newly invented Happy Families. Home concerts were frequently organised, comprising musical items, amateur theatricals and recitations.

Many of the musical items sung in drawing rooms were the popular tunes of the day. Thousands of copies of the sheet music for songs such as *My Old Man Said Follow the Van*, *I Dreamt that I Dwelt in Marble Halls*, and *Ta-ra-ra-Boom-de-ay* were produced and sold for enthusiastic performances to family and friends at home.

When guests came, everyone joined in party games like charades, and danced to music by a hired orchestra, if the hosts were very rich, or a piano in less exalted homes. Dancing was a skilled business, and no one would dream of taking the floor without having practised in private first.

At Christmas time, new carols were gaining popularity, and old carols such as *Silent Night* made their way across Europe. Christmas became sentimentalised and commercialised. The first Christmas card, a lithograph coloured by hand and costing one shilling, was produced in 1843, the same year in which Dickens wrote *A Christmas Carol*. Christmas trees were introduced from Germany, and in the 1870s Father Christmas became Santa Claus – an immigrant to Britain from the United States, while on the Continent St Nicholas prevailed.

COUNTRY AIR AND SENTIMENTAL SONG

On a fine day, late Victorians could take their bicycles into the country, or they could go for a picnic, taking a substantial meal in a wicker hamper complete with china and cutlery. A picnic in such style was for the better-off, but almost anyone could afford to spend an evening at a music hall. Early music halls were simply rooms in pubs, but by the 1880s many of them were luxurious venues with fixed seating, draped velvet curtains, gilding, and scroll work decorating every surface. The audience were still allowed to drink at their seats as they joined in the choruses of sentimental songs, laughed at the bawdier ones and, like those in the upper balcony, waved to and cheered on the performers through a haze of tobacco smoke. Acts by scantily clad dancers were always hits, but it was singers such as

Marie Lloyd and comedians such as Dan Leno and George Robey who became the household names. One popular act was the French trapeze artist, Jules Léotard, who gave his name to the gymnasts' costume, and inspired the song *The Flying Trapeze*.

Picnic basket for two

Poster advertising cycling

OPERATIONS AND DOSES TO CURE – OR KILL

To undergo a surgical operation in the early decades of the 19th century called for a high degree of fortitude. Blindfolded and tied to a stretcher, with no anaesthetic, the patient could only hope that the surgeon would be brisk. 'Half-a-dozen strokes and the limb is in the sawdust,' reported an observer of a leg amputation in 1846. From start to finish, the removal of a limb usually took 28 seconds; some surgeons laid claim to 19 seconds.

Its swiftness notwithstanding, the shock and pain of such an operation without anaesthetics often proved fatal. Even more deadly were the dangers of septicaemia and gangrene.

Until the 1840s, a survival rate of six out of ten among serious surgical cases was considered satisfactory by most hospitals. Even those who felt it unsatisfactory thought that there was little they could do to improve matters. Few surgeons had much idea about hygiene, and before an operation the only precaution they would take would be to don a blood-spattered overall and give their instruments a swift wipe.

Many of the city hospitals of Europe – such as Hotel-Dieu in Paris, Santo Spirito in Rome, St Bartholomew's in London – had been founded in the Middle Ages. In the early 19th century they were still sadly primitive, despite attempts at reform since the middle of the previous century. Hospital wards were crowded with unwashed patients still wearing the clothes they arrived in, food was at starvation level and alcohol freely available. According to Florence Nightingale, who visited hospitals in the 1840s, large wards were heated by tiny fires at the end of each room.

'It was common practice to put a patient into the same sheets used by the last occupant of the bed, and mattresses were generally of flock, sodden, and seldom, if ever, cleaned.'

FLORENCE NIGHTINGALE, c.1860

Yet there was nothing new about hygiene in medical treatment, or in using anaesthetics during surgery. Physicians in ancient India and Egypt had emphasised the importance of meticulously scrubbing their hands before touching the patient. Opium and laudanum had been used as anaesthetics in various parts of the world for centuries, and in the 1830s James Esdaile, a surgeon with the East India Company, operated painlessly on patients under hypnosis.

During the 1840s surgeons started to use first ether and then chloroform to dull patients' pain and put them to sleep during surgery. With the patient unconscious, the surgeon could now work more slowly and carefully, and perform more complicated operations. Patients, however, were still vulnerable to infection, and many of them died.

An early victory against the spread of disease in hospitals occurred in 1846: it was demonstrated in Vienna that childbed fever, which killed many young mothers, was spread by doctors moving from one bed to another without washing their hands. At that time it was not understood that the bacteria on the doctors' hands and clothes were the cause of the spread of infection.

In the 1860s the battle against infection started in earnest. In France, Louis Pasteur established that the bacteria visible under a microscope were the cause of infections following surgery, and recommended scrupulous

Night refuge *The poor, and particularly their children, were the most vulnerable to disease. The casual ward of the workhouse, whose queue here in 1871 includes several children, provided a night's shelter, but only in overcrowded and insanitary conditions where diseases spread quickly.*

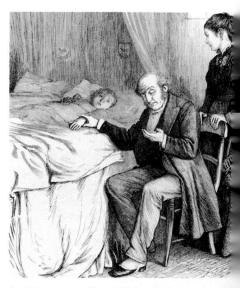

Bedside manner *The medicines that doctors prescribed, and their presence at the patient's bedside, provided comfort and hope even at a time when knowledge of disease and suitable treatment was limited.*

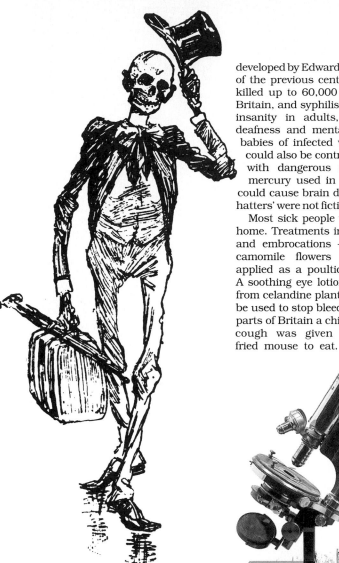

Lethal visitor 'King Cholera', as portrayed in a contemporary caricature, called often in the early 19th century, and killed 72,000 people in Britain in 1848-9. Epidemics were less common after it was shown that the disease was spread by infected water.

cleanliness in hospitals, an idea taken up by Joseph Lister in Britain. A further boost to hospital standards came from improvements in nursing. Until the mid-19th century, nursing was not considered a suitable job for a respectable woman, for nurses had a reputation for drunkenness and low morals. Far reaching changes came through nurses' training for women of high moral character, as in the school set up by Florence Nightingale, whose methods were taken to other hospitals.

Major illness was a constant threat to every household. Smallpox was still common, in spite of the vaccine

developed by Edward Jenner at the end of the previous century; tuberculosis killed up to 60,000 people a year in Britain, and syphilis was rife, causing insanity in adults, and blindness, deafness and mental defects in the babies of infected women. Diseases could also be contracted by working with dangerous substances. The mercury used in making felt hats could cause brain damage, and 'mad hatters' were not fictional characters.

Most sick people were cared for at home. Treatments included poultices and embrocations – an infusion of camomile flowers and hops was applied as a poultice to ease pains. A soothing eye lotion could be made from celandine plants, cobwebs could be used to stop bleeding, and in some parts of Britain a child with whooping cough was given a fried mouse to eat.

On view A microscope made tiny bacteria visible.

People also tried to prevent illness: mothers regularly dosed children with castor oil, and carrying a nutmeg was thought to ward off rheumatism.

As well as homemade cures, there were plenty of remedies for sale. One popular ingredient was sarsaparilla, the dried root of an America plant which was claimed to purify the blood, and some medicines contained opium, including Godfrey's cordial which was used to soothe babies. Advertisements promoted remedies vigorously – the fumes of a Carbolic Smoke Ball would, the makers claimed, 'positively cure' 15 different ailments, including loss of voice and headache, with the Bishop of London's testimony to back it.

If all this failed, or in serious cases such as that of a child with diphtheria, the doctor might be called. By the middle of the 19th century, doctors rarely practised bleeding or used leeches; their approach to disease was to do the least possible damage, while keeping the patient comfortable.

Childbirth, often an annual event, also took place at home, supervised by a midwife who might have no formal training. It was a hazardous business. Stillbirth was common, and one new-born child in six died along with many mothers. A few contraceptives were available for those who could afford them – quinine pessaries and rubber condoms, and gold, silver, wood or ivory intrauterine devices.

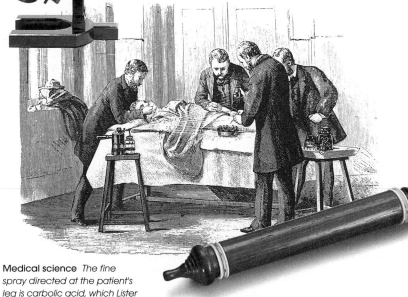

Medical science The fine spray directed at the patient's leg is carbolic acid, which Lister used as an antiseptic to rid the air of bacteria. He also used carbolic acid to disinfect bandages. The frock-coated surgeons might also have used stethoscopes; the rounded end of this wooden model of the 1830s picked up sounds from the lungs.

Street battle A Salvation Army procession is mobbed by the crowd – a frequent experience in the movement's early years. By combining a practical approach to poverty with evangelism, the movement gradually gained respect.

QUESTIONS OF FAITH

New ideas in science ruffled the surface of 19th-century religious belief. In 1830, Charles Lyell's Principles of Geology declared that the world had been created not in six days, as the Bible said, but over millions of years. Then in 1859 Charles Darwin, in his Origin of Species, suggested that the diversity of living things had evolved by natural selection to their present form – a concept of survival of the fittest that presented a direct challenge to the belief that God had created every living creature in its final form.

The Victorian era was, in Britain, a time of great religious debate and revival; Sunday was more strictly observed than before, and many churches were rebuilt. The Church of England was in a state of upheaval. Within it there were different groups: the Oxford Movement, which leaned towards Rome, opposed the idea that Parliament should reform the Church; the Evangelicals, who detested ritual, wanted to take the Gospel to the poor; and the Christian Socialists wanted to bring Christianity into industrial relations. In the new factory towns the Methodists had a wide following among better-off workers. Among the poor of the cities, however, there was indifference, and even hostility, to religion. Missionaries were sent to the slums as though to some distant colony, and new churches and chapels were built. In 1878 William Booth started the Salvation Army, which gave food and shelter to the needy, and tackled such problems as prostitution and drunkenness.

EMPIRES AT THEIR SUNSET

Throughout the 19th century the Russian Empire steadily grew, until it stretched from the Baltic in the west to the Pacific in the east, from the Arctic in the north to the Hindu Kush in the south. Many intelligent Russians recognised that their country, despite its immense size, was backward and needed fundamental changes, but they were divided on how this aim could be achieved. Reform was made additionally difficult by the diversity of Russia's peoples. In the 18th century she had absorbed, through annexation, the bulk of Poland's Jewish population. The pious and impoverished Jews of the Pale of Settlement doggedly resisted change and clung to a culture and way of life that remained shut off from external, modernising influences. In the Austrian Empire, the Habsburg dynasty faced similar problems to those of the Romanovs in Russia. In seeking to maintain control they too had become increasingly entrenched in their unyielding rule over a discontented, multinational population.

EASTERN EUROPE AD 1800–1900

STIRRINGS IN THE RUSSIAN VILLAGE

Towards the end of the 1870s a group of young Russian idealists sat round a table planning a new future for their giant country. The men were bearded, and dressed in the typical baggy trousers and boots of the Russian peasant, while the girls wore faded cotton skirts and rough, crumpled peasant jackets. Men and women alike rolled and smoked cigarettes of coarse tobacco. As the smoke grew thicker and the vodka bottle passed from hand to hand, their arguments grew steadily wilder and their theories less likely of achievement.

Although they affected the clothes of the peasants and tried to imitate their way of life, all came from comfortable middle-class city families and were out of touch with the harsh realities of Russian peasant life. In any case, it was impossible for any one person to claim a knowledge of the Russian people, since Russia was home to more than 200 different nationalities.

Among them were Finnish and Germanic peoples from the Baltic, a Greek community living in the Crimea, nomadic tribes who roamed across the wasteland of Siberia and gypsies from Bessarabia. Their religions were almost as varied as their national origins. The Armenians and Georgians had their own ancient forms of Christianity, the Mongolian peoples of central Asia were Buddhists, while the Kazakhs of the steppes were Muslims.

The problem that faced successive tsars was how to govern such a vast, backward, multinational empire. They also had to bring Russia into line, economically at least, with the rapidly developing industrialised West. The extremes of climate and distance had always made communications in Russia difficult, and the centuries-old

Patchwork of peoples *From the Caucasus Mountains to the Baltic Sea stretch the wide plains of eastern Europe, distinct in history and character both from western Europe and from Asiatic Russia. The gypsy with his tame baboon is one of the human tide of nomads who have ebbed and flowed over these vast lands, regardless of borders.*

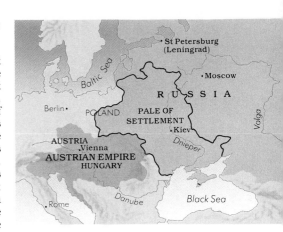

system of serfdom, which kept people tied to the rural areas, meant that potential labour for new industry was very thinly scattered. It was not until the growth of a railway network in the 1860s and 1870s that Russia's natural resources could be exploited. These included minerals in the Urals, coal in the Donets Basin, oil in the Caucasus, and in the Russian heartland vast forests of timber and prairies of fertile black earth.

A century earlier, during the reign of Catherine the Great, many wealthy, educated Russians had adopted French clothes, language and culture, hoping by so doing to change Russia's image as a feudal, semi-Asiatic backwater. Outsiders, however, regarded such changes as being little more than skin deep. One 18th-century traveller from England wrote of the Russians: 'They are neither well-bred nor agreeable,

capitalist principles of the West. The commune was a gathering of all heads of peasant households within a village. They would meet together, under the elected leadership of a village elder, or *starosta*, usually in the open air, on holidays or Sundays when they were free from their labours. Here they would discuss village matters, such as the time for haymaking or ploughing fallow land. The commune was also responsible for tax-gathering, and for the selection of quotas for the army; and a peasant could not leave his area without the commune's permission.

Missions to the villagers

Many communes vigorously resisted attempts by central bureaucracy to regulate them, and it was for this reason that they were seen by many young revolutionaries as a pattern for ideal constitutional government. As

the expanding industrial proletariat in the towns and cities. In spite of the repression, censorship and dissent that marked 19th-century Russia, there was an enormous flowering of the arts. Inevitably, most of the artists and their patrons came from the landowning classes, cushioned as they were by education and leisure. Among them were the composers Glinka, Mussorgsky and Tchaikovski; but it was in literature that Russia reached its highest achievements. The poet Pushkin, son of an old aristocratic family, established a literary voice for Russia in the 1820s, to be followed in the 1830s by writers such as Lermontov and Gogol.

They in turn paved the way for Russia's three literary giants – Tolstoy, Dostoyevsky and Turgenev – to earn the Russian novel a place in the mainstream of world literature. These writers reflected the issues of their time, and the anguish and turmoil that went into Russia's struggle to come of age. Tolstoy especially tried to come to terms with the peasants' outlook and aspirations. As an idealistic landowner, Tolstoy, born in 1828, was strongly attached to the Russian soil, and took a keen interest in rural concerns. He cared deeply about the living conditions of the serfs on his estate, setting up a school for their children, and even wrote reading primers for them. In his later years he sought to lead

Imperial sway *By the mid-19th century, eastern Europe was divided between the rival empires of Russia and Austria.*

Muslim miss *Asiatic Russia embraced Muslim Tatars such as this pigtailed girl.*

Hopeful hunter *A Yakut from north-east Siberia sets off for the hunt, armed with spear and bow.*

Long haul *Life for the peasant in Tsarist Russia was a round of backbreaking toil. A painting by Ilya Repin, The Volga Boatmen, shows human beings doing the kind of work for which horses were used in other countries. This glimpse of the reality of bargemen's lives caused a sensation when it was exhibited in 1873.*

but obvious imitators and as such overacting the externals without having the slightest pretensions to that soothing suavity of manner which pleases so universally in France.'

In the rout of Napoleon's army in 1812, the Russians revealed their patriotic enthusiasm and national pride. Many young Russians insisted that Russia's salvation lay in fostering her own unique 'Slavic' qualities. The Russian peasant, in his Orthodox piety and simplicity, seemed to them to be the embodiment of many of Russia's ancient, fundamental traditions. They saw the village commune, or *mir*, as a uniquely Russian institution, which could serve as the basis for a new economic system, avoiding the selfish

the 19th century progressed, young radicals continued their attempts to raise the consciousness of the peasant masses, embarking on evangelical-style missions to the villages, in the naive hope of converting the peasants to the idea of a new social order. Most peasants, however, were illiterate and therefore could not understand the language of revolution.

After the assassination in 1881 of the reforming Tsar Alexander II – ironically, the tsar who had emancipated the serfs 20 years previously – there was a backlash against any further movement for change. The radicals evolved new political theories. Abandoning their attempts to convert the peasants, they directed their activities towards

a life of simple peasant values, dressing in peasant clothes and toiling with his peasants at mowing, ploughing, haymaking and lugging timber. His rejection of material values ultimately led Tolstoy to turn his back on his home, his family and his wealth. His lonely death in 1910, at a far-off railway station with the world's Press gathered outside, marked the end of an era.

Worlds apart *By the late 19th century, students who were learning about a wider world began to urge their fellow Russians to demand reforms. The immensity of their task was compounded by the empire's huge racial 'mix' of more than 200 different peoples, differing in race and religion.*

LANDLORD AND SERF UNDER THE TSARS

On an estate somewhere in central Russia, a landowner sits in the early morning sun on his verandah, sipping endless glasses of tea from his samovar as he sends his serfs off to their work. As the last of them plods down the path to a day of drudgery in the fields the landowner relaxes and looks forward to his lunch. He may start with a dish of tasty *zakuski* pickles, washed down with a tumbler or two of vodka. Then will come the universal cabbage soup, followed by sturgeon, sucking pig or saddle of mutton, accompanied by pies and pasties, tarts and potato cakes.

After lunch it is time for a snooze, with the dogs sprawled around and the house servants snoring in their quarters. Towards evening, after more glasses of tea, the landowner will drive round the fields in his horse-drawn droshky, and later consult with his steward about how the farm work is progressing, or listen to complaints and petitions from his serfs. The long evening may be enlivened by a game of cards, a pipe of tobacco and more vodka with landowning neighbours.

Unlike the aristocracy of western Europe, few of Russia's landowners had either real landed wealth or blue blood. The nobility acquired their land and the serfs on it only by service to the ruling tsar. Promotion to the ranks of the nobility was granted automatically to those who had reached certain

Idle hours *During the last decades of tsarist rule, upper-class life in the Russian countryside was a ceaseless quest for diversions to fill the long idle hours. The family group in Ilya Repin's* On the Banks *could have stepped from the stage of one of Anton Chekhov's plays.*

ranks in the army and Civil Service, irrespective of family pedigree. Moreover, every member of a titled family had the right to use that title, which meant that there were thousands of princes and counts who were in fact landless and penniless. There were only about 1400 really wealthy families who owned more than 1000 serfs, while one-third of Russia's landowners had fewer than ten. The average landowner did not have a palatial mansion with grand avenues and ornamental gardens. His estate was often little more than a haphazard collection of wooden buildings ringed by peasant huts. The landowner and his family lived in a modestly furnished one-storey house, with a verandah, barn, stables and granary. A kitchen garden provided staple foods such as cabbages, onions and beetroot, while an orchard yielded cherries, apples and pears. There was usually also a summerhouse, where the landowner himself could retire for a quiet smoke.

Cut off from their neighbours by miles of bad roads, which became a quagmire during the rains of spring and autumn,

Country retreat *In summer, wealthy families from Moscow or St Petersburg would leave the heat of the city for a dacha, often built of wood in the traditional Russian fashion, in the countryside.*

such landowners often turned to drink as a relief from the deadly monotony of their daily routine. Sometimes they adopted the more desperate measure of waylaying travellers on the road and bringing them home, more or less forcibly, for a few hours of company.

Summer in the country

Life was very different for the small number of wealthy families. They spent little time on their estates, arriving mainly in summer in order to escape the oppressive heat of Moscow or St Petersburg, with a vast retinue of friends and relatives, servants, French tutors and English governesses. In the country they enjoyed their favourite open-air pursuits – hunting elk, bears and wolves with borzoi dogs, shooting, fishing, swimming, picnicking, and gathering mushrooms and berries.

Once winter threatened, however, they decamped back to the cities, where they enjoyed the brilliant social life that centred round the imperial Russian family. Or they spent their time abroad in the fashionable spas and casinos of Europe, where many of them gambled away both their estates and the serfs who lived on them.

Serfs on private estates, who made up 20 million of Russia's population of

Lives on the cards *Russian landowners' powers over their serfs is grimly satirised in a cartoon by Gustave Doré in which landlords use their peasants as gambling chips.*

36 million, were entirely at their landowner's disposal. They could be sold at auction in the marketplace and their families might be broken up. Many of them lived in squalid conditions. The huts of the poorest among them had floors thick in grime, and soot-covered walls and ceilings. Pigs' bladders were stretched over the windows, which kept out most of the draught but admitted hardly any light, even at midday. They drank their watery cabbage

soup from wooden bowls and ate their solid food from wooden trenchers, on rough-hewn tables which were scraped clean only at holiday times. Serfs, pigs and calves slept under the same roof, in an atmosphere so smoke-filled that a burning candle looked as though it was shrouded in mist.

Talented serfs, such as coachmen or skilled craftsmen, were a valuable asset and treated accordingly. But a serf who proved troublesome could be flogged, conscripted into the army for 25 years, or even exiled to Siberia. A landowner could refuse his serf the right to marry the girl of his choice; or he could compel him to marry young, in order to produce more children who would work on the estate. The serf also had to repay the landowner for the small piece of land he was allowed to

Boots of bark *Peasants in the Russia of the 1880s set off for the fields, carrying rakes over their shoulders, and wearing boots and leggings made of birch bark. They come from the village on the Volga where Lenin was born in 1870.*

Chain gang *Exile to Siberia was the fate of thousands of revolutionaries, and even of some peasants whom flogging failed to keep subservient to their landlords. These 19th-century convicts work chained to their barrows.*

till for himself, either by giving his labour for three days a week – a system known as *barshchina* – or else by *obrok*, a quit-rent paid either in money or in produce. Payment of obrok enabled a serf to apply for permission to go and work in a city or factory, where the enterprising person could sometimes save enough money to buy his own serfs. Those on barshchina often had to work more than three days a week during harvest time, and their wives and children had to work alongside them.

For years the tsars had realised that liberty for the serfs was essential if Russia was to take her place in the modern world. But it was not until 1861 that they were finally liberated by Tsar Alexander II. Under the terms of their freedom they were allowed to purchase allotments of land from their previous landlords.

Flagrant overpricing of land, however, meant that the former serfs, now free peasants in name at least, were shackled with huge loan repayments. Moreover, the size of each peasant's piece of land was reduced to about half what it had previously been, and proved too small to be economic. This led to great hardship, as the peasants, poorly fed and living in insanitary

conditions, succumbed in ever greater numbers to disease, epidemics, and a catastrophic famine in 1891-2.

Many landowners proved incapable of running their estates at a profit. As one of them remarked, bemoaning the passing of the good old days: 'Then we didn't keep accounts and we drank champagne. Now we do keep accounts and have to make do with beer.' In the first 30 years after the serfs were freed, 20,000 estates were sold, as the landowners gave up the unequal struggle and headed for life in the city.

'To be sold. Three coachmen, well-trained and handsome; and two girls, one 18 and the other 15 years of age... In the same house there are for sale two hairdressers; one of them, 21 years of age, can read, write, play on a musical instrument, and act as huntsman.'

MOSCOW GAZETTE, 1801

Patriarchal family *Old-established merchant families, such as the group below, were deeply religious, narrow-minded, and implacably opposed to any change. In this family, from the Nizhny Novgorod region east of Moscow, the men wear top hats and long black coats saved from an earlier age, in contrast with the women in their brightly coloured silks and brocades.*

Versatile wood *In the forested regions of north-west Russia, wood was the material for many household objects. A scoop for gathering berries stands beside valued pottery, broken then mended with strips of birch bark.*

TALES FROM THE VIENNA WOODS

Even after intervening wars had made it seem as remote as Nineveh, old people glowed a little when they remembered the great ballroom of the Imperial Palace in Vienna. The walls soared cream and gold, banked with flowers, to the lofty ceiling, from which hung chandeliers in long rows ablaze with a thousand candles. They struck fire from a king's ransom of diamonds, emeralds and rubies onto an opulence of snow-white bosoms, shimmering on the richness of silk. Yet however gorgeous their ball gowns, the women were only pale shadows in contrast with the men. There were hussars wearing scarlet shako hats and fur-trimmed cloaks, bearing sabres with scabbards of gold.

Crusty promise *A baker's sign lures the Viennese passer-by.*

There were officers in the silver and green of the Rifles, the royal blue and saffron of the Lancers, the black and gold of the Halberdiers. There were Hungarians in tight blue breeches embroidered with gold, Poles in their astrakhan headgear ornamented with diamond sprays – everywhere a glitter of decorations, a nodding of plumes, all whirling and gliding to the waltzes of Johann Strauss, which filled the room with a brilliance that matched the sparkle of the chandeliers.

The gaiety of the ballroom for which Vienna became renowned in the 19th century was, however, no more than the froth on the surface of one of the intellectual capitals of Europe. Its character was made up of ingredients that had been many centuries in the blending, and sprang in part from the city's location at a crossroads between East and West. Blond Nordic Germans mixed with dark Jews from Galicia; hot-blooded gypsies from Hungary rubbed shoulders with Poles, Russians and Italians. Fine Baroque buildings, over which towered the spire of the 15th-century St Stephen's Cathedral, were the backdrop for an extravagant cast of pedlars from Slovakia, soldiers from Bosnia, Czech pastrycooks and Magyar dancers and musicians. One result was that the Viennese spoke a dozen different languages, including their own dialect, *Wienerisch* – which, along with French, was the language of the emperor and his court.

From the middle of the 16th century until 1806, the city was the capital of the Holy Roman Empire, whose lands stretched from Switzerland to Muslim Montenegro and deep into Italy. Then, until 1918, it was the seat of the mighty Habsburg dynasty and capital of the Austro-Hungarian Empire. At the end of the Napoleonic Wars, the crowned heads of Europe, or their first ministers, met at the Congress of Vienna to settle Europe's frontiers and to try to return the Continent to the state it enjoyed before the revolutions that had disrupted it.

'Cosiness', the Viennese virtue

No one was more assiduous in this work than the courtly and charming Chancellor of Austria, Prince Clemens von Metternich. With the approval of Emperor Franz Josef, he established a system of censorship and secret police to stamp out the embers of liberal sympathies. It was, said the Viennese, a system enforced by 'a standing army of soldiers, a seated army of officials, a kneeling army of priests and a creeping army of informants'.

Counterpointing the serious work of the Congress, music swirled ceaselessly through the city's ballrooms and palace reception halls and the Winter Riding School. Asked how the Congress was marching forward, one diplomat replied: 'It doesn't march, it dances!'

Despite its intentions, the regime which resulted from the Congress was far from harsh. Frequently it became submerged beneath its own paperwork, and was renowned mostly for 'muddling through'. If it did nothing else, it promoted stability, and the Viennese virtue of *Gemütlichkeit*. This is generally translated as 'cosiness', but implies many other things as well – charm, fondness for the good and simple things of life, an easy fatalism that shrugs off the worst of news. For relaxation, citizens took to the nearby Vienna Woods, celebrated in waltz by Strauss, or made summer outings to old inns among the vineyards in the hills where they could dine and dance to gypsy music on zither and harp.

In Vienna itself, people went to the Volksgarten, or People's Garden, to listen to the band, or to the funfair at the Prater – with its giant Ferris wheel added in 1873 – where royalty, nobility and gentry paraded in carriages with gilded spokes. The higher the rank of the carriage's owner, the more gilding he was entitled to display. Visitors said that the Viennese always looked as though they were going to a party – and they not infrequently were.

In addition, they had the theatre of the streets, free entertainment such as the emperor's Silver Wedding Pageant in which the leading citizens dressed up as Renaissance princes. They also had probably the finest hospitals and best-trained doctors and nurses in Europe. The excellence of the medical care gave rise to the saying: 'If you must fall ill, then do so in Vienna!'

Just as much appreciated were the city's coffee-houses. Everybody had his favourite establishment, whether it was the Kaiserbründl, with tall mirrors and red plush alcoves, or the Central,

Music in the woods *Even picnics in the forested hills of the Wiener Wald, or Vienna Woods, had a musical accompaniment.*

Winter reflections *Even on a wet winter evening, Vienna's fashionable Ringstrasse, which replaced the city's medieval walls, is thronged with cabs taking pleasure seekers to dates in ballroom, theatre or café. Strollers pause to admire the brilliant window displays.*

which the writers patronised. Male customers gazed at the voluptuous waitresses and listened to the worldly wisdom of the waiters. They ordered a *Mokka*, black coffee, a *Melange*, half and half, or an *Einspanner*, black coffee topped with whipped cream, before getting down to the serious matter of

Fragile elegance
Beakers and goblets display the rich colours and elaborate engraving of the Biedermeier style.

choosing a pastry. Viennese pastries soon acquired their reputation as spectacular flights of fancy created by craftsmen. There was *Sacher torte*, named after Metternich's chef and consisting of chocolate sponge with apricot jam and chocolate icing, Hungarian *Dobstorte* with its covering of caramel, and all the strudels from apple to black cherries with cream.

Poor people in Habsburg Vienna, however, saw very little Strauss or strudel, and in 1848 there was a brief and bloody revolution. Its only lasting effect was the destruction of the walls

of the Old City, making way for a fine new thoroughfare, the Ringstrasse. There the financiers and industrialists built their magnificent mansions and entertained intellectuals, musicians, writers, actors and artists. New stars in the firmament included the composers Mahler and

Bruckner, maintaining the Viennese musical pre-eminence established by Mozart and Beethoven; the playwright Arthur Schnitzler; the controversial Art Nouveau painter Gustav Klimt; and Sigmund Freud, later renowned as the 'father of psychoanalysis'.

Meanwhile, the fates were gathering about the ageing Emperor Franz Josef. In 1898, his beloved Empress Elisabeth was assassinated, and in 1914 his new heir, Archduke Franz Ferdinand, was murdered at Sarajevo – setting in train a world war that would bring many European monarchies to an end.

Makers of music *The Viennese composer Franz Schubert was the hero of a lively group of the city's young, who met to hear him play in their homes.*

Tragedy queen
Sophie Schröder brought melodrama to the Viennese stage.

COMFORT AND CONFORMITY

Life in the early 19th-century Viennese home was dominated by the Biedermeier style, which found its expression in solid villas, carved and inlaid furniture with fringed tablecloths, and encrusted vases containing bouquets of peacock feathers and palm leaves. At the heart of the Biedermeier household was the living room, with its large sofa where the *hausfrau* sat as a queen on her throne. The style was named after a fictitious schoolmaster and figure of fun in whose character were mixed a desire for comfort and a quiet life, a dislike of intellectuals, and a love of the status quo.

Stylish seating *This curved chaise longue is typical of the later stages of Biedermeier furniture.*

Coffee craze *The Viennese addiction to coffee dates from the 1680s, when the Turks, fleeing from their siege of the city, abandoned sacks of green beans. The beans were then roasted and brewed to make coffee. Soon the coffee house was the centre of Vienna's social life – a place for spirited debate on social and political issues, for reading the newspapers, or simply for having a quiet doze.*

303

POVERTY AND JOY IN THE JEWISH SHTETL

Across the flat expanses of Russia's western borderlands, with their vast forests and rolling fields of grain, the horizon is broken here and there by a scattering of small, often dilapidated towns. These are the *shtetl* – the homes in which the Jews of eastern Europe maintained in the 19th century an isolated way of life little changed since medieval times.

Before the mid-18th century there had been few Jews in the Russian Empire, since permanent residence had been denied them by law. But three successive partitions of Poland during the reign of Catherine the Great had by 1800 brought 1 million Jews from the eastern provinces of Poland into the Russian Empire. The Russians quickly took advantage of this new ethnic group, calling on their services as commercial middlemen, craftsmen and traders. But they hedged their lives around with restrictions, and confined them to a so-called Pale of Settlement outside which residence or travel was rarely permitted.

Throughout this swathe of territory, running from the Baltic to the Black Sea, the wooden houses of the shtetl were surrounded by winding alleys and unpaved, muddy streets, where sewage ran in open drains. The people who lived here fought a day-to-day battle against poverty, hunger and oppression. Yet the vibrant, tenacious life of the shtetl shone through on any market day, with its noise, smells and colour, as the inhabitants set up their booths, stalls and butchers' blocks.

Jewish pedlars are dressed in the traditional long gaberdine coat and skullcap. Women bear baskets of eggs and bundles of old clothes. Barefoot peasants offer goats, cows, geese and chickens. Wagonloads of grain, beans, pears, melons, sunflower seeds, garlic, parsley and radishes are laid out for sale. Here, in exchange for the staples of life, the Jews trade and barter the produce of their artisans – shirts, boots, shoes, spades, mattocks, lamps and household goods.

By the time the market is in full swing, crowded with peasants and Jews from the surrounding areas, the

Tough survivors *Rough cobbled streets separate the wooden houses of Kaunas, in Lithuania. Hundreds of such settlements made up the shtetl – a Yiddish word based on the German* stadt, *'little town', describing Jewish communities in eastern Europe.*

noise is deafening. The sound of voices haggling in Russian and Yiddish is accompanied by the loud braying of donkeys, the gentle mooing of cows, the clucking of hens, and above all the bleating of goats, which are to be found everywhere, leaping onto roofs and pulling at the thatch, or lying in the sun and chewing the cud. Sometimes a group of street musicians will arrive and play their cheerful traditional melodies. Always in the background is the sound of children chanting their lessons in the one-roomed *cheder*, or Hebrew school.

Everything to maintain and enrich the Jewish way of life is found nearby – a bathhouse, where the men go to

Holy light *The menorah holds eight candles, lit one by one over the eight days of Chanukkah, the Festival of Lights. The two larger candles light the others.*

wash on Sabbath evenings, a prayer house, and a cemetery where people venerate the graves of dead ancestors. The larger towns have a *yeshiva*, or rabbinical school, and a Jewish hospital. The focal point of Jewish life is the wooden synagogue, where three times a day the men assemble to pray, donning their prayer shawls and strapping scriptural texts to their foreheads and arms. If there is time, they may stop later to discuss meanings of the Torah, their sacred book, with the rabbi, or to seek his advice on questions of religion and the proper upbringing for their children.

Although there were some Jewish merchants who succeeded in larger cities such as Moscow, Vilna and St Petersburg, the majority of Jews were artisans and traders who just about made a living, including woodworkers, weavers, tailors, carters,

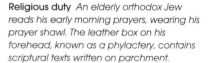

Religious duty *An elderly orthodox Jew reads his early morning prayers, wearing his prayer shawl. The leather box on his forehead, known as a phylactery, contains scriptural texts written on parchment.*

cobblers, tinsmiths and glaziers. There were also milkmen like Tevye, the main character in the musical *Fiddler on the Roof*. This was based on a story by the Yiddish humorous writer Sholem Aleichem (1859-1916), the son of a Russian storekeeper, who came from the shtetl.

The daily struggle for survival was exacerbated by the constant threat of anti-Semitic violence. Some townlets in the shtetl were almost exclusively Jewish, but in others, where the Jews coexisted with the peasants, a crude class hatred manifested itself in a resentment of the Jews' talent for enterprise and hard work.

Jews were excluded from a number of professions and trades, and were severely restricted in their opportunities for further education outside the shtetl. But there were ways round the laws. For those with money, police and government officials could be bribed into giving residence permits. Some young women, desperate to pursue academic studies in St Petersburg or Moscow, obtained residence permits by registering as prostitutes.

By a law of 1827 Jewish boys as young as 12 might be drafted into the army for 25 years, though parents with money could purchase their release. For other young men, the only solution was the cutting of beards and sidelocks – the first step towards assimilation and conversion to Christianity.

In general, though, the Jews of the Pale strongly resisted tsarist attempts to make them conform, convert or in any way relinquish their traditional way of life. The daily preoccupation of feeding and clothing their usually large families was bound up closely with the strict observance of dietary laws, the Sabbath and religious festivals.

Burdens of education and marriage

For the Jew, poverty was no excuse for not marrying, and childlessness was thought a tragedy. But the educating of sons and the marrying of daughters could be an enormous burden. Somehow the money had to be found for a son to attend school. This Jewish thirst for knowledge meant that a boy as young as three would have to sit for up to ten hours a day, six days a week, studying the Hebrew of the Bible and the Aramaic of the Talmud, and then translating them into Yiddish, the language of his everyday speech.

Yet extreme poverty did not prevent many Jewish boys from going on to the rabbinical school. Well-to-do Jews might marry off their daughters to promising

With fiddle and harp *Street players kept alive the strong musical traditions of the people of the shtetl.*

students and subsidise their studies: to do so was both an honour and an act of personal redemption. For a poor Jew, however, the marriage of a daughter could be a nightmare. Where was he to find the money for the trousseau and dowry? Then there was the *chuppa*, or wedding canopy, and food and musicians for the wedding feast. The dream of a rich son-in-law was a major preoccupation for men like Tevye who had seven daughters.

The *shadchen*, or matchmaker, had an essential, though interfering, role in shtetl life, and even the poorest of families had marriages arranged for them. The shadchen gathered facts about potential couples, researching their family backgrounds for respected ancestors such as rabbis or scholars, often exaggerating their virtues and their good points while concealing inadequacies and shortcomings.

Although some attempts were made throughout the 1850s and 1860s to improve the lot of the Jews and to relax the restrictions put upon them, the assassination of Tsar Alexander II in 1881, and the implication of the Jews in the revolutionary movement, unleashed a huge anti-Jewish backlash and the beginning of a series of pogroms over the next 25 years. As persecution and a desire for educational and intellectual advancement grew, many Jews decided to emigrate. At the end of the 19th century there were as many as 5 million Jews in Russia; but by 1910 one in three of all the Jews of eastern Europe had moved on – the majority of them to begin a new life in the United States.

Festive occasion *The hardships which the people of the shtetl suffered were relieved by joyous celebrations and continual re-telling of traditional tales. The artist Marc Chagall, who was born in Russia in 1887, adds a touch of mysticism to his scene of a village wedding.*

Folk dress *Polish garb includes a bright plastron, or bodice, and a headband of velvet and pearls.*

Day dress *Boys often wore a fur-trimmed shtreimel over the yarmulke, or skullcap.*

WHEN CLOTHES WERE IMPOSED BY LAW

Since the Middle Ages, the Jews of Russia's empire had been compelled to wear their own distinctive costume, which varied greatly from one region to another. For example, in Poland the men wore *caftans*, or full-length robes with long sleeves; in Lithuania men wore long tunics of black silk with broad silk sashes round the waist, while the women wore silk gowns beneath fur cloaks. Jews, especially in the Polish shtetl, grew so attached to these styles that in the 1850s the Russians passed laws to ban extreme types of clothing and the wearing of sidelocks by men.

WARRIORS, SLAVES AND SETTLERS

Civilisations flourished in Africa south of the Sahara centuries before Europeans set foot in the continent. From the 8th century, a series of powerful kingdoms arose in West Africa at the southern end of camel-caravan routes across the Sahara, and the Arabs who came to trade converted the inhabitants to Islam. It was not until the 15th century that Europeans established themselves on the coast and began to trade in gold, ivory and slaves. Slave-trading wars led to the rise of strong military kingdoms, both as protectors and raiders.

The interior of Africa remained largely unknown to Europeans until the 19th century. Vast areas were occupied by deserts and forests, and the climate, with the diseases that thrived in it, proved lethal to Europeans. Only on the southern tip of the continent were Europeans able to establish themselves; a Dutch settlement established in the 1650s spread steadily northwards, at first in search of hunting and herding lands, and later in search of farm land, farm labour and mineral wealth. In time, the incentives of curiosity, evangelical zeal and the desire for greater wealth drove Europeans to journey deep into the interior, and as a result large parts of Africa came to be partitioned between different European powers.

AFRICA AD 1400 – 1900

KINGDOM OF BRONZE AND PALM WINE

At festival times, a vast assemblage of courtiers, officials, priests, slaves and craftsmen thronged the palace at Benin, the hub of a West African empire that reached its height in the 16th century. The city was rimmed by 3 miles (5 km) of walls, within which 30 broad avenues, each over 100 ft (30 m) wide, intersected at right angles.

The wood and clay houses were spacious, and the palace itself was a labyrinth of apartments, courtyards, shrines and galleries. Here, presiding over all, lived the Oba, an absolute monarch revered by his people as the earthly representative of Benin's gods.

Swathed in robes and hung with outsize coral necklaces, the Oba of Benin spent a great deal of his time performing ceremonies and sacrifices, or relaxing in the company of his hundred or more wives. At annual festivals, however, he would make a public progress through his palace followed by a retinue of courtiers, with drummers beating rhythmic tattoos while other musicians played bells, rattles and elephant-tusk trumpets.

On some occasions the Oba would be preceded by a courtier carrying a box of kola nuts – which were chewed as stimulants – for distribution to his people. These were joyful occasions, on which much palm wine was drunk.

The Oba maintained a large and disciplined army, and ruled through an array of chiefs and subchiefs who handled the day-to-day affairs of state – a system which provided an efficient set of checks to prevent the abuse of power. Although European visitors might disapprove of the sight of young women walking naked through the streets of Benin, they were impressed by the city's atmosphere of stability. A 17th-century visitor reported: 'The citizens of Benin are good people who have good laws and a well-organised

Music at the fingertips *The thumb piano, in various forms, has long been a popular instrument in many parts of Africa. The thin metal bars were thumbed to create a melody, and the beautifully decorated, flat-bottomed bowl acted as a resonator.*

police force; they live on good terms with the Dutch and other foreigners who come to trade among them.'

Trade with the Europeans began in the 15th century, by which time Benin was already a thriving commercial centre dealing in goods ranging from tools and weapons to such delicacies as fried lizards. The city's merchants were known for their shrewdness, and used as currency cowrie shells, or bracelet-shaped gold or copper ingots known as manillas. The Portuguese were the first Europeans to begin regular trading with them. They came looking for gold – which Benin did not have – but were happy to accept slaves to use as commodities when dealing with the African kingdoms that did have gold to offer.

Warriors with a civil service

One of the West African kingdoms that prospered from the slave trade was Ashanti, founded in the 17th century. Rich in gold and mighty in battle, the Ashantis spread from the area around their capital, Kumasi, to control a large part of what is now Ghana. Whatever prisoners they took became slaves to be sold to European traders.

By the 19th century, the Ashantis' battles with the British had brought them much fame as warriors, but their achievements during peacetime were impressive as well. Their realm was administered by a literate civil service staffed by Muslim and Arab clerks, and a courier system carried the king's commands to every part of the state.

New laws were promulgated at a great annual yam harvest, when all the provincial rulers gathered for several days of religious ceremonies.

White visitors were astonished by the quantities of gold worn by Ashanti chiefs. In the early 18th century, an English traveller, T.E. Bowdich, wrote: 'Manillas and rude lumps of rock gold hung from their left wrists, which were so heavily laden as to be supported on the head of one of their handsomest boys. Gold and silver pipes, and canes dazzled the eye in every direction. Wolves' and rams' heads as large as life, cast in gold, were suspended from their gold-handled swords.'

The cleanliness of the Ashantis was renowned too. The wide streets of Kumasi were regularly swept, and the house walls of red and white clay were polished. Important buildings had internal lavatories whose sewage pipes were cleansed daily with boiling water. Even outlying villages had public lavatories, one for each sex, taking the form of a trench with poles laid across it, set in a palm-roofed hut. Special huts were set aside for women who were menstruating – a condition surrounded by many taboos.

Religion was an all-pervading force, not only within the West African kingdoms, but with the remote peoples of the forests and the pastoral peoples of sub-Saharan and Eastern Africa as well. Although forms of worship varied,

Benin bronze *The people of Benin were skilled in the art of casting bronze, and their reliefs and figurines give a graphic impression of life in the court of the ruling Oba. Music played an important part in all ceremonies.*

Kingdoms and colonies *Europeans believed they were bringing civilisation to Africa through settlements such as the Cape Colony, which by 1847 extended as far as the Orange River. However, major African cultures flourished in 14th-century Benin and 17th-century Ashanti, while the settlers were soon to feel the might of the Zulu people.*

Worth their weight in gold
The only form of currency used by the Ashantis was gold dust. The weights used to measure quantities of gold dust were cast in brass, and sometimes depicted animals, plants, people, or even proverbs.

most Africans believed in a benign creator who could be influenced through lesser deities – in order to boost crops, for instance, or to promote fertility. The spirits of the animals and ancestors were often depicted in art, and many cults invoked them through dance, rituals, and the wearing of masks. Diviners, having the powers to heal or harm through their herbs and spells, were held in awe.

Lucky charms and amulets – known as juju in West Africa – were widely thought to possess magical powers. And when the first conversions and baptisms were carried out by visiting missionaries, crucifixes were carried by a few chiefs as emblems of power much like their own fetishes.

Pastoral life *Most Africans lived in small farming communities scattered across the grasslands or cut deep into forests. They lived in houses of clay or mud and thatch, fenced against raiders and predators.*

Such a palaver *'Had Job amongst his other trials,' said a 19th-century English explorer, 'been exposed to the horrors of an interminable African palaver, his patience must have forsaken him.'*

LONG MARCH TO SLAVERY OR DEATH

Chained together from neck to neck, chafed and bleeding from their bonds, slaves captured in the East African interior were force-marched to the Indian Ocean coast in conditions of extreme suffering. If they uttered so much as a complaint, slaves might be gagged by having a piece of wood like a snaffle fixed into their mouths.

Slaves suspected of trying to escape were shackled at the neck with a beam of wood forked at one end and secured with an iron rod. A lighter version was used to yoke two slaves together. If the party made a stop to trade or get more slaves, the prisoners would be herded together in a hastily built stockade.

Slaves who proved too weak or ill to keep pace with the column were killed on the spot and left to rot by the side

Africa robbed of Africans *Slave traders burned villages, pillaged crops and left corpses strewn upon the ground. Slavers in eastern and southern Africa generally captured women and youths, causing greater depopulation than in West Africa, where the women were left behind.*

of the path. And if the caravan passed through a part of the country that was suffering a famine, groups of slaves might be left to starve – often still chained together.

The march frequently lasted three months or more – an ordeal made even harder for the slaves by the trading goods they were forced to carry. Some 2 million Africans are estimated to have been taken as slaves in East Africa, but for every one who reached Zanzibar's slave market, four or five died on the way. And if the people killed during village raids are taken into account, the cost in human life for one slave was probably considerably more than that.

The traffic in East Africa was largely in the hands of Arabs and Swahilis, or coastal Africans, and managed by the subjects of the Sultan of Zanzibar – an island just off the coast which was the destination of most slave caravans. In the early days, slavery had been a by-product of the ivory trade; slaves were captured to carry the tusks back to the coast. Later, however, the demand grew and raiding parties were sent into the African interior to attack villages. Those men, women and children who had neither fled nor been slaughtered were rounded up – unless they were too old or decrepit to be saleable.

The slave traders did not usually endanger their lives in the fighting. More often they would incite one chief

to attack another's village, giving their ally guns and gunpowder, and loaning him armed men in exchange for the captives. An inevitable result of this was a catastrophic increase in inter-tribal warfare, which only served to increase the carnage the slave trade had already caused. Vast areas were left devoid of people. Travellers could journey for weeks without encountering a single living human being, even though the region may have been well populated just a few years previously.

The slave caravan itself was usually headed by two or three Swahili or Arab merchants, supported by a retinue of

Ship of slavers *Dhows were used by the slave traders to transport their human cargo to Zanzibar. The voyage lasted about three days, and the slaves got little food or water.*

attendants, armed guards and a large number of porters who might themselves be slaves. The traders were keen to pick up slaves at any stage along the route, but their routes quickly became so depleted of human life that only organised raids, pushing ever farther inland, could supply their needs.

'Our captors then separated babies from their mothers, tied them into bundles like maize and hung them up on trees. Babies remained crying hysterically while their mothers were led away.'
MAMA MELI, SLAVE

The march towards the coast ended at the ports of Kilwa, Lindi or, most often, the town the Africans called Bagamoyo – 'throw away your heart'. To transport the slaves to Zanzibar, they were crammed into lightly built

Trappings of captivity *Once slaves had reached the ports of the African coast, they were tethered in heavy chains and herded into 'barracoons', or pens, to await the arrival of the ships that would transport them to the slave markets.*

Bound for America *Although Arabs dominated the slave trade on the east coast of Africa, European traders conducted a flourishing business on the opposite side of the continent. With the opening up of the Americas, vast numbers of human beings were transported across the Atlantic Ocean to work on sugar, tobacco and cotton plantations.*

Truth and light *Magic lanterns – primitive slide projectors lit with candles – were used by the first missionaries to illuminate their Bible message.*

Saving a life *Some African practices shocked the European travellers. John Hanning Speke, explorer of Lake Victoria, saved one of the wives of Mtesa, King of Buganda, from being clubbed to death at the young monarch's whim.*

ships known as dhows and stowed there in bulk. The first batch went along the floor of the vessel, in pairs of adults with a child between them. When one tier had been completed in this way, a deck was laid down an inch or two clear of their bodies, and a second tier was stowed above them – and so on until the gunwale of the vessel was reached.

Those who died of starvation on the lower decks could not be removed, and remained side by side with the living. The landing of slaves at Zanzibar was a grim business, in which corpses were unloaded alongside the famished and dysentery-ridden survivors who sometimes dropped dead in the customs house, or in the street.

At this stage, however, some meagre comforts were to be found. Lodged for some days in the dealers' houses, the slaves were at last fed and watered so that they should gain strength and look more presentable for the slave market. In spite of this, Europeans who visited the market were appalled by the condition of the slaves that were on offer: starved and demoralised creatures, with sunken chests, hollow cheeks and protruding eyes, some of whom were too weak to stand up.

The market was held in the cool of the evening, when the slaves were arranged in a number of semicircles, divided into groups of men, women and children, inside which the Arab traders stood, chatting, haggling and discussing the captives' good and bad points as if they were animal stock. When deals were agreed the slaves might be taken off to work on their new masters' plantations in Zanzibar, or perhaps to serve in homes in Swahili towns along the African coast.

Others, though, faced the ordeal of a second and even longer voyage to Mauritius, Arabia or the East Indies – and so the nightmare of shipment began once again. However, those who survived the hideous rigours of the slave trade might find a reasonable life at the end of their journey. Humane treatment of slaves was recommended by the Koran, and all evidence suggests that those kept in Arab homes or on Arab plantations were treated with more paternal care than, for example, their counterparts working in the cotton fields of America's Deep South.

Reports by European adventurers brought the East African slave trade to the world's attention, and David Livingstone was particularly successful in campaigning to stamp out the traffic. Livingstone was convinced that Christianity would only take root in Africa when the slave trade had been abolished and European merchants were able to penetrate what journalist and explorer Henry Morton Stanley called the 'Dark Continent'. It was not, however, until the beginning of this century, 30 years after the Scottish missionary's death, that the trade in Africa's human resources eventually came to an end.

INTO THE UNKNOWN

To explore and map the interior of the African continent, 19th-century European writer-explorers braved the little-known hazards of Africa's rivers and huge forests, deserts and high grasslands. Few of them travelled alone. Most were accompanied by guides and by armies of bearers to transport their cumbersome equipment: provisions, tents, folding beds, medicine chests, tools, ropes, collapsible boats, guns and ammunition. For clothing, the explorers believed in the merits of flannel worn next to the skin, and in long woollen socks – the thicker the better, whatever the heat. Knee-high boots protected their legs in swamps and kept out mosquitoes, while their leather belts were festooned with whistles, canvas water bottles, knives and other tools. A helmet-like hat known as a sola topi was often worn for protection against sunstroke, though some travellers preferred straw hats with veils hanging from the brim to ward off insects. In the evening, the important task of writing up the travel diary would require a hurricane lamp and folding writing table.

SETTLERS WHO TAMED SOUTH AFRICA'S CAPE

Bracing himself against the Atlantic swell, Jan van Riebeeck stands at the rail of the *Drommedaris* and peers through a telescope at the great flat-topped mountain with its shroud of white cloud. The Dutchman is both excited and apprehensive: will the Cape of Good Hope live up to its name?

As befits the founder of the Dutch East India Company's settlement at the south-western tip of Africa, Van Riebeeck is decked out in his finest doublet and breeches, his lace-edged collar fastened with a cord ending in tassels. He has a droopy moustache and his hair, whipped by the south-easter, cascades to his shoulders.

Beside him is his wife, and mother of his two children, the former Maria de la Quellerie. A gentle woman of great charm and tact, she is to prove a valuable asset to Van Riebeeck as he tackles the most challenging job of his career – the taming of the Cape.

The Cape peninsula in the 1650s was a wild and beautiful region. Its backbone of rugged mountains was flanked by lush, sweeping valleys and crisscrossed by rivers and streams. Antelope grazed the mountain slopes and lions prowled the thick bush.

Soon after the Van Riebeeck party's arrival at the Cape in April 1652, work began on the fort that would protect the victualling station the commander had been instructed to establish. The directors of the Dutch East India Company were acutely aware of the Cape's strategic importance for their fleets, particularly since diplomatic relations between the English and the Dutch had become increasingly tense.

There was a further and equally practical reason for constructing the fort. The Khoikhoi people had long resisted the intrusions of visiting sailors, and were described by Van Riebeeck as savage, untrustworthy and without conscience. What the Khoikhoi thought of Van Riebeeck is not recorded. But whatever his personal view, the Dutch commander followed his superiors' instructions to treat the Khoikhoi fairly, though he did not concede their title to any land.

For a long time, life at the Cape revolved around the fort – later to be replaced by a five-cornered stone castle – and there were few other dwellings in the settlement. By 1656 the only buildings in existence were the fort, the smithy, a few small fortifications and a thin scattering of dwellings for the company's workmen. Houses were built from wattle and daub, stone or wood; furniture was handmade or imported from Holland, depending on the occupant's status. Determined to set up gardens at the Cape as quickly as possible, the new commander ordered a large quantity of seeds and plants. These duly arrived, and in spite of an initial struggle during the winter months the gardens began to produce increasingly large crops of fruit and vegetables, and soon there was more than enough food. After ten years the gardens extended for 45 acres (18 ha), and contained a variety of fruit crops and vegetables such as sweet potatoes, beetroots, turnips, cabbages, lettuces, cucumbers, pumpkins, cauliflowers, carrots, beans and peas. There were also maize and tobacco plantations.

Wine soon became a product of the Cape: three years after the founding of the settlement, the first vines arrived, and in 1659 Van Riebeeck was able to record in his journal: 'Today, praise be to God, wine was made for the first time from Cape grapes...' No mention was made of the quality, probably because it was virtually undrinkable.

Van Riebeeck was aware that he needed to gain the trust of the Khoikhoi, since the success of the settlement depended on bartering for cattle, from which the company's own flocks and herds would grow. He developed good relations with them, even raising a Khoikhoi girl, whom he named Eva.

The Khoikhoi living near the Dutch fort seized the opportunity to trade and prosper. Sheep and cattle were in constant demand by settlers and sailors, who were now calling at the Cape more often. Trade with these Khoikhoi opened up inland trade too, the Peninsular groups exchanging their copper or tobacco for cattle from the interior. To ensure their grip on trade with the Europeans, the Peninsular Khoikhoi did their best to prevent contact between inland clans and the Dutch, discouraging visits to the fort with horrific tales about the settlers.

The monopoly of the Peninsular Khoikhoi on trade was finally broken by Eva, who was descended from an

Cattle on parade *A large, flat area outside the Castle of Good Hope served as a parade ground for the castle garrison. The castle was completed in 1679 to replace the original fort of Van Riebeeck. Built to protect the colony from invasion, it never fired a shot in anger and functioned largely as the centre of social life at the Cape – and occasional grazing for cattle.*

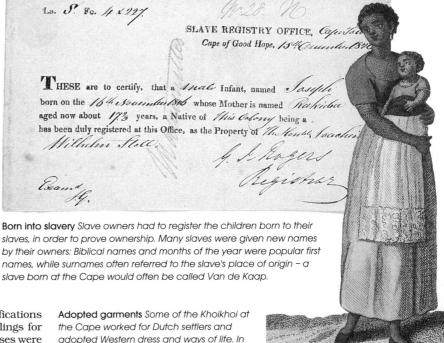

Born into slavery *Slave owners had to register the children born to their slaves, in order to prove ownership. Many slaves were given new names by their owners: Biblical names and months of the year were popular first names, while surnames often referred to the slave's place of origin – a slave born at the Cape would often be called Van de Kaap.*

Adopted garments *Some of the Khoikhoi at the Cape worked for Dutch settlers and adopted Western dress and ways of life. In February 1713 a smallpox epidemic broke out at the Dutch settlement, and spread to the Khoikhoi. Having less resistance to the disease than the settlers, and no medical lore against a totally foreign illness, the Khoikhoi died in their hundreds.*

African town *Black peoples occupied large areas of the Cape before white settlers came. They had cattle and crops, and lived in grass houses. Europeans crossing the Orange River in the early 1800s found this town, called Lattakoo, as big as Cape Town.*

Trekboers at rest *By the early 1700s, some Dutch settlers had started a hard, nomadic life of cattle farming and hunting beyond the Cape Colony's boundaries. They called themselves trekboers, or travelling farmers and some gathered substantial wealth.*

inland group called the Cochoqua, and encouraged contact between her clan and the Dutch. Soon the Cochoqua were trading regularly with the Dutch, and moving closer to the fort – grazing their cattle on land once claimed by the Peninsular Khoikhoi as their own. The pressure thus placed on the available land was increased a few years later when nine men were released from the service of the Dutch East India Company and granted land on which to establish farms. This finally resulted – in May 1659 – in an uprising by the Khoikhoi, an unsuccessful attempt to drive the Dutch settlers away.

Van Riebeeck had been issued with explicit instructions by the company not to enslave the African people of the Cape. Slaves from other regions, however, were quite permissible, and within a few weeks of arrival the commander had sent off his first request for slaves to assist in building the fort and tilling the soil. The company replied that slaves could not be spared. In 1658, however, fate obliged with a cargo of some 75 slaves captured by the Dutch ship *Amersfoort* from a Portuguese slave ship bound from Angola to Brazil. Of these, 21 men and 22 women were sent to work in the fields and gardens, while the rest were assigned to company officials. Later that year another 228 slaves, purchased on the West African coast, arrived on the Hasselt, though many soon died from disease.

Disease was only one of the many torments faced by slaves in the service of their Dutch masters. Degradation, ill-treatment and humiliation caused many to run away. Punishment of slaves was the responsibility of the owners – Van Riebeeck made it a condition of ownership that settlers kept a whip in their houses for this purpose. Determined to end a spate of escapes, he even allowed owners to chain up recaptured slaves. A slave's second escape attempt might result in his ears or right hand being cut off, or the tip of his nose being severed.

The whites' fear of an uprising was reflected in a law which prohibited more than two slaves belonging to different owners from meeting at any time. A curfew required any slaves out of doors after 10 pm to carry a lantern, unless accompanied by a member of the owner's family. In practice, though, slaves often disregarded these rules and pursued amusements such as gambling, cockfighting, smoking opium and drinking – anything in order to dull the pain.

In the early years of the Cape settlement, when men substantially outnumbered women, several marriages took place between Dutch settlers and slave women. Subsequently, sexual liaisons occurred between whites and slaves outside wedlock, and the company's slave lodge became, in effect, the colony's leading brothel.

By the time Van Riebeeck left the Cape of Good Hope to take up the post of Governor of Malacca in 1662, the Dutch settlement had become firmly established at the Cape of Good Hope. It would continue to grow, both in size and stature, after his departure, as interest in the colony increased and many people arrived at the settlement to start a new life at the Cape.

Wine on the wagon *The wines of the Cape Colony had acquired a formidable reputation by the early 1800s. Wines from the Constantia estate were particularly popular among buyers overseas – and even drunk by Napoleon during his exile on St Helena.*

WARRIORS OF SHAKA'S ZULU KINGDOM

Discipline was strict and justice swift and final in the kingdom of Shaka in 1820. Mercurial, emotionally insecure and implacably cruel, the Zulu king ruled as absolute monarch, with the power of life and death over every one of the hundreds of diverse communities that made up the Zulu nation.

Death was the standard punishment for a host of offences, including adultery, and offenders were taken by soldiers to a special killing field near the royal kraal and clubbed or impaled on sharpened stakes.

But Shaka was more than just a cruel despot. He was a born leader, and a military genius who was well respected far beyond the boundaries of the Zulu empire he created through his wars of conquest. He equipped his warriors with short-handled, broad-bladed stabbing spears, clubs and oxhide shields about 4 ft (1.2 m) in height. The Zulus scorned footwear in battle, as it slowed them up, and could traverse the roughest and thorniest ground on their toughened soles. Their headdresses and armbands were made from the pelts of antelopes and other animals – only Shaka and his chiefs were entitled to wear leopard skin. The king's highest award for bravery was a necklace of olive wood.

The Zulu army's method of attack proved brutally effective. Called the 'bull-and-horns' formation, it combined a frontal assault on the enemy position with diversions on the flanks by units of the fastest runners. Once the enemy was surrounded, the Zulus closed in on the foe. Clan after clan succumbed to the Zulu war machine, which united thousands of homesteads under Shaka and drove thousands of others to flight.

Shaka, legend said, was the offspring of a casual liaison between Senzangakona, heir to the throne of the Zulus when they were still an unimportant chiefdom, and Nandi, a member of the Langeni clan. The marriage that resulted embarrassed the Zulus, who before long cast out Nandi and Shaka. Later they were both rejected by the Langeni clan as well. Shaka was never to forget these early humiliations, and later exacted his own terrible vengeance.

The centre of the Zulu people's social structure and traditions was the homestead. The production of food,

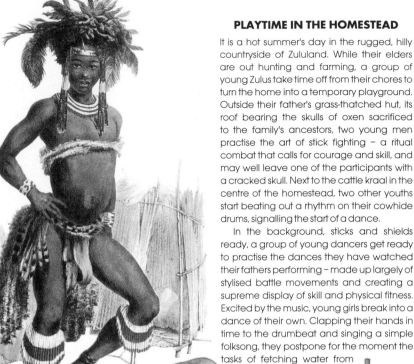

Dance wear *A young Zulu dons ostrich plumes as part of his regalia for a ritual dance.*

PLAYTIME IN THE HOMESTEAD

It is a hot summer's day in the rugged, hilly countryside of Zululand. While their elders are out hunting and farming, a group of young Zulus take time off from their chores to turn the home into a temporary playground. Outside their father's grass-thatched hut, its roof bearing the skulls of oxen sacrificed to the family's ancestors, two young men practise the art of stick fighting – a ritual combat that calls for courage and skill, and may well leave one of the participants with a cracked skull. Next to the cattle kraal in the centre of the homestead, two other youths start beating out a rhythm on their cowhide drums, signalling the start of a dance.

In the background, sticks and shields ready, a group of young dancers get ready to practise the dances they have watched their fathers performing – made up largely of stylised battle movements and creating a supreme display of skill and physical fitness. Excited by the music, young girls break into a dance of their own. Clapping their hands in time to the drumbeat and singing a simple folksong, they postpone for the moment the tasks of fetching water from the river and preparing food for the evening meal which have to be done before the adults return.

Village brew *A beer called* tshwala *was prepared from sun-dried sorghum or millet. This was ground and mixed with water, after which the mixture was boiled and blended with malted meal, more millet and salt. The beer would begin to ferment after a day or two.*

clothing, implements and virtually all other needs was concentrated in the circle of huts that made up the homestead, and livestock was kept in a brushwood enclosure at its centre. The husband's hut always stood at the opposite end of the homestead to the gateway, with his wives' huts arranged along the sides according to seniority.

Each hut was built in the shape of a beehive, with a low, arched doorway, and a removable door made from a lattice of wattle branches. Ventilation was provided by air flowing in through the door and filtering out through the thatch; smoke from the concave fire-place on the floor escaped the same way. A coating of soot on the ceiling discouraged vermin and insects. The floor was plastered with a mixture of mud – usually made from the soil of an ant hill – and cow dung. Sometimes animal fat was added to give it a sheen.

Furnishings were very spartan. The Zulus sat on goatskin rugs and slept on mats of river rushes or under 'blankets' of animal skins. Their staple food was millet – or maize if the year's harvests were good enough – prepared in a number of ways. After grinding it into meal on a concave stone, they made a lumpy porridge which they ate with their hands. They also enjoyed a sour milk drink called *amasi*. Custom, however, sometimes obliged them to

Re-usable weapon *The Zulu assegai was a stabbing spear developed by Shaka to replace the traditional throwing spear, which a warrior could use only once in battle. One assegai, by contrast, could be used to stab again and again.*

forgo this particular treat. A number of occurrences such as menstruation or contact with death were believed to be sources of contamination that required certain procedures to ensure purification – and one of these was abstention from amasi. People washed in their houses – or, in the case of children, in the open air – and cleaned their teeth with ash from the previous night's fire.

The well organised society of the Zulus assigned carefully defined roles to men and to women. Zulu women accepted their inferior status from early childhood. Children of five or six years underwent a ritual in which their ears were pierced, and after this girls were drawn increasingly into what were regarded as 'women's duties', working in the fields and carry-ing out a variety of domestic chores, while the boys tended livestock. Females had to be avoided by boys undergoing puberty rituals, by herbalists, and by any man who intended going on a hunt or performing a ritual sacrifice.

Marriage in the Zulu state was subject to the absolute authority of the king, who was unlikely to grant permission for the men of his regiments to marry before they were well into their thirties, with women about 10 to 15 years younger. When a Zulu man married, he left his father's homestead and set up his own family, often augmenting it with more wives and children. The number of wives a man might have was determined by the number of cattle he could afford in *lobola*, or bride price – a system that had evolved to cope with the shortage of men that battles and hunting had caused. By controlling marriage in his kingdom, the king determined

Moment of glory *In 1879, the warriors of chief Cetshwayo destroyed a British force at Isandlwana, but the British retaliation spelt the Zulus' downfall.*

the number of children born and who had them. The husband was the sole arbiter of disputes and dispenser of favours in the Zulu household, and his control of the relative ranking of wives allowed him to discriminate in favour of an obedient wife.

Zulu women did, however, enjoy certain rights. Fathers were obliged to support their unmarried daughters, husbands were expected to look after their wives, and sons were responsible for the well-being of their widowed mothers. Older women often wielded great influence in their sons' homes, and in the case of royalty, wives or close female relatives were sometimes appointed to influential positions as heads of households.

Killing of a king

In his ascent to supremacy, Shaka eliminated anyone he thought might challenge his throne, but he overlooked his half-brother Dingane, a devious and cunning man. On September 22, 1828, Dingane, with the assistance of another half-brother, Mhlangane, stabbed Shaka to death.

Shaka's murder led to far-reaching changes in Zululand. Dingane, though just as ruthless as his half-brother, was an incompetent military tactician. Defeated by the Boers at the Battle of Blood River in December 1838, he fled Zululand and later died in exile. After

Changing sides *Many refugees from the Zulus fled south, where they were given protection by the British. Later, they fought with the British against other Africans.*

Dingane's defeat, the whites set up a small settlement to the south named Natalia, which under Boer and later British rule was to grow and further challenge Zulu power. Helped by the Boers, Mpande, another of Shaka's half-brothers, became the Zulu king, and for a while there was peace.

The succession to the throne of Mpande's son Cetshwayo, however, saw the start of a new conflict – this time with the British. In the war of 1879 the new king's bid to revive Zulu power was to bring about the downfall of his nation as a military power and the eventual division of Zululand into 13 chiefdoms, with no king.

A DAY IN THE LIFE OF A VOORTREKKER

As dawn breaks across the sun-burnt veld, a burly man in one of the wagons in the trekker camp pulls on his coat and peers through a gap in the canvas. His wife is already up and dressed, preparing breakfast – her *kappie*, or poke bonnet, chintz dress and layers of petticoats look out of place in the dusty veld. Pulling on his *riempieskoene*, or leather-thong shoes, he goes in search of coffee, one of the Boers' most valued imports. He has slept in his woollen shirt and brown corduroy trousers, for fear of night attack.

Holding a steaming mug of coffee, he gazes across the laager. Tendrils of smoke still rise from the ring of fires built the night before to keep lions away. Reaching into his pocket, he produces a homemade soap-stone pipe and a tobacco pouch made from the skin of a dassie, or rock rabbit. Striking a spark from a tinderbox, he lights up. Inside the wagon his daughter is unpicking the seam of a worn jacket: the thread will be saved for use in a new garment.

Soon the camp breakfasts on freshly baked bread, maize and venison left over from the previous day's hunt. The young men are sent off to tend the sheep and cattle, while the older men hunt for the pot, discuss progress and mend equipment. At the end of the day, the trekkers hold a prayer meeting to give thanks, before gathering around the fire to talk and tell stories to the children. After topping up the fires and posting guards, the trekkers retire to bed.

Uphill task *An artist captures in heroic style the legendary ability of the trekker wagons to withstand South Africa's rugged terrain.*

Source of inspiration *The Voortrekkers were a devout and staunchly Calvinist people, and the Bible was often the only book a family had in its possession.*

BY OX-WAGON ON THE BOERS' GREAT TREK

In the mid-1830s, a number of groups of Afrikaner families set off in ox-wagons from the eastern Cape region of South Africa, bound for the sketchily mapped interior of the country. They later became known as Voortrekkers, meaning 'forward journeyers', and the expedition they undertook became known in retrospect as the Great Trek.

These Boers, or farmers, were angry at what they saw as a violation of their rights by the British. Competition for good grazing land was fierce, and the Boers felt that the British system of justice threatened the independent lifestyle which they treasured and took away their right to defend themselves. Furthermore, the increasingly important role of cash in the economy was ruining the barter system with which the Boers were familiar. Then there was the abolition of slavery and the return to the indigenous Xhosa of annexed land – territory which the Boers had helped to capture. While most Boers were prepared to accept the new order, a significant number of them were not.

Once over the colony's borders and beyond British control, they reasoned, they would be able to establish their own state. They were wrong, however, in believing that vast expanses of territory north of the Orange River and east of the Drakensberg mountains had been depopulated by wars, and that they would be welcomed by the survivors as allies. In reality, inter-African conflicts had by no means emptied the land of people.

Laden with their possessions, the trekkers and their African servants set out on the epic journey that was to become a treasured part of Afrikaner history. The trekkers found that no Dutch Reformed Church minister from the Cape colony was prepared to accompany them. The church synod

Jawbone wagon *The Voortrekkers' kakebeenwa, or 'jawbone wagon', resembled in shape the lower jawbone of a horse or ox. It could carry a heavy load of equipment.*

Ready for an attack *The typical trekker was not a career soldier. Most were hunters, herders or farmers, who took up arms only when danger threatened. They were fine scouts and superb marksmen.*

opposed the expedition, saying it would lead to 'godlessness and a decline of civilisation'. So the pioneers relied on Erasmus Smit, a lay preacher; the American Congregational missionary Daniel Lindley and James Archbell, a Wesleyan missionary.

Their home, their transport and their fortress was the ox-wagon. The typical trekker wagon was about 15 ft (4.5 m) long, 3 ft (1m) wide and tented throughout its length. The spokes of the wheels were made from assegai-tree wood and the axles from ironwood. Inside was a *wakis*, or wagon chest, on which the driver sat, and a bed frame with mattress. Chicken coops, pots and pans were carried on a timber grating under the rear of the wagon. The oxen were yoked together in pairs to a draw-rope made from plaited hide, later replaced by chains.

The trekkers used skids behind the rear wheels to brake the wagons on steep slopes. Occasionally they took the rear wheels off altogether and tied branches in their place. In this way they protected the axles while 'tobogganing' down the mountains.

A people's army goes to battle

Military prowess was of paramount importance to the trekkers, for they were invading and conquering lands to which African societies laid claim. They were truly a people's army, with the whole family, servants included, being drawn into defence and attack.

The trekkers would ride into battle in formidable groups, equipped with their muskets, *kruithorings*, or powder horns, and bandoleers – bullet pouches made from hartebeest, kudu or ox-hide and usually strapped to the belt. Bullets were frequently sliced almost through to make them split and fly in different directions, and buckshot was prepared by casting lead in hollow reeds and then chopping it up. To harden the lead, the trekkers added tin from discarded tableware.

The trekkers were forced to become medically self-sufficient, because they were roaming far from doctors. By the time they left, they had acquired an impressive knowledge of the medicinal uses of herbs and other plants of South Africa's open grassy veld, and by 1850 more than 100 different plant species were being used regularly. All trekker parties carried small medicine chests containing bottles of medicine, ointments and plasters.

Some of the Voortrekkers' medical practices, though, were bizarre. When the nephew of a trekker leader lost three fingers in a shooting accident, his son-in-law amputated the shattered remains with a hammer and chisel before applying a dressing of cobwebs combined with sugar. When another trekker hurt his leg with an axe, self-styled doctors applied burnt aloe and a guinea coin to the wound. Then a goat was slaughtered and the unfortunate man was told to drink an infusion of its bowel contents.

Vulture or iguana fat was used to treat lumbago, goat fat was applied on chapped hands and children's faces, and measles was treated by giving the patient an infusion of goat's dung to drink. Yet despite these unconventional treatments, the trekkers were a remarkably healthy people. This was due at least in part to their sanitary safeguards; refuse and excreta were properly disposed of, while the water supplies were always protected from pollution by animals or humans. The laager – the protective ring into which the trekkers drew their wagons when they camped – would always be located below the water source.

Trekker women were a hardy breed accustomed to privation and danger. The wives and older daughters had to provide meals for the family in the most difficult of circumstances, often without firewood for cooking. They used a three-legged, cast-iron pot for cooking over the fire, and placed cow-dung embers on the lid for baking. They dressed the meat, baked bread and griddle cakes, and made their own soap from the *ganna*, or lye-bush, and the fat from sheep's tails. They were also responsible for the repairing and laundering of clothes. Needles were particularly valuable items, sometimes being loaned from person to person for months and being filed sharp every time they were broken until they were no longer than a fingernail.

If their husbands were ill or hurt, the women would take over the reins of the ox-wagons. They often had to carry small children or even help with heavy wagon wheels and other equipment when the party made steep climbs or descents. In the absence of teachers, they taught their offspring to read. These were strong women: one widow raised nine children without help. She employed just two teaching aids – a leather strap and strong language.

Combined operation *Flint-lock muskets were cumbersome to load, and each family would use two or more weapons in turn. While the husband aimed and fired one musket, his wife and children loaded the next in readiness.*

Place of tears *A surprise Zulu attack on a Boer camp in Natal in 1838 resulted in the deaths of 500 Boers and their servants. The location of the attack was named Weenen, 'weeping', to commemorate the event. The trekkers used the laager – usually effective, though it failed this time – as their principal defensive tactic. It involved drawing the wagons into a circle, then filling the gaps between the wheels with branches to provide cover. Cattle and other livestock were driven into the circle for protection.*

DIGGING FOR DIAMONDS IN THE 'BIG HOLE'

Thieves and vagabonds prowled the diamond diggings of early Kimberley. Desperate men fought and died over the little shiny stones that would one day sparkle on the necks of beautiful women in Europe and America. Nature, too, was implacable: the searing sun drained moisture and energy like a sponge, while stray whirlwinds sucked up the ubiquitous red dust and disgorged it on tents and people.

Only the most ruthless survived the harsh reality of the mining settlement, a brash crucible of fresh beginnings, wealth beyond avarice and shattered dreams. In the early days, claims were up for grabs, and success belonged to the toughest and meanest. One of the 'diggers' – as small claim-owners came to be called – later recounted how he climbed Colesberg Kopje before dawn one day to guard his claim, to prevent it from being appropriated by the thieves who roamed the settlement.

This seemingly endless sprawl of tents and shanties was the birthplace of Kimberley (named after the British Colonial Secretary of the day), the haunt of diamond magnates such as

Cecil Rhodes and Barney Barnato, and a turbulent frontier town the like of which South Africa had never seen. The Kimberley story began in 1871 when a man named Fleetwood Rawstorne staked his claim to the hill that was destined to become the wealthiest diamond mine in the world, and named it after his home town of Colesberg. That simple act was to change the lives of countless people. In those halcyon days, diamonds were there for the taking. A digger could be poor in the morning and rich that afternoon. He took his find to one of the numerous diamond merchants near the diggings, who having examined and weighed the stone would make an offer and, after the obligatory exchange of insults or expressions of disbelief, hand over a wad of banknotes.

Happy, the digger might head for The Hard Times, one of the many establishments dedicated to soothing diggers' dusty throats – and parting customers from their money.

A contemporary account describes a typical hostelry: 'Around the bar were detectives mingling and drinking with the fish they hoped to catch; broken down, grandiose captains; jewelled gamblers stinking of scent; liquor-loving lawyers; Irish patriots of combative and fiery inclinations; a few flabby actors, unwashed and unabashed, with last night's triumphs plastered on their faces; newspaper reporters, down at heel; unemployed nondescripts...' Diggers recalled only too well the greed, terror and boundless excitement of those early days, and how they stared in disbelief at their first diamond. A handful of gravel would be scattered on a crude sorting table, then spread out with a scraper so that each individual pebble became visible – and suddenly there glittered a diamond. Others, however, toiled for weeks on end without finding a diamond and were finally reduced to living on handouts.

Striking it rich

There were success stories aplenty, though, and when diggers struck it lucky they wanted the whole world to know it, dispensing cigars to everyone and sometimes using banknotes to light them. One man invited a lady of the night to share his good fortune, but insisted that she first take a bath in the best champagne.

Later, he invited his friends to join him on one of the merry-go-rounds in the town. He climbed onto one of the wooden horses, waving a whisky bottle and shouting ribald remarks to passers-by. He knew his money would soon be gone but he didn't care. He was rich for now...

Fond though they were of sharing a drink with friends, the diggers were aware of the cutthroat nature of their

business and kept a watchful eye on their claims. The labourers whom the diggers employed to do the actual spade work often helped themselves to some of the shiny stones, and they found ready buyers in a town where illicit diamond dealing was just another form of free enterprise.

Although the Diggers' Committee imposed harsh penalties, including public floggings, for this illegal trade, the temptation to make easy money spawned a variety of ingenious smuggling methods. It was estimated that anything up to 50 per cent of the mine's production was being spirited away by wily criminals.

'May his soul, released from this low Babel, Be found a gem on God's great sorting table.'
– EPITAPH TO ALBERT BRODRICK, DIGGER

Workers hid diamonds in decayed teeth, in self-inflicted gashes in their legs or even in the quicks of their toenails. More often they swallowed the stones for recovery later. A corps of diamond police was established, and African labourers were forced to live in compounds surrounded by wire fences.

Working at the mine was extremely hard. Weaving his way between a

Homes at the mine *The first homes at the diggings were tents and wagons. However, these were soon replaced by wooden-frame houses covered with canvas as the tents were often flattened by the wind. Even the lieutenant-governor of the region lived in these humble conditions.*

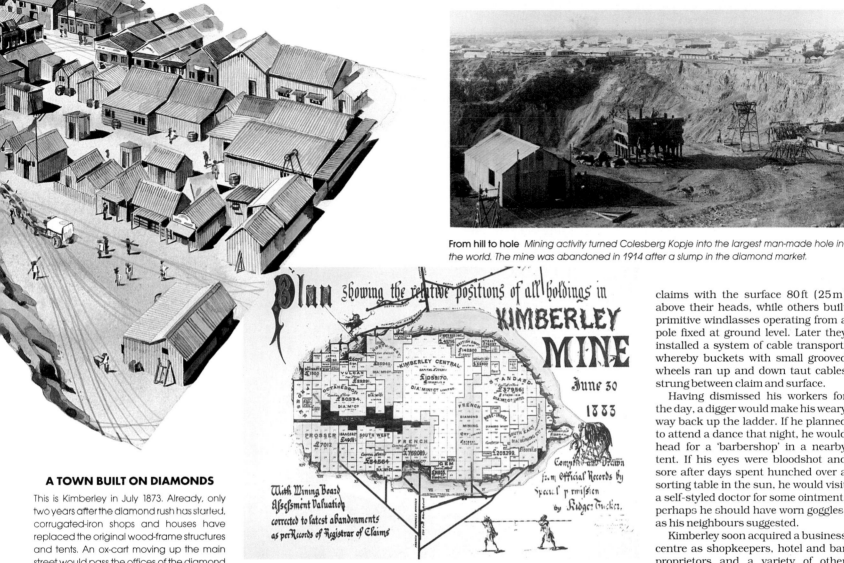

From hill to hole *Mining activity turned Colesberg Kopje into the largest man-made hole in the world. The mine was abandoned in 1914 after a slump in the diamond market.*

Mine on paper *As the years passed, the expense and technical difficulty of working on different levels forced many independent diggers to sell out to small mining companies. These sold to ever bigger companies, until one company held a monopoly of production.*

A TOWN BUILT ON DIAMONDS

This is Kimberley in July 1873. Already, only two years after the diamond rush has started, corrugated-iron shops and houses have replaced the original wood-frame structures and tents. An ox-cart moving up the main street would pass the offices of the diamond merchants Danziger and Company – their name displayed on the large gabled sign above the door to attract the successful digger who wishes to sell his findings for a reasonable price. The digger trying for a higher price can move up the street to the rival merchants Koefoed's, flying a red flag. Beyond, on the corner of a side street, is a third merchant, Tonesca's.

Opposite Tonesca's is Norris's Hotel, a favourite place for diggers to gather to moisten their parched throats with generous helpings of Cape Smoke, a cheap brandy. More sober diggers, meanwhile, will be stocking up at the gabled trading store of Wallace and Company – just off the public square, with the flags flying over it. Drunk or sober, all will finally head for home for a night's sleep, before plunging again down the gaping maw of the ever-expanding Big Hole that has given birth to Kimberley.

motley assortment of tents, wagons and sorting equipment, a digger would have to keep his eyes on the ground, aware that one false step could send him plummeting to injury or even death. Around him would be a tangle of steel cables and frayed ropes, resembling the web of a deranged spider. As he descended to his claim, he would glance upwards several times as he climbed cautiously down the swaying rope ladder.

Diggers had reason to be cautious, for on several occasions ropes snapped and dropped loads of rubble onto the heads of the men toiling below, some-times killing or maiming them. As the workings penetrated ever deeper into the earth, such accidents became more and more frequent. In the early days the diggers built wooden ramps up which the diamond-bearing rubble was wheeled to the surface in carts and barrows. Sometimes they had tunnels cut to their claims from outside the workings. Once the workings had sunk far below ground level, however, labourers were obliged to haul sacks or buckets up with knotted ropes that hung over the edge of the pit.

Some diggers provided ladders, or cut steps and terraces linking their claims with the surface 80 ft (25 m) above their heads, while others built primitive windlasses operating from a pole fixed at ground level. Later they installed a system of cable transport, whereby buckets with small grooved wheels ran up and down taut cables strung between claim and surface.

Having dismissed his workers for the day, a digger would make his weary way back up the ladder. If he planned to attend a dance that night, he would head for a 'barbershop' in a nearby tent. If his eyes were bloodshot and sore after days spent hunched over a sorting table in the sun, he would visit a self-styled doctor for some ointment; perhaps he should have worn goggles, as his neighbours suggested.

Kimberley soon acquired a business centre as shopkeepers, hotel and bar proprietors and a variety of other professional men flocked to meet the needs of the burgeoning population.

Weekends were far from dull. A racecourse laid out just outside town attracted large crowds of punters, and prizes often amounted to £1500. There were picnics on the banks of the Vaal River, game shooting, and cricket and football matches.

Every Sunday there were church services. While not devout by nature, the diggers felt this was one essential concession to civilised norms: so each Sunday they scrubbed off the week's accumulated dirt, donned their cleanest clothes and filed into a wattle-and-daub 'church'. There they would sit, faces shiny, heads still spinning from the previous night's revelry, and launch into a ragged chorus: 'Oh God, our help in ages past...'

HINDUS AND THE RAJ

India has always been a magnet to invaders from Central Asia and beyond. The long arc of the Himalayas is almost impregnable, but the mountain passes of Afghanistan have allowed waves of invaders to break out onto the fertile northern Indian plain. Muslim incursions from the 11th century led to conquest of much of northern and central India, and to the founding in 1526 of the Mughal dynasty, which by the end of the 17th century controlled most of India. By this time colonists from Portugal, the Netherlands, Britain and France had established footholds in India, and by the mid-18th century the French and the British were contending for power.

British success gave government over India to the merchant adventurers of the East India Company. They in turn were succeeded by the civil administrators and military officers who formed the backbone of the Raj – a society within a society, governed by the morality of Victorian England, and having almost no social contact with the millions whose lives they controlled.

INDIA AD 1600–1900

HOW CASTES SHAPED LIFE IN THE VILLAGE

Successive waves of conquest left the fundamental patterns of Hindu society unchanged. Life went on as it always had, governed by what really mattered: the coming of the monsoon rains, the predictions of horoscopes, the pleasing of the gods through the intercessions of the Brahmin priests and the offering of sacrifices, the busy annual round of festivals, obligations to one's caste, duties to one's family, the avoidance of pollution and, above all, the constant cycle of birth, marriage and death.

This pattern became fixed as early as 1000 BC, after Aryan invaders had migrated into India from Iran and conquered the aboriginal dark-skinned Dravidian inhabitants. From the Aryan word for the Indus region, home of India's earliest civilisation, came the names 'Hindu' and 'India'. The Aryans imposed their own rules in the form of a caste system dividing Hindu society into four *varna*, likened to the human form. At its head were the Brahmins, priests and scholars; the warrior caste or *Kshatriyas* provided the arms; the *Vaishyas*, or farmers and merchants, were the stomach; and the *Shudras*, labourers and serfs, were the legs. A fifth category was formed by the *Panchama*, who had no place in this caste system and were categorised as 'untouchable'. Caste was an inherited status, which referred to an order of duties in which everyone had a particular role to play, and which was conceived as separate from wealth or power. A caste's varna status was not rigid, and a family's standing was partly influenced by changing conditions:

Dancing girl *Eastern allure pervaded a Western artist's image of a girl at the Mughal court. Hindus had their own dance traditions, but life for most women was less glamorous.*

nevertheless the system bound Hindu society together and enabled it to resist pressures for change from outside. Though life did change in rural India, many customs were very long-lived.

Settled life in Hindustan was based on villages and not on towns. It was a society rooted in shared tradition, although each region had its own local customs. In the sun-baked Punjab, dwellings had flat roofs and walls of brick and mud, whereas in the Bengal wetlands houses had thatched roofs and wickerwork walls plastered with mud and cow dung. What united both regions was the Hindu social order.

One common pattern of village took its shape from the various castes that lived there. Every caste had its own enclave where its community lived and carried on its hereditary occupation. Each enclave consisted of dwellings facing each other across an open yard. It was surrounded by a wall, broken by a gated entrance, closed at night.

Relations between the villagers were based on caste rules, mostly linked to the need to avoid ritual pollution. The higher the caste of a Hindu the more threatened he felt by the presence of lower castes who might make him spiritually unclean. The 'untouchables' at the bottom of the social order were the weavers, basket-makers, leather workers, washermen, refuse sweepers and potters. They were forced to live on the outskirts of the village, while the high-caste Kshatriyas and Brahmins lived conveniently near to the temple, by the communal shade tree, or close to the village well.

Simple homes and complex lives

Domestic life also followed strict rules that governed relations between the sexes and between old and young. Within the extended family, property and income were shared, but all knew their place according to a strict order of seniority, dominated by the family elder. Loyalty to family came first, then caste loyalty. As a result, marriages were arranged often while couples were still children, on the basis of what was best for the family.

Dwellings were simple. The verandah at the front was the men's area and the front room the main working area. The back room was for the women and cooking, the main stove being kept well away from sources of pollution such as open doors. Because food was a source of spiritual purity, all activities to do with food preparation and eating were surrounded with various precautions

to avoid contamination. The vegetarian diet was based on boiled rice, wheat or, for the poorer people, millet and other inferior grains. There were often pulses, fried vegetables spiced with chillies, and pickles and onions. The men were fed first, before they set to work in the morning, and again at sunset. They ate with their right hands, avoiding the use of the unclean left hand, and seated cross-legged on the floor. Cow dung was used as a plaster to coat the floor; this gave it sanctity, as the cow was a symbol of purity. Tables and chairs had no place here, the main items of furniture comprising the multi-purpose *charpoy*,

or cot, the iron-bound chest for the household's jewellery and best clothes, and containers for grain.

In summer, sun and dry winds might bring drought and famine. Rains usually followed, regenerating the land. The cycle of death and rebirth lay at the heart of the Hindu philosophy of *karma*. Gods and goddesses of nature had to be propitiated; trees, snakes and cows were sanctified as being givers of life and death. Spiritual values, alongside material concerns, were part of life in the Hindu village.

Centres of control *Rajputana, in north-west India, was the home of the Rajput rulers. British settlers arrived by sea, through the ports of Calcutta, Bombay and Madras. Yet outside such centres, traditional Indian life showed little change.*

Dancing deity *Shiva the destroyer was, with Brahma the creator and Vishnu the preserver, one of the chief gods of Hinduism. The four-handed Shiva was also 'Lord of the Dance'.*

Holy contortions *The Hindu religion has great respect for the ascetic lives of holy men, or fakirs – from the Arabic word for 'poor men' – who hold poses of extreme discomfort for so long that their bodies become locked in contorted positions.*

Model village *The bustle of a typical Indian village is shown in this model of a Bengal bazaar. Goods were exchanged, sometimes for money and sometimes by barter, in a jigsaw of local self-sufficiency. Each caste had its own role and contributed special skills, such as basket-weaving, handloom weaving, wood-carving or pottery.*

HIGH LIVING BY THE 'SONS OF KINGS'

In 1806 a 24-year-old captain in the East India Company's Bengal Army named James Tod journeyed into the Indian interior as part of a political mission. The East India Company had just triumphed over its principal main political rivals, the Marathas, to win military control over much of northern India. Tod's mission was to win over the many local kings and chieftains who ruled over the area known as Rajputana, the 'country of kings'.

What Tod discovered was a warrior caste consisting of royal clans who called themselves Rajputs, or 'sons of kings', and claimed descent from the sun and the moon. Their ancestors may have been Scythians, Huns and other nomadic tribes from Central Asia who had swept into India between the 4th century and the 7th century AD. These warlike tribes carved out kingdoms for themselves and were quickly absorbed into the cultural framework of Hindustan. Over the next 1000 years the Rajput clans held sway over much of northern and central India as local rulers, known by titles such as maharajah or rajahs.

The Rajputs were a proud, warlike people who followed a strict code of chivalry, similar to that of the knights of medieval Europe. They saw themselves as the defenders of Hinduism against the Muslim invaders from the west, but much of their violence, in fact, was directed against themselves, as Rajput fought Rajput.

Rajputs were powerful in many regions, but in Rajputana they ruled over territories that were more or less independent of the Mughal or British empires. The Rajput chieftains erected large forts to house and protect their dependants. Each ruler expanded and beautified these structures, turning

Fly remover *A rajah's horsehair fly whisk was brandished by an ornate silver handle.*

them into huge fortified palaces. With success came new pleasure palaces, summer palaces, temples, hunting lodges, memorial cenotaphs – and a style of life that, even in times of peace, reflected their warrior culture.

In the Rajput world, loyalty to the clan chief was everything. His nobles attended him at his *durbar*, or court, and paid tribute in gold coins. The nobles held durbars in their dukedoms where their vassal knights were required to pay homage, and these knights had their own manors where they ruled as local lords.

Rajput royalty and nobility followed a way of life that revolved around the warrior code. The men lived in the world of the *mardana*, the open part of the palace-fort. This had its public hall of audience, where the durbars were held with great pomp and ceremony, and a private hall of audience where affairs of state were discussed. The women of the palace lived at the back of the complex in an enclosed world behind walls and guarded doors. To this *zanana*, all men except the ruler and the more immediate members of his family were forbidden access.

> *'Those were the days which the Rajput yet loves to talk of, when three things alone occupied him: his horse, his lance and his mistress.'*
>
> LT COL JAMES TOD, 1829

Other parts of the palace complex were used to store food, weaponry and supplies, the ruler's treasury and state jewellery, and stabling for his horses, camels, elephants and oxen. An army of retainers, fighting men and servants had also to be accommodated. These were drawn from all castes: from the Brahmins, who presided over religious rites in the palace, down to the original tribal people of the area, who acted as guards and foot soldiers, and performed all the menial tasks.

Though its public rooms were rich in frescoes and miniatures, the overriding atmosphere in the palace was spartan. James Tod noted that there were no chairs or couches, 'though the painted and gilded ceiling may be supported by columns of serpentine, and the walls one mass of mirrors, marble or china'. As Tod records, hunting was the Rajput's chief pastime, with wild boar, lions and tigers as his main

prey. 'It would appal even an English fox-hunter to see the Rajpoot driving their steeds at full speed, bounding like the antelope at every barrier with their lances balanced in the air, or leaning on the saddle-bow slashing at the boar. The royal kitchen moves out on this occasion, and in some chosen spot the repast is prepared, of which all partake, for the hog is the favourite food of the Rajpoot.'

The way of the warrior

Hunting was only one of the ways in which the Rajput copied the warrior's way of living. 'Everything around him speaks of arms and strife,' recorded Tod. 'Riding in the ring with the lance in tournaments, defence of the sword against the lance, firing at a mark with a matchlock and, in some parts of the country, throwing a dart or javelin from horseback, are favourite amusements. The practice of the bow is likewise a main source of pastime. In these martial exercises the youthful Rajpoot is early initiated and, that the sight of blood be familiar, he is instructed, before he has strength to wield a sword, to practise with his boy's scimitar on the heads of lambs and kids. In this manner the spirit of chivalry is continually fed.'

For high-born Rajput women and their attendants, life was much more restricted. Their world was confined to the zanana, where the maharani, the senior wife of the local chieftain, ruled her own private world of junior wives, concubines, female relatives, children, female attendants and eunuchs. Even when they moved from one residence to another – in summer to palaces set on water to cool the hot winds – and went out on picnics or to take part in hunts, Rajput ladies remained at all times in *purdah*, or 'behind the curtain', and out of sight of prying male eyes. For them, the occasions to look forward to were marriages arranged between clans, with the glad proceedings spread out over many days, and the many religious festivals. The most lively of these was the spring festival of Holi. Then the women could see the men celebrate by looking down through the latticework screens of marble in the zanana before holding a private party in their own area. Tod describes how men patrolled the streets,

Ruler in procession *A rajah rides out on his charger, surrounded by a military escort. In front of him march a picked guard of lancers, while behind him are borne in procession his standards, including a ceremonial umbrella. In the long term, such troops succumbed to British Indian armies.*

Upper caste *A Rajput prince and his wife were at the summit of the local caste system.*

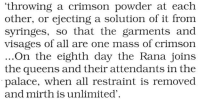

'throwing a crimson powder at each other, or ejecting a solution of it from syringes, so that the garments and visages of all are one mass of crimson ...On the eighth day the Rana joins the queens and their attendants in the palace, when all restraint is removed and mirth is unlimited'.

Death before capture

As Tod's account of Rajput history testifies, Rajput courage was second to none. His *Annals of Rajasthan* are filled with stories of terrible sacrifices made in the name of Rajput honour – and none are more terrible than the accounts of *johur*, when the women committed mass suicide rather than fall into the hands of the enemy. The ancient Rajput capital of Chittor was sacked three times in its 1000-year-long history, and each time many thousands of Rajput women died by fire in underground caverns while their men went out to die in battle. Chittor fell for the last time in 1568 after it was besieged by the Mughal emperor Akbar, who killed 35,000 of its inhabitants, including the heads of all the clans, nine queens and five princesses.

After Chittor had fallen, the kings of Rajputana were forced to admit the supremacy of the Mughal emperors. Many of the Rajputs came to accept the Mughal rulers and were influenced by them, just as in later years they cooperated with the British, adopting some European tastes and styles. They kept their titles under the Raj – and to some extent they have endured even to the present day.

WIVES WHO DIED ON THE PYRE

When a prominent Rajput died, his widow or widows were expected to hurl themselves into the flames of his funeral pyre. This terrible ritual, known as *suttee* or *sati*, was the ultimate proof of a woman's devotion to her husband. A wife who had immolated herself in this way was greatly honoured after her death. Though the practice, also associated with other high castes, was outlawed by the British in the 19th century, it still occurs occasionally to the present day.

Prints of honour *These handprints were carved on the walls of a Rajasthan palace to honour wives who had committed suttee.*

Ladies only *Only women and eunuchs were allowed into the zanana, where gossip and games filled the idle hours of a Rajput ruler's wives and concubines.*

Sporting prince *The rulers of Rajasthan were enthusiasts for every kind of sport. In a painting of around 1740 (left) a rajah has just released a hawk from his gloved fist. It attacks and brings down one of a flock of herons, while other birds fly away in terror.*

Lower caste *This group includes a peasant and a teacher.*

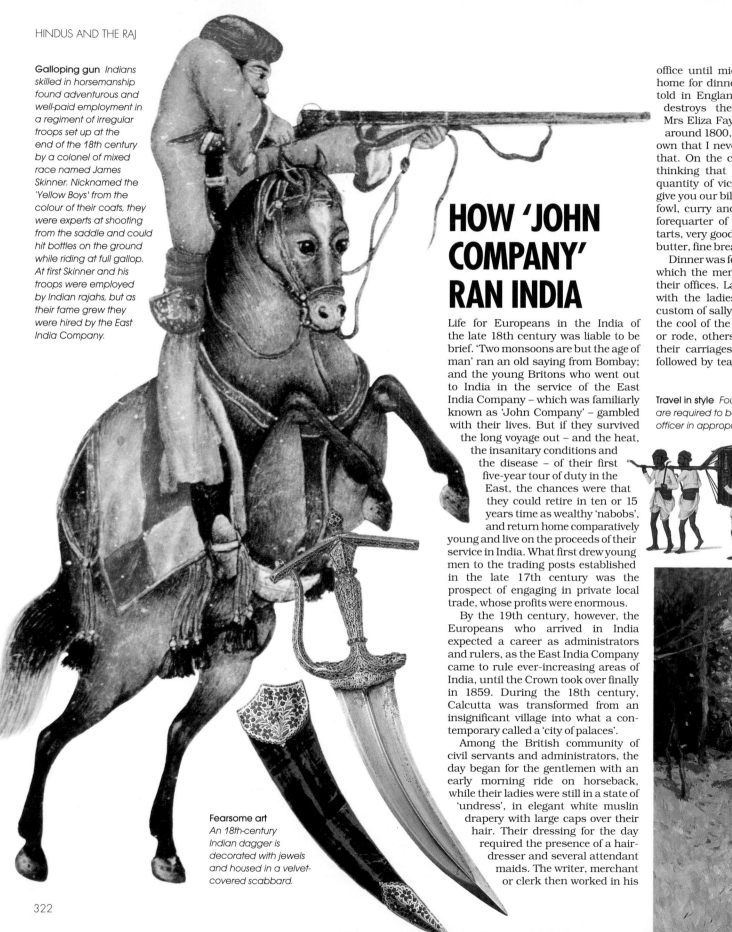

Galloping gun *Indians skilled in horsemanship found adventurous and well-paid employment in a regiment of irregular troops set up at the end of the 18th century by a colonel of mixed race named James Skinner. Nicknamed the 'Yellow Boys' from the colour of their coats, they were experts at shooting from the saddle and could hit bottles on the ground while riding at full gallop. At first Skinner and his troops were employed by Indian rajahs, but as their fame grew they were hired by the East India Company.*

Fearsome art *An 18th-century Indian dagger is decorated with jewels and housed in a velvet-covered scabbard.*

HOW 'JOHN COMPANY' RAN INDIA

Life for Europeans in the India of the late 18th century was liable to be brief. 'Two monsoons are but the age of man' ran an old saying from Bombay; and the young Britons who went out to India in the service of the East India Company – which was familiarly known as 'John Company' – gambled with their lives. But if they survived the long voyage out – and the heat, the insanitary conditions and the disease – of their first five-year tour of duty in the East, the chances were that they could retire in ten or 15 years time as wealthy 'nabobs', and return home comparatively young and live on the proceeds of their service in India. What first drew young men to the trading posts established in the late 17th century was the prospect of engaging in private local trade, whose profits were enormous.

By the 19th century, however, the Europeans who arrived in India expected a career as administrators and rulers, as the East India Company came to rule ever-increasing areas of India, until the Crown took over finally in 1859. During the 18th century, Calcutta was transformed from an insignificant village into what a contemporary called a 'city of palaces'.

Among the British community of civil servants and administrators, the day began for the gentlemen with an early morning ride on horseback, while their ladies were still in a state of 'undress', in elegant white muslin drapery with large caps over their hair. Their dressing for the day required the presence of a hairdresser and several attendant maids. The writer, merchant or clerk then worked in his office until midday, before returning home for dinner. 'We were frequently told in England that heat in Bengal destroys the appetite', comments Mrs Eliza Fay, who lived in Bombay around 1800, in a letter home. 'I must own that I never yet saw any proof of that. On the contrary, I cannot help thinking that I never saw an equal quantity of victuals consumed. I will give you our bill of fare: a soup, a roast fowl, curry and rice, a mutton pie, a forequarter of lamb, a rice pudding, tarts, very good cheese, fresh churned butter, fine bread, excellent Madeira...'

Dinner was followed by a siesta, after which the men generally returned to their offices. Later they again met up with the ladies to follow the Indian custom of sallying into the fresh air in the cool of the evening. Some walked or rode, others drove out in style in their carriages. The promenade was followed by tea and coffee and calling

Travel in style *Four bearers and an escort are required to bear a red-coated army officer in appropriate style in his palanquin.*

on friends and acquaintances. Callers who were asked to lay aside their hats knew this to be an invitation to stay to supper, which rarely began before 10 pm. These were occasions for heavy drinking and boisterous behaviour. The men usually drank two bottles of wine at a sitting, while the women did not hold back either. Mrs Fay noted that 'every lady (even your humble servant) drinks at least a bottle'. The lawyer and man-about-town William Hickey, whose memoirs give a vivid picture of the nabobs' life, disliked the 'barbarous custom of pelting each other with bread pills' in which the ladies indulged as keenly as the men. Europeans and Indians tended to lead separate lives, but occasionally a rich Indian might invite a group of guests to attend a *nautch* – an entertainment given by Indian singers, dancers and musicians, which most Europeans found very unmusical. Getting home in the early hours presented no problem, as many of the guests had palanquins, with teams of six bearers and a torch-bearer to light them on their way.

The gossipy memoirs of William Hickey show a society of extravagant living, where corruption was rife. Vast retinues of servants were employed to support English manners with Indian methods. Hickey, as a bachelor, paid off 63 servants when he first left Calcutta in 1808, each of whom had cost him on average ten rupees, or 25 shillings a week. Included among this enormous retinue was his own personal hairdresser. British social life in Calcutta was hampered by a chronic shortage

Taking it easy *British officers relax on the terrace outside their bungalow. One officer called his servants 'very smart', and mentioned coffee-making as one of their main duties and accomplishments.*

Sportsman's return *A British official rides back from a tiger shoot, attended by a team of hunters and bearers. Tigers were usually driven by a line of beaters towards the guns, safely ensconced on elephants.*

of European women. In Bengal in 1800 there were no more than 250 British women and about 4000 men. Once a year 'cargoes of females' from England came to Calcutta looking for husbands, and most of the women were married off within days by special licence. But many British traders took Indian *bibis*, or wives, in addition to taking up such customs as wearing pyjamas or smoking hookas.

Just as important to the East India Company as its administrators were its army officers, who led their *sepoys*, or Indian soldiers, into battle with great success. The armies adopted various Indian practices, and took on mainly high-caste Indian recruits. However, they imposed strict European standards of discipline. The young men who went out to join the East India Company's armies as cadets became deeply attached to the men under their command.

Maintaining the regiment's honour

'There are no soldiers more faithful, more brave, or more strongly attached to their colours and officers,' recorded a young captain in the 40th Madras Native Infantry named Albert Hervey. The number 40, he went on to say, is 'engraven on my heart. 'Tis a number which will ever be foremost, whenever the standard which bears it, and the gallant *sipahees* (sepoys) who own it, may be called upon to maintain its honour'.

Hervey arrived in south India as a 16-year-old John Company cadet in 1833, and spent the next 40 years serving as an officer in the field. Every so often the regiment, together with its families, baggage, livestock, camp followers and servants, would be sent to a new station some 300 or 400 miles (480 or 640 km) away. This involved routemarches that lasted for weeks, with thousands of people moving over the country like a swarm of locusts. Sometimes the regiment went on a campaign as part of

Crime of passion *An East India Company official listens to lawyers at a murder trial. The accused, held by a policeman, is said to have beheaded his wife after a bearded priest had seduced her. The wife's decapitated body is shown.*

a field force. When such armies took the field, their marching columns stretched for many miles. 'A line of march in India is a sight replete with interest and novelty,' recorded Hervey in his memoirs. 'The quantity of living souls in motion, the train of baggage, the quantity of cattle, the body of troops, small in comparison to that of the followers, the proportion being of three or four to each individual fighting man, this vast concourse of human beings moving together renders the whole an exciting scene.'

Household brass *Tea was India's staple drink, while a gong summoned the family to meals.*

323

Cool elegance *The 'bungalow' of a British colonel in Bengal is an elegant and spacious country house, with a colonnade open to the breeze but giving shelter from the sun. The bungalow's name comes from the Indian word bangla, meaning Bengali. Around it are clustered thatched cottages where dozens of house servants, gardeners and grooms live with their families.*

RED TAPE, PICNICS AND ADULTERY

In the 1880s, the way of life of the Indian Raj was laid bare by a young journalist named Rudyard Kipling, who was working on newspapers in Lahore and Allahabad. His verses and short stories, revealing a world of 'duty and red tape, picnics and adultery', scandalised his fellow Anglo-Indians – British-born government officials and their families, who spent their working lives in India but invariably returned to Britain when they retired.

Kipling's pen immortalised a rigid, protocol-ridden but vulnerable society whose members were advised to 'fear the sun' and protected themselves with pith helmets, spine pads, cholera belts, mosquito nets and daily doses of quinine. Its chief institutions were the station club, where the 'civil and military' officers got together in the evening, and the hill stations to which their wives and children fled with the approach of the hot weather.

The British Raj had arisen from the ashes of the Indian Mutiny. In the summer of 1857 a revolt by sepoys of the East India Company's Bengal Army grew into a full scale uprising against the British. The rebellion was savagely suppressed, but it ended a century of government by the East India Company. It was replaced with a Viceroy who governed India in the name of Queen Victoria, soon to be proclaimed Empress of India.

By the time Kipling was writing, the Raj was entering a golden age. The coming of the railways, the telegraph, the steamer and in 1869 the opening of the Suez Canal had all helped to bring

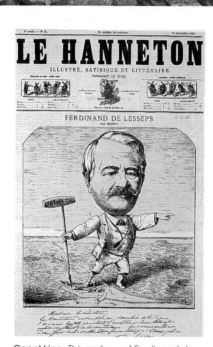

Canal king *This cartoon of Ferdinand de Lesseps, builder of the Suez Canal, appeared in a French satirical magazine in 1867. Before the canal was opened in 1869, travellers to India had to travel either round the Cape, or up the Nile from Alexandria to Cairo and then by land across the desert to Suez to join another ship.*

England and 'Home' that much closer. India had become less of a place of exile, with the result that many more British women came to live in India. The *bibi*, or wife, of the *sahib*, or master, was now the *memsahib*, the queen of the bungalow, requiring creature comforts and bringing with her from Britain her Victorian conventions that did not always match the realities of the Indian scene.

The Anglo-Indians' social round was governed by the seasons. In the hot weather those who could not escape to the hills worked as best they could

with the aid of *punkahs*, or fans pulled by servants, sheltering from the sun behind screens of wet grass – and waiting for the rains that preceded the arrival of the cold weather. For the Anglo-Indians the Indian winter was a time of relaxation, of *Burra Khanas*, or big suppers, theatricals, fancy-dress parties, balls, picnics, boar spearing from horseback, tiger shoots, horse races, polo matches, gymkhanas and touring. This was the world of a ruling class that rarely made friends with Indians. The languages of the subcontinent, however, had a considerable

influence on English. Many familiar words such as verandah, bungalow, pyjamas, thug and khaki are of Indian origin, while Anglo-Indians used Hindi terms for their *tiffin*, or snack, and the *chota peg*, or small drink, that they enjoyed while writing a *chitty*, or note.

The map of India under the viceroys showed two distinct Indias. One-third of the country was a yellow patchwork of 562 Princely and Native States where local rulers governed with advice from British Political Agents. The remaining two-thirds was coloured pink and represented British India. The main

Happy family *Enjoying the high living standard of an official of the Indian Civil Service, a family relaxes on the verandah of their bungalow. A butler brings whisky and water, while a house servant circulates the air by pulling on the cord of a punkah – a large fan made from a palm frond or strip of cloth suspended from the ceiling. The ayah, or nursemaid, carries the youngest child. Chairs are lightweight for coolness.*

gaols and courts of justice. He levies the rent of their fields, he fixes the tariff and he nominates every appointment.'

The young civilian who won a place in the ICS was called a 'competition-wallah'. He was expected to spend his first 'tour' of five years 'up-country', leading an isolated bachelor existence in the district. When one young recruit, Alban Way, joined the ICS in 1890 he was soon trying his first court case as a junior district magistrate. When the cold weather began in November he followed the custom of touring the countryside, sleeping under canvas.

'I am going out by myself on a tour of inspection,' wrote Way to his parents in November, 1891. 'I have to inspect everything: schools, roads, hospitals, dispensaries, ferries, police stations

and, most important of all, the records of fields and cultivators kept by the village accountants...I am by myself, and on my own resources.'

Supporting the District Officer in his district was a whole range of professional services from the Indian Police to the Public Works Department. The senior officials in all these services were British. They referred to themselves as 'civilians', and each one had his place in the ruling hierarchy, laid down in the government handbook known as the Warrant of Precedence.

A single district could be larger than an English county and contain a million or more inhabitants. It had a district headquarters and subdivisional headquarters, each with its little community of British officials. In these 'stations'

the 'civilians' lived apart from the local population in an area of well laid out avenues known as the 'civil lines'. This was usually separated from the local town or bazaar by open ground used for recreation and military parades. The troops lived apart in the station's 'military cantonment'.

India's complex taboos and caste prohibitions, coupled with the high standard of living required of a civilian in government service, meant that even a bachelor had to have a host of servants. 'It is one of the social follies of Indian life that you must keep three servants to do the work of one,' declared a woman writer in 1882. A 'tolerably well-to-do' family required at least 25 servants, while a bachelor could hardly get by with less than 14.

A MEMSAHIB AT HOME

Maud, the wife of an official of the Indian Civil Service, is awakened at dawn as the *khitmutgar*, or butler, pours her a cup of tea. The *ayah*, or maid, helps her with her toilet and into her muslin morning dress. Her husband Henry joins her on the verandah for a full English breakfast, before the pony and trap come round to drive him to work.

During the morning Maud attends to the household duties. She first receives the *khansamah*, or cook, to check his accounts and fix the day's menu. Next the *mali*, or head gardener, comes for his instructions, followed by the *darzi*, or tailor. As Maud has no calls to make, she spends the morning writing letters until Henry returns for *tiffin*, or a light lunch, at midday. After tiffin, Maud rests, then puts on a tea gown to receive visitors.

At dusk Henry drives her in the trap down to the club. They play a set of mixed doubles on the clay tennis court, and adjourn for drinks. Then it is back to the bungalow to change into formal evening wear for a supper party given by the wife of one of Henry's colleagues. It is a long evening, but as they drive back to their bungalow, in the cool night air under the stars, Maud feels that a memsahib's life has its compensations.

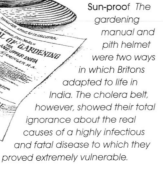

administrative area of the Raj was the District, the key figure of which was the District Officer or Collector, who came from the ranks of the country's powerful élite – the Indian Civil Service, or the ICS. 'To the people of India the Collector is the Imperial Government,' wrote George Aberigh Mackay, a member of the ICS, in 1880. 'He watches over their welfare... He establishes schools, dispensaries,

Regular briefing *A senior British official's wife gives the instructions for the day to her large household staff.*

Sun-proof *The gardening manual and pith helmet were two ways in which Britons adapted to life in India. The cholera belt, however, showed their total ignorance about the real causes of a highly infectious and fatal disease to which they proved extremely vulnerable.*

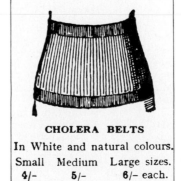

CHOLERA BELTS
In White and natural colours.
Small   Medium   Large sizes.
4/-   5/-   6/- each.

Well attended *Some families had more nurses and domestic servants than children.*

GREAT SOUTH LAND

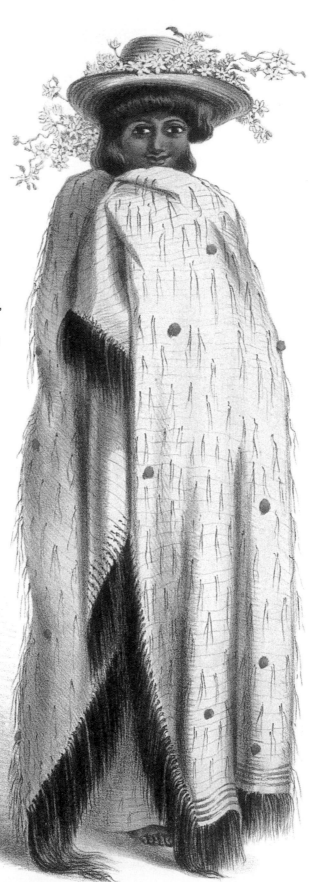

Inspired by accounts from early explorers of the islands that dot the vastness of the Pacific, the British Government in 1769 gave to a scientific expedition led by Lieutenant James Cook the further objective of finding the fabled 'Great South Land' that had long fired people's imaginations. Dutch mariners had reached Australia a century earlier and mapped much of its west coast, but the British believed that a still larger continent existed. Cook's expedition disproved this theory, and revealed the broad outlines of Australia and New Zealand.

Less than 20 years after Cook's arrival, British settlers began to colonise Australia, driving the indigenous Aborigines out of the best land. By the 1860s settlers in New Zealand, too, were fighting bitter battles over territory. Traders and whalers brought their alien customs, and devastating diseases, to most of the islands of the South Pacific, where traditional ways of life came under increasing threat from the technologically more advanced European newcomers.

AUSTRALIA, NEW ZEALAND AND THE PACIFIC ISLANDS AD 1750–1900

SETTLERS OF THE SOUTH SEA ISLANDS

At sunset on June 18, 1767, the captain of HMS *Dolphin*, Samuel Wallis, dropped anchor in a harbour of the Polynesian island of Tahiti. When he and his scurvy-ridden crew awoke the next morning, they found themselves in a paradise inhabited by good-looking, hospitable people whose customs and easy life entranced the sick and weary sailors.

One year later, the French explorer Louis-Antoine de Bougainville also fell under the Polynesian spell. Finding 'hospitality, ease and innocent joy, and every appearance of happiness' among the people, he named the island New Cythera, after the birthplace of Venus. He also took a Tahitian, Ahutou, to Paris, where society treated the man as a celebrity, seeing him as the 'noble savage' who conformed to the ideal described by the philosopher Jean-Jacques Rousseau.

In the island world of Oceania, tropical seas and lush inland forests provided a comfortable life. The people filled their leisure with music, dancing and social ceremony, and sports such as wrestling, surfboard riding and mock armed combat. Only occasional wars over territory, caused by over-population and the ambitions of chiefs, disturbed the easy life.

The 3000 or more islands that constitute Oceania can be divided into three broad regions: Polynesia, meaning 'many islands'; Melanesia, or 'black islands'; and Micronesia, 'small islands'. The peoples of these three island groups vary widely in appearance and speak hundreds of different languages.

Their traditional ways of life were, however, similar in many respects. They cultivated their food plants on

Changing fashions *The European hat worn by this Maori girl above her traditional robes symbolises the many changes which the arrival of the Europeans brought to the way of life of the peoples of the South Pacific. Even in hot, wet climates missionaries often forced women to cover themselves from head to foot, which promoted the spread of European diseases.*

the mountainous islands and coral atolls of the tropics, growing sweet potatoes, bananas, pumpkins, breadfruit, yams and a tropical plant with an edible rootstock called taro.

The Oceanic peoples were skilled carvers of wood into beautiful idols and ancestral figures. The working of stone reached high levels on many islands – notably on Easter Island, where huge statues of human heads were hewn from volcanic rock and erected on coastal platforms.

The Pacific islanders were also accomplished boat builders, and they sailed enormous distances in their craft using only natural navigational guides. Sun, clouds, moon and stars, winds, currents and the flight of birds all helped sailors to determine their direction. For often-used routes, Micronesians constructed charts using sticks bound together to illustrate routes and currents, and small shells and stones to indicate islands.

Enter the Europeans

Europeans first reached Oceania in 1520, when three Spanish ships under the command of Ferdinand Magellan passed through the region on the way to the Philippines, encountering people only on the Mariana Islands. During the next two centuries, Spanish and Dutch sailors discovered many islands, though they were more interested in finding the elusive 'Great South Land', which was supposed to exist in the South Pacific.

In 1769 the Royal Society sent an expedition under James Cook to Tahiti to observe the passing of Venus in front of the Sun. After completing his sightings, Cook, acting on secret Admiralty orders, sailed south-west. He sailed round New Zealand, then proceeded westwards and charted the east coast of Australia before returning home. On a second voyage, which began in 1772, he gave the Tongans and New Caledonians their first look at white men, and took a Tahitian named Omai home with him. Omai returned to Tahiti on Cook's third voyage, during which the explorer was killed by Hawaiians in February 1779.

European settlers and missionaries followed the explorers into the Pacific. Settlement began in January 1788, when 11 British ships carrying 736 convicts reached the eastern coast of Australia and founded Sydney, in the colony of New South Wales. Escaped convicts from New South Wales were the first white settlers on many of

the Pacific islands – including Tonga in 1796 and New Zealand in 1806. Missionaries reached some islands to find white men already living with the natives. A number of the missionaries gave up religion to become beachcombers too.

In 1797, shocked by tales of cannibalism, promiscuity, human sacrifice and killing of babies in the islands of the South Pacific, the London Missionary Society, a Protestant organisation, landed missionaries in Tahiti, the Marquesas Islands and Tonga. Eventually they eradicated all the traditional rites and customs, including cannibalism, the killing of chiefs' widows in Fiji and infanticide in Tahiti. Religious sites were destroyed and idols were burned.

Christianity prevailed throughout the Pacific by 1870, and some bleak regimes were imposed in its name. In Hawaii, American missionaries forbade cooking on Sunday but gave the Hawaiians five church services to attend, and on Managareva a French priest forced Gambier islanders to build a huge cathedral. Whalers and sealers began operating in the Pacific in the 1790s, and traders in timber and New Zealand flax added to the influx of

Europeans early in the next century. Settlement in Australia expanded in the 1830s under new land policies and assisted immigration, and by 1850 settlers had founded most of the main towns of Australia and New Zealand. Native peoples throughout the South Pacific were gradually dispossessed by Europe or America until, by the outbreak of the First World War, every one of the islands of Oceania was under foreign control.

Peril at sea *Explorers whose imagination was fired by the South Seas included the British adventurer William Dampier, who faced storms in a canoe during voyages north of Australia in 1699.*

South lands *Migrants from South-east Asia were almost certainly the first settlers of Australia and the South Pacific islands.*

Island-hoppers *The peoples of Oceania hollowed logs to make canoes – generally outrigger canoes with sails. They were able to navigate over great distances, and maintained contact between islands.*

Nautical deity *The chief deity of the peoples of western and central Polynesia was Tangaroa, god of navigators and the ocean. He was also believed to be the ancestor of the first people to arrive on the islands.*

Appeasing the gods *Human sacrifice was still being practised in Tahiti when the explorer James Cook visited the island in 1774. The victim, strapped to a pole, had been clubbed to death as an offering to the gods.*

NOMADS WHO INHERITED A DREAMTIME

Australia's Aborigines lived a life of outward simplicity, but one that was sustained inwardly by rich spiritual beliefs. They believed in a period known as the Dreamtime, a golden age when the earth had been created and supernatural beings roamed its surface. All men, they believed, were related to these creatures and the land they had created. Mountains, water holes and other features of the Aborigines' domain were all seen as the creations or embodiments of these Dreamtime beings.

Aborigines were nomadic peoples, shifting camp whenever local foods became scarce. Their movements followed a seasonal cycle, timed by the ripening of plant foods and the migrations of birds and fish. In fine weather, Aborigines camped in the open around a fire, sheltered only by a windbreak of bushes. On cold or rainy nights, or at long-term campsites, they would build low huts made of bark sheets, grass or palm fronds tied to a framework of

saplings. In western Victoria some huts were made of stone, while whale ribs served as rafters along parts of Australia's south coast. The larger homes could shelter up to ten people, who would sleep around a central fire, with blankets made from the fur of kangaroos or possums for extra warmth. Often they would snuggle against the camp dingoes – the dogs they brought with them from Asia.

The Aborigines had no need of clothes – except during winter in southern Australia, where cloaks of possum skin or seaweed were often worn – but the men and women of most tribes did wear a few simple adornments, such as possum-fur strings around

Hunting boomerang

Many uses *This Aborigine spear thrower also served as a dish, and has a cutting edge. A knife could be fixed to the wax at the tip. Only men fished with a spear; women used nets, or hooks and lines.*

Fishing party *The lithe action of a fisherman preparing to hurl his many-pointed spear is caught by one of the first English artists to meet the Aborigines. The fire gave warmth, and warded off mosquitoes.*

THE HUNT FOR FOOD

The Aborigines were skilled hunters, adept at tracking their prey. Hunting was done by the men, and boomerangs, throwing clubs and woomeras, or spear throwers, were used to hunt kangaroos, emus and wallabies. Some boomerangs were made to return to the hand of the thrower; these were usually lighter models, and used for play or to frighten birds into nets. Stone axes allowed Aborigines to hew open hollow tree limbs to reach bees' nests, and cut steps into trunks to help them take possums, phalangers, fledgling birds and eggs. From their bark canoes they dived for shellfish and sea turtles, or caught fish using line and hooks, spears or nets. They also built fish traps: these were stone dams just below the high-water level in rivers and along the coast in which fish were trapped when the water receded.

Clash of cultures *Proud and independent, the Aborigines of Australia fought against the efforts of the European newcomers to explore and colonise their land. Eventually the Aborigines' spears, ideal for their traditional way of life, proved no match for the sophisticated arms of the Europeans.*

Artistic insight *Aborigine artists did not paint only the external frame of an animal or human; sometimes they looked beneath the skin to show the bones and vital organs.*

Song and dance *Only rarely were Europeans able to witness and paint a corroboree, a festival of singing and dancing by hundreds of warriors, closed to women and children.*

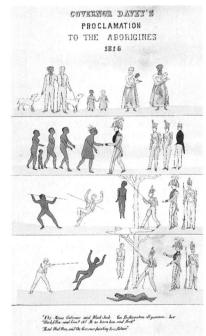

Equal rights *Since the Aborigines could not read, picture posters were used to give warning that a murderer of either race would be arrested and brought to trial.*

the waists of the men, feathers attached to the hair and bracelets made of reeds. The Aborigines were hunter-gatherers, dependent upon nature for their needs, and they knew the land and its resources intimately. They used fire to manage their territory, burning the undergrowth to encourage food plants to grow, to trigger new grass for game, and to make travelling easier. Hunting was the domain of the men, but it was the women, travelling in separate groups, who gathered the small animals and plant foods such as fruits, tubers and seeds, which gave up to 80 per cent of the diet. The woman's tool was the digging stick, a stout pole up to 6 ft (2 m) long, used to root up tubers, lizards and grubs. Plant foods were carried home in baskets of reeds or bark, or in shallow wooden bowls.

Although snacks were taken during the day, the principal meal was the evening feast around the campfire – a time to relax and tell jokes and stories. Most of the food was roasted, although certain tubers and seeds needed long grating, soaking and baking by the women to remove the toxins. The available food was shared out between families, and the sick and elderly were well provided for. In fertile regions, where hunting was easy, the Aborigines found time for recreation. In one game teams vied for possession of a ball made of kangaroo skin stuffed with grass. There were mud fights, accompanied by much laughter, and mimicking games in which players attempted to imitate the antics of friends. On hot days children took to the water, swimming, diving after white stones, or chasing pranksters pretending to be turtles or swans. They also enjoyed skipping with a vine, and played cat's cradle with string.

The availability of food determined the size of Aboriginal groups. In the deserts a foraging party might consist only of a couple and their children, though older men often had several wives, betrothed to them according to tribal rules. In fertile areas the groups were often considerably larger, and brought together a number of related families. When food was especially abundant, hundreds of Aborigines would camp together for weeks at a time to trade and exchange news. On special days corroborees would be held. Dances were often accompanied by a hollow wooden tube called a didgeridoo, which was blown to produce a continuous droning sound.

At meetings of the elders, stories would be told and insults occasionally traded – leading to a fight with spears and shields the next day. Although very fierce, these fights were ordered affairs, and usually ended when one of the participants was seriously injured or killed. The meetings were also occasions for initiating young men to manhood, and teaching them the secrets of the land and the rituals of the tribe. Many tribes scarred the skin of the initiates as part of the rites, though sometimes this was done simply for decoration.

Important persons at these rites were the diviners. These wise and venerable men, steeped in tribal lore, were believed to possess great spiritual powers, and the ability to visit the skies, dive into the earth, bring rain, talk to spirits, and cure disease.

One task for diviners was deciding the cause of injuries, illness or death. Aborigines believed that these could only be caused by malevolent people or spirits, and the diviner had to find the culprit so he could be punished. To the Aborigines, life was too rich in meaning for anything to happen by accident.

FROM CONVICT SETTLEMENT TO RICH CITY

On a bright morning in September 1819, the lookouts on the Heads of Sydney harbour signalled the arrival of ships from Britain. As the fleet beat its way up the length of the great harbour, most of the residents of the settlement converged on the foreshore.

Ships meant news, even if it was nine months old – the time taken for the voyage from England. They also meant letters from home, and goods both for the government store and the general shops. Perhaps most importantly, they meant an infusion of new blood, and the possibility of servants and labourers. This particular fleet brought a commissioner sent by the government of Britain to determine whether the colony of New South Wales was meeting in the most appropriate and economical fashion the purposes for which it was established.

The crowds made a colourful sight in the southern sunshine, the scarlet and navy blue of the garrison uniforms standing out in contrast to the yellow convict clothing with its distinctive arrow. The emancipists – convicts who had served their terms but who lacked the means or will to return to England – were more variously, if rather poorly, dressed. Here and there, the cool white finery of a settler's wife in a carriage or the gaudier apparel of a female servant stood out.

A number of the younger men and women were notable for their height and build: these were the Cornstalks – the children born and bred in the colony and provided with abundant food. On the edge of the crowd loitered

Reluctant job-hunters Convicts from England provided much needed skilled labour. Outside Sydney's barracks, a newly arrived batch of convicts await employers.

a few Aborigines, survivors of the devastation that European disease had wrought but themselves destroyed by their newfound addiction to alcohol.

Goats and ownerless dogs added to the confusion. Vendors of fish, oysters, cakes and pies cried their wares – in sharp contrast to the landfall of ships in earlier days when semi-starving hordes had eagerly awaited the arrival of food. Convict settlement though it was, Sydney had become a capitalist society, in which earlier methods of payment in goods such as rum had being replaced by coinage and more-or-less trustworthy credit notes. Grain still had to be imported, but otherwise food was plentiful, as sheep and cattle multiplied and fruit and vegetables became established and flourished.

Nevertheless, the commissioner who had just arrived from England, John Thomas Bigge, was soon to become horrified by many aspects of Sydney society. He was aghast at the amount of freedom given to the convicts, who were kept in the city more by fear of what lay beyond the settlement than by barrack walls. He deplored the continuing corruption among the officers – even though the wings of the notorious 'Rum Corps', who had enriched themselves with land and goods by selling illicit spirits, had been clipped. He looked with contempt on efforts at road-building by gangs of the most insolent and stubborn convicts.

Bigge's report, critical as it was, marked a change in the settlement's direction. Immigration by free settlers

Seat of power Taking ten years to build, Government House in Sydney was completed in 1845, above the harbour where settlers arrived.

ROOFTOPS AND WINDMILLS IN EARLY SYDNEY

By 1842 the settlement of Sydney as seen from its hilltop observatory has already grown into a sizeable town, with houses in orderly rows on the British pattern. On a grass verge beside the road, a governess pauses with her charge to watch the newly established gentry of the colony going about their social engagements. Larger buildings have sprung up as the result of a programme begun by Lachlan Macquarie, governor from 1809 to 1821.

Among them are the graceful St James's Church and the nearby convict barracks, both designed by the ex-convict architect Francis Greenway. Officers of the New South Wales Corps are housed in simple cottages, some with verandahs to provide shelter from the sun. Windmills dot the surrounding hilltops, turning corn into flour: the colony's fast-expanding population has created a demand for bread that the early hand-mills can no longer meet.

Flight of fancy *A cartoon satirises a bid to lure unmarried women to Australia, to redress the imbalance between the sexes.*

Old habits *Christmas lunch in the Australian summer, in the relative cool of a scenic mountain setting, was a novelty for new settlers. Even after the turn of the century, many still donned the formal wear customary in Europe.*

Skin treatment *In an attempt to keep their skin fashionably pale, women had parasols imported to hide their faces from the sun.*

Catches the Germ as well as the Fly

Sanitary and Non-Poisonous

BOOMERANG FLY-PAPER

MANUFACTURED IN AUSTRALIA

Sticky end *Flypaper eventually provided some relief from the ever-present problem of bush flies and other insect nuisances.*

Banks were established, and breweries, cloth factories and foundries were set up. Entrepreneurs brought in steam engines and pumps, modern milling equipment and power looms. The town still depended heavily on European goods, however, and to pay for them Australia had to export. By the 1820s the early staple exports of whale and seal products, and bêche-de-mer – a kind of slug considered a delicacy in China – were already giving way to wool. Sydney society followed the pattern that most of its members had known in Britain. Even if the only claim that many people could lay to gentility came from their commercial success, the rich behaved like gentry nevertheless. Men of leisure organised cricket matches and race meetings on weekdays, when ordinary people were at work. Their wives rode in private carriages to each other's homes – often making several calls in an afternoon.

Regimental bands entertained the public with frequent open-air recitals, provided music for church services and played for the gentry at balls. Bandmasters composed music for the latest dance crazes from Europe; the quadrilles, the polka and the waltz. Soldiers could remain in Australia on completion of their service, and until 1835 most professional musicians in Sydney were former army bandsmen.

The more respectable members of the poorer classes centred their social lives around the Church or took up worthy causes like the Temperance Movement. Rougher characters had a choice of pubs and illicit grog shops. There newspapers were read aloud, for the illiterate or impoverished, illegal bets lodged and news of illicit dog fights and other doubtful entertainments circulated.

The gold rushes of the 1850s marked the beginning of a new era in the development of New South Wales. As prosperity and self-confidence grew, moves towards independence gradually gathered strength.

was encouraged, and trade with the remainder of the world was opened up. Although convicts were brought to the colony for 20 more years, and the taint remained, the town grew by leaps and bounds. Property values and rents soared, and crowding, speculation in land and jerrybuilding became rife. The government struggled to improve the water supply and pave the roads.

Sydney's society was surprisingly wealthy. Merchants, frequently former convicts, had a sharp eye for profit.

Hat badge *A hat made from leaves of cabbage-tree palms was the Australian-born male's own chosen badge.*

SQUATTER FARMERS OF THE OUTBACK

Driving his few sheep ahead of him with the aid of his trusty dog, the foot-sore pioneer neared the end of his long journey over the Blue Mountains. Ahead lay broad plains, new grazing lands on which to stake his claim and cash in on the worldwide demand for fine Australian wool.

He wore rough cotton or canvas 'slop' clothing – a badly cut jacket and trousers held together with twine and distinguished from convict garb only by the absence of a stencilled arrow. Other pieces of twine, known as bowyangs, were used to tie up the bottom of each trouser leg, to keep out mud and snakes. A hat of cabbage-tree leaves shielded his face from the burning sun, a large cotton neck scarf protected his nose and mouth from the clouds of fine dust kicked up by travelling stock, and a pair of stout boots protected his feet.

East of the Blue Mountains, 25 years of European settlement had created a shortage of land. The best land around the seaports was practically monopolised by established property owners, so there was only one place for younger sons, ex-convicts and the like to go: into the bush. There they could hope to eke out a living as smallholders, timber getters, horse breeders – or graziers of sheep and cattle.

A worldwide boom in the wool trade during the early 19th century coincided with the discovery that vast areas of inland Australia were suitable for farming huge numbers of the wool-producing merino sheep that had been brought to Australia in 1797. The route across the Blue Mountains, discovered in 1813, gave access to this land, and although the British Government would make no grants, men started driving their flocks over and laying unofficial claim to the land.

The squatter's first task on arriving in empty land was to blaze trees on every horizon to indicate the 'run', or piece of land claimed. He needed as

Syrup dispenser

much land as he could get, for here the carrying capacity of land was measured in acres per sheep rather than sheep per acre. It was also essential that the land have a permanent water supply. By night he gathered his sheep in a fold, for sheep meant food to the Aborigines – and the Aborigines knew that the land and what it supported had been theirs since the Dreamtime.

At first this was land where there was no government; no authority to verify the squatter's claim to his land. Soon, however, the British Government accepted that there was no stopping the tide, and that demand for fine Australian wool was at last making the colony self-sufficient, so squatters were made legal with the issue of a £10 annual licence.

Meanwhile, the squatter had pitched his canvas tent or built a rough bush hut. This first homestead might be made entirely from logs, or else of wattle and daub – moistened clay forced into a framework of wattle-tree twigs and then dried to make solid walls. Sometimes a log palisade would be built around the homestead for protection.

Windows and doorways were small, with hardwood shutters on leather hinges to cover them. Floors were usually left as muddy or dusty earth, at best lined with hardwood slabs laid directly on the ground. In some areas, though, the earth from termite hills was moistened and pounded flat onto the floor, where it set like concrete. A fireplace of rough stones sealed together with clay was built at one end of the hut. The chimney was the weakest point, often built only of hardwood planks lined inside with flattened tins.

Furniture was made from bush timber and packing cases. The bed might be a large sheet of flattened bark raised on two billets of wood, or a springy construction of thin boughs covered with sheepskins. Seats were simply logs sawn to a suitable length.

The only illumination at night came from tins filled with solidified mutton fat with a wick of twine or thread. An essential possession was a flint and steel, from which sparks could be struck to ignite dry shredded bark.

For food, new squatters brought flour, tea and sugar; later golden syrup would become an indispensable part of the larder. These were used to vary a

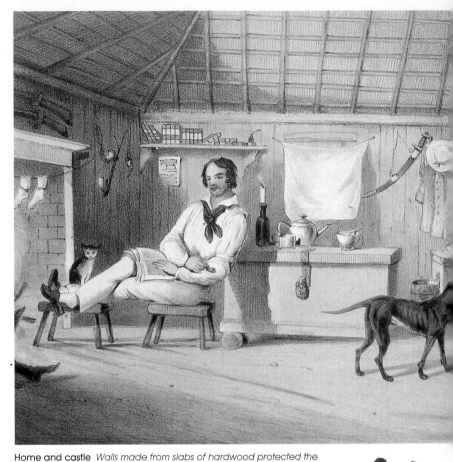

Home and castle *Walls made from slabs of hardwood protected the squatter from attack by Aborigines. Within, as comfort increased, books, calendars and engravings from journals decorated the walls.*

meat-laden diet, which often involved eating mutton in various guises up to three times a day. The flour was used to make 'damper' – a kind of unleavened bread, baked on the ashes of an open fire, which was often eaten smeared with fat or wild honey. Ordinary tea was often supplemented by an infusion made from the strong leaves of the wild Australian 'tea-tree'. Fruit was universally shunned, as it was wrongly believed to

White gold *High-quality merino wool gave Australia economic independence, and sheepshearers became the folk heroes of the outback. Shearers would spend months 'on the track', following the shearing cycle from station to station across the country.*

cause dysentery. Few squatters were willing to learn anything from the Aborigines about the wild fruits, roots and berries that were safe to eat and full of nourishment, and the settlers' badly balanced diet often resulted in skin eruptions known as 'Barcoo rot', or even scurvy.

Early days were hard; but soon the money came in from the first wool clips and the squatters could afford to engage shepherds and manage their 'runs' more efficiently. Gradually the homesteads became more settled and prosperous. Wooden fences were built around the home paddocks – vast areas of 100 acres (40 ha) or more. Pumps were bought to provide water more easily, and barbed wire, introduced in the 1870s, offered the prospect of a fully fenced estate.

Shortage of labour was a serious problem. Aborigines provided part of the answer, as they proved to be excellent horsemen. They were employed as boundary riders, taking weeks at a time away from the station to check and repair fencing. Aboriginal women helped around the homestead, and the number of part-Aborigines grew. Labour was also supplied by itinerant workers, who moved from farm to farm. These included drovers, who took the flocks on the road when drought had exhausted the station's grass, horse breakers, sheepshearers, carpenters, blacksmiths and stonemasons.

As one area after another became prosperous, newcomers were forced ever farther into the increasingly marginal land. The coming of canning and, later, refrigeration, made large-scale cattle-ranching profitable, and areas of Queensland as large as Wales became single ranching stations. Herds were allowed to wander wild and breed at will until it was time to round them up and drive them on the hoof to the slaughter yards.

Encouraged by the belief that rain followed the plough, men tried to farm areas which did not have a sufficiently high annual rainfall. Here they were to find that a few years of good rains could be followed by long droughts, which killed their flocks and destroyed their crops. Eventually, mortgaged to the hilt, they were forced to walk off their farms carrying no more than the clothes on their backs, and leaving the land to the banks.

'The ways of the Bush are most marvellously changed since this time twelve months. We now have young ladies, forsooth, and pianos.'

HENRY MEYRICK, SQUATTER, 1841

Rags to riches *As the wealth of some farmers grew, they built larger homesteads with timber floors and glazed windows – which allowed rooms to be decorated and kept reasonably clean. To reduce the risk of fire, kitchens were set apart from the main house. The original hut of this successful owner has become the kitchen for his new home.*

At the mine
Prospectors lured into the outback by the promise of gold lived under a sapling framework covered with sheets of bark.

Into the Iron Age *Corrugated iron reached Australia in the mid-1800s, and gained tremendous popularity because of its lightness and durability. Initially it was used simply as a roofing material, but in country areas corrugated-iron walls soon became common, and corrugated-iron water tanks collected valuable rain water.*

Tools of the trade
Hand shears were kept clean and oiled, as a shearer depended on them to earn his living in the outback.

A SWAGMAN'S LIFE ON THE ROAD

Swagmen, or 'swaggies', were men and occasionally women who travelled the roads, often with a dog, with all their worldly goods in a bundle or 'swag' – originally a convict term meaning the proceeds of a successful robbery. The swag was a calico bag or waterproof sheet which could also act as a ground sheet or roof. Inside were blankets – dark blue so as not to show the dirt – clothes, and a needle and thread. Occasionally a tattered book or faded, dog-eared photographs – fragments from another life – would also be packed. An axe was stuck in the strap of the swag, while a 'nose-bag' containing rations, tobacco and a tin mug hung from the top of the pack onto the swaggie's chest. In his hand he carried a 'billy', or can, of water.

Swagmen walked from station to station, sometimes covering as much as 40 miles (60 km) in a day, looking for casual work such as driving cattle or sheep, or chopping firewood in return for rations and a little money. Even if there was no work available, the swaggie would usually be given enough meat, flour, sugar and tea to take him to the next property, which might be up to 50 miles (80 km) away. Any squatter who failed to feed a swaggie might find his bush set alight, his fencing destroyed or his sheep stolen.

The number of swaggies varied according to the state of the economy, but there were always some who found that the lifestyle provided all they wanted. Though life was a constant battle to get enough work and food, few swaggies were prepared to swap their freedom to take the chance of a quieter life in the city.

THE TATTOOED WARRIORS OF NEW ZEALAND

The Maoris arrived in New Zealand around AD 800 from somewhere in tropical Polynesia, bringing with them little rats called *kiore*, dogs known as *kuri* and a variety of food plants. These included the *kumara*, a sweet potato that was so important to the Maoris that one of their deities had charge of it. Steamed kumara were dried and stored to be brought out for important people and guests.

Kumara flourished in much of the North Island, but farther south crops were unreliable, and the Maoris who lived on the southern half of the South Island fished, caught birds and gathered wild plants for their food. The staple food of Maoris everywhere was a starchy paste made from the rootstock of bracken which had been first dried, soaked in water, roasted and then beaten to clean it of fibres. Other wild vegetable foods eaten included various seaweeds, young fern fronds, the taproots and leaf shoots of cabbage trees and bulrush pollen, which was made into cakes and steamed.

Northern Maoris created extensive gardens in clearings on the fringe of the forest, sheltering them with fences and stone walls. Men worked the ground over with digging sticks, and women broke up the lumps of soil to plant various vegetables.

The Maoris' protein foods were bats, kiore, seafoods and, on occasion, the bodies of their enemies. The huge flightless moa and a dozen other bird species had been hunted to extinction by 1800, but there was still abundant prey for hunters. They hunted flightless birds such as the kiwi with kuri dogs, and snared others, or speared them with lances up to 30 ft (9 m) long.

In the fresh waters there were eels and crayfish, and people at the coast gathered sea-birds' eggs and shellfish such as lobsters and sea urchins. They fished with huge seine nets – up to half a mile (800 m) long and 33 ft (10 m) deep – which they carried to sea on a platform spanning two large canoes. Surplus foodstuffs were kept in storehouses raised off the ground for safety. In cold weather the Maoris wore skirts and large, shaggy capes made from New Zealand flax. Frequently, however, both men and women went nearly naked. Men's faces and thighs were often tattooed with patterns cut into the skin using bone chisels and made permanent with soot. Women also were often tattooed, on the chin and lips. Necklaces made of the teeth of sharks, kuri dogs or even dead relatives were worn as ornaments, as were feathers or whalebone combs in the hair.

Prestige was extremely important to the Maoris, and any insult or injury was violently avenged. Wars were fought on points of honour, and every adult male was a warrior, adept at hand-to-hand combat with traditional clubs. Insult or injury to one person would be seen as an insult to his whole tribe and vengeance would be sought, usually by means of a military raid. This, in turn, would be avenged by those attacked. Constant warfare was the result of this system; pitched battles, however, were rare, as the maximum honour was gained from destroying one's enemies at minimal cost – as, for instance, by slaughtering them at a peace conference.

As war was so much a part of the Maori way of life, a well-fortified settlement known as a *pa* was built along with the peaceful open village known as the

Maori warrior

Woodwind *This wooden flute shows the Maoris' skill at carving. Music was always a part of Maori culture, with various flutes and whistles of wood or bone, trumpets made out of triton shells and wooden gongs – though not drums – being played.*

Formal greeting *The traditional Maori greeting was a ceremony known as hongi, in which two people meeting would, after a preliminary word of greeting, press their noses together. The storage hut in the kainga, or village, is raised high on stilts to keep food out of the reach of dogs, rats and the flightless birds, some of which were inveterate thieves.*

Built for war *Maoris paddled into battle in war canoes up to 70 ft (21 m) in length, carved from a single tree trunk. Some 20 warriors could travel in a single craft, both prow and stern of which sported elaborate carvings. Rolling eyes and protruding tongues added to the menacing impression given by the warriors. The streamers of feathers hanging from the stern were supposed to be resting places for the spirits to whom the Maoris entrusted themselves when they went on a voyage. The lower streamer was for the spirits of the water, and the upper one for the spirits of the air.*

kainga. The pa was surrounded with palisades and often earthworks, and sited to make the best defensive use of the land's features. Some Maoris moved to the pa when they felt there was danger of being attacked, and then returned to the kainga as soon as the threat had passed.

The houses in a kainga faced the rising sun and a plaza which was known as the *marae*. Each kainga had a meeting house which, like the houses of important families, had wooden bargeboards, posts, door jambs and panels coloured with red ochre; these were sometimes elaborately carved to represent guardian ancestors.

The Maori home comprised a single room, and a front porch where women worked during the day. The roof and low walls were thickly thatched, while the doorway, just big enough to crawl through, had a sliding panel to keep in heat. Smoke from the hearth escaped through a small vent in the roof and a tiny window in the front wall. The Maoris never took food into the house. They ate outside or in the open-sided shed where the food was roasted over a fire or steamed, wrapped in leaves, in an earth oven called a *hangi*.

The arrival of the *pakeha*, the name the Maoris gave to the Europeans, abruptly altered traditional ways. Foreign foods were introduced, and the Maoris became increasingly dependent on them. As early as 1804, Maoris were selling potatoes to the British whalers at the North Island's Bay of Islands, and within a few years the vegetables could be obtained throughout New Zealand in exchange for iron nails, fish hooks or other implements. By 1830 the Maoris were supplying ships with pigs and fruit, and trading their flax in return for blankets, tomahawks, knives and clothes.

Iron tools enabled woodcarvers to elaborate their decorative styles, and meeting houses became increasingly ornamented. Young Maori women were attractive to the newcomers, and many whalers and sealers settled down with Maori wives.

Soon the tribal chiefs were demanding firearms. As early as 1815, Maori tribes were waging war against each other with muskets. The massive destruction that resulted from these wars – aggravated by the spread of European diseases – provided fertile ground for the doctrines of peace brought by Christian missionaries. In 1840, by the Treaty of Waitangi, the Maoris ceded sovereignty to Queen Victoria, and New Zealand was made a dependency of New South Wales. With the organised colonisation of the islands, Maori life faced new pressures.

WHALES AND SEALS ATTRACT THE FIRST SETTLERS

It was during the 1790s that mariners first told of thousands of whales in the waters around New Zealand, and of huge colonies of seals on the shores of South Island. A sealing gang, New Zealand's first European residents, landed in 1792, and soon Australians, British and Americans were slaughtering seals so freely that by the 1820s few survived. British and American ships in pursuit of sperm whales began calling at northern harbours from the late 1700s, and soon settlements sprang up. Whale Island, in the Bay of Islands, became a centre at which whalers from all over the world could rest and take on water. Hunting for sperm whales reached its peak in the 1830s, and whaling for species closer inshore expanded. By 1839 some 30 whaling stations enjoyed the protection of Maori chiefs, who supplied the whalers with men and food in exchange for guns. Young Maori warriors were excellent sailors, and were often recruited onto whaling ships. Within 50 years of the arrival of the first sealing gangs, there were some 1400 white settlers in the North Island and 600 in the South Island. The Maori way of life was to change even faster.

Hunting the whale

Ornate oar *The paddles of Maori canoes were often painted and carved.*

Source of power *Carving was a skill believed to have come from the gods, and sculpted objects were seen as being sources of mana, or spiritual power.*

Symbol of authority *Carved adzes with jade blades were carried by chiefs and priests as symbols of their rank.*

Wooden bowl

Whalebone comb

FAR EAST MEETS WEST

At the end of the 18th century, China was perhaps the most powerful state on earth, with a population of 300 million, a sophisticated bureaucracy, and more than 2000 years of tradition behind it. The neighbouring states of Vietnam, Korea and Japan had long taken China as their model. By the 1870s, however, China was lurching into chaos, and Japan was introducing a Western-style constitution as a symbol of its modernity.

To the south lay peninsulas and islands vulnerable to foreign invasion by sea. By 1800 the Dutch had control of much of present-day Indonesia. The British established a trading base on the island of Singapore, and gradually brought the whole Malay peninsula under their control. The French established their own empire of Indochina, in the face of violent resistance, but Thailand maintained its independence, forming a buffer between rival Western interests.

THE FAR EAST AD 1800–1900

Chinese migrant *The shaved head and pigtail of the Chinese was originally a sign of subservience to their Manchu rulers, but even as they spread all over South-east Asia most Chinese continued the custom. Both men and women carried fans. The silk robe is the original form of the cheongsam, 'long gown', later adapted as a woman's dress.*

GODOWNS, TRIADS AND GAMELANS

When the young Stamford Raffles landed on the tiny, swampy island of Singapore in 1819 it had a population of 150. Within a year it had risen to 5000; within another year to 10,000. The directors of the British East India Company put a great deal of trust in Raffles' judgment when they gave him the go-ahead to buy Singapore from the Sultan of Johore, and it was not misplaced. Singa Pura – 'Lion City' in Malay – soon came to dominate the shipping lanes of the entire region.

The island was cosmopolitan from the start. Malays flocked in, along with Thais, Europeans, Javanese and Arabs. The biggest group, however, were the Chinese, the richest of whom promoted further immigration of their countrymen by extending credit to start them in business.

New arrivals brought with them the culture of their native country. One of Singapore's earliest buildings was an Armenian church. The site for a cathedral was marked out in 1823; wealthy Chinese businessmen paid to build a lavish temple, with ornamental carvings brought from China; Arab immigrants built a mosque. The town had its first newspaper by 1824, and in the 1830s Europeans established a billiards club and enjoyed amateur theatricals and an annual regatta.

In its early days Singapore was a turbulent, even dangerous, place to live. In 1823, four years after Raffles arrived, it had its first riots. Its first major fire occurred in 1830, and its first organised vice-ring flourished by 1843. Tigers or crocodiles were reported to kill a man a day between them, and British expatriates formed a Tiger Club to hunt down the marauders.

The British were less successful in eliminating the triads – Chinese secret

Fine art *Court ladies in Java dyed fabrics for their robes by the batik method: dyes were applied one at a time to chosen parts of the cloth, while wax masked surrounding areas. Other arts of Java included shadow puppets, and gamelan orchestras of gongs, drums and heavily carved percussion instruments with tuned metal bars.*

societies associated with prostitution and organised crime on the island. The triads originated in China itself as conspiracies against the ruling Manchu dynasty. In Singapore they easily found recruits among immigrant youths, for whom they arranged protection and employment – in return for absolute obedience. Violence was part of their way of life; in the 1850s some 500 Chinese Christians were slaughtered by their non-Christian compatriots, and a ten-day inter-triad conflict left 600 people dead.

Attempts were made to grow cloves, cotton, coffee and sugar on the island, but they were frustrated by the poor soil. The island flourished, however,

on freedom; Singapore was an open port, without dues and with few taxes of any kind, where everything came from somewhere else and was bound for somewhere farther on. Europe sent manufactured goods; from India came peppers, opium and cotton cloth; from China tea, porcelain and dried fish, and from Indonesia sago, rattan canes and gutta-percha.

> *'Here you will see at the same time Chinese, Siamese, Malay, and Sumatra vessels bringing cargoes, and taking away European and American goods.'*
>
> AMERICAN IN SINGAPORE, *c.*1850

By 1860 the island's population had risen to 100,000. The opening of the Suez Canal in 1869 gave a further boost to trade, and from the 1870s the advent of steamships made it possible to trade over long distances in bulky commodities such as tin and timber, rather than in small cargoes of high-value spices which had previously dominated the area's commerce. At the end of the century, Singapore was the seventh largest port in the world.

Away from Singapore and the other great ports of the region, life was very different. Beyond villages which were barely touched by Western ways lay vast tracts of tropical forest and uplands where people lived unaware of the new world closing in on them.

The Chinese way of life permeated the entire region. In contrast, the

impact made by Westerners – in spite of imperial interests – was local, and most obvious in the great ports where the *godowns*, or dockside warehouses, were stuffed with the bales and bundles of goods produced 'up country'.

Vast plantations of sugar, coffee and tobacco were created to supply Western markets, and were often tilled by imported labourers, such as the Tamils who worked on coffee plantations in Malaya. But they were islands of commerce in an ocean of traditional farming. The missionaries who worked in South-east Asia had considerably less impact than those who went to Africa, and schooling on a large scale was scarcely attempted outside the cities.

Wedding belle *The young bride wears her traditional Javanese finery, although she sits on a Western-style chair for a photograph.*

Shipping lanes *Strung around the South China Sea were great ports such as Canton, Batavia and Singapore that thronged with ships of many nationalities. From the 1850s, Japan's ports were also open to trade.*

Taming the lion *Settlers of many nationalities look down on a Singapore which by the 1860s had become a thriving settlement. Most sightseers look out across the European-style buildings to the ships coming and going in the harbour, but the attention of one settler's daughter is fixed on a tropical plant closer at hand.*

Home from home *In Asian cities such as Hanoi, Saigon and Rangoon, colonial administrators laid out tree-lined boulevards, squares and gardens in the style of the day in their own countries, and lined them with law courts, cathedrals, hotels, post offices and villas . This tree-lined street in Saigon could easily be mistaken for a scene in a French provincial town.*

CHINA FACES THE 'FOREIGN DEVILS'

Correct procedure at the start of an audience with the Emperor of China was to *kowtow* – to kneel and knock the forehead on the ground as a sign of submission. Lord Macartney, the leader of a British embassy to China in 1793 refused to kowtow, although he was quite happy to fall on one knee and kiss the emperor's hand, in the way he would greet his own sovereign. After long argument, the emperor allowed his visitor to bow instead, but Lord Macartney left empty handed.

Lord Macartney's brief was to try to extend trading links with China. In Britain the Industrial Revolution was well under way, and merchants' mouths were watering at the thought of selling goods to the vast markets of China. The Chinese, however, had no interest in trading with the West. As the emperor saw it, he ruled a land which had everything that anyone could reasonably require; anyone not Chinese was 'barbarian', and anything that Macartney could offer would be inferior to China's own produce.

Westerners had no intention of going away. As well as wanting to sell the products of their own countries to the Chinese, customers at home in Europe and America craved Chinese goods – tea, silk, rhubarb, porcelain, lacquerware and other crafts.

In the early years of the 19th century the only port open to Westerners was Canton. Traders were confined to a small area of land where they lived, worked and stored their merchandise in 'factories'. Their lives were ruled by irksome restrictions imposed by the Chinese government. No women were allowed – families had to be left in Macao – and traders were forbidden to learn Chinese, to row freely on the river, or to sit in sedan chairs. They were allowed to visit the nearby Flower Gardens – in small groups of ten or less – but only on three days each month.

At first Westerners paid for Chinese goods with silver, but then they found that opium – long used medicinally in China – was more acceptable. Even as the emperor and Lord Macartney met, shiploads of opium sent by the British from India were arriving in China, and the evils of drug addiction were spreading rapidly. When the Chinese government took steps to stop the opium trade, the result was a war that ended in 1842 in defeat for the Chinese.

To pay for war, the government raised taxes, which led to poverty and discontent, and to resentment of the ruling dynasty. Manchu rulers had forced Chinese men, as a symbol of servility, to shave the hair at the front of

From bush to buyer *Tea merchants flocked to Canton in the early years of the 19th century to satisfy Western thirsts; Britain alone imported more than 25 million pounds (11.5 million kg) each year. The artist has shown all the stages in tea production, from the picking of the leaf to sealing it in chests for purchase by tail-coated buyers.*

Taking a letter *Western ways made no difference to many aspects of Chinese life. A woman with bound feet dictates to a professional letter-writer, in the year known to the foreigners as 1873.*

their heads and to grow it at the back as a pigtail. Now rebellious groups cut off their pigtails. Uprisings, and foreign incursions, continued throughout the 19th century, sapping the strength of the once proud Manchu empire.

Several ports, Shanghai, Amoy and Foochow among them, were opened to Western traders in the 1840s. While the more remote parts of China were almost unaffected by the presence of Europeans and Americans, areas near the coastal and river trade centres were transformed by contact with the West.

Though visitors in European clothes were sometimes pursued with the cry of 'foreign devil', agricultural workers from the surrounding areas poured in to work in the new industries. A new class of businessmen and engineers came into being, and a minority of Chinese became very wealthy from commerce. Far more Chinese, however, displaced by fighting and poverty, were persuaded – or kidnapped – into becoming 'coolies', vast hordes of whom provided cheap labour for tin mines in Malaya, sugar plantations in Cuba or railways in Canada.

From the 1860s the Chinese made a tentative start at introducing Western

Seeking oblivion *Opium addicts heated a mixture made from fresh opium and ashes of the drug, then inhaled the vapour through the long pipe that the reclining addict is using. His companion is smoking tobacco through a metal pipe which has water in the bottom to cool and purify the smoke.*

Trade war *Chinese junks were the targets of the British steamship Nemesis in 1841, during the war triggered off by the opium trade.*

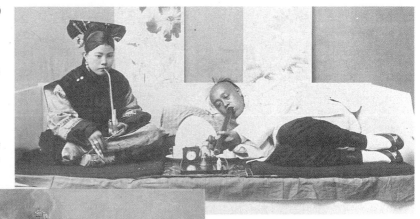

THE ENEMY OF CHINA

The opium pipe was a feature of life at all levels of society – even among government officials. Addiction resulted in aching bones, drowsiness and trembling; the drug took its toll on the economy, as addicts worked less efficiently and spent money on opium rather than on other goods. The opium, mostly from east India, soon became widely available, particularly in the cities: by the 1890s, some 80 per cent of Chinese men, and many women, were using the drug to some degree.

technology. They manufactured guns, built steamships, opened coal mines and textile mills, and introduced the telegraph and railway lines. Foreign language schools were set up, books on scientific and military matters were translated and students sent to the United States, Germany, France and Britain to study Western technology and military methods. Western goods started to appear in the shops – kerosene lamps and matches to light them, soap, tinned food and sewing machines. The new industries made little impact on most people's lives, and where they did there was sometimes local opposition. Railway lines disturbed ancestors' graves, cut through fields and took traffic away from the canals and trading roads, putting bargemen and roadside innkeepers out of work. A railway track built by the

British near Shanghai was destroyed by the Chinese in the 1870s.

Christian missionaries came in increasing numbers, and as well as trying to gain converts they set up schools and hospitals. Isabella Bird, a late 19th-century traveller to many countries, visited a mission hospital at Hangchow, near the mouth of the Yangtze. She saw a waiting room decorated with 'scripture pictures' and a drugstore stocking meat extract and condensed milk, which, she said, had caught on firmly.

'Folk would cry after the missionary, "There goes the foreigner that eats children," and children would be hurriedly hidden.'

AUSTRALIAN TRAVELLER, c. 1890

Missionaries attracted increasing hostility, and not only because of the rumours that were spread linking Westerners to the murder of children. Mixed congregations ran counter to the Chinese tradition of segregating men and women at public gatherings. There were also feelings that missionaries upset the social order, because new converts no longer took part in local festivals and ancestor worship.

Flying the flag *On an 18th-century painted fan, flags of several nationalities fly in front of the Canton 'factories' where Western merchants based their trade. All business was conducted through Chinese intermediaries, using pidgin English.*

Public humiliation *While he wore the cangue, a heavy wooden collar, the petty criminal could neither lie down nor reach his mouth. It had to be worn in public during the day, but was removed at night.*

JAPANESE SET OFF ON NEW TRACKS

When passengers boarded the first trains to run in Japan, many of them took off their shoes – as they were accustomed to do whenever they went indoors. Then they watched, aghast, as their footwear was left behind when the train steamed out of the station. All kinds of oddities such as this arose when Western ways were introduced to Japan in the mid-19th century.

For more than 200 years Japan had, as a principle of government policy, isolated herself from the rest of the world, allowing only a small Dutch trading station to operate at Nagasaki, in the south of the country. During the first half of the 19th century, traders from Europe and America arrived in the Far East in increasing numbers, putting Japan under pressure to open up for trade and to provide harbour facilities for ships. At the same time, scholars and intellectuals inside Japan were hungering to extend their contacts with Westerners.

A new era began in 1853 with the arrival of America's envoy, Commodore Matthew C. Perry. Soon afterwards, Japan opened up her ports to foreign traders, and commenced a determined embrace of the ways of the Westerners. More changes to the old order were to come in 1868 when the last military overlord,

Axe

or shogun, was overthrown. In his place came imperial government under an emperor who took the title of Meiji, meaning 'Enlightened Government'. Feudalism was abolished, restrictions on foreign travel were removed, and Christians, formerly the victims of persecution and torture, were allowed to practise their religion.

To find out how Western countries were organised, parties of Japanese men and women visited the United States and Europe. They studied state institutions, then chose the methods that suited them best and adapted them to Japan's needs. The country's constitution was largely influenced by that of Germany, and its legal system was an adaptation of that of France.

'We will become like a great wharf in the Pacific, a wholesaler of international commerce; the sun will be darkened by the smoke rising from thousands of smokestacks.'

JAPANESE JOURNALIST, c. 1880

The Japanese made a concerted effort to bridge the technological gap between their own country and the West. Foreigners were brought in and paid huge salaries to pass on their knowledge of agriculture, engineering and technology, while groups went abroad to learn all they could of a wide variety of subjects. The building of the first railway was a great symbolic event, and steamships, telegraphs and postal services all soon arrived. Cities

Camera

Umbrella

Bearing gifts *The first camera seen in Japan, tools and the new telegraph system were among gifts brought by America's envoy. They were drawn as curiosities by local artists, and soon adopted by an enthusiastic public.*

Industrial revolution *Yokohama, described as a 'populous village' by Perry in 1854, had by 1870 expanded to form Japan's most important port. It was here that the first iron bridge was built to take pedestrians, horse-drawn vehicles and sedan chairs from one part of the harbour to another.*

Rifle

Telegraph key and wire

Sickle

WHEN GEISHAS LEARNED TO PLAY THE VIOLIN

Commodore Perry arrived in Japan with four gunboats and a letter from the President of the United States to the emperor. It assured him of friendly relations but also indicated – with veiled threats of force – that the United States was resolved to win access to Japan.

From the outset, the Japanese showed intense curiosity about the newcomers. Perry described how they 'followed the officers and men about, examining every part of their garments, and showing the strongest desire to obtain one or more of their buttons'. Those who were allowed on board ship 'peered into every nook and corner, measuring this and that, and making sketches'.

For his part, Perry was struck by children made from their earliest years to bow their shaven heads, by the women's blackened teeth, and by socks 'made to allow the great toe to be separated from the other four'. He noted that oiled paper took the place of glass in windows, that the Japanese rarely

sat on chairs or benches, and that Sumo wrestlers were like 'stall-fed bulls'. The cuisine, he felt, deserved 'no very great praise', and seemed to consist chiefly of fish-based 'thick soups or rather thin stews' and such oddities as 'a small, square pudding, the consistency of blancmange'; this was probably tofu, made from bean curd. Before long, there was a craze for Western ways among better-off Japanese. Sewing machines were imported to make clothes in the Western fashion. The man of progress might sport a Western suit, haircut and shoes, and merchants who clung to the kimono took to wearing foreign hats. Daughters of wealthy families took up ballroom dancing, geishas learned the violin – and baseball became popular.

Pick-axe

Trowel

Amusing storeys *With bars, theatres, restaurants and shops at every level, Tokyo's first skyscraper was wholly devoted to entertainment. Shoes were left outside.*

were transformed, as brick–built shops began to intrude among the traditional structures of wood and bamboo; in 1890 Tokyo even acquired a skyscraper rising to 12 storeys, complete with an elevator that carried visitors up to the eighth floor.

Above all, industrialisation was the great goal of Japan's new leaders, for they saw in factory production the secret of the power of the West. The government set up textile mills, mines, and factories making glass, bricks,

cement and tiles. The new silk and cotton factories, staffed by battalions of factory girls, were a favourite subject of Japanese printmakers. Merchant contractors known as *seisho* then proceeded to develop the industries as independent corporations, resulting in several mighty industrial combines under tight family control. Famous names included Mitsubishi, and Mitsui who owned the first commercial bank. For much of the Meiji period, however, large factories remained the exception, and smaller workshops were far more common.

To school at drumbeat

Improved education was one of the most important goals of the Meiji reformers. Teachers were brought from abroad to teach science and technology to a high level. Isabella Bird, a British traveller who visited Japan in 1878, described a school in a provincial city where teachers in European clothes taught in European-style buildings which housed well-equipped science laboratories. In one village Miss Bird visited, a drum beaten at 7am summoned children to a school equipped with blackboards and maps. The children, she noted, 'looked very uncomfortable sitting on high benches in front of desks, instead of squatting, native fashion'. All

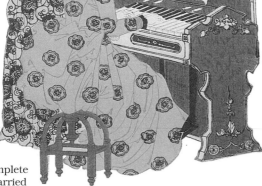

Parisian style *Wives of government officials and ladies of the imperial family took with enthusiasm to the foreigners' musical instruments and fashions, including hats generously laden with flowers. Some ladies found Western clothes so uncomfortable, however, that they swiftly abandoned them.*

Rural reality *In country areas, house and barn were frequently under the same deep thatched roof. A stream, often enclosed in a stone channel, was crossed at intervals by planks. When the stream overflowed in heavy rain, the street became a quagmire.*

the same, the pupils were exceptionally attentive, obedient and docile as they pored over their school books. At noon they marched out of the grounds, the boys in one division and the girls in another, to disperse quietly to their homes for their midday meal. Then came homework: 'In nearly every house,' she stated, 'you hear the monotonous hum of the preparation of lessons.'

Women of the upper classes came more to the fore in society, as wives were now required to help to entertain foreigners alongside their husbands, in European style. Many Western ways, however, affected only the families of courtiers, businessmen and officials. They did not undermine traditional features of Japanese culture such as Shinto worship, Noh drama, tea houses and Sumo wrestling, which survived alongside advancing technology.

The countryside was less affected by change than the bustling cities. Wheeled transport played little part in Japan's development; off the main highways the roads were very poor, and many villages and hamlets were remote from the capital, ports and thriving provincial towns and cities.

In such out-of-the-way places the poor often wore few clothes, and living standards were low, and even squalid. A Western visitor to Japan in the 1870s described children suffering from scalp, skin and eye diseases, and the poor condition of many houses where, during bitterly cold winters, families wrapped in wadded quilts huddled around smoky fires.

Age of steam *America's gifts to Japan included a miniature train, and before long there were plans for railways in Japan. The first track, 19 miles (30km) long and opened in 1872, ran between Tokyo and the port of Yokohama and was soon carrying 2 million passengers a year. As in the West, telegraph lines ran alongside railways.*

THE NEW AMERICA

At the start of the 19th century the newly independent United States was a predominantly rural society which moved by the rhythms of the sun and the year. As the century progressed, the advent of factories and cities transformed the way Americans lived. Urban life, encouraged by new industrial technology and by improved transportation and communication, helped to break the tyranny of nature; it also brought exposure to new styles, new customs, new ideas and new modes of behaviour.

As some Americans moved to the cities, others moved to the West. Both groups were seeking to improve their lot, and in their quest they created new patterns of life. Meanwhile, in a broad belt across the Southern states, another society built on slavery and cotton took shape. Between 1861 and 1865 the free labour and slave labour systems resolved their differences by a resort to arms. The North was victorious, and by the end of the century the north-east had become the creative dynamo of the nation, its urban, industrial culture the predominant pattern for the whole of America.

NORTH AMERICA AD 1830–1900

PIONEERS ON THE MOVE WESTWARDS

On the bare floor inside the cramped log cabin there is just room for a table, half-a-dozen chairs and a few chests for storage. Against the bare walls stand beds or simple pallets for the family. Some crude pots, kettles, cutlery, buckets and bowls are the only utensils. Around the house are a few shabby outbuildings, and bare earth without trees or even grass. The log cabin, introduced by Swedish settlers in Delaware as early as 1638, became the common type of dwelling in the newly settled regions of the infant and rural United States. In the 1830s two out of every three Americans still earned their living by tilling the soil. They used the daylight as much as possible, rising at dawn and going to bed soon after sunset. The sun also moulded the countrymen's year. The months between spring ploughing and autumn harvest was a time of frantic activity on the farm. Men and boys ploughed and planted, tilled and weeded, picked and threshed.

Within the confined space of the typical rural farmstead, the woman of the house plied her skills – helped by her grown daughters or, in more prosperous families, by someone else's daughter hired out specially for the occasion. Here, until the advent in the 1830s of the cast-iron stove, she cooked with heavy skillets and pots placed directly on the hearth fire or suspended over it.

Here the family also washed. This was not a sanitary age. Even a weekly bath was rare. People were usually content to sprinkle water on their hands and face. They seldom used soap. But clothes, stiff with grime and sweat, had to be laundered, and that

Breaker of boundaries *The coonskin-hatted trapper typified the enterprising spirit which inspired America's expansion westwards. Armed with rifle, knife and hatchet, and with pack on back, the trapper looks ahead to the animals he will snare, the pelts he will sell, and the frontiers he will conquer.*

Cutting the corn *The introduction of the McCormick horse-drawn reaping machine in the 1840s helped farmers to work the vast, flat prairie faster and with less labour, producing cheaper grain. The reaper's rotating paddles held the stalks against two rows of blades, the upper row moving back and forth against the fixed lower row.*

Cutting the sod
The John Deere plough, with its polished steel share, sliced cleanly through the hardened prairie sod. Early ploughs of cast iron often clogged in the tough soil.

Settling the continent *Throughout the 19th century, settlers and prospectors headed west to the Great Plains and California, while cities such as Chicago and San Francisco sprang up as rivals to New York. Farther north, settlements such as Winnipeg grew into the cities of modern Canada.*

meant a long day, usually Monday, slaving over a huge kettle of boiling water, followed by a frenzy of hanging, ironing and starching.

In this period women spun flax, cotton, wool into yarn and wove cloth. They also sewed, altered and repaired their family's clothes from either their own fabric or cloth bought at the store. Much of a farm woman's labour involved bringing food to the family table. But despite her best efforts, rural diet was monotonous. Maize and pork were staple foods across most of rural America. In the North, however, farm people ate more beef, bread and dairy products than those in the South and West. By the middle of the century more fruits and vegetables were being added to the diet, and 'Irish potatoes' had become common, particularly in the cooler North.

The great move West

Changes, however, were on the way. Between 1830 and 1860 the area under the plough more than doubled, with most of the expansion occurring in the states adjacent to the Mississippi River. The settlers in this new region came mostly from the states immediately to the east. A number, however, were from regions farther afield unable to compete with the superior fertility of Illinois, Iowa, Arkansas or east Texas. The tide of westward-moving farmers also included Europeans, particularly Germans, who were eager to trade their few worn acres in Central Europe for the cheap, virgin lands of America.

The vast torrent of newcomers reached their destinations in various ways. The majority came on foot and

horseback, their possessions piled in farm wagons or handcarts, their livestock driven before them. By then the pioneers could use the macadamised National Highway, completed as far as mid-Ohio by 1833. Thousands more moved west by steamboat on the Ohio and Mississippi rivers or the Great Lakes. Still more came by the network of artificial waterways built in the wake of New York State's spectacularly successful Erie Canal. By the 1850s many immigrants were using the swift railway cars to reach the rich prairies and rivers of the new West.

To begin with, life in the pioneer farm communities was primitive. Settlers lived in tents, lean-tos and log cabins. They used the simple tools and utensils they had brought with them, leaving behind heavier equipment. However, the new farm technology, though eastern in origin, often found its biggest market in the West. The horse-drawn

reaper, for instance, invented by the Virginian Cyrus McCormick, was better suited to the sparsely populated, broad and level prairies of the West than to the densely peopled and wooded East. The steel plough, too, was better suited to the heavy soils of the West than to the sandy loams of the East. By 1857 some 10,000 steel ploughs each year were being turned out at one factory alone. Factory workers and farmers had forged a lasting bond – one that was literally to change the faces of rural and urban America, and to benefit both.

Cast-iron cooker
Industry created the free-standing stove of cast iron which replaced the open fire in the homes of pioneer families. The wood-burning stoves made cooking easier and heated farms and cabins more efficiently.

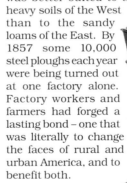

Bleak house *Lacking bricks and an adequate supply of timber, many pioneers – such as this family in Nebraska in 1890 – made their single-storey homes of sods cut from the ground. It was a hard and lonely existence, with water drawn laboriously from the well, and the nearest neighbours often a long, bumpy carriage-ride away.*

MASTER AND SLAVE IN THE DEEP SOUTH

At a rice plantation in South Carolina, a wealthy planter engages a guest in learned talk about literature and art. Across the room, his daughter sings, accompanying herself on the harp. Mahogany furniture stands upon deep carpets; paintings and finely bound books line the walls; chandeliers glitter overhead; and priceless silver and porcelain gleam from within glass-fronted cabinets.

The scene was repeated in the 1850s in scores of homes in the Southern states, where the plantation owners entertained with the lavish display of hospitality that their social code demanded. Many of these homes were showplace plantations, maintained by the revenues gained from working plantations in the cotton belt, the rice coast, or the sugar lands of Louisiana – all of them dependent on the labour of slaves.

Not all planters, however, lived in such grandeur. Many lived in simple frame houses or even in a 'double cabin', two adjacent log structures with a 'breeze way' between, joined by a

The Big House *Some plantation owners lived in pillared homes built on classical lines, in a style that came to be known as Greek Revival. This elegant Mississippi house, with its sweeping drive, dates from the 1850s.*

Slaves for sale *As the supply of new slaves from Africa ceased, top-hatted plantation owners in the Southern states bought and sold their existing hands for ever higher prices at auction, and even used them as 'currency' to pay their bills and to meet gambling debts. But already the issue of slavery was dividing the nation into two bitterly opposed political camps.*

VALUABLE GANG OF YOUNG NEGROES

By JOS. A. BEARD.

Will be sold at Auction,

ON WEDNESDAY, 25TH INST.

At 12 o'clock, at Banks' Arcade,

17 Valuable Young Negroes, Men and Women, Field Hands. Sold for no fault; with the best city guarantees.

Sale Positive and without reserve!

☞ TERMS CASH.

New Orleans, March 24, 1840.

continuous roof. Some of these so-called 'plain folk' devoted more time to raising pigs and cattle than to cultivating the land. There were other planters who, rather than attending to work, indulged in horse racing, hunting, dancing, drinking and love affairs. However, far more common was the hard-working, conscientious planter who paid close attention to his crops, his labour force and his accounts. Planters with fewer than 30 slaves often personally supervised the tasks of planting, cultivation and harvesting, coming daily to the fields to inspect the work and check the drivers and foremen – who were usually trusted slaves. Planters who had larger estates generally hired an experienced overseer, but gave him detailed written instructions about how to manage the slaves and run the plantation.

Working for profit-hungry masters, slaves often worked in gangs and followed rigorous routines. Roused by a bell or a horn, field hands by dawn

Slave gang *Clutching their few possessions, gangs of slaves were herded like cattle across country to work on the plantations of their new owners.*

Corporal punishment *Under the eye of the cigar-smoking owner, a female slave tied to a post receives a flogging, as her family look on in numbed resignation. As many as 20 lashes were the common penalty for offences such as shirking or disobedience.*

were in the fields where, depending on the crop and the season, they planted, weeded, fenced, picked, manured, ditched, hoed, cleared and performed the whole range of tasks needed to make the enterprise succeed.

With a short break at midday for lunch and rest, the hands laboured until it was dark and then returned to their cabins. There they often devoted time to their garden plots, cultivating vegetables to add to the sack of maize meal and the three or four pounds of fat bacon allotted per person each week. Slave women as well as men worked as field hands, though women also did most of the family's cooking, cleaning and child care. Children were working in the fields by the age of ten, and old women and men were employed at spinning, fence mending and keeping a watchful eye on the young children while they were playing.

Not all plantation slaves were field hands. Many worked in the 'Big House' as maids, cooks, laundresses, butlers and coachmen. These house servants

were better clothed and fed than the field hands, and saw themselves as a slave aristocracy. The larger plantations also employed skilled masons, carpenters, blacksmiths and coopers.

Slavery was a coercive system that encouraged inhuman behaviour. Slaveholders controlled their charges by public floggings. Other punishments included chaining, confining to stocks, incarceration in private or public jails, or humiliation – for example by forcing male slaves to wear women's clothes, or to perform women's tasks.

Some masters also sought to control their slaves by way of rewards – these included days off at Christmas; more status as drivers or skilled workers; extra clothing, food or tobacco; larger garden plots in which to raise crops for sale; passes for occasional visits off the plantation; and access to formal education, though many states forbade the teaching of slaves to read or write.

In some ways the cruellest feature of slavery was the utter disruption of family life. Masters could break up families by sale, with children, parents

'That's him!' Dogs and horsemen were used to hunt down slaves who escaped from the plantations. An owner could reclaim a runaway slave simply by saying in effect, 'That's him!'

and spouses separated, never to be reunited. Such sales were sometimes meant to punish; but more often than not they were prompted by the owners' financial circumstances.

Many slaves who found conditions on the plantations too grim to bear fled to the freedom of the Northern states and Canada. Many of them travelled on the so-called 'Underground Railroad'. This was a secret organisation of private citizens and church members which helped the runaway slaves to escape from their pursuers, provided them with food, clothes and shelter, and enabled them to forge new and unshackled lives.

The fugitives made their way mostly under the cover of darkness and were frequently disguised with moustaches, wigs, veils, and even face powder to make them appear white. Using railroad terms, they were known as 'passengers' or 'freight'; the houses, stores, farms, caves and barns in which they took shelter were called 'stations'; and those who bravely assisted them were aptly referred to as 'conductors'. The railroad was at its busiest in the 1840s and 1850s, when about 1000 slaves a year – men, women and children – travelled

along its network of routes through 14 Northern states, including Illinois, Indiana and Ohio – whose southern borders formed a rough dividing line between North and South. Sometimes the fugitives actually did travel by train, but most went on horseback or in wagons, complete with guides.

The railroad 'employed' some 3000 people and had many more supporters, among whom was the novelist Harriet Beecher Stowe, whose experiences with the fugitives inspired her powerful anti-slavery novel, *Uncle Tom's Cabin, or, Life Among the Lowly*, first published as a newspaper serial in 1851-2. The book's powerful propaganda message awoke the conscience of the nation and made slavery one of the main issues of the Civil War.

A particular source of Mrs Stowe's anger was the infamous Fugitive Slave Act of 1850, under which anyone aiding a fugitive could be jailed for up to six months and heavily fined. US marshals could be fined $1000 for refusing to arrest a fugitive and return him to his 'rightful' owner. If he was caught, a fugitive could not testify on his own behalf and was denied the right of trial by jury.

'Whenever I hear anyone arguing for slavery, I feel a strong impulse to see it tried on him personally.'

ABRAHAM LINCOLN, 1865

The act was roundly condemned by liberals everywhere, and was exploited by greedy bounty hunters, who were well rewarded for every slave they recaptured. Even after slavery was officially abolished in 1865, blacks still suffered coercion through statutes such as the so-called Jim Crow laws, designed to maintain racial segregation, and through organisations such as the Ku Klux Klan.

Founded in Tennessee in 1866 as a social club for Confederate veterans, the Klan reformed along political and racial lines the following year to uphold the supremacy of whites in the South. Its white-sheeted members ruthlessly tracked down black freedmen, whipping and killing them in a succession of savage nighttime raids.

However, the Klan's regime of murder and kidnapping led to it being disbanded in 1869, and banned two years later under an act which made it illegal to deny any citizen – white or black – his civil rights.

Sun and shade Heads covered against the burning Louisiana sun, a group of cane-cutters rest their machetes and take a brief pause during their arduous 12 hour shift. At dusk such slaves returned wearily to their cabins, usually single-storey, one-room structures made of logs and sometimes bricks – like these neat but regimented cabins on a cotton plantation in Savannah, Georgia. Designed to shelter a single family, they sometimes housed several families – men, women and children – crammed unhealthily together under one roof.

JOHNNY REB VERSUS BILLY YANK

Johnny Reb and Billy Yank went off to war in early 1861 fired with much the same enthusiasms and emotions. Both Confederate (Southern) and Union (Northern) soldiers were young men between 18 and 30, filled with patriotism and zeal for adventure. As war fever soared, the young volunteers were cheered into battle by all the important people in their lives. Women especially – wives, sisters, mothers, and girl friends – made their patriotic feelings known.

Johnny Reb and Billy Yank came from similar social backgrounds. Some six out of ten Rebel recruits for the Confederate cause were farm lads, and more than 47 per cent of Union troops were farmers or farm labourers. Many more Yankees than Rebels, however, were foreign born: about a quarter were predominantly German and Irish. By the end of the war, nearly 180,000

The blue and the grey *Blue was the colour normally worn by Union officers and men, while the Confederates generally favoured grey. Both sides had muskets and bayonets – but the Unionist troops were usually better equipped.*

black soldiers, mostly slaves recently recruited in the South, had fought for the Union.

Life for the Civil War soldier was harsh. Winters were spent in log cabins, tents or dugouts, heated by smoky fires. Lighting was often a candle on a bayonet attached to the wall or thrust into the dirt floor. On the march, the Union army lived largely on coffee, salt meat and hardtack – tough squares of wheat flour often called 'teeth-dullers' or 'sheet-iron crackers'. The Rebs did without the coffee, substituting brews made of acorns, peas or dried apples. Standard rations in both armies included potatoes, sugar, vinegar, beans, rice, salt and other condiments. But breakdowns in food supplies meant that few soldiers ever received their full rations. However, packages from home or purchases from camp followers added cakes, pies and sweets to the diet. Union troops in particular, who were fighting largely in Confederate territory, seized local farmers' pigs, chickens, cattle, apples, peaches and maize. Tedium was the severest trial to most troops, who spent much of their time preparing for action. In camp they had to endure a continuous round of drill, parades, inspections and exercises. Inevitably, Johnny Reb

and Billy Yank both sought diversions. Religious services and revivals were particularly popular in the camps of the Confederates. The men read a lot, mostly newspapers and 'dime novels'. They also enjoyed singing and putting on plays and skits.

Gambling, especially poker, filled time for a large proportion of the men. Swearing was endemic, as in every army. Alcohol was scarce – though in 1862 one Union general, George McClellan, observed that 'no one evil agent so much obstructs this army... as the degrading vice of drunkenness'.

The chief weapon of both forces was the single-shot, muzzle-loading rifle, mostly made either by the Springfield arsenal in Massachusetts, or by the Enfield company of Britain. It was an accurate but cumbersome weapon with a range of 600 yds (550 m). To load it the rifleman emptied powder from a cartridge into the gun's muzzle. Then he inserted the lead ball and pushed both down the barrel with a ramrod. Finally, he used a percussion cap, so that when the hammer was activated by means

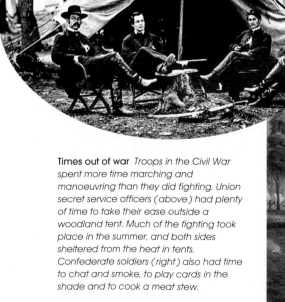

Times out of war *Troops in the Civil War spent more time marching and manoeuvring than they did fighting. Union secret service officers (above) had plenty of time to take their ease outside a woodland tent. Much of the fighting took place in the summer, and both sides sheltered from the heat in tents. Confederate soldiers (right) also had time to chat and smoke, to play cards in the shade and to cook a meat stew.*

of the trigger the powder would explode, so expelling the bullet. The process took even the most expert marksman 20 seconds to complete.

The common soldier of the Civil War dreaded battle. Fighting, when it came, was chaos. Rifle and cannon smoke obscured vision and made eyes water. Shouts, screams, roars, blasts, bugle notes and drumbeats filled the air. Officers urged their men to keep cool. But many were afraid, and scores of stragglers and skulkers drifted away from the scenes of carnage.

> 'There is many a boy here today who looks on war as glory, but, boys, it is all hell!'
>
> GENERAL SHERMAN (1820-91)

Fear was often worst at the start of an engagement, while the men moved into position. Their mouths were dry, their breathing laboured, their bodies wet with perspiration. Once the actual fighting started, adrenalin pumped into young arteries kept men going, and time went by at breakneck speed.

On many occasions the fighting was savage and hand-to-hand. The men of both sides were issued with bayonets, but they were seldom used. The usual weapon used in close action was the rifle swung as a club. The worst horror of battle was its sheer butchery.

The war transformed everyday life for civilians as well. While the soldiers of both forces were surviving largely on hardtack, fighting and dying at Gettysburg, the New York newspapers were reporting crowds of well-dressed folk flocking to the shops and new department stores on Broadway to buy imported foods and wines, bonnets, silks and cloth. But the war brought out the best in other Northerners, who met in church groups and charity organisations to provide medical services, reading matter, spiritual comfort and warm clothing for the boys in blue. On the farms, meanwhile, high prices for grain, meat and produce helped to wipe away debt and encouraged the purchase of farm machinery to make up for the absent farm boys.

For the South, the war's principal battlefield, the impact was far more painful. Invasion by marauding armies disrupted civilian life. Thousands fled before the advancing troops; others stayed, living under Yankee rule. Most Southerners experienced severe shortages of food, clothing, medicines and raw materials, owing to the Union naval blockade and the breakdowns in internal transportation. Violent food riots broke out in Atlanta, Richmond and Mobile. The rioters, armed with knives and hatchets, broke into stores and warehouses and pillaged their

Hardtack

contents. Far more than the Union, the Confederacy suffered from inflation. Using paper money to finance its huge outlays, the Richmond government pumped up prices to an absurd level. In October 1863 the head of the Confederate Bureau of War noted that his annual salary of $3000 went about as far as $300 had gone before hostilities started. The war at first scarcely changed the lives of the 4 million Southern slaves, and to the end many of them stayed on the land producing the Confederacy's vital crops. However, even before their emancipation was officially declared, on January 1, 1863, slaves in contact with Union forces had begun to defect. Many of these 'contrabands' worked for Union troops as labourers, woodchoppers, cooks, orderlies and servants – who for the first time ever received their wages in money.

Once the Union armies began to penetrate the enemy's territory, slaves threw down their hoes and flocked whole-heartedly to the Yankee lines. For every mile that General Ulysses Grant advanced through Mississippi, a chronicler recorded, 'ten thousand freedmen drop their chains'.

By the last period of the war, slavery had fallen apart in the South, although it was still not officially illegal everywhere. During these final few months, and for a long time to come, many former slaves took to the road to test their new freedom and to look for long-lost friends and relatives. It was a time of necessary experiment, but this further disrupted Southern life and work. The biggest and most difficult task was determining what role the freed slaves would play in the postwar world. No one could foresee how long it would take for this to fully unfold.

DEATH BY SURGERY AND DISEASE

Despite the efforts of army doctors, disease killed more Rebels and Yankees than enemy fire. Of an overall death toll of some 620,000, more than half were the victims of dysentery, typhus, typhoid fever, malaria and measles. Sanitation in the camps was revolting, even by the standards of the day. Conditions were little better in field hospitals, where wounds frequently became infected, leading to death by septicaemia. Abdominal wounds were considered a virtual death sentence, and surgery was primitive.

One Northern soldier due for treatment in hospital wrote that: 'I insisted on taking to the field...thinking that I had better die by rebel bullets than Union quackery.' When not in the field, many officers took mistresses, while enlisted men met their needs with prostitutes. Richmond, the headquarters of Confederate government, was notorious for its brothels, and the Union capital, Washington, D.C. had its full share of 'scarlet women'. Venereal disease was a scourge in many commands.

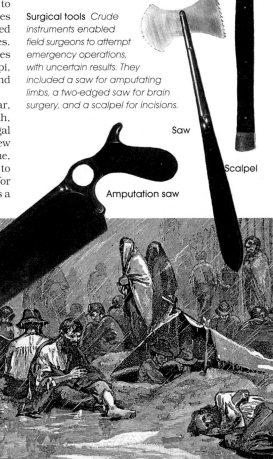

Surgical tools *Crude instruments enabled field surgeons to attempt emergency operations, with uncertain results. They included a saw for amputating limbs, a two-edged saw for brain surgery, and a scalpel for incisions.*

Saw

Scalpel

Amputation saw

Martial music *Ballads and patriotic songs were played and sung by soldiers of both sides at the front, and by their folks at home. Troops were exhorted to 'rally round the flag', and their thoughts were with mother, wife and family. In the North, posters appeared showing emotional farewells.*

Legal tender *To raise money for the war, the Northerners issued the one-dollar bill in 1862. The so-called 'greenback' was the first US paper money.*

Prison hell *Capture on the field of battle often meant a lingering death in a prison camp. Unionist prisoners were held without proper sanitation, food or shelter in a Confederate military prison at Andersonville, Georgia, from February 1864 to May 1865. Some 13,000 Northerners died there of disease and exposure.*

A COWBOY'S LIFE IN THE SADDLE

The rancher and the cowboy are central figures of American legend. Their era was the generation following the Civil War; their setting was the Great Plains. It was then and there that the open-range cattle industry briefly flourished, leaving behind a wealth of dramatic stories. Some of the cowboys came from Mexico; some were blacks. The Texans who manned the 'long drives' to railheads in the late 1860s and the 1870s included many Civil War veterans wearing traces of Confederate grey. To begin with the ranchers were mostly Texans, but as news of profits from grazing cattle on government land spread, easterners, Scots, Englishmen, and even Frenchmen and Germans, flocked to the Plains. From Mexico came the lariat, leather chaps, the broad-brimmed hat and high-heeled boot, the branding iron, the round-up. Most of the cattle that stocked the Plains were originally Mexican longhorns – a tough, wiry, long-legged breed that could live without shelter or fodder through the bitter winters. The classic Plains cattle industry began in 1866 when Texas ranchers, learning of the North's depleted stockpile of meat and hides, launched the first drive of surplus cattle – herds of around 2000 to 3000, each bearing the brand of their ranch or territory – to the nearest terminal along the routes of the new railways going westwards across the Plains. A typical drive crew was made up of a trail boss – often the owner – some half-dozen cowboys, a cook, and one or two wranglers to look after the extra horses, which gave each man a choice of six or seven mounts.

Double X, a Mexican cattle brand

Such a band would set out from southern Texas, usually in the early spring when the grass was beginning to get lush. At the head of the column was the cook driving his chuck wagon containing the supplies. These were made up largely of staples such as canned tomatoes, flour, beans, coffee, bacon, dried fruits, and strings of onions, together with jugs of vinegar and kegs of molasses. Behind the cook

Ride him cowboy!
Broncos, or half-tamed horses, were broken in by cowboys, who spent much of their lives in the saddle. Riders had to provide their own gear, and their hats, boots, bridles and saddles cost in total much more than the horses on which they rode.

A COWBOY'S DAY ON THE LONG DRIVE

Before dawn, the cowboy crawls out of his bedroll in the bunkhouse. He puts on his collarless cotton shirt, kerchief, leather vest, trousers, chaps – the Spanish *chaparrejos*, or leather leggings – and well-oiled leather boots. He then checks that his Smith and Wesson or Colt 'Peacemaker' pistol, with wooden butt, are in working order, in case an emergency arises on the cattle drive ahead. After a breakfast of bacon and beans, the trail boss gives the signal to start. The cowboy keeps alert for straying cattle and for hostile Indians and rustlers. At noon the column halts for the cowboys to have a dinner of leftovers, while the cattle graze. Dusk brings an end to the day's drive of up to 20 miles (32 km). After supper the cowboy does two hours' guard duty, riding around the perimeter of the sleeping herd. If the animals are nervous he sings gently to calm them. To keep awake, he chews wads of tobacco. Once guard duty is over he sleeps under the stars, with blankets and a tarpaulin against the cold and rainy prairie night.

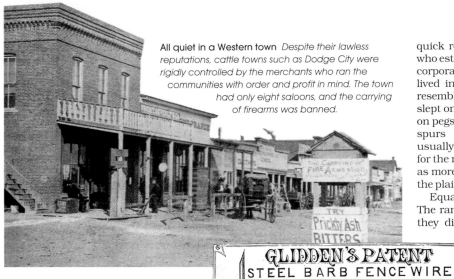

All quiet in a Western town *Despite their lawless reputations, cattle towns such as Dodge City were rigidly controlled by the merchants who ran the communities with order and profit in mind. The town had only eight saloons, and the carrying of firearms was banned.*

and his wagon came the wranglers and their horses, followed by the cattle. These were guided by two 'point' men in front, several 'swing' men and flank riders at the sides, and 'drag' men at the rear. There were moments of high excitement when storms blew up, stampeding the cattle, or when Indians attacked. Every drive had its anxious moments at a river crossing, when the cattle had to swim to the far side guided by the cowboys on horseback.

At the trail's end were the bustling cow towns. There the herds were put in pens and sold to dealers, who shipped the cattle off to the Midwest or to the butchers and packers in Chicago and Milwaukee. The men were paid off with a hundred dollars or more spending money in their pockets.

They lost no time in hitting the bars or saloons, dance halls, gambling dens and brothels. Few of the saloons came close to Abilene's 'Alamo', with its triple set of glass doors, brass-mounted long bar, felt-topped gambling tables and

GLIDDEN'S PATENT STEEL BARB FENCE WIRE GALVANIZED OR JAPANNED

Barbed warfare *Mass-produced barbed wire was used to fence off areas of cattle land. This led to range warfare between farmers and the cattle barons, who had driven their herds across the country at will.*

ornate mirrors. Most of them were little more than disreputable and squalid holes-in-the-wall.

By the mid-1870s the railways had come to Texas, making unnecessary the 1500 mile (2414 km) drive to terminals. Texas cattle continued to be herded north, mostly to stock the plains there. Once the buffaloes had been exterminated and the Indians confined to reservations, the northern region was open to cattle, and ranching gradually spread through western Kansas and the Dakotas, Nebraska, Colorado, Wyoming and Montana.

The rancher either squatted on land belonging to the government or homesteaded a 'quarter section' of 160 acres (65 ha) near a stream. Before building a permanent dwelling, he lived in a dugout or tent. A few hundred head of longhorns allowed to graze cost-free would, with luck, multiply quickly.

During the 1880s, growing markets in the East and Europe for Western beef converted the herds into cash. The

Bringing home the beef *Running a gauntlet of rustlers, Indians, storms and stampedes, cowboys helped to supply America with beef. They drove herds of longhorns along the cattle trails to railhead towns such as Cheyenne, Kansas City and Abilene.*

quick returns attracted businessmen who established generously capitalised corporate cattle ranches. The cowboys lived in a one-room bunkhouse that resembled an army barracks. The men slept on bunks and hung their clothes on pegs alongside the saddles, bridles, spurs and other gear. There was usually a cook, who prepared meals for the rancher and cowboys alike. But as more and more stock crowded onto the plains, prices slumped.

Equally serious was overgrazing. The ranchers relied on natural grass; they did not supply fodder, even in the wintertime. Once past a certain number of cattle per acre the food supply became precarious. The bitter, sub-zero winter of 1886-7, when cattle by their thousands froze to death, meant the end of the classic cattle kingdom. Ranching continued, but it was much changed. Ranchers had to provide fodder for the animals and also had to reduce the number grazed per acre. Fewer animals meant better animals, providing higher-quality beef.

Increasingly the cowboy became a hired hand who spent more time mending fences than roping steers. 'Nesters', dry-farmers, in ever-growing numbers nibbled at the edges of the plains. Sheep, better suited to harsh climates than cattle, also began to encroach on the grasslands. An era had died – but a legend had been born.

Black cowboy *An ex-slave named Nat Love was among some 5000 Negro cowboys who rode the cattle trails. He was famed as a gunslinger and Indian fighter.*

'Come and get it!' *Working at his chuck wagon, a cook makes a pie for the men on a 'long drive'. Trail food was washed down with black coffee so strong, it was said, that a pistol would float in it. For their skills, cooks were paid more than the cowboys.*

OVERLANDERS ON THE LONG TRAIL WEST

A distance of 2000 miles (3200 km) separates the Missouri River from the Pacific coast of the United States, and before the first transcontinental railway was completed in 1869 the way was hard. Fur traders, explorers and Indians had long used the overland trails from the settled parts of the United States, but these had been rough men who carried little more than the clothes on their backs, their guns, and trading goods. Not until the early 1840s did the first parties of settlers

Leaving the old homestead *Families who had sold their farms and homes to pay the cost of moving west were often broken-hearted when it was time to go. Departures were tearful as the travellers embraced relatives whom they might never see again.*

cross overland by wagon, with their worldly goods and the basic elements of a settled agricultural society.

Most of the overlanders were farm people from the Midwest, fired by the quest for cheap land, for adventure, for a second chance, and – at the end of the decade – an opportunity to get rich quick by digging for gold in California.

From a trickle the movement soon became a flood. In 1843 about 1000 Americans reached Oregon by the overland route. Between 1849 and 1860 another 53,000 travelled by wagon to Oregon, while 200,000 took

the turn-off to California. In all, during the pre-Civil War period, more than 250,000 Americans travelled the overland route to the Pacific coast.

The trails to Oregon and California both started at one of three Missouri River ferry crossings: Independence, St Joseph, or Council Bluffs. Small wagons held the family's food, clothing, farm tools, weapons, children's toys, dolls and books, household gear, valued furniture, prized possessions such as china, linen and silverware, and any members of the party unable or unwilling to walk.

At night the wagons served as shelters for the heads of households and their wives, while the children and others slept in tents. The wagons were pulled along the trails by sure-footed oxen, guided by a man or an older boy walking alongside them, or else by horses and mule teams, which were driven from the wagon.

A case of cannibalism

As the trip took from four to five months, it had to begin in the early spring if the overlanders were to avoid snow in the mountains. The convoys were often highly organised, with an elected trail captain and bylaws to govern the members. Even so, in 1846 one group of emigrants to California, the Donner party, fell behind schedule and became trapped by early blizzards high in the Sierra Nevada. By the time rescue came, about 40 of the party had died; of the 47 who survived, some did so by eating human flesh.

The first portion of the route, shared by all, crossed the high plains across north-eastern Kansas and then along the south fork of the shallow Platte River. Here the way, clearly marked by deep wagon ruts, was level and well watered. After covering 500 miles (805 km) in 40 days from the Missouri, the wagons forded the south fork of the Platte and angled north-east to

Fancy quilt *Women used their long days in the wagon to turn odd scraps of material into colourful, hard-wearing quilts for warmth on mountain nights.*

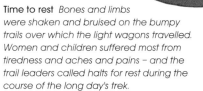

Time to rest *Bones and limbs were shaken and bruised on the bumpy trails over which the light wagons travelled. Women and children suffered most from tiredness and aches and pains – and the trail leaders called halts for rest during the course of the long day's trek.*

Mobile home *Home for an entire family for months on end, the lightweight farm wagon known as a 'prairie schooner' had a waterproofed canvas roof supported on a frame of bent hickory-tree branches. On its sides were fastened articles for the overlanders' future use on their farms.*

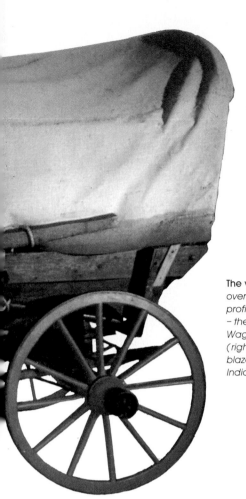

Travelling clock *Many overlanders took family heirlooms – such as this ornate clock with brass works – with them on the trail. Despite their weight, even items such as pianos were found space in the wagons.*

The way ahead *The overlanders inspired a profitable new business – the publication of Wagon Road Guides (right), following trails blazed by buffaloes, Indians and traders.*

Gateway to the West *Pioneers in their thousands stream over South Pass, cutting through the Rocky Mountains on the Oregon Trail. Here wagon drivers faced a continual 'traffic jam' – though in less congested areas they usually travelled three or even four abreast, rather than in single file, to try to avoid the choking dust billowing up from wagons in front of them.*

the whites' arrogance, their spreading of disease and their slaughter of the buffalo, these attacks multiplied in number and ferocity. Even so, there were few of those scenes so beloved of Western writers in which desperate white men in circled wagons fend off shouting, feathered warriors on ponies – often suffering grisly deaths in the process. Indeed, of 10,000 or so overlanders who died on the trail, probably no more than 300-400 were victims of the Indians. By the late 1850s the trails had been improved and support and rescue services, both private and public, were provided. By the end of the overland trail era, the number of merchants busily providing food, shelter, ferry services, repair facilities and a variety of supplies had become so many that the old trails took on something of the character of modern highways, with well-stocked service stations and refreshments at regular intervals.

Looking back with pride

The wardrobe of the typical overland family was limited but extremely practical. Men took with them three or four shirts of cotton, linen or wool, cotton socks, several pantaloons of linsey-woolsey (a mixture of linen and wool), and an overcoat made of coarse, thick cotton or fustian, a similar hard-wearing fabric.

A woman needed two or three dresses, usually of dark gingham or wool, two or three petticoats of linen, several aprons, a kerchief, a warm shawl, and perhaps an outer coat. Men wore broad-brimmed straw or felt hats; women fastened on their heads sunbonnets made of calico stretched over wire. In addition, palm-leaf hats and green-shaded goggles were used against the sun.

Few overlanders ever forgot their rugged time on the trail. Years later those who had survived remembered with pride the sights, the dangers, the shared adventures. In both California and Oregon during the 1870s the overlanders formed pioneer societies to commemorate the experience and to preserve memories about the epic event of their lives.

Fort Laramie, a major fur-trading post. Here the overlanders usually got their first glimpse of proud and warlike Plains Indians such as the Sioux. Many had heard stories of Indian savagery and thievery and felt uneasy. In fact, many more overlanders died of disease – cholera on the Plains and tick-borne fevers in the mountains – than from attacks by Indians.

Some of the overlanders, however, did run into attackers, especially on the western part of the route. In the later years, when Indians came to resent

A FRONTIER WIFE'S DAY ON THE TRAIL

It is 4am and still dark, as the frontier wife wakes in her family wagon and goes quietly outside. There she stokes the fire, pours out water, and puts out plates and cutlery. She then prepares a breakfast of coffee, fried bacon, hot beans and baked bread. Her husband rises an hour later and, after eating, yokes the oxen to the family wagon. By 7am the train is on its way. As the man and his two older boys walk beside their team, the wife rides in the wagon, looking after her two younger children, mending a torn shirt for her husband, or making a quilt for their bed.

At noon the train halts and the oxen are unhitched, watered, and set to graze. Now the wife prepares a lunch of cold leftovers.

Gathering fuel *A frontier wife collects 'chips', dried buffalo droppings, on a treeless plain and wheels them back to use as fuel.*

An hour later the journey resumes and continues until dusk, by which time the train has covered 15 miles (24km) since dawn. The party then makes camp on a wooded slope. After hauling water from a nearby stream and gathering branches and other fuel for a fire, the wife gets ready to cook a substantial supper, occasionally consisting of meat stew, over an open fire. The food ready, the members of the family sit on the ground and eat hungrily off tin plates, ending the meal with hot cakes and coffee.

It is soon time to turn in, heads of household sleeping in the wagons and children and others bedding down in tents. Tomorrow is washday, when the wife will rinse, boil and beat the accumulated dirt of two weeks' wear from the family's clothes.

THE WAY THEY GO TO CALIFORNIA.

Off to California *As the Gold Rush reached its height, cartoons poked fun at the fortune-seekers, showing them using every means available – and some that were not, such as futuristic flying machines – to make their way to California.*

Panning for gold *A prospector fills his shallow pan with gravel from a riverbed and carefully washes it out with water. Any heavy, gold-bearing flakes that may be there will sink to the bottom of the pan.*

FORTY-NINERS IN A RUSH FOR GOLD

On a cold, clear morning in January 1848, James Marshall, a construction foreman working for mill-owner John Sutter, saw something glittering on the bed of the water channel by Sutter's new sawmill on the south fork of the American River in central California.

Dipping his hand in the chilly water, Marshall lifted out a yellow pebble about half the size of a pea. He quickly gathered several more fragments and examined them closely. He had long suspected that there was gold in the Sierra foothills. But were the pebbles real gold or iron pyrites, 'fool's gold'? He put his yellow pebble on a hard surface and hit it with a rock. It was malleable; it must be gold. Pyrites were brittle and would have shattered.

Putting the flakes and pieces on the dented crown of his old white felt hat he rushed off to show them to his work-mates. 'Boys,' he shouted, 'by God, I believe I have found a gold mine!'

The men hurried down to the channel and gathered other flakes and pieces. They repeated this for the next two days, and when they had accumulated two or three ounces of the findings Marshall rushed off to tell his employer. Sutter borrowed a set of scales from a nearby apothecary, and behind closed doors the two men tested the yellow fragments in every way they could. There could be no doubt: it *was* gold. Even so, Sutter was

a worried man. Would his workers stay? Or would they drop their tools and go off prospecting? Sutter made Marshall and his men promise to remain on the job for another six weeks. He also implored them to keep the discovery secret.

Despite this, by mid-April a head-long exodus from Sutter's ranch was underway – and in a few months the news of the gold find had crossed continents and oceans and spread around the world. By the end of 1848 there were 6000 men working at the diggings along the major rivers and streams running from the Sierras to the Pacific. The next year saw the arrival of the 'forty-niners', as the

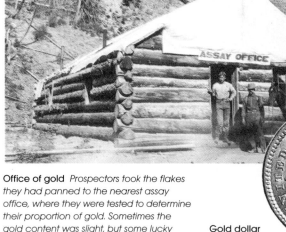

Office of gold *Prospectors took the flakes they had panned to the nearest assay office, where they were tested to determine their proportion of gold. Sometimes the gold content was slight, but some lucky miners became fabulously rich. In one day, a team of four miners, working from dawn to dusk on the Feather River, gathered $50,000-worth of high-quality gold.*

Gold dollar *Many miners spurned the gold dollars minted in 1849. Instead, they used their own gold nuggets as ready money.*

A DAY IN THE LIFE OF A MINER

At daybreak the 'forty-niner' rolls out of his blankets and pulls on soggy jeans, flannel shirt and heavy boots. He breakfasts quickly on coffee and pancakes, then hurries off to the gold streams. He spends the morning doggedly panning for gold – the lure of which had made him give up his job in the stockyards of Chicago and join in the stampede to California. By noon he still has not struck lucky, and he takes a break for dinner. The afternoon passes slowly as he continues the back-breaking labour of scooping up earth and flushing it for the signs of the precious metal. But by sundown his luck has not improved. He returns to camp for a filling supper of beans, potatoes, bread and dried apples. Tomorrow, he tells himself as he turns in, will be the day that he finally strikes it rich.

first prospectors were dubbed. By the end of 1849 almost 90,000 of them had reached California by land or sea.

The classic phase of the California gold rush lasted little more than two years. By late 1850 the most accessible gold was already skimmed off, and further exploitation required capital and high-grade skill. The diggings were also congested. In October 1850 some 57,000 miners toiled along the gold-bearing streams that flowed down the western slopes of the Sierras.

After that, however, the numbers quickly dwindled. Many miners left to sample life in the booming California cities of Stockton, San Francisco and Sacramento. Others went back home to the east. But for a brief but hectic period the gold miners created a vivid and memorable way of life.

The miners were a very mixed social and cultural lot. Virtually all of them were males, of whom about one-third came from abroad. Among the non-Americans the largest group was the British, with smaller contingents of Frenchmen, Mexicans, Hawaiians, Australians and Chileans. The miners came from every class of Euro-American society. One party of 60 would-be prospectors from Michigan – fancifully known as the Wolverine Rangers – included farmers, doctors, carpenters, blacksmiths, mechanics, lawyers, merchants, school teachers, artists and public officials.

Those who crossed by land – about half the total – were toughened by the journey; those who came by sea had grown soft and puffy after weeks aboard crammed ships, and suffered accordingly. The miners lived in camps with colourful names such as Red Dog, Rich Bar and Hang-dog, consisting of clusters of canvas tents, lean-tos of branches, shacks made of logs or of rough boards. Fortunately for them the California winters were mild. They were also rainy, however, and the men were often drenched to the skin and covered with mud.

Determined to make their fortunes quickly and then return home, the miners subordinated everything to finding and collecting 'pay dirt'. The day's labour was interrupted by dinner at noon. Supper at sundown consisted of beans, potatoes, dried beef or salt pork, hardtack bread, and dried apples. The absence of dairy products, fresh fruit and vegetables in the miners' diet, along with poor sanitation, led to scurvy, dysentery and other diseases. Even so, some of the miners resented the time spent in preparing food and gladly paid local cooks, often Chinese, to supply meals.

Fleeting friends and hard drinkers

Though claims were usually worked by groups of several men, ties within the larger community were generally weak. As one forty-niner wrote: 'Here all know and feel that our acquaintance is of short duration.' A mining camp friend or partner was 'something like a stage-coach or steamboat acquaintance'.

Hard drinking was a common affliction. 'The President of the Miners' Association,' one prospector reported, 'was helped up the fork [of the river] the other day so drunk that he went down every five yards in spite of all that a man hardly half as drunk as himself could do.'

At first the crime rate at the diggings was low. Men left their possessions unguarded while they worked their claim. But this state of affairs did not last much beyond the middle of 1849.

After that, as competition for limited gains grew stiffer, petty theft, as well as more serious crimes, proliferated. So the miners formed their own informal law-enforcement bands.

'You can scarcely form any conception of what a dirty business this gold digging is and of the mode of life which a miner is compelled to lead. We live more like brutes than humans.'

CALIFORNIA MINER, 1850

When news reached the men of some dishonest act they gathered to listen to the facts and to mete out punishment to the offender. At times the whole group acted as a collective jury. On other occasions they chose judge and jury from among their number. Punishment ranged from banishment from the diggings through whipping to hanging. The sentences were imposed quickly; there were no jails for the convicted. The miners then had a round of drinks and returned to work.

Most California gold-seekers did not become rich. The earliest groups of miners were the luckiest. Some made as much as $500 a day – this at a time when the typical skilled worker in the eastern states earned about $2 a day. The prospectors who arrived towards the end of 1849 seldom did as well as their predecessors. But even those who materially had little to show for months of danger and hard work took pride in their participation in one of their country's great epics.

Team work *Working in a group, one miner shovelled earth into a long, topless box on rockers. A second miner poured water into the box while a third miner rocked it to and fro, so that any gold flakes would be trapped on ridges at the bottom.*

'May I have the pleasure...?' *Wearing a skirt and lady's jacket, a husky, bearded miner takes the female role at a Saturday night dance in a mining camp. Women were in short supply in the camps: indeed, they formed only 7.5 per cent of the population of California in 1850.*

FROM WELLS, FARGO TO THE IRON HORSE

'I felt like a mess of eggs being scrambled – I was bounced and tossed all over.' So said a traveller describing a trip on a frontier stagecoach. For more than half a century the coach was the chief form of overland transport in the American West, and even after the railroad linked the east and west coasts, coaches still served a vital function in the remote frontier areas.

Wells, Fargo and Company is the name forever associated with stagecoaches. The firm was founded in 1852 to provide banking and mail services for men in the Californian gold camps, and over the coming years the stage routes followed the paths of the miners wherever they settled: over plains, mountains and deserts strewn with rocks, buckthorn and other shrubs.

By the 1870s, Wells, Fargo monopolised the express business throughout the West. The company's classic vehicle was the flat-topped Concord coach, made at Concord, New Hampshire, with an open driver's seat at the front. As well as mail and baggage, coaches

carried a mixed bunch of people. The prim schoolmarm or Bible-carrying preacher might face being confined for many days in the company of rough-hewn prospectors, saloon fancy girls or tobacco-spitting cowhands.

'Passengers becoming crazy with whiskey, mixed with want of sleep, are often obliged to be strapped to their seats,' wrote one traveller. 'Their meals, dispatched during their ten-minute halts, are simply abominable.'

Shotgun-riders and hold-up men

The roads were bone-shakingly bad, the heat was often sweltering and at night lamps could not be used for fear of Indians, who often attacked stagecoaches crossing their territory. Among the most celebrated of the coach routes was the Deadwood Stage which ran from Cheyenne, Wyoming, to Deadwood, South Dakota, through Sioux territory. Here, as elsewhere, a hawk-eyed assistant 'rode shotgun' beside the driver, or 'ribbon-handler'.

Stagecoaches were a regular target for hold-up men, who included the notorious Charles E. Bolton, known as 'Black Bart'. He began his criminal career in 1877, and always wore a flour

RIDERS OF THE PONY EXPRESS

In the early 1860s the call went out for 'young, skinny, wiry fellows, not over eighteen' to become cross-country riders for the newly established Pony Express. As well as being expert horsemen, the youngsters must be prepared to 'risk death daily'. In view of the danger from outlaws and hostile Indians, said the company, orphans were preferred. Among those prepared to risk death by answering the call was the young William F. Cody, who later became famous as 'Buffalo Bill', frontiersman and Wild West showman.

Long-distance coach *Anything from eight to 14 passengers crammed into the Wells, Fargo Concord coaches, with their luggage piled on the roof. The coaches were drawn by teams of four to six horses, which covered an average of 5 miles (8 km) an hour.*

sack with eyeholes over his head. It was Bart's custom to leave a signed scrap of doggerel behind him, a typical example being:

'I've labored long and hard for bread,
For honor and for riches,
But on my corns too long you've tred,
You fine-haired sons of bitches...'

The Wells, Fargo story was matched for drama and excitement by that of the Pony Express, a horseback relay mail service that ran for almost 2000 miles (3200 km) between St Joseph in Missouri, and Sacramento, California. Though it operated for less than 20 months in 1860-1, it was to become an undying legend of the Old West.

Relays of up to 200 Pony Express riders galloped hell-for-leather between relay stations which were set up some 5 to 20 miles (8 to 32 km) apart, taking just two minutes to change riders or horses before setting off again. The whole romantic enterprise was made obsolete by the coming of the coast-to-coast telegraph, which bankrupted the Pony Express's backers but made the fortunes of the rising new experts in communications. Samuel Morse is

At the depot *The scream of the whistle brought passengers and onlookers hurrying to the platform in settlements along every railway line. The depot was a focus of interest for local people, a magic place of arrivals and departures, a point of contact between different worlds.*

credited with the invention of electric telegraphic communications, for which he used the ingenious 'Morse Code' of dots and dashes to represent letters of the alphabet. By 1861 a nationwide network was in operation and the 'talking wires', as they were dubbed by the Indians, were carrying messages across the country at speeds that no rider could possibly hope to match. As well as this, river-boatmen and gangs of canal-builders helped to unite the fast-growing nation. Between 1830 and 1850 some 7000 miles (11,200 km) of canal were built. The waterways were plied by long, flat cargo barges and packet boats which provided passenger travel in greater comfort than the stagecoaches offered. Thousands of immigrant families travelled inland along the canals, while vast tonnages of grain and other farm produce came along the waterways to the east coast.

The engineer Robert Fulton's steamboat *Clermont* established the first regular passenger service in 1807, and

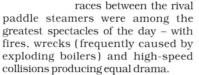

Morse telegraph key

splendid vessels, built like floating palaces, later churned up and down the Mississippi – which, with more than 40 tributaries, became one of the nation's great highways.

A new and special type of steamer was developed for sailing along the Mississippi, where sandbars were a recurrent problem; it was a double-decked and flat-bottomed vessel with large side paddles. As richly filigreed with ornament as a wedding cake, the Mississippi steamboat was decorated in the height of luxury with thick carpets, gilded mirrors and carved panelling. Although the ladies kept mainly to their own quarters, all the cabin passengers sat together for meals, when rich ten-course dinners were routine fare. All-out races between the rival paddle steamers were among the greatest spectacles of the day – with fires, wrecks (frequently caused by exploding boilers) and high-speed collisions producing equal drama.

It was the iron horse that eventually supplanted the steamboat. Railway building was well under way by 1860, when some 30,000 miles (48,000 km) had already been laid and a distinctively American type of locomotive had evolved. This was heavier and slower than its European counterpart, but it pulled longer trains. The chimneys

Riverboat casinos *The well-appointed riverboats were noted for their whiskey-drinking passengers, often playing poker games for high stakes far into the night. These attracted professional gamblers and cardsharpers, and provided material for the humorous writer Mark Twain, a former steamboat pilot on the Mississippi.*

were shaped like inverted funnels, and equipped with 'spark-arresters' designed to prevent sparks from the wood-burning engines from starting grass fires in prairie regions. In addition, 'cow-catchers' at the front of the locomotives coped with cattle or bison that strayed onto the railway line.

After the Civil War, an era of hectic railway expansion began, boosted by the completion of the first transcontinental link on May 10, 1869. On that day, lines built by the Central Pacific and Union Pacific companies met at Promontory, Utah, and the tracks were joined by a golden spike. The link-up cut coast-to-coast travelling time to days instead of weeks, and inventions such as the Westinghouse air-brake – which worked all a train's brakes at once – improved safety. Comfort was enhanced too, from 1864, when George Pullman built a new kind

of car with plush, sliding seats, more efficient heating and foldaway berths. Pullman's luxurious sleeper cars also had washrooms for passengers, and dining cars were later added.

Along the railroads, as they pushed out across the country, settlements sprang up. Some of these vanished as quickly as they had appeared, but some lasted and became permanent communities. In these, the railway depot retained an aura of excitement. Here newcomers from the east stepped straight into the raw realities of life on the frontier, and the poor farm boy might set out to meet some fantastic destiny waiting far along the line.

A SHRIEKING CART FOR THE METIS FARMER

The trail lay under a sky so wide it looked like a great, blue bowl inverted over the prairie. A banshee shriek tore through the air: but the wiry, dark-complexioned man on horseback did not even look around. He knew the sound well. It was just a Red River cart, one of the horse-drawn wagons that were the freighters of the Canadian West. The shriek came from axles that were never greased, because grease would hold the prairie dust and grind away at the hubs.

Like the wide sky and the cart, the rider was very much a part of the Canadian West. More than 70 years earlier, in 1812, poverty had forced his father out of his home in the Scottish Highlands. With the aid of a charitable laird, he and others had crossed the Atlantic, gone south from the St Lawrence region and then farther south still across the plains to settle at a point on the Red River that would become the city of Winnipeg.

Like the Scots and French fur traders of the region, the rider's father had taken an Indian wife. The children of those unions became a new people of the plains, the Métis, whose name meant 'charred wood' – a reference to their dark skins.

In his youth, the boy had, like most Métis, lived by mixed farming. He also hunted the buffalo, joining other Métis for daredevil horseback charges into wildly stampeding herds of 100,000 animals and more. Each hunter would gallop up to a plunging buffalo, level his carbine across the saddle at the animal's shoulder and fire. Then, still at full gallop, he would pour fresh powder down the barrel, spit a musket ball from the dozen or so in his mouth, ram home the charge, and fire into the next buffalo.

The last of the big herds

Buffalo hides made warm coats for winters dropping to 50 degrees below zero. They also made tents and blankets. Cut into strips, they made tough machine belts for eastern factories. Dried buffalo meat, pounded with berries and fat, then stored in a sack made from the buffalo's stomach, became pemmican, a meat that could be kept for months without refrigeration. Buffalo hair was woven into ropes, and sinew made thread.

In early times, the buffalo were so numerous that a single herd might take days to pass. By 1884, however, they had been all but annihilated by hunters. Even the tough prairie grass – called buffalo grass – that grew under the snow was quickly being torn up by

Off to the hunt *Twice a year the Métis joined forces, under the command of a 'war chief' to guard them against Indians, to seek the dwindling buffalo herds. In two hours, 400 hunters might kill 1500 animals, returning with carts piled high with meat and skins.*

LIFE IN A HUNTER'S LOG CABIN

It is late spring, and a Métis sits mending his net outside his log cabin home. A birch-bark canoe is drawn up on the lake shore; lakes and rivers provided the easiest routes through thick forest. The cabin is built in French-Canadian style, with horizontal squared logs fitted into grooved upright supports and a shingle roof with a stone chimney. Snowshoes, ready for the winter, hang on the cabin's side wall, near the hunter's axe, rainwater barrels, fencing posts, firewood and chopping block. Inside, his wife sews by the foot of their bed, on which are an Indian-style blanket and a buffalo skin. A meal cooks in an iron pot over the blazing log fire. Above the fireplace hang a musket and powder horn, and to the side are a hide coat and hat.

- Fall and Winter Catalogue -

T. EATON & CO.
- IMPORTERS -

Nos. 190, 192, 194, 196 ... STREET, TORONTO, ONT.

Mail order *One feature of European life carried west by the Canadian Pacific Railway was the mail-order catalogue. From what the Indians called the 'Wishing Book' they ordered household goods on a sale-or-return basis – and at the same time learned the white people's names for them.*

Dual purpose *The Red River cart was simply a two-wheeled, wooden platform drawn by horses or oxen. It could be quickly dismantled for use as a raft when transporting loads across rivers or lakes.*

Man of the Mounties *The men of the early North West Mounted Police wore informal slouch hats and fringed, leather jackets on their long and arduous patrols in the West.*

the ploughs of farmers from eastern Canada. What brought the farmers west was the Canadian Pacific Railway – tracks of steel, still glistening with newness, that stretched for more than 3000 miles (4800 km) from the Atlantic to the Pacific. Completed in 1885 – largely by using cheap Chinese labour – the railway for ever ended the isolation of the plains, opening them up to more than a million settlers within two decades.

The railway took away the wheat that grew so richly in the prairie soil. In return it brought new machines such as the steam-powered thresher. In a land where farms were big and labour

scarce, the Métis farmer needed machinery: but he knew it would put him into debt to the bank for many years to come. The railway was also bringing more settlers. Métis and Indians were still a majority on the plains: but it was obvious that this would not last. Already, Indians were being confined to reservations, to clear the land for European settlers. Weakened by diseases brought by the Europeans, demoralised by whiskey and starving now that their staple food of buffalo was gone, they were in no condition to resist.

Huts made from slabs of sod cut from the prairie soil were the first homes of settlers. Sod was a fine protection against summer heat and winter cold, but the huts were cramped and, under melting snows, dreadfully damp. As soon as possible, settlers replaced them with wooden houses of cut lumber from the mills of eastern Canada. The city of Winnipeg, already home to more than 5000 people and growing fast, actually had some houses made of stone and brick.

Keeping the law on horseback

The Métis farmer might see, beyond the sod huts, the conical shapes of the Cree tepees. Made of canvas, now that buffalo hides were no longer available, the high tents were airy, with ventilation flaps at the top that could be moved to suit any shift of wind. The open fire in the centre of each tepee was fed by outside air through a small tunnel, another aid to keeping air inside the tent fresh.

Between the huts and the tepees a group of horsemen rode by, each with a carbine slung from his saddle, a revolver on his hip and a sword at his side. They were part of a small force, some 300 in all, that policed hundreds of thousands of square miles in weather that ranged from fierce heat and choking dust in summer to raging

Whiskey trade *White traders peddled fake whiskey to the Indians. A buffalo skin bought one drink of 'whiskey', and a horse was the price of a gallon. The liquor consisted mainly of alcohol, tobacco juice and water, and was spiced with ginger.*

blizzards in winter. These were the men of the North West Mounted Police, as it was then called. The Mounties, a combined military and police force, were stationed in posts scattered throughout the West. Many young Englishmen as well as Canadians had joined the force, looking for a life of excitement and adventure. They found it by doing battle with armed traders preying on the weaknesses of the Indians, by keeping order in towns and Indian reservations, or by riding long patrols between isolated farms and remote settlements.

By early evening, the Métis would return to his farm. His grandchildren and some friends might be playing a game with a bat and ball. The English settlers called it rounders, but everyone else called it baseball. A carriage with its horse hitched to the verandah might announce the arrival of a visitor – perhaps the Presbyterian minister.

Seeing the cleric's black-clad figure, the Métis would nervously touch the small bag that hung from his shoulder under his coat. Most of the Métis were Christians, but they hung onto some of the religion of their Indian heritage. Many of them carried a medicine bag – a leather pouch containing a piece of animal bone, the ear of a fox and a feather – given to them by their Indian mothers to protect them from harm.

A date for the wedding

The minister, however, might have come to talk not about Indian beliefs but about marriage. Most plainsmen never bothered with the formality of a wedding ceremony. But now life in the West was changing. Remembering the freer days of the Old West, the Métis had no love for the severe ways of eastern churches; but many were reluctantly agreeing that it was time to conform. As he helped the minister into his carriage, the farmer promised to set a date for the wedding and to ask him to officiate over it.

At last he walked into the house and threw his fringed jacket across a chair. Fringes were another inheritance from his Indian ancestors. More than a decoration, fringes drew off rainwater that would otherwise seep through the seams of a coat, wetting its wearer. Looking out of the door, he could see that night had come. The astonishingly wide sky of the prairies stretched in every direction. There were millions of stars spread out – almost as many stars, it seemed, as there had once been buffaloes on the plains.

IMMIGRANTS IN THE MELTING POT

Bearded men bent under the weight of giant sea chests filled with household goods. Women wearing headscarves clutched babies and fretful children. Skinny adolescents with ill-fitting, homemade garments scrambled down the gangways. From Ireland, Scandinavia, Germany, Hungary, Italy and Poland, immigrants in their thousands poured off the boats onto the harboursides of New York, Philadelphia and Boston. Shipowners grew fat on the passage money paid out by their human cargo, crammed tightly in every corner. Through the late 19th and into the early 20th century, some 13 million Old World immigrants, most of whom did not speak any English, flowed into the vast melting pot that was North America. In these bustling eastern cities, the newcomers clustered in brick tenements, rising high over narrow streets. Irish men found work driving wagons drawn by teams of sturdy horses, or hammering and sawing to raise buildings to house the swelling population of America.

Working parties lived for months in camps thrown up near swamps, as they dug the canals that linked America's rivers to the seaports. Mule teams hauled the barges along the canals they built. Singing songs from the homeland and making up new ones, they eased the heavy work of building the new industrial world: 'I've a mule and her name is Sal. Fifteen miles on the Erie Canal. She's a good ole' worker and a good ole' pal.'

Irish women emigrated, too, pushed out by the potato famine and changes in land ownership. Many of them found employment as cooks, nurses and housekeepers. Both men and women toiled in the textile and shoe industries sprinkled throughout the cities and towns of the north-east. The 12 hour or 14 hour working day began before dawn. Posted on the wall of the factory, the immigrants could read rules and

'Welcome ashore!' *Tired and bewildered after the rigours of the Atlantic crossing, immigrants clutch their few belongings and taste their first New World authority – policemen ordering them to line up for inspection.*

warnings such as, 'Washing must be done outside of working hours', or 'Notice! Time is money'. At noon a blast of the factory whistle brought smaller children running to the factory gates carrying dinner pails for their fathers, brothers and sisters.

Often financial panics shut down industries for months, and whole towns grew lean and hungry waiting for the giant machines to clatter again. Employers constantly tried to squeeze more work out of their employees, and as industry grew the workers formed unions, both in the factory towns and in the growing cities. Because pogroms and official discrimination made life unbearable for Jews across Poland, the Austro-Hungarian Empire and Russia, they too set out for the New

World. In lower Manhattan the streets rang with the cries of pushcart pedlars hawking pots and pans, fruit, clothing and shoelaces. The ghetto's street children scavenged in rubbish dumps for broken goods and rags. They combed the railway tracks for coal and the streets for bits of wood to use as fuel. They hawked newspapers at streetcar stops, so earning as much as a quarter of a family's income. But they kept some tips for themselves, to spend on bars of chocolate and, by the turn of the century, on flickering picture-shows at the crowded nickelodeons – cinemas which charged no more than five cents, a nickel, for admission.

With beds, sofas and chairs rented to boarders, tenement apartments had little room for high-spirited children to play. Hot nights made sleep in the overcrowded tenements impossible, and whole families took cushions and

slept out on the rooftops. At mealtimes the network of family, relatives and boarders took turns eating at the kitchen table. At other times the table became a little home factory, covered with paper roses or cuffs, buttonholes and sleeves assembled by the women of the house, ready for delivery next day to subcontractors. Although this 'homework' earned women only a few dollars a week at piecework rates, even then dishonest jobbers often cheated them of their pay, claiming that the work had been badly done.

In the coalfields and mill towns of Pennsylvania, Slavs also took in as many boarders as their cramped frame houses could fit. Giant pots of borscht – a hearty Russian soup of beetroot or cabbage, often served with sour

Saluting the flag *Under the approving gaze of their teachers, immigrant children stand to attention and salute the Stars and Stripes at a New York industrial school – so taking their place as patriotic Americans.*

City of high hopes *Bristling with power, wealth and energy – as well as with some of America's first skyscrapers – New York in the 1880s seemed like a dream come true to the new arrivals. But they soon found that life for the lowly was hard, and that their presence was not always welcome. For many, the dream ended in disillusionment.*

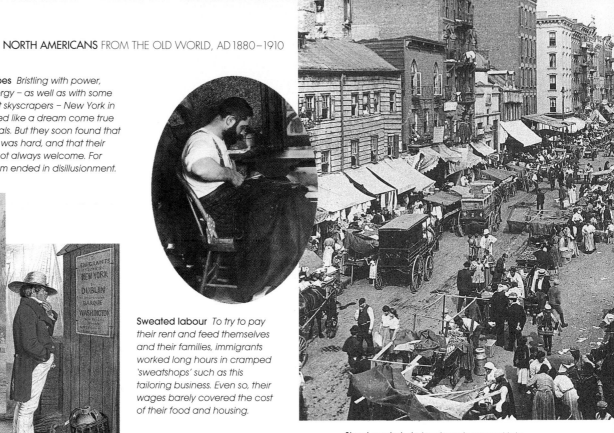

Sweated labour *To try to pay their rent and feed themselves and their families, immigrants worked long hours in cramped 'sweatshops' such as this tailoring business. Even so, their wages barely covered the cost of their food and housing.*

cream – bubbled on the stoves to be ladled out at all hours of the day and night to miners and ironworkers returning home tired and hungry. The immigrants lived modestly, sending as much money as possible back home. To help in times of need, they put their small coins into mutual aid societies which cared for the sick, fed widows and orphans, and paid for burials. Other immigrants spent their first savings on tickets to bring their wives, brothers, sisters and parents to the New World.

Savings could also enable a factory worker to open one day his own small neighbourhood business, such as a tobacconist's, pawnbroker's or green-grocery store. The habit of cooperation helped the immigrants to band against

Rags to riches *Lured by the vision of work, money and good living, many immigrants set out from Ireland in tatters. Their dream was to make their pile, then return in style to the 'old country' to buy land or a home.*

Coast to coast *Immigrant families travelled across America on wooden-seated trains to start new lives on the West coast. Little conversation relieved the tedious journeys, as passengers came from different countries and spoke different languages.*

the brutal conditions of early industrial life. News of factory closings or wage cuts spread like wildfire through the immigrant districts, bringing crowds out to public squares to call for strikes and mass protests. Newspapers for unions of the cigar-makers, the textile workers or the miners appeared in Italian, German, Polish and Yiddish.

On the plains and prairies, where Scandinavians grew wheat and raised pigs, immigrant farmers came up against the power of the great grain merchants as well as the railways that shipped their crops. Located next to the rail lines were the skyscrapers of the plains: the huge grain elevators. At first the poor peasants of Sweden and Norway dreamed of simply raising food for themselves on family farms. But the richness of the plains – and the generous size of the plots granted to encourage the immigrants – led them to plant acres of grain to sell. In

Street market *As immigrants poured into New York they formed their own close-knit communities, with their customs brought from Europe. Many Jews settled in and around Hester Street on the Lower East Side, turning it into a clamorous marketplace.*

good years, they packed their cellars with canned beets and carrots, and wheels of cheese. In bad years grass-hoppers descended on the fields and the families had to rely on store credit until the next year's crops came. Many of the western farmers formed grain, dairy and food cooperatives to market their harvest together, to fight for fair rates on the railways and to help each other through hard times.

Outside New York, one of the largest concentrations of immigrants settled in Chicago. In the 1890s the city was said to have more Germans than any German city but Hamburg and Berlin, more Swedes than any Swedish city but Stockholm and Göteborg, and more Norwegians than any Norwegian city but Christiana and Bergen.

In town and country many native Americans mocked the immigrants' accents and customs and cheated the newcomers – who were bewildered by the sheer pace and hurly-burly of daily life in the growing nation. But with hard work and perseverance, the immigrants often managed to gain a foothold in their new home.

Ticket to ride *The railways offered cut-price tickets to immigrants bound for California.*

COMFORT AND SQUALOR IN THE BIG CITY

As the newly independent United States entered the 19th century, its entire population numbered around 3½ million people. By the end of the same century, the same number of people lived in the single city of New York. This was the gateway to the continent, its glory made possible by the wonders of technology – by steam power, the 'genie' of the 19th century, and by electricity, which would rule the 20th century.

One sign of the city's success, by around 1900, was the thrusting upwards of apartment blocks five or six storeys high, as land prices forced buildings to rise rather than to spread. A successful professional worker or businessman expected his apartment building to have such conveniences as electric lights, and gas for cooking. He would have hot air or steam heat from a coal-fired basement furnace, and hot and cold running water.

In poorer districts, by contrast, as many as 40 large families of low-paid manual workers lived packed into one five-storey building, sharing a single privy set in a central courtyard. The businessman in the wealthier part of the city rose early and dressed himself in long-sleeved, long-legged underwear, a cotton shirt with detachable Celluloid collar and cuffs, uncreased trousers made of wool, high-buttoned shoes of leather and fabric, a cravat, a waistcoat, and a sober jacket. In 1900 he might shave his chin, but leave a moustache and sideburns. His wife was swathed in a chemise, dark cotton stockings, knee-length drawers, a corset and a petticoat over which was a floor-length skirt and a 'shirtwaist', or dress with a bodice styled like a shirt.

Working men wore coarse cotton shirts and trousers or overalls, and caps instead of the 'derbies' or bowler hats favoured by their bosses. Except for the very rich, everyone wore clothes ready-made and mass-produced in factories, and widely advertised. Wives, however, often had a sewing machine for repairs, and sometimes made their own or their children's clothes from widely available paper patterns.

Every American with a job was likely to have a hearty breakfast of ham, eggs, or porridge, doughnuts, biscuits, beef, potatoes, buttered bread and jam, washed down with coffee. Butter and eggs from local dairies were kept fresh in an 'icebox' – an insulated wooden chest with a tin-lined top compartment, containing blocks of ice carried up on the strong shoulders of ice men. Dinner consisted of more meat and potatoes, with some fruits and vegetables brought from outlying market gardens. Processed foods such as cereals and custard, and canned meat, fruit and vegetables were also becoming common.

Although most food was still bought from the small, family owned grocery, butcher's shop, bakery or vegetable market, a few large chain groceries such as the Great Atlantic and Pacific Tea Company appeared on the scene. Each morning businessmen and factory hands took the new electric 'street cars' as far as 6 miles (10 km) to their work. However, there were still thousands of horses pulling delivery wagons, or hauling loads of coal which were shovelled through openings into basements. There were also elevated railways that rumbled noisily overhead at second-storey level; but the first subway, or underground electric railway, was not completed until 1904.

Another novelty was the department store, such as Wanamaker's in New York, Marshall Field's in Chicago and Filene's in Boston. In this four or five-storey palace of merchandising, only a few light, strong pillars were needed to support upper floors, leaving room for sweeping vistas of aisle and counter space. Huge plate-glass windows let daylight stream in. On the ground floor, show windows held striking fashion displays or holiday tableaux. Inside, armies of managers kept careful track of inventories and accounts; change was paid from a central location linked to the sales counter by pneumatic tube; electric elevators took customers from floor to floor. In the poorer

'Which floor Madame?' *With the invention of the elevator by Elisha Graves Otis in 1857, tall blocks sprouted where previously people's unwillingness to climb stairs had kept buildings low. This early 'water lift', operated by hydraulic ram, was soon followed by the electrically driven elevator.*

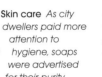

Skin care *As city dwellers paid more attention to hygiene, soaps were advertised for their purity.*

Working women *In the 1870s the Sholes typewriter helped to revolutionise women's role in society. Increasingly they obtained work in offices, shops, department stores and schools.*

Aladdin's cave *Well-to-do women flocked to the department stores, whose shelves and counters were stacked with everything for the family, all at fixed prices and sold with courtesy. Delivery boys were on hand to take heavy loads to the shoppers' homes.*

Child of the slums *A crop-headed infant stands forlornly under a water pump on the wall of a dark, unswept, tenement landing. One pump often supplied the water for every family in the building.*

THE TWO FACES OF NEW YORK

New York at the end of the 19th century showed two contrasting faces to the world. The 'downtown' financial and shopping districts were urban showplaces, with steel-framed skyscrapers in which office workers pounded typewriters and telephones rang constantly. The canyon-like streets were crowded and noisy, especially at junctions where carts and trams jammed up while their drivers impatiently clanged bells and shouted with frustration. At lunchtime, office clerks dashed into quick-service restaurants and bolted down sandwiches, pie and coffee before hurrying back to work. By contrast, the outlying factory districts and slums were dismal, garbage-choked places packed with unsavoury saloons, sweatshops and fire-trap buildings, and overrun by vermin, thieves and vicious street gangs. Prostitutes plied their trade, and vice and crime were rampant.

quarters, Woolworth's 'five-and-dime' stores sold cheap, good-value items. At home, a middle-class wife was helped by one or more maids who worked for 80 or 90 hours a week for little more than their board. Women who did not go out to work coped with household tasks themselves, often in addition to caring for several children in cramped living quarters.

On fine Sundays, many New York families sallied forth to Central Park and Prospect Park. There they strolled

Street scene
Crammed one on top of each other like modern cliff dwellers, slum families lived largely in the streets, their washing strung out overhead.

on tree-shaded pathways, looked at the monuments and statues, listened to bands performing popular marches and airs, and admired the scenery. In hot weather even more people flocked to beaches such as Coney Island to bathe in the sea, eat 'hot dogs', and take 'white-knuckle' rides on the roller coaster or Ferris wheel. Some, seeking fresh-air exercise, took advantage of another new engineering marvel – the safety bicycle, which was the fore-runner of the motor car. The bicycle craze of the 1890s led to an increased concern with personal health, good roads and lighter clothing.

Almost everyone could record these hard-earned moments of leisure with another revolutionary invention, the pocket Kodak camera. Made by the thousands and widely sold, it was light-weight, inexpensive and easy to use, and so allowed ordinary men and woman to become their own artists and archivists.

Household names *As marketing became big business, factory-made products carrying national brand names were a familiar part of American life.*

Web of wires *The rapid spread of the telephone and the telegraph created a complex web of electric wires above the New York streets. The wires collapsed during a snowstorm in 1888, after which they were laid underground.*

361

The way it is now

This book has told the story of the lives of ordinary men and women through 30,000 years of history. From the earliest human beings, living in caves and surviving on the animals they hunted and the plants they gathered, it has carried the human story up to the point when in late 19th-century North America people were beginning to live in skyscrapers and shop in department stores. At the same time, immigrants from many nations were joining the quest for the new prosperity which the Industrial Revolution, cradled in Britain, had made possible.

In America and in continental Europe, as well as in the British Empire, the death of Queen Victoria on January 22, 1901, seemed like the end of an era. Pointers to a new age were soon apparent. On October 16, 1901, the President of the United States entertained a black man to dinner in the White House for the first time. Two months later, the young Italian inventor Guglielmo Marconi transmitted the first wireless signal across the Atlantic, the forerunner of far-reaching developments in communications. The first motor cars had been luxury objects, but in 1908 Henry Ford produced his first Model T, 'a motor car for the great multitude'; by 1927, more than 15 million Model Ts had been built.

These huge strides in communication and transport which ushered in the new century brought peoples all over the world closer together, and lessened the differences between them. The term 'global village' was later coined to describe this breaking down of barriers between people of different cultures, and the mingling of their ways of life. It is for this reason that this book ends its account of everyday life at the turn of the century: henceforward, while distinctions in the ways of life of different peoples persisted, people everywhere began to share common aspirations. The 20th century was hailed at its very start as 'the century of the common man'– and the concept of this 'common man' was a global one.

As the years passed, the expectations of the common man were to rise. There were still social differences, particularly marked during the first years of the new century, but there were already signs that for large numbers of people over large areas of the world, yesterday's luxuries were becoming today's necessities. By 1901 there were already significant numbers of women anxious to ensure that this should be their century, too. Jobs came before votes, but both were in demand. Women were to become increasingly emancipated as the century went on – at least in most parts of the world.

Further changes were to come, not only in the factory and the voting booth but also in the home and in the shop, and in leisure as well as in work. The first domestic electric appliances were being advertised in 1900, along with an increasing range of branded foods and ready-made clothes. There was one brand new leisure activity, also. In 1903 there were huge audiences for one of the longest 'moving pictures' yet made, The Great Train Robbery. It lasted for eight minutes, and at its climax the moustachioed robber-in-chief fired a pistol point-blank at the audience.

More than pistols were to be fired in the 20th century. The century began with the Boer War continuing in South Africa and the violent Boxer Rebellion in China. Later there were to be two world wars, great divides in human experience, with consequences for every man and for every woman, many of them unforeseen. The heavy price of the First World War, which grew out of Europe's divisions, *was 10 million dead. The Second World War lasted longer, cost 64 million dead and brought about more profound changes; it affected people's lives not only in Europe's cities but in tropical islands, and ended with the explosion of an atomic bomb on Japan, ushering in a nuclear age.*

The origins of the nuclear age can be traced back to the beginning of the 20th century, when the science of physics underwent a radical revolution. Few ordinary people understood it. For the 20th century was not only to be the century of the common man and woman: it was also to be the century of the scientist – and of the expert. The first Nobel prizes, paid for out of a fortune made in the production of explosives, were awarded in 1901.

There were Nobel prizes in medicine, however, as well as in physics, and it was through the development of scientific medicine, including the discovery of new drugs, that human life in peace-time conditions was to be significantly prolonged. The contraceptive pill, too, was to be an innovation with potentially far-reaching consequences, in a world whose population had risen at an unprecedented rate from 2000 million in 1930 to 3000 million a generation later, in 1960.

There were to be political revolutions, too – revolutions which profoundly affected the patterns of everyday life, particularly in Russia, which had its first revolution as early as 1905, and in China, where things for so long had remained unchanged. Such revolutions were to divide the world into different camps during the second half of the century. Yet there was an increasing sense that there was only one world. There was an increasing recognition also that the world had common problems, including problems of the environment – an environment that almost everywhere had changed significantly since 1901 and, in changing, had directly affected people's everyday lives. Nonetheless, it was a triumph for mankind as a whole when in 1961 a Russian astronaut orbited the earth, and eight years later when an American set foot on the moon. The time scale was for many people alarmingly fast: the first manned landing on the moon came only 60 years after Louis Blériot had become the first man to cross the English Channel in an aeroplane.

The moon landings were as far removed from everyday life as anything could possibly be. Yet they were seen by millions of ordinary people on television. In 1900 few people could have foreseen either the moon landings or the accomplishments of radio and television in revealing events on earth and beyond it to a global audience. History never stands still. Nor do people's thoughts and feelings about what is happening now. Yesterday's newspaper is out of date before today begins.

Asa Briggs

A–Z OF EVERYDAY THINGS

Through the ages, human ingenuity has excelled at finding ways of making life more comfortable, and taking the drudgery out of day-to-day existence. This selection shows how 100 amenities which today we take for granted came about, some by happy accident, others by a long process of trial and error.

Adhesives

Everyday articles such as clothes and writing paper have been joined together by adhesives since earliest times. The Ancient Egyptians made glue by boiling animal skin, bone and sinew. The first adhesive bandage, too, seems to have been used in Ancient Egypt: records mention soft poultices and harder plaster made from myrrh and honey spread on linen.

Advertisements

The oldest-known advertisement was issued by the English printer William Caxton in 1479, to publicise books from his press. Two centuries later playbills were printed to lure the public to the London theatres. Advertising became widespread in the 18th century, when newspapers began to advertise luxury goods, articles lost and found, and servants for hire. In America, early advertising was fostered by Benjamin Franklin, who bought the *Pennsylvania Gazette* in 1729. His contemporary, the 18th-century patriot Paul Revere, used advertising to persuade Boston

Sandwichman of 1828

residents to buy his own brand of hand-fashioned false teeth. By 1820 more than 500 American newspapers advertised snuff, shoes and slaves. In 1886 a painting by Sir John Millais showing a child blowing soap bubbles became the classic advertisement for Pears Soap.

Anaesthetics

The Ancient Egyptians inhaled the fumes of Indian hemp or cannabis as a painkiller, and the Greeks used opium. At much the same time the South American Indians were using cocaine.

Salicin, or natural aspirin, occurs in the willow, and its pain-reducing properties were known in the Middle Ages. Willow bark was chewed to relieve toothache, and willow leaves and roots were boiled to make concoctions for a variety of complaints. Nitrous oxide, or 'laughing gas', was used for a tooth extraction in America in 1844, and three years later Sir James Simpson applied chloroform to reduce the pain of childbirth.

The first synthetic aspirin was produced in Germany in the 1890s by the Bayer company.

Antiseptics

The germ-killing power of certain substances was widely recognised in the ancient world. The Egyptians used honey, myrrh and various spices; the early Indians used honey and sesame oil; and the Ancient Greeks used urine, wine or vinegar on open wounds. The Arabs cauterised to control infection. In 1867 Joseph Lister used carbolic acid in the first antiseptic surgery.

Ball games

By 2000 BC the Ancient Egyptians were playing a game resembling bowls using stones, and the Persians had invented a game similar to hockey. By 500 BC the Chinese played a version of football, and the Ancient Greeks used inflated pigs' bladders in a similar game.

Football became popular in Britain after the Romans introduced it around AD 200. The

9th-century Maya of central America played a game called *pok-a-tok*. Players were allowed to hit the ball only with buttocks, fists and elbows. The Maya took their national game seriously – losers were sometimes sacrificed.

A game resembling tennis was brought back from the Holy Land by the Crusaders, who had seen the Saracens playing it. Refined in the 12th century by French monks, it was played by several French kings, and reached Italy and Britain by the late 14th century.

Golf became popular on the sand dunes of Holland and Scotland in the 15th century.

Baths

As long ago as 20,000 BC people were throwing water onto heated stones to create steam baths. Communal baths have been built since 4000 BC, but it was the Egyptians who invented the first bathrooms – small waterproof rooms built of stone.

In Ancient Greece men had steam baths after exercising at a gymnasium, while women enjoyed scented baths which were believed to cure ailments and benefit the skin. The Romans followed the Greek fashion and built vast public baths that could hold up to 1600 people.

After the collapse of Rome in the 5th century, bathing became rare. This state of affairs continued in Europe throughout the Middle Ages and later. Until the 1860s few ordinary homes had bathrooms; when Queen Victoria came to the throne in 1837 there was no bathroom in Buckingham Palace. Only from the 1870s did bathrooms become common.

Beds

A pit dug into the earth and lined with springy vegetation provided a bed for early people. At night, hunting tribesmen cloaked themselves with animal skins; the Eskimos slept on communal beds covered in animal fur.

The earliest off-the-ground bed consisted of four forked branches stuck into the ground, supporting a wooden frame latticed with

thongs. A mattress of skins was laid over it. The Egyptians used wooden headrests and latticed beds covered in long linen sheets which were folded back and forth to form a mattress.

The Greeks had ornate bronze beds, latticed with leather thongs and draped with heavily embroidered counterpanes. Their pillows were filled with wool, feathers and vegetable fibres. The Romans preferred wooden pillows covered in cloth, and invented the first mattress using hay, wool and feathers.

By the end of the Middle Ages huge wooden beds were being built with canopies, but until the 1600s beds were owned only by the wealthy. Four-poster beds were popular in Elizabethan England. Elizabeth I received ambassadors and discussed state affairs from her bed.

In 1871 the coiled bed spring, invented in 1850, was combined with the padded base to produce the first interior-sprung mattress.

A 19th-century maharajah ordered a silver bed from Paris with each of its four posts carved in the form of a life-size nude woman. His weight activated a music box, which played God Save The Queen.

Beer

A crude form of ale made from barley was first brewed in Mesopotamia about 10,000 years ago. The Egyptians drank large quantities of ale; mothers even gave their children a daily ration to take to school. A papyrus written around 1400 BC warns: `Do not get drunk in the taverns in which they drink ale, for fear that words may go out of your mouth without your being aware of having uttered them.'

By AD 900 English monks discovered that the addition of hops gave beer an improved bitter flavour, and by 1086 Domesday Book listed more than 40 breweries in England.

Birth control

Artificial contraception was practised before 2000 BC, when barriers were made of lint and

coated with ground acacia root, which is acidic and therefore a spermicide. Egyptians made barrier creams from mustard seeds, beeswax, dried figs and even crocodile dung. Some primitive tribes ate dead bees.

Male contraceptives made from goats' bladders are mentioned in the Talmud. Condoms were popular in 17th-century France; they were described by Mme de Sévigné as `an armour against enjoyment and a spider web against danger'.

Condoms made of sheep gut were widely used in England during the 18th century; they needed soaking in water before use, and were often tied at the base with a pink ribbon. Because they were porous, men were advised to wear two. Rubber sheaths date from the 1870s.

Board games

By 3000 BC the Mesopotamians had developed many board games, most of them involving dice. A rectangular board with a patterned circuit or track dating from 2600 BC was found in the royal tombs at Ur in ancient Sumeria. With it were seven black figures, seven white figures, three white dice and three made of lapis lazuli. The dice were shaped like four-sided pyramids.

Backgammon is probably the oldest board game still played. The Egyptians played it on a board with 30 squares. The Romans reduced the number of squares (or triangles) to 20, and took the game to Scandinavia, Germany and England. Chess derives from an Indian war game called *chaturanga* played before AD 6. The Persians re-named some moves – the term `checkmate' comes from the Persian *shah mat*, `the king is dead'.

Bridges

Simple bridges made by fixing tree trunks across a stream were probably made before 10,000 BC. Larger and more complex bridges were being constructed by the Sumerians by 3200 BC, and the Egyptians built a multi-span bridge over the Nile in 2650 BC. Bridges were an essential part of the Romans' road network, but after the fall of Rome bridge-building practically disappeared except for crude wooden constructions.

Stone bridges with small spans and massive piers started to be built again during the Renaissance, but it was not until the late 18th century, with the discovery of steel, that spans could be greatly lengthened, making dramatic improvements possible.

Calendar

Early peoples relied on the 29 day cycle of the moon to measure time; but by 3000 BC Sumerian scribes had divided the year into 12 months, each with 30 days.

The Egyptians formulated a calendar based on a year of 365 days, further refined to keep it in step with the annual flooding of the Nile. In 46 BC the Egyptian calendar was modified by Julius Caesar, who added an extra day every fourth year, making a `leap' year.

In 8 BC August was named after Emperor Augustus. Previously it had been called Sextilis, then the sixth month. Sextilis, however, had only 30 days – one fewer than July, named after Julius Caesar – and Augustus could not bear to be outdone; so he decreed that August should be extended by one day and February reduced to 28 days.

Over the centuries the Julian calendar was proved slightly inaccurate, and Church festivals timed from the spring equinox fell earlier and earlier each year. In 1582 Pope Gregory XIII corrected these discrepancies by dropping ten days from the calendar and decreeing that a centennial year would not be a leap year unless it was divisible by 400: for example, 1600 and 2000 count as leap years, whereas 1900 did not.

Canned food

The principle of canning was invented by a Frenchman, Nicolas Appert, in 1795. He placed the food in loosely sealed jars, heated them by boiling, then sealed them to prevent the contents going bad.

Jars soon gave way to cans made of tin plate, after the first canning factory was opened in Bermondsey, London, in 1811. Canned meat, soup and vegetables were supplied to the Royal Navy during the war of 1812 against the Americans, and proved highly successful.

Canning was not used extensively in America until the Civil War in the 1860s, when millions of cans were supplied to both sides. Enormous meat-packing industries using the latest canning techniques began in Chicago in the 1880s. In 1888 H.J. Heinz started his '57 Varieties' of canned food.

Veal canned in 1825

Cats

In Ancient Egypt a whole family would go into mourning and shave their eyebrows when a pet cat died. Dead cats were embalmed and buried in special vaults; killing a cat, even by accident, was punishable by death. Romans, Chinese and South American Indians all revered cats. Medieval Europe thought less highly of them, as they were believed to be the familiars of witches, and it was further believed that the devil took the form of a cat.

At the end of the 15th century the pope ordered the Inquisition to hunt down cat worshippers, and thousands of cats were destroyed. Among the cat lovers of later centuries were the writers Honoré de Balzac, the Brontë sisters and Mark Twain. Charles Dickens's cat used to sit by him while he worked, and snuff out the candle when it was time for him to stop.

The Prophet Muhammad was so fond of his cat that one day, while it was sleeping against his arm, he cut his sleeve rather than disturb his pet.

Central heating

The Ancient Greeks built rooms over flues warmed by outside furnaces. The Romans evolved the hypocaust, by which heat from a furnace was fed into a space below floor level, connected to flues in the wall.

The modern principle of hot-water heating was pioneered in 1716 by the Swedish engineer Martin Triewald, who used it to heat a greenhouse in Newcastle upon Tyne, in northern England. The idea was taken up to heat a chicken house in Paris.

In 1793 the English engineer Joseph Green patented a method using air heated by pipes running through a fire. In the 1840s central steam heating was installed in London's Houses of Parliament. The modern system, evolved with the production of cast-iron radiators in the 1880s.

Chairs

Ceremonial high-backed chairs were used by exalted persons in Egypt by 3000 BC, while the lowly slumped on stools or on the floor.

Stools long remained the principal form of seating, and seats with backs were rare before the Middle Ages. Upholstered chairs became popular in 18th-century France, and rocking chairs appeared in England and the United States in the 1840s.

Children's games

The first detailed descriptions of children's games come from the Ancient Greeks, whose children played games such as hide and seek, ducks and drakes, tug of war, leapfrog and blind man's buff. Countless generations of children have handed down these games virtually unaltered.

The swinging 1450s

Shakespeare refers to '*All hid, all hid*', '*Hoodman-blinde*' and '*Leape-frogge*'. By the 18th century these were joined by marbles and cricket for boys, and hopscotch and skipping for girls.

Gymnastic games date back to the time when Stone Age children swung from creepers. The swing must have been known in ancient times, though it was first mentioned in England as recently as 1678.

Cigars

Cigars get their name from the Mayan Indian word *sik'ar*, meaning smoking. Mayas had been smoking cigars for 1500 years when the Europeans first saw them rolling tobacco leaves.

In the 16th century planters began exporting tobacco leaves to France, Spain, Portugal and later England. It was not until the 19th century, however, that the habit spread to America – where smoking was prescribed as a cure for sore throats, lockjaw and bad breath.

Cigarettes

A Turkish cannonball was responsible for the invention of the first paper-wrapped cigarette in 1832. It smashed a communal clay pipe belonging to a group of Egyptian artillerymen, who then stuffed their tobacco into the hollow paper torches they used to touch off their guns.

Cigarettes were first mass-produced in Cuba in 1853, but smoking cigarettes rather than clay pipes remained the pleasure of the rich until the Crimean War of 1854-6, when British soldiers acquired the habit from their Turkish allies.

Clocks

Around 330 BC the Greeks invented the *clepsydra*, a water clock consisting of linked water-filled cylinders operating a pointer which marked the hours on a graduated scale. But accurate timekeeping did not come for another 600 years.

Towards the end of the 13th century the first clocks were installed in monastery towers: their name comes from the medieval Latin *clocca*, meaning a bell. The first clocks marked the hours by means of the regulated descent of a stone on the end of an unwinding rope. When the stone reached a certain point, a man would ring the church bell as a signal for prayer.

By 1335 Milan, in Italy, had a public clock that automatically struck the hours, and by 1350 most European cities had tower clocks, with faces, hour hands and a bell.

In 1656 the Dutch astronomer Christian Huygens adapted the pendulum to the clock's mechanism. From about 1700 the grandfather or longcase clock was an essential item of furniture in the middle-class home.

Greek water clock

Compass

The Chinese discovered that an iron needle, magnetised by rubbing it with a lodestone – a naturally magnetic mineral of iron – would point north if floated in a straw on a bowl of water. The first mention of the invention appears in essays by Shen Kua around AD 1060. Such simple compasses were in use by Chinese navigators in the 12th century. Originally, the needle was thrust through a straw floating in a bowl of water, but by 1300 it was mounted on a pivot and combined with the compass card. The great age of exploration in medieval Europe relied on such simple compasses.

Concrete

A form of concrete was used by Ancient Egyptians when they discovered the use of gypsum to bind stone and brick to make a waterproof building material.

In 150 BC the Romans discovered that volcanic dust from Pozzuoli near Vesuvius, when mixed with lime and water, set hard to create a material which they called *caementum*. This was the forerunner of modern cement. Elsewhere the Romans made a similar material by mixing clay, limestone and gypsum; when gravel, crushed stone, sand and water were added, the mixture set as hard as natural stone. Concrete enabled the Romans to build their systems of roads, sewers and aqueducts.

In England in 1824, Joseph Aspdin patented synthetic cement – a mixture of limestone and clay, heated to a high temperature and then ground into powder.

Crane

The first clear description of a crane comes from the Roman architect Vitruvius, writing around 10 BC, though Archimedes in the 3rd century BC is said to have devised a crane with three pulleys. For powering their cranes,

the Romans used treadmills – huge wheels inside which slaves walked around, driving the wheel with their weight.

The derrick crane as used today, with a pulley at the end of a slanting arm, was developed in Italy in the 1400s.

Dentistry

Dental specialists were practising in Ancient Egypt as early as 3700 BC, and Sumerian tablets found in the River Euphrates contain advice on tooth decay. By AD 2 the Greek doctor Galen had recognised the difference between gum disease and tooth decay, speculating that decay was caused by a blood disorder.

After the fall of Rome, the Arabs took the lead in dentistry and began to use gold to fill cavities. In medieval Europe, monks carried out most dental work.

It was not until the 19th century that the Americans identified bacteria as the cause of tooth decay. Anaesthetics were not officially advocated until 1840.

Dogs

The longest-established of all domesticated animals, dogs are descended from a variety of wolf that lived 15 million years ago. Stone Age man 20,000 years ago trained wolf cubs for tracking game and as guard dogs.

The Ancient Egyptians are credited with developing the first true breed, the saluki. The Romans had names for six distinct kinds, which they subdivided into different breeds. The Gauls around the time of Christ used

armoured fighting dogs in war, while the medieval Crusaders had fighting dogs that could distinguish between Christians and infidels by scent.

A dog's faithfulness has long been legendary. When Homer's hero Odysseus returned home after 20 years' absence, his old dog Argus recognised him, wagged his tail – and died.

Dolls

In Ancient Greece children played with clay dolls. A girl kept her dolls until marriage, when she sacrificed them to the goddess Artemis. Roman children played with rag dolls.

During the Middle Ages, children of rich families had wooden dolls with movable limbs. Poor children had to make do with dolls made of straw, rags or clay. The 14th century saw the first dolls with carved faces and proper clothes.

Until the 19th century dolls' bodies were usually made of leather or cloth, but after 1850 rubber-like gutta-percha, stuffed with sawdust, was used instead. Arms, hands and feet became more realistic, and heads were often made of porcelain, with real hair attached.

In 1827 the German Johann Nepomuk Maelzel, inventor of the metronome and a friend of Beethoven, patented a doll's voice box which said 'Papa' or 'Mama' when squeezed.

Doors

Prehistoric people made the doors of their huts from animal hides, cloth or woven twigs. When temporary homes gave way to fixed settlements, doors became more solid. In Rome, the bronze doors of the Pantheon are still intact after 1800 years. Many houses in Pompeii, destroyed by Vesuvius in AD 79, had folding doors. Wooden doors large enough to let carts and animals through had smaller doors cut into them for pedestrians to use.

At the dentist, 1773

Dyes

Traces of indigo, a blue dye obtained from the indigo plant, have been found in clothing woven in Egypt 5000 years ago. Saffron, turmeric and henna were used by the Egyptians to create yellow and orange fabrics.

By Roman times dyeing had become a large and profitable business. A purple dye obtained by the Phoenicians from the gland of a Mediterranean shellfish was adopted as the imperial colour, and its production was strictly controlled.

The cochineal, an insect of Mexico and central America, was the source of a scarlet dye. The European woad plant yielded a blue dye, but its production caused a repellent stench, and Elizabeth I forbade woad mills within 5 miles of her country homes. A Dutch trade in indigo flourished during the 16th and 17th centuries.

Envelopes

Babylonians protected inscribed tablets within a thin sheet of clay which they wrapped round the message, crimped together and baked. Other early peoples enclosed records made on cloth, animal skins or reeds within coverings of the same materials.

The first recorded use of an improvised envelope in Europe came in 1696; it was used by the Scottish Secretary of State to enclose a letter to his English counterpart. A Brighton manufacturer made envelopes in 1830 – but sales were slow at first as the user had to pay the extra postage charge. The first prepaid envelope came with the introduction of the English Penny Post in 1840, and four years later the General Post Office issued gummed envelopes.

Factory

When Venice was at war with the Turks at the beginning of the 16th century, 100 war galleys were built in as many days at the Arsenal. Standardisation of parts such as sternposts and rudders made production-line assembly possible

on a massive scale. The factory (originally 'manufactory') of today developed in the late 18th century, when the water wheel and the steam engine were applied to the spinning of yarn. Electric conveyor belts were first used in the 1850s for meat-packaging in Chicago. But it was not until 1913 that Henry Ford perfected the assembly line, cutting the time it took to turn out a Model T Ford from 13 hours to one.

False teeth

The earliest-known set of false teeth belonged to a Phoenician man of 1000 BC; his four lower incisors had been replaced by four teeth taken from another person's jaw, joined with gold wire and strung round four canines.

Partial false teeth made from bone or ivory were used by 700 BC, but the earliest-known set of dentures date back only to 1450. Found in Switzerland, the teeth were carved from bone and attached by gut to a hinged side-piece. Dentists of 1600 wired loose teeth with gold, and made false teeth from hippo or walrus ivory. The first porcelain dentures were manufactured in Paris in 1770.

In the 16th century, Elizabeth I put her false teeth in when receiving dignitaries, but took them out to eat.

Fingerprinting

Fingerprinting was first used by the Indian Civil Service in 1877 to ensure that people did not draw their pension more than once. At the end of the 19th century the technique was improved by the English scientist Sir Francis Galton and the policeman Edward Henry to help identify criminals. Scotland Yard opened a fingerprint department in 1901.

Firefighting

The world's first firefighting forces were organised 2000 years ago in Rome by Emperor Augustus. Rome had at least 20 fire brigades, whose members fought blazes using crude water pumps and blankets soaked in vinegar. Medieval Europe had groups of fire-fighters paid for by their community. They used fire engines with simple water pumps, and were equipped with long rakes to pull down burning thatch from roofs. The Great Fire of London in 1666 revealed the lack of efficient firefighting equipment. The first official fire brigade was established in Britain by Nicholas Barbon, of the Phoenix Fire Office, in 1684. He created a group of men, probably Thames watermen, who fought fires for the sum of one shilling for the first hour, sixpence for succeeding hours, and unlimited beer. They wore a bright tunic and breeches, and were given immunity against being pressed into service by the Royal Navy.

In 1813 Captain George Manby from Yarmouth designed a portable extinguisher consisting of a copper canister holding four gallons of water and charged with compressed air.

Water pump of 1660s London

Fireworks

As early as the 9th century the Chinese were using fireworks for their military signals and celebrations, making them with black powder – a mixture of saltpetre (potassium nitrate), sulphur and charcoal.

The first Europeans to produce fireworks were the Italians, who used them in the 16th century during theatrical performances. By the beginning of the 17th century firework displays were a regular climax to coronations, royal weddings and victories.

To accompany a display in London's Green Park, held in 1749 to celebrate the peace of Aix-la-Chapelle which ended the War of the Austrian Succession, Handel

Fireworks to end a war

wrote his *Music for the Royal Fireworks*. By 1785 a French chemist had discovered how to make coloured fireworks by the addition of metallic salts. By the middle of the 19th century magnesium and aluminium were giving a vast increase in brilliance. London's Crystal Palace became world famous for its displays of landscapes, battle scenes and emblems, 'painted' with fireworks.

Flags

As long ago as the 5th century BC Chinese warriors flew silk flags in the form of dragons, which fluttered and writhed in the wind, guiding troops in the heat of battle. The Romans evolved a type of flag called a *vexilla*, which was a square of purple or fringed cloth hanging from a lance.

In early medieval times kings and generals had their own flags for use on the battlefield. These gradually gave way to national flags; among the earliest was that of the Italian city-state of Genoa, which in the 12th century took the St George's cross (a red cross on a white background) as its symbol.

From about 1400, until the development of electric signalling, flags were used for daytime communication at sea. In the 1770s Admiral Howe issued the first-ever printed signal book, and at much the same time Admiral Sir Home Popham perfected a complete flag alphabet. Nelson's last signal at the Battle of Trafalgar in 1805 was No 16 in Popham's code: `Engage the enemy more closely.' In 1817 Captain Marryat, naval officer and author, produced the first internationally accepted flag code.

Forks

Although by AD 100 the Byzantines were using small gilt forks to eat their food, it was not until the 11th century that two-pronged forks came into use in Italy. Some households in 15th-century England possessed forks, but it was years before poorer people used them. For centuries a curious stigma remained attached to forks: a preacher sermonised that it was `an insult to Providence not to touch one's meat with one's fingers'. As late as 1897 British sailors were forbidden to use forks because it was considered unmanly.

Funerals

The earliest-known grave, in China north of Beijing, dates back 400,000 years. The cult of the dead reached its height in Ancient Egypt, where elaborate tombs, notably the pyramids, were built for the pharaohs, their wives and leading citizens.

Some African tribes smoked the corpse and displayed it in the place where death occurred. The Australian aborigines ate their dead, hoping to absorb their good qualities.

Gardens

By about 2000 BC the gardens of Babylon contained at least 70 different aromatic herbs. A Roman fresco from a 1st-century BC villa shows pomegranates, poppies, violets, roses and an oak tree. Byzantine gardens featured artificial trees of silver and gold, and mechanical birds.

During the Middle Ages, most gardens belonged to monasteries, with the emphasis on herbs and vegetables. In Tudor times, formal knot gardens were laid out with foliage plants such

as lavender, thyme and box. By the 17th century, the Italians had developed a distinctive style, with grottoes, terraces and fountains. The art of formal gardening reached its height at the end of the 17th century, at Versailles, near Paris, which was laid out with sculpture, topiary, tall hedges and avenues of trees. At much the same time the Dutch were concentrating on the more domestic and decorative art of raising flowers, notably tulips.

In the 18th century the concept of formal gardening was challenged, especially in England, where garden designers such as Lancelot 'Capability' Brown sought to break down the boundaries between the garden and the landscape.

Glasses

The Roman emperor Nero, in the 1st century AD, held a faceted jewel to his eye to make out the details of the gladiatorial games in the arena below. The earliest-known depiction of an aid to sight comes from 1200 years later. This is a stone statue, at Constance in Germany, showing the Greek physician Hippocrates looking through a glass held by its stem.

By the end of the 13th century spectacles with convex lenses were being worn in places as far apart as Venice and China; and by the mid-15th century concave lenses to correct short sight had appeared in Italy. Paired lenses, linked by bridges, were roughly graded in intensity, and a customer experimented until he found a pair that suited him.

The first bifocals were made in America by Benjamin Franklin in 1775. Contact lenses were first suggested in 1827 by the English astronomer Sir John Herschel, but it was not until 1887 that Dr Eugen Frick of Zurich produced contact lenses of sufficient precision to be worth wearing.

Guidebooks

Temples, battlefields and other historical sites give the very first guidebook a recognisably modern look. It was written in

AD 22 by the Roman writer Pausanias for his fellow countrymen who were touring Ancient Greece.

The first printed guidebook, Benedict's *Mirabilia Romae* ('The Wonders of Rome'), was printed in Rome in 1473. In 1577 William Harrison wrote a *Description of England*, with practical hints for travellers. The first restaurant guide, *Almanach des Gourmands* printed in 1804, listed no fewer than 500 Paris restaurants.

In Karl Baedeker's first guide to European travel, printed in 1830, St Peter's in Rome and the Mona Lisa scored his top two-star rating. Rembrandt and the Arc de Triomphe rated only one star.

Hairstyles

Greek women curled their hair with terracotta rollers. Roman women twisted their hair into ringlets around hollow tubes heated internally by rods, piling it high and fixing it with precious combs or gold nets. The wealthiest women powdered their heads with gold dust. The most exaggerated hairstyles ever created were worn by wealthy European women in the 18th century. At the court of France's Louis XV, women piled their hair high into structures 3ft (0.9m) high, which obliged them to sleep sitting up. They kept their hair in position sometimes for several months, providing nests for insects and even mice.

Cupid's Tower of 1828

Horses

Around 2000 BC nomads on the steppes of central Asia domesticated the descendants of the earliest horse, *Eohippus*. This animal, which lived about 50 million years ago, browsed on undergrowth rather than eating grass. It was about the size of a large dog and had a long nose, like a tapir. Instead of hooves, it had four toes on the front feet and three on the back feet. The Greeks, and later the Romans, raced both chariots and ridden horses. About 200 BC nomadic tribes from the east introduced into Europe iron horseshoes fastened with nails. These gave a far better grip, both for riding and for pulling loads.

While Europe relied on the often vicious primitive horse, the gentler and more controllable Arabian horse was being developed in North Africa, where it had been bred since Old Testament times. It was brought back to Europe by returning Crusaders and crossed with native horses to produce the modern breeds.

In the 4th century BC Alexander the Great named a town after his battle-charger Bucephalus. In the 1st century AD the Roman Emperor Caligula built his horse Incitatus a marble stable with an ivory manger.

Hospitals

Both the Ancient Egyptians and the Greeks had healing centres. A public hospital was established in Rome in AD 362, but in medieval Europe the only medical treatment available was in hospital wings attached to monasteries. The Arabs were far more advanced: in the 13th century the Al Mansur hospital, in Cairo, had spacious wards cooled by fountains, where patients could listen to musicians and storytellers. Yet at much the same time the Hotel Dieu, in Paris, crammed six patients into a bed.

In England, the squalid conditions found in most hospitals improved in the 19th century with the reforms pioneered by Florence Nightingale. New hospitals were built, nurses were properly trained, and efficient antiseptics and anaesthetics began to be used.

About AD 920 the Arab physician Rhazes was looking for a healthy site in Baghdad to build a new hospital. He chose the part of the city where meat took the longest time to rot.

18th-century warming pan

Hot-water bottles

The ancestor of the hot-water bottle was the warming pan, used in Europe since the 15th century. The long-handled pan, filled with hot coals and covered by a hinged lid, was pushed between the sheets to air the bed.

Towards the end of the 18th century water-filled warming pans began to be used, made water-tight by a screw stopper. After about 1820 the handle was dispensed with, and metal pans were replaced by earthenware bottles known from their shape as 'pigs'. From the 1890s, earthenware gave way to rubber.

Before the warming pan came into use, a servant had to climb into the bed to warm it before the master or mistress retired for the night.

Ice cream

The home of dairy ice cream may well have been China, for Marco Polo brought recipes for making ice cream from milk to Venice in 1295.

By the 1550s ice cream was established in France, after Catherine de Medici had brought *gelatieri*, Italian ice-cream makers, to the French court on her marriage to the future Henry II in 1533. In 17th-century England, Charles I's chef, Gerald Tissain, made dishes from ice, milk and cream. So appreciated were these puddings that he was awarded a £20 a year pension for life – on condition that he kept his recipe secret.

The ice came from ice houses – huge larders, often underground, which were filled with ice in winter and were sufficiently well insulated to keep it solid through the summer.

Mass-produced ice cream had to wait for the invention of refrigeration. Jacob Fussell, a Baltimore dairyman, started

producing ice cream in 1851 as a way of reducing wastage of cream. He sold it at the low price of 25 cents a quart (1136 ml).

In 1790 George Washington, the first President of the United States, spent $200 on ice cream in just two months. History does not record his favourite flavour.

Kites

Kites were first flown in China as long ago as 1080 BC, and were brought to Europe from the Far East by the Dutch around 1600. In the early 1800s kite power was used by a Bristol schoolmaster, George Pocock, to pull a lightweight carriage, carrying four passengers, at 20 mph (32 km/h).

At the same time kites were used in Western experiments in manned flight. The invention of the box kite in 1893 by Lawrence Hargrove, in Australia, inspired the aircraft designs of the Wright Brothers and other pioneers.

Knives

Flint knives were used by Stone Age people for killing animals and carving them up for meat. Bronze knives were used by 3000 BC. The first steel knives were made by the Romans, who had specialised knives for such tasks as shoemaking and, by the 1st century AD, folding knives.

In the 14th century specially made sharp-pointed knives began to be used at the table. Previously, medieval knights had used their hunting knives to spear food from the serving dishes.

Round-ended knives began to be used in the 17th century, after the French Cardinal Richelieu was so disgusted at the sight of his guests picking their teeth with their knife-points that he ordered all his household knives to be ground to rounded ends. By 1669 pointed table knives were illegal in France.

Lamps

In the Stone Age, the first simple lamps were made by dipping a strand of moss, rush or twisted grass into an open dish of tallow, or animal fat. Tallow lamps, or rushlights, survived until the

Industrial Revolution. Rushes were sometimes doubled over to provide extra light – hence the expression 'burning the candle at both ends'.

Tallow was also used to make candles; beeswax candles burned brighter and smoked less, but were more expensive. In the late 18th century, sperm oil from the whaling industry came into use for candles. Whale oil was also used for oil lamps, together with vegetable oils.

Gas lighting, developed in Europe early in the 19th century, was vastly improved by the invention of the gas mantle in 1887. Made of cotton impregnated with metal oxides, the mantles glowed when heated by the flame, producing a more brilliant light.

In 1879 both Thomas Edison in the United States and Joseph Swan in England produced the first incandescent electric lights, evacuated glass globes inside which a fine filament glowed as current flowed through it.

Lathe

Egyptian furniture from before 3000 BC bears the marks of shaping by a lathe. By 500 BC Greek carpenters were using a pole lathe, in which one end of a cord was attached to a foot treadle and the other end to a springy pole. Wheel-driven lathes, where the treadle turns a wheel, rotating the workpiece continuously, came into general use in the 14th century.

Lavatory

The Ancient Egyptians, the Cretans and the Romans evolved methods of waste disposal connected to sewers, while medieval monasteries built 'reredorters' above flowing streams. In medieval towns toilet seats were fitted over cesspits, from which the night soil, or waste, was removed in barrels to be used as fertiliser. Buckets were usually emptied into the street.

The first water closet, flushed from a mains water supply and connected to a sewer, was

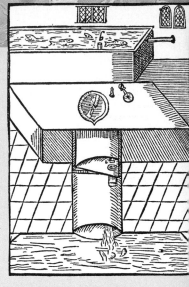

Water closet of 1589

designed in 1589 by Sir John Harington, Elizabeth I's godson. In the 1770s Alexander Cummings invented a WC incorporating water released from an overhead tank. Joseph Bramah further improved the system by adding a water-filled U-bend, which acted as an efficient barrier to the smell from the cesspit or sewer.

Early lavatory bowls were generally made of metal, but from about 1870 the cheaper ceramic bowls replaced them.

Libraries

The first libraries, established 4000 years ago in Ancient Egypt and Mesopotamia, housed hand-baked clay tablets and papyrus scrolls which were consulted by scholars and officials.

The library at Alexandria in Egypt, founded in the 4th century BC, was estimated to house up to 700,000 scrolls and papyri. Alexandria's great rival was the library at Pergamum, in modern Turkey. When the jealous Alexandrians cut off the supply of papyrus to Pergamum, the librarians there used parchment made from dried animal skins instead. Parchment had the advantage over papyrus that both sides could be used.

By the Middle Ages scrolls had been superseded by books, which were so rare that they were kept chained to the shelves, as in the medieval library at Hereford Cathedral. Britain's first public library was established in Norwich in 1608, and in 1852 Britain's first free public lending library opened in Manchester.

Lighthouses

The earliest-known lighthouse was the Pharos of Alexandria, one of the Seven Wonders of the Ancient World. Built in the 3rd century BC, it was 350ft (107m) high, and the fire in the metal basket at the top was said to be visible from 30 miles (48km) away. The Romans built lighthouses round their empire, from the Black Sea to the Atlantic.

Most early lighthouses were built on commanding headlands, but developing engineering skills enabled some to be built on rocks at sea, such as the successive Eddystone lighthouses off Plymouth, from 1698.

The light from the earliest lighthouses came from wood or coal in open baskets, gradually replaced by candles and oil lamps. In 1782 the Swiss scientist Aimé Argand produced an oil lamp with a ring-shaped wick, which burned ten times brighter than earlier lamps.

By the end of the 18th century the light was further intensified by curved metal reflectors.

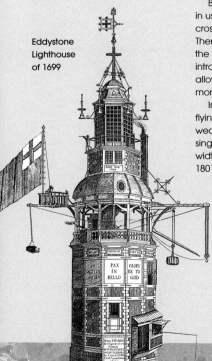

Eddystone Lighthouse of 1699

Locks

An ancient ruined palace near Nineveh, Iraq, dating from about 2000BC, has a wooden locking device attached to a door. The Ancient Egyptians had ingenious wooden locks and keys, and the Romans used iron locks and bronze keys. Medieval and Renaissance locks were sometimes made with extra devices to deter thieves, such as sharp blades that could slice off fingertips when the lock was tampered with.

Viking lock and key

In 1778 Robert Barron devised the tumbler to make lock-picking more difficult, and in 1788 Joseph Bramah patented a safety lock with a cylindrical key, still in use today. In 1861 the American inventor Linus Yale patented the lock which bears his name.

Loom

The principle of weaving cloth on a loom – that is, interlacing the warp or lengthwise threads with the weft or horizontal threads – was known in Turkey and Palestine as long ago as 5000BC.

By 1400 BC vertical looms were in use, with the warp strung to crossbars at the top and bottom. There was little improvement until the Middle Ages, when the introduction of the treadle allowed weavers to create far more intricate patterns.

In 1733 the invention of the flying shuttle by the English weaver John Kay enabled a single worker to weave varying widths of cloth at a rapid rate. In 1801 a French silk weaver, Joseph Marie Jacquard, invented the Jacquard loom, in which perforated cards guided hooks to lift the warp threads.

Lucky charms

The lives of the Ancient Egyptians were largely governed by charms and talismans. Among them were the scarab, or dung beetle, regarded as the symbol of resurrection. Immortality was symbolised by the ankh, a T-shaped cross with a loop at the top, and the salamander, a small lizard believed to have the power to live in fire.

Many objects have been credited with the power of bringing health or good luck. The 'adder stone' was a coloured, glass-like stone, prized as a charm against ague, whooping cough and nightmares. It was believed to be produced from petrified snake saliva – hence its name.

The 'lucky bone', a small T-shaped bone found in the skulls of sheep, was believed to protect against witchcraft and bring good fortune.

Maps

The first-known map, on a clay tablet from Mesopotamia, was made around 1000BC. It shows the world as a disc surrounded by water, with Babylon at its centre. The Ancient Greeks conceived the world as a sphere, placing orientation lines, and horizontal and vertical grids, on their maps. The Romans improved on the Greeks' methods, producing road maps or 'Itineraries', with towns clearly marked.

The Middle Ages were more concerned with piety than with scientific accuracy, and so all maps of Christendom – like the Mappa Mundi, or 'map of the world', in Hereford Cathedral – have Jerusalem at the centre. East was always placed at the top, as the direction in which paradise was thought to lie.

By 1480 there were 27 known maps of the world. In 1569 the Flemish geographer Gerardus Mercator produced a world map which solved the problem of how to plot a straight line on a curved surface. Towards the end of the 17th century the invention of accurate chronometers and the sextant led to huge improvements in mapping.

Scientific surveying began in the 18th century. In Britain, the first Ordnance Survey map produced to a scale of 1in to 1mile (1cm to 0.64km) was drawn by military engineers in 1801.

The world map of the Greek geographer Ptolemy, made around AD150, was used by Columbus in 1492, and misled him into thinking that he had reached the Indies after crossing the Atlantic.

Matches

The first attempts to make a match go back to 1680. Pieces of wood were dipped in sulphur and struck against phosphorus until they flared up. However, until the 19th century the usual method was to use flint and steel to produce a tinder-igniting spark.

In 1826 an English chemist, John Walker, produced a match by accident. A stick with which he was stirring a mixture of potash and antimony burst into flame when he scraped it against the stone floor to remove the blob of chemical on the end.

The safety match was invented in Sweden 30 years later by John Lündstrom. Non-safety matches will ignite when struck against any rough surface, whereas safety matches will only light against a chemically treated surface, invariably sandpaper.

Measurement

The Egyptians built their temples and pyramids using a standard of length derived from their own pharaoh. The Royal Cubit of 20.6in (523mm) was the length of his forearm from elbow (*cubitum* in Latin) to the tip of the middle finger. A standard cubit was made of a block of black granite, used as the basis for further rules made of stone or wood.

In England Edward I, in 1305, defined the yard as the distance from the tip of his nose to the tip of his outstretched thumb, giving the yard of 3ft (0.9m). A foot was originally the length of a man's foot from heel to big toe. The Romans divided the foot into 12 *unciae,* or 'inches'.

The Roman mile was 1000 double paces, or about 1665yds (1522m). The acre was the area a yoke of oxen could plough in a day.

The French, after the Revolution, devised a new system of measurement based on the metre, named after the Greek word for 'measure' and defined as one ten-millionth of the distance from the North Pole to the Equator.

Mills

Water mills were used by the Greeks and improved by the Romans, who devised the vertical water wheel with gearing to transmit its drive to the millstones. By 1086, Domesday Book recorded 5000 water mills operating in England.

The windmill made its first appearance in Persia in the 7th century AD, reaching Europe about 1180. The first mills were post mills, built around huge posts so that the entire mill could be turned into the wind. Later the tower or smock mill, in which only the cap rotates, was developed.

By 1840 there were 10,000 windmills working in England and 8000 in Holland, where mills were used for sawing wood, papermaking, and grinding oil seeds as well as corn.

18th-century windmill grinding sugar cane on Antigua.

Mirrors

The Ancient Egyptians used mirrors of polished brass. About 300 BC the Greek mathematician Euclid worked out the optical laws that govern mirrors. These laws were applied by Archimedes against a Roman fleet that attacked his native city, Syracuse in Sicily, at the end of the 3rd century BC. He used concave mirrors of polished metal to concentrate the rays of the sun in an attempt to set the Roman ships on fire.

In the early 14th century the Venetians vastly improved the reflecting properties of glass by means of the silvering process, applying tinfoil and mercury to the back of the mirror.

In the 15th century, German glass-blowers developed convex mirrors which reflected almost everything in a room.

The Ancient Chinese fixed mirrors of polished brass on the outside of their doors, so that marauding spirits would frighten themselves away.

Money

The word `money' comes from the Romans, who in 269 BC established their first mint in the temple of Juno Moneta. But some form of money as a means of exchange goes back to the Stone Age, as is shown by a cache of cowrie shells from a prehistoric site in Iraq, dating from 20,000 BC.

Coins of standard value were pioneered about 700 BC in Lydia, western Turkey. Small bean-shaped slugs of electrum, a gold and silver alloy, were stamped with the figure of a lion, and with punch marks certifying the weight of the metal.

The Greeks minted large numbers of coins. At first they bore the heads of the gods, but after 320 BC, when Alexander the Great had his own head portrayed on coins, portraits of the current ruler became common. This practice was followed by the Romans, and is still prevalent.

Coins have been debased from the earliest times, either by shaving or clipping their edges, or by shaking them in a bag, so as to knock off tiny scraps of metal. Paper money originated in China in the 6th century AD and was issued in large quantities by the Mongol emperor Kublai Khan. The first European banknotes were issued in Stockholm in 1661.

In the Middle Ages, money used to be kept in purses hanging at the belt. Pockets made their debut when Charles IX of France forbade tailors to continue making purses, for fear they could conceal assassins' daggers.

Mousetraps

Several different designs of mousetrap were illustrated in a 13th-century book of Hebrew parables. A German version of this book shows a metal contraption with a large spring and serrated jaws, and also a wooden trap with its upper jaw clamped down on a mouse.

At much the same time the Italians used cages of wicker and wood. The bait was attached to a lever which let down a 'portcullis' across the entrance, trapping the mouse inside. In the 15th century Italian bankers were obliged by their contracts to keep down the mice which might damage the pledges deposited with them.

18th-century mousetrap

Nails

The earliest nails, dating from 3500 BC, were found in a statue of a bull in Mesopotamia. In the Middle Ages the nail-maker became a specialist, pulling rods of iron through a graded series of holes until he reached the required diameter, then flattening out a lump at one end to make the head. The first reliable machine for the mass-production of nails was patented in 1786 by Ezekiel Reed, in America.

Newspapers

The first newspapers were hand-written news reports passed from person to person: the first English example is an account of the Battle of Flodden, in which Henry VIII defeated the Scots, in 1513.

Printed newspapers appeared early in the 17th century. Rivals for the accolade of being the very first are the Antwerp *Nieuwe Tijdinghen* (1605), the *Aviso Relation oder Zeitung,* published at Wolfenbuttel in Lower Saxony in 1609, and the *Relation* of the Strasbourg printer Johann Carolus of the same year.

Paint

The earliest-known paintings, representing animals hunted for food, were made by Stone Age artists on the walls of caves at Lascaux, in France, around 25,000 BC.

The first colours were such naturally occurring pigments as red made from iron oxide, yellow and brown from clay ochre, and black from soot. It was not until 3000 BC that blue and green were obtained by grinding up lapis lazuli and malachite.

The first synthetic pigments were developed after a British chemist, William Perkin, discovered a dye called mauveine. The first truly synthetic medium, based on coal tar, was developed in Germany towards the end of the 19th century.

Paper

The first writing was done on animal skins, or on papyrus made from reed fibre, by the Egyptians as long ago as 3000 BC.

The invention of proper paper is attributed to a Chinese court official, Tsai Lun, who in AD 105 steeped a mixture of rags, hemp, mulberry bark and old fishing nets in water, and spread the mixture across a sieve to drain. He dried the resulting sheet of pulp, producing a perfectly smooth writing surface.

Paper came to the West centuries later. In AD 751, during a battle in central Asia between the Arabs and Chinese, the Arabs captured two Chinese paper-makers. They passed their secret to the Arabs, who in the 12th century opened Europe's first paper mill in Spain.

During the 19th century wood pulp rather than cotton rags began to be used as the basic material for paper.

Passport

Passes granting safe conduct were issued as early as the reign of the Roman emperor Augustus in the 1st century BC. Their wording ran: `If there be anyone on land or sea hardy enough to molest this traveller, let him consider whether he be strong enough to wage war with Caesar.' English passports, first recorded in 1414, were handwritten permits allowing the bearer to `pass the port' out of the country.

In Shakespeare's Henry V, *the king, before the Battle of Agincourt in 1415, tells his army:* `He which hath no stomach to this fight/Let him depart; his passport shall be made/And crowns for convoy put into his purse.'

Pens

The word 'pen' comes from the Latin *penna,* meaning a feather. From about 500 BC until the 19th century the quill or feather, shaved to a fine point, was the principal writing implement, followed by the steel nib dipped into an inkpot.

A quill with an ink tank attached was made in the mid-17th century. But the fountain pen did not become practicable until the 19th century, when the steel nib superseded the quill. In 1884 Lewis Edson Waterman produced the first workable fountain pen, with a feed-bar to maintain a steady flow of ink.

Perambulators

Although from ancient times children were pulled about in simple carts, the development of the pram of today required smooth roads and sound pavements, which were non-existent before the 18th century.

The first tiny baby carriage was built in 1733 at Chatsworth, the Derbyshire seat of the Duke of Devonshire. Designed by the architect and decorator William Kent, it was built in the shape of a scallop shell, with a folding hood, and was carried on an undercarriage of curved bronze snakes. Like all early prams it was designed for an infant large enough to sit up, and was pulled, not pushed. The first modern prams, in which tiny babies could lie full length, appeared in 1876.

Perfume

Before a social gathering, wealthy women in Ancient Egypt put cone-shaped pomades of flowers steeped in wax on top of their heads. As the atmosphere grew warmer, the wax melted, trickling down their faces and necks and scenting their skin.

The Greeks used perfume for medicinal purposes, believing that wearing rose petals round the head would prevent the onset of hangovers.

The Romans were obsessed by perfumes. In the 1st century AD the luxury-loving Emperor Nero slept on a bed of rose petals, and his palace contained hidden pipes from which his unsuspecting guests were sprayed all over with exotic scents.

The Romans put on perfume before going into battle — a custom revived centuries later by the Crusaders, who believed perfumed clothes would bring them luck. The French perfume industry dates back to Queen Catherine de Medici, who in the 16th century ordered her chemist to concoct as many scents as there were types of flower in southern France.

Plates

In the Middle Ages, large stale loaves were cut into thick slices known as trenchers, which were used as plates. Each slice had a depression in the centre, where the diner piled the meat taken from a communal dish set in the middle of the table. After the meal, the gravy-soaked bread was distributed to the poor. By 1500, bread trenchers had been superseded by wooden slabs. These gave way to plates made of pewter or silver, followed in the early 18th century by china, such as the blue-and-white ware of the Staffordshire potteries.

Playing cards

First mentioned in China in AD 969, playing cards arrived in the West around 1300. The earliest European cards were made in France around 1440: there were four suits, and the court cards – Ace, King, Queen and Jack or Knave – were the same as today.

Spades (from the Italian *spada*, 'a sword') resembled the swords of the nobles, hearts the shields of the Knights of the Church, and diamonds the tiles that paved the exchanges where merchants traded. The club or clover leaf symbolised the peasant's life.

In 1486 England banned the use of imported cards, to protect English card manufacturers. The game of piquet dates from the 15th century, while whist and cribbage were first mentioned by writers in the 17th century.

Columbus's men played cards on their voyage of 1492. After one storm, which they thought had been sent by God to punish them for card-playing, they threw their packs overboard, but as soon as they reached land they made new cards out of dried leaves.

In 1685 the French military commander in Quebec ran out of coins to pay his troops. So he cut playing cards into quarters, signed the pieces and issued them as money.

Playing cards from East and West

Postage

Postal services take their name from the Roman system of routes followed by couriers and marked with wooden posts. For the most part, private individuals had to find their own couriers, or bribe government messengers to carry their letters. Rich families, like the Medicis in Italy, organised their own private services.

Things changed in the 18th century, with the coming of the mail coach. John Palmer of Bath organised a service in 1784 in which mail and passengers were carried from London to Bristol by stagecoach in just 17 hours.

Letters were paid for by their recipients, not their senders, until the introduction of the postage stamp in Britain in 1840. In the golden age of the Penny Post, and the railways, letters within cities were often delivered on the day they were posted.

Postcards

The first picture postcard was engraved by Franz Rorich of Nuremberg in 1872. It showed six small views of Zurich. In Britain the picture postcard was delayed by Post Office regulations, but when these were eased in 1894 publishers immediately began to produce cards. To begin with, the message had to share the front of the card with the picture, but in 1902 the modern postcard finally emerged, with the front occupied by the picture, and the back split between message and address.

Puzzles

Verbal puzzles include acrostics, which go back to the time of the Ancient Greeks. In an acrostic, the first letter of each line of a poem, when read downwards, forms a word. Today's crosswords derive from the acrostic. Palindromes, in which the letters can be read both ways, have an equally long history. Puzzles involving manual dexterity include the cat's cradle, in which a loop of string is formed into various patterns between the two hands. The

Chinese invented the tangram, in which black paper is cut into seven geometrical shapes. These can be put together to form a vast number of silhouettes of people, boats, houses or birds.

Razor

The Ancient Egyptians used flint blades to scrape off facial hair, while in Europe by 1000 BC men were using slivers of bronze. Native Americans, by the same period, were using sharp chips of a rock called obsidian. The earliest safety razor was the invention of Jean Jacques Perret, a master cutler in Paris, in 1762 he added a wooden guard to a straight razor. The disposable safety-razor blade was the brainchild of King Camp Gillette in 1895.

'Cutthroat' razor, 19th century

Refrigeration

The use of ice to preserve food was well known from ancient times. Probably even Neanderthal Man, who lived through the glaciations, realised that meat left in the ice would remain fresh.

For many centuries there was a trade in ice, delivered daily from large underground storehouses, and used to keep food cool in ice boxes. Refrigerated and frozen food spread after mechanical refrigeration was invented in Australia and the US in the 1850s.

James Harrison, a Scot who had emigrated to Australia to edit the *Melbourne Gazette*, in 1873 served a public banquet with meat, poultry and fish, which had been frozen for six months. The domestic refrigerator was a 20th-century invention.

Roads

The greatest road-builders of the ancient world were the Romans, who brought superb surveying

and engineering skills to their construction. It was possible to cross the Roman Empire from Hadrian's Wall in northern England to the distant borders of Ethiopia, using a network of 53,000 miles (85,000 km) of main highway and 100,000 miles (160,000 km) of secondary roads.

Long before the Romans, Bronze Age traders in amber travelled along well-defined trackways between the Baltic and the Mediterranean. Farther east, there was a well-maintained system of roads between China and Persia, Syria and Asia Minor.

Road-building did not reach Roman standards again until the early 19th century, when the Scots engineer John McAdam devised a method of construction using a layer of large rocks below a layer of smaller stones, with gravel as a binding agent.

Roller skates

In 1760 Joseph Merlin, a Belgian musician, constructed a pair of skates on wheels and wore them to a masked ball in London. He glided into the ballroom playing his violin, but as he was unable to stop or change direction, he crashed into a mirror, seriously injuring himself.

In 1863 an American, James Plimpton, patented a four-wheel skate with cushioned mountings, which enabled the skater to shift his weight and to steer. By the end of the 19th century roller-skating had become a craze in America.

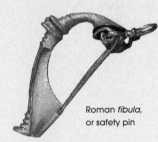

Roller skates of 1790

Rubber

The Mayas and the Aztecs of central America played games with balls made from the substance that oozed from the bark of a local tree, and waterproofed their clothing with sheets of the melted material. In 1736 a French naturalist took the substance to Europe. It was given the name 'rubber' by the British chemist Joseph Priestley in 1770, because it could be used for rubbing out pencil marks.

In 1823 Charles Macintosh made raincoats using dissolved rubber sandwiched between two layers of cloth. In 1841 Charles Goodyear vulcanised rubber, by impregnating it with sulphur, so making it stronger and more elastic.

Roman *fibula*, or safety pin

Safety pins

Bronze brooches much like today's safety pin were in use in Western Europe by around 1200 BC. Roman men and women used a *fibula*, often elaborately decorated, to fasten their cloaks and other garments.

The modern safety pin, with its coil spring and concealed point, was developed by a New Yorker, Walter Hunt, in 1849. He failed to capitalise on his invention, however, as he handed the patent over to a colleague to pay off a 15 dollar debt.

Scissors

The oldest type of scissors, consisting of two blades of bronze joined by a spring, were widely used by 5000 BC. The Ancient Romans also used pivoted scissors of bronze and iron. Scissors for domestic use became more common in the late 16th century. From the 1760s, the use of cast steel produced stronger blades.

Sewerage

The town of Mohenjo Daro, in the Indus Valley of what is now Pakistan, boasted the world's first sewerage system, in about 2500 BC. Waste from the houses was carried by clay pipes into covered channels running along the streets and discharging onto the fields outside the city.

The Romans were great sewer builders, and Rome had a system of small sewers from houses feeding into a massive one, the Cloaca Maxima, that stretched from the Forum to the Tiber. It is still in use 2500 years later. After the Roman Empire fell, sewers were neglected, resulting in epidemics. It was not until the latter half of the 19th century that the cities of Europe were provided with proper sewers, most of which are in use to this day.

Signals

The arrival of the Spanish Armada off the coast of Britain in 1588 was signalled by a series of hilltop beacon fires. A more advanced system was designed by the Frenchman Claude Chappe in 1790. His semaphore consisted of a chain of hilltop towers, equipped with wooden pivoted arms that could be placed in 196 different positions for signalling.

The first successful electric telegraph was invented in England in 1837. Laid alongside the Great Western Railway, in 1845 it was instrumental in capturing a suspected murderer.

At much the same time, the American Samuel Morse devised his code of dots and dashes, ideal for the new telegraph.

Silk

For 3000 years silk was the world's best-kept secret. Discovered by the Chinese in 2640 BC, the method of spinning the finest yarns from the cocoons of silkworms was unknown to the outside world until it was betrayed to the Japanese around AD 300.

The Chinese discovery is said to have been made in the garden of the emperor Huang-di, who had asked his wife Xi Lingshi to find out what was eating the leaves of the mulberry trees. Picking off some white worms that spun shiny cocoons, she dropped one of them by accident into warm water, then found that she could draw from it a fine filament and wind it onto reels.

Soap

A recipe from Mesopotamia dating from 3000 BC describes a cleaning solution composed of one part oil and 5.5 parts potash. The Ancient Egyptians washed with soda and scented oils, while the Greeks and Romans covered themselves with a paste of olive oil and pumice, which they removed with a *strigil*, or bronze scraper, along with the dirt and the sweat on the body.

The Gauls used cleaning pastes made from animal fat and potash to make their hair glossy, and introduced it to the Romans, who found it cured 'scrofulous sores'. Soap was not heard of again until the 10th century. By about 1250 soap-makers were established in London. Their crude product was cut from a block kept in the shop.

The first individually wrapped cakes of soap were made at Newburgh, New York, in 1830, and the first packaged soap powder appeared 15 years later.

Spinning wheel

To be useful as a continuous thread, the short fibres of wool from a sheep's fleece must be spun together. This was done from earliest times, but the first machine to speed the job was the spinning wheel, which reached Europe during the 14th century, perhaps from India.

Spinning was regarded as women's work – hence the term 'spinster'. The spinning wheel remained a vital tool until the invention of the spinning jenny in England in the 1760s. The jenny spun yarn on eight or more spindles at the same time, greatly speeding up the process.

Spirits

Alcohol was not distilled until around 1100, when the school of medicine at Salerno, in Sicily, heated wine or beer to give off vapour, which was then condensed back into liquid of greater alcoholic strength. Regarded as a medicine, it was called *aqua vitae*, `water of life', and was considered a panacea for dropsy, gout, toothache and other physical complaints, and as a preserver of youth. Distilled liquid was referred to by the Arabs as *al-kohl*, from which the word alcohol is derived. The Dutch called it *brandewijn*, 'burnt wine', the origin of the word brandy.

From the 16th century, northern Europeans distilled their own spirits, producing whisky, gin and vodka from grain, and rum from the molasses of the West Indian sugar plantations.

In 1493 a Nuremberg doctor warned brandy drinkers: `Now that everyone is in the habit of drinking aqua vitae, it is necessary to learn to drink it according to one's capacity, if one wishes to behave like a gentleman.'

Distilling whisky in the 16th century

Spoons

Primitive man ate sloppy or liquid food with spoons made of seashells, bone or baked clay. By the time of the Ancient Greeks, wooden spoons had evolved. During the Middle Ages, spoons were used during cooking for stirring and ladling, and at table for retrieving small pieces of meat from the communal dish. By the mid-17th century, the spoon had joined the knife and fork on the dining table.

Stirrups

The stirrup was first used by barefooted Hindu warriors in the late 2nd century BC. It took the form of a loop which fitted round the rider's big toe. By about AD 300 the Chinese had adapted it to take the whole width of a booted foot. Its introduction into Europe in the 8th century revolutionised the nature of warfare. Along with the saddle, it gave horsemen far greater stability, allowing them to use long, heavy lances, and hold their spears under their arm.

Sugar

India seems to have been the home of the sugar cane. As early as 1000 BC the people of the Indus Valley had devised a means of crushing the juice from the cane and boiling it to make sugar. In about 327 BC an officer who accompanied Alexander the Great to India remarked on 'a reed that yields honey without the help of bees' – honey then being the usual method of sweetening food and drink.

The cultivation of sugar cane spread westwards with the Arabs, who introduced it into southern Europe in the 8th century AD. The descendants of the Crusaders grew it in Cyprus, while the Spaniards planted it in the Canary Isles, out in the Atlantic.

Throughout the Middle Ages, however, honey remained the principal sweetener. Sugar did not come into its own until Columbus took it to the Caribbean on his second voyage in 1493. The conditions there proved ideal for it, and slaves, shipped from Africa in appalling conditions, cultivated the crop. In northern latitudes sugar remained an expensive imported luxury until in the 1740s the German chemist Andreas Marggraf found a way of making sugar from sugar beet.

Tea

Chinese legend says that in 2737 BC, while the Emperor Shen Lung was sitting by a cauldron of water boiling on a camp fire, leaves from a nearby tea plant fell into it. Shen Lung drank the aromatic water and found it delicious, and tea has been drunk ever since.

The first tea to arrive in Europe was imported by the Dutch in 1610, and tea drinking soon became popular. In 1657 it reached Britain, where the diarist Samuel Pepys drank his first cup three years later.

In the 18th century, after the family had drunk the first brew, the servants poured more hot water on the tea leaves and made a second brew. Finally, the twice-used leaves were bought from the back door by the poor.

Toothbrushes

Long before toothbrushes were invented, toothpicks were used for cleaning teeth. By 3000 BC the Sumerians were using gold toothpicks. The earliest recognisable toothbrush, with bristles set at right angles into a handle, appeared in China in 1500. In 1780 a prisoner in London's Newgate jail, William Addis, bored tiny holes into bone salvaged from prison suppers and filled them with bristles. On his release, he founded Britain's first toothbrush manufacturing firm.

Toothpicks were widely used in the Middle Ages. In Spain, young women seldom removed them from their mouths, regarding them as useful deterrents to unwanted kisses.

Toys

Ancient Egyptian craftsmen made wooden toys such as tigers with string-operated jaws. Greek and Roman children played with hobbyhorses, hoops and tops. Between Roman times and the 17th century there was little advance in toymaking. In his play *Bartholomew Fair*, written in 1614, Ben Jonson mentions miniature animals, dolls, hobbyhorses and gingerbread sold at the fair.

In the 18th century toys began to be made of metal and paper, as well as the traditional wood and earthenware. Dolls' houses and model farms became popular, as did educational toys such as pictorial alphabet cards.

The 19th century saw an enormous expansion in toy production, with musical boxes, wooden soldiers, working train models and optical gadgets added to long-established toys.

Trousers

Long before the time of Christ, tribes from central Asia had adapted long-flowing garments for riding astride a horse. The custom spread through northern Europe, and was noted by Julius Caesar when he landed in Britain in 55 BC. However, the Romans regarded trousers as fit only for barbarians and slaves, and stayed loyal to their togas, though they allowed soldiers serving in the chillier provinces to wear leather breeches.

By the 18th century the tights worn by men in medieval and Tudor times had evolved into knee breeches; and towards the end of the century loose-fitting pantaloons became popular. Modern trousers for men came into fashion during the early years of the 19th century. By the end of the century women had begun to wear divided skirts and knickerbockers for cycling and other sporting activities.

Umbrellas

The earliest umbrellas gave shelter from the sun rather than from the rain. The pharaohs of Ancient Egypt are depicted sitting beneath ceremonial umbrellas. In Ancient China, umbrellas conferred such prestige that only royalty or high officials were allowed to use them; they were made of gold

cloth and studded with gems. Roman women were probably the first to use umbrellas to keep off the rain; they preferred purple models. After Roman times, the umbrella seems to have been ignored until the 16th century, when the clergy rehabilitated it as a symbol of honour.

The first-known waterproof umbrella was made in 1637 for Louis XIII of France. Nearly a century passed before another Parisian designed the first folding umbrella. In the early 18th century umbrellas were held over people as they walked from their doors to their carriages, but it was not until 1750 that John Hanway, a London philanthropist, popularised the carrying of an umbrella, in spite of the insults of coachmen, who saw it as a threat to their trade.

By 1820 heavy oak or cane frames were replaced by whalebone and steel ribs, and 30 years later coverings of sticky oiled silk or linen gave way to cotton and alpaca. A lightweight fluted steel rib was the useful addition of Samuel Fox in 1852.

Underwear

The oldest undergarments for both sexes were briefs derived from the loincloth, with the ends drawn up between the legs. The Greeks controlled women's figures with a band of linen bound round the waist and torso. A Roman mosaic shows women athletes wearing two-piece garments very like bikinis.

During the Middle Ages both sexes and all classes wore underwear derived from the tunic – the shirt for men and the shift for women. Wealthy women wore an underbodice stiffened with paste, which was known as a 'cotte'.

In Tudor times men and women pinched in their waists with iron corsets, or wore contraptions of leather and whalebone. Again in the late 19th century women were corseted so tightly to create tight 'egg-timer' figures that it was not uncommon for them to suffer broken ribs and punctured lungs. Padding was also much used. Around 1800, women often wore

'breast-improvers', made of wax or stuffed cotton. Men with skinny calves padded out the stockings below their knee breeches.

Elizabethan women wore three layers of petticoat. The outer one was known as 'the modest', the middle one was 'the rascal', and the inner one 'the secret'.

Decorated French watch, 1660

Watch

The oldest-known watch, made in 1504 by Peter Henlein of Nuremberg, was a pocket-sized clock, driven by a coiled spring. It was not very accurate, as its single hand tended to creep ahead or lag behind.

By the 18th century Switzerland had become the centre of watchmaking. But watches remained a luxury item until 1865, when the Swiss Georges Rosskopf designed the world's first cheap pocket watch, with simpler gearing than earlier watches.

By the 1880s miniaturisation had made possible the production of cheap wristwatches. They were at first worn only by women, as men thought them effeminate. But the stigma faded when the German Navy ordered its officers to wear wristwatches, rather than fumbling in their pockets while striding around the quarter-deck.

Wigs

The men of ancient Babylon wore wigs, saving themselves hours of hairdressing time. But the heyday of the wig came 3000 years later, in the Europe of the 17th and 18th

centuries. By about 1680 it had become huge and elaborate, with a mass of intricate curls sometimes reaching the waist.

During the 18th century wigs became smaller, and were tied back. A fashionable English fop might pay up to £300, or at least £3000 in today's terms, for a wig made of female hair rather than horsehair or wool. He would comb his wig in public, sitting in a theatre box or drawing room.

Wigs were powdered with starch or flour in special 'powder closets', usually attached to the bedroom. In England, a powder tax introduced in 1798 enraged the wearers of wigs – but by then the vogue of the wig had passed.

During the 18th century, British soldiers received 1 lb (450 g) of flour each week to powder their wigs. Officers received 2 lb (900 g), as their wigs were much larger.

Windows

Although glass was discovered around 3000 BC, and was used by wealthy Romans to glaze at least some of their windows, it long remained a luxury.

The origin of the word window is 'wind eye', for that is exactly what most medieval windows were – gaps through which the wind could blow. Where windows were cut, they were provided with shutters to keep the weather out, and for security during the night.

Before glass became widespread, waxed parchment, linen or even the placenta of cattle might be stretched over a window to admit some light but exclude draughts. In Tudor England glazed windows were designed as removable casements that could be taken away if the occupants moved.

Only in the 17th century, as developing technical skills allowed larger panes of glass to be made, did glass windows become more widespread. In 1696 the English Parliament introduced a window tax, designed to hit the rich; many people saved money by blocking up windows. The tax was doubled in 1784, and abolished only in 1851.

Wine

The vine comes originally from Asia Minor, now Turkey. The Hittites, who flourished there from 2000 BC, were enthusiastic wine producers, and the Ancient Egyptians imported wine from Syria and Palestine.

The Greeks loved wine, to which they sometimes added a lump of dough kneaded with honey. The Romans drank wine at all their formal meals, normally diluting it, like the Greeks. They introduced wine to Gaul, where the vineyards of Burgundy and Bordeaux were producing wine by the 1st century AD, and to Britain.

By the 16th century wine was being drunk in Europe in large quantities, but as the casks used to hold it were not air proof, the wine had to be drunk young. Not until around 1750, with the development of the cylindrical wine bottle with a cork, did it become possible to age wines for long periods. In the 1780s, each Parisian drank on average 26 gallons (120 litres) of wine a year.

Yoke

As long ago as 300 BC, pairs of oxen joined by a yoke were pulling ploughs in Mesopotamia. The earliest yokes were fastened round the animals' necks and tied by leather straps to their horns. Ropes were attached to the ends of the yoke and draped along the animals' flanks, for pulling ploughs or sledges. Later came the yoke made from a baulk of timber, curved in the middle to fit across the animals' shoulders. This enabled them to pull loads using the full power of their shoulders, rather than that of their neck muscles alone. Yokes were not only borne by animals. Until the end of the 19th century, milkmaids in Europe wore wooden yokes to carry pails of milk from farm or field to dairy.

Milkmaid with yoke, in 1805

INDEX

Page numbers in **bold** type indicate an entire chapter or a two-page spread devoted to a subject. Page numbers in *italics* indicate an illustration. The panels provide quick reference to some of the major themes of everyday life occurring throughout the book

F

G

ACKNOWLEDGMENTS

The publishers have made every effort to trace the copyright owners of the illustrations in this book, but the nature of the material has meant this has not always been possible. Any person or organisation we have failed to reach, despite our efforts, is invited to contact the Picture Editor at Reader's Digest General Books, Berkeley Square House, Berkeley Square, London W1X 6AB.

The sources of the illustrations are listed below. Work commissioned by Reader's Digest is credited in italics. The following short forms have been used; pictures marked BA–are from the Bridgman Art Library, BL–reproduced by permission of the Board of the British Library, BM–reproduced by permission of the Trustees of the British Museum, BN–from the Service Photographique of the Bibliotheque Nationale, Paris, EA–from Ekdotike Athenon, Athens, ET–from ET Archive, London, HP - from the Hulton Picture Company, London, MH–from Michael Holford, London, ME–from the Mary Evans Picture Library, London, PN–from Peter Newark's American Pictures, Bath, RMN–photos © Réunion des Musées Nationaux, Paris, V & A–reproduced by permission of the Board of Trustees of The Victoria and Albert Museum. Abbreviations: T=Top; C=Centre; B=Bottom; R=Right; L=Left.

ANCIENT WORLDS **12** J.D. Lajoux. **13** (TR) *Malcolm Porter.* (CL) Musée de l'Homme, Paris/J. Oster. (CR) *Vana Haggerty.* (flint workers) *Ivan Lapper.* (BR) *Vana Haggerty.* **14** (TR) Jean Vertut. (BL) *Richard Bonson.* (BC) *Richard Bonson* after an illustration in *The First Civilisations*, Giovanni Casselli (Macdonald 1983). (BR) *Richard Bonson* after an illustration in *The First Civilisations*, Giovanni Casselli (Macdonald 1983). **14-15** *Ivan Lapper.* **15** (TR) *Gino D'Achille.* (L) Hans Hinz. (R) *Richard Bonson* after an illustration in *Early People* (Eyewitness Guides, Dorling Kindersley 1989). **16** (TR) Musée des Antiquities Nationale, Paris/© RMN. (BL) *Ivan Lapper.* (BC) *Richard Bonson* after an illustration in *The First Civilisations*, Giovanni Casselli (Macdonald 1983). **17** (T) Begovan Collection/Photo Jean Vertut. (L) Archiv für Kunst und Gesischte, Berlin. (R) Jean Vertut. **18** (TL) *Malcolm McGregor* after an illustration in *Excavations at Hacilar*, James Mellaart (Edinburgh University Press 1970). (B) *Richard Bonson.* **19** (R) *Richard Bonson.* (C) *Richard Bonson.* (BR) *Richard Bonson.* **20** Erich Lessing/Magnum. **21** (TL) *Richard Bonson.* (TR) *Malcolm Porter.* (C) Emmett Bright. (R) Museum of London. (B) MH. **22** (TL) From *The Emergence of Man; The First Cities* © 1973 Time-Life Books Inc/Aldo Durrazzi. (C) *Malcolm McGregor.* **23** (strainer) *Edward Williams*/Ashmolean Museum, Oxford. (L) *Edward Williams.* (TR) BM. (C) *Richard Bonson.* (BR) *Gino D'Achille.* **24** (L) Claus Hansman, Munich. (R) *Steve Smith.* **25** (TR) Gilgamesh, Musée du Louvre, Paris/© RMN. (BC) Hirmer Verlag, Munich. (CR) *Richard Bonson.* (BR) BM. **26** (T) *Ivan Lapper.* (B) *Edward Williams* after an illustration in *Further Excavations at Mohenjo-Daro;* E. MacKay (Archaeological Survey of India). **27** (TR) *Edward Williams* after an illustration in *Further Excavations at Mohenjo-Daro;* E. MacKay (Archaeological Survey of India). (BL) National Museum Delhi. (BC) *Edward Williams* after an illustration in *Further Excavations at Mohenjo-Daro;* E. MacKay (Archaeological Survey of India). **28** Roger Wood. **29** (TR) *Malcolm Porter.* (L) BM. (BR) BN/Librairie Hachette. (boat) MH. **30** (TL) BM. (harvest) BM copy by N. De Garis Davies. (oxen) MH. (B) BM. **31** (T) Musée Guimet, Paris/Librairie Hachette. (CL) Erich Lessing/Magnum. (B) BM. (C) BM. **32** (TR) Musée du Louvre, Paris/© RMN. (BL) Librairie Hachette. (earring) BM. (CR) *Richard Bonson*/BM. **33** (C) MH. (BL) MH. (BR) *Richard Bonson*/BM. (sandals) BM. **34** (TL) *Brian Delf* after an illustration in *Rapport sur le Fouilles de Deir el Medinah*, B. Bruyere (Cairo 1939). (C) *Richard Bonson* after an illustration in *Ancient Egypt* (Eyewitness Guides, Dorling Kindersley 1990). (B) MH. **35** (TL) Egypt Exploration Society. (pigments) BM. (CL) BM. (B) BM. **36** (TL) BM. (B) BM. (C) *Richard Bonson* after an illustration in *Ancient Egypt* (Eyewitness Guides, Dorling Kindersley 1990). **37** (TL) *Richard Bonson.* (CR) MH. (B) BM. **38** (T) BM. (B) BM. **38-39** (T) BM. (B) MH. **39** (BR) BM. **40** (T) F.L. Kennet/Robert Harding, George Rainbird collection. (L) Erich Lessing/Magnum. **40** (B) *Gino D'Achille.* **40-41** BM. **41** (C) *Richard Bonson.* (CL) *Richard Bonson.* (R) BM. **42** EA. **43** (TR) *Malcolm Porter.* (CL) EA. (CR) *Richard Bonson*/EA. (vase) *Richard Bonson*/Heraklion Museum. (BL) EA. (BR) EA. **44** (L) *Richard Bonson* after an illustration in *The First Civilisations*, Giovanni Casselli (Macdonald 1983). (R) *Richard Bonson.* **44-45** *Ivan Lapper.* **45** (L) EA. (C) *Richard Bonson.* (ewer) EA. (CR) C.M. Dixon. (BC) *Richard Bonson* after an illustration in *Gournia* (Boyd-Hawes 1908). (BR) *Richard Bonson.* **46** *Richard Bonson*/EA. **46-47** EA. **47** (TR) EA. (CL) EA. (C) EA. (CR) EA. (B) EA. **48** (T) By permission of the artist, Alton S. Toby. (C) EA. (BC) EA. (BR) *Richard Bonson.* **49** (TL) *Richard Bonson.* (BL) Alison Frantz, Dept of Classics, University of Cincinnati. (BC) *Luise Roberts.* (margin) *Luise Roberts.* (BR) *Gino D'Achille.* **50** Oriental Institute, University of Chicago. **51** (TL) *Richard Bonson*/Erich Lessing/Magnum. (TR) *Malcolm Porter.* (BC) Mansell Collection, London. (BR) Musée du Louvre, Paris. **52** (C) *Steve Smith.* (BR) ET. **52-53** BL. **53** (CL) Erich Lessing/Magnum. (BL) Sonia Halliday. **54** (TL) Woodfin Camp Assoc./Nathan Benn. (BL) 'La Filleuse', Musée du Louvre, Paris/© RMN - Larrieu. **55** (T) Grose Thurston Partnership. (C) *Edward Williams*/Israel Museum, Jerusalem/D. Harris. (CR) Israel Museum, Jerusalem/D. Harris. (BR) Erich Lessing/Magnum. **56** (T) ET. (L) Musée du Louvre, Paris/© RMN. **56-57** Musée du Louvre, Paris/© RMN. **57** (TR) MH. (BR) BM. (BC) *Richard Bonson.* **58** BM. **58-59** BM. **59** (TR) *Edward Williams*/MH. (CR) *Gino D'Achille.* (BR) Reader's Digest. **60-61** *Ivan Lapper.* **61** (TL) Erich Lessing/Magnum. (BR) MH. **62** (L) Erich Lessing/Magnum. (R) *Terence Dalley.* **63** (TL) Musée du Louvre, Paris/© RMN. (C) *Gino D'Achille.* (BR) William MacQuitty. **64** Courtesy of the Cultural Relics Bureau, Beijing and the Metropolitan Museum of Art, New York. **65** (TL) Institute of History and Philology, Academia Sinica, Taipei. (TR) *Malcolm Porter.* (C) William Macquitty. (BR) Andromeda. **66** (TL) Royal Ontario Museum. (TR) BM. (C) Wan-Go H.C. Weng/Ezekiel Schloss Collection. **67** (TR) Royal Ontario Museum. (BL) Wan-Go H.C. Weng/Nelson-Atkins Museum of Art. (C) Courtesy Museum of Fine Arts, Boston, Denman Waldo Ross Collection. (BR) (both) *Richard Bonson*/BM. **68** (T) Courtesy Ministry of Culture, Beijing and the Shaanxi Archaeological Corporation, Shaanxi. (C) *Richard Bonson* after an illustration in *Science and Civilisation in China*, Joseph Needham (Cambridge University Press 1965). **68-69** St Louis Art Museum. **69** (T) Andromeda. (CL) Society for Anglo-Chinese Understanding. (CR) Pitt Rivers Museum, Oxford. **70** (L) Institute of History and Philology, Academia Sinica, Taipei. (BC) Private Collection. **70-71** Robert Harding Picture Library. **71** (TC) *Luise Roberts.* (C) Courtesy Museum of Fine Arts, Boston, Archibald Gary Coolidge Fund. (BL) from *A History of Far Eastern Art*, Sherman Lee (Abrams). (BC) Andromeda. (R) M.H. Hackforth-Jones/Robert Harding Picture Library. **72** Courtesy of Museum of Fine Arts, Boston, Francis Bartlett Fund. **73** (TR) *Malcolm Porter.* (RC) *Richard Bonson.* (BL) Mansell Collection. (Greek letters) *Luise Roberts.* (BR) Robert Harding Picture Library. **74** (L) Bildarchiv für Preussischer Kulturbesitz. (TR) Ancient Art & Architecture Collection. (BL) *Gino D'Achille.* **74-75** *Ivan Lapper.* **75** (TR) J. Pierpont Morgan Collection © Wadsworth Atheneum. **76** (TL) *Grose Thurston Partnership.* (C) MH. (BC) *Richard Bonson*/BM. (BC) BM. (BR) *Richard Bonson*/BM. (potty in use) BM. **77** (L) *Edward Williams.* (CL) Stadtische Museum, Frankfurt. (BC) Museo Archeologico Nazionale, Taranto/Frederico Garolla. (R) Courtesy of Museum of Fine Arts, Boston. H.L. Pierce Fund. **78** (TL) L.A. East. (BR) Musée du Louvre, Paris/© RMN. **78-79** BN. **79** (BC) Museo Mandralisca/Scala. (BR) Ashmolean Museum, Oxford. **80** (T) *Richard Bonson* after an illustration in *The Horizon Book of Ancient Greece* (American Heritage 1965). (BL) Bibliotheque Nationale (Paris). **80-81** BM. **81** (TR) EA. (BR) *Edward Williams*/EA. (Hippocrates) Museo Ostiense/Sergio Rossi. **82** (C) Mansell Collection. (BL) Fitzwilliam Museum, Cambridge. (BR) *Richard Bonson.* **83** (BL) The Metropolitan Museum of Art, Gift of John D. Rockefeller Jr. 1932. (BC) BM. (TR) EA. (BR) Staatliche Museum, Berlin. (CR) *Ivan Lapper.* **84** (TC) BM. (BL) *Richard Bonson.* (BC) Martin von Wagner Museum, University of Wuerzburg photo/K. Oerhlein. (BR) *Richard Bonson.* **85** (TL) Ashmolean Museum, Oxford. (string instruments) *Edward Williams.* (TR) BM. (lyre player) Musée du Louvre, Paris/© RMN. (BR) BM. **86** Giraudon. **87** (TR) *Malcolm Porter.* (C) Leonard von Matt. (RC) Brian Brake/John Hillelson Agency. (BL) Erich Lessing/Magnum. (BC) Vatican Museo Greg. Profano, Rome/P. Zigrossi. **88** (TL) Mauro Pucciarelli. (TR) *Edward Williams*/Museum of London. (C) *Steve Smith.* (lamp) Peter Clayton. (god) MH. (shrine) Scala. **89** (TL) Ancient Art & Architecture Collection. (TR) G. Dagli Orti. (C) *Edward Williams*/(adults) Josephine Powell/(child) after an illustration in *Ancient Rome* (Eyewitness Guides, Dorling Kindersley 1990). (BL) Museum of London. (BC) G. Dagli Orti. (BR) Erich Lessing/Magnum. **90** (TL) BM. (TC) BM. (BR) Giraudon. **90-91** *Edward Williams*/Musée du Louvre, Paris. **91** (TL) Giraudon. (TR) Scala. (CR) V & A. (BR) Mansell Collection. **92** (T) Musei Vaticani, Rome/Icona. (B) C.M. Dixon. **93** (TL) *Richard Bonson* after an illustration in *Roman Family Life*, P. Hodge (Longman). (TC) *Gino D'Achille.* (TR) C.M. Dixon. (strigils & dice) *Edward Williams.* (C) G. Dagli Orti. (CR) Neil Holmes. (BR) BM. **94** (TR) Scala. (CL) L.A. East. (C) Musée du Petit Palais, Paris. (CR) BM. **95** (T) *Ivan Lapper.* (CL) St Germain-en-laye/© RMN. (BL) Musées Departementaux de la Seine-Maritime/Francois Dugue. (BC) Archivi Alinari. **96** (C) Museum of London. (BL) Erich Lessing/Magnum. (BC) Josse/Librairie Hachette. **96-97** Brian Brake/John Hillelson. **97** (plough) Ancient Art & Architecture Collection. (sickle) BM. (C) C.M. Dixon. (BL) Erich Lessing/Magnum. (BR) *Edward Williams.* **98** (TL) Scala. (C) MH. (spear, sandal, purse) *Edward Williams* after an illustration in *Ancient Rome* (Eyewitness Guides, Dorling Kindersley 1990). (BR) G.M. Kam/Rijksmuseum, Nijmegen. **98-99** Scala. **99** (TR) Museum of London/Woodmansterne. **100** (TL) Bad Kreuznach Museum. (C) Roger Wood. (B) BM. **100-101** Roger Wood. **101** (TC) BM. (TR) Erich Lessing/Magnum. (C) Musei Capitolini, Rome/Scala. (BR) (both) BM. **102** (dancer) Musée Archeologique, Orleans/Bulloz. **103** (L) *Richard Bonson* after an illustration in *The Celtic World*, Barry Cunliffe. (TR) *Malcolm Porter.* (C) Silkeborg Museum/Lars Bay. (BR) Landesmuseum Joanneum. **104** (L) BM. (C) BM. (R) BM. **104-105** *Richard Bonson.* **105** (TR) Georg Gerster/John Hillelson Agency. (C) *Richard Bonson*/BM. (BR) Erich Lessing/Magnum. (CR) Bern History Museum/S. Rebsamen. **106** (T) *Malcolm McGregor.* (BL) (all) Museum of London. **106-107** *Richard Bonson*/National Museum of Wales. **107** (TR) BM. (TL) *Richard Bonson.* (CR) *Richard Bonson.* (BR) BM. **108** BM. **109** (TL) Werner Forman Archive. (TR) Lee Boltin. (BC) *Gino D'Achille.* (BR) Lee Boltin.

OLD WORLDS, NEW WORLDS **112** Hans Hinz. **113** (TR) *Malcolm Porter.* (coins) *Richard Bonson*/BM. (BR) Werner Forman Archive. (BC) BM. **114** (TL) Werner Forman Archive. (B) *Terence Dalley* after original drawings by Rowland Mainstone in his *Hagia Sophia* (Thames and Hudson 1988). **115** (TC) Scala. (C) (all) Werner Forman Archive. (BC) Werner Forman Archive. (BR) Werner Forman Archive. **116** Photo, Studio Rapuzzi. **116-117** Geoffrey House. **117** BN. **118** Biblioteca Nacional, Madrid (Vit 26-2 54v). **119** (TL) *Gino D'Achille.* (TR) Biblioteca Nacional, Madrid (Vit 26-2 157va). (BC) Rapho. **120** BM. **121** (TL) Ashmolean Museum, Oxford. (TR) *Malcolm Porter.* (CR) Keith Morris. (BL) BL (Add ms 39942 f2). (BC) MH. **122** (TC) (coin) L.A. East. (TC) (die) *Richard Bonson*/York Archaeological Trust. (TR) Jim Hancock. (B) Colour Centre Slides. **123** (TC) *Richard Bonson* after an illustration in *Early Christian Times*, Charles Thomas (Thames and Hudson). (TR) Patrick Thurston. (counter) Robert Micklewright. (C) (both) Robert Micklewright. **124** (T) Anthony Weir/Janet and Colin Bord. (BL) Scala. **124-125** Eric Meacher. **125** (TL) *Richard Bonson.* (TR) Scala. (BL) Librairie Hachette/BN. (BR) Trinity College, Dublin (Ms. 58 f.5r). **126** (T) BN. (C) Benediktinerstift, St Paul. (horn) Artephot/Brumaire - C.D.R.I. (BR) Österreich Nationalbibliothek, Vienna (Ms Salz. 9 Jh.Cod.387 f90v). **127** (TL) Archiv des Domstifts, Merseberg (Ms 136 fol.16). (TC) Shiftsbibliothek St Gallen (Cod. 22 S141). (C) Bildarchiv Preussischer Kulturbesitz. (R) Kunsthistorisches Museum, Vienna. **128** (TC) Universitetets Oldsaksamling, Oslo/Ove Holst. (C) *Gino D'Achille.* (BL) Universitetets Oldsaksamling, Olso/Eivik I. Johnson. (weapons) *Edward Williams.* **128-129** (T) Universitetets Oldsaksamling, Olso. (B) *Edward Williams* after an illustration in *The Ship*, Bjorn Landstrom (Allen and Unwin). **129** (TL) © The Pierpoint Morgan Library 1991 (Ms.M.736 f.9v). (BC) National Museum, Reykjavic. (BR) ATA Stockholm/S. Hallgren, SHM. **130** (C) Patrick Thurston. (BR) Arhus University Museum, Moesgard. (BC) Patrick Thurston. **130-131** *Ivan Lapper.* **131** (TR) National Museum of Ireland. (glass & bowl) *Edward Williams*/Kulturan, Lund. (lamp) Universitetets Oldsaksamling, Olso/Ove Holst. (BR) Lund Historiska Museum/Kulturen/Lars Westrup. **132** (coins) BM. (BL) *Gino D'Achille.* (BR) ATA Stockholm. **132-133** (scales) Historisk Museum, Bergen/Ann-Mari Olsen. (bag) Historisk Museum, Bergen/Ann-Mari Olsen. **133** (TR) Christian Krohg 'Leif Eiriksson discovers America' 1893, oil on canvas, 313x470cm NG 558/photo Jacques Lathion, © Nasjonalgalleriet, Oslo. (CR) Frances Lincoln/Lennart Nilsen. (BR) Tromso Museum. **134-135** El Escorial, Madrid/MAS. **135** (TC) L.A. East. (TC) (drawn coins) *Richard Bonson*/BM. (moneylenders) E.T. Archive/BL. (TR) *Malcolm Porter.* (BR) G. Dagli Orti. **136** V & A. **136-137** MH. **137** (CR) Society of Antiquaries, London. (C) Public Record Office, London. (B) *Richard Bonson.* **138** (TR) Dominique Martinez, Strasbourg. (BL) ET. **139** (TL) Giraudon. (C) Stadtmuseum, Munich/Claus Hansmann. (BR) *Ivan Lapper.* **140** (TC) Public Record Office, London. (TR) BN. (B) BN (Ms Arsenal 5062/0149). **141** (TL) Museo Civico Medievale, Bologna (Ms 93f.1). (CR) BN/Librairie Hachette. (BR) Bibliotheque St Genevieve, Paris/BA. **142** (TL) BN (Ms 5.7 f.220v). (TR) Bodleian Library, Oxford (Ms. Douce 208). (BL) *Steve Smith.* (CR) The Museum of London. **142-143** *Richard Bonson.* **143** (TL) © The Pierpont Morgan Library 1991 (M.399 f 2v). (BR) BN. **144** (TL) BL. (BR) Österreische Nationalbibliothek, Vienna. **145** (TR) BN. (CR) BN. (BL) MH. (BR) Science Museum, London. **146** (TR) Musée du Louvre, Paris/© RMN. (BL) Universitat Bibliotek, Heidelberg (Ms Manesse Cod. 848 f 149). **146-147** Universitat Bibliotek, Heidelberg (Ms Manesse Cod. 848 f 52r). **147** (TC) & (TR) Universitat Bibliotek, Heidelberg (Ms Manesse Cod. f 395 & f 256 v). (BR) *Gino D'Achille.* **148** (TL) © The Pierpont Morgan Library 1991 (Ms. 638 f28). (B) © The Pierpont Morgan Library 1991 (Ms. 638 f23). **149** (TR) HP. (BC) *Richard Bonson.* (BC) The Metropolitan Museum of Art, Rogers Fund, 1925. (BC) (halberd) *Richard Bonson.* (BR) Musée de L'Armée, Paris. **150** (C) *Sarah Fox-Davies.* (CR) *Peter Ward.* (BL) Bibliotheque Royale, Brussels. **150-151** (T) Private Collection. (B) ME. **151** (T) BN. (BR) Weidenfeld Archives/Bibliotheque Royale, Brussels. (BC) BL. **152** (TL) MH. (TR) Bodleian Library, Oxford. (CR) Bibliotheque Saint-Genevieve (Ms 143)/Studio Ethel. (BR) Bibliotheque de Dijon (Ms 170 f 59r). **153** (TL) BL (Ms Roy. 10 E.IV f 187r). (TR) BL (Ms Add 39843 f 6v). (BL) Royal Commission for Historic Monuments. (BR) *Gino D'Achille.* **154** (T) Southampton City Museums. (BL) BL (Ms Add. 42130 f 186v). (BR) The Mansell Collection. **155** (TR) Scala. (CR) David Lees. (BR) Giovanni Bellini 'The Assassination of St Peter' (detail) The National Gallery, London. **156** HP. **157** (TL) Roger Wood. (TR) *Malcolm Porter.* (CR) BN (Ms. 5847 f 94v). (BC) BN (Ms. Arabe 385 f 123v). **158** (TL) BN (Ms. 495 Arabe 5847 f 120v). (BL) BN (Ms. Arabe 5867 f 11v). (C) Courtesy of the Freer Gallery of Art, Smithsonian Institution, Washington D.C. **158-159** *Ivan Lapper.* **159** (TR) BN (Ms 5847 f 105). (BR) The Metropolitan Museum of Art, Bequest of Horace Havemeyer, 1956. The H.O. Havemeyer Collection (56.185.22). **160** (TL) BN (Ms. Arabe 5847 f 5v). (BL) MH. (BR) MH. **161** (TR) BN (Ms. Arabe 2964 f 22). (C) Horniman Museum/Godfrey New. (CR) BN (Ms. Arabe 2953 f 79v). (BR) *Luise Roberts.* **162** (T) BN (Ms. FR 5594 f 213). (C) *Richard Bonson*/Public Record Office, London. (BL) BN (Ms. Fr. 5594 f. 213). **162-163** BN. **163** (TR) Caisse Nationale de Monuments Historiques, Paris. (C) (both) L.A. East. (BR) Topkapi Museum, Istanbul. **164** BN. **164-165** Julia Temple/Susan Griggs. **165** (TL) BN (Ms Fr 2630 f 22v). (L) Mansell Collection. (C) Museo del Ejercito. **166** (T) Victor Englebert/Susan Griggs. (BL) (shells & salt) Pitt Rivers Museum, Oxford. (BL) (drawings) *Richard Bonson*/Royal Museum of Central Africa, Brussels. **166-167** BN (Ms. Arabe 5847 f 143). **167** (TC) *Richard Bonson*/Professor Thurston Shaw. (TR) BL (Ms. Or. 718 127v). (BC) BM, Department of Ethnography. (BR) *Gino D'Achille.* **168** Red Fort Museum, Delhi/Laurie Platt Winfrey, Inc. **169** (TC) Courtesy of the Cultural Relic Publishing Company, Beijing. (TR) *Malcolm Porter.* (BC) Erich Lessing/Magnum. (BR) Sonia Halliday. **170** (TL) *Richard Bonson.* (C) Roland and Sabrina Michaud/John Hillelson. **170-171** (T) Topkapi Museum, Istanbul. (B) V & A. **171** BM. **172** (C) *Richard Bonson.* (BR) Chester Beatty Library, Dublin/BA. **172-173** (BL) (Ms. Add 25900 231v). **173** (TR) Topkapi Museum, Istanbul. (CR) Gabriele Mandel University Selcukide Konya/Mahmed Khan Foundation. **174** Reproduced by courtesy of the Trustees of the Chester Beatty Library, Dublin (Ms. No439 f 9). **175** (TR) BL/Laurie Platt Winfrey, Inc. (CR) Historisches Museen, Vienna. (BL) BA. (ewer) *Richard Bonson*/John Carswell. (BR) Sonia Halliday.

176 (TR) Victoria & Albert Museum/BA. (spinning & weaving) New York Public Library. (BL) Courtesy Museum of Fine Arts, Boston. (BR) Aldus Archive, Syndication International. **177** (L) BM. (TR) William Macquitty. (CR) By Permission of The Board of Trustees of the Royal Armouries/Godfrey New. (BC) New York Public Library, Spencer Collection. **178** (TL) Prince of Wales Museum, Bombay/Laurie Platt Winfrey, Inc. (BL) BL (Johnson Album XIII f 6 extra 299). **178-179** Reproduced by courtesy of the Trustees of the Chester Beatty Library, Dublin. **179** (TL) V & A. (TR) Erik Pelham/The National Trust. (BR) Bodleian Library, Oxford. **180** Adam Woolfitt/Susan Griggs. **181** (T) Scala. (BR) Scala. **182** (TL) From *The Age of the Renaissance* (Thames and Hudson, London). (coins) *L.A. East.* (B) Scala. **183** (TR) BL (Add 24189 f16). (CR) V & A. (L) Scala. (BC) *Richard Bonson.* **184** (T) *Gino D'Achille.* **184-185** Roma, Galleria Doria Pamphili/photo A. De Luca. **185** (TL) Gabinetto Nazionale delle Stampe, Rome. (BL) Scala. (BR) *Edward Williams* after an original in the Metropolitan Museum of Art, New York. **186** (T) V & A. (BL) V & A. (BR) Scala. **187** (TL) BL. (C) Scala. (BR) Scala. **188** (T) HP. (C) Bodleian Library, Oxford. (BR) BL. **188-189** Ambrosius Holbein 'Aushangeschild eines Schulmeisters', Oeffentliche Kunstsammlung, Kunstmuseum, Basel. **189** (T) Jon Stephan van Calcar 'Von des menschen cörpers Anatomey', woodcut, title page, Oeffentliche Kunstsammlung, Kupferstich Kabinett, Basel. (C) Scala. (BR) Herzog Anton Ulrich-Museum/Keiser1986. **190** (TL) The *Grose Thurston Partnership.* (TR) *Richard Bonson.* (C) BM. (B) Museum Boymans-Van Beuningen, Rotterdam/BA. **191** (C) Giraudon Paris/BN. (BR) Kunsthistorisches Museum, Vienna. **192** (R) Bibliotheque Publique et Universitaire, Geneva/Jean Arlaud. (L) Kunsthistorisches Museum, Vienna/BA. **193** (T) Musée Historique de la Reformation, Geneva. (B) Kunsthistorisches Museum, Vienna/BA. **194** (TR) MH. (BL) (drawings) *Edward Williams.* (BL) (photograph) *Adam Woolfit.* **194-195** *Richard Bonson.* **195** (T) Mansell Collection. (L) MH. (BR) Syndication International/Aldus Archive. **196** MH. **197** (TR) *Malcolm Porter.* (figure) MH. (disc) MH. (BL) BM. (BC) BM. (BR) © Pierpont Morgan Library, New York 1991 (MA 3900, f 100). **198** (T) Museum für Volkerkunde, Basel/Werner Forman Archive. (B) Bibliotheca Nazionale, Florence/Scala. **198-199** BM Department of Ethnography. **199** (TR) Coyote feathered shield, gift to Cortes for the Bishop of Palencia not for the King of Spain/Museum für Volkerkunde, Vienna. (vessels) *Edward Williams*/Werner Forman Archive. (BL) *Luise Roberts* after an illustration in *The Aztecs of Mexico*, G.C. Valliant (Pelican). (BR) Lee Boltin. **200** (TL) MH. (R) Lee Boltin. (BC) Christopher Donnan. **201** (TL) Aldus Archive, Syndication International. (TR) Royal Library Copenhagen. (quipu) *Edward Williams*/American Museum of Natural History. (CL) Royal Library Copenhagen. (CR) Museum für Volkekunde, Berlin. (BR) South American Pictures. **202** (T) *Steve Smith* after an illustration in *America's Fascinating Indian Heritage* (Reader's Digest 1978). (BL) *Gino D'Achille*/National Anthropological Archives, Smithsonian Institute, Washington. (BC) Bradford Collection, gift of W.R. Coe Foundation/Werner Forman Archive. (BR) Buffalo Bill Historical Center/Werner Forman Archive. **202-203** (T) Museum für Völkerkunde, Berlin/Werner Forman Archive. (B) (bow) Werner Forman Archive. **203** (TR) MH. (BL) New York Public Library, Rare Book Division. (BC) Museum für Volkerkunde, Berlin/Werner Forman Archive. (BR) *Edward Williams*/Peabody Museum, Harvard University. **204** (TL) Library of Congress, Washington. (TR) BL (De Bry 'America' XIII). **204-205** (T) Montreal Military & Maritime Museum. (B) C. Smyth, 'Indians Bartering', Public Archives of Canada (c-1026). **205** (BL) Royal Ontario Museum. (BR) Buffalo Bill Historical Center, Cody, WY, Gift of Mrs Karl Frank. **206** (T) Maryland Historical Society. (CR) ME. (BR) Aldus Collection, Syndication International. **206-207** Private Collection. **207** (CR) CAA/Gibbes Museum of Art. (BR) 'Sea Captains Carousing in Surinam' by John Greenwood, Saint Louis Art Museum. **208** (TL) The Granger Collection. (TR) BL (De Bry 'America' XIII). (B) (both) ME. **209** (TR) *Ivan Lapper.* (BR) (all) Reproduced by permission of the American Museum in Britain, Bath. **210** Collection of the National Palace Museum, Taiwan. **211** (TC) Metropolitan Museum of Art, New York. Gift of Heber R. Bishop 1902 (02.18.385). (TR) *Malcolm Porter.* (B) Courtesy of Beijing Museum. **212** (TL) BL. **212-213** Metropolitan Museum of Art, New York. Fletcher Fund gift of A.W. Baha 1947 (47.18.50). **213** (TL) Courtesy Department of Library Services, American Museum of Natural History, Photo Julius (314313). (TR) Courtesy of the Freer Gallery of Art, Smithsonian Institute, Washington. (C) Percival David Foundation. (CR) Percival David Foundation. (bowl) *Richard Bonson*/Percival David Foundation. **214** (TL) *W.M. Cai.* (TR) *W.M. Cai.* (CL) BM. (C) Percival David Foundation. (BL) Werner Forman Archive. (BR) Ch'en Chih-Mai, *Chinese Calligraphers and their Art* (Melbourne University Press). **215** (TR) Wan-Go H.C. Weng. (CR) Percival David Foundation. (BL) Collection of the Nelson-Atkins Museum of Art. (BR) (plate) *Richard Bonson*/Percival David Foundation. (BR) Percival David Foundation. **216** (TL) Michael Nichols/Magnum. **216-217** Zhu Junbi, Chinese (attrib. to) 'Street Scenes in Times of Peace' (Taiping fenghui tu), handscroll, ink and colour on paper, Ming, 15th-16th centuries, 26 x 790 cm, Kate S. Buckingham Fund, 1952.8 detail: view #14; The puppet show © 1991 The Art Institute of Chicago, All rights Reserved. **217** (BR) Private Collection. **218** (C) *Richard Bonson.* (TR) V & A/Ian Thomas. (BL) James A. Michener Collection, Honolulu Academy of Arts, Hawaii. (BR) Okura Shukokan Museum/Laurie Platt Winfrey. **218-219** Christie's Colour Library. **219** (TR) Werner Forman Archive. (BR) Kennin-Ji Temple, Kyoto, Japan. **220** (C) *Richard Bonson.* **220-221** (T) Narai-Ji, Kyoto National Museum/Andromeda. (B) Local History Museum, Tokyo/International Society for Educational Information. **221** (TC) National Museum, Tokyo. (CR) Werner J. Koppitz Collection/Ernest Coppolino. (plate & decanter) Munsterberg Collection, New York. (BR) *Richard Bonson*/Munsterberg Collection, New York. **222** (TR) Hikone Castle Museum/Andromeda. (C) Kunitochi College of Music. (BR) Suntori Museum of Art, Tokyo. **223** (TR) Kiyomizudera Temple, Kyoto. (mask) Zefa/Orion. (CR) L.J. Anderson Collection/Werner Forman Archive. (BL) MH. **224** Private Collection. **225** (T) ME. (TR) *Malcolm Porter.* (B) Prado, Madrid/BA. **226** Kunsthistorisches Museum, Vienna. **226-227** Aldus Archive, Syndication International/Rijksmuseum, Amsterdam. **227** (C) Aldus Archive, Syndication International. (BL) Aldus Archive/Syndication International/Rijksmuseum, Amsterdam. **228** (T) Prado, Madrid. (B) Mansell Collection. **229** (TL) & (C) BL. (BL) Prado, Madrid/MAS. (coin) *L.A. East.* (TR) MH/Gerry Clyde. **230** (T) Fotomas Index. (BL) *Ivan Lapper.* **231** (TR) *Brian Delf.* (BL) *The Accomplisht Lady's Delight*, 1677. (C) Museum of London. (CR) *Richard Bonson.* **232** (T) Canaletto 'St Paul's and the Thames from Somerset House' (detail) Royal Collection, St James's Palace © Her Majesty the Queen. (BL) Museum of London. (BR) Museum of London. **233** (TL) HP. (CL) Weidenfeld Archives. (BR) (all) Museum of London. **234** (BL) *Richard Bonson*/Bolton Museum and Art Gallery. (BC) Museum of Rural Life, Reading. **234-235** Arthur Lockwood. **235** (TR) HP. (BL) BL (W.H. Pyne 'Microcosm' 1802). **236** (BL) Mansell Collection. **236-237** (pikemen) Board of Trustees of the Royal Armouries/Godfrey New. (musket) Board of Trustees of the Royal Armouries/Godfrey New. **237** (TR) National Gallery, London/BA. (B) BM. **238** (B) Van der Meulen 'Versailles under Construction' (detail) Royal Collection, St James's Palace © Her Majesty the Queen. **238-239** Versailles/RMN. **239** (L) BN/Bulloz. (CR) Bulloz. (BC) BN. **240** (TL) Tate Gallery, London/BA. (CR) ET. (B) Jean-Loup Charmet, Paris. **240-241** Museum of the History of Science, Oxford. **241** (T) Ashmolean Museum, Oxford. (C) Archiv für Kunst und Geschichte, Berlin. (BR) V & A. **242** (TL) Holkham Hall, Norfolk/BA. (C) Society of Apothecaries/Godfrey New. (books) *David Sheppard.* (BR) Canaletto, 'Rome', Royal Collection, St James's Palace © Her Majesty the Queen. **243** (TL) Towneley Hall Art Gallery and Museum, Burnley/Bridgeman Art Library. (TC) V & A. (BR) Fotomas Index. **244** (BL) (J. Atkinson 'Manners and Customs of the Russians' 1804). **245** (all) BL. (TR) *Malcolm Porter.* **246** (C) *Richard Bonson*/(bowl) Erich Lessing, Magnum /(mug) State Historical Museum, Moscow. (BR) BL. **246-247** A. Vasnetsov/Novosti. **247** (R) Loukomski 'La Vie et les Moeurs en Russie'. (BL) Weidenfeld Archives. **248** (TL) *Brian Delf.* (BL) MH. (BC) MH. **248-249** MH. **249** (TR) *Richard Bonson*/Novosti. (BR) BL. **250** (TL) & (TR) BL. (C) Horniman Museum/Godfrey New. **250-251** BL. **251** BL.

THE MODERN WORLD **254** BN/Bulloz. **255** (maps) *Malcolm Porter.* (flag) *Edward Williams.* (CR) Bulloz. (BL) Fred Sieb. (B) Wellcome Institute. **256** (T) National Army Museum, London. (CR) *Richard Bonson*/Wallis and Wallis Military Heritage Museum, Lewes. **257** (TR) Library Company of Philadelphia. (C) Culver. (BL) Library of Congress, Washington. (BR) Courtesy of the John Carter Brown Library at Brown University. **258** (TR) ME. (C) *Edward Williams.* (BL) Jean-Loup Charmet, Paris. **258-259** (T) *Richard Bonson.* (B) BM. **259** (TL) HP. (C) BN. (CR) *Richard Bonson*/Musée de Mognenan, Portets. (BR) Jean-Loup Charmet, Paris. **260** (TL) Historisches Museum, Frankfurt. (C) V & A. (battle) Musée de l'Armée, Paris. (B) ME. **261** (TR) Anne S.K. Brown Military Collection, Brown University Library. (C) ME. **260-261** Chateau de Versailles, Paris/BA. **262** (TL) National Maritime Museum, Greenwich. (BL) ET. (L) National Maritime Museum, Greenwich. **262-263** *Richard Bonson*/Pitkin Pictorials. **263** (TR) National Maritime Museum, Greenwich. (C) National Maritime Museum, Greenwich. (barrel) *Richard Bonson*/Pitkin Pictorials. **264** Ann Ronan Picture Library. **265** (T) Ann Ronan Picture Library. (C) National Trust. (CR) Science Museum, London. (BR) BM. **266** (T) BM. (BL) Fine Art Photographic Library. (stools) *Edward Williams*/Wenderton Antiques. **266-267** (T) *Richard Bonson.* (B) ET. **267** (TC) Lincoln Museum/ET. (all mono drawings) *Robert Micklewright.* (BR) Museum of Rural Life, Reading. **268** (TL) *Richard Bonson.* (TR) Welsh Industrial & Maritime Museum. (C) Ironbridge Gorge Museum Trust. (B) Pehr Hillström, 'In The Foundry', National Museum, Stockholm/Statens Konstmuseer. **269** (C) Ironbridge Gorge Museum Trust. (BL) ET. (BC) MH. (BR) Henry Perlee Parker, 'Miners Playing Quoits', Courtesy Tyne & Wear Museums. **270** (R) *Edward Williams.* (token) *L.A. East.* (BL) Manchester City Art Gallery. **270-271** Sheffield City Museum. **271** (TR) Mansell Collection. (BL) Ann Ronan Picture Library. (BC) MH. (BR) *Martin Cameron.* **272** (BL) ME. (C) *Patrick Thurston.* **272-273** Royal Holloway & New Bedford College, Surrey/BA. **273** (TR) Roger Viollet. (CL) *Edward Williams.* (C) *Patrick Thurston*/Railway Museum, York. (CR) *Edward Williams.* (BR) Ann Ronan Picture Library. **274** (BL) Brunel University Library. (BC) TUC Library, London. **274-275** (T) Ann Ronan Picture Library. (B) ET Archive. **275** (CL) ET. (BR) Fred Olsen. **276** (T) ET. (C) Jean-Loup Charmet, Paris. **276-277** (T) Roger Viollet. (B) Mansell Collection. **277** (L) Jean-Loup Charmet, Paris. (C) *Edward Williams.* (R) Mansell Collection. **278** ME. **279** (TC) (both) ME. (TR) *Malcolm Porter.* (BL) The Museum of London. (BR) Harlingue-Viollet. **280** Bibliotheque Historique, Paris/Chavanne, Studio des Grands Augustins. **280-281** Harrogate Museums & Art Gallery. **281** (TR) Mansell Collection. (CL) V & A. (BC) Marshall Cavendish. (BR) Illustrated London News. **282** (L) *Grose Thurston Partnership.* (BR) HP. **283** (T) HP (C) Marshall Cavendish/Ray Duns. (iron) *Edward Williams.* (BR) BA. **284** (L) Von Menzel 'Pariser Wochentag', Kunstmuseum, Dusseldorf. **285** (TL) BA/Musée Carnavalet, Paris/Lauros Giraudon. (glasses) Christie's Colour Library. (fan) *Richard Bonson*/Marshall Cavendish/Dennis Barnard. (BL) ME. (BR) Bulloz/Musée Carnavalet. **286** (T) Staatliche Museen Preussischer Kulturbesitz, Nationalgalerie, Berlin/Jörg P. Andeus. (B) Private Collection. **287** (TL) Archiv für Kunst und Geschichte, Berlin. (TR) Private Collection. (BL) Stadtmuseum, Munich/Claus Hansmann. (CR) Archiv für Kunst und Geschichte, Berlin. (BR) Claus Hansmann. **288** *David Sheppard.* (BR) ME. **288-289** Tate Gallery, London. **289** (BL) Collection Sirot Angel, Paris. (TR) (all) HP. **290** (TR) Roger Viollet. (BL) ME. **290-291** Museum of London. **291** (TR) ME. (print) Harlingue-Voillet. (C) Roger Viollet. (BL) HP. (BC) ME. **292** (C) National Postal Museum, London. (B) Museum of London. (BR) Barnaby's Picture Library. **292-293** *David Sheppard*/John Frost. **293** (TR) HP. (CR) MH. (BR) Jean-Loup Charmet, Paris. (BL) Barnaby's Picture Library. **294** Jean-Loup Charmet, Paris. **294-295** Museum of London. **295** (TL) Musée du Petit Palais, Paris/Bulloz. (TR) Marshall Cavendish/Dennis Barnard. (C) Jean-Loup Charmet, Paris. (BR) *Ivan Lapper.* **296** (T) Royal Holloway & Bedford New College, Surrey/BA. (B) ME. **297** (TL) BN. (TR) Mansell Collection. (C) Jean-Loup Charmet, Paris. (Lister) Wellcome Institute, London. (stethoscope) Science Museum, London. **298** From *Russia in Original Photographs*, Marylin Lyons, (Routledge & Kegan Paul 1977). **299** (TR) *Malcolm Porter.* (CL) I. Repin/Novosti. (CR) (both) BL. (BR) Novosti. **300** (TR) Society for cultural relations with the USSR. (BL) Popperfoto. **300-301** BL. **301** (TR) HP. (C) Collection Raoult, Musée de l'Homme, Paris. (BL) Collection Raoult, Musée de l'Homme, Paris. (BR) *Richard Bonson*/H.V. Opolovnikiv, *Wooden Architecture of Russia* (Thames and Hudson 1989). **302** (C) Werner Forman Archive. (BL) Graphische Sammlung Albertina, Vienna/Lichtbildwerkstätte Alpenland. (BR) Graphische Sammlung Albertina, Vienna/Lichtbildwerkstätte Alpenland. **302-303** Stadtische Museum, Vienna/BA. **303** (TL) BA. (TR) ET. (C) Marshall Cavendish. (BR) Museen der Stadt, Vienna. **304** (T) Bildarchiv Preussischer Kulturbesitz. (B) *Edward Williams*/Jewish Museum, New York. (CR) Collection Raoult, Musée de l'Homme, Paris. **305** (BR) Chloe Obolensky, 'The Russian Empire'. (T) Marc Chagall, 'The Wedding', c1992 ADAGP, Paris and DACS, London/Private Collection/BA. (C) V & A. (BR) From A. Rubens *A History of Jewish Costume* (Weidenfeld 1973). **306** Royal Geographical Society, London. **307** (T) *Malcolm Porter.* (TC) BM Department of Ethnography. (BL) Octopus Picture Library. (C) Frans Lanting/Bruce Coleman. (weights) BM Department of Ethnography. **308** (BL) Mansell Collection. (CR) *Edward Williams.* **308-309** Royal Geographical Society, London. **309** (C) The David Livingstone Centre, Blantyre. (TC) Edimedia, Paris. **310** (TL) South African Cultural History Museum, Cape Town. (CR) Eckley Dykman/Library of Parliament, Cape Town. (BR) Africana Museum, Johannesburg. **311** (TR) *David Sheppard.* (CL) Africana Museum, Johannesburg. (BR) Eckley Dykman/Library of Parliament, Cape Town. **312** (C) BL. (BL) BL. **312-313** *Ivan Lapper*/Aubrey Elliot, *Zulu, Heritage of a Nation* (Struik 1991). **313** (L) BM Department of Ethnography/Godfrey New. (TR) National Army Museum, London. (CR) William Fehr Collection, Cape Town. **314** (TL) Mansell Collection. (C) Voortrekker Museum, Pietermaritzburg. (BR) Voortrekker Museum, Pietermaritzburg. **315** (TL) Peter Newark's Historical Pictures. (B) Voortrekker Museum, Pietermaritzburg. (BR) Africana Museum, Johannesburg. **316** Africana Museum, Johannesburg. **316-317** *David Thorpe.* **317** (TR) Cape Archives, Cape Town. (C) De Beers. **318** Paul Mellon Collection, Yale Center for British Art. **319** (TR) *Malcolm Porter.* (CL) ME. (C) MH. (BR) Peabody Museum of Salem/Mark Sexton. **320** (BL) Marshall Cavendish/Lyndon Parker. (BR) Mansell Collection. **321** (CR) Douglas Dickins. (BL) National Museum, New Delhi. (BC) Mansell Collection. (BR) V & A. **322** (L) BL India Office Library. (CR) ET. (BR) Wallace Collection. **322-323** Fine Art Photo Library. **323** (TR) ET. (CL) The National Army Museum, Chelsea. (BC) Marshall Cavendish/Ray Duns. (BR) *Richard Bonson*/Marshall Cavendish/Ray Duns. **324** (TL) BL India Office Library/Marshall Cavendish. (C) Mansell Collection. **324-325** ME. **325** (C) ET. (BL) *Richard Bonson.* (BC) Private Collection. (BR) Private Collection. **326** Mitchell Library, State Library of NSW. **327** (T) Rex Nan Kivell Collection, National Library of Australia, Canberra. (C) MH. (TR) *Malcolm Porter.* (BC) BM. (BR) BM/Werner Forman Archive. **328** Mitchell Library, State Library of NSW. **328-329** (T) *Richard Bonson*/Axel Poignant. (B) Axel Poignant. **329** (TR) Private Collection, Prague/Werner Forman Archive. (C) ET. (CR) Mitchell Library, State Library of NSW, Sydney. **330** (T) Mitchell Library, State Library of NSW, Sydney. (BL) Mitchell Library, State Library of NSW, Sydney. **330-331** (T) Dixson Galleries, State Library of NSW, Sydney. (C) *Richard Bonson.* (B) Mitchell Library, State Library of NSW. **331** (TC) La Trobe Collection, State Library of Victoria, Melbourne. (C) Private Collection. (BC) Private Collection. **332** (TL) Private Collection. **332-333** (T) National Library of Australia, Canberra. (B) National Gallery of Victoria, Melbourne. **333** (TR) ET. (CL) Private Collection. (BR) (shears & can) Private Collection. (hut) The La Trobe Library, Victoria, Australia. (BR) Government Printing Office Collection, State Library of NSW. **324** (TR) Mitchell Library, State Library of NSW, Sydney. (TL) ET. (BL) Pitt Rivers Museum, Oxford. **334-335** (BL) (Ms ADD 23920 f50). **335** (CR) ME. (C) BM Department of Ethnography/Godfrey New. (bowl) Axel Poignant Archive. (comb) *Richard Bonson.* (CR) Axel Poignant Archive. **336** Courtesy of the Martyn Gregory Gallery. **337** (TL) BA. (TR) *Malcolm Porter.* (C) Private Collection. (BR) Popperfoto. (BL) APA Photo Agency, Singapore. **338** (TR) Berry-Hill Galleries, New York. (BL) Popperfoto. **338-339** Laurie Platt Winfrey/Mr & Mrs Rafi Y. Mottahedeh/Otto Nelson. **339** (TR) Topham. (C) National Maritime Museum, Greenwich. (BC) Popperfoto. **340** (T) *Kanagawa Prefectural Museum.* (object drawings) Laurie Platt Winfrey. **341** (TL) Laurie Platt Winfrey. (TR) Popperfoto. (C) Laurie Platt Winfrey. (BR) BM/Andromeda. **342** ME. **343** (TL) Ann Ronan Picture Library. (TR) *Richard Bonson*/Deere and Company. (map) *Malcolm Porter.* (CR) Old Sturbridge Village Collection/Henry E. Peach. (BC) HP/Bettman Archive. **344** (T) PN. (C) PN. (BL) PN. (BR) Private Collection. **344-345** Taylor, 'The American Slave Market' 1852, Courtesy Chicago Historical Society. **345** (T) PN. (C) PN. (B) PN. **346** (T) PN. (CR) HP/Bettman Archive. (BR) HP/Bettman Archive. **346-347** New York Public Library. **347** (T) *Richard Bonson*/PN. (instruments) Armed Forces Institute of Pathology. ('Off for the War') Library of Congress. (dollar) *L.A. East.* **348** (L) HP/Bettman Archive. (TR) *Vanessa Marsh.* **348-9** W.H.D. Koerner. **349** (TC) PN. (TR) HP/Bettman Archive. (C) PN. (BR) PN. **350** (TR) Harald Sund © 1974 Time-Life Books Inc, Courtesy Oregon Historical Society. **350-351** Harald Sund © 1974 Time-Life Books Inc, Courtesy Oregon Historical Society. (CL) James Wilkins 'Leaving the Homestead', Art Collection Missouri Historical Society. (B) PN. **351** (TL) (clock) Harald Sund © 1974 Time-Life Books Inc, Courtesy Oregon Historical Society. (C) Denver Public Library. (CR) HP. (BL) H.W. Jackson, 'South Pass', Utah State Historical Society. **352** (TL) Granger Collection. (CR) PN. (C) Library of Congress. (BR) *L.A. East.* **353** (CL) California State Library. (BR) Granger Collection. **354** (TC) HP/Bettman Archive. (CR) HP/Bettman Archive. (B) PN. **355** (T) Metropolitan Museum of Art, New York, Bequest of Moses Tanenbaum, 1937 (39.47.1). (BL) *Richard Bonson.* (BR)

ME. **356** (CR) Archives of Ontario (F229-10-1). (BL) *Steve Smith*/Manitoba Museum of Man and History, Winnepeg. (BR) Archives of Ontario (F229-1-017). **356-357** (T) Paul Kane, 'Half Breeds Travelling', Royal Ontario Museum (912-1.24). **357** (TC) Lorne Coulson. (BL) RCMP Archives. (BC) New York Historical Society from Frank Leslie's Illustrated Newspaper, Sept 23, 1871. **358** (C) ME. (BR) Jacob A. Riis Collection, Museum of the City of New York. **358-359** Eno Collection, New York Public Library. **359** (TR) PN. (C) (both) Laurie Platt Winfrey/New York Historical Society. (tailor) HP. (BL) PN. (BC) PN. **360** (TR) ME. (C) Smithsonian Institution, Washington. (BL) Bettman Archive. (BR) PN. **360-361** PN. **361** (TL) Bettman Archive. (C) George Wesley Bellows, 'The Cliff Dwellers' (detail), Los Angeles County Museum of Art. **361** (Heinz) Robert Opie Collection. (BL) Hershey Foods Corporation/James McInnis. (BR) New York Historical Society. **362** ME. **363** (T) Bodleian Library, Oxford (Ms Bod 264 pt 1 f90). (C) Tin Research Institute. (BR) *Richard Bonson* after an illustration in *The Greeks*, A. Millard and S. Peach (Usborne 1990). **364** ME. **365** (TL) *Eileen Tweedy*. (R) ME. (BC) ET. **366** (TL) *Richard Bonson.* (TR) HP. **367** (TC) *Patrick Thurston*. (BL) HP. (BR) ET. **368** *Richard Bonson* after an illustration in *Trapping and Poaching*, Arthur Ingram (Shire Publications). **368-369** Permission of the Worshipful Company of Playing Card Makers/BA. **369** (TC) Marshall Cavendish/Ray Duns. (CR) *Patrick Thurston*. (BL) (both) MH. (skater) ME. **370** ET. **371** (T) BA. (B) ET.

The publishers also acknowledge their indebtedness to the following books and journals which were consulted for reference or as a source of quotations:

GENERAL *America's Historylands* (Reader's Digest); *Discovering Costume*, A. Barfoot (University of London); *Discovery and Exploration* (Reader's Digest); *Encyclopaedia Britannica*; *The Emergence of Man* (Time-Life); *The Faber Book of Reportage*, ed. J. Carey (Faber); *Food* (English Heritage); *Great Ages of Man* (Time-Life); *Great Civilisations* (Thames and Hudson); *Hamlyn History of the World in Colour*; *A History of Everyday Things in Britain*, M. and C.H.B. Quennell (Batsford); *History of Food*, R. Tannahill (Penguin); *A History of Private Life*, ed. Aries and Duby (Belknap and Harvard); *History Today*; *History of the World*, J.M. Roberts (Pelican); *Houses*, M. and A. Potter (Murray); *An Illustrated History of Medicine* (Hamlyn); *The Last Two Million Years* (Reader's Digest); *Library of Modern Knowledge* (Reader's Digest); *The Life History of the United States*; *Life Through the Ages*, G. Casselli (Dorling Kindersley); *Men at Arms* (Osprey); *Milestones of History* (Reader's Digest); *Money*, J. Cribb (British Museum); *National Geographic*; *Penguin Dictionary of English and European History*; *The Roots of Evil*, C. Hibbert (Penguin); *The Story of America* (Reader's Digest); *Structures of Everyday Life*, F. Braudel (Collins); *Wonders of Man* (Reader's Digest); *World History Factfinder*, C. McEvedy (Cresset Press); *The World's Last Mysteries* (Reader's Digest).

ANCIENT WORLDS *The Ancient Olympic Games*, J. Swaddling (British Museum); *Athenian Red Figure Vases*, J. Boardman (Thames and Hudson); *Atlas of Ancient Civilisations*, K. Branigan (Heinemann); *Atlas of Ancient Egypt*, J. Baines and J. Malek (Phaidon); *Atlas of the Bible*, J. Rogerson (Phaidon); *Atlas of Early Man*, Jacquetta Hawkes (Macmillan); *Atlas of the Greek World*, P. Levi (Phaidon); *Atlas of the Roman World*, T. Cornell and J. Matthews (Phaidon); *BC: The Archaeology of the Bible Lands*, M. Magnusson (Bodley Head); *The Cambridge Encyclopaedia of China*, ed. B. Hook (Cambridge University Press); *The Canaanites*, J. Gray (Thames and Hudson); *China, a Concise Cultural History*, A. Cotterell (John Murray); *China, an Integrated Study*, A. Cotterell and D. Morgan (Harrap); *Cultural Atlas of Mesopotamia*, M. Roaf (Facts on File); *The Dawn of Civilisation* (Thames and Hudson); *Egyptian Life*, M. Stead (British Museum); *Egyptian Painting*, T.G.H. James (British Museum); *Everyday Life in Babylonia and Assyria*, H.W.F. Saggs (Batsford); *Everyday Life in Bible Times* (National Geographic); *Everyday Life in Prehistoric Times*, M. and C.H.B. Quennell (Batsford); *Everyday Life in Roman and Anglo-Saxon Times*, M. and C.H.B. Quennell (Batsford); *The First Settlements*, J. Robottom (Watts); *The First Merchant Venturers*, W. Culican (Thames and Hudson); *The Greek Armies*, P. Connolly (Macdonald); *Greek and Roman Life*, I. Jenkins (British Museum); *The Greeks*, S. Peach and A. Millard (Usborne); *The Heart of the Dragon*, A. Clayre (Collins); *Half the World*, A. Toynbee (Thames and Hudson); *The Hittites*, O.R. Gurney (Pelican); *How People Lived*, A. Millard (Dorling Kindersley); *Illustrations of Old Testament History*, R.D. Barnett (British Museum); *Images of the Ice Age*, P.G. Bahn and J. Vertut (Windward); *Iron-Age Farm*, P.J. Reynolds (Colonnade); *Linear B and Related Scripts*, J. Chadwick (British Museum); *The Mycenaeans*, Lord William Taylour (Thames and Hudson); *Ancient Empires*, ed. S.G.F. Brandon (Weidenfeld and Nicolson); *The Minoans*, S. Hood (Thames and Hudson); *The Roman Army*, P. Connolly (Macdonald); *Roman Britain*, K. Branigan (Reader's Digest); *The Roman World*, M. Vickers (Phaidon); *The Search for Early Man* (Cassell); *Sport and Recreation in Ancient Greece*, W.E. Sweet (Oxford); *Vanished Civilisations* (Thames and Hudson).

OLD WORLDS, NEW WORLDS *The Age of Chivalry*, C.T. Wood (Weidenfeld and Nicolson); *The Age of Expansion* (Thames and Hudson); *The Age of Sultan Süleyman the Magnificent* (National Gallery of Art, Washington); *Amsterdam in the Age of Rembrandt*, J. Murray (David and Charles); *Art of the Renaissance*, P. and L. Murray (Thames and Hudson); *Art of the Dark Ages*, M. Backes (Abrams); *Art of Warfare in Biblical Lands*, Y. Yadin (International Publishing); *Atlas of the Islamic World*, F. Robinson (Phaidon); *Atlas of Medieval Europe* (Phaidon); *Atlas of Russia*, R. Milner-Gulland (Phaidon); *The Barbarian West*, J.M. Wallace-Hadrill (Hutchinson); *The Beginnings of English Society*, D. Whitelock (Pelican); *The Birth of Western Civilisation* (Thames and Hudson); *The British and the Grand Tour*, J. Black

(Croom Helm); *Byzantium*, R. Loverance (British Museum); *Byzantium, City of Gold, City of Faith*, P. Hetherington (Orbis); *Charlemagne and his World*, F. Heer (Weidenfeld and Nicolson); *China – A History in Art* (Gemini Smith); *The Christians*, B. Gascoigne (Cape); *Cities of Destiny* (Thames and Hudson); *The Conquest of the Incas*, J. Hemming (Macmillan); *Cortes and the Aztec Conquest*, I. Blacker (Cassell); *Cultural Atlas of China*, C. Blunden (Phaidon); *Cultural Atlas of Japan*, M. Cullcutt (Phaidon); *The Crusades*, M. Holden (Wayland); *Daily Life of the Aztecs*, J. Soustelle (Weidenfeld and Nicolson); *Daily Life in England in the Reign of George III*, A. Parreux (Allen and Unwin); *The Dark Ages* (Thames and Hudson); *English Life in Chaucer's Day*, R. Hart (Wayland); *Early Christian Ireland*, M. and L. de Paor (Thames and Hudson); *Early Medieval Art*, J. Beckwith (Thames and Hudson); *The Eighteenth Century* (Thames and Hudson); *Elizabethan England*, A. Plowright (Reader's Digest); *English Social History*, G.M. Trevelyan (Penguin); *The English Village*, R. Muir (Thames and Hudson); *Everyday Life in Medieval Times*, M. Rowling (Batsford); *Everyday Life in Ottoman Turkey*, R. Lewis (Batsford); *Everyday Life of the Incas*, A. Kendall (Batsford); *The Evolution of Russia*, O. Hoetzsch (Thames and Hudson); *The Flowering of the Middle Ages* (Thames and Hudson); *The Georgian Gentleman*, M. Brander (Saxon House); *The Georgian Triumph*, M. Reed (Routledge and Kegan Paul); *The Grand Tour*, C. Hibbert (Spring Books); *The Great Moghuls*, B. Gascoigne (Cape); *Heritage of Canada* (Reader's Digest); *A History of Japan*, Sir G. Sansom (Dawson); *Holland*, A. Hopkins (Faber and Faber); *Horizon Book of the Arts of China*; *Horizon Book of the Elizabethan World*; *Horizon Book of the Middle Ages*; *Horizon Book of the Renaissance*; *Horizon History of China*; *In Search of Canada* (Reader's Digest); *Ireland: A Cultural Encyclopaedia*, ed. B. de Breffiny (Facts on File); *Japan: A History in Art*, B. Smith (Weidenfeld and Nicolson); *Life in Anglo-Saxon England*, R.I. Page (Batsford); *Life in Georgian England*, E.N. Williams (Batsford); *Life of the Aztecs*, P. and J. Soisson (Minerva); *Lost City of the Incas*, H. Bigham (Greenward); *Montezuma and the Aztecs*, N. Harris (Wayland); *The Making of Medieval Spain*, G. Jackson (Thames and Hudson); *The Medieval Establishment*, G. Hindley (Wayland); *The Medieval Machine*, J. Gimpel (Gollancz); *Medieval Warfare*, G. Hindley (Wayland); *Mexico*, M.D. Coe (Thames and Hudson); *Mysteries of the Ancient Americas* (Reader's Digest); *Moorish Culture in Spain*, T. Burckhardt (Allen and Unwin); *Oxford Illustrated History of Ireland*, ed. R.F. Foster; *Princes of Jade*, E. Capon and W. Macquitty (Cardinal); *Rome: Biography of a City*, C. Hibbert (Viking); *Spain: The Root and the Flower*, J.A. Crow (Harper and Row); *Atlas of Medieval Civilisations* (Times); *Taming of the Canadian West*, F. Rasky (McClelland and Stewart Ltd); *The Vikings* (Cassell); *The Vikings* (Nordbok); *The Vikings and Their Origins*, D.M. Wilson (Thames and Hudson); *A walk through the Dark Ages*, F. Delaney (Collins); *The Way of the Samurai*, R. Storry (Orbis); *Wooden Architecture of Russia*, A.V. and Y.A. Opoluvnikov (Thames and Hudson).

THE MODERN WORLD *African Art*, Frank Willett (Thames and Hudson); *The African Past*, ed. B. Davidson (Penguin); *The Age of Paradox*, J. Dodds (Gollancz); *The American Civil War*, E. Meyers (Golden Press); *The American Cowboy in Life and Legend*, B. McDowell (National Geographic); *American Heritage Histories of the Civil War, the Great West, and the Indians*; *The Asante*, M. McLeod (British Museum); *An Australian in China*, G.E. Morrison (Angus and Robertson); *Chronicle of the French Revolution* (Chronicle); *Citizens*, S. Schama (Penguin); *Concise History of India*, F. Watson (Thames and Hudson); *Cook's Tours*, E. Swinglehurst (Blandford); *Cook's Voyages and Peoples of the Pacific* (British Museum Publications Ltd); *Chronicles of America*, Currier and Ives (Promontory); *The Dragon Wakes*, C. Hibbert (Longmans); *Exploration of Africa*, T. Sterling (Cassell); *The Fall of Paris*, A. Horne (Macmillan); *Great Exhibition of 1851*, C.H. Gibbs-Smith (Victoria and Albert Museum); *A History of African Exploration*, D. Mountfield (Hamlyn); *Human Documents of the Victorian Golden Age*, E. Royston-Pike (Allen and Unwin); *Illustrated History of South Africa* (Reader's Digest); *Illustrated London News Social History of Victorian Britain*, C. Hibbert (Book Club Associates); *Life Below Stairs*, F.E. Huggett (Murray); *London – 2000 years of a City and Its People*, F. Barker and P. Jackson (Book Club Associates); *Napoleon*, C, Barnett (Allen and Unwin); *The Naval Heritage*, D. Mathew (Collins); *The Personal Journal of Commodore Perry*; *Plain Tales from the Raj*, C. Allen (A. Deutsch); *A Portrait of Britain 1851-1951*, D. Lindsey (Oxford); *Raj – A Scrapbook of British India 1877-1947*, C. Allen (A. Deutsch); *The Rise of Modern China*, I.C.Y. Hsü (Oxford); *The Seaside Holiday*, A. Hern (Cresset); *Shops and Shopping*, A. Adburgham (Allen and Unwin); *The Siege of Paris*, R. Baldick (Batsford); *Social History of England*, A. Briggs (Penguin); *A Social History of Housing*, J. Burnett (Methuen); *Social History of the Navy*, M. Lewis (Allen and Unwin); *The Story of Africa*, B. Davidson (Mitchell Beazley); *Unbeaten Tracks in Japan*, I. Bird (Virago); *Victorian Pubs*, M. Girouard (Yale); *The Victorian Country Child*, P. Horn (Roundwood Press); *Victorian England as seen by Punch*, F. Huggett (Book Club Associates); *Victorian Entertainment*, A. Delgado (David and Charles); *The Victorians*, H. and M. Evans (David and Charles); *The Victorians at Home and Away*, J. and P. Phillips (Croom Helm); *The Victorian Home*, J. Calder (Batsford); *The Victorian House*, J. Marshall and I. Willox (Sidgwick and Jackson); *The Victorian Railway*, J. Simmons (Thames and Hudson); *The Victorian Scene*, N. Bentley (Weidenfeld and Nicolson); *The Yangtze Valley and Beyond*, I. Bird (Virago); *The Wooden World*, N. Badger (Collins).

Index compiled by Michèle Clarke. Many writers, consultants and researchers, as well as those named on pages 4-5, helped in the preparation of this book. The publishers wish to thank them all, particularly: Sally Bamber; Dr M.L. Bierbrier; D.F. Cheshire; James Cox, FRCGP; Ellen Gillis; Nichola Johnson, MA; Kevin McRae; Katherine Polanski; Peter J. Reynolds; Geoffrey Ross; Joseph Sarkis; Keith Spence; C.B.F. Walker; Rosemary I. Weinstein, BA, FSA; Dr Francis Wood.